# Lecture Notes of the Institute for Computer Sciences, Social Informatics and Telecommunications Engineering

**634**

The LNICST series publishes ICST's conferences, symposia and workshops.
LNICST reports state-of-the-art results in areas related to the scope of the Institute.
The type of material published includes

- Proceedings (published in time for the respective event)
- Other edited monographs (such as project reports or invited volumes)

LNICST topics span the following areas:

- General Computer Science
- E-Economy
- E-Medicine
- Knowledge Management
- Multimedia
- Operations, Management and Policy
- Social Informatics
- Systems

Ahmet Soylu · Fan Liu · Karan Mitra ·
Yan Zhang · Tor-Morten Grønli
Editors

# Mobile and Ubiquitous Systems

## Computing, Networking and Services

21st EAI International Conference, MobiQuitous 2024
Oslo, Norway, November 12–14, 2024
Proceedings

 Springer

*Editors*
Ahmet Soylu
Kristiania University of Applied Sciences
Oslo, Norway

Fan Liu
Southeast University
Nanjing, China

Karan Mitra
Luleå University of Technology
Luleå, Sweden

Yan Zhang
University of Oslo
Oslo, Norway

Tor-Morten Grønli
Kristiania University of Applied Sciences
Oslo, Norway

ISSN 1867-8211        ISSN 1867-822X  (electronic)
Lecture Notes of the Institute for Computer Sciences, Social Informatics
and Telecommunications Engineering
ISBN 978-3-032-10553-0        ISBN 978-3-032-10554-7  (eBook)
https://doi.org/10.1007/978-3-032-10554-7



This Springer imprint is published by the registered company Springer Nature Switzerland AG
The registered company address is: Gewerbestrasse 11, 6330 Cham, Switzerland

If disposing of this product, please recycle the paper.

# Preface

We are thrilled to present the proceedings of the 21st EAI International Conference on Mobile and Ubiquitous Systems: Computing, Networking, and Services (EAI MobiQuitous 2024). Hosted by Kristiania University of Applied Sciences in Oslo, Norway, the conference was held from November 12–14, 2024. Continuing the rich tradition of MobiQuitous, this year's proceedings offer a platform for researchers, industry professionals, and students from across the globe to share ideas, explore innovative techniques, and discuss cutting-edge tools.

The technical program of MobiQuitous 2024 consisted of 32 full papers, selected from 73 submissions. Each submission was reviewed following a single-blind process with a minimum of 3 reviews per paper. The technical program also featured two keynote speeches. The two keynote speakers were Radu Prodan from University of Klagenfurt, Austria and Sabita Maharjan from University of Oslo, Norway. This year's program reflected the diversity and innovation within the field, with accepted papers covering a wide range of topics. Highlights included advancements in novel frameworks for mobile edge and fog computing, innovative applications of mobile augmented reality in healthcare and education, and groundbreaking interaction technologies leveraging AI and IoT. The contributions demonstrated not only technical excellence but also a strong focus on real-world applications, addressing challenges in scalability, sustainability, and user experience in mobile and ubiquitous systems.

Coordination with the steering chair, Tao Gu, and members Takahiro Hara and Max Mühlhäuser was essential for the success of the conference. We sincerely appreciate their constant support and guidance. It was also a great pleasure to work with such an excellent organizing committee team for their hard work in organizing and supporting the conference. We are also grateful to the Conference Manager, Lenka Vatrtova, for her support and to all the authors who submitted their papers to the MobiQuitous 2024 conference.

We strongly believe that MobiQuitous 2024 provided a good forum for all researchers, developers, and practitioners to discuss all science and technology aspects that are relevant to mobile and ubiquitous computing. We also expect that future MobiQuitous conferences will be as successful and stimulating as indicated by the contributions presented in this volume.

Ahmet Soylu
Fan Liu
Karan Mitra
Yan Zhang
Tor-Morten Grønli

# Organization

## Steering Committee

Tao Gu                                Macquarie University, Australia
Takahiro Hara                      **Osaka University, Japan**
Max Mühlhäuser                **Technische Universität Darmstadt, Germany**

## Organizing Committee

### General Chair

Yan Zhang                          University of Oslo, Norway

### General Co-chair

Tor-Morten Grønli            Kristiania University of Applied Sciences, Norway

### TPC Chair and Co-chairs

Ahmet Soylu                    Kristiania University of Applied Sciences, Norway
Fan Liu                               Southern University of Science and Technology, China
Karan Mitra                      Luleå University of Technology, Sweden

### Local Chair

Huamin Ren                      Kristiania University of Applied Sciences, Norway

### Workshops Chairs

Xiaomeng Su                   Norwegian University of Science and Technology, Norway
Deepak Mishra                University of New South Wales, Australia

| | |
|---|---|
| Tianyi Li | Aalborg University, Denmark |

**Web Chair**

| | |
|---|---|
| Changkyu Choi | UiT The Arctic University of Norway, Norway |

**Publicity Chairs**

| | |
|---|---|
| Changqing Luo | Virginia Commonwealth University, USA |
| Jia-chun Lin | Norwegian University of Science and Technology, Norway |
| Yin Zhang | University of Electronic Science and Technology of China, China |
| Chiara Bordin | UiT The Arctic University of Norway, Norway |
| Hongyang Chen | Zhejiang Lab, China |
| Xiaokang Zhou | Shiga University, Japan |

## Technical Program Committee

| | |
|---|---|
| Abhishek Kumar | University of Helsinki, Finland |
| Afrand Agah | West Chester University of Pennsylvania, USA |
| Akif Quddus Khan | Norwegian University of Science and Technology, Norway |
| Álvaro Suárez Sarmiento | University of Las Palmas de Gran Canaria, Spain |
| Amiya Nayak | University of Ottawa, Canada |
| Ana Patrícia Rocha | University of Aveiro, Portugal |
| André Constantino da Silva | IFSP & NIED/UNICAMP, Brazil |
| Antonio Brogi | University of Pisa, Italy |
| Arda Goknil | SINTEF AS, Norway |
| Beihong Jin | Institute of Software, Chinese Academy of Sciences, China |
| Brano Kusy | CSIRO, Australia |
| Brent Lagesse | University of Washington Bothell, USA |
| Bruno Dzogovic | Oslo Metropolitan University, Norway |
| Chandra Krintz | UC Santa Barbara, USA |
| Chiara Bordin | UiT The Arctic University of Norway, Norway |
| Chiu Tan | Temple University, USA |
| Christoph Stach | University of Stuttgart, Germany |
| Cornelia Aurora Győrödi | University of Oradea, Romania |
| Cristian Borcea | New Jersey Institute of Technology, USA |
| Daniela Micucci | University of Milano-Bicocca, Italy |

| | |
|---|---|
| Dimitrios Tomaras | Athens University of Economics and Business, Greece |
| Dimitris Chatzopoulos | University College Dublin, Ireland |
| Federica Rollo | University of Modena and Reggio Emilia, Italy |
| Floriano Scioscia | Polytechnic University of Bari, Italy |
| Francesca Martelli | Istituto di Informatica e Telematica (CNR), Italy |
| Francisco Falcone | ISC-UPNA, Spain |
| Franco Frattolillo | University of Sannio, Italy |
| Frode Eika Sandnes | Oslo Metropolitan University, Norway |
| Fusang Zhang | Institute of Software, Chinese Academy of Sciences, China |
| George Xylomenos | Athens University of Economics and Business, Greece |
| Giuseppe D'Aniello | University of Salerno, Italy |
| Giuseppe Loseto | Polytechnic University of Bari, Italy |
| Gopika Premsankar | Aalto University, Finland |
| Gui Zhou | Friedrich-Alexander University of Erlangen-Nürnberg, Germany |
| Gyu Myoung Lee | Liverpool John Moores University, UK |
| Habib Mostafaei | Eindhoven University of Technology, Netherlands |
| Hamza Ouarnoughi | Université Polytechnique Hauts-de-France, France |
| Haoqiu Xiong | KU Leuven, Belgium |
| Hem Regmi | University of South Carolina, USA |
| Hongfei Xue | University of North Carolina at Charlotte, USA |
| Honghao Gao | Gachon University, South Korea |
| Huber Flores | University of Helsinki, Finland |
| Imed Ben Dhaou | University of Turku, Finland |
| Ismail Hassan | Oslo Metropolitan University, Norway |
| Ivan Pires | University of Beira Interior, Portugal |
| Jacek Izydorczyk | Instytut Elektroniki Politechniki Śląskiej, Poland |
| Javier Berrocal | University of Extremadura, Spain |
| Javier Gozalvez | Universidad Miguel Hernández de Elche, Spain |
| Jingao Xu | Tsinghua University, China |
| Jordi Mongay Batalla | Warsaw University of Technology, Poland |
| K. Subramani | West Virginia University, USA |
| Kaitao Meng | University College London, UK |
| Kawon Han | University College London, UK |
| Kevin Lee | Deakin University, Australia |
| Kevin Matthe Caramancion | University of Wisconsin-Stout, USA |
| Lei Yang | Hong Kong Polytechnic University, China |
| Leo Zhang | Griffith University, Australia |

| | |
|---|---|
| Luca Bedogni | University of Modena and Reggio Emilia, Italy |
| Luca Reggiani | Politecnico di Milano, Italy |
| Marcin Woźniak | Silesian University of Technology, Poland |
| Maria Luisa Damiani | University of Milan, Italy |
| Mesut Güneş | Otto von Guericke University Magdeburg, Germany |
| Michael Sheng | Macquarie University, Australia |
| Michele Ruta | Politecnico di Bari, Italy |
| Minmei Wang | University of Connecticut, USA |
| Nebojsa Bacanin | Singidunum University, Serbia |
| Nikolay Nikolov | SINTEF AS, Norway |
| Oladayo Bello | New Mexico State University, USA |
| Pari Delir Haghighi | Monash University, Australia |
| Peiyuan Guan | University of Oslo, Norway |
| Pierre Leone | University of Geneva, Switzerland |
| Prem Prakash Jayaraman | Swinburne University, Australia |
| Przemysław Falkowski-Gilski | Gdańsk University of Technology, Poland |
| Radu Prodan | University of Klagenfurt, Austria |
| Rakib Abdur | Coventry University, UK |
| Rang Liu | University of California, Irvine, USA |
| Renato Ferrero | Politecnico di Torino, Italy |
| Rute C. Sofia | fortiss GmbH, Germany |
| Safiqul Islam | Oslo Metropolitan University, Norway |
| Sajib Mistry | Curtin University, Australia |
| Sandeep Singh Sandha | University of California, Los Angeles, USA |
| Sanjay Madria | Missouri University of Science and Technology, USA |
| Satoshi Kurihara | Keio University, Japan |
| Sergio Ilarri | University of Zaragoza, Spain |
| Serhiy O. Semerikov | Kryvyi Rih State Pedagogical University, Ukraine |
| Shihang Lu | Southern University of Science and Technology, China |
| Shouqian Shi | University of California, Santa Cruz, USA |
| Shuangyang Li | TU Berlin, Germany |
| Stefan Fischer | University of Lübeck, Germany |
| Stephen Lee | University of Pittsburgh, USA |
| Suprio Ray | University of New Brunswick, Canada |
| Tao Chen | University of Pittsburgh, USA |
| Tetiana A. Vakaliuk | Zhytomyr Polytechnic State University, Ukraine |
| Thierry Villemur | University of Toulouse, France |
| Tomasz Pieciak | Universidad de Valladolid, Spain |
| Tomasz Rak | Rzeszow University of Technology, Poland |

# Contents

## Health, Biomedical Applications, and Human-Centric Computing



## IoT, Cybersecurity, and Wireless Communication

## Machine Learning, AI, and Smart Systems

**Robotics and Autonomous Systems**

**Simulation, Optimization, and Specialized Techniques**

# Health, Biomedical Applications, and Human-Centric Computing

# A Preliminary Study on Core Temperature Estimation Using a Neonatal Thermal Model via Backpropagation Algorithm


Natsumi Sakamoto[1]([✉]), Hiroki Kudo[1,2], Keisuke Hamada[3], Eiji Hirakawa[4], and Akira Uchiyama[1]

[1] Osaka University, Osaka, Japan
n-sakamoto@ist.osaka-u.ac.jp
[2] Kyoto Tachibana University, Kyoto, Japan
[3] Nagasaki Harbor Medical Center, Nagasaki, Japan
[4] Kagoshima City Hospital, Kagoshima, Japan



**Abstract.** Neonates require precise temperature management in incubators due to their immature thermoregulatory functions. Traditional methods which use skin-attached probes, are challenging because of the neonates' delicate skin. Therefore, efforts are underway to develop non-contact temperature measurement using thermography. However, thermography can be obstructed during medical procedures by factors such as the medical staff's hands. To address this issue, we employ Gagge's two-node model, a human thermal model, to simulate body temperature changes. Our method integrates real-time sensor data, including thermography and incubator conditions, to estimate skin and core temperatures. We utilize backpropagation for rapid parameter optimization within the model. Importantly, the proposed method is not a black-box approach; it ensures explainability, providing a clear understanding of how temperature estimates are derived. Evaluation results based on data from five cases demonstrated that the accuracy is comparable to that of the probes currently used in NICUs, with the method achieving core temperature estimation with an average absolute error of 0.075 °C, even 10 min after thermography data becomes unavailable.

**Keywords:** Neonates · Human Thermal Model · Gagge's Two-Node Model · Backpropagation · Parameter Estimation · Core Temperature · NICUs


## 1 Introduction

In Japan, birth rates have been declining every year since 1980. According to Ref. [10], the proportion of low-birth-weight neonates (birth weight less than 2500g) [16] has been increasing since 2010 and has remained at the same level since then. With the rise in the number of low-birth-weight neonates, there has




A. Soylu et al. (Eds.): MobiQuitous 2024, LNICST 634, pp. 3–21, 2026.
https://doi.org/10.1007/978-3-032-10554-7_1

been an increasing demand for neonatal medical devices, such as incubators. Neonates have immature thermoregulatory functions and, compared to adults, a disproportionately large body surface area relative to their weight. These factors make neonates more prone to heat loss and hypothermia than adults [13,21]. Research indicates that neonates who develop hypothermia face a significantly higher mortality rate than those with normal body temperatures [20]. Therefore, there is a critical need for systems capable of long-term monitoring of neonatal core temperature to ensure accurate management of neonatal body temperature.

In current NICU (Neonatal Intensive Care Unit) settings, neonatal body temperature is measured by attaching probes (contact sensors) to their skin. However, the delicate nature of neonatal skin and their active limb movements often cause these probes to detach, complicating long-term monitoring. This invasive measurement method places a significant burden on the neonate's body, increasing the risk of skin diseases and other complications [6].

To address this problem, the use of thermography for non-invasive body temperature measurement is gaining attention [8,24]. This approach leverages the strong correlation between the neck skin temperature and the core temperature for accurate estimation. Using thermography to measure skin temperature at the neck offers a non-invasive method for estimating core temperature.

However, during interventions, medical personnel can inadvertently obscure the camera, as shown in Fig. 1b, temporarily preventing the measurement of the neonate's body temperature. This presents a significant barrier to continuous temperature monitoring. Additionally, there are scenarios where the neonate moves out of the camera's view or becomes obscured by blankets, leading to potential delays in medical response.

In light of these challenges, this study aims to develop a model capable of estimating core temperature as a complementary method when neonatal temperature cannot be measure using thermography. Given the medical context, the system must utilize an explainable model. To meet these requirements, we propose a method for core temperature estimation by applying a human thermal model called Gagge's two-node model [17] to neonates.

The human thermal model can simulate the production, movement, and dissipation of heat in the human body. It consists of physical equations that represent heat transfer among body parts and between the body and the ambient air, ensuring the model's explainability. However, existing human thermal models are designed for adults and include some equations that are either different from or not applicable to neonates. Neonates differ from adults in thermoregulation processes and skin maturity [3,14], making these models unsuitable for direct application. Therefore, in this study, we employ the error backpropagation method as a parameter optimization technique to adapt the model for neonates, thereby constructing a neonatal core temperature estimation model.

A key component of this method is the parameter optimization process utilizing backpropagation. In NICUs, neonates vary widely in gestational age and days old, leading to significant differences in physical maturity. Additionally, a neonate's maturity level changes over time, making it challenging to use the same core temperature estimation model for an extended period. To address this issue, we aim to develop a model that can be continuously updated through real-time parameter adjustments using the backpropagation method.

In this study, we evaluated the performance of the proposed method using data from neonates (n = 5) obtained in an actual NICU. The results showed that even 10 min after thermography data was no longer available, core temperature could still be estimated with high accuracy. Specifically, a mean absolute error of 0.075 °C was achieved, which is comparable to that of a contact-type probe [12]. Given that 10 min is a standard duration for medical procedures in the NICUs, these findings suggest that the proposed method is highly effective.

(a) Clear thermal image without medical intervention

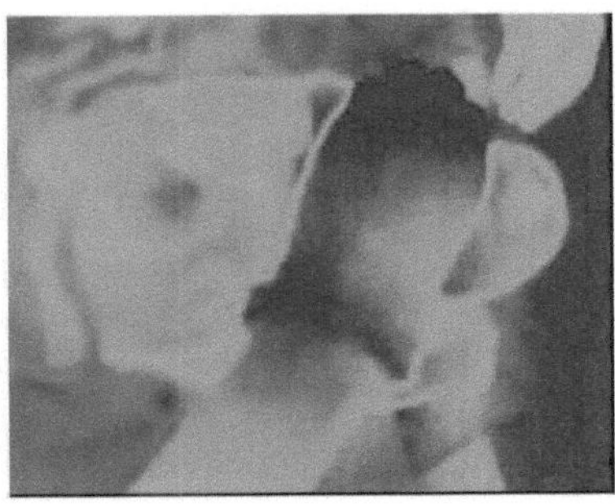

(b) Neonate obscured during medical
intervention

**Fig. 1.** Examples of thermography images of neonates in incubators.

## 2    Related Work

### 2.1    Human Thermal Model

Numerous human thermal models have been proposed to assess changes in body temperature [17,22]. These models, grounded in physical equations, trace heat generation, movement, and exchange processes, providing clear explainability of their operations.

Gagge's two-node model [17] stands out as one of the simplest and most comprehensible human thermal models. It divides the human body into two nodes: the skin and the core, and performs thermal calculations at each node to model the expulsion of heat from the core through the skin. More complex human thermal models, such as that by Strojwik et al. [22], divide the body into six parts, including the head, torso, and limbs, enhancing simulation accuracy with additional complexity.

These models, however, are based on adult physical benchmarks and assume a uniform thermal environment, leading to issues when applied to neonates.

Neonates differ significantly from adults in their physiological characteristics and thermoregulatory processes. For example, neonates have thinner subcutaneous fat and immature skin that lacks sweating capability [9]. They also possess unique heat generation mechanisms, such as brown adipose tissue [5]. Additionally, these models do not account for the unique environmental conditions within incubators, which are warmer and more humid than ambient air and involve different heat exchange mechanisms.

To address these issues, research has been conducted to develop human thermal models tailored for neonates. Ying et al. [27] modified and integrated Gagge's two-node model with Stolwijk's multi-node model to incorporate neonatal thermoregulatory processes. Pereira et al. [18] also used Stolwijk's model as a foundation to develop a neonatal model that adapts to individual differences. Despite these advancements, challenges remain, such as effectively modeling low-birthweight neonates and adapting to the daily growth of neonates. Moreover, the complexity of multi-node models necessitates extensive data input and parameter optimization, which hinders real-time updates.

For these reasons, our proposed method adopts Gagge's two-node model. The model is the simplest among human thermal models, making it particularly suitable for representing the unique physiological characteristics of neonates and enabling rapid parameter updates. Our method also incorporates features that adapt to daily growth changes specific to neonates.

## 2.2 Parameter Optimization Using Backpropagation

Our proposed method performs parameter optimization when applying the human thermal model to neonates. Techniques like exhaustive search and grid search identify optimal solutions through comprehensive searches but require significant computational resources. Consequently, rapid optimization techniques that fine-tune parameters around initial values using training data have been developed.

One such technique is the backpropagation method, which is widely incorporated into various approaches due to its efficiency and speed. Physics-Informed Neural Networks (PINNs), proposed by Raissi et al. [19], build neural networks that adhere to physical laws and optimize parameters through backpropagation, thereby constructing models that comply with physical constraints while using training data. Wu et al. [26] also advocate for backpropagation in mathematical model optimization, highlighting its efficiency in solving complex problems.

In this paper, we leverage backpropagation for parameter optimization, given its capability for real-time updating with stream data obtained from continuous monitoring of a target neonate in an incubator.

# 3  Proposed Method

## 3.1  Usage Scenario

The overview of the proposed method is shown in Fig. 2. The model simulates temperature changes using the human thermal model when the surface temperature of a neonate cannot be measured with thermography.

If a neonate is visually obscured due to medical intervention, our method initiates a core temperature estimation process. The estimation begins by inputting initial data such as the neonate's height, weight, the most recent skin temperature recorded by thermography, and the most recent core body temperature. The most recent core temperature, although ideally estimated from the neck skin temperature obtained through thermography in future applications, was measured using esophageal temperature probe in this study to ensure an accurate evaluation of the proposed method's performance. Meanwhile, the most recent average temperature of the torso area is used as the skin temperature. To identify body parts in thermal images, we employ the segmentation method proposed by Asano et al. [2].

By setting up the human thermal model with this initial information, it is possible to reflect the current internal thermal state of the neonate in the model. Temperature and humidity data from the incubator, given at each time step, enable the model to simulate heat transfer, producing outputs of core body and skin temperatures.

Additionally, as a preliminary step of the simulation, optimization of the model parameters is performed using the data collected up until the start of the simulation from the target neonate. The data used for real-time optimization is collected from the system's operation prior to the medical intervention. This parameter optimization allows for estimations tailored to the individual differences and maturity level of the target neonate.

## 3.2  Neonatal Human Thermal Model

Figure 3 illustrates the human thermal model for neonates. In this study, we adopt Gagge's two-node model [17]. Gagge's two-node model represents the human body as a sphere that comprises two nodes: a core node and a skin node. The model simulates the heat exchange among these two nodes and the ambient air. To apply the Gagge's two-node model to neonates, we have made three modifications:

- Sweating model
  Preterm neonates, born before 36 weeks of gestation, lack fully developed sweating capabilities and do not sweat during their initial weeks of life [9]. Consequently, in our method, the equations related to sweating in the model have been excluded.
- Body surface area formula
  Gagge's two-node model uses the Dubois-BSA formula [7], which is intended for adults, to calculate body surface area $A_{body}$ based on height [cm] and

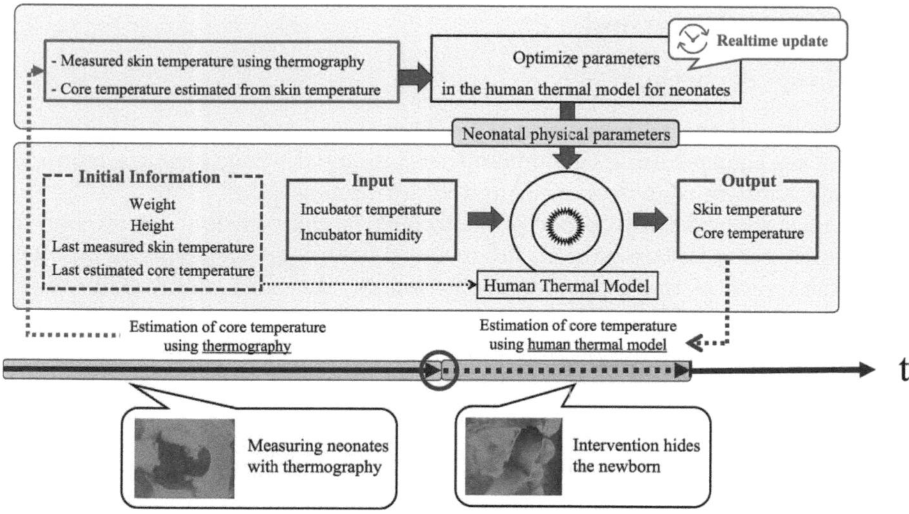


**Fig. 2.** Overview of proposed method.

weight [kg]. However, neonates have a larger body surface area relative to their weight compared to adults, rendering the Dubois-BSA formula inappropriate. Therefore, we employ a neonate-specific formula called Neo-BSA [1], which is expressed by the following equation:

$$A_{body} = 5.52005 \cdot weight^{0.5526} \cdot height^{0.3800} \tag{1}$$

– Resting metabolic rate formula

The formula for calculating the resting metabolic rate corresponds to the metabolic heat produced in the core node. Gagge's model calculates resting metabolic heat $M_{rest}$ based on oxygen consumption at rest. However, due to varying maturity levels of neonates based on gestational age and postnatal age, it is inappropriate to use the same formula as adults. Thus, we have adopted the formula for neonates' resting metabolic heat as suggested by Bruck [4], which is defined as below:

$$M_{rest} = weight(0.0522 \cdot \tau_{PA} + 1.64) \tag{2}$$

This formula incorporates two critical variables, weight and postnatal age $\tau_{PA}$, which are particularly important for neonates.

In the simulation, at each time step, the model calculates the changes of the core temperature and the skin temperature from time $t$ to $t+1$. We denote the temperatures of the core node and the skin node at time $t$ as $T_{core}(t)$ and $T_{skin}(t)$, respectively. Given the change rate of the core temperature $\Delta T_{core}(t)[°C/hr]$ from time $t$ to $t+1$, the model calculates $T_{core}(t+1)$ using the following equation:

$$T_{core}(t+1) = T_{core}(t) + \frac{1}{60} \cdot \Delta T_{core}(t) \tag{3}$$

In the same manner, the model calculates $T_{skin}(t+1)$, given the change rate of the skin temperature $\Delta T_{skin}(t)[°C/hr]$ and $T_{skin}(t)$ as below:

$$T_{skin}(t+1) = T_{skin}(t) + \frac{1}{60} \cdot \Delta T_{skin}(t) \tag{4}$$

Iterating the above calculation of core and skin temperatures every minute simulates long-term temperature changes.

$\Delta T_{core}(t)$ and $\Delta T_{skin}(t)$ are defined by the following equations:

$$\Delta T_{core}(t) = \frac{M_{rest} - q_{res} - (q_{cond} + q_{blo})A_{body}}{m_{core} \cdot c_{core}} \tag{5}$$

$$\Delta T_{skin}(t) = \frac{(q_{cond} + q_{blo} - q_{diff} - q_{conv} - q_{rad})A_{body}}{m_{skin} \cdot c_{skin}} \tag{6}$$

where $m_{core}$, $m_{skin}$, $c_{core}$, and $c_{skin}$ are the mass [kg] and specific heat [J/(kg·°C)] of the core and skin nodes, respectively.

Equation (5) represents the heat production $M_{rest}$ in the core node, a part of which is transferred to the skin node through conduction $q_{cond}$ and blood flow $q_{blo}$, while another part is expelled to the ambient air through respiration $q_{res}$. The remaining energy in the core node is then converted into the temperature change $\Delta T_{core}(t)$. Similarly, Eq. (6) demonstrates how energy received from the core node is partially released through insensible perspiration $q_{diff}$, convection $q_{conv}$, and radiation $q_{rad}$, with the remaining energy contributing to the temperature change $\Delta T_{skin}(t)$. These calculations utilize the incubator's internal temperature $T_{air}$ and humidity $\phi_{air}$. The details of each component are described in Ref. [17].

## 3.3   Optimization of Parameters Using Backpropagation

Gagge's two-node model incorporates multiple parameters that influence the output (i.e., skin and core temperature). These parameters fall into two categories: physical (e.g., the conversion coefficient from [J] to [cal]) and physiological (e.g., the specific heat capacity of blood). Due to significant differences in tissue and skin maturity between adults and neonates [11], these physiological parameters cannot be directly applied to neonates. Therefore, we optimize these parameters using pre-acquired case data to minimize the error between the model's outputs and the ground truth. The list of the physiological parameters subject to optimization is shown in Table 1.

In the optimization of parameters within the human thermal model, backpropagation is employed. The advantage of using backpropagation lies in its ability to effectively handle large datasets. As the proposed method operates over an extended period, the amount of data obtained from the neonates increases over time. Therefore, it is crucial for the optimization process to remain fast, regardless of the dataset size.

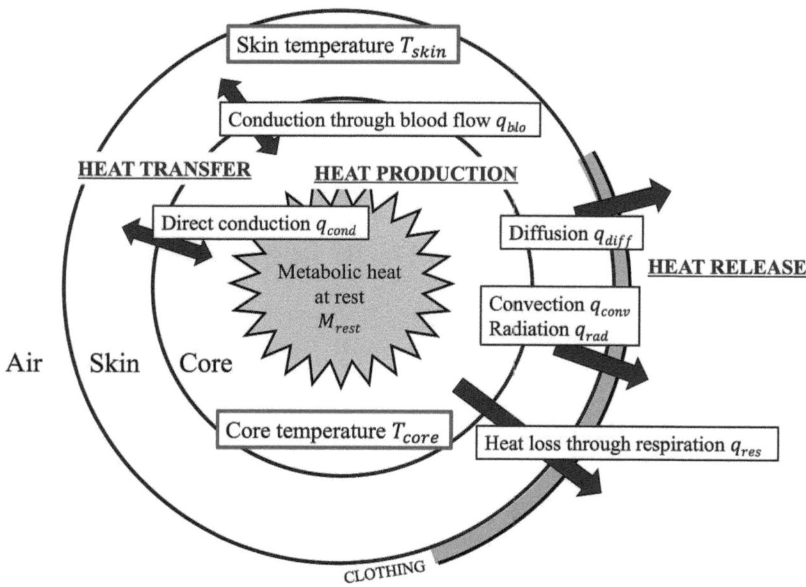



**Fig. 3.** Human thermal model for neonates.

To perform parameter optimization using the backpropagation method, the physical equations of Gagge's two-node model are mapped onto the computational graph of a neural network. This mapping ensures that the parameters targeted for optimization are represented as weights of the nodes within the graph. A graphical representation of the computational graph for the core node is shown in Fig. 4. The same approach is also applied to the skin node, resulting in computational graphs for each node. Consequently, a comprehensive computational graph for the entire Gagge's two-node model is constructed.

For optimization, we use all the collected data prior to any medical intervention. The initial values for the parameters in this computational graph are set to those of adults. Updates to the parameters are made based on the discrepancies between the simulated outputs and their actual values, using backpropagation. The loss functions for the core $\mathcal{L}_{core}$ and skin $\mathcal{L}_{skin}$ nodes are defined as follows:

$$\mathcal{L}_{core} = \frac{1}{N} \sum_{i=1}^{N} \frac{1}{t'} \sum_{t=1}^{t'} \left( \hat{T}_{core}(t)_i - T_{core}(t)_i \right)^2 \tag{7}$$

$$\mathcal{L}_{skin} = \frac{1}{N} \sum_{i=1}^{N} \frac{1}{t'} \sum_{t=1}^{t'} \left( \hat{T}_{skin}(t)_i - T_{skin}(t)_i \right)^2 \tag{8}$$

Here, $N$ represents the size of the dataset. By adjusting the value of $t'$ in Eq. (7) and (8), the time horizon over which errors are considered in the loss function can be modified. As $t'$ increases, the parameter optimization process can account for more long-term temperature changes. In this work, $t'$ is set to 10 min, aligning with the typical duration of medical interventions in NICUs.

By iteratively updating the parameters using the aforementioned computational graph, neonatal-specific parameters can be estimated. The parameters related to the core node are optimized through the loss associated with $L_{core}$, those related to the skin node through the loss associated with $L_{skin}$, and those related to both the core and skin layer through the combined loss of $L_{core}$ and $L_{skin}$. In this process, focusing the exploration around the adult physiological parameters allow for efficient and reliable optimization.

**Table 1.** Physiological parameters in human thermal model.

|  | Parameter | Core or Skin Node |
|---|---|---|
| $W_1$ | Convective heat transfer coefficient ($h_{conv}$) | Skin |
| $W_2$ | Radiation heat transfer coefficient ($h_{rad}$) | Skin |
| $W_3$ | Skin minimum thermal conductance ($K_{min}$) | Core/Skin |
| $W_4$ | Skin blood flow ($V_{blo}$) coefficient 1 | Core/Skin |
| $W_5$ | Skin blood flow ($V_{blo}$) coefficient 2 | Core/Skin |
| $W_6$ | Coefficient of respiratory heat loss ($q_{res}$) | Core |
| $W_7$ | Effective heat transfer coefficient ($F_{cl}$) | Skin |
| $W_8$ | Specific heat of blood ($c_{blo}$) | Core/Skin |
| $W_9$ | Effective physical movement coefficient ($F_{pcl}$) | Skin |
| $W_{10}$ | Convective heat transfer coefficient for insensible heat loss ($q_{diff}$) | Skin |

## 4    Evaluation

### 4.1    Dataset

**Data Collection.** Data collection for this study took place in the NICU at Nagasaki Harbor Medical Center in Japan, with IRB approval obtained for the experiment (Approval No. NIRB No. R02-006). The research was carried out in accordance with the Declaration of Helsinki. The collected data included images from a thermographic camera (FLIR A35; Teledyne FLIR LLC, Wilsonville, OR, USA), temperature and humidity inside the incubator, and core body temperature measured by an esophageal temperature probe (Atom Medical Corporation, Tokyo, Japan). The thermographic camera was installed in a convective neonatal incubator (Incu i; Atom Medical Corporation, Tokyo, Japan), which was equipped with sensors to record internal temperature and humidity. Each sensor recorded data every minute. Figure 5 illustrates the data collection environment.

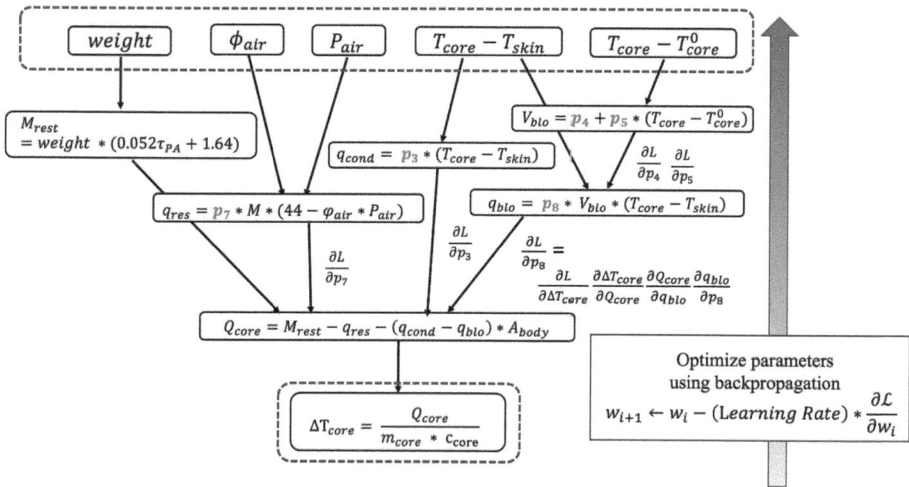

**Fig. 4.** Computational graph of core node.

Additionally, we recorded clinical information on the neonates, including gestational age, number of days postpartum, birth weight, and gender.

In this study, five cases were examined, including both low birth weight and normal birth weight infants, as well as both male and female neonates. Table 2 presents the information on the neonates used in the evaluation.

**Data Preprocessing.** Preprocessing steps were applied to the collected data. First, thermal images were segmented into the head, torso, and limbs using the method proposed by Asano et al. [2], with the average torso temperature extracted as the skin temperature. Next, temperature corrections were made using the method proposed by Hamada et al. [8], and the corrected temperature was used as the skin temperature in the proposed method. Analysis of the trends between skin and core body temperatures revealed significant instantaneous noise and extreme outliers. To address this, outliers were removed using a threshold, and a moving average was calculated over a 5-minute window for both core and skin temperatures. The preprocessed data were used for the evaluation.

## 4.2   Performance of Core Temperature Estimation

In this section, we evaluate the accuracy of the optimized human thermal model in predicting core and skin temperatures within a critical 10-min window, the standard time frame for neonatal interventions.

We optimized the model parameters using the first 70% of the time-series data for each neonate as the training dataset. The remaining 30% of the data was used to evaluate the model's performance. For the evaluation, the test data were input into the human thermal model, which had been personalized with

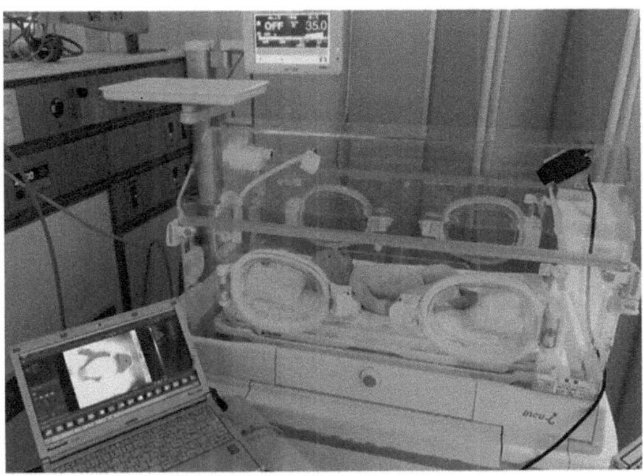

**Fig. 5.** Data collection environment.

**Table 2.** Patients information.

| Patient | Gestational age[week] | Weight[kg] | Sex | Time[min] |
|---|---|---|---|---|
| A | 38 | 3.651 | F | 4000 |
| B | 34 | 2.235 | M | 380 |
| C | 35 | 2.081 | M | 1020 |
| D | 35 | 2.207 | M | 980 |
| E | 34 | 2.155 | M | 3125 |
| MEAN (SD) | 35.2 (1.47) | 2.4658 (0.59) | – | 1901 (1481.2) |

subject-specific parameters, and the core and skin temperatures were estimated up to 10 min later.

Figure 6 presents an example of the simulated results for core and skin temperature estimations up to 10 min for Patient A (a normal birth weight infant), and Patient B (a low birth weight infant). Additionally, Fig. 7 shows the distribution of absolute errors in core temperature estimation at each time up to 10 min for all test data from Patients A and B.

As seen in Fig. 6, the estimated results closely track the measured values. However, while the overall trend of skin temperature shows a decrease, the model struggles to capture finer fluctuations, resulting in larger errors compared to core temperature estimations. This is likely because the skin, being the outer node, is more affected by outside factors. In Fig. 7, it is evident that the error in core body temperature increases over time. This occurs because the output of the human thermal model is always dependent on the model's previous state, and once an error occurs, it influences subsequent estimations.

For all patients, we performed core temperature estimation and calculated the absolute error 10 min after the simulation began. The evaluation was conducted separately for both adult parameters (from the original thermal model) and optimized neonatal parameters. The results are presented in Table 3. As shown in Table 3, the proposed neonatal thermal model significantly outperformed the estimations using adult parameters. This trend was observed across all cases, with a 21.3% reduction in mean absolute error compared to the original model. This demonstrates that the proposed method effectively optimizes the parameters of the human thermal model to align with the unique characteristics of neonates. Additionally, focusing on the estimation results with the neonatal parameters, all patients achieved a mean absolute error of less than $0.1\,^\circ$C in terms of accuracy. When evaluating the overall performance across the five cases, the mean absolute error was $0.075\,^\circ$C. Considering that the accuracy of contact-type probes used in NICU is within $\pm 0.1\,^\circ$C [12], the proposed model estimates core temperature with sufficient accuracy. This suggests that the proposed method is capable of maintaining adequate accuracy within the 10-minute time frame, which is critical for medical interventions in NICUs.

**Table 3.** Absolute error at 10 min after the start of simulation for each case.

| Patient | Adult parameters (Original) | | | | *Optimized neonatal parameters (Proposed method) | | | |
|---|---|---|---|---|---|---|---|---|
| | Mean | Median | Min | Max | Mean | Median | Min | Max |
| A (3651g) | 0.35226 | 0.34667 | 0.02149 | 0.95619 | 0.09596 | 0.08507 | 0.00082 | 0.55399 |
| B (2235g) | 0.36237 | 0.35554 | 0.30824 | 0.48267 | 0.03214 | 0.03134 | 0.00028 | 0.08611 |
| C (2081g) | 0.35719 | 0.32457 | 0.00688 | 0.79064 | 0.07975 | 0.03854 | 0.00009 | 0.42028 |
| D (2207g) | 0.34334 | 0.34642 | 0.26372 | 0.41232 | 0.02248 | 0.01611 | 0.00001 | 0.08262 |
| E (2155g) | 0.34438 | 0.34953 | 0.17621 | 0.45945 | 0.08806 | 0.08119 | 0.00075 | 0.26128 |
| All | 0.34946 | 0.34572 | 0.00688 | 0.95619 | **0.07467** | 0.05977 | 0.00001 | 0.55399 |

## 4.3   Reliability Evaluation

In this section, we conduct a detailed comparison between standard adult parameters and the optimized parameters for neonates using our method. This analysis aims to evaluate whether our parameter optimization aligns with established medical insights. Our evaluation focuses on two specific cases: Patient A (a normal birth weight infant) and patient B (a low birth weight infant). The comparative results between the post-optimization parameters for neonates and the standard adult parameters are detailed in Table 4.

Upon comparing adult and neonatal parameters, we observed significant differences. Notably, the radiative and convective heat transfer coefficients are lower in neonates than in adults. This suggests that neonates experience less heat loss, likely due to their different environmental exposures. The adult parameters typically assume open environments that promote heat loss through convection, whereas neonates are situated in the more controlled, enclosed settings of

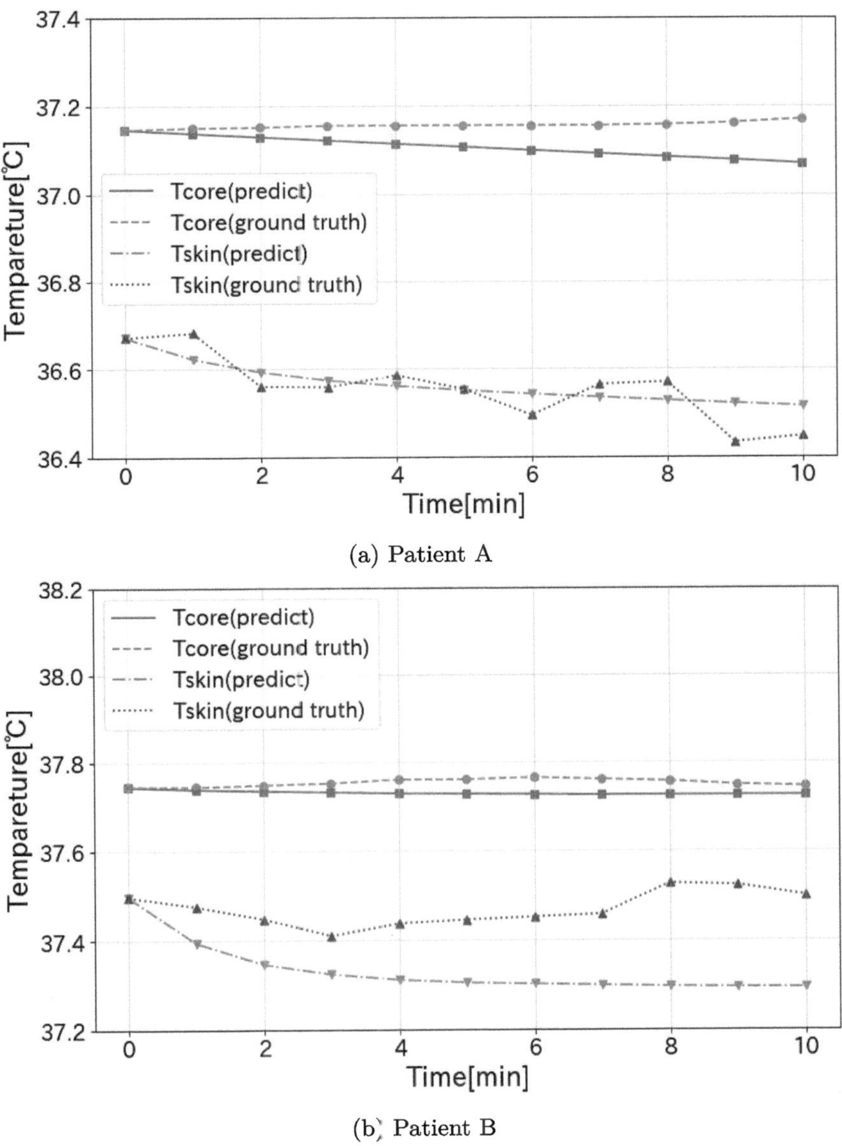

(a) Patient A

(b) Patient B

**Fig. 6.** Example of estimated skin and core temperature.

incubators. Given that incubators minimize convective heat loss, this observed reduction in the heat transfer coefficients is reasonable.

Another difference is in the specific heat of blood, denoted as $c_{blo}$, which is higher in neonates. This adjustment is medically intuitive as it reflects the

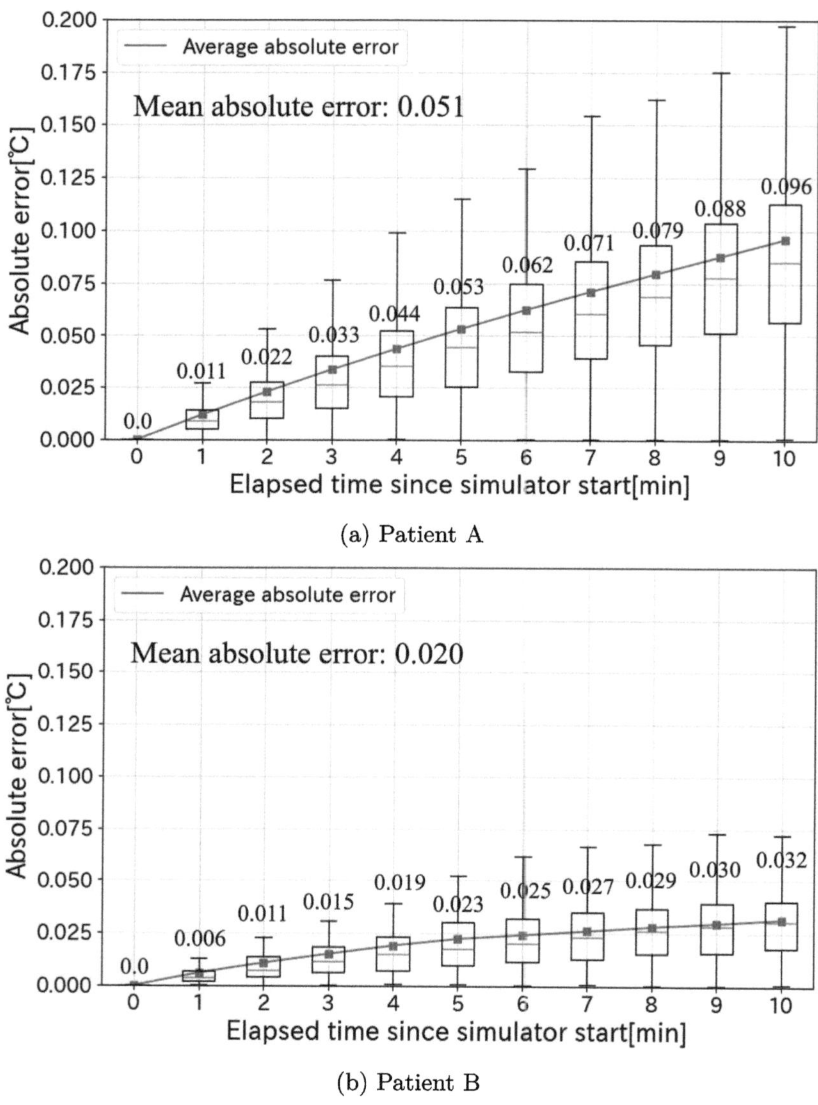

(a) Patient A

(b) Patient B

**Fig. 7.** Absolute error distribution of estimated core temperature.

neonates' immature cardiovascular systems, which are slower to respond to temperature shifts at the skin's surface compared to adults [15].

Additionally, the coefficient for heat loss due to respiration, $q_{res}$, is adjusted to a relatively higher value in neonates compared to adults. Neonates have an immature thermoregulation system, making them more susceptible to environmental influences and more reliant on respiratory heat adjustment. This observation is supported by findings from Sulyok et al. [23], who reported that respiratory heat loss in neonates is relatively higher than in adults. Therefore, the observed changes in the respiratory heat loss coefficient align well with these established medical insights.

These distinctions between adult and neonatal parameters indicate that the proposed method accurately captures the unique physiological characteristics and thermoregulatory processes of neonates. Furthermore, this comparison underscores the medical relevance of the adjustments made during the optimization process.

Next, a comparison of parameters between Patient A (a normal low birth weight infant) and Patient B (a low birth weight infant) was conducted. The differences in physiological structures due to birth weight have not been sufficiently studied, leaving many aspects yet to be elucidated. However, it has been reported that insensible water loss is higher in premature infants, which is attributed to their thinner, more immature skin, leading to greater water evaporation, as noted in Ref. [25]. This tendency is reflected in the results of this evaluation, suggesting that the proposed method may effectively model the maturity of neonates.

**Table 4.** Physiological parameters after optimization. (The values are rounded to match the number of decimal places used for adult parameters.)

| Parameter | Adult | Patient A | Patient D |
|---|---|---|---|
| Convective heat transfer coefficient ($h_{conv}$) | 2.91 | 2.51 | 2.61 |
| Radiation heat transfer coefficient ($h_{rad}$) | 5.23 | 4.56 | 4.74 |
| Skin minimum thermal conductance ($K_{min}$) | 5.28 | 5.85 | 5.74 |
| Skin blood flow ($V_{blo}$) coefficient 1 | 6.3 | 7.48 | 7.17 |
| Skin blood flow ($V_{blo}$) coefficient 2 | 0.5 | 0.49 | 0.50 |
| Coefficient of respiratory heat loss ($q_{res}$) | 0.0023 | 0.0622 | 0.0791 |
| Effective heat transfer coefficient ($F_{cl}$) | 0.143 | 0.149 | 0.149 |
| Specific heat of blood ($c_{blo}$) | 1.163 | 2.017 | 1.840 |
| Effective physical movement coefficient ($F_{pcl}$) | 0.155 | 0.840 | 0.681 |
| Convective heat transfer coefficient for insensible heat loss ($q_{diff}$) | 0.06 | 7.4e-06 | 0.0002 |

# 5  Discussion

Our proposed method is characterized by its high accuracy and its capability to estimate core temperature while ensuring explainability. Evaluation experiments demonstrated that the proposed method achieves core temperature estimation accuracy comparable to that of contact-type probe currently used in NICUs. Additionally, we showed that it is possible to construct models aligned with medical knowledge.

Our proposed method uses a human thermal model, an area that remains largely unexplored in neonatology. Specifically, applying Gagge's two-node model to neonates is a novel approach that has not been extensively researched before. The following challenges of the proposed method have emerged from our evaluation results:

(1) The estimation accuracy cannot be guaranteed after a significant error occurs. As shown by the maximum absolute error 10 min after the start of the simulation in Table 3, significant errors have occurred in some cases. This issue arises because the proposed method carries over the estimated values from the previous time step to the next, meaning that once an error occurs, it may propagate and affect subsequent estimations. In medical models, such outliers pose a serious risk. Therefore, it is necessary to develop methods that detect statistically improbable values and either exclude or correct them.

(2) Extended estimations over a prolonged period using the same model may lead to reduced accuracy. Table 3 shows that there are both cases with high accuracy and cases with poor accuracy. Focusing on the configuration information of these cases, it becomes evident that cases with longer measurement periods tend to correlate with lower accuracy. In this study, the first 70% of the time-series data is used for optimization, and the remaining 30% is used for test using the optimized model. Since neonates grow rapidly, the physiological maturity observed in the earlier data might differ significantly from that in the later data used for evaluation, especially in longer-term data. To ensure accurate long-term estimations, it is necessary to re-optimize the model in real-time, adjust the weighting of the data used for optimization, or implement other strategies, and then reassess the results.

A challenge of this study is the insufficiency of available datasets. The only reliable method for measuring body core temperature in neonates is through contact-type probes, which creates a significant barrier to obtaining measurements and makes dataset acquisition difficult. This is due to the fact that neonates have immature skin, which makes the probes prone to detachment and results in unstable measurements. Moreover, neonates in NICUs vary significantly in birth weight and maturity level, contributing to potential dataset imbalance. Very low birth weight infants, despite their small numbers, often require medical interventions post-birth, making long-term data collection challenging. There are also privacy concerns associated with data collection. The dataset includes sensitive information such as thermographic images of the neonates, treatment details, birth weight, gender, and other personal data. In our proposed approach, model construction is based on datasets provided by medical institutions, necessitating careful consideration in handling personal information to gather more extensive data. Methods such as anonymization and augmentation are important for protecting personal information, and evaluating their effectiveness within the proposed system is also valuable.

Future work will focus on exploring methods to overcome barriers in data collection and attempting to acquire a larger set of case data. To enhance the statistical reliability of the findings obtained in this study, we plan to use an expanded dataset and validate the versatility of the proposed method. Additionally, we will work on developing a system capable of real-time model construction and consider strategies such as adjusting the weighting of data used for optimization to further validate the method's generalizability. Moreover, we aim to build a generalized model that can accommodate neonates with varying levels of maturity.

## 6 Conclusion

In this study, we proposed a human thermal model capable of estimating core temperature as a complementary measure when thermography is unable to measure neonatal body temperature.

Our method applies Gagge's two-node human thermal model to neonates and optimizes the parameters using backpropagation, enabling highly accurate core temperature estimation.

We validated the effectiveness of the proposed method using data collected from 5 neonates in NICU. The result demonstrated that within the 10-min time frame, which is a critical intervention window in NICUs, the method achieved a mean absolute error of $0.075\,^\circ$C. This indicates that core temperature can be estimated with a level of accuracy comparable to that of contact-type probes.

**Acknowledgment.** We would like to express our sincere gratitude to Atom Medical Corporation for their invaluable support throughout this research.

## References


1. Ahn, Y.: Formula and scale for body surface area estimation in high-risk infants. Collegium Antropologicum **34**, 1273–1280 (2010)
2. Asano, H., et al.: A method for improving semantic segmentation using thermographic images in infants. BMC Med. Imaging **22** (2022). https://doi.org/10.1186/s12880-021-00730-0
3. Braun, F., Lachmann, D., Howanietz, H.: The use of synthetic skin cleansers in neonates and infants. In: Braun-Falco, O., Korting, H.C. (eds.) Skin Cleansing with Synthetic Detergents, pp. 164–170. Springer, Heidelberg (1992). https://doi.org/10.1007/978-3-642-50146-3_20
4. Brück, K.: Temperature regulation in the newborn infant (part 1 of 3) regulation thermique chez le nouveau-né. Neonatology **3**(2–3), 65–81 (1961)
5. Cannon, B., Nedergaard, J.: Brown adipose tissue: function and physiological significance. Physiol. Rev. **84**(1), 277–359 (2004). https://doi.org/10.1152/physrev.00015.2003. pMID: 14715917
6. Chung, H.U., Rwei, A.Y., et al.: Skin-interfaced biosensors and pilot studies for advanced wireless physiological monitoring in neonatal and pediatric intensive care units. Nat. Med. **26**, 418–429 (2020). https://doi.org/10.1038/s41591-020-0792-9

7. Du Bois, D., Du Bois, E., Du Bois, D., Du Bois, E.: A formula to estimate the approximate surface area if height and weight be known. 1916. Nutrition **5**(5), 303 (1989). https://eurekamag.com/research/039/063/039063801.php
8. Hamada, K., et al.: Infrared thermography with high accuracy in a neonatal incubator. Ann. Biomed. Eng. **50**(5), 529–539 (2022). https://doi.org/10.1007/s10439-022-02937-w
9. Harpin, V., Rutter, N.: Sweating in preterm babies. J. Pediat. **100**(4), 614–619 (1982). https://doi.org/10.1016/S0022-3476(82)80768-3. https://www.sciencedirect.com/science/article/pii/S0022347682807683
10. Ministry of Health, L., Welfare: Live birth, specified report of vital statistics in fy2021 (2021). https://www.mhlw.go.jp/english/database/db-hw/FY2021/live-births.html
11. Hoeger, P.H., Enzmann, C.C.: Skin physiology of the neonate and young infant: a prospective study of functional skin parameters during early infancy. Pediatric Dermatol. **19**(3), 256–262 (2002). https://doi.org/10.1046/j.1525-1470.2002.00082.x. https://onlinelibrary.wiley.com/doi/abs/10.1046/j.1525-1470.2002.00082.x
12. Jirapaet, V., Jirapaet, K.: Comparisons of tympanic membrane, abdominal skin, axillary, and rectal temperature measurements in term and preterm neonates. Nurs. Health Sci. **2**(1), 1–8 (2000). https://doi.org/10.1046/j.1442-2018.2000.00034.x. https://onlinelibrary.wiley.com/doi/abs/10.1046/j.1442-2018.2000.00034.x
13. Knobel, R.B.: Thermal stability of the premature infant in neonatal intensive care. Newborn Infant Nurs. Rev. **14**(2), 72–76 (2014). https://doi.org/10.1053/j.nainr.2014.03.002. https://www.sciencedirect.com/science/article/pii/S1527336914000233, thermoregulation
14. Lidell, M.E.: Brown adipose tissue in human infants. Handb. Exp. Pharmacol. **251**, 107–123 (2019)
15. Norman, M., Gu, L., Herin, P., Fagrell, B.: Reactive hyperemia in term neonates and adults-a laser doppler fluxmetry study of skin microcirculation. Microvasc. Res. **41**(2), 229–38 (1991). https://doi.org/10.1016/0026-2862(91)90024-6
16. Organization, W.H.: Who recommendations for care of the preterm or low-birth-weight infant (2022). https://www.who.int/publications/i/item/9789240058262
17. P., G.A.: An effective temperature scale based on a simple model of human physiological regulatory response. ASHRAE Trans. **77**, 247–262 (1971). https://cir.nii.ac.jp/crid/1573668923915679104
18. Pereira, C.B., Heimann, K., Czaplik, M., Blazek, V., Venema, B., Leonhardt, S.: Thermoregulation in premature infants: a mathematical model. J. Therm. Biol. **62**, 159–169 (2016). https://doi.org/10.1016/j.jtherbio.2016.06.021. https://www.sciencedirect.com/science/article/pii/S0306456516300286
19. Raissi, M., Perdikaris, P., Karniadakis, G.: Physics-informed neural networks: a deep learning framework for solving forward and inverse problems involving nonlinear partial differential equations. J. Comput. Phys. **378**, 686–707 (2019). https://doi.org/10.1016/j.jcp.2018.10.045. https://www.sciencedirect.com/science/article/pii/S0021999118307125
20. Silverman, W.A., Fertig, J.W., Berger, A.P.: The influence of the thermal environment upon the survival of newly born premature infants. Pediatrics **22**(5), 876–886 (1958). https://doi.org/10.1542/peds.22.5.876. https://cir.nii.ac.jp/crid/1362262943487614464
21. Singer, D.: Pediatric hypothermia: an ambiguous issue. Int. J. Environ. Res. Public Health **18**(21) (2021). https://doi.org/10.3390/ijerph182111484. https://www.mdpi.com/1660-4601/18/21/11484

22. Stolwijk, J., Hardy, J.: Temperature regulation in man–a theoretical study. Pflüger's Archiv für die gesamte Physiologie des Menschen und der Tiere **291**(2), 129–162 (1966)
23. Sulyok, E., Jéquier, E., Prod'hom, L.: Respiratory contribution to the thermal balance of the newborn infant under various ambient conditions. Pediatrics **51**(4), 641–50 (1973). https://doi.org/10.1542/peds.51.4.641
24. Voss, F., Brechmann, N., Lyra, S., Rixen, J., Leonhardt, S., Hoog Antink, C.: Multi-modal body part segmentation of infants using deep learning. BioMed. Eng. OnLine **22** (03 2023). https://doi.org/10.1186/s12938-023-01092-0
25. Wu, P.Y.K., Hodgman, J.E.: Insensible water loss in preterm infants: changes with postnatal development and non-ionizing radiant energy. Pediatrics **54**(6), 704–12 (1974). https://doi.org/10.1542/peds.55.5.737
26. Wu, X.: Application of bp neural network algorithm in solving mathematical modeling optimization problems. In: 2022 International Conference on Knowledge Engineering and Communication Systems (ICKES), pp. 1–6 (2022). https://doi.org/10.1109/ICKECS56523.2022.10059599
27. Ying, B., Kwok, Y., Li, Y., Yeung, C., Li, F., Li, S.: Mathematical modeling of thermal physiological responses of clothed infants. J. Therm. Biol. **29**(7), 559–565 (2004). https://doi.org/10.1016/j.jtherbio.2004.08.027. https://www.sciencedirect.com/science/article/pii/S0306456504001068

# A Two-Step Deep Neural Network Approach for Real-Time Context-Aware Health Monitoring of Hajj Pilgrims

Nazim Ahmed Belabbaci[1,2,3] and Mohammad Arif Ul Alam[1,2,3]([envelope])

[1] Richard A Miner School of Computer and Information Sciences,
University of Massachusetts Lowell, Lowell, USA
nazimahmed_belabbaci@student.uml.edu, mohammadariful_alam@uml.edu
[2] University of Massachusetts Chan Medical School, Worcester, MA, USA
[3] National Institute on Aging, National Institute of Health, Bethesda, MD, USA

**Abstract.** Monitoring the health of Hajj pilgrims is challenging due to the intense physical and emotional demands of the pilgrimage. Existing solutions often fail to accurately integrate diverse physiological data and adapt to dynamic conditions. We propose a two-step LSTM-TabNet model that first captures temporal dependencies with an LSTM and then uses TabNet for robust feature selection and classification. This approach effectively addresses these challenges, providing real-time, context-aware health monitoring for pilgrims using wearable devices. Data collected from 19 participants demonstrated that our model achieves high accuracies of 97.0% for physical tiredness level, 95.0% for emotional mood level, and 95.0% for rukun (Hajj ritual) activity classification, outperforming existing frameworks. To promote reproducibility, the code and anonymized dataset are publicly available.

## 1 Introduction

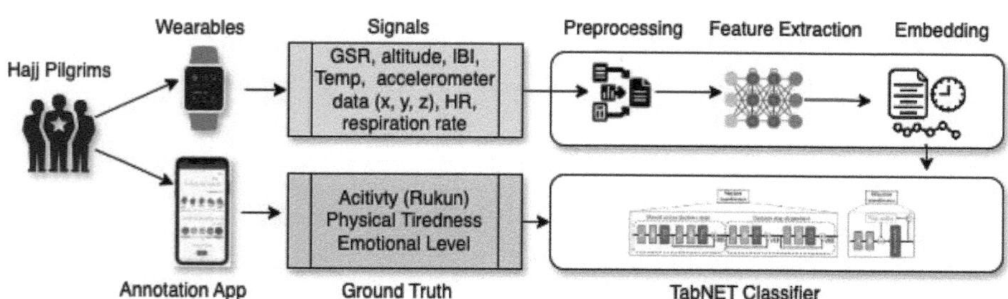


**Fig. 1.** Overview of the Proposed Method: Predict Physical Tiredness Level, Emotional Mood Level, and Rukun (Hajj Ritual) Activities using LSTM and TabNet models.

Supported by organization x.


A. Soylu et al. (Eds.): MobiQuitous 2024, LNICST 634, pp. 22–36, 2026.
https://doi.org/10.1007/978-3-032-10554-7_2

Ensuring the health and well-being of Hajj pilgrims is of paramount importance due to the immense physical and emotional demands of the pilgrimage [7]. Each year, approximately 2.5 million Muslims from around the world gather in Mecca, making Hajj one of the largest annual gatherings globally [21]. This convergence poses significant health management challenges, including the prevention of incidents such as stampedes, heat stress, and exacerbations of chronic conditions [8]. For instance, cardiovascular diseases alone account for over 60% of ICU hospitalizations during Hajj, with older pilgrims being particularly vulnerable [4]. In 2002, it was reported that 31% of pilgrims aged 65 to 74 had diabetes, 27.5% had hypertension, and 11.4% had hypercholesterolemia, highlighting the prevalence of chronic diseases among participants [4].

Real-time health monitoring using wearable devices presents a proactive solution to these risks by continuously tracking vital signs and physiological parameters, allowing for timely interventions and informed decision-making. One recent study [3] demonstrated the use of mobile GPS and physiological data from wearable sensors to classify Hajj activities, fatigue levels, and emotional states with promising accuracy levels. This system achieved a minimum of 75% accuracy for activity recognition and fatigue detection [3,6]. Our research builds upon this foundation by employing a two-step deep neural network to further enhance prediction accuracy for real-time health monitoring of Hajj pilgrims. This integration of advanced machine learning techniques with wearable technology not only improves the precision of health assessments but also ensures that potential health issues are detected early [13,16].

Recent advancements in wearable signal processing and deep learning techniques offer significant potential in mitigating the health risks associated with large gatherings like Hajj. Modern wearable devices can now capture a wide range of physiological signals, such as heart rate variability, skin temperature, and electrodermal activity, with high precision [18]. These signals can be processed using sophisticated algorithms to detect early signs of fatigue, stress, and other health issues. Deep learning techniques, particularly those involving recurrent neural networks (RNN) and convolutional neural networks (CNN), have shown remarkable success in analyzing time-series data from wearables [11,17,25]. Studies have demonstrated that these models can accurately predict mental and physical states, enhancing the ability to provide timely health interventions [17,25]. Nakisa et al. [17] utilized multimodal deep learning to achieve high accuracy in emotion recognition from physiological signals, while Zhang et al. [25] developed a deep temporal model for mental fatigue detection. By leveraging these advanced techniques, our research aims to deliver a robust health monitoring system that not only tracks real-time physiological data but also provides actionable insights to improve the safety and well-being of Hajj pilgrims.

Despite these advancements, there are still significant limitations in the current state-of-the-art wearables and deep learning technologies [14]. Many existing systems struggle with the complexity and variability of physiological signals, leading to issues such as overfitting, poor generalization across different individuals, and limited accuracy in real-world settings. Furthermore, most models do not adequately address the integration of diverse physiological data streams or fail to adapt to the dynamic conditions experienced by Hajj pilgrims [7,15].

To overcome these challenges, we propose a two-step deep neural network technique that enhances the robustness and accuracy of health monitoring for Hajj pilgrims. In the first step, advanced pre-processing methods are employed, incorporating deep neural embedding to effectively represent complex physiological data. This is followed by the second step, where a complex neural network model, Attentive Interpretable Tabular Learning (TabNet) [9], is fine-tuned to predict three major health outcomes: (a) physical tiredness level, (b) emotional mood level, and (c) Rukun (Hajj ritual) activity. TabNet's ability to handle tabular data with high interpretability and accuracy makes it an ideal choice for this application. Our proposed framework was validated on a real-time wearable sensor dataset collected from 19 individuals actually performing Hajj rituals in Mecca. This validation demonstrated significant improvements in prediction accuracy and model robustness compared to existing methods. By addressing the limitations of previous approaches, our model provides a comprehensive solution that effectively monitors the health status of pilgrims, ensuring timely interventions and enhancing overall safety.

## 2   Related Work

### 2.1   Wearable-Based Fatigue Detection

Recent research on wearable-based fatigue detection frameworks has shown significant advancements in monitoring physiological sensor signals (such as smartwatches, fitness trackers, and specialized medical sensors used to collect data on heart rate, electrodermal activity, and skin temperature). Studies have utilized electroencephalograms, electrocardiograms, and photoplethysmograms to develop models that can accurately predict fatigue levels based on changes in these physiological parameters [1]. Techniques such as supervised machine learning and deep learning have been predominant, with SVM and CNN frequently employed to enhance the accuracy of fatigue detection [11,13]. Most wearable-based fatigue detection models focus on binary classification, while some studies have explored multilevel classification, aiming to differentiate between various levels of fatigue intensity [19]. Despite the progress, existing models often face challenges such as variability in individual physiological responses and environmental factors affecting the reliability of the collected data. The integration of multimodal data and real-time processing capabilities has shown promise in improving the robustness and applicability of these models in real-world settings [17,26]. Proposed model addresses these issues by incorporating advanced pre-processing methods with deep neural embeddings and utilizing the Attentive Interpretable Tabular Learning (TabNet) model.

### 2.2   Wearable Based Activity Recognition

Wearable based Human Activity Recognition (HAR), particularly using Inertial Measurement Units (IMUs), has seen significant progress in recent years

[2, 10, 12, 20, 24]. IMU-based HAR approaches utilize accelerometer and gyroscope data to monitor and classify human activities. Studies such as Wang et al. have demonstrated the effectiveness of CNN combined with Bi-LSTM models in capturing spatial and temporal features from IMU data for activity recognition [22]. Additionally, researchers like Yu et al. and Ihianle et al. have shown that integrating data from multiple IMUs can enhance the accuracy of HAR systems by providing more comprehensive movement data [12, 24]. More recently, Gao et al. introduced a dual attention network that integrates both channel and temporal attention to capture complex patterns from accelerometer and gyroscope data [10]. Similarly, Tang et al. proposed a triple cross-domain attention framework to enhance feature extraction across sensor dimensions [20]. Another notable approach by Al-qaness et al. incorporated RNNs with attention modules to improve time-series feature extraction for wearable HAR [2]. Despite these advancements, existing models often struggle with handling the variability in sensor data across different individuals and activities. Our proposed method improves upon these limitations by utilizing a two-step deep neural network approach that incorporates advanced preprocessing and the TabNet model, leading to more accurate and generalized activity recognition. The process flow of our proposed method is illustrated in Fig. 1.

## 3   Data Acquisition

### 3.1   Wearable Physiological Sensor Data Collection

In this study, the acquisition of physiological data was facilitated using commercially available wearable sensors, specifically the Zephyr belt-type BioHarness and the Empatica E4 wristband. These sensors were chosen based on their compatibility with Android APIs, which allowed seamless integration with our developed mobile application, and their capability to continuously and in real-time monitor a broad spectrum of physiological signals. The Zephyr BioHarness sensor, worn on the chest, is particularly effective in measuring respiration rate, though it requires direct skin contact for accurate readings, making it suitable for contexts where bare-chest conditions are acceptable. The Empatica E4 wristband, on the other hand, measures various physiological parameters including skin temperature and blood volume pulse using an infrared thermopile sensor with high sensitivity.

A bespoke mobile application was developed for Android devices using Java. This application was designed to record and synchronize location data, raw physiological signals, and user inputs related to their activities and physical and emotional states during the Hajj pilgrimage. The app continuously collected data via Bluetooth connections with the sensors, ensuring real-time monitoring. The collected physiological data was securely stored in the mobile devices and periodically uploaded to a central server for further analysis. The data included signals such as heart rate (HR), heart rate variability (HRV), respiration rate, skin temperature, and electrodermal activity (EDA), where applicable. This setup ensured comprehensive monitoring of the participants' physiological states during the Hajj rituals.

### 3.2   Data Annotation

In addition to physiological data collection, the study involved extensive data annotation to contextualize the physiological readings. A dedicated demographic user interface (UI) within the mobile application captured essential demographic details from each participant, including their name, gender, nationality, and responses to health-related questions such as their history of chronic diseases, frequency of exercise, and prior experience with Hajj or Umra.

Furthermore, the application featured an annotation user interface (UI) designed for participants to log their activities and subjective experiences. This interface allowed participants to record specific Hajj activities such as Tawaf, Saai, various types of prayers (Sunna and Fard), and supplications (Doaa). They also provided self-assessments of their fatigue levels on a visual discrete scale from 1 (not tired) to 5 (extremely tired) and their emotional status on a continuous scale from 0 (extremely negative) to 100 (extremely positive). This annotation process was integral to the study, as it enabled the correlation of physiological signals with specific activities and emotional states, thus providing a richer understanding of the participants' experiences during the Hajj pilgrimage. All annotated data were timestamped and synchronized with the physiological data, ensuring a cohesive dataset for subsequent analysis.

## 4   Two-Step Deep Learning Approach for Prediction

### 4.1   Sensor Signals

The final dataset comprises meticulously cleaned physiological data collected during the Hajj pilgrimage from 19 participants. This dataset includes features such as galvanic skin response (GSR), altitude, peak acceleration, inter-beat interval (IBI), temperature (TEMP), three-axis accelerometer data (X, Y, Z), heart rate (HR), respiration rate, and heart rate variability (HRV). These features were collected under diverse conditions, providing a robust dataset for comprehensive analysis. The Empatica E4 wristband was equipped with four sensors, each operating at different sampling frequencies: Blood Volume Pulse (BVP) sensor at 64 Hz, Temperature sensor at 4 Hz, Accelerometer at 32 Hz, and Electrodermal Activity (EDA) sensor at 4 Hz. Conversely, the Zephyr Bio-Harness belt logged data at a frequency of 1 Hz. Additionally, location data was recorded at a frequency of 0.1 Hz. Given the varied sampling rates, a specialized protocol for handling missing values and aligning the timestamps of different signals was formulated. This involved techniques such as linear interpolation, data resampling, and the use of imputation algorithms to ensure temporal alignment and data integrity across all sensors.

### 4.2   Preprocessing

Preprocessing is essential to ensure data quality and involves several steps. Initially, we handle anomalies by identifying and addressing outliers and missing values. Using a Z-score normalization method, we standardize the physiological measurements to ensure consistency. Anomalies in the physiological data (e.g., temperature, heart rate, and respiration rate) were identified and corrected, with outliers replaced by the mean of the 10 nearest non-anomalous values to maintain data integrity and minimize noise. The data is then grouped by participant IDs, selecting the ID with the least amount of anomalies for further analysis. Features are aggregated into sequences for each participant, using the numerical features: GSR, altitude, peak acceleration, IBI, TEMP, X, Y, Z, HR, respiration rate, and HRV. This preprocessing step ensures that the dataset is clean and standardized, ready for use in the subsequent stages of our proposed method.

## 4.3    Data Labels Definition

**Physical Tiredness Level.** The Physical Tiredness Level classification task involved predicting one of five possible values, ranging from 1 (not tired at all) to 5 (extremely tired).

**Emotional Mood Level.** The Emotional Mood Level classification task aimed to predict the emotional status of the participants, categorized into three classes: 0 (very negative and negative), 1 (neutral), and 2 (positive and very positive).

**Rukun (Hajj Ritual) Activity.** The Rukun (Hajj Ritual) Activity classification task involved predicting one of 16 specific Hajj-related activities performed by the participants.

By ensuring the consistency of the classification tasks across the data acquisition and processing stages, we ensure that our analysis accurately reflects the diverse physiological states and activities of the participants during the Hajj pilgrimage.

## 4.4    Feature Extraction and Embedding Generation Using LSTM

We utilize a Long Short-Term Memory (LSTM) model to capture temporal patterns in the physiological data. The LSTM model is chosen due to its capability of learning complex patterns in time series data, making it ideal for extracting features that encapsulate temporal dynamics. These embeddings represent the underlying physiological state of each participant over time, providing a rich feature set for subsequent classification tasks.

**Problem Formulation.** Given a set of time-series physiological data $X = \{x_1, x_2, \ldots, x_T\}$, where $x_t$ represents the physiological measurements at time $t$, our objective is to learn a function $f : X \rightarrow E$, where $E$ is the embedding space. The LSTM model is employed to map the input sequence $X$ to a fixed-length embedding vector $e \in \mathbb{R}^d$, which encapsulates the temporal dependencies and underlying patterns in the data.

**LSTM Architecture.** The LSTM architecture consists of several layers designed to capture different aspects of temporal relationships within the data. Specifically, our LSTM model includes:

- **Input Layer:** Takes in the standardized physiological features $X = \{x_1, \ldots, x_T\}$.
- **LSTM Layers:** Two LSTM layers with 16 units each, formulated as follows:

$$h_t = \sigma(W_{ih}x_t + W_{hh}h_{t-1} + b_h)$$

where $h_t$ is the hidden state at time $t$, $W_{ih}$ and $W_{hh}$ are the weight matrices, and $b_h$ is the bias term.
- **Dropout Layer:** A dropout layer with a rate of 0.2 to prevent overfitting.
- **Dense Layer:** A fully connected layer that produces the embeddings $e$:

$$e = W_{ho}h_T + b_o$$

where $h_T$ is the hidden state of the last LSTM unit, $W_{ho}$ is the weight matrix, and $b_o$ is the bias term.

The training procedure involves splitting the dataset into training and validation sets, optimizing hyperparameters such as learning rate and batch size to achieve the best performance. The model is trained using the Adam optimizer and mean squared error loss.

**Utilization of LSTM-Generated Embeddings.** Embeddings generated by the LSTM model encapsulate the temporal features extracted from the physiological data. These embeddings serve as compact and informative representations of the data, which are then used for classification. The embeddings $e$ are passed to a downstream classification model, where they are used to predict various outcomes, such as activity recognition, fatigue level, and emotional status. This approach leverages the temporal dynamics captured by the LSTM to enhance the performance of the classification tasks.

### 4.5  TabNet Model for Classification

To build robust classification models for physical tiredness level, emotional mood, and the type of ritual performed, we employed TabNet, a deep learning model specifically designed for tabular data. TabNet was chosen for its ability to integrate attention mechanisms to select relevant features, making it particularly effective for handling diverse and high-dimensional tabular datasets, such as the physiological data embeddings generated in the previous section.

TabNet employs sequential attention to select which features to process at each decision step, effectively combining the interpretability of decision trees with the representational power of neural networks. Given the embeddings $e$ generated by the LSTM model, the objective of the TabNet model is to map these embeddings to three different classification outputs: physical tiredness level, emotional mood, and the type of ritual performed. Mathematically, this can be defined as:

$$f_{\text{TabNet}} : e \rightarrow \{y_1, y_2, y_3\}$$

where $e \in \mathbb{R}^d$ represents the LSTM-generated embeddings, and $y_1, y_2, y_3$ are the classification outputs for physical tiredness level, emotional mood, and the type of ritual performed, respectively. Each output is determined through a series of decision steps, with attention mechanisms dynamically selecting the most relevant features from $e$ at each step.

The TabNet model addresses several limitations of existing classification methods. Traditional classifiers often struggle with high-dimensional and complex data, failing to capture intricate feature interactions. TabNet's use of attention mechanisms ensures that only the most relevant features are considered at each decision step, reducing overfitting and enhancing interpretability. Additionally, the model's sequential processing of features allows it to handle missing values more effectively and to provide insights into feature importance, which is crucial for understanding the physiological factors influencing each classification task. By combining the temporal embeddings from the LSTM with TabNet's robust feature selection and classification capabilities, we achieve a comprehensive and accurate classification system for monitoring the health and activities of Hajj pilgrims.

## 5 Experimental Evaluation

This section describes the experiments conducted to evaluate the effectiveness of the proposed method.

### 5.1 Data Description

The dataset used in this study comprises physiological data collected from 19 participants during the Hajj pilgrimage. The participants included a diverse demographic, with ages ranging from 20 to 65 years, representing different nationalities and genders. The physiological measurements captured include galvanic skin response (GSR), altitude, peak acceleration, inter-beat interval (IBI), temperature (TEMP), three-axis accelerometer data (X, Y, Z), heart rate (HR), respiration rate, and heart rate variability (HRV).

The data collection was facilitated using the Zephyr BioHarness belt and the Empatica E4 wristband. The Zephyr BioHarness, worn on the chest, provided measurements at a frequency of 1 Hz, including respiration rate and heart rate. The Empatica E4 wristband, worn on the wrist, captured data at varying frequencies: Blood Volume Pulse (BVP) at 64 Hz, Temperature at 4 Hz, Accelerometer at 32 Hz, and Electrodermal Activity (EDA) at 4 Hz. Additionally, location data was recorded at a frequency of 0.1 Hz.

## 5.2  Models Development

Our proposed two-step algorithm involves feature extraction using an LSTM model followed by classification using the TabNet model. The LSTM model is designed to capture the temporal dependencies in the physiological data, generating embeddings that encapsulate the dynamic nature of the signals. These embeddings are then utilized by the TabNet model, which leverages attention mechanisms to select relevant features and perform robust classification.

We developed three classifiers using this two-step approach:

- *Physical Tiredness Level Classification*: Predicts one of five fatigue levels, ranging from 1 (not tired at all) to 5 (extremely tired).
- *Emotional Mood Level Classification*: Predicts one of three emotional states: 0 (very negative and negative), 1 (neutral), and 2 (positive and very positive).
- *Rukun (Hajj Ritual) Activity Recognition*: Predicts one of 16 specific Hajj-related activities performed by the participants.

This method ensures that the temporal patterns in the physiological signals are effectively captured and used to enhance the accuracy and robustness of the classification models, thereby providing comprehensive monitoring of the participants' health and activities during the Hajj pilgrimage.

## 5.3  Evaluation Metrics

To evaluate the performance of our models, we used accuracy, precision, recall, and F1-score. These metrics were calculated and optimized during the model training process using techniques such as hyperparameter tuning and cross-validation to ensure the robustness and reliability of our predictive models. The evaluation metrics are defined as follows:

Accuracy: Measures the overall correctness of the model by calculating the ratio of correctly predicted instances to the total instances.

$$\text{Accuracy} = \frac{TP + TN}{TP + TN + FP + FN} \tag{1}$$

where TP is the number of true positives, TN is the number of true negatives, FP is the number of false positives, and FN is the number of false negatives.

Precision: Indicates the model's ability to avoid false positives by calculating the ratio of true positive predictions to the total predicted positives.

$$\text{Precision} = \frac{TP}{TP + FP} \tag{2}$$

Recall (Sensitivity): Reflects the model's capability to identify all relevant instances by calculating the ratio of true positive predictions to the total actual positives.

$$\text{Recall} = \frac{TP}{TP + FN} \tag{3}$$

F1-score: Provides a balanced measure of performance by considering both precision and recall. It is calculated as the harmonic mean of precision and recall.

$$\text{F1-score} = 2 \cdot \frac{\text{Precision} \cdot \text{Recall}}{\text{Precision} + \text{Recall}} \tag{4}$$

These metrics were optimized through hyperparameter tuning and validated using cross-validation techniques to enhance model robustness and ensure reliable performance across different data splits.

## 5.4   Model Training

The LSTM model was trained with two layers, each containing 16 units, over a maximum of 10 epochs with early stopping based on validation loss and a patience of 10 epochs, and a batch size of 32. The model demonstrated a good fit, with training and validation accuracy curves closely following each other, indicating minimal overfitting. The embeddings extracted from the LSTM model were then used as input for the TabNet classifier. The TabNet classifier was trained with $n_d$ and $n_a$ set to 8, three decision steps (two independent and two shared), and a maximum learning rate of 0.01 with a batch-level scheduler, over a maximum of 30 epochs with early stopping based on the validation set and a patience of 10. The dataset was divided into 67% for training, and 33% for testing, ensuring that data from each participant was contained only within one of these splits to prevent data leakage. This approach guarantees that no participant's data appears in both the training and testing sets, reducing the risk of overfitting and improving the model's ability to generalize to unseen data. We took specific precautions to avoid data leakage by ensuring that the data splitting was done at the participant level. This means that all time-series data from a single participant were included in either the training, validation, or testing set, but never in more than one. This approach prevents any overlap between training and testing data, which is crucial in time-series data to maintain the integrity of the evaluation.

## 5.5   Results and Discussion

**Physical Tiredness Level Classification.** The physical tiredness level classification task involved predicting one of five possible values, ranging from 1 (not tired at all) to 5 (extremely tired).The results demonstrate high precision, recall, and F1-scores across most classes, particularly for classes 1 and 2. However, the performance drops for classes 4 and 5, which have fewer samples, suggesting the need for more balanced data collection (Fig. 2, left). These findings indicate that while the model is highly effective in distinguishing lower tiredness levels, it struggles with higher tiredness levels due to sample imbalance.

**Emotional Mood Level Classification.** The emotional mood dataset was mapped into three classes for better distribution: 0 (very negative and negative),

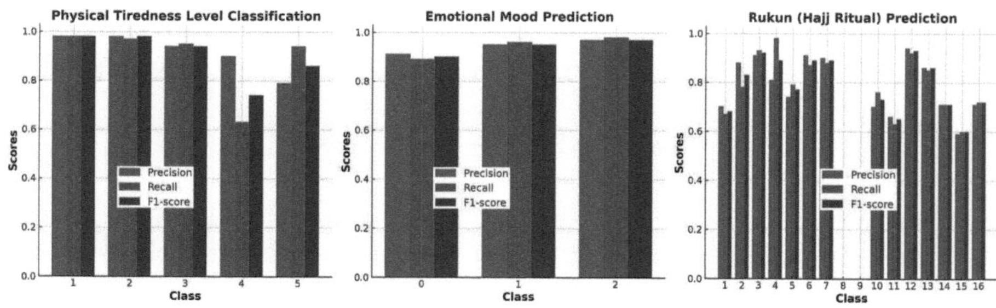

**Fig. 2.** Classification Results: (left) Physical Tiredness Level Classification, (middle) Emotional Mood Classification, and (right) Rukun (Hajj Ritual) Activity Prediction. The bar charts display the Precision, Recall, and F1-score for each class. Our model's performance is indicated in red, and Al-Shaery's model in green.

1 (neutral), and 2 (positive and very positive). Our model achieved an average accuracy of 95%, with high precision, recall, and F1-scores across all classes (Fig. 2, middle).

The results highlight the model's strong performance in predicting emotional mood, with high precision, recall, and F1-scores across all classes. The slightly lower precision and recall for class 0 indicate that the model may occasionally confuse very negative/negative moods with neutral or positive moods, likely due to the inherent subjectivity and variability in mood data.

**Rukun (Hajj Ritual) Activity Recognition.** The rukun classification task involved predicting one of the 16 activities (rukun) performed by participants. Our model achieved an average accuracy of 95%, with varying performance across different classes.

The results (Fig. 2, right) show high variability in the model's performance across different classes. For example, classes 8 and 9 have very low precision and recall due to the small number of samples, highlighting the need for more data in these categories. The model performs well for more common activities, such as classes 3, 4, and 12, indicating its effectiveness in recognizing frequently performed rituals. The lower performance in less common activities suggests that further data collection and model refinement are necessary.

## 5.6   Comparisons with State-of-the-Art

To evaluate the performance of our proposed two-step LSTM TabNet model, we compared it against several baseline state-of-the-art algorithms across three classification tasks: fatigue level, emotional status, and activity recognition (Fig. 1)

Our proposed LSTM TabNet model outperforms several state-of-the-art algorithms in both emotional status and activity recognition tasks and shows competitive performance in fatigue level classification. For fatigue level classification,

**Table 1.** Comparison of classification performances with state-of-art. CAE-M - Convolutional Autoencoding Memcry network, OCSVM - One-Class Support Vector Machine, OCSLT - One-Class Single Layer LSTM.

| Task | Study | ML Model | Acc (%) |
|---|---|---|---|
| Fatigue | Zhang et al. [26] | CAE-M | 82.9 |
| | Zhang et al. [26] | OCSVM | 53.9 |
| | Zhang et al. [26] | OCSLT | 71.85 |
| | **Al-Shaery** [3] | **Bidirectional LSTM** | **98.5** |
| | Our Model | LSTM TabNet | 97.0 |
| Emotion | Nakisa et al. [17] | ConvNet LSTM | 71.61 |
| | Xing et al. [23] | LSTM | 81.1 |
| | Alhagry et al. [5] | LSTM RNN | 72.06 |
| | Al-Shaery et al. [3] | Bidirectional LSTM | 64.5 |
| | **Our Model** | **LSTM TabNet** | **95.0** |
| Activity | Al-Shaery et al. [3] | Bidirectional LSTM | 83.0 |
| | **Our Model** | **LSTM TabNet** | **95.0** |

our model achieved an accuracy of 97.0%, which is slightly lower than the Bidirectional LSTM model [3]. However, it significantly outperforms other models like the CAE-M, OCSVM, and OCSLT models by Zhang et al. [26], which achieved accuracies of 82.9%, 53.9%, and 71.85% respectively. The superior performance of the Bidirectional LSTM can be attributed to its ability to capture bidirectional dependencies in the data, which might be critical for accurately predicting fatigue levels.

In the emotional status classification task, our model achieved an accuracy of 95.0%, outperforming other models such as the ConvNet LSTM by Nakisa et al. [17], LSTM by Xing et al. [23], and LSTM RNN by Alhagry et al. [5], which achieved accuracies of 71.61%, 81.1%, and 72.06% respectively. The higher accuracy of our model can be attributed to the combination of LSTM for capturing temporal dependencies and TabNet for feature selection, which allows for a more nuanced understanding of the emotional states reflected in the physiological data. The significantly lower performance of the Bidirectional LSTM model by Al-Shaery et al. [3], with an accuracy of 64.5%, suggests that our model's integration of TabNet provided substantial improvements in handling the complex emotional data.

For activity recognition, our model achieved an accuracy of 95.0%, outperforming the Bidirectional LSTM model by Al-Shaery et al. [3], which achieved an accuracy of 83.0%. This improvement can be attributed to TabNet's ability to dynamically select relevant features at each decision step, which enhances the model's ability to accurately classify a diverse set of activities.

# 6    Discussion and Future Works

The results of our study demonstrate the potential of the LSTM-to-TabNet model in effectively predicting physical tiredness level, emotional mood level, and rukun (Hajj ritual) activities using physiological data. While the dataset consists of 19 participants, the demographic diversity (ages 2065, various nationalities, and health statuses) helps to generalize the model to different physiological states. The selection of participants was based on data quality considerations; only those with the least amount of unclean or misleading data (e.g., negative heart rates, negative temperatures, or significant periods of missing recordings) were included to ensure the integrity and reliability of the model's training. This approach aimed to maximize the model's performance by focusing on high-quality, consistent data. Our model achieved high accuracy in both physical tiredness and emotional mood classification, suggesting that the physiological signals captured are strong indicators of these states. However, the moderate performance in rukun classification highlights the need for further refinement, possibly through the inclusion of additional features and/or participants, and more sophisticated modeling.

One of the primary challenges observed was the imbalance in class distributions, particularly for certain rukun activities, which adversely affected the model's performance. Addressing this imbalance through more diverse data collection is essential to enhance model generalization. Additionally, the inherent subjectivity and variability in mood data pose challenges that require further exploration of supplementary contextual or behavioral data to improve emotional state predictions.

Future work will focus on overcoming these limitations by exploring advanced deep learning architectures and data augmentation techniques, thereby enhancing the predictive capabilities, robustness, and reliability of the model in real-world applications. By improving our models, we aim to develop a comprehensive health monitoring system that can provide timely interventions, enhancing the overall safety and well-being of Hajj pilgrims. Another important avenue for future research is the development of a mobile application that integrates the three classifiers—physical tiredness, emotional mood level, and ritual performed (rukun)—to provide real-time recommendations to pilgrims. This advisory tool will help individuals understand their readiness to perform Hajj tasks, minimizing risks of injuries, deaths, and other health-related issues during the pilgrimage, significantly enhancing the safety and experience of millions of Muslims undertaking the Hajj pilgrimage each year.

# 7    Conclusion

We presented a novel approach for predicting physical tiredness level, emotional mood, and rukun (Hajj ritual) activities using physiological data from the Hajj Crowd Activity dataset. By combining LSTM and TabNet models, we effectively captured temporal dependencies and leveraged feature selection to achieve high classification accuracy. The model demonstrated balanced performance in emotional mood classification with a validation accuracy of 84.3% and an F1-score of 84.2%. This method addresses challenges in classifying complex physiological signals and highlights its potential in real-world applications, particularly in enhancing safety and wellbeing during the Hajj pilgrimage. Future work aims to develop a mobile application integrating these classifiers to provide real-time recommendations, minimizing health risks and improving the overall Hajj experience for millions of Muslims annually.

## 8  Reproducibility

We made the data and code public in github following the NeurIPS 2019 Reproducibility program guidelines: https://github.com/NazimBL/A-Two-Step-DNN-Approach-for-Real-Time-Context-Aware-Health-Monitoring-of-Hajj-Pilgrims.

**Acknowledgement.** The source codes and the de-identified data will be publicly shared upon acceptance.

## References


1. Adão Martins, N.R., AnnaLeim, S., Spengler, C.M., Rossi, R.M.: Fatigue monitoring through wearables: a state-of-the-art review. Front. Physiol. **12** (2021). https://doi.org/10.3389/fphys.2021.790292
2. Al-qaness, M.A., Dahou, A., Abd Elaziz, M., Helmi, A.: Multi-resatt: multilevel residual network with attention for human activity recognition using wearable sensors. TII **19**(1), 144–152 (2022)
3. Al-Shaery, A.M., et al.: Real-time pilgrims management using wearable physiological sensors, mobile technology and artificial intelligence. IEEE Access **10**, 120891–120900 (2022). https://doi.org/10.1109/ACCESS.2022.3221771
4. Al Shimemeri, A.: Cardiovascular disease in hajj pilgrims. J. Saudi Heart Assoc. **24**(2), 123–127 (2012). https://doi.org/10.1016/j.jsha.2011.12.005
5. Alhagry, S., Aly, A.: Emotion recognition based on EEG using LSTM recurrent neural network. Int. J. Adv. Comput. Sci. Appl. **8**(10), 1–4 (2017)
6. Alhawsawi, A.N., Ahmad, A., Rehman, F.U., Qamar, A.M., Qadah, T.M., Yasein, M.S.: Surveying challenges for enhancing precision in hajj crowd simulation. Preprint (2020). https://ssrn.com/abstract=4645327
7. Alhawsawi, A.N., Ahmad, A., Rehman, F.U., Qamar, A.M., Qadah, T.M., Yasein, M.S.: Surveying challenges for enhancing precision in hajj crowd simulation. Preprint (2021). https://ssrn.com/abstract=4645327
8. Arabi, Y.M., Sameer, M.A.H.: Emergency room to the intensive care unit in hajj. The chain of life. Saudi Med. J. **27**(7), 937–941 (2006)
9. Arik, S.Ö., Pfister, T.: Tabnet: attentive interpretable tabular learning. In: Proceedings of the AAAI Conference on Artificial Intelligence, vol. 35, no. 8, pp. 6679–6687 (2021). https://doi.org/10.1609/aaai.v35i8.16826

10. Gao, W., Zhang, L., Teng, Q., He, J., Wu, H.: Danhar: dual attention network for multimodal human activity recognition using wearable sensors. Appl. Soft Comput. **111**, 107728 (2021)
11. Hossain, M.S., Muhammad, G., Guizani, N.: Explainable AI and mass surveillance system-based healthcare framework to combat covid-19 like pandemics. IEEE Network **34**(4), 126–132 (2019). https://doi.org/10.1109/MNET.011.2000174
12. Ihianle, I.K., Usman, M., Olaleye, S.A., Iheabunike, C., Aniyikaiye, T.E.: A deep learning approach for human activities recognition from multimodal sensing devices. IEEE Access **8**, 179028–179038 (2020)
13. Islam, S.M.R., Kwak, D., Kabir, M.H., Hossain, M., Kwak, K.S.: The internet of things for health care: a comprehensive survey. IEEE Access **3**, 678–708 (2021). https://doi.org/10.1109/ACCESS.2021.3010557
14. Lopez, G., Rios, V.H., Fuentes, J.M., Civit, A.: Wearable technologies for health monitoring of elderly people: a review. Int. J. Comput. Appl. **68**(21), 21–25 (2019). https://doi.org/10.5120/ijca20217914
15. Mohammad, G., Mostafa, A., Hossain, M.S.: Enabling explainable AI in healthcare through blockchain and smart contracts. IEEE Access **6**, 14650–14658 (2018). https://doi.org/10.1109/ACCESS.2018.2813490
16. Mukhopadhyay, S.C.: Wearable sensors for human activity monitoring: a review. IEEE Sens. J. **19**(3), 1324–1337 (2018). https://doi.org/10.1109/JSEN.2018.2873240
17. Nakisa, B., Rastgoo, M.N., Rakotonirainy, A., Maire, F., Chandran, V.: Automatic emotion recognition using temporal multimodal deep learning. IEEE Access **8**, 225463–225474 (2020)
18. Patel, S., Park, H., Bonato, P., Chan, L., Rodgers, M.: A review of wearable sensors and systems with application in rehabilitation. J. Neuroeng. Rehabil. **9**, 21 (2020). https://doi.org/10.1186/1743-0003-9-21
19. Maman, E.S., Sandars, J., Cheung, B., Fowler, P., Darzi, A., Patel, R.: Wearable-based fatigue detection frameworks for sports and workplaces: state-of-the-art and research needs. IEEE Sens. J. **20**(15), 8454–8467 (2020). https://doi.org/10.1109/JSEN.2020.2992105
20. Tang, Y., Zhang, L., Teng, Q., Min, F., Song, A.: Triple cross-domain attention on human activity recognition using wearable sensors. TETCI **6**(5), 1167–1176 (2022)
21. Turan, K.: It is time to reform the management of the hajj. Technical report, Brookings Inst., Washington, DC, USA (2020). https://www.brookings.edu/opinions/it-is-time-to-reform-the-management-of-the-hajj/
22. Wang, J., Chen, Y., Hao, X., Peng, X., Hu, L.G.: Deep learning for sensor-based activity recognition: a survey. Pattern Recognit. Lett. **119**, 3–11 (2019)
23. Xing, X., Li, Z., Xu, T., Shu, L., Hu, B., Xu, X.: SAE+LSTM: a new framework for emotion recognition from multi-channel EEG. Front. Neurorobot. **13**, 37 (2019)
24. Yu, S., Qin, L.: Human activity recognition with smartphone inertial sensors using BIDIR-LSTM networks. In: ICMCCE, pp. 219–224. IEEE (2018)
25. Zhang, Y., Chen, Y., Pan, Z.: A deep temporal model for mental fatigue detection. In: Proceedings of the IEEE International Conference on Systems, Man, and Cybernetics (SMC), pp. 1879–1884 (2018)
26. Zhang, Y., Chen, Y., Pan, Z.: A deep temporal model for mental fatigue detection. In: Proceedings of IEEE International Conference on Systems, Man, and Cybernetics (SMC), pp. 1879–1884 (2018)

# Environment Independent Fall Detection with WiFi Streams

Rui Zhou[✉], Yue Luo, Chenxu Liu, and Songlin Li

University of Electronic Science and Technology of China, Chengdu, China
ruizhou@uestc.edu.cn

**Abstract.** Fall detection is of great importance for elderly care. WiFi-based fall detection has advantages over visions and wearables wrt. privacy protection, convenience, low-cost and ubiquity. However, environment dependence is a major challenge that hinders the real-world deployment of such systems. In this paper, we investigate the problems and present an environment independent fall detection method exploiting WiFi Channel State Information (CSI). To achieve environment independence, we propose a feature disentanglement neural network to separate the motion-related features and the environment-related features. Only the motion-related features are extracted to classify falls and non-falls. To achieve real-time fall detection, we propose an online data segmentation method to detect and extract the motion segments from continuous CSI streams automatically. To mitigate the scarcity of fall data and improve the robustness of the model, we design a composite Autoencoder to generate virtual fall samples by adding random noise to real fall samples. Extensive real-world evaluations show that the proposed method is free of training in new environments and achieves real-time fall detection independent of users, locations, rooms, and times.

**Keywords:** Channel State Information · Environment independence · Fall detection · Feature disentanglement · Virtual data generation

## 1 Introduction

Falls are major safety threats to the elderly. It is of great significance to detect falls automatically and take timely rescue. In the past years, a large number of studies on fall detection have been carried out, which can be categorized as vision-based, wearable-based and ambient sensor-based. Vision-based approaches deploy cameras to detect falls by analyzing the images [2,17]. Wearable-based approaches attach specific wearable sensors to the users to detect falls by analyzing the sequential sensor data [13,16]. Ambient sensor-based solutions detect falls by analyzing the ambient wireless signals or sounds [19,21]. Fall detection based on wearables requires the users to carry the wearables all the time, which may cause inconvenience and reluctance. Fall detection based on visions may incur privacy violations, hence is not suitable for private places.

© ICST Institute for Computer Sciences, Social Informatics and Telecommunications Engineering 2026
Published by Springer Nature Switzerland AG 2026. All Rights Reserved
A. Soylu et al. (Eds.): MobiQuitous 2024, LNICST 634, pp. 37–57, 2026.
https://doi.org/10.1007/978-3-032-10554-7_3

Ambient sensor-based solutions require to install a number of sensors in the environment, incurring high cost. Free of these limitations, wireless fall detection has attracted growing attention in recent years. Many studies on wireless fall detection as well as wireless sensing have emerged [6,11].

Wireless fall detection can be realized through a variety of technologies, such as millimeter wave [18], acoustic [10] and WiFi [19,21]. Due to ubiquity and low-cost, WiFi is considered as one of the most promising technologies. Compared with visions, WiFi fall detection avoids privacy violations and can work under any light conditions. Compared with wearables, WiFi fall detection is contactless and more friendly to the elderly. Compared with ambient sensors and other wireless solutions, WiFi fall detection has a lower cost and longer range. WiFi fall detection systems usually exploit Channel State Information (CSI) to detect falls. CSI depicts the amplitude and the phase on different frequency channels [5,22], providing finer-grained information of the propagation environment. Investigating CSI, we can capture the changes in the surrounding environment accurately. Although promising results have been achieved by WiFi fall detection, there still are a few unsolved challenges.

(1) *How to achieve environment independence?* Most WiFi fall detection systems build the fall detection model with supervised learning. Although performing well in the training environments, they degrade significantly in different environments due to the shift of feature distributions. To achieve robustness, the fall detection model should be environment independent and work properly in unseen environments without re-training.

(2) *How to achieve real-time fall detection from WiFi streams?* Many WiFi fall detection systems work in offline mode. As falls may happen at any time, it is important to detect falls in real-time and take timely rescue. Some systems try to achieve fall detection in real-time, but they often involve complex computation and assume high stableness of the WiFi devices and the surroundings. In reality, there may be packet losses, device jams, and various interferences from the environment, making it difficult to segment the motion data from WiFi streams.

(3) *How to overcome the scarcity of fall samples?* Compared with daily activities, fall data are much more difficult to collect, resulting in the lack of them. Fall detection can be regarded as binary classification. The imbalance of positive and negative samples may degrade the performance. However, collecting a large number of fall samples is impractical.

In this paper, we focus on these problems and propose an environment independent fall detection method. We propose a feature disentanglement network based on Convolutional Neural Networks (CNN), to separate the motion-related features and the environment-related features and diminish the influence of the environments. We take CSI amplitude as the measurement and propose an online data segmentation method to capture the motion segments from continuous CSI streams. For the scarcity of fall samples, we design a composite Autoencoder (AE) to generate virtual fall samples by adding random Gaussian noise to real fall samples. We conducted extensive evaluations on fall detection with different users at different locations in different rooms across different days. The results demonstrate that the proposed method can segment continuous CSI streams online in real-time and achieve robust fall detection in new domains free of re-training. The contributions of the paper are summarized as follows.

(1) Proposes an online environment independent fall detection method with WiFi CSI streams. The key modules include a feature disentanglement network, an online CSI stream segmentation method, and a virtual sample generator. After training with source environments, the fall detection model performs well in new environments without re-training.

(2) To achieve domain independence in wireless sensing, most existing works require some data in the target domains, while our method requires no data in the target domains. To this end, we devise a feature disentanglement network, composed of a feature extractor, a fall classifier, and a domain classifier. It disentangles motion-related features and environment-related features, classifies falls and non-falls using only the motion-related features, hence mitigates the problem of environment dependence.

(3) To ensure the motion segments to be captured correctly in the face of unstable WiFi signals and meanwhile to finish the computation in real-time, we propose an online CSI stream segmentation method. It selects the most sensitive subcarrier, detects the motions through a sliding window with adaptive thresholds, and checks the quality of the segments to keep the ones containing the complete motions. Such a design enables the online method to tolerate unstable WiFi signals, achieve fast data processing, and reduce false detection.

(4) Proposes a composite Autoencoder to generate virtual fall samples. It divides a fall sample into multiple sub-samples according to the antenna pairs, adds Gaussian noise to each sub-sample, reconstructs them by the corresponding Autoencoder, and concatenates them to form a virtual fall sample, thus balancing fall and non-fall samples and improving the diversity.

## 2   Related Work

Since the release of CSI tools [5,22], a large number of CSI-based sensing systems have been proposed [6,11,12]. In this review, we focus on CSI-based fall detection. WiFall [21] extracted features from CSI amplitude and classified falls with one-class Support Vector Machine (SVM) and Random Forest (RF). SMFDS [3] applied Discrete Wavelet Transformation (DWT) to denoise CSI amplitude and leveraged binary Long Short Term Memory (LSTM) to classify falls and non-falls. These systems did not consider the environment dependence issue. They performed well in the training environments, but could not achieve proper detection accuracy in unseen environments.

Environmental robustness is essential for practical fall detection systems. Researchers have made some progress on this issue. One way is extracting environment independent features by signal processing techniques. FallDeFi [15] applied Short Time Fourier Transform (STFT) to extract time-frequency features from CSI amplitude to detect falls, and leveraged a sequential forward selection algorithm to single out features resilient to environments. Domain adaptation is another way to increase the generalization capability to unseen environments. TL-Fall [23] utilized Principal Component Analysis (PCA) to obtain the second principal component and applied DWT to extract the features. It leveraged a binary SVM classifier to train the fall detection model in the source domains and transferred it to new domains by fine-tuning. Nguyen et al. [14] made use of the Adversarial Data Augmentation (ADA) method to improve the generalization of learning-based fall detection methods to unseen domains. These methods required some samples in the new environments to participate in the training, hence could not meet the real-world demands of no data in the new environments. Detecting falls in real-time is also essential for practical systems. RT-Fall [19] made use of the variance of phase difference to segment the motions from continuous streams in real-time, and extracted features in both the time and the frequency domains to differentiate falls from other motions with SVM. Keenan et al. [9] determined the motion segments by the deviation of phase difference, extracted features from the amplitude and the phase difference to detect different types of falls with SVM and a Bagged Tree classifier. These segmentation methods were based on fixed thresholds. But environmental dynamics and interferences have a great impact on CSI streams, which will cause the thresholds inapplicable, resulting in inaccurate segmentation and detection. Considering both domain independence and real-time, FallViewer [20] improved the robustness of fall detection in various environments by a few methods. It first calibrated CSI phase and amplitude, and then eliminated multipath interference by antenna power adjustment. The motion segments were determined by the variance of CSI data with flexible thresholds, which were adjusted according to the real-time CSI data. DeFall [7] consisted of an offline template-generating stage and an online decision-making stage, using speed and acceleration patterns as the templates of falls. It collected CSI data at a low sampling rate and switched to a high sampling rate once a motion was detected. However, if the users fall from a static state, the fall data obtained by this method may be incomplete, which will degrade the detection accuracy.

Compared with the existing works, firstly, our method achieves environment independent fall detection through a feature disentanglement neural network, hence it does not require any data from the new environments. Secondly, it can achieve real-time motion segmentation and fall detection in the face of noisy and unstable WiFi signals. Thirdly, it overcomes the scarcity of fall samples by leveraging a composite Autoencoder to generate virtual fall samples, which reduces the effort of data collection and improves the diversity of training data.

## 3  Methodology

The proposed method of fall detection consists of the training stage and the detection stage. In the training stage, as illustrated in Fig. 1(a), the method

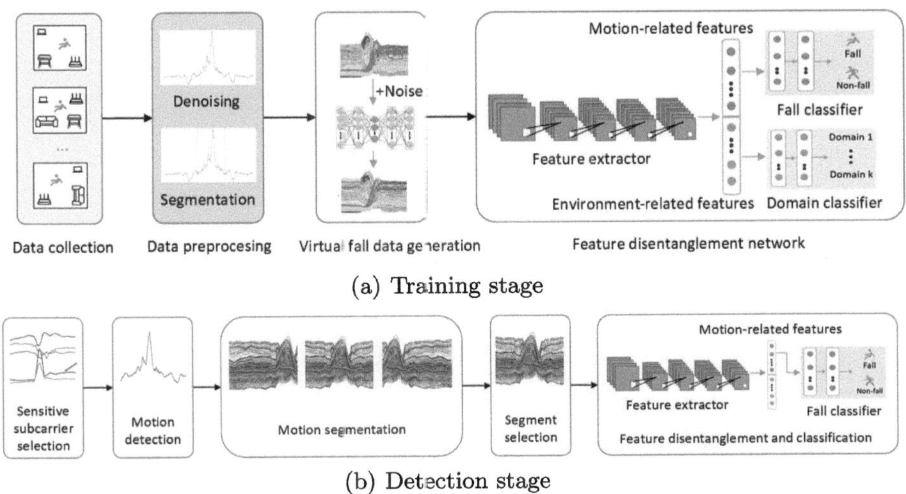



(a) Training stage



(b) Detection stage

**Fig. 1.** The proposed method of fall detection.

goes through data collection in multiple training environments (called source domains), data preprocessing (including denoising and segmentation), virtual fall data generation, and training of feature disentanglement neural network. In the detection stage, as illustrated in Fig. 1(b), with continuous CSI streams, the method automatically goes through the selection of the most sensitive subcarrier, motion detection, motion segmentation, segment selection, feature disentanglement and fall classification.

The CSI data of falls and non-falls (i.e. daily activities) are collected in several training environments. We first adopt the Moving Average Filter (MAF) to smooth the amplitude waveforms and remove the high frequency noises. As the activities are depicted by the slow frequency trend, the smoothing will not filter the useful information in activity patterns. After data segmentation according to the amplitude variance, we obtain the motion segments of falls and non-falls as the training samples. Each training sample is labeled with a binary motion label representing fall or non-fall, and a domain label representing the training environment. As fall samples are non-trivial to collect, we design a composite Autoencoder to generate virtual fall samples. The real and the virtual samples are joined together to train the feature disentanglement network, which can separate the motion-related features and the environment-related features. For real-time fall detection, the CSI streams are constantly monitored. When a motion is detected, the motion part will be segmented from the CSI stream automatically, which will be fed to the feature disentanglement network to extract the environment independent features and classified by the binary fall classifier.

We take the CSI amplitude as the measurement. The CSI phase on commercial WiFi devices cannot be measured accurately due to phase synchronization errors between the transmitter and the receiver, and the time complexity of generating spectrogram is high, making it difficult to achieve real-time detection. The CSI amplitude is easy to collect and sensitive to the surrounding changes, therefore, we take it to detect falls. A labeled sample can be represented as $(\boldsymbol{x}, y, z)$, where $\boldsymbol{x}$ denotes the CSI sample, $y$ denotes the motion label (fall or non-fall) and $z$ denotes the domain label. A fall takes some time, hence a CSI sample is a time sequence of CSI vectors, and each CSI vector contains the amplitude of all the subcarriers. Formally, a CSI sample can be denoted as:

$$\boldsymbol{x} = (\boldsymbol{x}_1, \boldsymbol{x}_2, \cdots, \boldsymbol{x}_j, \cdots, \boldsymbol{x}_t) \tag{1}$$

where $t$ is the time length and $\boldsymbol{x}_j$ represents the CSI vector at time $j$, which can be expressed as:

$$\boldsymbol{x}_j = (x_{j1}, x_{j2}, \cdots, x_{ji}, \cdots, x_{js}) \tag{2}$$

in which $s$ is the number of subcarriers and $x_{ji}$ represents the CSI amplitude of subcarrier $i$ at time $j$.

### 3.1   Building the Fall Detection Model

The building of the fall detection model is illustrated in Fig. 1(a). We first collect motion data from multiple training environments, including falls and daily activities (as non-falls), to constitute the training set. Apart from data denoising and segmentation, we propose the methods to tackle the problems of scarcity of fall samples and environment dependence.

**Generating Virtual Fall Samples.** The training set contains fall and non-fall samples collected in multiple environments. However, fall samples are more difficult to collect, thus much less than non-fall samples. Binary classifiers normally require the balance of positive and negative samples to achieve proper performance. Therefore, we design an Autoencoder-based generator to generate virtual fall samples. Observations showed that human motions affect different antenna pairs differently [21]. The subcarriers in the same antenna pair show similar patterns, whereas the subcarriers in different antenna pairs show different patterns, as illustrated in Fig. 2. To keep the specific information in each antenna pair, we train an Autoencoder for each antenna pair and assemble them as a composite Autoencoder, as shown in Fig. 3. Each encoder and decoder is a 3-layer fully-connected neural network. The virtual samples generated by the composite Autoencoder preserve the specific features of each antenna pair.

We take a real fall sample $\boldsymbol{x}$, denoise it and divide it into a group of sub-samples according to the antenna pairs as:

$$\boldsymbol{x} = (\boldsymbol{x}_1^g, \boldsymbol{x}_2^g, \cdots, \boldsymbol{x}_v^g, \cdots, \boldsymbol{x}_u^g) \tag{3}$$

where $u$ represents the number of antenna pairs. We then add Gaussian noise ($\mu = 0, \sigma = 0.005$) to the sub-sample $\boldsymbol{x}_v^g$ of each antenna pair $v$, input it into its Autoencoder, and reconstruct the sub-sample as:

$$\hat{\boldsymbol{x}}_v^g = decoder_v(encoder_v(\boldsymbol{x}_v^g + noise)) \tag{4}$$

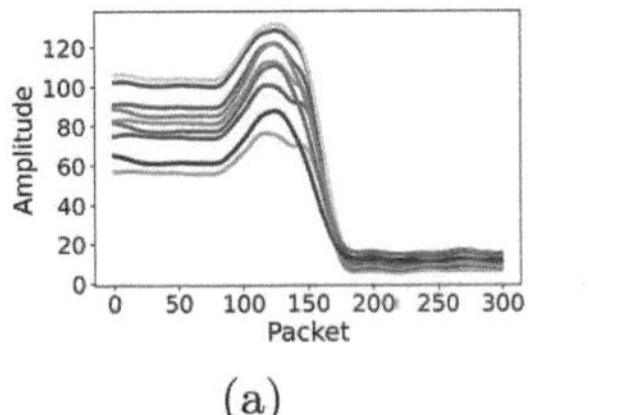
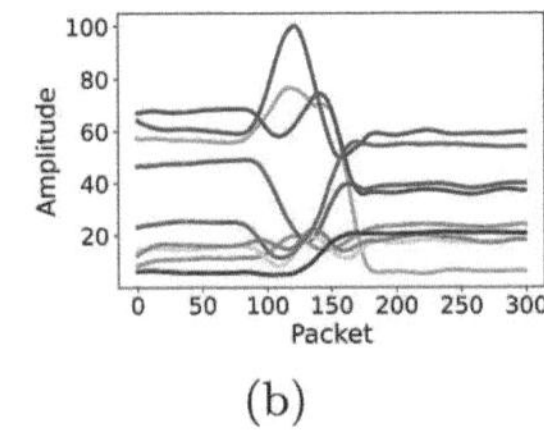

(a)                                         (b)

**Fig. 2.** (a) Subcarriers in the same antenna pair show similar patterns. (b) Subcarriers in different antenna pairs show different patterns.

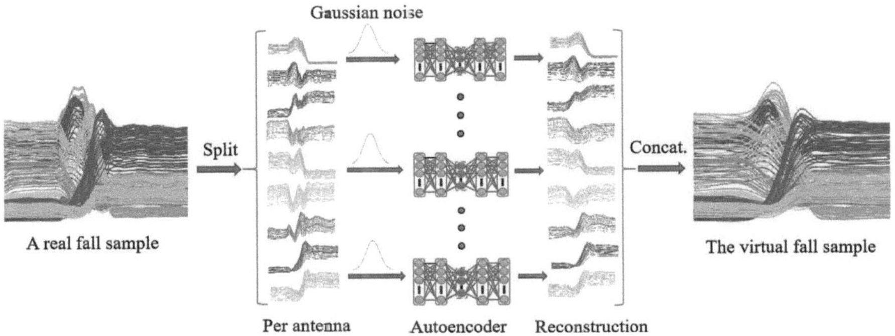


**Fig. 3.** Composite Autoencoder.

The reconstructed sub-samples of all the antenna pairs are concatenated to form the complete virtual sample and smoothed as:

$$\hat{x} = (\hat{x}_1^g, \hat{x}_2^g, \cdots, \hat{x}_v^g, \cdots, \hat{x}_u^g) \tag{5}$$

A real fall sample and its virtual sample are shown in Fig. 3 as the input and the output. The virtual sample has slight difference but retains the trend of the real fall sample, thus can be used in the subsequent model training. By this way, we can generate a large number of fall samples to compensate for the lack of them.

**Feature Disentanglement Network.** The CSI samples are affected by both the motions and the environments, so they contain both the motion-related and the environment-related information. If we use such samples to train the fall detection model, the environment-related features will be mis-regarded as part of the motion features, making it difficult to generalize to unseen environments. As illustrated in Fig. 4, if the person is different or the person is in a different room, the CSI samples of the same motion will be quite different, causing the fall detection accuracy to decline. It is necessary to remove the environment-related features and use only the motion-related features to detect falls.

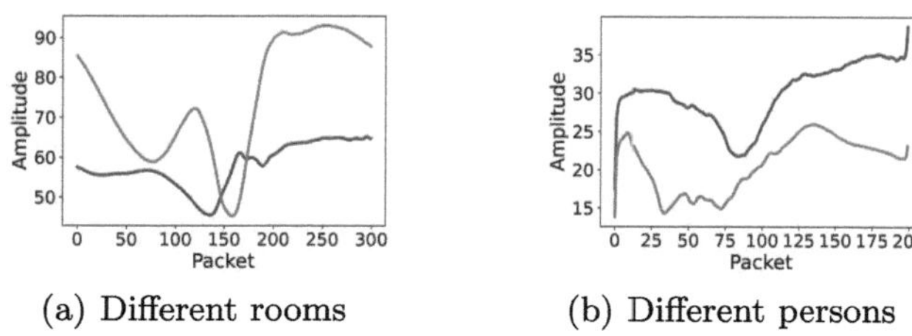

(a) Different rooms          (b) Different persons

**Fig. 4.** CSI samples of the same motion in different environments (rooms or persons), each curve represents an environment.

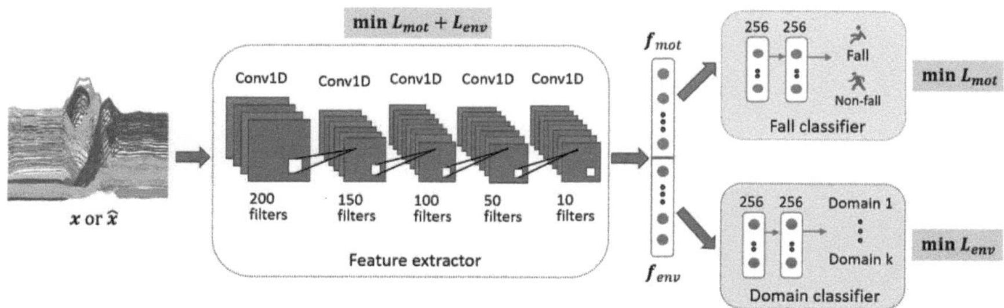


**Fig. 5.** Feature disentanglement network.

To address this issue, we propose a feature disentanglement network, aiming to learn the robust feature representations across different environments. The basic idea is to disentangle the motion-related features and the environment-related features during feature extraction and use only the motion-related features for fall classification. After the environment-related features are removed, the detection model can generalize well to unseen environments. The feature disentanglement network is composed of a feature extractor, a fall classifier, and a domain classifier, as shown in Fig. 5. The feature extractor is a Convolutional Neural Network (CNN), composed of 5 convolutional blocks. Each block consists of a one-dimensional convolutional layer and a max-pooling layer. Both the fall classifier and the domain classifier are 2-layer fully-connected neural networks. In the feature vector extracted by the feature extractor, half of the elements are for fall classification, and the other half are for domain classification.

The virtual samples and the real samples are used together to train the feature disentanglement framework. Let $f$ denote the extracted feature vector, which is split into $f_{mot}$ and $f_{env}$, representing the motion-related features and the environment-related features, with the dimensions of $d$ respectively:

$$f = (f_{mot}, f_{env}) \tag{6}$$

$f_{mot}$ is classified by the binary fall classifier, and $f_{env}$ is classified by the domain classifier. The loss of the fall classifier can be defined as:

$$\min L_{mot} = \frac{1}{n} \sum_{i=1}^{n} (-(y_i log(\bar{y}_i) + (1 - y_i)log(1 - \bar{y}_i))) \tag{7}$$

where $n$ is the number of training samples, $y_i$ is the real label of sample $i$, $\bar{y}_i$ is the predicted label of the sample. The loss of the domain classifier is defined as:

$$\min L_{env} = -\frac{1}{n} \sum_{i=1}^{n} \sum_{j=1}^{k} z_{ij} log(\bar{z}_{ij}) \tag{8}$$

where $k$ is the number of domains, $z_{ij}$ is the real domain label of sample $i$ wrt. domain $j$, and $\bar{z}_{ij}$ is the predicted domain label of the sample. The total loss of the feature disentanglement network is then defined as:

$$\min L_{total} = L_{mot} + L_{env} \tag{9}$$

During model training, the feature extractor extracts the features and separates them as motion-related and environment-related. The motion-related features are classified by the fall classifier, minimizing the fall detection loss $L_{mot}$, thus the motion-related features aggregates to $f_{mot}$. The environment-related features are classified by the domain classifier, minimizing the domain classification loss $L_{env}$, thus the environment-related features aggregates to $f_{env}$. After iterations of training, the feature extractor obtains the ability to disentangle the motion-related and the environment-related features. We can use it to detect falls in new environments, free of re-training.

Compared with the domain adaptation methods based on Generative Adversarial Network (GAN) [8] or Domain Adaptive Neural Network (DaNN) incorporating Maximum Mean Discrepancy (MMD) [4], our method requires no data in the new environments, whereas GAN-based and DaNN-MMD-based domain adaptation methods require some unlabeled data from the new environments and can not generalize well to unseen environments.

### 3.2   Online Segmentation and Fall Detection

Detecting falls from CSI streams online demands tolerance of the unstableness of WiFi signals and fast data processing. Comparing the variance of amplitude with the threshold is a common method to segment the motions in continuous streams. However, environmental dynamics and interferences will cause the threshold inapplicable in the changed environment, resulting in inaccurate segmentation and detection. For online motion segmentation, a sliding window is often utilized to capture the CSI streams. During wireless transmission, the cases like packet losses or device jams may happen. To tolerate the unstableness, the size and the update frequency of the sliding window should be set to ensure that the complete motion segments can be captured in the face of the unstableness,

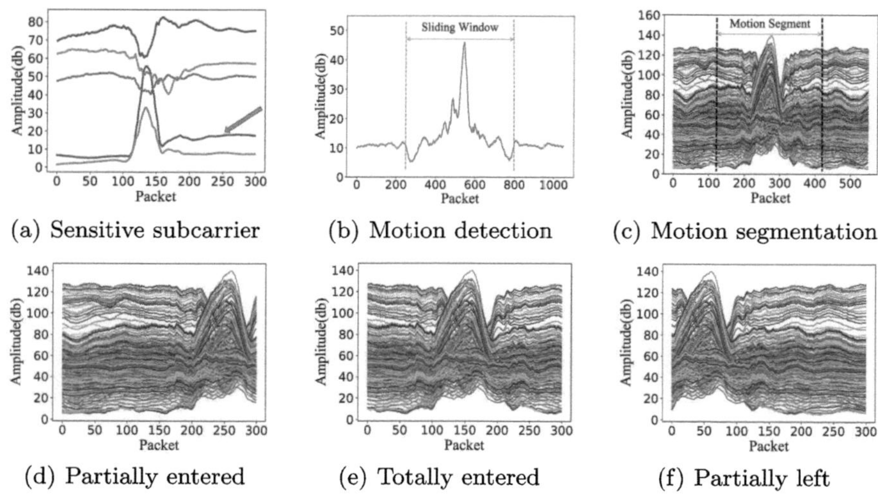

(a) Sensitive subcarrier    (b) Motion detection    (c) Motion segmentation

(d) Partially entered    (e) Totally entered    (f) Partially left

**Fig. 6.** Online motion detection and segmentation.

meanwhile the computation should be in real-time. To address these issues, we propose a method to detect and segment motions automatically from continuous CSI streams under the circumstance of unstable WiFi signals and meanwhile achieve fall detection in real-time. The method consists of 5 steps: selection of the most sensitive subcarrier, detection of motions, segmentation of motions, selection of eligible motion segments, and fall classification, as shown in Fig. 6.

**Step 1: Selection of the Most Sensitive Subcarrier.** When no motion occurs, the CSI amplitude waveforms are relatively stable. When motions occur, the CSI amplitude waveforms will fluctuate due to the interference of motions on WiFi signals. Based on these observations, we calculate the amplitude variance in a sliding window of the continuous CSI streams. If the amplitude variance exceeds the threshold, it indicates the occurrence of motions. Our configuration has 270 subcarriers. If the amplitude variances of all the subcarriers in the sliding window are calculated, the calculation speed may not keep up with the arrival speed of the CSI data, resulting in miss alarms. Through observations, it is found out that not all subcarriers are subject to the same degree of interference. Some subcarriers are more sensitive than the others, hence their amplitude variances are larger than the others, as shown in Fig. 6(a). To reduce the calculation time and ensure real-time, we select the subcarrier that is the most sensitive to environmental changes. When motions occur, the amplitude of this subcarrier changes most obviously. If the amplitude variance of this subcarrier exceeds the threshold, we consider that a motion occurs.

To select the most sensitive subcarrier, the CSI streams are monitored for a short period of time in the static environment, denoted as:

$$\boldsymbol{x} = (x_{ji})_{T \times s} \tag{10}$$

where $T$ is the time length of the monitored data, $s$ is the number of subcarriers, $x_{ji}$ represents the amplitude of subcarrier $i$ at time $j$. We calculate the amplitude variance of each subcarrier $i$ $(i = 1, 2, \cdots, s)$ as:

$$\sigma_i^2 = \sum_{j=1}^{T} (x_{ji} - \overline{x}_i)^2, \quad \overline{x}_i = \frac{\sum_{j=1}^{T} x_{ji}}{T} \tag{11}$$

The subcarrier with the largest amplitude variance is selected as the most sensitive subcarrier, denoted as subcarrier $I$:

$$I = \arg\max_i(\sigma_1^2, \sigma_2^2, \cdots, \sigma_s^2) \tag{12}$$

**Step 2: Motion Detection.** After finding the most sensitive subcarrier, we set a sliding window of size $w$ $(w = 550)$ to capture the CSI streams, which has a time length of 5.5 s. We calculate the amplitude variance of the subcarrier $I$ in the sliding window as:

$$\sigma_I^2 = \sum_{j=1}^{w} (x_{jI} - \overline{x}_I)^2, \quad \overline{x}_I = \frac{\sum_{j=1}^{w} x_{jI}}{w} \tag{13}$$

If $\sigma_I^2$ exceeds the threshold, a motion is detected, as shown in Fig. 6(b). As only one subcarrier is involved, the calculation time is trivial. The threshold is flexible and adjusted with real-time CSI data. The size and the update frequency of the sliding window are critical. If the window is too small, it can not contain the complete motion segments, while if the window is too large, the calculation time will increase. If the update frequency is too slow, the motions may not be detected promptly, while if the update frequency is too fast, the calculation time will increase. As the duration of a motion is no more than 3 s, we set the sliding window size as 5.5 s and update it per second.

**Step 3: Motion Segmentation.** When a motion is detected in the sliding window, we need to intercept the segment containing the motion. We set the motion segment size as $m$ $(m = 300)$, which is a time length of 3 s, to contain the complete motion. For each subcarrier $i$, we choose the part with the largest amplitude variance within the sliding window as its motion segment:

$$\sigma_i^2(p) = \sum_{j=p}^{p+m-1} (x_{ji} - \overline{x}_i(p))^2, \quad \overline{x}_i(p) = \frac{\sum_{j=p}^{p+m-1} x_{ji}}{m} \tag{14}$$

$$q_i = \arg\max_p(\sigma_i^2(1), \cdots, \sigma_i^2(p), \cdots, \sigma_i^2(w - m))$$

The segment $(x_{q_i,i}, x_{q_i+1,i}, \cdots, x_{q_i+m-1,i})$ has the largest amplitude variance for the subcarrier $i$ and is regarded as its motion segment. For each subcarrier, we find its motion segment. As shown in Fig. 6(c), the final motion segment for all the subcarriers $(j = 1, 2, \cdots, s)$ is calculated as:

$$(x_{start,j}, x_{start+1,j}, \cdots, x_{start+m,j}), \quad start = \frac{\sum_{i=1}^{s} q_i}{s} \tag{15}$$

**Step 4: Selection of Eligible Motion Segments.** Experiments showed that under daily data flow, one motion might be intercepted multiple times by the proposed method, thus multiple segments might be obtained for the same motion. We take a fall as example. A sudden fall lasts no more than 1.5 s, while the sliding window can store 5.5 s of data. When a fall occurs, multiple sliding windows with amplitude variance exceeding the threshold will be obtained. From these sliding windows, we intercept multiple motion segments, as shown in Fig. 6(d)–6(f). The segments that do not contain the complete motion should be discarded. For this purpose, we find the position of the 100 continuous packets with the largest variance in each segment. If the position is too forward or too backward, we discard the segment. The remaining motion segments are eligible. Figure 6(e) is an eligible segment, while Fig. 6(d) and Fig. 6(f) are ineligible.

**Step 5: Fall Classification.** The eligible motion segments are input to the feature extractor to obtain the environment independent features, which are classified to falls or non-falls by the fall classifier. If there are multiple eligible motion segments, a max-voting algorithm is adopted to make the final decision, because different motion segments may have different predictions.

## 4   Evaluations

### 4.1   Experimental Setup

We conducted experiments in four scenarios using commercial off-the-shelf WiFi devices. Scenario 1 and scenario 2 were in the different regions of a laboratory of size 8.5 m × 6 m, as shown in Fig. 7(a)–7(b). Scenario 3 and scenario 4 were in the different regions of another laboratory of size 8 m × 7 m, as shown in Fig. 7(c)–7(d). The laboratories were cluttered with computers, tables, cupboards and constant network traffics. We deployed one pair of WiFi transmitter and receiver in these scenarios. The transmitter was a commercial router TP-LINK WDR7660 and the receiver was a laptop equipped with Intel WiFi Link 5300. Both the transceivers were equipped with 3 antennas, forming 9 antenna pairs. Each antenna pair contained 30 subcarrier groups, hence each data packet contained 270 dimensions. The sampling rate was 100 packets per second. We exploited the CSI tools [5] to obtain the CSI data. Apart from our own datasets, we recruited the public dataset of Baha et al. [1]. Its experimental scenario was a laboratory of size 4.7 m × 4.7 m, deploying two computers with Intel WiFi link 5300, as shown in Fig. 7(e). The transmitter sent 320 packets per second with one antenna, the receiver had 3 antennas, hence each packet had 90 subcarriers.

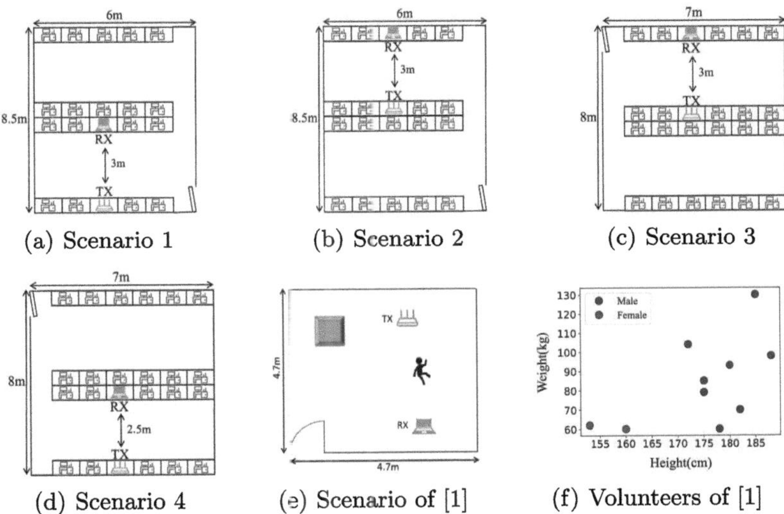

(a) Scenario 1          (b) Scenario 2          (c) Scenario 3

(d) Scenario 4          (e) Scenario of [1]          (f) Volunteers of [1]

**Fig. 7.** Experimental setup.

## 4.2 Data Collection and Model Training

We recruited extensive datasets to evaluate the performance and generalization of the method, including our own datasets in four scenarios and the public datasets from [1], as listed in Table 1. We leveraged the composite Autoencoder to generate virtual fall samples to augment the training set, until the number of falls was close to the number of non-falls. The falls included forward falls, backward falls, leftward falls, and rightward falls. Daily activities included walk, squat down, stand up, sit down, jump, bend, etc.

We trained two models: the virtual data generator and the feature disentanglement network. The virtual data generator consists of 9 Autoencoders. Each encoder/decoder is a 3-layer fully-connected neural network. The encoder has the nodes of [512, 256, 64] and the decoder has the nodes of [64, 256, 512], taking ReLU as the activation. The loss is defined as the Mean Square Error (MSE) between the real samples and the constructions. By minimizing the loss, the virtual data generator can be trained. The learning rate is set as $10^{-3}$, and the optimizer is Adam. The training took about 30 min. The feature disentanglement network is composed of a feature extractor, a fall classifier, and a domain classifier. The feature extractor is composed of 5 1D convolutional layers, each layer containing [200, 150, 100, 50, 10] kernels with the kernel size of 20, and one fully-connected layer with 2050 nodes. ReLU is the activation. Both the fall classifier and the domain classifier are 2-layer fully-connected neural networks, with the nodes of [256, 64], taking ReLU as the activation. The learning rate is $10^{-3}$, and the optimizer is Adam. The training of the feature disentanglement network took about 60 min.

**Table 1.** The datasets.

| Dataset type | Dataset | Motion | Motion count |
|---|---|---|---|
| Scenario | Scenario 1–4 | Squat down, stand up, stand still, walk | 30×4×4 |
| | | Fall | 60×4 |
| Location | 8 locations in Scenario 1 | Squat down, stand up, walk, jump | 10×8×4 |
| | | Fall | 20×8 |
| Time | 14 days in Scenario 4 | Squat down, stand up, walk, jump | 870 |
| | | Fall | 590 |
| Person | 10 persons [1] | Stand up | 20×10 |
| | | Sit down | 20×10 |
| | | Walk | 20×10 |
| | | Pick up a pen | 20×10 |
| | | Fall from standing | 20×10 |
| | | Fall from sitting | 20×10 |
| Misc fall | 6 locations in Scenario 4 | Squat down | 10×6 |
| | | Sit down | 10×6 |
| | | Bend | 10×6 |
| | | Walk | 10×6 |
| | | Forward fall | 5×6 |
| | | Backward fall | 5×6 |
| | | Leftward fall | 5×6 |
| | | Rightward fall | 5×6 |

**Table 2.** Performance of fall detection in invariant domains.

| Dataset type | Datasets | Train samples | Test samples | Accuracy | Precision | Recall |
|---|---|---|---|---|---|---|
| Scenario | 3 scenarios | 432 | 108 | 95.2% | 94.8% | 95.7% |
| Location | 6 locations | 288 | 72 | 96.3% | 96.0% | 96.7% |
| Time | 12 days | 1024 | 256 | 97.1% | 96.5% | 97.4% |
| Person | 8 persons | 768 | 192 | 96.7% | 96.1% | 97.1% |
| Misc fall | 4 locations | 192 | 48 | 95.0% | 94.1% | 95.4% |

## 4.3   Evaluations in Invariant Domains

We use accuracy, precision and recall as the metrics. Accuracy is defined as the ratio of correctly identified events out of all events, precision is defined as the proportion of actual falls out of detected falls, and recall is defined as the proportion of correctly identified falls out of actual falls. We first evaluated the performance of the method in invariant domains involving multiple scenarios, locations, persons and days, i.e. the testing environments were the same with the training environments. We used the datasets in Table 1 to evaluate, taking 80% of the data randomly as the training set and the remaining 20% as the testing set. We also evaluated the method with different types of falls and similar motions, using the dataset type of *Misc fall* in Table 1, taking 80% of the data randomly for training and the remaining 20% for testing. The evaluation results are shown in Table 2. For almost all the testings, including different types of falls and similar motions, the accuracy, the precision and the recall were above 95%. It demonstrated high performance of fall detection in invariant domains.

## 4.4   Evaluations Across Domains

To evaluate the generalization of our method to new domains, we trained the model with source environments and tested it in unseen environments.

**In New Scenarios.** We tested in 4 scenarios shown in Fig. 7(a)–7(d). In each scenario, the volunteer performed 4 daily motions of squat down, stand up, stand still and walk, each repeated 30 times, and performed falls for 60 times. The datasets are listed in Table 1. We took 3 scenarios to train the model and tested in the other scenario, which was not involved in the training. The evaluation results in each unseen scenario are listed in Table 3. Without any data from the new scenario and without re-training, the accuracy, precision and recall could achieve more than 80% in the new scenarios.

**At New Locations.** The person's location has an impact on wireless propagation, thus falling at different locations often produces different signal patterns. To evaluate the generalization of the method to different locations, we tested at 8 locations in Scenario 1. The volunteer performed 5 types of motions at each location: squat down, stand up, walk, jump and fall, each repeated 10 times except for fall 20 times. The dataset is listed in Table 1. We took 6 locations as source domains to train the model and tested at the other 2 locations, which were not involved in the training. The evaluation results are listed in the upper part of Table 4. Without any training data from the testing locations, the average accuracy, precision and recall could achieve 87.8%, 87.3% and 90%. We also evaluated the method with different kinds of falls and similar motions. We tested at 6 locations in Scenario 4. The volunteer performed 4 non-fall motions and 4 different types of falls at each location: squat down, sit down, bend, walk, forward fall, backward fall, leftward fall and rightward fall. Each non-fall motion was repeated 10 times and each type of fall was repeated 5 times. The dataset is listed in Table 1. We took 4 locations as source domains to train the model and tested on the other 2 locations, which were not involved in the training. The evaluation results are listed in the lower part of Table 4. Without any data from the new locations, the average accuracy, precision and recall could achieve 84.7%, 83.9% and 85.9% for similar motions and different types of falls.

**By New Users.** Individuals perform motions with unique styles. To evaluate the generalization of the method to different users, we recruited the public dataset of Baha et al. [1]. In the dataset, 10 volunteers participated in the data collection, including males and females, with quite different weights and heights, as shown in Fig. 7(f). The motions were stand up, sit down, walk, pick up a pen, fall from standing and fall from sitting, each repeated 20 times. The dataset is listed in Table 1. We took 8 volunteers to train the model and tested on the other 2 volunteers, who were not involved in the training. The results are listed in Table 5. Without any data from the new users, the average accuracy, precision and recall could achieve 86.9%, 86.5% and 88.4%.

**On New Days.** The temperature, humidity, and network traffic vary with time. They all have impacts on wireless propagation. Automatic gain control in WiFi devices imposes another major influence on WiFi signals. To evaluate the generalization of the method to different times, we tested in Scenario 4 for 14 days, spanning over one month. The motions were squat down, stand up, walk, jump and fall. A total of 590 fall samples and 870 non-fall samples were collected. The dataset is listed in Table 1. We took 12 days to train the model and tested on the other 2 days, which were not involved in the training. The

**Table 3.** Performance in new scenarios (%).

| Scenarios | | Performance in new scenarios | | |
| --- | --- | --- | --- | --- |
| Training (Source) | Testing (Target) | Accuracy | Precision | Recall |
| 2, 3, 4 | 1 | 80.0 | 78.1 | 83.0 |
| 1, 3, 4 | 2 | 82.5 | 80.9 | 85.0 |
| 1, 2, 4 | 3 | 83.3 | 83.3 | 83.3 |
| 1, 2, 3 | 4 | 85.8 | 87.7 | 83.3 |
| **Average** | | **82.9** | **82.5** | **83.6** |

**Table 4.** Performance at new locations (%)

| Locations in scenario 1 | | Performance at new locations | | |
| --- | --- | --- | --- | --- |
| Training (Source) | Testing (Target) | Accuracy | Precision | Recall |
| 3–8 | 1, 2 | 87.5 | 92.8 | 82.5 |
| 1, 2, 5–8 | 3, 4 | 92.5 | 92.6 | 92.5 |
| 1–4, 7, 8 | 5, 6 | 83.7 | 76.5 | 97.5 |
| 1–6 | 7, 8 | 87.5 | 87.5 | 87.5 |
| **Average** | | **87.8** | **87.3** | **90.0** |
| Locations in scenario 4 | | Performance at new locations | | |
| Training (Source) | Testing (Target) | Accuracy | Precision | Recall |
| 3, 4, 5, 6 | 1, 2 | 86.1 | 84.9 | 88 |
| 1, 2, 5, 6 | 3, 4 | 85 | 85 | 85 |
| 1, 2, 3, 4 | 5, 6 | 83.1 | 82 | 84.7 |
| **Average** | | **84.7** | **83.9** | **85.9** |

**Table 5.** Performance by new users (%).

| Users | | Performance for new users | | |
|---|---|---|---|---|
| Training (Source) | Testing (Target) | Accuracy | Precision | Recall |
| 3–10 | 1, 2 | 88.7 | 87.7 | 91.2 |
| 1, 2, 5–10 | 3, 4 | 81.8 | 80.4 | 87.5 |
| 1–4, 7–10 | 5, 6 | 91.8 | 93.1 | 90 |
| 1–6, 9, 10 | 7, 8 | 87.5 | 87.5 | 87.5 |
| 1–8 | 9, 10 | 84.9 | 84.2 | 86.2 |
| **Average** | | **86.9** | **86.5** | **88.4** |

**Table 6.** Performance on new days (%).

| Days | | Performance on new days | | |
|---|---|---|---|---|
| Training (Source) | Testing (Target) | Accuracy | Precision | Recall |
| 3–14 | 1, 2 | 96.5 | 96.9 | 96.5 |
| 1–4, 7–14 | 5, 6 | 82.5 | 81.6 | 83.7 |
| 1–8, 11–14 | 9, 10 | 86.8 | 84.1 | 91.2 |
| 1–12 | 13, 14 | 83.8 | 84.7 | 83.7 |
| **Average** | | **87.4** | **86.8** | **88.7** |

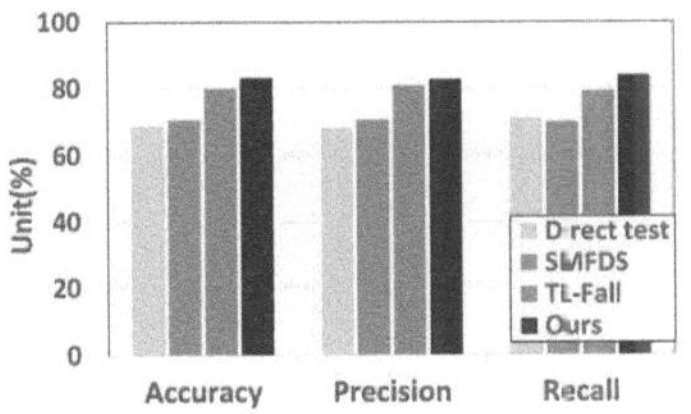
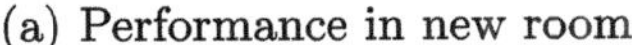

(a) Performance in new rooms

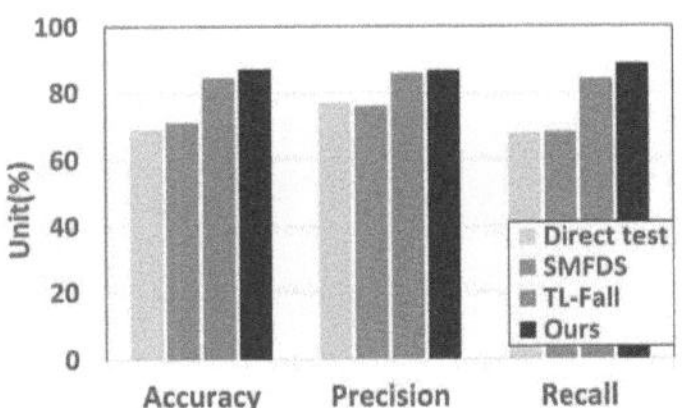

(b) Performance by new users

**Fig. 8.** Comparison with existing works.

results are listed in Table 6. Without any data from the new days, the average accuracy, precision, and recall could achieve 87.4%, 86.8%, and 88.7%.

## 4.5  Comparison with Existing Works

We carried out comparisons with the existing fall detection systems. We compared our work with *direct test*, *SMFDS*, and *TL-Fall*. The method *direct test* applied the fall detection model trained in source domains to new domains directly. *SMFDS* [3] applied DWT to denoise CSI amplitude and leveraged binary LSTM to classify falls and non-falls. *TL-Fall* [23] utilized PCA and DWT to extract the features, leveraged binary SVM to train the fall detection model in source domains, and transferred it to new domains by fine-tuning with a small amount of labeled data in the new domain. *Our method* does not require any target domain data and uses only source domains to extract the domain-independent features. We compared these methods wrt. generalization to new rooms and new users, using the datasets in Table 1. Figure 8(a) shows their comparison of performance in new rooms, taking 3 rooms as the training set and 1 new room as the testing set. Figure 8(b) shows their comparison of performance for new users, taking 8 users as the training set and 2 new users as the testing set. In all the testings, our method achieved the best performance. SMFDS performed well in the training environments, but could not achieve satisfactory detection performance in new environments. The performance of TL-Fall was close our method, but it required some labeled data in the new domains.

### 4.6   Ablation Study

**Effect of Feature Disentanglement and Virtual Data Generation.** Feature disentanglement (FD) and virtual data generation (VDG) are the key modules in the method. To verify their effect, we conducted experiments to compare the fall detection performance with or without them when generalizing to new rooms, locations, times, and users. The results are shown in Fig. 9. With feature disentanglement, the performance was improved, and with both feature disentanglement and virtual data generation, the performance was improved further.

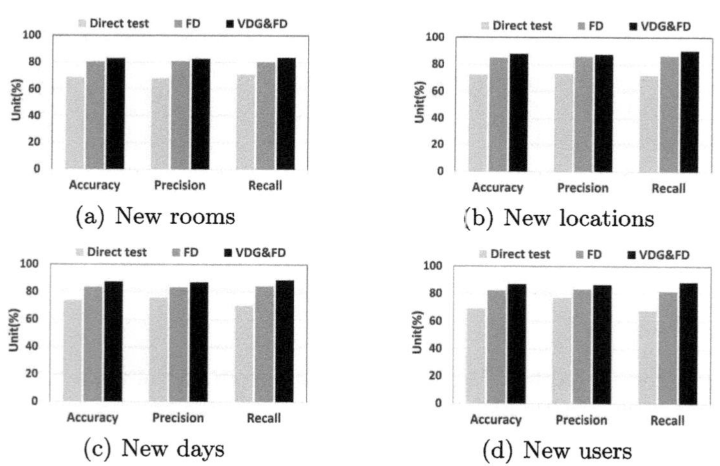


**Fig. 9.** Effect of feature disentanglement and virtual data generation.

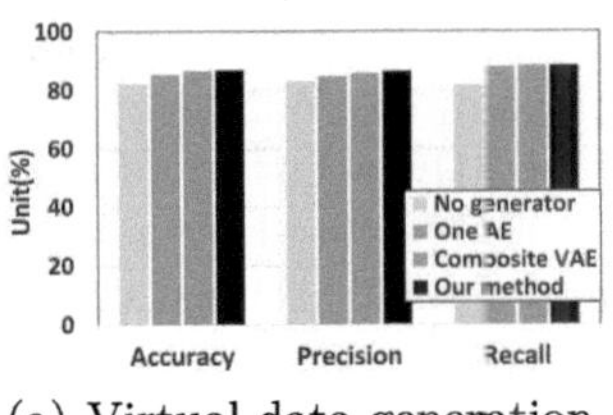
(a) Virtual data generation

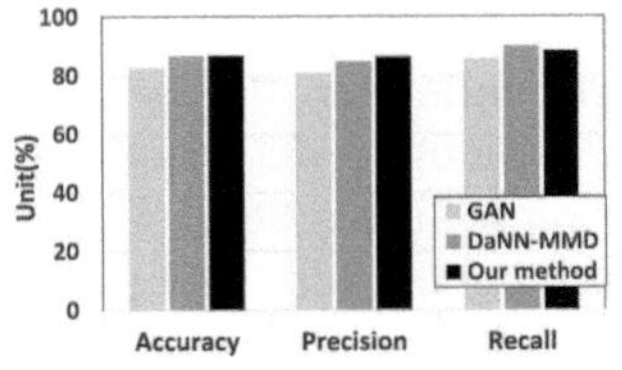
(b) Domain adaptation

**Fig. 10.** Comparison of different methods.

**Effect of Virtual Data Generation Method.** We employ a composite Autoencoder to generate virtual fall samples. To verify its effect, we compared it with a single Autoencoder and a composite Variational Autoencoder (VAE) as well as no generator. The composite VAE contains a separate VAE for each antenna pair. As shown in Fig. 10(a), compared with not using virtual fall data, all the generators improved the performance. The improvement of the single Autoencoder was marginal, while the composite VAE and our composite Autoencoder enhanced the performance. The composite VAE and our composite Autoencoder had similar performance, but ours took less time.

**Effect of Domain Adaptation Method.** To prove the effect of the feature disentanglement network, we compared it with *GAN*-based and *DaNN-MMD*-based domain adaptation methods. The *GAN*-based method [8] consists of a feature extractor, a classifier, and a domain discriminator. Through adversarial training, the domain-independent features are extracted. *DaNN-MMD* [4] is a feature distribution alignment method, which extracts the features from the source and the target domains, minimizing the MMD distance between them. GAN-based and DaNN-MMD-based methods require some target domain data to train the network. For them, we took 30% of target domain unlabeled data for training, and the remaining 70% for testing. Our method does not require any target domain data. We used all the target domain data for testing. The comparison is shown in Fig. 10(b). Although the performance of GAN-based and DaNN-MMD-based methods were close to our method, their disadvantage is that they required some target domain in the training, which is impractical.

### 4.7 Real-Time Evaluation

We evaluated the real-time performance of the fall detection system in Scenario 2 under the circumstance of daily network traffic and interferences. We trained the model with the data of 12 days, including 500 falls and 780 non-falls. The testing was conducted online on a different day. Hence the real-time issue and the environment dependence issue were both involved. During testing, the volunteer conducted motions continuously, including 30 falls from standing, 20 falls from walking, 20 walking, 20 squatting down and 20 standing up. From online

CSI streams, the fall detection system segmented the motions automatically and detected the falls in real-time. In the face of unstable WiFi signals, the accuracy of online motion detection achieved 96% and the accuracy of online motion segmentation achieved 98%. The errors were mainly caused by noise, automatic gain control, device jams and packet losses. Under such circumstances, the accuracy, precision and recall of fall detection still reached 84.5%, 87.2%, and 82%. The system ran on a desktop equipped with a GPU of Colorful RTX 3090 and a CPU of Intel i5-12600K. The method took 0.1 s to detect a motion, 0.3 s to segment the motion, 0.2 s to select the eligible segments, and 1.1 s for feature extraction and fall detection. Altogether, it took 1.7 s for an online detection, which satisfied the real-time demand.

## 5   Conclusions

Due to non-contact, low-cost and no privacy concern, WiFi-based fall detection has attracted much attention. However, it still suffers from the scarcity of fall samples, low generalization to new environments, and non-real-time. In this paper, we propose a fall detection method based on WiFi CSI, aiming to solve these problems. To remove environment dependence, we propose a feature disentanglement network to extract the environment independent features. For real-time, we propose an online real-time motion detection and segmentation method from unstable continuous CSI streams. For the scarcity of fall samples, we propose a composite Autoencoder to generate virtual fall samples. Extensive experiments showed that our method can achieve real-time fall detection and can generalize well to unseen environments, such as rooms, locations, times and users.

## References


1. Alsaify, B., Almazari, M.M., Alazrai, R., Daoud, M.I.: A dataset for Wi-Fi-based human activity recognition in line-of-sight and non-line-of-sight indoor environments. Data Brief **33** (2020)
2. Auvinet, E., Multon, F., Saint-Arnaud, A., Rousseau, J., Meunier, J.: Fall detection with multiple cameras: an occlusion-resistant method based on 3-d silhouette vertical distribution. IEEE Trans. Inf. Technol. Biomed. **15**(2), 290–300 (2011)
3. Ding, J., Wang, Y.: A wifi-based smart home fall detection system using recurrent neural network. IEEE Trans. Consum. Electron. (2020)
4. Ghifary, M., Kleijn, W.B., Zhang, M.: Domain adaptive neural networks for object recognition. In: Pham, D.-N., Park, S.-B. (eds.) PRICAI 2014. LNCS (LNAI), vol. 8862, pp. 898–904. Springer, Cham (2014). https://doi.org/10.1007/978-3-319-13560-1_76
5. Halperin, D., Hu, W., Sheth, A., Wetherall, D.: Predictable 802.11 packet delivery from wireless channel measurements. In: ACM International Conference on Applications, Technologies, Architectures, and Protocols for Computer Communication (SIGCOMM), pp. 159–170. ACM (2010)

6. He, Y., Chen, Y., Hu, Y., Zeng, B.: WiFi vision: sensing, recognition, and detection with commodity MIMO-OFDM WiFi. IEEE Internet Things J. **7**(9), 8296–8317 (2020)
7. Hu, Y., Zhang, F., Wu, C., Wang, B., Liu, K.J.R.: DeFall: environment-independent passive fall detection using wifi. IEEE Internet Things J. **9**(11), 8515–8530 (2022)
8. Jiang, W., et al.: Towards environment independent device free human activity recognition. In: 24th Annual International Conference on Mobile Computing and Networking (MobiCom). ACM (2018)
9. Keenan, R.M., Tran, L.N.: Fall detection using wi-fi signals and threshold-based activity segmentation. In: IEEE 31st Annual International Symposium on Personal, Indoor and Mobile Radio Communications, pp. 1–6 (2020)
10. Lian, J., Yuan, X., Li, M., Tzeng, N.F.: Fall detection via inaudible acoustic sensing. Proc. ACM Interact. Mob. Wearable Ubiquitous Technol. **5**(3) (2021)
11. Liu, J., Liu, H., Chen, Y., Wang, Y., Wang, C.: Wireless sensing for human activity: a survey. IEEE Commun. Surv. Tutor. **22**(3), 1629–1645 (2020)
12. Ma, Y., Zhou, G., Wang, S.: WiFi sensing with channel state information: a survey. ACM Comput. Surv. **52**(3) (2019)
13. Melillo, P., Castaldo, R., Sannino, G., Orrico, A., de Pietro, G., Pecchia, L.: Wearable technology and ecg processing for fall risk assessment, prevention and detection. In: 37th Annual International Conference of the IEEE Engineering in Medicine and Biology Society (EMBC), pp. 7740–7743 (2015)
14. Nguyen, T.D.H., Nguyen, H.N.H.: Towards a robust wifi-based fall detection with adversarial data augmentation. In: 54th Annual Conference on Information Sciences and Systems (CISS) (2020)
15. Palipana, S., Rojas, D., Agrawal, P., Pesch, D.: FallDeFi: Ubiquitous fall detection using commodity wi-fi devices. Proc. ACM Interact. Mob. Wearable Ubiq. Technol. (2018)
16. Pierleoni, P., et al.: A wearable fall detector for elderly people based on AHRS and barometric sensor. IEEE Sens. J. **16**(17), 6733–6744 (2016)
17. Stone, E.E., Skubic, M.: Fall detection in homes of older adults using the microsoft kinect. IEEE J. Biomed. Health Inf. **19**(1), 290–301 (2015)
18. Wang, B., Zhang, H., Guo, Y.X.: Radar-based soft fall detection using pattern contour vector. IEEE Internet Things J. **10**(3), 2519–2527 (2023)
19. Wang, H., Zhang, D., Wang, Y., Ma, J., Wang, Y., Li, S.: RT-Fall: a real-time and contactless fall detection system with commodity wifi devices. IEEE Trans. Mob. Comput. (2017)
20. Wang, Y., Yang, S., Li, F., Wu, Y., Wang, Y.: FallViewer: a fine-grained indoor fall detection system with ubiquitous wi-fi devices. IEEE Internet Things J. (2021)
21. Wang, Y., Wu, K., Ni, L.M.: WiFall: device-free fall detection by wireless networks. IEEE Trans. Mob. Comput. (2017)
22. Xie, Y., Li, Z., Li, M.: Precise power delay profiling with commodity wifi. In: 21st Annual International Conference on Mobile Computing and Networking, MobiCom'15, pp. 53–64. ACM (2015)
23. Zhang, L., Wang, Z., Yang, L.: Commercial wi-fi based fall detection with environment influence mitigation. In: 16th Annual IEEE International Conference on Sensing, Communication, and Networking (SECON) (2019)

# Real-Time Mobile Health Analytics and Interventions Pipeline to Detect Acute Events in COPD


Heet Sankesara[1]([envelope]) [ORCID], Yatharth Ranjan[1]([envelope]) [ORCID], Pauline Conde[1] [ORCID], Malik Althobiani[4] [ORCID], Zulqarnain Rashid[1] [ORCID], Akash Roy Choudhury[1] [ORCID], Callum Stewart[1] [ORCID], Yuezhou Zhang[1] [ORCID], Joanna Porter[3] [ORCID], John Hurst[2] [ORCID], Richard JB Dobson[1] [ORCID], and Amos Folarin[1] [ORCID]

[1] Department of Biostatistics and Health Informatics, King's College London, London, UK
{heet.sankesara,yatharth.ranjan,pauline.conde,zulqarnain.rashid,
akash.roy_choudhury,callum.stewart,yuezhou.zhang,richard.j.dobson,
amos.folarin}@kcl.ac.uk

[2] Royal Free Campus, University College London Respiratory, University College London, London, UK
j.hurst@ucl.ac.uk

[3] Respiratory Medicine, Division of Medicine, Faculty of Medical Sciences, University College London, London, UK
joanna.porter@ucl.ac.uk

[4] Department of Respiratory Therapy, Faculty of Medical Rehabilitation Sciences, King Abdulaziz University, Jeddah, Makkah, Saudi Arabia
malik.althobiani.20@alumni.ucl.ac.uk



**Abstract.** We developed a real-time mHealth anomaly detection pipeline using wearable data to identify chronic obstructive pulmonary disease (COPD) exacerbation events. A scalable framework implemented on the RADAR-base platform integrates data from questionnaires, smartphone sensors, and wearables for building models and running real-time inference. This case study was designed to check the feasibility of a COPD real-time intervention system, focused on technical and engineering feasibility rather than on the performance of analysis methods. In this paper, we applied an unsupervised Long-Short-Term Memory Autoencoder model trained on physiological data to detect deviations from normal health states. In this six-month study with 20 COPD patients, the system's real-time predictions triggered exacerbation rating scale(ERS) questionnaires. The results showed that the system could detect anomalies up to nine days before patients began medication, with ERS reports indicating normal exacerbation ratings but elevated symptom levels. The results thus proved that the system captured the worsening of symptoms before exacerbation onset, showing the potential of real-time mHealth data in health monitoring, enabling timely intervention and, thus, improved management and prognosis.


---


H. Sankesara and Y. Ranjan—The authors contributed equally to the manuscript.




A. Soylu et al. (Eds.): MobiQuitous 2024, LNICST 634, pp. 58–77, 2026.
https://doi.org/10.1007/978-3-032-10554-7_4

**Keywords:** remote-monitoring · mHealth · intervention · real-time · copd

# 1   Introduction

The mobile health (mHealth) domain has immense potential for real-time applications that would improve healthcare, e.g. just-in-time interventions such as pre-empting an adverse event [5, 16]. Real-time mHealth capabilities allow (near)instantaneous monitoring, analysis, and response to health data, enabling timely interventions and decision support (e.g., risk assessment). This is particularly useful for continuous health monitoring of chronic conditions for both acute adverse events and longer-term trajectories. Just-in-time interventions leverage contextual information to deliver personalised and timely support, such as medication reminders, health tips, and behaviour change prompts. With the growing ubiquity of wearable sensors and smartphones, these capabilities have the potential to revolutionise healthcare delivery, inverting the present paradigm and moving towards a proactive, personalised healthcare system which leverages this automation.

Integrating mHealth platforms with machine learning (ML) and deep learning (DL) models enables real-time data analysis and personalised patient healthcare services. RADAR-base is a mHealth platform built around Apache Kafka to provide event-by-event real-time data processing as core capability [22]. We have additionally implemented a scalable framework that provides flexible real-time ML, data analysis and effectors coupled with the existing RADAR-base components. Our framework utilises streams of passive sensor data from wearables and mobile devices and applies ML algorithms to perform actions based on the model results. This framework was applied in a real-world case study of chronic obstructive pulmonary disease (COPD), a common chronic respiratory disease that affects millions of people worldwide [20]. Exacerbations are significant acute events which are debilitating for these patients; low-burden, cost-effective methods for identification, early treatment, and monitoring of these events have the capability to significantly improve patient quality of life.

# 2   Background

## 2.1   RADAR-Base

RADAR-base is an open-source platform to leverage data from wearables and mobile technologies. It provides scalable and customisable capabilities for remote real-time data collection from a wide range of sources and apps, providing a unified system for researchers to store, manage and analyse the collected data [22].

The RADAR-base passive app collects background data from several sensors on modern smartphones, such as ambient noise, ambient light, phone usage information (e.g., which apps have been used and for how long), passive audio, Global Positioning System location, local bluetooth device connectivity, battery life, gyroscope, steps, and acceleration from smartphone sensors.

Alongside passive smartphone data, RADAR-base also collects data from the wearables. The data is collected via plugin integration to the passive app offering a native SDK integration (e.g., Empatica E4) or through third-party vendors' REST-API (e.g., Fitbit, Garmin). Continuous physiological data such as heart rate, respiratory rate, wrist acceleration, physical activity, and sleep are collected via the wearables.

The active app collects data requiring conscious effort (e.g., questionnaires and other tasks), which are customisable according to study requirements. The platform sends notifications via the active app to remind study participants to fill out the questionnaires and other prompts; related timestamps are recorded when the notification is delivered when participants start filling out the questionnaires and finish them.

Data previously collected using RADAR-base have shown that the phone-derived mobility features have the potential to predict future depression, which may provide support for future clinical applications, relapse prevention, and remote mental health monitoring practices in real-world settings [31]. the RADAR-CNS long-term remote monitoring project [15] on adults with major depressive disorder (MDD) revealed digital biomarkers that have the potential to predict depression severity. Digital Biomarkers like Homestay (time at home), Location Entropy (time distribution on different locations), and Residential Location Count (reflecting travelling) were significantly correlated with the subsequent changes in the PHQ-8 (Patient Health Questionnaire) score [14], while changes in the PHQ-8 score significantly affected the subsequent periodicity of mobility.

Furthermore, a study looking at individuals with multiple sclerosis using the RADAR-base platform demonstrates the utility of wearable devices in assessing ambulatory impairments in people with MS in free-living conditions and provides a basis for future investigation into the clinical relevance [25]. In the study, 96 features in different temporal granularities (from minute-level to day-level) from wearable data have been extracted, and their utility in estimating 6-Minute Walk Test scores (6MWT) [8] has been explored. The applied Random Forest model could distinguish the participants with low disability from those with high disability. Furthermore, it is observed that the minute-level ($\leq 8$ min) step count, particularly those capturing the upper end of the step count distribution, had a stronger association with 6MWT. The use of a walking aid was indicative of ambulatory function, measured through 6MWT.

The RADAR-base platform has real-time data collection capabilities and is designed to manage data at any scale. The collected data can be used for various disease cohorts; however, the utilisation of the real-time intervention was limited. Therefore, there was a requirement for the development of a comprehensive end-to-end, real-time pipeline for RADAR-base, intended to facilitate data processing and analysis in diverse manners.

## 2.2 End-to-End Machine Learning Lifecycle Platform Streaming Frameworks

We have researched various machine learning lifecycle platforms to integrate them with our real-time prediction framework. An ML lifecycle platform aims to provide users with the tools to develop, deploy, experiment and improve machine learning and deep learning algorithms. We require a lifecycle platform that can work seamlessly with various machine learning and deep learning frameworks, has a well-defined workflow, is easier to deploy and provides an intuitive UI to track experiments. We evaluated four popular frameworks: Amazon SageMaker, Google AI, TensorFlow Serving, and MLflow. We have listed the advantages and disadvantages of all the platforms.

*The Amazon SageMaker platform* is advantageous for its rapid prototyping capabilities, offering an integrated notebook environment that facilitates swift model development and experimentation. It provides an extensive library of pre-trained models, comprehensive example notebooks, and an optimised development environment with preconfigured kernels, all of which streamline model implementation and deployment. Additionally, SageMaker supports scalable inference through distributed computing. However, it has notable cost implications and imposes workflow constraints that may limit flexibility in complex projects.

*Google AI Platform* offers significant flexibility and portability, allowing seamless deployment of machine learning (ML) pipelines both on-premises and in the Google Cloud environment, which helps avoid vendor lock-in. It strongly integrates with TensorFlow and tools like Google Cloud Dataflow and TensorFlow Extended (TFX) for scalable pipeline management. The platform's disadvantages include challenges in customising modules, nascent support for PyTorch, potential cost escalations, and a steep learning curve requiring substantial time and effort to master.

*TensorFlow Serving combined with TensorBoard* is a cost-effective, open-source solution that eliminates licensing fees and offers optimised performance, particularly for GPUs. It supports model versioning and efficient communication through gRPC and Protobuf. However, it is limited to TensorFlow models, and integrating TensorBoard requires additional configuration efforts.

*MLflow* is also an open-source platform which offers cost-efficiency and excels at experiment tracking, model lifecycle management, and code reproducibility. It provides a modular and independent workflow, facilitating customisation and integration with other tools. Nonetheless, MLflow has limitations in code integration compared to commercial platforms like SageMaker or Google AI and has a steeper learning curve due to its open-source nature.

We decided to integrating MLflow with the real-time platform as it makes tracking different experiments and hyperparameters easier, supports all machine learning frameworks, and packages the machine learning code with its corresponding environment, making it reusable and ideal for inference. Furthermore, MLflow is open-source software that philosophically aligns with the RADAR-base platform.

### 2.3   Chronic Obstructive Pulmonary Disease (COPD)

COPD is a common lung condition often caused by smoking, leading to daily symptoms and frequent chest infections called exacerbations, which can be severe enough to require hospitalisation. Early treatment of exacerbations helps in faster recovery and reduces hospital admissions [29]. Monitoring heart rate and oxygen saturation, especially overnight, can assist in early detection [2]. Combining these signals with symptom data such as COPD Assessment Test (CAT) scores and advanced analysis methods enhances early detection and disease assessment.

### 2.4   Real-Time Intervention Systems for COPD Exacerbations

There is very limited evidence of real-time mhealth systems applied to COPD. One study uses deep neural networks for the prediction of exacerbations [19]. The authors used data from daily measurements of symptom-specific questionnaires, pulse, and peripheral capillary oxygen saturation (SpO2) of the blood. It did not involve spirometry, wearable devices, or smartphone sensors. They used data augmentation to artificially increase the size of the dataset. The data analytics methods included feed-forward neural network (FFNN) and Long-Short-Term Memory (LSTM). This was, however, not a real-time analysis and was done after the data collection. In another study, the author designed a risk assessment dashboard for early interventions in COPD [3]; however, it was an algorithm tested on simulated data and not evaluated in the real world. The authors used a single data type questionnaire, the Clinical COPD Questionnaire (CCQ), and the multi-layer Artificial Neural Network (ANN) method.

There is a lot of interest in using machine learning in real-time to treat COPD, but the platform's lack of availability provides a significant barrier to these types of work, as signified by the lack of literature around this. [23,26]

### 2.5   Autoencoders

The Autoencoder architecture is an unsupervised learning network that aims to learn efficient data representations from unlabelled data [4]. Autoencoder contains an encoder and a decoder network. The encoder reduces the dimensionality of the input data to create a latent space representation of the input. This latent space representation is passed through the decoder model to regenerate the input data. Hence, the model can learn the latent space representation by minimising the loss between the reconstructed tensor and the input tensor.

LSTM-AE uses LSTM architecture [10] as both encoder and decoder networks. LSTM is a Recurrent Neural Network (RNN) that can retain long-term dependencies in sequential data such as time series or text data. LSTM-AE have been prominently used for time series anomaly detection and forecasting [18,28,30]. Since the model can learn accurate input data projection into another vector space, it is possible to detect anomalies by observing deviation in the latent space.

## 3    Aims and Objectives

The objective is to utilise the RADAR-base real-time pipeline in a real-world case study to assess whether the end-to-end apparatus performs as expected in a real-world scenario. This case study aims to determine the feasibility of real-time detection and prediction, providing data to detect anomalies and have participants score these exacerbation predictions when they occur.

## 4    Methods

### 4.1    COPD Case Study

We demonstrate the use of a real-time data processing and analysis framework in a mobile health platform in a real-world COPD patient monitoring scenario with a cohort of 20 COPD patients with a history of 2 or more exacerbations in the last year followed for 6 months [21]. Participants who fit the inclusion/exclusion criteria will be identified from the respiratory outpatient clinics at the University College London Hospital(UCLH) and Royal Free Hospital(RFH) in London. The aim was to simulate an intervention for exacerbations in COPD and study the efficacy of the apparatus and algorithms used. We send an exacerbation rating scale(ERS) questionnaire [7] on detecting an exacerbation from passive wearable data, asking patients to rate their exacerbation state in near real-time. The ERS would later enable us to evaluate the performance of the real-time framework and exacerbation detection algorithm. In future, the ERS could be replaced with an actual intervention (e.g. medication, additional testing, notifying medical team). Data in the study was collected using Garmin Vivo active 4 [9] wearable device, finger pulse oximeter, App-based questionnaires and Nuvoair AirNext Spirometer devices. This tests the apparatus and infrastructure rather than the algorithms used for exacerbation detection in COPD.

### 4.2    Real-Time Analytics and Interventions Framework

The real-time mHealth data processing, model training, and inference pipeline comprises three major components: the model class, the model builder, and the model invocation endpoint, as shown in Fig. 1. The model class library is a customisable data processing class that stores necessary queries to create training, validation, testing, and inference datasets. The model builder has been implemented to adaptively train custom ML/AI-based models that can read incoming data and run training sessions. The trained model and hyperparameters are stored in the MLflow server. The server also stores a packaged inference module that can be accessed to create inferences using a specific model. The model invocation endpoint is a REST API connection capable of reading trained models from the MLflow server and making inferences on exacerbations.

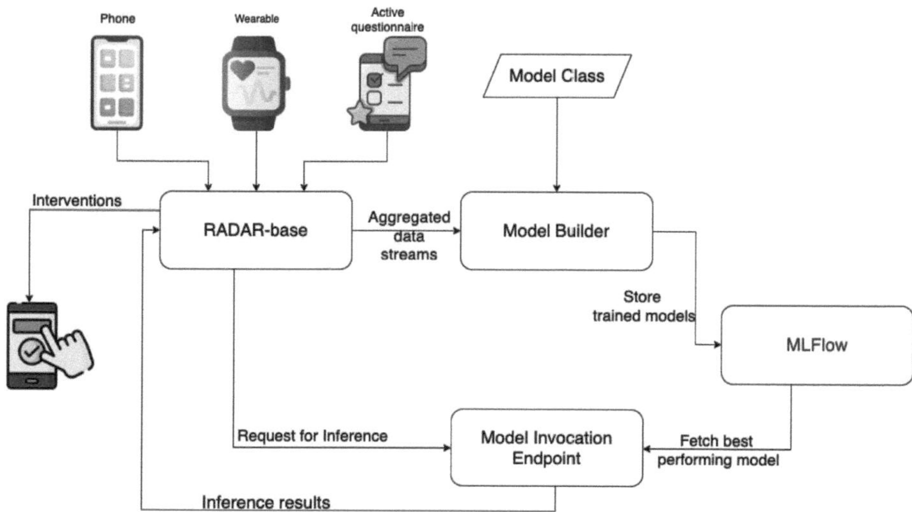


**Fig. 1.** Summarised architecture of the real-time framework. The active and passive smartphone data, along with data from the smartwatch, is collected via RADAR-base. Then, the aggregated data goes to the model builder to train the model. The trained model is stored in the MLflow server, from where the Model Invocation Endpoint module fetches the best-performing model to make inferences and send intervention notification back to the participant's smartphone via RADAR-base

**Model Class.** The Model Class is a blueprint for data preparation and management within the real-time pipeline. It is designed as an abstract class, meaning it cannot be instantiated directly but provides a structure for concrete subclasses to inherit and implement. The core functionalities of the Model Class include the following.

1. *Data Querying*: Defines methods like get-query-for-training and get-query-for-prediction to generate SQL queries for extracting data required for model training and inference, respectively.
2. *Data Preprocessing*: Incorporates a preprocess-data method to handle data cleaning, transformation, and feature engineering necessary for model input.
3. *Output Formatting*: Includes a create-return-obj method to structure inference results into a standardised output format, often accompanied by metadata.

The Model Class utilises the Query Builder class to facilitate efficient SQL query construction. This utility offers a range of functions for creating different query components, such as selecting specific columns, applying grouping and ordering operations, and constructing complex queries.

The system ensures consistency in data handling processes across different ML models by establishing a common interface through the Model Class. This abstraction promotes code reusability, maintainability, and flexibility in the pipeline.

**Model Builder.** The Model Builder executes the model training process. Figure 2(a) shows the architecture of Model Builder. As shown in the figure, The KSQL module aggregates data from the Kafka streams and stores it in the Timescale DB. Afterwards, the necessary model code utilises the data loader component of the Model class to fetch data from the database based on the provided queries. The extracted data is subsequently preprocessed by the Model class.

Once the data is prepared, the Model Builder executes the MLflow training pipeline to construct and train the machine learning model. Upon successful training, the model's hyperparameters, evaluation metrics, and other relevant metadata are recorded in the MLflow server. To ensure model reproducibility and deployment, the trained model, along with the necessary Python environment and Model Class, are packaged and stored in the MinIo object storage.

**Model Invocation Endpoint.** The Model Invocation Endpoint is the crucial interface for real-time inference on the trained machine-learning models. Upon receiving a REST API request, the endpoint initiates the inference process by dynamically determining the appropriate model. This selection can be based on various criteria, such as the latest trained model, the model with the highest performance metrics for a specific task, or a user-specified model version as shown in Fig. 2.

To ensure accurate and relevant predictions, the endpoint leverages the Model Class to construct a tailored prediction query. This query is then executed against the underlying database to retrieve the necessary data for the inference. The extracted data undergoes preprocessing using the Model Class to prepare it for consumption by the model.

Once the data is ready, the endpoint feeds it into the selected model, which generates the desired predictions. The inference results are then returned to the client in a suitable format. Additionally, the endpoint can optionally persist the inference details, including input data, model version, and predictions, in a database for subsequent analysis or auditing purposes.

### 4.3   Unsupervised LSTM Architecture for Anomaly Detection

We have created an unsupervised LSTM-based anomaly detection algorithm to detect exacerbation using physiological signals (Fig. 3). To do that, we have

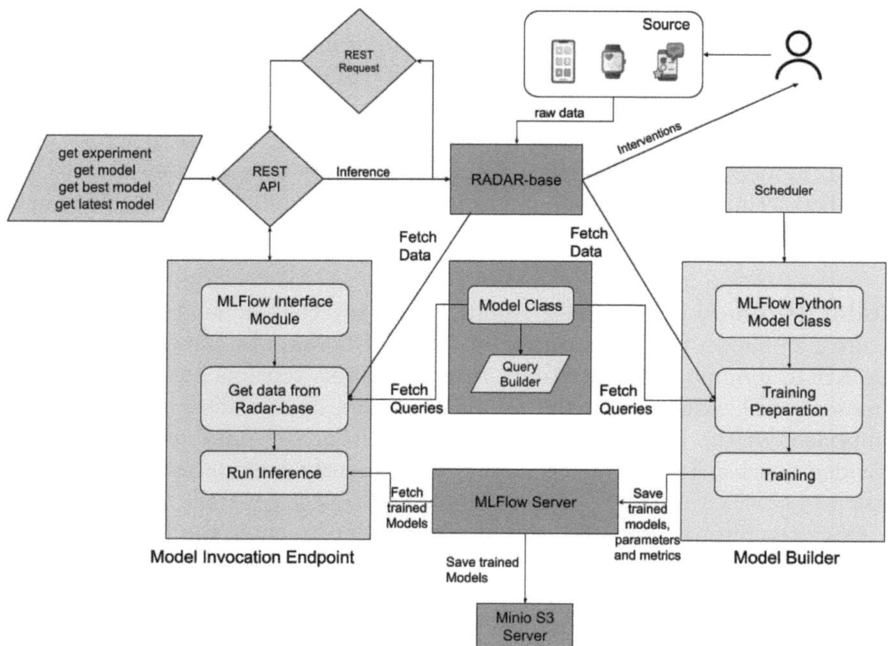



**Fig. 2.** The framework architecture includes the Model Builder, Model Invocation Endpoint, and Model Class. The Model Class handles data queries and preprocessing. Both the Model Builder and Invocation Endpoint access data from the RADAR-base. The Model Builder trains models and stores them on the MLflow server. When the Model Invocation Endpoint receives a REST request, it retrieves the model, processes data from RADAR-base, runs inference, and returns the results with metadata to RADAR-base.

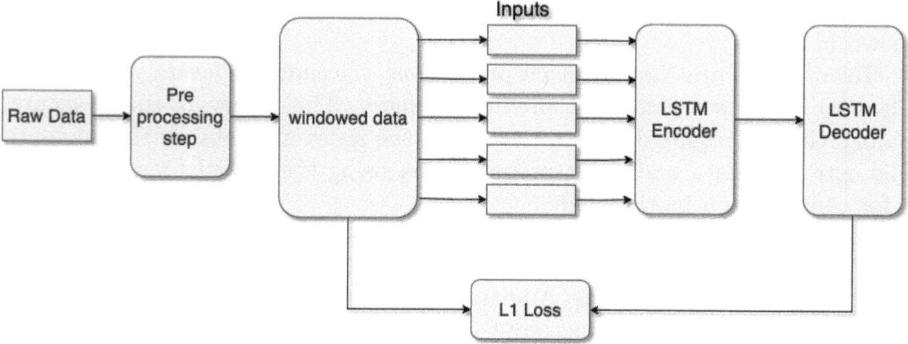



**Fig. 3.** Raw data undergoes preprocessing to transform it into five-day windows. These windows are fed into an LSTM encoder, which generates a latent vector representation. Subsequently, an LSTM decoder reconstructs the input data from this latent vector. The model is trained to minimise the L1 loss between the original and reconstructed data, thereby learning a meaningful latent space representation.

used the self-reported CAT at the baseline to create a training dataset. The idea behind this anomaly detection approach is to use the encoder-decoder model, which can learn latent and salient features by reconstructing the initial input using the output from the encoder function. This would help the model to learn what normal (i.e. without exacerbation episodes) 5 days of physiological data looks like. During the just-in-time inference/prediction, if the model fails to reconstruct the input data with a loss under a certain threshold, we call it an anomaly event and send the participant a notification asking if they are feeling exacerbation episodes. This threshold is the final validation loss we obtained during the training.

**Training and Validation Data.** We used the 5-day windowed data for variables relevant to the cardiopulmonary and other physiology: heart rate, Garmin body battery, Garmin Pulse rate, Garmin Respiration Rate, Garmin Stress, Garmin summary of daily activity, Garmin Sleep data, and CAT score. For every physiological feature, we computed hourly counts, minimum, maximum, average, standard deviation, median, mode, interquartile range, and skewness, yielding 63 hourly physiological characteristics. The CAT score is the gold standard for assessing the severity of COPD, and we used it during the baseline to detect events when participants were not exacerbating. During the training process, we aim to train the model only on the baseline health data so that the model can infer deviations from the normal state. In the literature, a change of more than 5 in the CAT score is considered an exacerbation state, so we excluded data where this is true [12].

**Preprocessing.** The data was preprocessed hourly. Only hours with at least 60 heart rate, 18 body battery, and 1 respiration count of data points were retained. Subsequently, daily data was included if it contained a minimum of 8 h of acceptable heart rate and body battery data and 6 h of acceptable respiration data. Missing values for all variables were imputed with −1, a clear indicator of missing data given the non-negative nature of the signals (Fig. 4).

**Encoder-Decoder Model.** We created an LSTM-based unsupervised model. The model takes 5 days of windowed data as input, with 54 daily psychological features. This data is then used as input for the encoder model, which contains two layers of the LSTM model. The ReLU activation function follows the first layer of the LSTM model, and the second layer follows this. The hidden output from the last vector from the LSTM model passes through the ReLU activation function. We named it the encoded vector.

In the decoder, the encoded vector is repeated five times. Then, it passes through the LSTM, followed by ReLU. Afterwards, it passes through the second LSTM layer. The last vector of the hidden output from the LSTM layer passes through the ReLU activation function, followed by the Dense Layer.

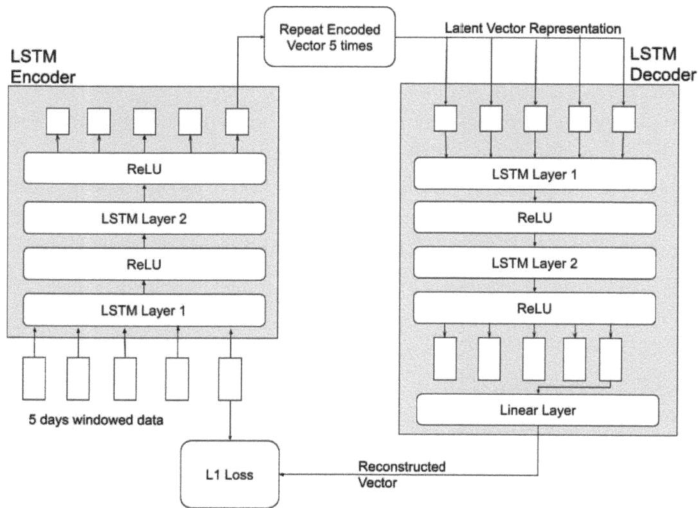


**Fig. 4.** Encoder-Decoder LSTM based model. The LSTM Encoder model contains two instances of LSTM layers, each followed by the ReLU activation function. It has 2,226,176 trainable parameters in total. The LSTM Decoder model has the same layers as the encoder model, followed by the Linear fully connected layer. It has a total of 1,464,432 trainable parameters. Therefore, the whole architecture has 3,689,528 trainable parameters.

We compare the output of the dense layer with the input data from the last day. We use the L1 Loss function to compare how much the reconstructed vector differs from the original one [11]. The L1 loss minimises the error, which is the sum of all the absolute differences between the actual and predicted values. Additionally, using L1 loss for reconstruction enhances the algorithm's robustness and stability compared to L2 loss. This is particularly advantageous due to L1 loss's superior ability to handle outliers [17]. The Adam optimiser [13] minimises the loss function, and the cyclical learning rate [24] method optimises the learning rate as the training progresses. The hyperparameters were selected early in the study by informal experimentations but were not methodically optimised as the aim of this experiment was to assess feasibility for the real-time framework.

During the inference, an anomaly is determined when the model fails to reconstruct the original vector under a certain threshold loss. This threshold loss is the final validation loss we obtained from the trained model.

## 5    Results

### 5.1    The Pipeline

We have used the best-performing model (i.e., the model with the lowest validation loss) to detect anomalies for the participant daily in real-time. When an anomaly is detected, we send the notification on the participant's smartphone to fill out the ERS questionnaire to assess the severity of their condition. Figure 5 shows an example of a change in physiological signals and questionnaire responses when the anomaly is detected. The increase in self-reported CAT score after the anomaly is detected shows that the model can detect the worsening of symptoms.

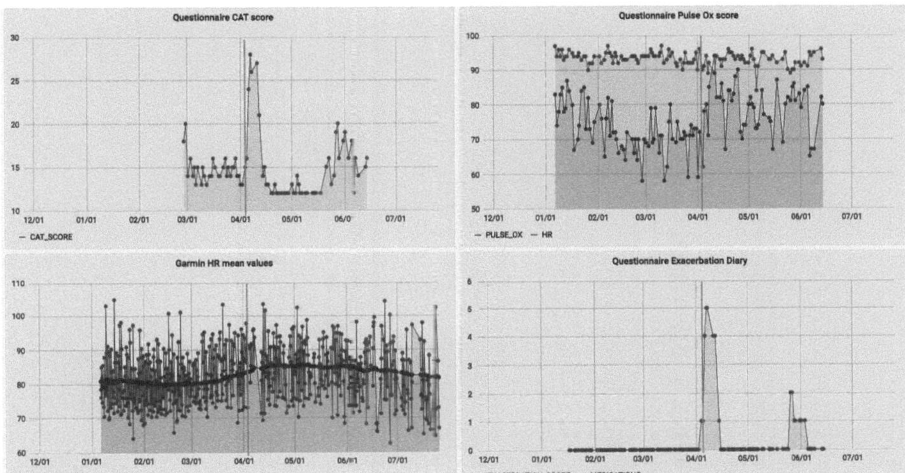

**Fig. 5.** Example changes in data when an anomaly is detected for a participant (blue line) shown in the live dashboard using the LSTM autoencoder-based anomaly detection method. The figure shows changes in the data in the COPD Assessment Test (CAT) questionnaire, Finger pulse oximetry, Garmin heart rate and exacerbation diary questionnaire when an exacerbation (anomaly) is detected based on a model trained only on Garmin wearable data (such as HR, pulse ox, sleep, activity). (Color figure online)

In the COPD case study, the framework ran inference for a total of 4706 times from "2022-02-17" to "2022-12-14", as can be seen in Fig. 6. Of these, 907 anomalies were detected for 15 users. Of the 907 detections, 61 responses were received from 6 users on the triggered on-demand ERS questionnaire since only one questionnaire was sent daily, even if there was more than one detection, resulting in 206 notifications. Some ERS data was missing due to technical glitches with the initial version of the apparatus, which are detailed in the discussion section. However, completion rates were higher for regularly scheduled daily questionnaires like medication (3333 responses), CAT and daily spirometry, which can be utilised as a proxy for ERS.

## 5.2  Primary Data

Figures 7 illustrate the aggregate changes in data after anomaly detection, averaged across all anomalies and users. Notably, medication peaks around 9–12 days

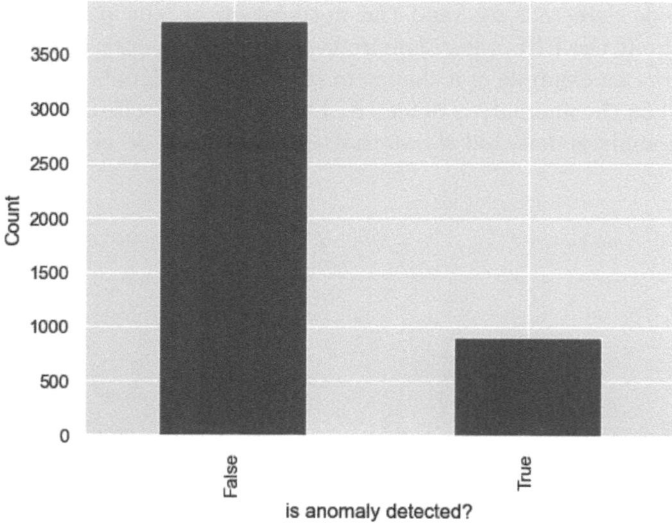



**Fig. 6.** Number of model runs and anomaly detections

after anomaly detection, indicating that the model using only passive wearable data can potentially predict exacerbation before patients start taking medication. FEV1 (Volume exhaled at the end of the first second of forced expiration) values from spirometry drop to the lowest right after anomaly detection and peak back up around the same time as medication peaks.

Next, we have checked the responses to the ERS questionnaire triggered on detecting anomalies in Fig. 8 and responses to validated questionnaires such as CAT when anomalies are detected in Fig. 9. The ERS exacerbation question scores had higher numbers of 0 and 1 responses from the patients, suggesting they were not experiencing exacerbations (very mild if so). The ERS symptom reports, on the other hand, show that most responses are at 1 (second last item on the scale), suggesting worsening symptoms.

As shown in Fig. 9, when anomalies are triggered, the $CAT_{anomaly}$ responses show a trend change from the $CAT_{non-anomaly}$ (CAT score when no anomaly is detected) distribution of the study, with higher values being reported more often when anomalies are detected. Although the p-value using the Mann-Whitney U-test was insignificant, it was trending towards significance with a p-value of 0.0625. Overall, these findings with ERS and CAT could suggest that the system detects an anomaly before the start of the exacerbation when the symptoms start worsening.

## 6  Discussion

The RADAR-Base real-time mHealth data processing and analysis pipeline with wearable data presented in this manuscript demonstrates a promising approach

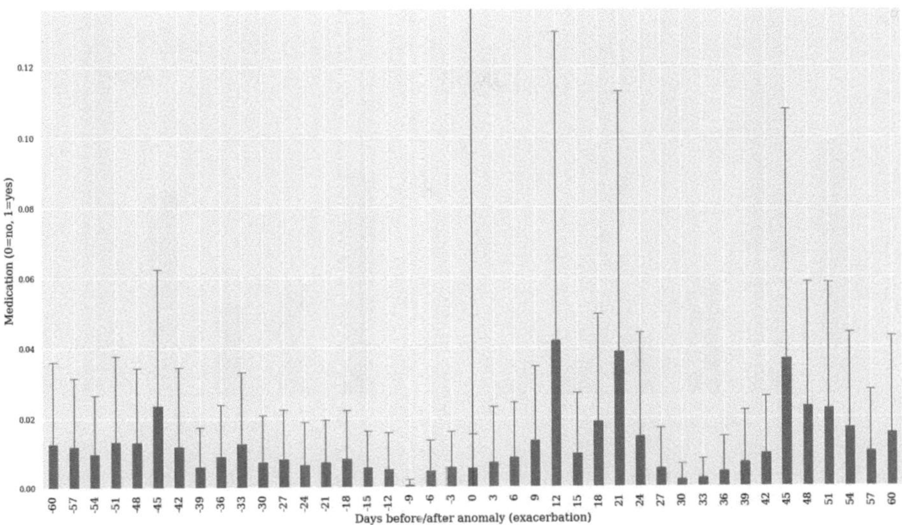

(a) Medication use vs Days before/after anomaly detection

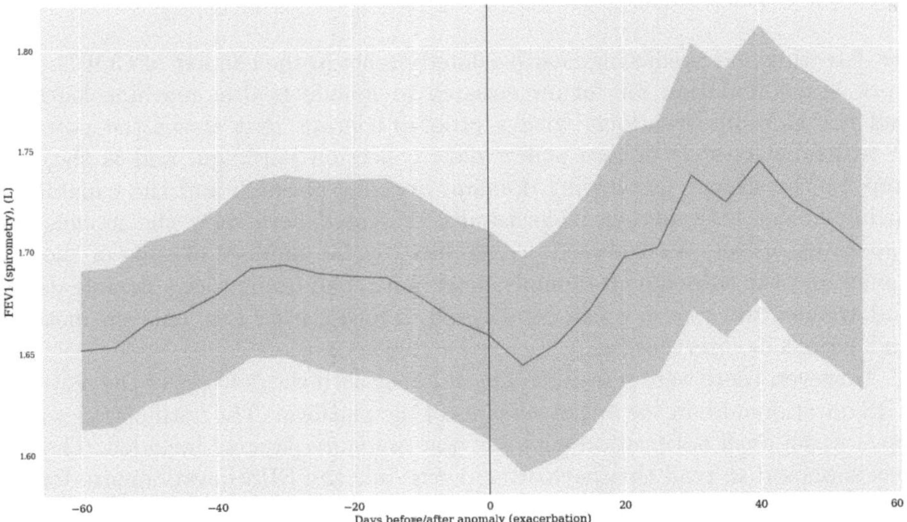

(b) FEV1 (Volume exhaled at the end of the first second of forced expiration)
values from spirometry vs Days before/after anomaly detection

**Fig. 7.** Aggregate medication use and FEV1 (spirometry) values reported around the
detection of anomaly (data types not used in the exacerbation detection LSTM model)
with 95% confidence intervals.

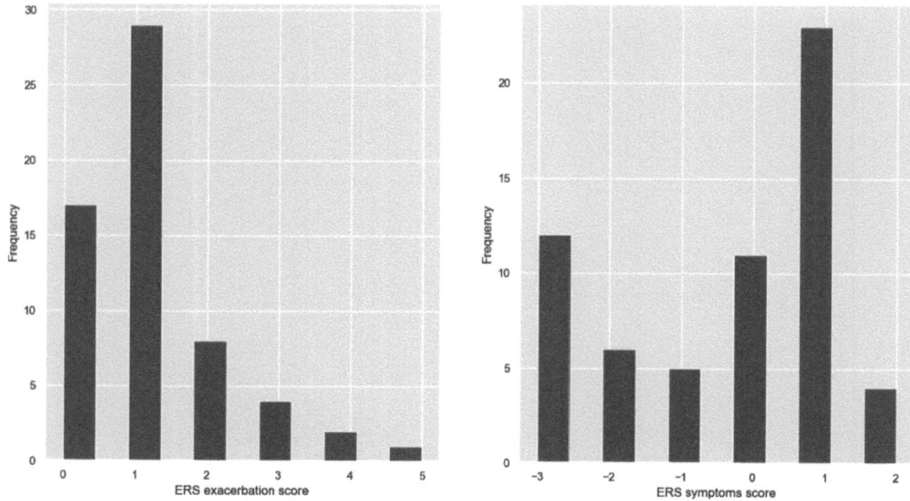

**Fig. 8.** Distribution of the real-time Exacerbation rating scale (ERS) triggered on anomaly detection. The left plot shows the exacerbation score (a higher value means worse exacerbations). The right plot displays the symptom scores (Higher means worsening symptoms).

for detecting and predicting health-related events in the context of COPD. This work is a foundation for future research in mobile health, machine learning, and real-time interventions, with a proof-of-concept that shows the potential of real-time data. It defines a new data collection paradigm and is the next step for the remote monitoring domain, bridging research and the capabilities to implement interventions. The results presented here show the models and apparatus operate as expected, as signified by the number of runs of the ML model and the subsequent anomaly detections. The framework's flexible design and architecture ensure it can be adapted to future use cases, analysis methods and actions or interventions.

However, there were certain technical issues with the delivery of the real-time ERS questionnaire in the initial versions of the platform. The notification sent to users was a push notification with the questionnaire payload included. The app was supposed to read this payload and schedule the ERS questionnaire for the user in the background. Due to restrictions on the amount of background processing and nuances of the Android and IOS operating systems, the scheduling was interrupted, and users were not presented with a questionnaire. The issue with background processing was fixed in the middle of the study by delegating the scheduling to a server backend. The system works well now, as indicated by the 61 responses received after the fixes were deployed, as shown in Fig. 10. This pilot study was designed specifically for this reason: to test the feasibility of the real-time inference apparatus and fix any bugs or issues it may have.

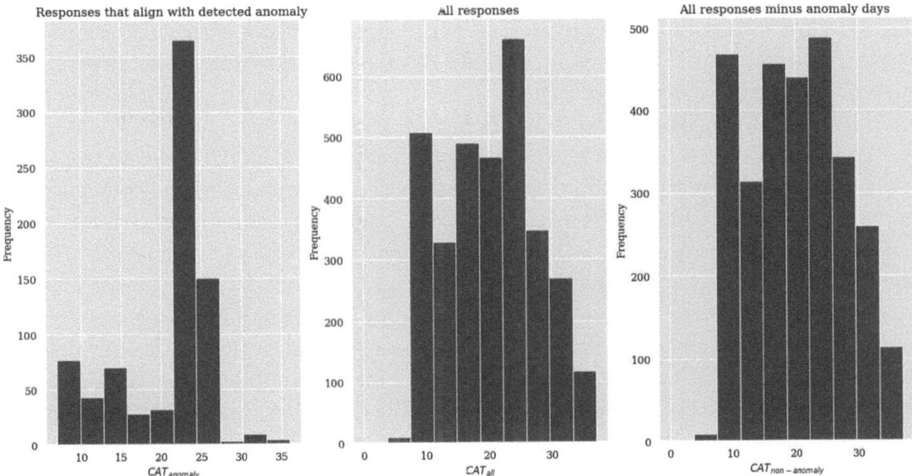

**Fig. 9.** $CAT_{anomaly}$ (daily) distributions on detection of anomalies (left), $CAT_{all}$ distribution in the study (middle) and $CAT_{non-anomaly}$ all responses except anomaly days distributions (right).

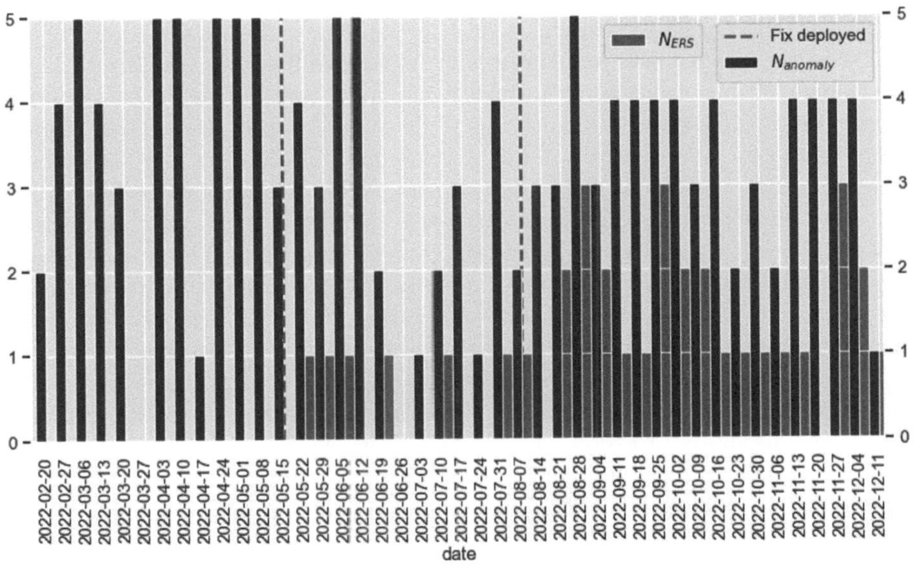



**Fig. 10.** Comparison of detected anomalies and ERS responses over time and the effect of technical fixes deployed. $N_{anomaly}$ (in blue) is the number of unique users for which the anomaly was detected, and $N_{ERS}$ (in red) depicts the number of unique users who completed the ERS questionnaire. The green dotted line shows when the fixes for the technical issues were deployed. (Color figure online)

The system presented demonstrates the potential for collecting multiple passive streams of data for the purpose of early identification of exacerbation; processing the range of passive data sources in near real-time goes beyond the current state of the art. Furthermore, the scope for using the developed system for different use cases and disorders is vital to consider.

This system's potential for generalisation beyond the COPD case with potential application in many chronic disease areas. The framework's flexibility allows us to implement machine-learning and non-machine-learning algorithms based on the problem statement. For instance, with trivial effort, a condition-based algorithm can be employed to notify participants if no passive sensor data is received for a certain period of time. This can improve future data collection and quality by reducing missing data. On the other end of the spectrum, deploying a large mHealth foundation model to predict personalised disease signals in real-time using N-shot learning and verify those predictions via questionnaires is possible. Moreover, a reinforcement learning algorithm can optimise and personalise the time to send questionnaire notifications to each individual based on passive sensor data such as GPS, nearby Bluetooth devices, etc. The model can tune the notification time to improve engagement by assessing participant's responses to those notifications.

COPD exacerbation symptoms can worsen rapidly in a short period of time therefore detecting early signals could provide crucial and life-saving support to individuals. Since it mainly affects middle-aged or older adults, an alert can be sent to the caregivers to check on the patients if we detect an early signal. This can provide essential support for elderly individuals who are living by themselves. From an economic perspective, such a system can be scaled up to provide better, low-burden monitoring. This type of approach can also improve the potential for home or community-based care and alleviate the need for the patients to be cared for in the hospital. Integration with health records would also allow efficient use of clinician/care-team time by helping prioritise participants who are at risk by notifying and prioritising this group. The framework can empower clinicians with valuable insights and decision support by implementing a comprehensive risk dashboard. By aggregating and visualising real-time data from wearable devices, the risk dashboard can give clinicians an actionable holistic view of their patient's health status, trends, and potential risk factors. This real-time risk assessment tool can aid clinicians in identifying high-risk patients, monitoring disease progression, and making informed treatment decisions. Moreover, the dashboard can incorporate predictive algorithms to alert clinicians to impending health events, enabling proactive interventions and personalised care delivery. By integrating machine learning models and evidence-based guidelines, the risk dashboard can enhance clinical decision-making and optimise resource allocation, ultimately improving patient outcomes and healthcare efficiency. A further benefit of these systems will be to improve over time by accumulating large amounts of labelled data as part of normal care pathways; these will be a powerful asset for improving models.

Several vital areas deserve attention in terms of future work. A follow-up study could further validate the system's performance and explore opportunities for improvement. Enhancing compliance in real-time data collection and refining the classification model for real-time analysis is essential to optimising the system's functionality. Additionally, exploring personalised/intelligent notifications could enhance the system's utility and user experience, ultimately improving healthcare outcomes. Moreover, the framework can be utilised for multiple diseases and health conditions. Anomaly detection while monitoring for chronic depression can detect the early onset of depression and can be used to provide appropriate early care [1]. Atrial fibrillation episodes can be detected in real-time by monitoring irregular heart rhythms [6], whereas irregular breathing and PPG signals can be used to detect Asthma attacks [27].

Addressing the ease of configuration, setup, and deployment of the real-time system is crucial for its widespread adoption. While a distributed microservices setup offers advantages in interoperability, flexibility, and scalability, it also presents challenges in installation and configuration. Overcoming these challenges and streamlining the setup process will be imperative for the system's practical implementation and utilisation in diverse healthcare environments. This also involves improving the system with prebaked analytics templates that can be configured through a graphical user web interface and a drag-and-drop configuration for non-technical users.

Finally, it is essential to reflect on the lessons learned from this study and outline how they will be applied in future, more extensive studies. The insights gained from this research will inform the design and implementation of future studies, guiding the development of more comprehensive and impactful healthcare solutions. In the future, we plan to expand our framework to include more ML algorithms and cohorts and validate its performance in more extensive studies. The framework should eventually enable guided clinical decision-making and early interventions in the long term. The framework presented in this manuscript holds promise for future applications in personalised health monitoring, predictive analytics, and clinical decision support. Through interventions targeted at both clinicians and patients, this approach can enhance healthcare delivery, improve patient outcomes, and contribute to the advancement of real-time, personalised healthcare solutions.

In conclusion, the real-time mHealth data processing and analysis pipeline with wearable data presents a promising approach for real-time detection, prediction, and potential intervention in healthcare. Its potential for generalisation, future work considerations, and the application of lessons learned will shape the direction of future research and contribute to the advancement of personalised, real-time healthcare solutions.

## References


1. Adler, D.A., et al.: Predicting early warning signs of psychotic relapse from passive sensing data: an approach using encoder-decoder neural networks. JMIR Mhealth Uhealth **8**(8), e19962 (2020)

2. Al Rajeh, A.M., et al.: Once daily versus overnight and symptom versus physiological monitoring to detect exacerbations of chronic obstructive pulmonary disease: pilot randomized controlled trial. JMIR Mhealth Uhealth 8(11), e17597 (2020)
3. Alharbey, R.: Predictive analytics dashboard for monitoring patients in advanced stages of copd. In: 2016 49th Hawaii International Conference on System Sciences (HICSS), pp. 3455–3461. IEEE (2016)
4. Bank, D., Koenigstein, N., Giryes, R.: Autoencoders. In: Machine Learning for Data Science Handbook: Data Mining and Knowledge Discovery Handbook, pp. 353–374 (2023)
5. Beratarrechea, A., Lee, A.G., Willner, J.M., Jahangir, E., Ciapponi, A., Rubinstein, A.: The impact of mobile health interventions on chronic disease outcomes in developing countries: a systematic review. Telemed. e-Health 20(1), 75–82 (2014)
6. Biersteker, T.E., Schalij, M.J., Treskes, R.W.: Impact of mobile health devices for the detection of atrial fibrillation: systematic review. JMIR Mhealth Uhealth 9(4), e26161 (2021)
7. Choi, H.S., et al.: Exacerbations of chronic obstructive pulmonary disease tool to assess the efficacy of acute treatment. Int. J. Chronic Obstruct. Pulmonary Dis. 471–478 (2019)
8. Enright, P.L.: The six-minute walk test. Respir. Care 48(8), 783–785 (2003)
9. Garmin, subsidiaries, G.L.O.I.: Garmin vívoactive 4: Smartwatch with gps: Fitness. https://www.garmin.com/en-GB/p/643382
10. Hochreiter, S., Schmidhuber, J.: Long short-term memory. Neural Comput. 9(8), 1735–1780 (1997)
11. Janocha, K., Czarnecki, W.M.: On loss functions for deep neural networks in classification. arXiv preprint arXiv:1702.05659 (2017)
12. Jones, P., et al.: Health status progression measured using weekly telemonitoring of copd assessment test scores over 1 year and its association with copd exacerbations. Chronic Obstruct. Pulmonary Dis. J. COPD Found. 11(2), 144 (2024)
13. Kingma, D.P., Ba, J.: Adam: a method for stochastic optimization. arXiv preprint arXiv:1412.6980 (2014)
14. Kroenke, K., Strine, T.W., Spitzer, R.L., Williams, J.B., Berry, J.T., Mokdad, A.H.: The phq-8 as a measure of current depression in the general population. J. Affect. Disord. 114(1–3), 163–173 (2009)
15. London, K.C.: RADAR-CNS (Remote Assessment of Disease and Relapse – Central Nervous System)—kcl.ac.uk. https://www.kcl.ac.uk/research/radarcns. Accessed 27 July 2024
16. Mao, Y., Lin, W., Wen, J., Chen, G.: Impact and efficacy of mobile health intervention in the management of diabetes and hypertension: a systematic review and meta-analysis. BMJ Open Diab. Res. Care 8(1), e001225 (2020)
17. Mu, J., Zhang, X., Zhu, S., Xiong, R.: Riemannian loss for image restoration. In: Proceedings of the IEEE/CVF Conference on Computer Vision and Pattern Recognition Workshops (2019)
18. Nguyen, H.D., Tran, K.P., Thomassey, S., Hamad, M.: Forecasting and anomaly detection approaches using LSTM and LSTM autoencoder techniques with the applications in supply chain management. Int. J. Inf. Manag. 57, 102282 (2021)
19. Nunavath, V., Goodwin, M., Fidje, J.T., Moe, C.E.: Deep neural networks for prediction of exacerbations of patients with chronic obstructive pulmonary disease. In: Pimenidis, E., Jayne, C. (eds.) EANN 2018. CCIS, vol. 893, pp. 217–228. Springer, Cham (2018). https://doi.org/10.1007/978-3-319-98204-5_18
20. Quaderi, S., Hurst, J.: The unmet global burden of copd. Glob. Health Epidemiol. Genom. 3, e4 (2018)

21. Ranjan, Y., et al.: Remote assessment of lung disease and impact on physical and mental health (ralpmh): protocol for a prospective observational study. JMIR Res. Protocols **10**(10), e28873 (2021)
22. Ranjan, Y., et al.: Radar-base: open source mobile health platform for collecting, monitoring, and analyzing data using sensors, wearables, and mobile devices. JMIR mHealth uHealth **7**(8), e11734 (2019)
23. Shah, A.J., Althobiani, M.A., Saigal, A., Ogbonnaya, C.E., Hurst, J.R., Mandal, S.: Wearable technology interventions in patients with chronic obstructive pulmonary disease: a systematic review and meta-analysis. NPJ Dig. Med. **6**(1), 222 (2023)
24. Smith, L.N.: Cyclical learning rates for training neural networks. In: 2017 IEEE Winter Conference on Applications of Computer Vision (WACV), pp. 464–472. IEEE (2017)
25. Sun, S., et al.: The utility of wearable devices in assessing ambulatory impairments of people with multiple sclerosis in free-living conditions. Comput. Methods Programs Biomed. **227**, 107204 (2022)
26. Taylor, A., et al.: Remote-management of copd: evaluating the implementation of digital innovation to enable routine care (receiver): the protocol for a feasibility and service adoption observational cohort study. BMJ Open Respir. Res. **8**(1), e000905 (2021)
27. Taylor, L., Ding, X., Clifton, D., Lu, H.: Wearable vital signs monitoring for patients with asthma: a review. IEEE Sens. J. **23**(3), 1734–1751 (2022)
28. Wei, Y., et al.: LSTM-autoencoder-based anomaly detection for indoor air quality time-series data. IEEE Sens. J. **23**(4), 3787–3800 (2023)
29. Wilkinson, T.M., Donaldson, G.C., Hurst, J.R., Seemungal, T.A., Wedzicha, J.A.: Early therapy improves outcomes of exacerbations of chronic obstructive pulmonary disease. Am. J. Resp. Crit. Care Med. **169**(12), 1298–1303 (2004)
30. Xu, X., Yoneda, M.: Multitask air-quality prediction based on LSTM-autoencoder model. IEEE Trans. Cybern. **51**(5), 2577–2586 (2019)
31. Zhang, Y., et al.: Longitudinal relationships between depressive symptom severity and phone-measured mobility: dynamic structural equation modeling study. JMIR Mental Health **9**(3), e34898 (2022)

# Wearable-Based Fair and Accurate Pain Assessment Using Multi-attribute Fairness Loss in Convolutional Neural Networks


Sharmin Sultana[1], Yidong Zhu[1], Shao-Hsien Liu[2],
and Mohammad Arif Ul Alam[1,2,3(✉)]

[1] University of Massachusetts Lowell, Lowell, MA, USA
{Sharmin_Sultana,Yidong_Zhu}@student.uml.edu
[2] University of Massachusetts Chan Medical School, Worcester, MA, USA
{ShaoHsien.Liu,MohammadArifUl.Alam1}@umassmed.edu
[3] National Institute on Aging, National Institute of Health, Bethesda, MD, USA



**Abstract.** The integration of diverse health data, such as IoT (Internet of Things), EHR (Electronic Health Record), and clinical surveys, with scalable AI(Artificial Intelligence) has enabled the identification of physical, behavioral, and psycho-social indicators of pain. However, the adoption of AI in clinical pain evaluation is hindered by challenges like personalization and fairness. Many AI models, including machine and deep learning, exhibit biases, discriminating against specific groups based on gender or ethnicity, causing skepticism among medical professionals about their reliability. This paper proposes a Multi-attribute Fairness Loss (MAFL) based Convolutional Neural Network (CNN) model designed to account for protected attributes in data, ensuring fair pain status predictions while minimizing disparities between privileged and unprivileged groups. We evaluate whether a balance between accuracy and fairness is achievable by comparing the proposed model with existing mitigation methods. Our findings indicate that the model performs favorably against state-of-the-art techniques. Using the NIH All-Of-US dataset, comprising data from 868 individuals over 1500 days, we demonstrate our model's effectiveness, achieving accuracy rates between 75% and 85%.

**Keywords:** CNN (Convolution Neural Network) · Fair-Loss ·
Privileged Group · Unprivileged Group · Protected Attribute. · Pain
Assessment


## 1 Introduction

The Intelligent Internet of Things (IIoT) is helping to improve healthcare by allowing for continuous monitoring of health vitals and behaviors, which can



A. Soylu et al. (Eds.): MobiQuitous 2024, LNICST 634, pp. 78–96, 2026.
https://doi.org/10.1007/978-3-032-10554-7_5

lead to just-in-time health interventions to the needful communities [1–3]. Given the hype and potential to revolutionize health assessment through IIoT coupling with hospital records, heterogeneous data availability has emerged as the largest dimension than ever and revolutionizes better health care by improving all aspects of patient care, including safety, effectiveness, patient-centeredness, education, and efficiency [4–6]. For all its potential, the use of Artificial Intelligence (AI) in healthcare also brings major risks and potential unintended harm by introducing biases in AI decisions. Such biased or unfair AI may discriminate its decisions based on persons' sensitive attributes also known as protected attributes (such as race, gender, ethnicity, and disabilities) which result in mistrust among clinicians and prevent AI systems to adopt in clinical settings [7,8]. Despite efforts to close these gaps, racial/ethnic minorities continue to have poorer healthcare and outcomes [9]. In AI, such discrimination is referred to as bias [10].

Bias indicates the inclination of judgment towards a certain group of people. Bias may arise from diverse origins, including unintentional errors by individuals, historical prejudices, and algorithmic parameters [11]. Measuring bias is challenging because it may occur explicitly or implicitly [12]. Explicit bias involves conscious attitudes that can be measured by self-report while implicit biases occur outside of conscious awareness and can result in a negative evaluation of a person based on protected attributes [13]. Protected attribute refers to the features that partition the entire population into groups and these groups influence the parity of the outcome. *Privileged Group* refers to the group of people in the protected attributes who are at systematic advantage level, generally having opportunities, benefits, or advantages in society that are not available to all groups. These privileges are often unearned and may be invisible to those who have them. *Unprivileged Group* is on the other side, refers to the group of people in the protected attributes who are at a systematic disadvantage level.

In a clinical context, the most effective approaches to evaluating an individual's health status are those that utilize straightforward and comprehensible questions and procedures. Self-reported questionnaires such as the Iowa Pain Thermometer (IPT) and Numeric Rating Scale (NRS) excel in assessing pain severity. However, the task of accurately diagnosing and managing pain remains challenging for healthcare providers due to its widespread occurrence and negative implications [14–18].

Additionally, the presence of racial bias in healthcare further complicates pain assessment and treatment. Medical professionals who endorse themselves false beliefs about biological differences between the two groups (Black or White) rate a Black patient's pain lower and provide less accurate treatment recommendations [19]. They also highlight existing research revealing disparities in pain treatment between Black and white patients, where Black patients are less likely to receive pain medications and are often given lower quantities. This concerning trend persists even in cases involving pediatric patients, revealing both overprescription for White patients and underprescription for Black patients. Furthermore, gender bias also plays a significant role in pain evaluation. A study reveals that female patients' pain tends to be underestimated due to ingrained gender stereotypes and biases [20]. Hence it's critical to understand the limitations of specific assessment techniques as well as the significant influence that biases have on the diagnosis and management of pain.

This paper introduces a research contribution centered on predicting patients' pain status using heart rate and step-count data obtained from wearable devices (Fitbit) and Electronic Health Records (EHR). The proposed approach utilizes a novel CNN method with Multi-attribute Fairness Loss (MAFL), incorporating all protected attributes (age, gender, race, ethnicity, cognitive ability) from the data and aiming to address disparities among protected attributes. The effectiveness of the fair pain assessment model is evaluated using NIH All-Of-US data [21], analyzing a cohort of 868 individuals' wearable and EHR data collected over 1500 days. The proposed model aims to promote fairness in classification by reducing differences between privileged and disadvantaged groups based on these attributes.

## 2   Literature Review

A lot of extraordinary work has been reported in the literature on pain assessment for wearable devices. However, to the best of our knowledge, there has been very limited work reported that uses bias detection and mitigation techniques to predict pain status. Below are some notable works which we studied in detail to understand the challenges in this research domain.

### 2.1   Clinical Pain Assessment Data Biases

Research has shown that racial, age-related, and socioeconomic biases exist in pain treatment, with nonwhite and older patients and those of lower socioeconomic status being less likely to receive pain medication [22,23]. Among others, age-related bias [24], (i.e., older adults being less likely to receive pain medications for pain compared to younger adults), socioeconomic bias [25] (i.e., lower socioeconomic status influencing clinician decision-making in pain treatment), have been observed significantly in clinical settings. Beside that, data may get biased to the light-skin-toned people over dark skin people in the publicly available datasets [45] whereas performance ML (Machine Learning) models also affect because of gender, age, and racial attributes [26]. Such biases skewed the decision of the models to the advantageous groups.

### 2.2   Wearable-Based Pain Assessment Automation

Wearable devices offer a promising opportunity to enhance pain assessment outcomes in clinical and research settings. The underlying concept is that pain triggers sympathetic physiological responses, reflected in increased heart and respiratory rates, blood pressure, and other measures' [27,28]. While wearable-based pain assessment research is limited, a study showed that biweekly coaching with wearables improved physical activity in knee osteoarthritis patients, potentially alleviating pain [29]. Correlation studies have explored pain biomarkers through wearables; for instance, Hallman et al. linked reduced neck/shoulder pain in males with less work-related sitting time [30], Jacobson and O'Cleirigh predicted pain levels (0–10) with 74.63% accuracy using minute-level activities for HIV patients [31], and Johnson et al. achieved 0.729 error rate in pain level prediction using Microsoft Band 2's accelerometer and heart rate data [32].

### 2.3   Bias in Wearables-Based Health Vitals Monitoring System

While earlier discussions hinted at wearables' potential for unbiased pain assessment, recent studies reveal that wearable sensors aren't immune to biases. These wearables offer a wealth of health-related data, encompassing heart rate anomalies, personal electrocardiogram (ECG) monitors, sleep trackers, and pulse pressure devices for a healthier lifestyle [33]. However, findings show that photoplethysmographic (PPG) green light signals lead to heart rate miscalculation in individuals with lighter skin tones, and galvanic skin response devices are less accurate for those with darker skin tones [34]. Despite limited coverage, the impact of dark skin tones on wearable accuracy remains a largely unaddressed issue necessitating industrial and scientific attention. Similarly, wearable-based health monitoring might engender disparities in older adults, and individuals with skin conditions, and possibly persist in wearable-based machine learning algorithms [35].

In this paper, we focus on pain progression alignment with the help of wearable (Fitbit) and EHR data. To predict pain status, we introduce MAFL, a novel loss function-based CNN model that incorporates all protected attributes present in the dataset. The aim of our implemented model is to reduce disparities among privileged and unprivileged groups.

## 3   Proposed Methodology

Our proposed framework consists of the following core modules, as depicted in Fig. 1:

1. **Data Collection:** In this module, we utilize the expansive NIH All-Of-Us dataset to query and select wearable sensor data, specifically data from Fitbit devices, in conjunction with corresponding EHR data. This step forms the foundational data source for our pain assessment framework.
2. **Time Series Feature Extraction:** This module focuses on the extraction of features from time-series data.
3. **Pain Assessment Ground Truth Extraction:** In this module, we perform ICD-10 code matching and interpretation to extract pain assessment ground truths from the All-Of-Us EHR database. These ground truths serve as the basis for training and validating our pain assessment model.
4. **Bias Detection** Five fairness metrics were used to estimate the intensity of bias. Identifying bias within pain assessment is crucial to ensure fairness and equity in our framework.

5. **Bias Mitigation:** To address identified biases, we introduce a Multi-attribute Fairness Loss (MAFL) based CNN model. This model is designed to detect pain levels using personalized features and pain assessment ground truth data. Its primary goal is to reduce disparities in pain assessment among privileged and underprivileged demographic groups.

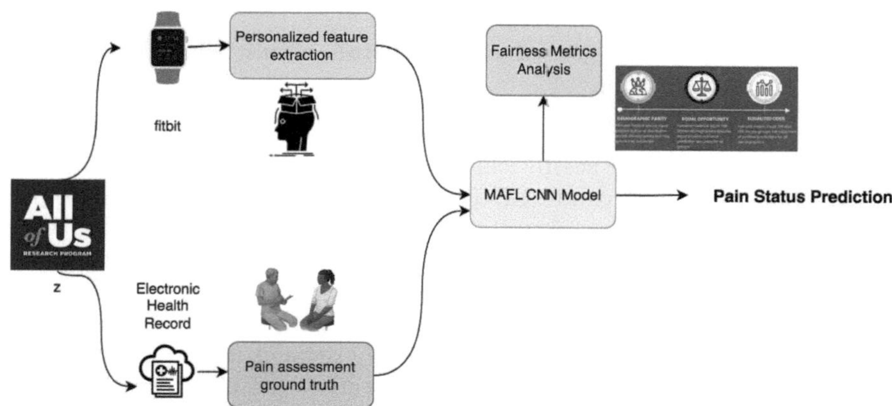


**Fig. 1.** Proposed Wearables and Electronic Health Record (EHR) based Fair Pain Assessment Automation Pipeline

## 3.1  NIH All-of-Us Data Collection

To access NIH All of Us data, we registered and signed a Data Use and Registration Agreement (DURA). Each member underwent the Collaborative Institutional Training Initiative (CITI Program) training and applied for Controlled Tier access. To date, the All Of Us Research Program collected diverse data from 327,000+ participants without missing values with the help of 100+ funded partner organizations from 460+ sites where 50% of them are racial and ethnic minorities. Among the entire data, 11,700 participants have wearable (Fitbit watch), EHR, and all forms of EMA (the basic, overall, health, lifestyle, pain assessment, personal medical history, etc.) surveys. The inclusion criteria of this paper are, that participants must have been evaluated with pain in the hospital visit at least twice in the same year and each of the wearable sensor values (Fitbit minute level step count and minute level average heart rate) should not have any missing values more than 10%. Among these 11,700 population of the whole dataset, only 636 (5%) match the inclusion criteria. We used the concept ID '3036453' from the EHR that provides a Visual Analog Score (VAS) of the pain assessment tool ranging from 0–10 where 10 is estimated as the highest level of pain and 0 is estimated as no pain.

## 3.2   Time Series Feature Extraction

Time series feature extraction serves as the initial stage in traditional machine learning methods. We analyze minute-level total step count and average heart rate data from the Fitbit wearable sensor, extracting more than 60 diverse features across temporal, statistical, and spectral domains for each individual data point. Table 1 shows the details of our extracted features in the above-considered domain.

**Table 1.** Statistical, temporal, and spectral domain feature details

**Statistical domain features**

Empirical Cumulative Distribution Function (ECDF), ECDF Percentile, ECDF Percentile Count, Histogram, Interquartile range, Kurtosis, Max, Mean, Mean absolute deviation, Median, Median absolute deviation, Min, Root mean square, Skewness, Standard deviation, Variance

**Temporal domain features**

Absolute energy, Area under the curve, Autocorrelation, Centroid, Entropy, Mean absolute diff, Mean diff, Median absolute diff, Median diff, Negative turning points, Peak-to-peak distance, Positive turning points, Signal distance, Slope, Sum absolute diff, Total energy, Zero crossing rate, Neighbourhood peaks

**Spectral domain features**

FFT mean coefficient, Fundamental frequency, Human range energy, Linear prediction cepstral coefficients (LPCC), Mel-frequency cepstral coefficients (MFCC), Max power spectrum, Maximum frequency, Median frequency, Power bandwidth, Spectral centroid, Spectral decrease, Spectral distance, Spectral entropy, Spectral kurtosis, Spectral positive turning points, Spectral roll-off, Spectral roll-on, Spectral skewness, Spectral slope, Spectral spread, Spectral variation, Wavelet absolute mean, Wavelet energy, Wavelet standard deviation, Wavelet entropy, Wavelet variance

In this paper, we did personalized feature extraction where only the total step count and average heart rate every minute are considered in our data set. We use the feature deviance method to extract personalized features for each individual. In this regard, at first, we extract statistical, temporal, and spectral domain feature $X_d^{fi}$ where $f$, $i$ and $d$ refer to the type of feature $f \in F = \{statistical, temporal, spectral\}$, index of feature $i \in N = \{1, 2..N\}$ (we have total N=60 features), day of the collected wearable data. We consider 4 different deviant functions on these 60 extracted features described as follows:

1. **Mathematical deviance:** This function directly subtracts previous day's features $X_{d-1}^{fi}$ from current day's, $X_d^{fi}$.

$$X_d^{fi}(1) = X_d^{fi} - X_{d-1}^{fi} \tag{1}$$

2. **Logarithmic deviance:** This function subtracts the previous day's logarithmic features from the current day's logarithmic features.

$$X_d^{fi}(2) = log(X_d^{fi}) - log(X_{d-1}^{fi}) \tag{2}$$

3. **Cosine deviance:** This function multiplies the previous day's cosine features with the current day's cosine features.

$$X_d^{fi}(3) = cos(X_d^{fi}) * cos(X_{d-1}^{fi}) \tag{3}$$

4. **LogCosh deviance:** This function can be defined as the following equation.

$$X_d^{fi}(4) = log(\frac{(e^x + e{-}x)}{2}) \tag{4}$$

where x is the mathematical deviance $X_d^{fi}(1)$ from Eq. 1.

Finally, we normalize all of the features thus they can be fed into the model.

### 3.3   Pain Assessment Ground Truth Extraction

These days, clinicians are more concerned about the changes (recovering or worsening) of pain rather than pure pain assessment with a scale ranging from 0 to 10, [36,37], we consider pain assessment as a pain recovery tracking progression (recovering or worsening than last assessment) to pace with the modern clinical pain progress tracking practice. In this regard, at first, we consider only the days when we have a ground truth of pain assessment using clinically validated tools extracted from EHR. Then, consider our problem as a binary classification, where the pain recovery will be labeled as 'True' if a patient's current state of pain is improved (pain level score gets reduced); and 'False' otherwise. To accommodate such pain recovery tracking problem, we require at least one prior pain assessment conducted by clinically validated tools. Such clinician/nurse evaluated prior pain assessment comparisons to enhance the 'human accountability' which is a core component of ML fairness [38].

### 3.4   Bias Detection

In this paper, we used 5 fairness metrics to check bias in our data and mitigation algorithm. Here, we use 'Unprv' to refer to the unprivileged group and 'Prv' to refer to the privileged group in all equations.

**Statistical Parity Difference** is the difference between the favorable outcome for unprivileged groups and privileged groups. Dwork et al.(2012) introduced the concept as "statistical parity" or "demographic parity" and defined it mathematically as below equation where A is the protected attribute [39], in our case the 'Prv'. The ideal value is 0 and this metric is considered fair for values ranging from $-0.1$ to $0.1$.

$$P(Y = 1|Unprv) - P(Y = 1|Prv) \tag{5}$$

**Disparate Impact** refers to the ratio of favorable outcomes for the unprivileged group to the privileged group. The ideal value for disparate impact is 1 and it is considered fair if the value ranges between 0.8 to 1.25. If the disparate impact value is less than 1, it gives benefits to the privileged group otherwise unprivileged group gets the advantage. Feldman et al.(2015) introduced the 80% rule from US labor law into algorithmic fairness and formalized the DI [40], in our case which can be written as:

$$\frac{P(Y = 1|Unprv)}{P(Y = 1|Prv)} \tag{6}$$

**Equal Opportunity Difference** computes the true positive rate difference between unprivileged and privileged groups whereas the true positive rate is the ratio of true positives to the total number of actual positives for a given group. The ideal value is 0 and the fairness range for this metric is -0.1 to 0.1. If the value is greater than 0, unprivileged groups are considered to benefit and if it is less than 0, privileged groups are the beneficiary. Hardt et al. (2016) introduced equal opportunity as TPR parity between groups and defined it mathematically [41], in our case can be presented as:

$$TPR = \frac{\#\text{True positive predictive values}}{\text{Total positive values}} \tag{7}$$

$$TPR(Unprv) - TPR(Prv) \tag{8}$$

**Theil Index** is a statistical measure of inequality that computes the distance away from the ideal value. The perfect value is 0, the lower value represents fairer metrics while the higher value indicates a problem. Speicher et al.(2018) adapted Theil index from economics to measure machine learning fairness and showed how it captures both individual and group unfairness [42].

**Average Odd Difference** is the average difference between the false positive rate and true positive rate between unprivileged and privileged groups. Hardt et al. (2016) introduced equalized odds, which average odds difference is based on and defined it using both FPR and TPR differences [41], the formula in our case is

$$\frac{(FPR_{Unprv} - FPR_{Prv}) + (TPR_{Unprv} - TPR_{Prv})}{2} \tag{9}$$

While the perfect value of this metric is 0, it is considered fair if the value ranges between -0.1 to 0.1. A value less than 0 implies benefit to the privileged group otherwise unprivileged group takes advantage.

We focused on Statistical Parity Difference (SPD) and Disparate Impact (DI) for initial bias detection due to their complementary nature [43]. SPD provides an absolute difference measure, while DI offers a ratio-based assessment, allowing us to capture both absolute and relative disparities in outcomes. For comprehensive evaluation, we employ all these five fairness metrics.

## 3.5  Bias Mitigation

Pain assessment is frequently influenced by a patient's demographic information, resulting in unequal care for certain groups. Hence, it's vital to establish a system free from bias to ensure equitable treatment for all segments of the population. In this paper, we designed a loss function MAFL that incorporates fairness constraints (demographic parity) alongside traditional binary cross-entropy loss. Then we train the CNN model with MAFL on our dataset. During training, the model will learn to minimize the disparities between privileged and unprivileged groups.

**Design of FairLoss**

---

**Multi_Attribute_Fair_Loss**($y_{\text{true}}, y_{\text{pred}}$):
    *unprivileged_indices* ← indices where *sensitive_attributes* equals 0
    *privileged_indices* ← indices where *sensitive_attributes* equals 1
    *loss_unprivileged* ← mean of $y_{\text{pred}}$ values at *unprivileged_indices*
    *loss_privileged* ← mean of $y_{\text{pred}}$ values at *privileged_indices*
    *disparity* ← *loss_privileged* - *loss_unprivileged*
    $\lambda$ ← 1.0
    *loss* ← Binary_Cross_Entropy($y_{\text{true}}, y_{\text{pred}}$)
    *loss* += $\lambda \cdot disparity^2$
    *regularization_loss* ← $0.01 \cdot \left| \sum_{k=1}^{n} (y_{\text{pred}} - mean y_{\text{pred}}) \right|$
    *total_loss* ← *loss* + *regularization_loss*
    **return** *total_loss*

---

MAFL adds fairness to the regular loss function. Initially, it takes the indices of the unprivileged and privileged groups within the sensitive attributes list and then calculates the mean prediction values for the unprivileged and privileged groups separately. The difference represents the disparity between the groups in terms of the predictions made by the model. A regularization term is added to the loss function to further promote fairness. The term penalizes large differences between individual predictions and the mean prediction of all samples. Finally, the total loss is calculated by summing the regular loss function (in this case, it is Binary Cross-Entropy) and the regularization loss. Here, a fairness score is applied to input and target for sensitive attributes (k = 1 to n). In our dataset, we have 5 protected attributes (gender, race, ethnicity, age, and cognitive ability (dementia)). MAFL avoids using sensitive attributes instead, focuses on other relevant factors (average heart rate and step count) to make predictions.

**Integrated CNN Framework to Predict Pain Status**
Figure 2 depicts the architecture of the deep convolution neural network for classification. It is made up of seven layers: an input layer, two 1D-convolutional

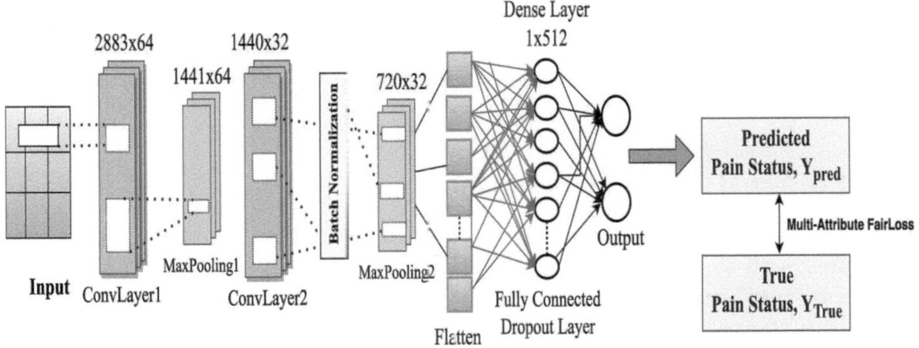


**Fig. 2.** The architecture of 1D deep Convolutional Neural Network (CNN) for pain level assessment

layers, two max-pooling layers, one flattening layer, one fully connected hidden layer, and an output layer. To predict the pain level, the softmax function is applied to the nodes in the output layer. The input layer contains 2883 input numbers that represent demographic features as well as heart rate and step counts for a day. The hidden features generated by the first convolution layer's 64 filters with window size three are used as input for the second convolution layer, which transforms them in the same way via convolution, batch-normalization, and non-linear transformation of its inputs with the rectified-linear unit (ReLU) activation function. Following that, a 1D max-pooling layer is added to convert the variable length hidden features in the previous convolution layer to a fixed number of features. The extracted features are then fed into a 512-node fully-connected hidden layer. To predict the probability of pain level, these 512 nodes are fully connected to two nodes in the output layer. The softmax activation function is used by the node in the output layer. The dropout technique is used in the hidden layer to prevent over-fitting (i.e., the 6th layer in Fig. 2).

## 4   Experiment Evaluation

### 4.1   Pre-process the Dataset

For any classification model to work, raw data must be converted into a clean data set, which means the data set must be converted to numeric data. In the beginning, we converted the string type date attribute to python supported DateTime module and then compared the previous date's pain with the next date's pain. If pain improves then we assign the pain level as 1 otherwise 0. After that, we included cognitive ability (dementia) column for each person based on the list of patients who have dementia. Numeric data conversion was accomplished by encoding all categorical features as binary column vectors. Since data on a person's heart rate and step counts for a day were in list format, we split the data into multiple columns (1440 columns for heart rates and 1440 columns for step counts for each day). If any rows are missing, we fill them with mean or interpolated values. Finally, we dropped columns that are not necessary to carry out our work after re-scaling them using the Min-Max normalization technique.

### 4.2  Protected Attribute Selection

The clean dataset we used, has 868 records. In our dataset, we have 5 protected attributes such as gender, race, ethnicity, age, and cognitive ability (dementia). The term "race" and "ethinicity" are often used interchangeably in everyday language, but they refer to different concepts in social science and identity studies. Banton [44] defines race as a category based on physical characteristics that are perceived as significant by society. The concept of race is seen as a way to categorize and often hierarchize individuals and groups based on superficial traits. While, ethnicity refers to the cultural factors that distinguish groups of people from one another. Ethnicity is viewed as a source of identity and belonging, often linked to cultural and social practices rather than physical characteristics.

To select privileged groups for each sensitive attribute, we determined which groups are rich subgroups i.e. who are most advantageous than others [45]. According to National Institutes of Health(NIH) [46,47] adults 65 or older are generally described as "elderly". For our dataset, we determined that males, Asians, not Hispanic or Latin, age less than 65, and people with no dementia are the rich subgroups for each protected attribute respectively which are called gender, race, ethnicity, aging, and cognitive disability biases respectively (Fig. 3).

### 4.3  Implementation Details

To evaluate our experiment, we conduct tests on our dataset using benchmark pre-processing, in-processing, and post-processing bias mitigation techniques suggested by AIF360 [48] to show that MAFL-CNN satisfies the tradeoff between fairness and accuracy. To begin, we transformed our dataset into Standard Dataset format and then partitioned it randomly by 80–20%; 80% training data, and 20% test data for each protected attribute. We calculated the dataset metrics i.e. statistical parity difference and disparity impact ratio for both training and test datasets. Then we assess the effectiveness of our MAFL-CNN model in terms of fair accuracy by comparing it to cutting-edge fairness-aware AIF360 bias mitigation techniques on Logistic Regression (LR), Random Forest (RF), Decision Tree (DT), Support Vector Machine (SVM), Naive Bayes (NB), and CNN models. For the *logistic regression*, we use liblinear solver and set the maximum iteration at 50,000. In *random forest*, we set maximum depth value 2. For the *decision tree* classifier, the entropy criterion is used to find the optimal split where entropy represents the disorder of features with respect to the target class. We used balanced class weight for *support vector machine* classifier that helps to reduce execution time. In *Naive Byes (NB)*, we use the Bernoulli NB model while binary cross entropy (BCE) was used as a loss function in the CNN model. For our **MAFL CNN** model, we set the two filter sizes (i.e. 64 and 32) for the

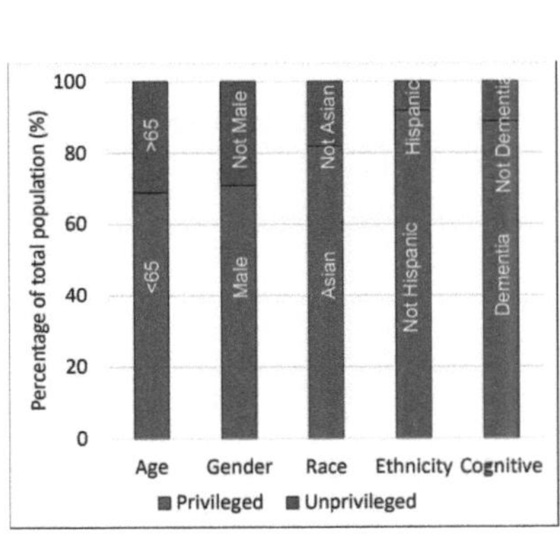

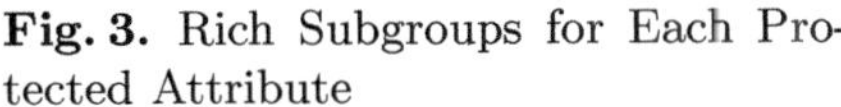

**Fig. 3.** Rich Subgroups for Each Protected Attribute

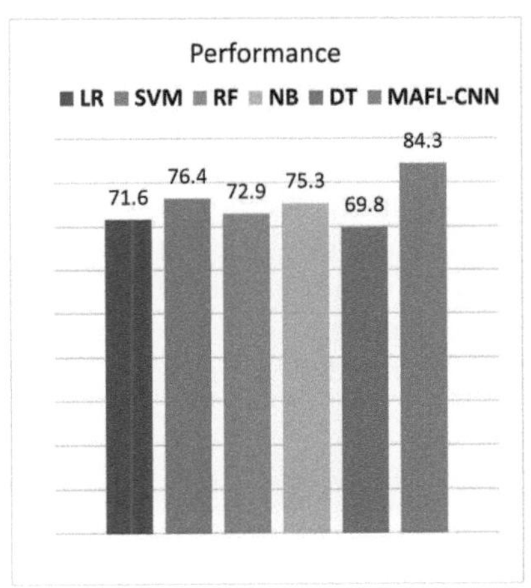


**Fig. 4.** Pain Assessment Performance for Classification Models

convolution layers and used 512 fully connected dense layers. We run our model for 20 epochs. We selected the best model based on the highest number of fair classification matrices (Statistical Parity Difference, Disparate Impact, Equal Opportunity Difference, Theil Index, and Average Odd Difference) to satisfy accuracy and fairness trade-off.

To carry on the whole experiment, a virtual environment has been created using python3.11. Our CPU configuration was Intel Xeon CPU (2.00GHz) processor with 12 GB of RAM and the GPU was Tesla K40c with 12 GB of RAM. It takes approximately 170 min to complete the task.

## 5   Results

### 5.1   Dataset Bias Detection and Mitigation

To assess the presence of bias in our dataset, we employed two fairness metrics, namely statistical parity difference and disparate impact, as described in the work by AIF360 [48]. If the unprivileged group receives a positive outcome of less than 80% of their proportion relative to the privileged group, it suggests a potential bias or disparate impact. In our original dataset, prior to any mitigation efforts, the disparate impact value was 0.72, and the statistical parity difference was 1.5, which ideally should range between −1 and 1. So clearly it indicates that our dataset is compromised in decision making. To address these biases, we made modifications to the original dataset using fair pre-processing procedures [48]:

Reweighing: We first assign weights to balance representation across(group, label) combinations, then maintain features while adjusting instance weights to ensure fairness [48]. Disparate Impact Remover: We use a repair level parameter(set to 1.0) to control the strength of the transformation and transform features to remove discriminatory information while preserving rank-ordering within groups, only modifies the features, labels or protected attributes are not affected [48].

To evaluate the impact of these pre-processing bias mitigation techniques on bias detection metrics, we computed fairness metrics both before and after the transformation. The results, shown in Fig. 5, indicate the extent of $\pm 1$ standard deviation using the bars. It is evident that the Reweighing and Disparate Impact Remover pre-processing techniques enhance fairness for all the datasets in terms of both provided measures.

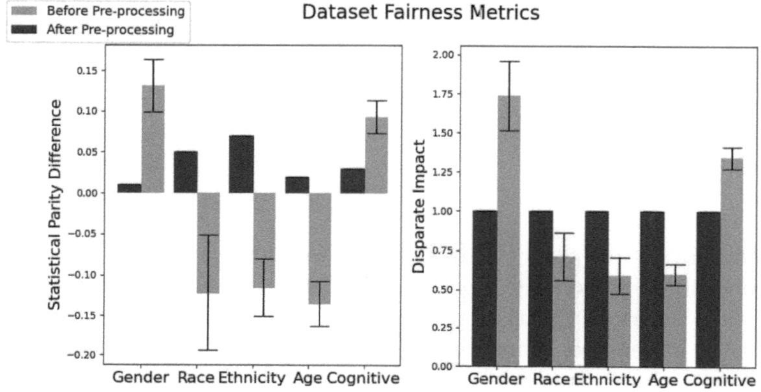


**Fig. 5.** Statistical Parity Difference (SPD) and Disparate Impact (DI) before and after applying pre-processing algorithms for different protected attributes. The black bars indicate the extent of $\pm 1$ standard deviation. The ideal fair value of SPD is 0 and DI is 1.

## 5.2   Performance of Mitigation Algorithm

To evaluate the efficacy of our mitigation algorithm, MAFL-CNN, we perform a comparative assessment of its classification accuracy against a selection of advanced mitigation algorithms provided by IBM, as detailed in [48]. As part of AIF360 mitigation techniques, we employed six state-of-the-art classification models, namely, Support Vector Machine (SVM), Random Forest (RF), Logistic Regression (LR), Decision Tree (DT), Naive Bayes (NB), and Convolutional Neural Network (CNN). Figure 4 illustrates the collective performance of the classification models. It is evident from the chart that MAFL-CNN consistently outperforms all other models, showcasing its superiority as a fairer classification technique.

We present a comprehensive summary of the classification model results in Table 2. In this table, we exclusively highlight the optimal model, characterized by its superior accuracy and reduced bias, for each mitigation technique. Our

**Table 2.** Bias detection and mitigation results for sensitive attributes: Age, Gender, Race, Cognitive Ability (Dementia), and Ethnicity. We compare MAFL-CNN with 5 state-of-art ML models and 1 NN model: SVM, RF, LR, DT, NB, and CNN referring to Support Vector Machine, Random Forest, Logistic Regression, Decision Tree, Naive Bayes, and Convolution Neural Network. We also evaluate MAFL-CNN with respect to AIF360 mitigation techniques (RW, DIR, EGR, AD, PR, and ROC referring to Reweighing, Disparate Impact Remover, Exponentiated Gradient Reduction, Adversarial debiasing, Prejudice Remover techniques, and Reject Option Classification).

| Mitigation | Age | | Gender | | Race | | Cognitive | | Ethnicity | | Altogether |
|---|---|---|---|---|---|---|---|---|---|---|---|
| | Model | Acc % | Model | Acc % | Model | Acc % | Model | Acc % | Model | Acc % | Acc % |
| Before Bias Mitigation | | | | | | | | | | | |
| Before Mitigation | LR | 82.0 | CNN | 78.74 | LR | 74.1 | RF | 70.4 | LR | 78.3 | – |
| MAFL-CNN Mitigation | | | | | | | | | | | |
| **MAFL-CNN** | - | 77.3 | - | **75.2** | - | 75.6 | - | **79.5** | - | 78.7 | **84.3** |
| AIF360 Mitigation | | | | | | | | | | | |
| RW-Preprocessing | SVM | 76.2 | SVM | 76.4 | LR | 69.8 | LR | 70.4 | CNN | 79.8 | – |
| DIR-Preprocessing | RF | 71.6 | LR | 67.6 | DT | 69.8 | RF | 70.6 | CNN | 72.9 | – |
| EGR-Inprocessing | LR | 71.6 | SVM | 65.7 | SVM | 72.7 | SVM | 62.2 | RF | 73.4 | – |
| AD-Inprocessing | – | 75.8 | – | **74.7** | – | 76.9 | – | 74.7 | – | 71.3 | – |
| PR-Inprocessing | - | **76.4** | - | 75.7 | - | 82.6 | - | 77.1 | - | 72.5 | – |
| ROC-Postprocessing | - | 73.3 | - | 75.2 | - | **80.6** | - | 77.5 | - | 72.3 | – |

analysis focuses on sensitive attributes such as gender, age, race, ethnicity, and cognitive ability, and their impact on classification fairness. It is evident from the table that, across these attributes, all state-of-the-art machine learning models exhibit unfairness in terms of bias detection metrics. However, MAFL-CNN stands out as a promising performer, displaying consistently strong performance across all individual or combined sensitive attributes. In the case of gender, cognitive ability, and $n$ sensitive attributes, MAFL-CNN surpasses other techniques by exhibiting superior performance in more than three fairness metrics. For age, ethnicity, and race, while the number of fairness metrics with superior performance is three or less, it remains noteworthy that MAFL-CNN consistently achieves higher accuracy compared to alternative mitigation methods.

Among the pre-processing techniques, SVM demonstrates the highest balance between accuracy and fairness metrics, achieving an accuracy of 76.4%. In the case of in-processing techniques, the Prejudice Remover (PR) technique performs well in terms of accuracy for the sensitive attribute 'Age', while the RF model shows fairness as a predictor for the Exponentiated Gradient Reduction (EGR) technique. The Reject Option Classification (ROC) technique exhibits an average accuracy of around 75% for each sensitive attribute. However, our MAFL-CNN model suppresses the performance of all the models, resulting in accuracy ranging from 75% to 85%. Furthermore, unlike the AIF360 mitigation techniques, our MAFL-CNN model can consider multiple sensitive attributes. Additionally, it is worth noting that AIF360 only includes one neural network (NN) model, which

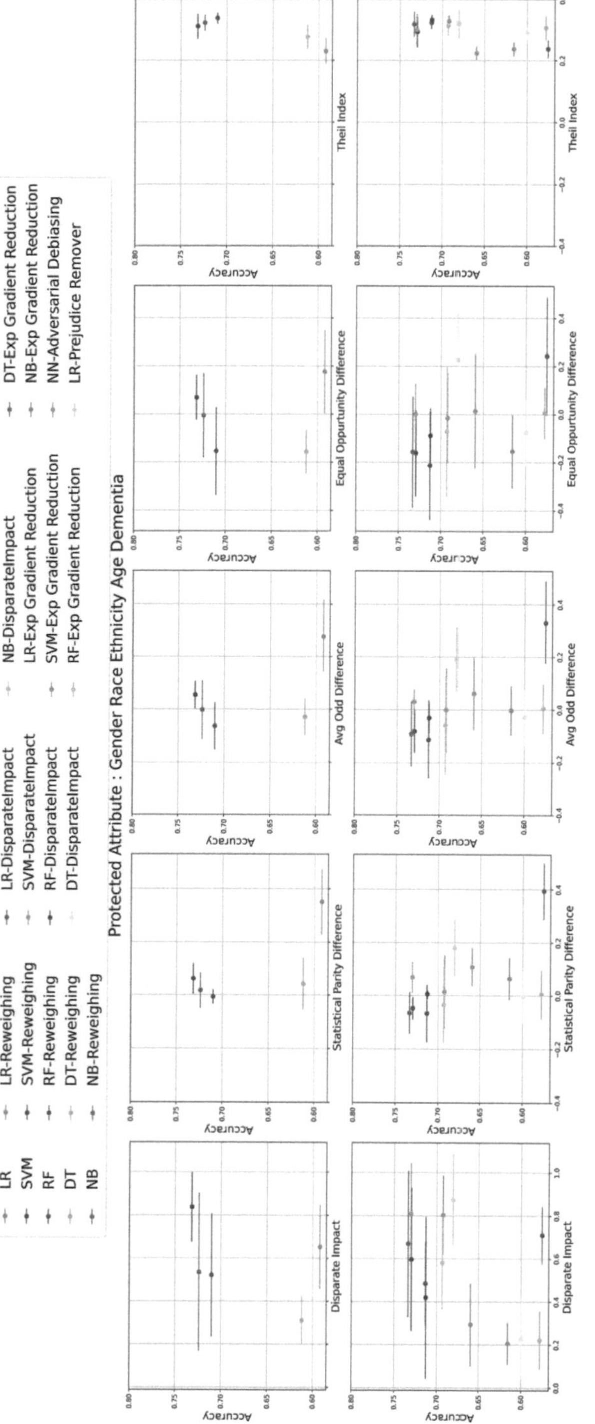

**Fig. 6.** Fairness vs. Accuracy before (top panel) and after (bottom panel) applying various bias mitigation algorithms. Five different fairness metrics are shown. The ideal fair value of disparate impact is 1, whereas for all other metrics it is 0. The circles indicate the mean value and the bars indicate the extent of ±1 standard deviation. Protected attributes: gender, race, age, ethnicity, dementia.

is the adversarial debiasing algorithm, and its performance is noticeably lower than our MAFL-CNN model. So we can say that MAFL-CNN is successful in balancing classification accuracy and fairness.

We report the bias detection and mitigation results more elaborately in Fig. 6 with details of bias metrics and accuracy changes for all algorithm-bias mitigation pairs. Here, we visualize a sample outcome of the bias mitigation process (before and after mitigation) to understand the impact of the bias mitigation technique on accuracy and bias detection metrics. The top panel of this fig depicts the classification metrics before bias mitigation for all classifiers and the bottom panel shows the metrics after using mitigation techniques. We can clearly see that bias mitigation techniques significantly change the bias metrics estimations as well as the accuracy.

## 6    Conclusion

This paper presents a cutting-edge model that not only provides accurate predictions of patients' pain status but also contributes significantly to the advancement of fairness and equity in decision-making systems. Our experimental results demonstrate the efficacy of our proposed approach. We observe significant reductions in disparity between privileged and unprivileged groups while maintaining competitive classification accuracy (Fig. 5). Furthermore, we analyze the impact of different protected attributes on the fairness metrics to gain insights into their influence on the classification process. By mitigating disparity in classification outcomes, our approach contributes towards promoting fairness and reducing bias in decision-making systems (Fig. 4) with accuracy ranging from 75% to 85% for existing protected attributes. This substantial accuracy range underscores the robustness and reliability of our proposed model. In summary, we have highlighted the current challenges and possible solutions to assess the pain automatically and ensure fairness. This work opens paths for future studies emphasizing exploring the generalizability of our method across different datasets and extending the approach to other deep learning architectures.

## References


1. Keogh, A., et al.: Assessing the usability of wearable devices to measure gait and physical activity in chronic conditions: a systematic review. J. NeuroEngineering Rehabil. **18**, 138 (2021)
2. Mosconi, P., et al.: Use of health apps and wearable devices: survey among Italian associations for patient advocacy. JMIR Mhealth Uhealth **7**(1), e10242 (2019)
3. Ferrell, B.A., Ferrell, B.R., Osterweil, D.: Pain in the nursing home. J. Am. Geriatr. Soc. **38**, 409 (1990)
4. Magni, G., Marchetti, M., et al.: Chronic musculoskeletal pain and depressive symptoms in the National Health and Nutrition Examination: Epidemiologic follow-up study. Pain **53**, 163 (1993)

5. Haendel, M.A., et al.: N3C consortium. The National COVID Cohort Collaborative (N3C): Rationale, design, infrastructure, and deployment. J. Am. Med. Inform. Assoc. **28**(3), 427–443 (2021)

6. Kulaylat, A.S., et al.: Truven health analytics marketscan databases for clinical research in colon and rectal surgery. Clin. Colon Rectal Surg. **32**(1), 54–60 (2019). Epub 2019 Jan 8. PMID: 30647546; PMCID: PMC6327721

7. Singh, R.P., et al.: AAO task force on artificial intelligence. Current challenges and barriers to real-world artificial intelligence adoption for the healthcare system, provider, and the patient. Transl. Vis. Sci. Technol. **9**(2), 45 (2020). PMID: 32879755; PMCID: PMC7443115

8. Davenport, T., Kalakota, R.: The potential for artificial intelligence in healthcare. Future Healthcare J. **6**(2), 94–98 (2019)

9. Maina, I.W., Belton, T.D., Ginzberg, S., Singh, A., Johnson, T.J.: A decade of studying implicit racial/ethnic bias in healthcare providers using the implicit association test. Soc. Sci. Med. **199**, 219–229 (2018)

10. Wan, M., Zha, D., Liu, N., Zou, N.: In-processing modeling techniques for machine learning fairness: a survey. ACM Trans. Knowl. Discov. Data (2022, just accepted ). https://doi.org/10.1145/3551390

11. Types of Bias in Statistics | Mailchimp (n.d.). Mailchimp. https://mailchimp.com/resources/data-bias-causes-effects/

12. Nelson, A.: Unequal treatment: confronting racial and ethnic disparities in health care. J. Natl Med. Assoc. **94**(8), 666 (2002)

13. FitzGerald, C., Hurst, S.: Implicit bias in healthcare professionals: a systematic review. BMC Med. Ethics **18**(1) (2017). https://doi.org/10.1186/s12910-017-0179-8. www.ncbi.nlm.nih.gov/pubmed/28249596

14. Hall-Lord, M.L., et al.: Pain and distress among elderly intensive care unit patients: comparison of patients' experiences and nurses' assessments. Heart Lung **27**, 123 (1998)

15. Kaasalainen, S.J., et al.: The assessment of pain in the cognitively impaired elderly: a literature review. Perspectives **22**, 2 (1998)

16. Rundshagen, I., et al.: Patients' vs nurses' assessment of postoperative pain and anxiety during patient- or nurse-controlled analgesia. Br. J. Anaesth. **82**, 374 (1999)

17. Weiner, D., et al.: Chronic pain-associated behaviors in the nursing home: resident versus caregiver perceptions. Pain **80**, 577 (1999)

18. Werner, P., et al.: Pain in participants of adult day care centers: assessment by different raters. J. Pain Symptom Manage. **15**, 8 (1998)

19. Hoffman, K.M., Trawalter, S., Axt, J.R., Oliver, M.N.: Racial bias in pain assessment and treatment recommendations, and false beliefs about biological differences between blacks and whites. Proc. Natl. Acad. Sci. U.S.A. **113**(16), 4296–4301 (2016). https://doi.org/10.1073/pnas.1516047113. Epub 2016 Apr 4. PMID: 27044069; PMCID: PMC4843483

20. Schoenthaler, A., Williams, N.: Looking beneath the surface: racial bias in the treatment and management of pain. JAMA Netw. Open **5**(6), e2216281 (2022). https://doi.org/10.1001/jamanetworkopen.2022.16281

21. The "All of Us" research program. N. Engl. J. Med. **381**, 668–676 (2019). https://doi.org/10.1056/NEJMsr1809937

22. Shah, A.A., Zogg, C.K., et al.: Analgesic access for acute abdominal pain in the emergency department among racial/ethnic minority patients: a nationwide examination. Med. Care **53**(12), 1000–1009 (2015)

23. Singhal, A., et al.: Racial-ethnic disparities in opioid prescriptions at emergency department visits for conditions commonly associated with prescription drug abuse. PLoS One **11**(8), e0159224 (2016)
24. Rasu, R.S., et al.: Determinants of opioid prescribing for nonmalignant chronic pain in US outpatient settings. Pain Med. **19**(3), 524–532 (2018)
25. Anastas, T.M., et al.: The unique and interactive effects of patient race, patient socioeconomic status, and provider attitudes on chronic pain care decisions. Ann. Behav. Med. **54**(10), 771–782 (2020)
26. Perez Alday, E.A., et al.: Age, sex and race bias in automated arrhythmia detectors. J. Electrocardiol. **74**, 5–9 (2022 ). https://doi.org/10.1016/j.jelectrocard.2022.07.007. Epub 2022 Jul 18. PMID: 35878534
27. Tousignant-Laflamme, Y., et al.: Establishing a link between heart rate and pain in healthy subjects: a gender effect. J. Pain **6**(6), 341–347 (2005)
28. Bendall, J.C., et al.: Prehospital vital signs can predict pain severity: analysis using ordinal logistic regression. Eur. J. Emerg. Med. **18**(6), 334–339 (2011)
29. Li, L.C., et al.: Efficacy of a community-based technology-enabled physical activity counseling program for people with knee osteoarthritis: proof-of-concept study. J. Med. Internet Res. **20**(4), e159 (2018)
30. Hallman, D.M., et al.: Association between objectively measured sitting time and neck-shoulder pain among blue-collar workers. Int. Arch. Occup. Environ. Health **88**(8), 1031–1042 (2015)
31. Jacobson, N.C., O'Cleirigh, C.: Objective digital phenotypes of worry severity, pain severity and pain chronicity in persons living with HIV. Br. J. Psychiatry (2019)
32. Johnson, A., et al.: Use of mobile health apps and wearable technology to assess changes and predict pain during treatment of acute pain in sickle cell disease: feasibility study. JMIR Mhealth Uhealth **7**(12), e13671 (2019)
33. Colvonen, P.J., et al.: Limiting racial disparities and bias for wearable devices in health science research. Sleep **43**(10), zsaa159 (2020)
34. Shcherbina, A., et al.: Accuracy in wrist-worn, sensor-based measurements of heart rate and energy expenditure in a diverse cohort. J. Pers. Med. **7**(2), 3 (2017)
35. Alam, M.A.U.: AI-fairness towards activity recognition of older adults. In: 17th EAI International Conference on Mobile and Ubiquitous Systems: Computing, Networking and Services (Mobiquitous 2020) (2020)
36. Tsai, P.F.: Assessing pain in older adults. J. Gerontol. Nurs. **37**(5), 3–4 (2011)
37. Tsze, D.S., von Baeyer, C.L., Bulloch, B., Dayan, P.S.: Validation of self-report pain scales in children. Pediatrics **132**(4), e971–e979 (2013)
38. Zhou, N., et al.: Bias, fairness, and accountability with AI and ML algorithms. CoRR abs/2105.06558 (2021)
39. Dwork, C., et al.: Fairness through awareness. In: Proceedings of the 3rd Innovations in Theoretical Computer Science Conference (ITCS), pp. 214–226 (2012). https://dl.acm.org/doi/10.1145/2090236.2090255
40. Feldman, M., et al.: Certifying and removing disparate impact. In: Proceedings of the 21st ACM SIGKDD International Conference on Knowledge Discovery and Data Mining, pp. 259–268 (2015). https://dl.acm.org/doi/10.1145/2783258.2783311
41. Hardt, M., Price, E., Srebro, N.: Equality of opportunity in supervised learning. In: Advances in Neural Information Processing Systems, NeurIPS 2016, vol. 29 (2016). https://papers.nips.cc/paper/2016/hash/9d2682367c3935defcb1f9e247a97c0d-Abstract.html

42. Speicher, T., et al.: A unified approach to quantifying algorithmic unfairness: measuring individual & group unfairness via inequality indices. In: Proceedings of the 24th ACM SIGKDD International Conference on Knowledge Discovery & Data Mining, pp. 2239–2248 (2018). https://dl.acm.org/doi/10.1145/3219819.3220046
43. Mehrabi, N., et al.: A survey on bias and fairness in machine learning. ACM Comput. Surv. (CSUR) **54**(6), 1–35 (2021). https://dl.acm.org/doi/10.1145/3457607
44. Banton, M.: What We Now Know About Race and Ethnicity. Berghahn Books, New York (2015)
45. Kinyanjui, N.M., et al.: Fairness of classifiers across skin tones in dermatology. In: MICCAI 2020, Part VI, pp. 320–329. Springer, Heidelberg (2020)
46. National Research Council (US) Committee on Population: Defining the Oldest Old. In: Manton, K.G., Soldo, B.J. (eds.) Demography of Aging. National Academies Press (US), Washington (DC) (1998). https://www.ncbi.nlm.nih.gov/books/NBK235450/. Accessed 26 Aug 2024
47. National Institutes of Health: Age. NIH Style Guide. https://www.nih.gov/nih-style-guide/age. Accessed 26 Aug 2024
48. Bellamy, R.K.E.: AI fairness 360: an extensible toolkit for detecting, understanding, and mitigating unwanted algorithmic bias. arXiv https://arxiv.org/abs/1810.01943 (2018)

# EEGAmp+: Investigating the Efficacy of Functional Connectivity for Detecting Events in Low Resolution EEG


Indrajeet Ghosh[1]([envelope]), Kasthuri Jayarajah[3], Nicholas Waytowich[4],
and Nirmalya Roy[2]

[1] Department of Information Systems, University of Maryland Baltimore County,
Baltimore, USA
`indrajeetghosh@umbc.edu`
[2] Center for Real-time Distributed Sensing and Autonomy,
University of Maryland Baltimore County, Baltimore, USA
`nroy@umbc.edu`
[3] Department of Computer Science, New Jersey Institute of Technology,
Newark, USA
`kasthuri.jayarajah@njit.edu`
[4] DEVCOM, Army Research Lab, Adelphi, USA
`nicholas.r.waytowich.civ@army.mil`



**Abstract.** Electroencephalography (EEG) has found many applications cutting across many domains, such as digital health, affective computing, and human-machine interfaces. However, its widespread adoption in practice has been primarily inhibited by its susceptibility to noise artifacts and the low spatial resolution of electrodes on commercial EEG sensors. While several prior works have investigated techniques for detecting and extracting noise, our understanding of performance degradation due to electrode sparsity remains limited. In this work, we explore the feasibility of using Functional Connectivity (FC) for improving the EEG sensing-based accuracy using two exemplars downstream, working memory-related tasks: (a) cognitive task load (CTL) assessment and (b) high attentional event-evoked potential (EEP) episodes detection. This paper proposes an integrated approach, **EEGAmp+**, that first utilizes channel-wise functional connectivity modules using independent component analysis (ICA) coupled with cosine distance for EEG signal reconstruction for cognitive task load assessment tasks. This is then coupled with a sliding window change point detection technique paired with continuous wavelet transformation (CWT) to extract high attentional EEP episodes. Our empirical results indicate that using independent component analysis (ICA) coupled with FC to improve spatial resolution increased cognitive load assessment accuracy by [5.6% $\pm$ 1.13] across four machine learning algorithms. Furthermore, after signal reconstruction, we introduce sliding window CPD coupled with CWT, which allows us to extract EEP segments legibly through decomposing the signals and the ability to capture both time and frequency representation from the reconstructed signal boosting detection accuracy by [11.1% $\pm$1.31].



© ICST Institute for Computer Sciences, Social Informatics and Telecommunications Engineering 2026
Published by Springer Nature Switzerland AG 2026. All Rights Reserved
A. Soylu et al. (Eds.): MobiQuitous 2024, LNICST 634, pp. 97–117, 2026.
https://doi.org/10.1007/978-3-032-10554-7_6

**Keywords:** Event-evoked Potentials · Functional connectivity ·
Visuospatial Working Memory · Electroencephalography · Affective
Computing · Cognitive Load Assessment

# 1    Introduction

Electroencephalography (EEG) has found many applications cutting across many domains such as digital health [7,41], affective computing [14,49], and human-machine interfaces [5,18,21]. EEG is a non-invasive method that records brain activity and offers high-temporal-resolution insights into neural dynamics related to cognitive functions. It has been widely used to study memory processes with specific brainwave patterns linked to memory encoding and retrieval phases [36]. Recent advancements in EEG analysis, including EEPs detection [25], cognitive task load assessment [3], etc., have enhanced the ability to decode and interpret the complex neural interactions involved in learning cognitive functions. However, its widespread adoption in practice has been largely inhibited by its susceptibility to noise artifacts as well as the low spatial resolution of electrodes present on commercial EEG sensors.

While several prior works have investigated techniques for detecting and extracting noise [38], our understanding of performance degradation due to such electrode sparsity remains limited. As our findings in Figs. 5a and 5b show (later in Sect. 5), 5-channel and 14-channel Commercial-Off-the-Shelf (COTS) EEG headset devices (such as Emotiv Insight and Epoc+[1]) perform significantly poorer in simple cognitive load classification tasks – for instance, suffering $\approx$ a 20% drop in accuracy on a 4 and 3-class task classification problem of remembering characters that appeared on screen and three subject-driven cognitive states (memory, music and subtraction tasks), respectively as compared to clinical grade sensors. We expect the accuracy to degrade even more in more complex, realistic scenarios such as search and navigation which involve visuospatial working memory processes [4].

Functional Connectivity (FC) [35] provides a deeper insight into the intricate interactions between different brain regions during memory processes, allowing researchers to observe how various factors influence these interactions. For instance, functional connectivity analysis can demonstrate the specific neural mechanisms triggered during tasks [48], highlighting the dynamic communication between brain regions such as the temporal, frontal, occipital and parietal lobes. Similarly, EEPs are time-locked EEG responses to specific sensory, cognitive, motor and visual events, providing high temporal resolution insights into the brain's processing stages [36]. Integrating functional connectivity analysis with EEPs detection enables a comprehensive understanding of how neural communication networks and event-specific brain responses interact to facilitate cognitive functions. Recent studies [12,13] show that a better understanding of memory processing mechanisms via FC techniques improves cognitive performance by examining how these factors influence neural connectivity and efficiency and also removing or suppressing the artifacts in the EEG signals.

---

[1] https://www.emotiv.com/.

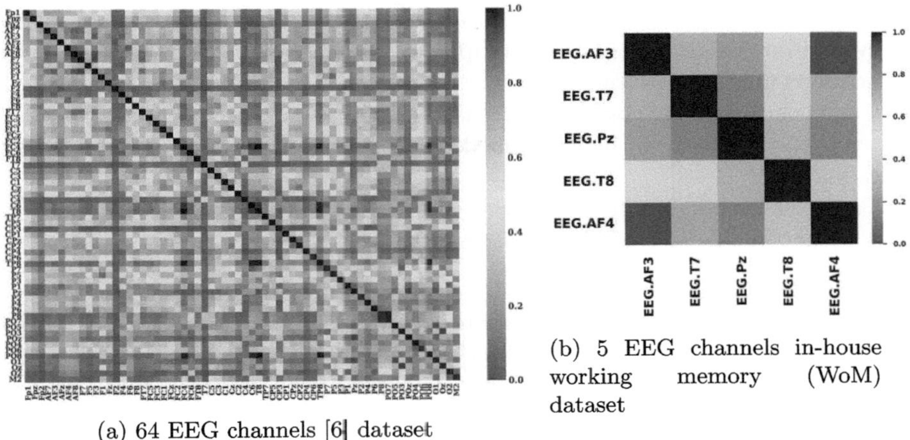

(a) 64 EEG channels [6] dataset

(b) 5 EEG channels in-house working memory (WoM) dataset

**Fig. 1.** Correlation between EEG channels across 64 and 5 electrodes, demonstrating functional connectivity and the ability to capture neural dynamics among specific EEG electrode locations.

**Challenges and Opportunities.** Here, we highlight and enumerate the key challenges and opportunities in using Commercial-Off-the-Shelf (COTS) EEG sensors for working memory-related applications. Empirical research [42] shows that the efficacy of signal capture in EEG studies depends more on the spatial specificity and placement of electrodes than on their number, demonstrating that just six strategically placed electrodes can achieve accuracy comparable to or even greater than a high-density setup with over 200 channels. Moreover, in addition to the lack of spatial resolution, EEG signals are also prone to artifacts such as eye blinks, eye and muscle movements and electrode contact issues [26]. Furthermore, while the lower spatial resolution of the electrodes is problematic, as we see in Fig. 1a. This lower resolution can cause electrodes positioned near both nearby and distant brain regions to exhibit high correlation levels, commonly referred to as functional connectivity (FC). The figure shows the pairwise Pearson's correlation values of the 64 and 5 channels in two datasets. The $x-$ axis denotes the channel names where similar prefixes indicate spatial proximity. The *blocky* nature of the matrix (e.g., AF4 to through Fz on the bottom right corner) shows a high signal correlation at proximity (0.9 and above). Figure 1b electrodes AF3 and AF4 exhibit strong correlations, demonstrating the high signal similarity between these adjacent electrodes. Similarly, T7 and Pz also show notable correlation, which may reflect functional connectivity between these regions (temporal-parietal and central-parietal regions of the scalp). This correlation can be leveraged to reconstruct signals with fewer electrodes while preserving relevant brain activity patterns.

Motivated by this, we pursue the following four lines of enquiry:

- When fewer electrodes are available, how much does the inference accuracy degrade in downstream tasks such as cognitive load assessment?

- Can fewer EEG electrodes capture relevant temporal visuospatial event-evoked potentials during more complex tasks such as navigation where noise artifacts are more prevalent?
- Can such functional connectivity-based signal reconstruction, leading to better pseudo-resolution, be performed efficiently to support real-time applications?
- Can user-friendly form factor, the COTS EEG headset devices match the accuracy of the best possible placements?

To address these research questions, we present *EEGAmp+* an end-to-end framework using COTS EEG sensors to classify cognitive task load assessment and subsequently capture high-quality attentional EEPs depicted in Fig. 2. We investigate (a) using FC techniques to augment the signal quality of EEG signals from low-density spatial resolution and (b) identifying high cognitive state (high-attentional) by extracting contextual information from the reconstructed EEG signals obtained through the FC module for memory logging.

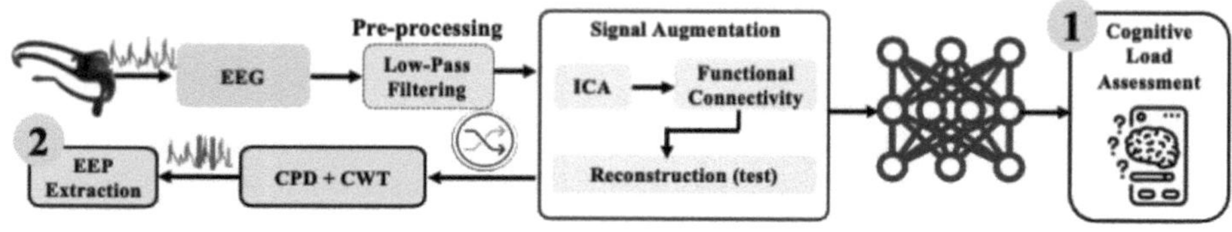


**Fig. 2.** EEGAmp+ : Overview of the overall pipeline for two downstream tasks: (1) cognitive task load (CTL) assessment and (2) extraction of event-evoked potentials (EEP) episodes.

The key contributions of the paper are summarized as follows:

- We studied the feasibility of using functional connectivity to improve accuracy and augment the quality of the EEG signal in working memory-related two downstream tasks: cognitive task load assessment (CTL) and event-evoked potential (EEP) episodes detection in low spatial-resolution commercial EEG devices through extensive studies.
- We propose a rigorous novel end-to-end methodological **EEGAmp+** framework, by incorporating channel-wise functional connectivity via independent component analysis (ICA) coupled with cosine distance to compute and augment the spatiotemporal information of the raw EEG signals and, subsequently integrated, a sliding window change-point detection coupled with continuous wavelet transformation for CTL assessment and high attentional EEP episodes detection, respectively.
- We compare the performance (macro-F1 score) against four state-of-the-art traditional algorithms for CTL assessment across two public-available datasets [6,46]. We also utilized in-house visuospatial working memory (WoM) datasets comprising 40 participants for high-attentional EEP

episode detection tasks. We noticed a substantial improvement in the CTL task by [5.6% ± 1.13] and in extracting EEP segments legibly, improving accuracy by [11.1% ± 1.31]. Additionally, we benchmark the time complexity of our EEGAmp+ EEPs pipeline (sliding CPD + CWT) across four CPD state-of-the-art approaches. Lastly, we conducted statistical tests, ensuring the reliability and validity of the results.

## 2   Related Work

This paper builds on summarizing and discussing the relevant literature contrast to the EEGAmp+ pipeline on: *(i)* cognitive task load assessment and (ii) event-related potential via electroencephalography. We mainly focus on the aspect of our utilized approach that contrasting from the state of art approaches.

### 2.1   Cognitive Task Load Assessment

Cognitive task load assessment involves analyzing and estimating the brain's electrical activity to determine the mental effort required for various tasks [11,20] offering valuable insights into cognitive processes and workload management. In [23], the authors employed Independent Component Analysis (ICA) to aid in cognitive load assessment by isolating brain-related components from artifacts in EEG data, enhancing the clarity of neural activity, and improving the reliability of EEG measurements through more accurate identification of spectral peaks and brain regions involved in cognitive load assessment. Similarly, in paper [27], the authors propose cognitive load prediction model by fusing spatial, tempo-ral, and spectral EEG features, including functional connectivity, microstates, and power spectral densities, demonstrating that this multidimensional approach significantly improves the accuracy of multilevel cognitive load prediction. Fur-thermore, in a similar study [17,33], the authors investigated tensor subspace analysis (TSA) to reduce the high-dimensionality of pairwise functional connec-tivity in EEG recordings during mental arithmetic tasks of varying difficulty, successfully predicting task difficulty levels from connectivity patterns.

### 2.2   Event-Evoked Potential Episodes Detection

Event-evoked Potential (EEP) [10] episodes detection involves identifying spe-cific brain responses to sensory, cognitive, or motor events, essential for under-standing the timing and neural mechanisms underlying cognitive processes. Recent studies highlight that change point detection methods have been investi-gated to learn the brain dynamic changes during stimulation. In [39], the authors introduce FreSpeD, a practical tool for detecting changes and change points in EEG-recorded brain activity, specifically to identify subtle disruptions preceding epileptic seizures and to trace seizure spread across brain regions. EEPs [33,47] have been investigated via the P3 and ERN components, which are not typi-cally lateralized but have broad scalp distributions with central maxima. The

P3 component, often elicited in oddball paradigms, is linked to cognitive processes such as attention and memory updating. In contrast, the ERN (Error-Related Negativity) is associated with error detection and is typically observed following an erroneous response in tasks requiring quick reactions. Furthermore, time-frequency analysis methods, such as short-time fourier transform (STFT) and traditional wavelet transforms, offer insights into the spectral content of ERPs over time [44]. These methods, however, face limitations in balancing time and frequency resolution due to the heisenberg uncertainty principle. STFT, for instance, uses a fixed window size, which may not be optimal for capturing both low-frequency components (requiring longer windows) and high-frequency transient events (requiring shorter windows) [16]. Our work is one of the few that have introduced a robust high-attentional EEPs detection approach via a sliding window approach coupled with CWT to detect brain dynamics responses (memory logging) episodes for visuo-spatial working memory tasks. This combination of CWT with CPD is superior because it effectively captures both abrupt changes and transient events, offering enhanced time-frequency localization and artifact mitigation compared to conventional methods.

## 3    Methodology

In this section, we discuss the overall methodology adopted in the work. Figure 2 highlights the EEGAmp+ pipeline, including two key modules for improving the quality of the low-density EEG signals: (a) signal reconstruction via channel-wise functional connectivity using ICA and cosine distance and (b) sliding window change-point detection and continuous wavelet transformation for extraction of high-attentional EEPs from the reconstructed signals.

### 3.1    EEG Signal Reconstruction via Functional Connectivity Module

COTS EEG headset devices with sparse electrodes suffer from degraded sensing fidelity [29,37]. However, a key insight from recent studies [35] is that EEG channels exhibit high cross-correlation among themselves, also referred to as *functional connectivity*. Motivated by this, we adopt a channel-wise functional connectivity-based approach to reconstruct signals with higher pseudo-density [35].

For the reconstruction of the EEG signals, we perform *Independent Component Analysis* (ICA) [43], commonly employed across various problems like Blind Source Separation (BSS). ICA allows the separation of multiple incoming signals into their respective sources by assuming all signals are non-Gaussian and statistically independent. Then, to leverage the high functional connectivity between EEG channels, we decompose the raw EEG signals into independent components. This transformation captures the underlying structure of the signals, facilitating better reconstruction even from a subset of electrodes. We infer the missing information from the sparsely placed electrodes by analyzing each component's relationships.

$$\mathbf{X} = \mathbf{AS} \tag{1}$$

Let $\mathbf{X} \in \mathbb{R}^{c \times t}$ be the raw EEG signal matrix, where $c$ is the number of channels and $t$ is the number of time points. The ICA decomposition of $\mathbf{X}$ is shown in Eq. 1, where $\mathbf{A} \in \mathbb{R}^{c \times c}$ is the mixing matrix and $\mathbf{S} \in \mathbb{R}^{c \times t}$ is the source matrix of independent components:

$$\text{cosine similarity}(\mathbf{M}, \mathbf{N}) = \frac{\mathbf{M} \cdot \mathbf{N}}{\|\mathbf{M}\|\|\mathbf{N}\|} = \frac{\sum_{i=1}^{n} M_i N_i}{\sqrt{\sum_{i=1}^{n} (M_i)^2} \sqrt{\sum_{i=1}^{n} (N_i)^2}} \tag{2}$$

$$\text{cosine distance} = 1 - \text{cosine similarity}(\mathbf{M}, \mathbf{N})$$

$$\text{Reconstructed Signals} = [\, \text{cosine distance}(\mathbf{M}_{\text{train}} \times \mathbf{N}_{\text{train}}), (\mathbf{M}_{\text{train}} \times \mathbf{N}_{\text{train}}),$$
$$\mathbf{M}_{\text{test}} \times \mathbf{N}_{\text{test}} \,] \tag{3}$$

Once we obtain the independent components using ICA, we use functional connectivity to determine a spatiotemporal similarity representation between the transformed signals and the raw signals. We compute the *cosine similarity* [8], as shown in Eq. 2, between the transformed matrix from the ICA and the subset of EEG signals. This cosine similarity helps quantify the resemblance between the reconstructed high-density signals and the original subset, ensuring that the reconstruction retains the essential characteristics of the EEG data. During the testing phase, the reconstructed EEG signals are estimated by combining the cosine distance and matrix products from training and testing data, as shown in Eq. 3. Specifically, we calculate the cosine distance between the training matrices $\mathbf{M}_{\text{train}}$ and $\mathbf{N}_{\text{train}}$ and incorporate the products $\mathbf{M}_{\text{train}} \times \mathbf{N}_{\text{train}}$ and $\mathbf{M}_{\text{test}} \times \mathbf{N}_{\text{test}}$ to align the reconstructed signals with the functional connectivity patterns observed in the raw EEG data. Here, $\mathbf{M}$ denotes the ICA-transformed matrix, $\mathbf{N}$ represents the subset of EEG signals, and $\times$ indicates element-wise multiplication. This approach ensures that the reconstructed signals retain the inter-channel relationships from training, preserving unique representation information crucial for downstream tasks while maintaining consistent dimensions across matrices over the downstream tasks, facilitating accurate alignment throughout the reconstruction phase.

### 3.2 Event-Evoked Potentials (EEP) Episodes Extraction Module

Extracting the high-attentional EEP episodes from the working memory task attained from the reconstructed EEG signals via the functional connectivity module, we employ change point detection (CPD) technique [2], which finds the abrupt changes in time-series data when a property of the time series changes. One of the key reasons for employing CPD is that EEG signals, being non-stationary and abrupt changes due to the susceptible property of the EEG to various factors such as eye blinks, muscle movements, eye movements, cardiac activity, etc. These non-stationary characteristics cause the signals to be prone to artifacts, interfering with accurate data interpretation, and CPD plays an essential in identifying temporal shifts within the signals [9].

Moving forward, we employ the *sliding window-based* CPD approach due to its lower complexity and comparable performance on similar time series tasks [40] is shown mathematically in Eq. 4. The cost function C(.) in our case, we employ $L1$ (least absolute deviation) shown in Eq. 5, the discrepancy measure is derived $d(...)$, where $(y_t)_t$ is the input signal and u $\leq$ v $\leq$ w index. The discrepancy is the cost gain of splitting the sub-signal $y_{u,...,v}$ at the index v. If the sliding windows $u...v$ and $v...w$ both fall into a segment, their statistical properties are similar and the discrepancy between the first window and the second window is low. If the sliding windows fall into two dissimilar segments, the discrepancy is significantly higher, suggesting that the boundary between windows is a change point.

$$d(y_{u,v}, y_{v,w}) = C(y_{u,w}) + C(y_{u,v}) - C(y_{v,w}) \tag{4}$$

$$C(y)_i = \sum_{t=i} ||y_i - \overline{y_i}|| \tag{5}$$

As discussed previously, sliding window CPD is used extensively in non-stationary temporal data to extract the abrupt in the time-series data [15,31]. However, the temporal artifacts encountered in EEG signals, such as eye blinks, muscle movements, etc., arise from external and internal sources, leading to temporal signal distortions that may interfere with interpreting the signals, causing hindrances in understanding and decomposing the local and global representation from the EEG signals. Therefore, it is critical to identify and mitigate these artifacts to ensure the validity of EEG findings. So, to capture EEPs and minimize such distortion, we employed wavelets-based analysis to decompose EEG signals into a set of wavelet functions, allowing for study in both time and frequency domains simultaneously.

$$CWT(a,b) = \frac{1}{\sqrt{|a|}} \int_{-\infty}^{\infty} x(t)\psi^* \left( \frac{t-b}{a} \right) dt \tag{6}$$

Motivated by the above challenges highlighted, we incorporate a *continuous wavelet transformation* (CWT) [19,30] coupled with the sliding window CPD approach to capture transient events in EEG signals, such as (EEPs) and artifacts removal, that occur at specific time segments [22,34]. The mathematical formulation of the CWT approach is highlighted in Eq. 6, where CWT(a,b) represents the CWT coefficients at scale $a$ and translation $b$, which quantify the similarity between the input signal $x(t)$, the analyzing wavelet $\psi^*(at - b)$ where $\psi^*$ and $t$ denotes the complex conjugate of the wavelet function and time, respectively. Additionally, sliding windows play a vital role in tackling three challenges: *detection of changes or peaks that occur at different time steps* (ii) *tackling time/response delay in response to stimuli across each working memory task* (iii) *identifying and potentially filtering out artifacts.* We showcase that combining the sliding window and CWT-based approach is more effective in removing artifacts such as eye blinks and random noise than detecting change points alone.

$$x_i(t) = x(t), \quad t \in [t_i, t_i + w]$$

$$EEGAmp+_i^{CWT+CPD}(a,b) = \frac{1}{\sqrt{|a|}} \int_{t_i}^{t_i+w} x(t)\psi^* \left(\frac{t-b}{a}\right) dt \tag{7}$$

The integrated approach for EEP episodes extraction via employing the continuous wavelet transform (CWT) coupled with the sliding window CPD is defined in Eq. 7, where $t_i = i \cdot \Delta t$, $\Delta t$ is the step size for sliding the window, $CWT_i(a,b)$ represents the CWT for the $i$-th window, $t_i$ is the start time of the $i$-th window, $w$ is the window length, and $x(t)$ is the signal. This approach leverages the sliding window's localized analysis and the wavelet transformation's multi-resolution capabilities on the reconstructed EEG signals. Lastly, we employed a grid-search method to fine-tune the optimal window sizes for the EEP episode extraction by exploring window durations from 0.1 - 1 s, enabling us to select the most suitable parameter i.e. *(0.75)* for the reconstructed signals.

$$\text{NED} = \frac{\sum_{i=1}^{N} X_i}{\sum_{i=1}^{N} X} \tag{8}$$

To quantify the accuracy of detecting high-attentional EEPs during working memory tasks, we utilized the **normalized EEP detection (NED)** metric, as defined in Eq. 8, where $N$ represents the number of instances, $X_i$ and $X$ represents the number of instances of fixations or periods of visual attention towards cued objects during tasks and the total number of attention-related change points and also including the artifacts (ocular and muscle movements), respectively.

## 4    Experimentation Pipeline

Our experiments were executed on a Linux server equipped with an Intel i7-6850K CPU, 4x NVIDIA GeForce GTX 1080Ti GPUs, and 64 GB RAM. For data preprocessing and deep learning tasks, we utilized Python. Due to the imbalance of class labels for the CTL classification task in most datasets, we use the macro-F1 score as the primary evaluation metric. The datasets were divided into training and testing sets with a split of 70:30%. It is also important to note that the test set was not used during the training phase.

### 4.1    Dataset Description

To achieve our goal and demonstrate the robustness of our end-to-end methodological framework, we categorize our experiments into two tasks using three

**Fig. 3.** Protocol followed for the WoM dataset

**Table 1.** Cued Objects for WoM dataset.

| Environment | Cued Objects |
| --- | --- |
| Indoor | Table, Laptop |
| Campus | Bus, Truck |
| Downtown Baltimore | Boat |
| New York City | Billboard |

different datasets: *cognitive task load (CTL) assessment* and *event-evoked potential (EEP) episodes extraction.*

## CTL Assessment

- **Cognitive Load Classification Dataset (CLC)** [6] comprises **15** participants (8 female); continuous EEG was recorded from 64 electrodes placed over the scalp at standard 10–10 locations with a sampling frequency of 500 Hz. The *classification task* is to recognize the *cognitive load levels* (1–4) corresponding to the set sizes from EEG recordings.
- **Test-retest resting, and cognitive state EEG Dataset (TrRCS)** [46] contains EEG data for resting (eyes closed, eyes open) and cognitive (subtraction, music, memory) states with 60 participants across three experimental sessions. The study involves short-term (within 90 min) and long-term (one month apart) designs. Each session includes EEG and behavioral data, along with comprehensive assessments covering demographics, sleep, emotion, mental health, and mind-wandering.

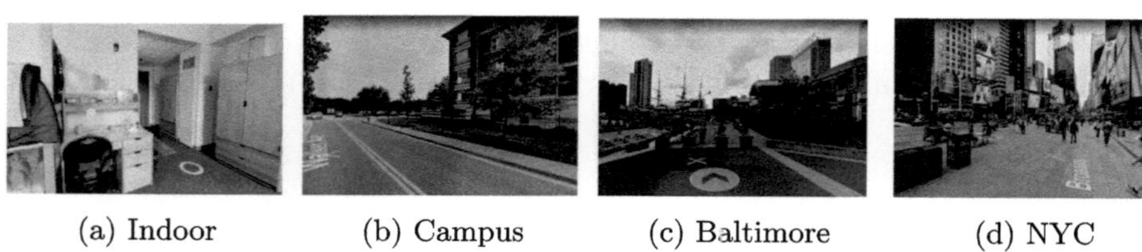

(a) Indoor        (b) Campus        (c) Baltimore        (d) NYC

**Fig. 4.** Virtual environments for in-house WoM datasets.

## High Attentional EEP Episodes Extraction

- **In-house working memory dataset (WoM)** collected which differs from the public datasets in that it (a) involves more cognitively demanding visuospatial tasks (as opposed to passive viewing) identifying episodes of *high cognitive state (EEPs)*. In desktop-based environments, participants were asked to navigate in different areas: (a) an indoor dorm, (b) a familiar, suburban campus area, (c) the downtown area of a mid-size US city, and (d) dense, cosmopolitan city (shown in Fig. 4) and increase cognitive stipulation. The dataset consists of recordings from 15 (7 male, 8 female, aged 18–29) participants performing each task for 1 min. Participants were *verbally cued* about different objects that they might encounter, and their recollection of *cued* objects shown in Table 1 and also additionally collected PAAS score [32] to determine the cognitive load. The institutional review board approved the studies and followed the protocol depicted in Fig. 3. We employed **Emotiv Insights** 5-channel headset for EEG brain signals and were collected at a sampling frequency of 128 Hz. While the navigation tasks were ongoing, we also captured the screen recording along with gaze fixations using the freely available Gaze Recorder[2] interface as ground truth of where the participants' visual attention was during the task and artifacts such as ocular or muscle and each data collection session was recorded through an action camera. In total, we recorded 1612800 data points available in the WoM dataset across 40 participants out of 58.28% clean segments (49.04% are high attentional EEPs segments), 27.75% are eye blink segments (ocular artifacts), and 13.97% are muscle movements, random noise irrelevant to the task and other noise sources such as poor scalp contact of a subset of channels. We also *partially released* the in-house **WoM dataset**[3] for the research community for reproducibility and engagement.

### 4.2  Data Preprocessing

We employ an anti-aliasing low pass filter, a 4th order Butterworth filter, with a cutoff frequency range of 23 Hz, 17 Hz and 14 Hz to avoid temporal shifts and signal distortion for the TrRCS, CLC and WoM datasets, respectively. Lastly, we removed nan values and the obtained filtered signal were normalized using a Min-Max scaler in the range [0–1].

## 5  Results and Discussion

In this section, we categorize our analysis into two main subsections: the effectiveness of *EEGAmp+* for (i) cognitive task load assessment task, and (ii) detecting visuospatial high attentional EEPs episodes.

### 5.1  Effectiveness of *EEGAmp+* for Cognitive Task Load Assessment

Here, we utilized the reconstructed signals for the CTL classification task for the CLC and TrRCS datasets to determine the effectiveness of the EEGAmp+ (channel-wise FC module). To accomplish our goal, we employed four ML algorithms to achieve our goal: decision tree, multi-layer perceptron, random forest and support vector machines across four scenarios highlighted in Figs. 5a and 5b. First of all, we noticed that **random forest** outperforms other ML algorithms

---

[2] https://gazerecorder.com.
[3] https://sites.google.com/umbc.edu/wmdataset/home.

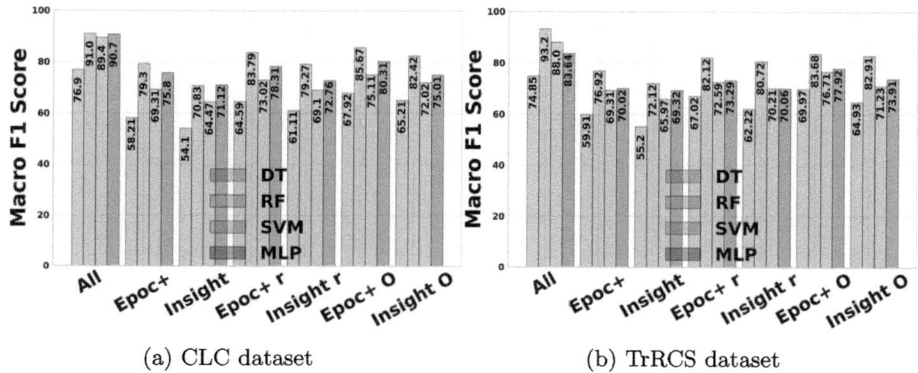

(a) CLC dataset

(b) TrRCS dataset

**Fig. 5.** Accuracy of classifying cognitive task load for CLC and TrRCS datasets using **Decision Tree (DT)**, **Multi-Layer Perceptron (MLP)**, **Random Forest (RF)** and **Support Vector Machines (SVM)** algorithms. <u>O</u>racle –the best accuracy over all combinations of N (5, 14) electrodes, **Insight <u>r</u>** and **Epoc+ <u>r</u>** – using reconstructed EEG signals from the same location 5 and 14 electrodes of the Insight and Epoc+ devices, respectively. **All** –all 64 electrodes available on the clinical-grade head cap.

in all the settings considered. *All* signifies the achieved accuracy using *all* the electrodes, the *Insight* and *Epoc* highlights similar location to COTS devices across 5 and 14 electrodes, respectively, *Oracle (O)* represents the best accuracy over all combinations of N (5, 14) electrodes and *Insight r* and *Epoc+ r* represented the accuracy achieved using reconstructed EEG signals via the FC module of EEGAmp+ . As anticipated, we observe that the COTS devices undergo significant degradation in accuracy. The Insight and Epoc incur a 10–20% loss in classification accuracy compared to the baseline (all electrodes) due to low spatial resolution.

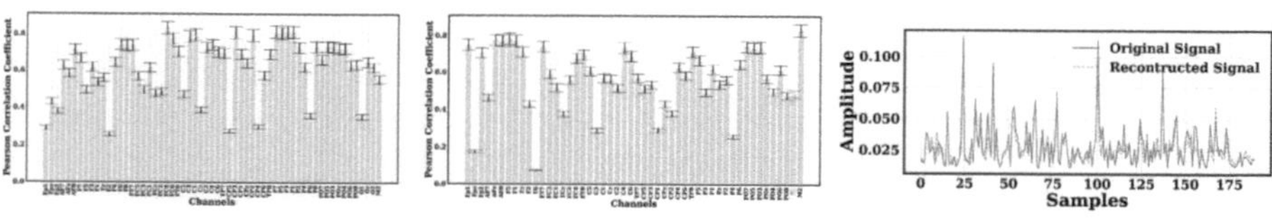

(a) Pearson Correlation Values using Insight r

(b) Pearson Correlation Values using Epoc+ r

(c) Original vs Reconstructed EEG signals

**Fig. 6.** Original vs reconstructed signals by employing our integrated reconstruction approach for CLC dataset.

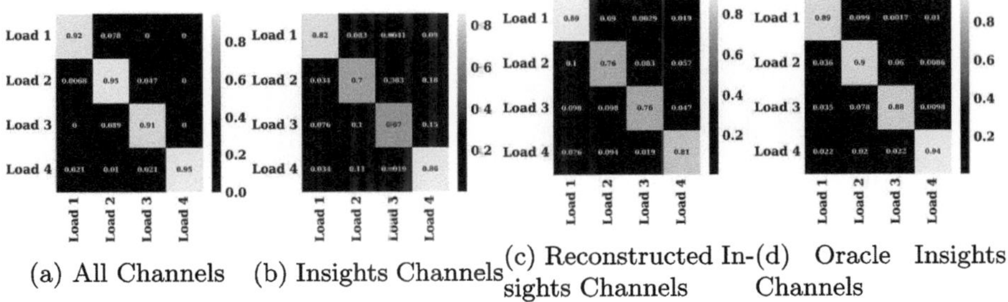

(a) All Channels    (b) Insights Channels    (c) Reconstructed In-  (d) Oracle Insights
                                             sights Channels        Channels

**Fig. 7.** Confusion matrices for the CLC dataset [6] in cognitive load classification using random forest (RF) algorithm. (a) All EEG channels; (b) Selected insight channels; (c) Reconstructed insight channels; (d) Oracle insight channels.

However, we notice an interesting phenomenon: when utilizing the EEGAmp+ (channel-wise FC module) for the classification, CTL task accuracy improved drastically for both datasets. We notice an average improvement of **5.1 ± 1.21%** and **6.1 ± 1.10%** accuracy for CLC and TrRCS datasets, respectively, between *Epoc+, Insight* vs *Epoc+ r, Insight r* settings, average macro F1-score **5.6% ± 1.13** both the datasets. Additionally, the reconstructed signals *(Epoc+ r, Insight r)* settings improvement is par with the *Oracle (O)* setting (combining of channels provides the best result for $N$ of channels) highlighted in Figs. 5a and 5b. Furthermore, to support our findings and results, we compute the pearson correlation coefficient for ($N = $ *(5,14)*) reconstructed signals to support our results and findings obtained by the EEGAmp+ pipeline highlighted in Figs. 6a and 6b to demonstrate correlation coefficient between each channel for the CLC dataset using the reconstructed EEG signal. Lastly, we plotted the original and the reconstructed signals for better representation, as shown in Fig. 6c.

Lastly, our experiments demonstrate that the functional connectivity module of the EEGAmp+ framework effectively captures high cross-correlation among EEG channels in low-density devices, significantly improving cognitive task load classification accuracy (Figs. 5a and 5b). The confusion matrices in Fig. 7 illustrate these improvements across four settings: (a) all EEG channels, (b) insight channels, (c) reconstructed insight channels, and (d) oracle insight channels for the CLC [6] dataset. These findings demonstrate the effectiveness of this reconstruction technique, substantially benefiting downstream cognitive task load classification tasks across benchmark datasets.

**Impact of COTS EEG Headset Electrode Locations:** Here, we examine how the location of EEG electrodes enhances the capture and comprehension of the spatiotemporal dynamics of the tasks. To illustrate this, we present the 64 COTS EEG headset along with the locations of each electrode as shown in Fig. 8. Here, we plot the **Oracle** electrodes (envisioning a completely custom hardware for the working memory task [6]) against the COTS electrodes (Insight

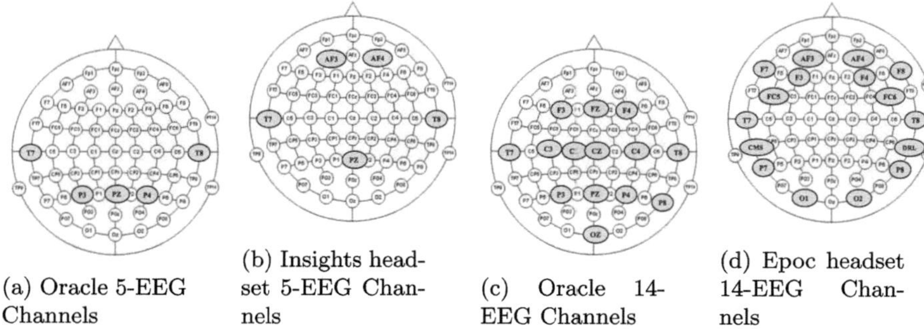

(a) Oracle 5-EEG Channels

(b) Insights headset 5-EEG Channels

(c) Oracle 14-EEG Channels

(d) Epoc headset 14-EEG Channels

**Fig. 8.** Oracle $N = (5/14)$ EEG channels yield high accuracy from 64 EEG channels scalp cap compared to the 5 and 14 channels on the Insight and Epoc devices, highlighted in Yellow highlighted in Figs. 5. The Oracle channels appear on the top of the scalp, whereas the COTS electrodes have more user-friendly placements wrapping around the scalp. We also noticed a higher overlap between the electrodes for both cases, with a minimal accuracy drop for the CTL assessment task. (Color figure online)

and Epoc), highlighted in yellow. Interestingly, we observe that the Oracle electrodes tend to be on the top parts of the scalp whilst the COTS devices are designed to *wrap around* the scalp, where the latter design is superior in comfort. We conclude that even with a more user-friendly form factor, the COTS devices can match the accuracy of the best possible placements using reconstruction techniques. This finding suggests that the trade-off between comfort and accuracy is minimized, making COTS devices a viable option for practical applications without compromising performance.

### 5.2   Effectiveness of *EEGAmp+* for Detecting Visuo-Spatial EEPs Episodes

We highlight and demonstrate the extended capabilities and boost the performance of *EEGAmp+* in extracting EEP episodes during visuospatial working memory tasks. The accuracy of EEP detection is evaluated using the **NED metric** as discussed in Subsect. 3.2. We employed the auxiliary gaze input from the recorder application to determine ground truth for visual attention and evaluated the framework's effectiveness on the WoM dataset. Furthermore, the gaze recorder application provides gaze data as heatmaps, where longer fixation dwell times result in redder and wider fixation points.

We report proportions for two cases: (a) raw EEG signals and (b) reconstructed EEG signals as shown in Fig. 10b. Reconstructed EEG signals significantly increase the number of instances capturing neural response spikes corresponding to **EEP cued attentional instances** compared to raw EEG signals. This indicates that the reconstruction process effectively highlights neural responses that may be less noticeable in the raw data. The reconstructed EEG (Recon EEG) integration captured EEPs for cue objects with an average score of

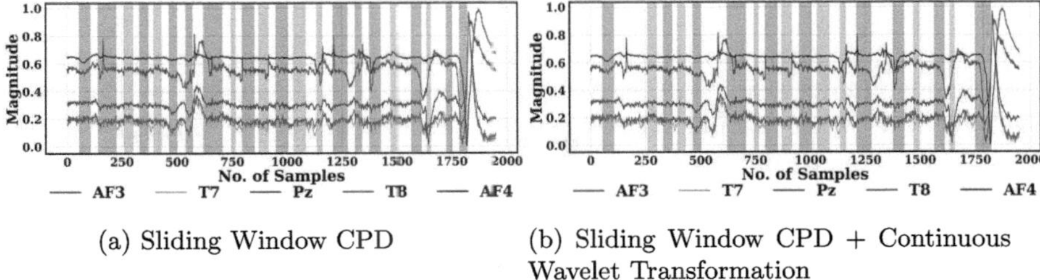

(a) Sliding Window CPD

(b) Sliding Window CPD + Continuous Wavelet Transformation

**Fig. 9.** Reconstructed EEG signal plots highlight various temporal information (cued EEPs and noise artifacts (eye blinks, random muscle movements)) where RED and GREEN highlight the detected segments corresponding to noise and EEP episodes, respectively. In Fig. 9a, the number of segments is 22, out of which EEPs are 8 and artifacts are 14, whereas in Fig. 9b, the number of segments for EEPs are 9 out of 17, total segments, i.e. the accuracy of detecting EEPs using CWT + sliding CPD is **52.94%** compared to sliding CPD is **36.36%**. We noticed some EEPs were not detected when using only the CPD technique. While coupling with the CWT technique, the EEPs were efficiently detected, and similar trends were observed across each participant in the WoM dataset; a similar trend was noticed in the figure as well. (Color figure online)

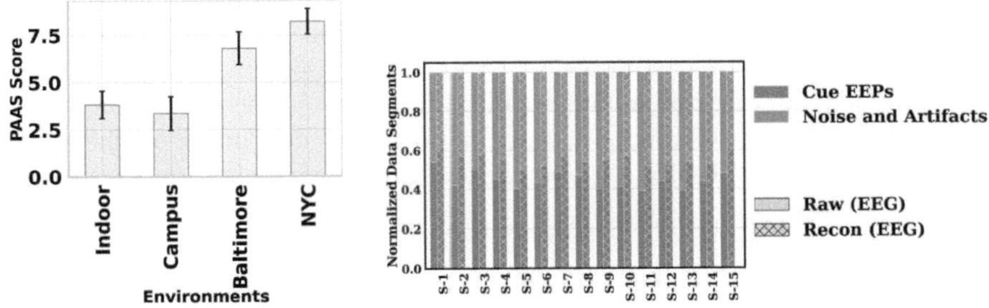

(a) Average PAAS score based on each participant's cognitive load during each environment

(b) Proportion of change point segments detected across four WM tasks using (a) raw EEG signals, (b) reconstruct EEG signals across all participants.

**Fig. 10.** Results of EEPs extraction module for the WoM dataset.

0.554%, compared to 0.443% for raw EEG per participant. Additionally, incorporating reconstructed EEG signals significantly reduced noise and artifacts, enhancing overall data quality. For raw EEG signals, at an average score **0.557%** of detections were noisy, whereas for Recon EEG, only **0.446%** were noisy. This reduction in noisy segments highlights the EEGAmp+ pipeline's effectiveness in increasing EEP detection and reducing noise. Lastly, in running a one-way ANOVA, with input data (EEG, Recon EEG) as the independent variable and the proportion of change points corresponding to cued objects as the dependent variable, showed significant differences in the proportion of cued moments captured ($F = 10.68$, $p < 0.0232$).

Moving forward, in Fig. 9b, we provide example illustrations of the outcome of two variations of the EEP extractor via: (a) using the sliding window approach for change point detection with EEG signals alone, (b) sliding window-based approach together with continuous wavelet transformation (CWT) on EEG signals. We observe a drastic decrease in the number of CPD segments of eye artifacts and random noise in the signals, with $\approx 52.94\%$ and $\approx 36.36\%$, in using the (a) and (b), respectively and overall improvement of $\approx\mathbf{16.58\%}$ using integrated approach for high-attentional EEP episodes extraction from low spatial-resolution COTS EEG headset as shown in Figs. 9b. The motivation behind utilizing the CWT technique [28] with sliding window CPD is that CWT provides a better representation of the whole signals and identifies broad frequency bands of interest. Additionally, sliding windowing includes information about the signal at a local level.

**Impact of Navigation Environments:** Here, we examine the impact of navigation task environments on the participant's cognitive states. While all participants recalled the cued objects better in most environments, interestingly, their recall performance was equal in the most cognitively loading environment, as evidenced by the PAAS scores (i.e., NYC with an average score of 7.6 high compared across all other environments) as shown in Fig. 10a. Lastly, we also run a one-way ANOVA to support, where the navigation environment is the categorical independent variable and recall performance is the dependent variable, we found significant differences in recall performance depending on the environment ($F = 8.57$, $p < 0.015$) supporting the impact of navigation environments on cognitive load.

**EEPs Episodes Extraction Module Runtime Complexity:** In Table 2, we tabulate the run time of **four** different state-of-the-art CPD algorithms and the combined time taken with the CWT-based approach. The experiments were run on a Macbook Pro laptop with an M1 chip with 8GB RAM and 512GB storage, showing that the techniques presented here can be efficiently run on mobile and edge platforms. Here, we demonstrate that by utilizing complex signal processing, the time complexity of the proposed integrated pipeline is par with the sliding-window CPD (lowest time complexity among the other CPD algorithms). Moreover, the results indicate that the EEGAmp+ pipeline (sliding window CPD and CWT) can be effectively scaled for real-time applications, underscoring its robustness and adaptability in dynamic environments.

<u>Key Takeaways:</u> Here, we highlight and summarize the key outcomes from the extensive experiments conducted:

- EEGAmp+ demonstrates that reconstructing the raw EEG signal and improving data quality drastically significantly enhances downstream tasks: CTL assessment and high attentional EEP episodes extraction.
- We also demonstrate that employing a functional connectivity module provides a more robust representation that augments and reconstructs EEG signal quality for low-resolution COTS EEG headsets.

**Table 2.** Profiling of EEGAmp+ (*CPD + CWT*) techniques based on computational time complexity (avg. execution time on CPU)

| CPD Algorithms | Computational Time Requirement |
| --- | --- |
| Sliding Window [45] | 2.21 s ± 5.3 milli-seconds per loop |
| Bayesian [1] | 4.32 s ± 9.4 milli-seconds per loop |
| SDAR [24,45] | 3.45 s ± 7.8 milli-seconds per loop |
| Binary Segmentation [45] | 2.82 s ± 4.1 milli-seconds per loop |
| **Sliding Window [45] + CWT** | **2.38 s ± 3.2 milli-seconds per loop** |

- We exhibit that the COTS EEG headset devices can achieve accuracy comparable to the best possible electrode placements.
- We illustrate that incorporating the sliding window CPD technique coupled with the CWT techniques enables the learning of broad frequency bands, boosting for high attentional EEPs episode extraction for visuospatial working memory tasks and also reducing/suppressing the impact of the noisy samples/segment in the EEG signals and also demonstrate that the EEPs extraction pipeline efficiently can run on mobile and edge platforms.

## 6  Conclusion

The **EEGAmp+** an end-to-end rigorous integrated approach, significantly advances affective computing and detects high attentional event-evoked potentials (EEPs) in visuospatial working memory (WM) tasks. Combining channel-wise functional connectivity via independent component analysis (ICA) and a sliding window CPD technique coupled with CWT improves cognitive load measurement and EEP extraction tasks, respectively. Empirical results show that our approach improves cognitive task load classification across four state-of-the-art machine learning algorithms by [**5.6% ± 1.13**]. Additionally, integrating both modules showed significant improvement in detecting EEP segments by [**11.1% (±1.31)**] and reduced noise and artifacts by [**11.2% (±1.16)**], thereby significantly improving data quality. This study underscores the effectiveness of EEG signal augmentation techniques in cognitive load assessment and EEP detection by learning complex correlation patterns of the brain signals.

## 7  Limitations and Future Work

To determine the computational cost of EEGAmp+, it is important to note that this framework may incur higher processing demands due to signal enhancement techniques such as functional connectivity analysis through Independent Component Analysis (ICA), coupled with sliding window Change Point Detection (CPD) and Continuous Wavelet Transform (CWT). Although these methods could potentially be deployed on edge platforms, such as mobile devices, further analysis is needed to assess real-time performance under varied conditions, including noisy, real-world environments. In future work, we aim to extend EEGAmp+ to explore multimodal physiological data integration and investigate task-agnostic data-driven deep learning approaches, such as variational autoencoders, transformers, self-attention mechanisms, etc., to improve signal reconstruction and reduce noise components. This effort will ultimately enhance the spatiotemporal information captured in the reconstructed signals, ensuring higher signal quality and robustness. by ensuring higher signal quality and robustness. We also intend to investigate advanced methods for accurate neural source localization, including beamforming, dipole modeling, and source separation techniques, to achieve precise mapping of neural activity patterns and brain wave dynamics (e.g., alpha, beta, and gamma waves). By characterizing these patterns more effectively, we can improve the quality and spatial resolution of signals, supporting a range of brain-computer interface (BCI) applications and enhancing performance in other downstream tasks.

**Acknowledgement.** This work has been partially supported by U.S. Army Grant $\#W911NF2120076$, NSF CAREER Award #1750936, ONR Grant $\#N00014\text{-}23\text{-}1\text{-}2119$, NSF REU Site Grant #2050999, and NSF CNS EAGER Grant #2233879. In addition, the authors would like to thank all our volunteers who provided the datasets at the University of Maryland Baltimore County.

# References

1. Adams, R.P., MacKay, D.J.: Bayesian online changepoint detection. arXiv preprint arXiv:0710.3742 (2007)
2. Aminikhanghahi, S., Cook, D.J.: A survey of methods for time series change point detection. Knowl. Inf. Syst. **51**(2), 339–367 (2017)
3. Antonenko, P., Paas, F., Grabner, R., Van Gog, T.: Using electroencephalography to measure cognitive load. Educ. Psychol. Rev. **22**, 425–438 (2010)
4. Baddeley, A.: Working memory. Science **255**(5044), 556–559 (1992)
5. Balanou, E., Van Gils, M., Vanhala, T.: State-of-the-art of wearable EEG for personalized health applications. Stud. Health Technol. Inform. **189**, 119–124 (2013)
6. Bashivan, P., Rish, I., Yeasin, M., Codella, N.: Learning representations from EEG with deep recurrent-convolutional neural networks. arXiv preprint arXiv:1511.06448 (2015)
7. Biondi, A., et al.: Noninvasive mobile EEG as a tool for seizure monitoring and management: a systematic review. Epilepsia **63**(5), 1041–1063 (2022)
8. Birvinskas, D., Jusas, V., Martisius, I., Damasevicius, R.: EEG dataset reduction and feature extraction using discrete cosine transform. In: 2012 Sixth UKSim/AMSS European Symposium on Computer Modeling and Simulation, pp. 199–204 (2012). https://doi.org/10.1109/EMS.2012.88
9. Boashash, B., Boubchir, L., Azemi, G.: A methodology for time-frequency image processing applied to the classification of non-stationary multichannel signals using instantaneous frequency descriptors with application to newborn EEG signals. EURASIP J. Adv. Signal Process. **2012**, 1–21 (2012)

10. Bressler, S.L., Ding, M.: Event-Related Potentials. Wiley Encyclopedia of Biomedical Engineering (2006)
11. Broadbent, D.P., D'Innocenzo, G., Ellmers, T.J., Parsler, J., Szameitat, A.J., Bishop, D.T.: Cognitive load, working memory capacity and driving performance: a preliminary fNIRS and eye tracking study. Transport. Res. F: Traffic Psychol. Behav. **92**, 121–132 (2023)
12. Capogna, E., et al.: Whole-brain connectivity during encoding: age-related differences and associations with cognitive and brain structural decline. Cereb. Cortex **33**(1), 68–82 (2023)
13. Castellanos, N.P., et al.: Reorganization of functional connectivity as a correlate of cognitive recovery in acquired brain injury. Brain **133**(8), 2365–2381 (2010)
14. Chen, J., Wang, X., Huang, C., Hu, X., Shen, X., Zhang, D.: A large finer-grained affective computing EEG dataset. Sci. Data **10**(1), 740 (2023)
15. Chu, C.S.J.: Time series segmentation: a sliding window approach. Inf. Sci. **85**(1–3), 147–173 (1995)
16. Cohen, M.X.: A better way to define and describe morlet wavelets for time-frequency analysis. Neuroimage **199**, 81–86 (2019)
17. Dimitriadis, S.I., Sun, Y., Kwok, K., Laskaris, N.A., Bezerianos, A.: A tensorial approach to access cognitive workload related to mental arithmetic from EEG functional connectivity estimates. In: 2013 35th Annual International Conference of the IEEE Engineering in Medicine and Biology Society (EMBC), pp. 2940–2943. IEEE (2013)
18. Ferreira, A., Celeste, W.C., Cheein, F.A., Bastos-Filho, T.F., Sarcinelli-Filho, M., Carelli, R.: Human-machine interfaces based on EMG and EEG applied to robotic systems. J. Neuroeng. Rehabil. **5**, 1–15 (2008)
19. Grossmann, A., Morlet, J.: Decomposition of hardy functions into square integrable wavelets of constant shape. SIAM J. Math. Anal. **15**(4), 723–736 (1984)
20. Hinss, M.F., Jahanpour, E.S., Somon, B., Pluchon, L., Dehais, F., Roy, R.N.: Open multi-session and multi-task EEG cognitive dataset for passive brain-computer interface applications. Sci. Data **10**(1), 85 (2023)
21. Hu, X., Chen, J., Wang, F., Zhang, D.: Ten challenges for EEG-based affective computing. Brain Sci. Adv. **5**(1), 1–20 (2019)
22. Kumar, J.L.M., et al.: The classification of EEG-based wink signals: a CWT-transfer learning pipeline. ICT Express **7**(4), 421–425 (2021)
23. Kumar, N., Kumar, J.: Measurement of cognitive load in HCI systems using EEG power spectrum: an experimental study. Procedia Comput. Sci. **84**, 70–78 (2016)
24. Lawhern, V., Kerick, S., Robbins, K.A.: Detecting alpha spindle events in EEG time series using adaptive autoregressive models. BMC Neurosci. **14**(1), 1–16 (2013)
25. Light, G.A., et al.: Electroencephalography (EEG) and event-related potentials (ERPs) with human participants. Curr. Protoc. Neurosci. **52**(1), 6–25 (2010)
26. Liu, Y., et al.: An efficient and robust muscle artifact removal method for few-channel EEG. IEEE Access **7**, 176036–176050 (2019). https://doi.org/10.1109/ACCESS.2019.2957401
27. Liu, Y., et al.: Fusion of spatial, temporal, and spectral EEG signatures improves multilevel cognitive load prediction. IEEE Trans. Hum.-Mach. Syst. **53**(2), 357–366 (2023)
28. Maddirala, A.K., Veluvolu, K.C.: Ica with cwt and k-means for eye-blink artifact removal from fewer channel EEG. IEEE Trans. Neural Syst. Rehabil. Eng. **30**, 1361–1373 (2022)

29. Montoya-Martínez, J., Vanthornhout, J., Bertrand, A., Francart, T.: Effect of number and placement of EEG electrodes on measurement of neural tracking of speech. PLoS ONE **16**(2), e0246769 (2021)
30. Morlet, J., Arens, G., Fourgeau, E., Glard, D.: Wave propagation and sampling theory–part I: complex signal and scattering in multilayered media. Geophysics **47**(2), 203–221 (1982)
31. Naqvi, S.F., et al.: Real-time stress assessment using sliding window based convolutional neural network. Sensors **20**(16), 4400 (2020)
32. Paas, F.G., Van Merriënboer, J.J., Adam, J.J.: Measurement of cognitive load in instructional research. Percept. Mot. Skills **79**(1), 419–430 (1994)
33. Proudfit, G.H., Bress, J.N., Foti, D., Kujawa, A., Klein, D.N.: Depression and event-related potentials: emotional disengagement and reward insensitivity. Curr. Opin. Psychol. **4**, 110–113 (2015)
34. Qassim, Y.T., Cutmore, T.R., James, D.A., Rowlands, D.D.: Wavelet coherence of EEG signals for a visual oddball task. Comput. Biol. Med. **43**(1), 23–31 (2013)
35. Ramakrishnan, A., Satyanarayana, J.: Reconstruction of EEG from limited channel acquisition using estimated signal correlation. Biomed. Signal Process. Control **27**, 164–173 (2016)
36. Rugg, M.D., Coles, M.G.: Electrophysiology of Mind: Event-Related Brain Potentials and Cognition. Oxford University Press (1995)
37. Sabio, J., Williams, N.S., McArthur, G.M., Badcock, N.A.: A scoping review on the use of consumer-grade EEG devices for research. PLoS ONE **19**(3), e0291186 (2024)
38. Sadiya, S., Alhanai, T., Ghassemi, M.M.: Artifact detection and correction in EEG data: a review. In: 2021 10th International IEEE/EMBS Conference on Neural Engineering (NER), pp. 495–498. IEEE (2021)
39. Schröder, A.L., Ombao, H.: Fresped: frequency-specific change-point detection in epileptic seizure multi-channel EEG data. J. Am. Stat. Assoc. **114**(525), 115–128 (2019)
40. Silva, R.P., Zarpelão, B.B., Cano, A., Junior, S.B.: Time series segmentation based on stationarity analysis to improve new samples prediction. Sensors **21**(21), 7333 (2021)
41. Singh, S., Bansal, D.: Design and development of BCI for online acquisition, monitoring and digital processing of EEG waveforms. Int. J. Biomed. Eng. Technol. **16**(4), 359–373 (2014)
42. Soler, A., Moctezuma, L.A., Giraldo, E., Molinas, M.: Automated methodology for optimal selection of minimum electrode subsets for accurate EEG source estimation based on genetic algorithm optimization. Sci. Rep. **12**(1), 11221 (2022)
43. Stone, J.V.: Independent component analysis: an introduction. Trends Cogn. Sci. **6**(2), 59–64 (2002)
44. Tallon-Baudry, C., Bertrand, O., Delpuech, C., Pernier, J.: Oscillatory $\gamma$-band (30–70 hz) activity induced by a visual search task in humans. J. Neurosci. **17**(2), 722–734 (1997)
45. Truong, C., Oudre, L., Vayatis, N.: Selective review of offline change point detection methods. Signal Process. **167**, 107299 (2020)
46. Wang, Y., Duan, W., Dong, D., Ding, L., Lei, X.: A test-retest resting, and cognitive state EEG dataset during multiple subject-driven states. Sci. Data **9**(1), 566 (2022)
47. Woodman, G.F.: A brief introduction to the use of event-related potentials in studies of perception and attention. Attention Perception Psychophys. **72**, 2031–2046 (2010)

48. Wu, L., Caprihan, A., Calhoun, V.: Tracking spatial dynamics of functional connectivity during a task. Neuroimage **239**, 118310 (2021)
49. Zhang, X., Yao, L., Zhang, D., Wang, X., Sheng, Q.Z., Gu, T.: Multi-person brain activity recognition via comprehensive EEG signal analysis. In: Proceedings of the 14th EAI International Conference on Mobile and Ubiquitous Systems: Computing, Networking and Services, pp. 28–37 (2017)

# IoT, Cybersecurity, and Wireless Communication

# Resilience Against APTs: A Provenance-Based IIoT Dataset for Cybersecurity Research

Erfan Ghiasvand[1], Suprio Ray[1]([✉]), Shahrear Iqbal[2], Sajjad Dadkhah[1], and Ali A. Ghorbani[1]

[1] Faculty of Computer Science, University of New Brunswick (UNB), Fredericton, NB, Canada
`{eghiasva,sray,sdadkhah,ghorbani}@unb.ca`
[2] National Research Council, Fredericton, NB, Canada
`shahrear.iqbal@nrc-cnrc.gc.ca`

**Abstract.** The Industrial Internet of Things (IIoT) is a transformative paradigm that integrates smart sensors, advanced analytics, and robust connectivity within industrial processes, enabling real-time data-driven decision-making and enhancing operational efficiency across diverse sectors, including manufacturing, energy, and logistics. IIoT is susceptible to various attack vectors, with Advanced Persistent Threats (APTs) posing a particularly grave concern due to their stealthy, prolonged, and targeted nature. The effectiveness of machine learning-based intrusion detection systems in APT detection has been documented in the literature. However, existing cybersecurity datasets often lack crucial attributes for APT detection in IIoT environments.

Incorporating insights from prior research on APT detection using provenance data and intrusion detection within IoT systems, we present the CICAPT-IIoT dataset. The main goal of this paper is to propose a novel APT dataset in the IIoT setting that includes essential information for the APT detection task. In order to achieve this, a testbed for IIoT is developed, and over 20 attack techniques frequently used in APT campaigns are included. The performed attacks create some of the invariant phases of the APT cycle, including Data Collection and Exfiltration, Discovery and Lateral Movement, Defense Evasion, and Persistence. By integrating network logs and provenance logs with detailed attack information, the CICAPT-IIoT dataset presents foundation for developing holistic cybersecurity measures. Additionally, a comprehensive dataset analysis is provided, presenting cybersecurity experts with a strong basis on which to build innovative and efficient security solutions.

**Keywords:** Industrial IoT · Advanced Persistent Threats · Data Provenance · Self-Supervised Learning


A. Soylu et al. (Eds.): MobiQuitous 2024, LNICST 634, pp. 121–144, 2026.
https://doi.org/10.1007/978-3-032-10554-7_7

# 1   Introduction

Advanced Persistent Threats (APTs) represent a sophisticated category of cyber-attacks, where an unauthorized user gains access to a network and remains undetected for a long period of time. Some attackers aim to harm organizations for financial motives or to gain notoriety by damaging a company's reputation, and they do not conceal their actions. However, in recent years, another type of attacker group has risen in prominence, which is characterized by a deliberate and methodical approach. They employ a "low and slow" strategy with the goal of either stealing sensitive data from their targets or disrupting their operations [4]. APTs represent a significant threat to critical infrastructure systems and have been responsible for numerous severe incidents. APT attacks are distinguished from typical cyberattacks by some key characteristics, such as complexity, persistence, being targeted, and elusiveness. APT attacks typically consist of several distinct phases, each with specific objectives and strategies. While the exact phases can vary depending on the attack group and campaign, the following [32] are common phases in an APT attack: (1) Initial Compromise, (2) Establishing a Foothold, (3) Privilege Escalation, (4) Reconnaissance, (5) Lateral Movement, (6) Maintaining Persistence, and (7) Data Collection and Exfiltration.

Indeed, Industrial Internet of Things (IIoT) networks represent a particularly vulnerable target for APT attacks. Originally centered around general applications, IoT has extended its influence to diverse sectors, including industry, where there is an increasing drive to interconnect previously isolated components, facilitating both intra-component communication and connections to the broader Internet [30]. Industrial IoT enables the seamless integration of several devices with sensing, identification, processing, communication, and networking capabilities [14]. Researchers use many system architectures for IIoT systems, such as Brown-IIoTbed [1], to develop an IIoT environment.

The security and safety of IIoT systems have been the subject of substantial research due to the essential importance and sensitivity of Industrial IoT applications. As demonstrated by historical occurrences like Stuxnet [29], the Ukrainian power plant attacks [45], and the TRITON incident [15], attacks on the IIoT can have significant consequences that go beyond the scope of a company's operations and may compromise the safety of citizens and even the entire nation. Research findings on the security of Industrial IoT reveal the disturbing fact that IIoT devices are susceptible to weaknesses, as described in [46] and [43]. This paints an alarming picture of the security environment used in current IIoT applications.

The convergence of critical infrastructure, interconnected devices, and often limited security measures within IIoT environments makes them an attractive and high-impact target for sophisticated and persistent adversaries like APT groups. These attackers seek to exploit vulnerabilities within IIoT systems to achieve their objectives, which can have significant consequences for industrial operations and, in some cases, national security. As a result, safeguarding IIoT networks from APT attacks is crucial in the realm of cybersecurity.

Traditional threat detection systems, including signature-based and anomaly-based approaches, face limitations in effectively detecting long-running APT campaigns [12]. Signature-based systems struggle to detect APTs that leverage zero-day exploits and new vulnerabilities [18]. Conversely, anomaly-based systems, that leverage network logs [48], system calls [11], and related system events [47], often encounter difficulties in modeling extended system behavior patterns. These systems are also vulnerable to evasion techniques since they primarily examine short sequences of system calls and events, thus limiting their ability to uncover sophisticated APT activities.

According to recent studies [8,10,23,25], data provenance may be a more reliable data source for identifying APTs. Data provenance depicts the flow of information between system entities, such as processes, and objects, such as files and sockets, as a directed acyclic graph (DAG), shows how a system is being used. Even when events are separated in time, this representation links the graph's causally connected events. Consequently, despite APT-affected systems often mimicking normal system behavior, the wealth of contextual information inherent in provenance data enhances the ability to distinguish between benign and malicious events [49]. Despite the demonstrated efficacy of utilizing provenance data in detecting APT attacks, researchers in the field encounter a significant challenge: the scarcity of available datasets. Moreover, the existing datasets frequently do not cover APT scenarios in IIoT environments, making it even more challenging to explore this problem In addition to that, the APT detection methods currently proposed often lack compatibility with some features of the ever-changing APT landscape.

In this research, we introduce CICAPT-IIoT[1], an APT attack dataset developed within an IIoT environment, to assist researchers in security analysis and developing detection methods. To achieve this, an IIoT testbed was established in a semi-controlled setting, mirroring real-world industrial operations. A realistic APT scenario, containing key APT phases like data exfiltration and defense evasion, was then implemented and executed. Raw and processed data collected during this scenario are also made available, enabling researchers to utilize and derive new features for enhanced security insights on using provenance data for the APT detection task. We also develop a self-supervised learning (SSL) model to process provenance data for APT detection tasks. This model is specifically designed to be compatible with the unique features of APT attacks and the heterogeneous nature of the provenance graphs.

The main contributions of our research are as follows:

- We introduce the CICAPT-IIoT dataset, a novel and comprehensive APT attack dataset captured within the IIoT environment. This dataset is generated using a hybrid testbed consisting of real and simulated IIoT components to demonstrate the complexity and diversity of modern technology systems;
- The dataset contains more than 20 distinct attack techniques divided into eight main attack tactics that map into the APT attack scenarios, inspired by the APT29 [33] campaigns. This APT scenario enhances the dataset's effectiveness in APT detection research;

---

[1] Canadian Institute for Cybersecurity Advanced Persistent Threats Dataset for IIoT.

- To evaluate the effectiveness of machine learning algorithms in APT-detection tasks, we applied several ML models on the CICAPT-IIoT dataset and analyzed their performance. Our evaluation uses a provenance-based detection framework offering insights into the practical challenges and considerations in deploying machine learning solutions for APT detection in the IIoT landscape;
- We propose a self-supervised based method and use the CICAPT-IIoT dataset to test and evaluate its performance in provenance-based APT detection. Our results show the effectiveness of the SSL-based model for the provenance graphs.

The rest of this paper is organized as follows. We discussed the related works in Sect. 2. Section 3 provides an overview of the testbed, its different components, and the APT attack emulation plan. we also explain the dataset generation experiments and the dataset properties in this section. Furthermore, a thorough analysis of the dataset is presented in the Sect. 4. Next, we describe predictive models for APT detection task in Sect. 5 and evaluate these models performance using CICAPT-IIoT dataset in Sect. 6. Finally, Sect. 7 presents the conclusion of this research.

## 2   Related Works

Recent research has explored the utility of provenance data across various domains, including security, reproducibility, data trustworthiness, and intrusion detection [28]. These studies have demonstrated its potential for improving the dependability and security of information systems against various threats such as APTs [31]. Datasets play a crucial role in any attack detection research, enabling the study and modeling of behavior to identify attack activities [44]. However, the majority of available datasets are generated for conventional intrusion detection rather than detecting Advanced Persistent Threats. Such datasets often lack the complexity inherent in APT cycle phases and typically comprise only network or system logs. In this section, we provide an overview of the datasets currently used in the literature for APT detection and general attack detection. Additionally, we offer a brief review of the literature on provenance data, methods for capturing provenance, and provenance-based attack detection techniques.

### 2.1   Related Datasets

The significance of datasets in attack detection research cannot be overstated, as they are fundamental to the development, testing, and refinement of detection algorithms. High-quality datasets provide a realistic representation of valuable data such as system logs and network traffic, and include both benign activities and malicious attacks, that are crucial for training and evaluating intrusion detection systems.

The TON IoT dataset [3] includes telemetry data from IoT/IIoT services and contains network traffic collected from a realistic representation of a medium-scale network at an IoT Lab. This dataset includes a variety of cyberattacks, including scanning attacks, Denial of Service (DoS) attacks, ransomware, and Man-In-The-Middle (MITM) attacks, among others, providing researchers with a comprehensive resource to study, understand, and develop countermeasures against these threats. The dataset is designed for multi-classification problems, incorporating labels for normal and attack classes, and sub-classes of attacks targeting IoT/IIoT applications. DAPT 2020 [34], is a benchmark dataset specifically designed to address the challenges in modeling and detecting APTs. This dataset includes attacks that are hard to distinguish from normal traffic flows and encompass both public-to-private interface traffic and internal network traffic. The APT stages that this dataset covers are Reconnaissance, Foothold Establishment, Lateral Movement, and Data Exfiltration which are all crucial steps in APT campaigns.

X-IIoTID [2] is a dataset for intrusion detection in the Industrial Internet of Things (IIoT) environment. IIoT systems, due to their vast connectivity and deployment of various protocols and devices, present significant security challenges. This dataset is designed to be both connectivity-agnostic and device-agnostic, thereby suitable for the heterogeneous and interoperable nature of IIoT environments. The authors state that X-IIoTD covers the Reconnaissance, Weaponization, C&C, and Lateral movement stages of an attack scenario. Edge-IIoTset [16], is a cybersecurity dataset designed for IoT and IIoT applications, useful for both centralized and federated learning intrusion detection systems. The dataset is generated from a custom-built IoT/IIoT testbed incorporating a wide range of devices, sensors, protocols, and cloud/edge configurations. Edge-IIoTset includes over 10 types of IoT devices that generate various types of data, such as temperature, humidity, and ultrasonic sensor readings, and contains data related to DoS, DDoS, MitM, Reconnaissance, and malware attacks.

The DARPA OpTC dataset [17] contains data from a pilot study aimed at testing the scalability of DARPA Transparent Computing technologies for cyber defense. This dataset, generated during a two-week evaluation in a highly instrumented environment, capturing both benign activities and malware injections across one thousand Windows 10 endpoints and serves as a critical resource for analyzing the effectiveness of scaled cyber defense technologies in detecting APTs within large-scale network environments. CICIoT2023 [36] is an IoT attack dataset designed to aid in the development of security analytics applications for real IoT operations by executing 33 attacks within an IoT topology of 105 devices, classifying these attacks into seven categories: DDoS, DoS, Recon, Web-based, brute force, spoofing, and Mirai, all executed by malicious IoT devices targeting other IoT devices.

Unraveled [35], one of the most recent datasets is a semi-synthetic dataset crafted to emulate APT attacks. In response to the scarcity of publicly accessible APT datasets, the creators endeavored to enrich this dataset with a range of sophisticated attack scenarios derived from the MITRE ATT&CK database. Additionally, they designed an Employee Behavior Generation model aimed at replicating typical employee activities. The dataset is collected during a 6-week period and contains data from Reconnaissance, Foothold Establishment, Lateral movement, and Data exfiltration stages of APTs.

## 2.2   Provenance Data and Provenance-Based Attack Detection

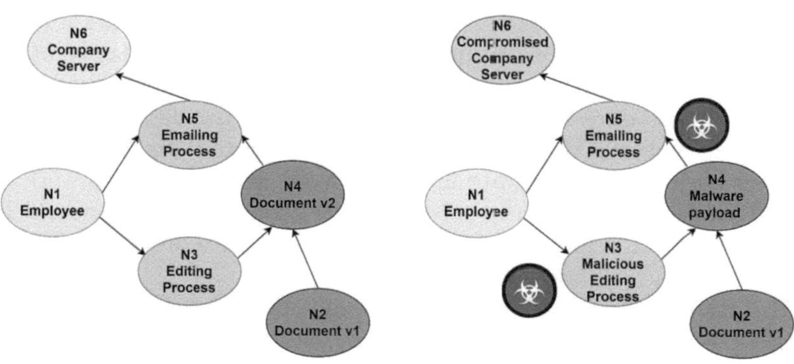

**Fig. 1.** Sample provenance graphs showing a benign scenario (Left) and an attack scenario (Right)

Data provenance refers to the documentation or record of the origin, lineage, and history of data. It includes every step of the creation, modification, and evolution of data over time [24]. Tracking the origins of data, such as where and how it was created and its evolution through various processing stages and transfers, are components of data provenance.

Bates et al. [9] introduced the Linux Provenance Modules (LPM), a framework designed for secure provenance collection on Linux operating systems. CamFlow [40], using a similar architecture, implemented a practical whole-system provenance system. This system leverages the Linux Security Module (LSM) and NetFilter hooks, capturing provenance data within the Linux environment. Some researchers developed cross-platform data provenance platforms that can collect provenance on different operating systems. For example SPADE [19] is a provenance solution capable of tracking and analyzing provenance from multiple possibly distributed sources including OS's auditing mechanisms. There has also been some research to introduce the concept of provenance to the IoT world and use its benefits to mitigate IoT security challenges [26]. Researchers in [5,6,38,42] have proposed various methods to collect and use provenance data in the IoT environment.

Since provenance data provides a thorough history and origin of any information within a system, it has become a valuable tool in intrusion detection systems. Cybersecurity researchers have explored provenance potential to improve security systems [39]. Works such as UNICORN [22] and ANUBIS [7] have utilized provenance data to train anomaly detection models for identifying APT activities within target environments.

UNICORN is an anomaly-based detection system designed to mitigate APTs that utilize data provenance by transforming system execution information into a directed acyclic graph (DAG). UNICORN employs graph sketching to create a scalable, incrementally updatable, fixed-size data structure. ANUBIS, another provenance-based framework for APT detection, is a machine learning-based system that uses a Bayesian Neural Network (BNN) for the classification of the system's events. This allows ANUBIS not only to detect APTs with high accuracy but also to explain its predictions, making it a valuable tool for cyber-response teams.

Figure 1 presents two different provenance graphs. The graph on the left depicts a benign scenario where a document is accessed, edited by a user, and subsequently sent to the company server. The graph on the right illustrates a simplified APT attack scenario: within a compromised system, a malicious editing process attaches a malicious payload to the file, which is then transmitted to the server, resulting in its compromise.

## 3  CICAPT-IIoT – A Semi-Synthetic IIoT APT Dataset

In this section, we present an overview of our data collection setup and the main components of our system. As APT detection research often suffers from the lack of realistic, open-source datasets, our research involves developing CICAPT-IIoT, a semi-synthetic dataset that imitates the characteristics of APT behaviors. The dataset generation design comprises diverse tools and devices, making it possible to gather a suitable dataset for APT detection within IIoT systems. Here we describe the data collection procedure and the various phases of the data generation process. Next, we explore our attack emulation plan and its different steps. Finally, we analyze the dataset and discuss the techniques we've used to distinguish between malicious and benign data.

### 3.1  System Overview

We have developed a simulation testbed to have a controlled environment that is useful for IIoT research and particularly beneficial for simulating APT scenarios. This testbed is based on the architecture of the Brown-IIoTbed framework [1]. Our testbed's structure integrates various virtual and physical components to mirror the complexity and interactions of real-world IIoT systems. Figure 2 illustrates an overview of the system.

At the heart of our testbed is the NS3 network simulator [37], running on an Ubuntu host. The NS3 is essential in bridging actual and simulated nodes through its tap bridge module, allowing us to coordinate a seamless integration between real and virtual network components. The testbed setup involves two Ubuntu VMs and two Kali Linux VMs hosted on a machine running NS3. Ubuntu VM1 acts as the gateway, managing network traffic, and is equipped with tools like Auditd and SPADE for logging and translating logs into provenance data, respectively. It also subscribes to MQTT topics, playing a critical role within the testbed's MQTT ecosystem. Ubuntu VM2 functions as an MQTT publisher and SCADA system via SCADABR software, interacting with a PLC simulated on Raspberry Pi1, which operates with OpenPLC and communicates

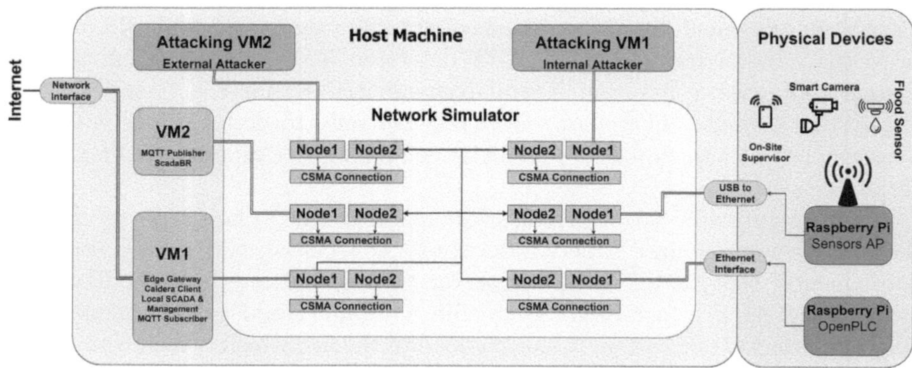


**Fig. 2.** Overview of the testbed

using the Modbus protocol. Raspberry Pi2 serves as a WiFi access point, enhancing the network's connectivity to IoT sensors. Kali VM1 and VM2 are set up as internal and external threat actors, equipped with MITRE Caldera and various attack tools, respectively. This sophisticated simulation environment not only generates comprehensive data including system logs, network traffic, and provenance data essential for APT research in IIoT environments but also mimics real IIoT operations to facilitate advanced IIoT security research. Adding devices like cameras, leakage sensors, and PLCs and using protocols such as MODBUS and MQTT helps the testbed more accurately replicate an IIoT environment [27]. PLCs enable realistic automation and control simulations typical in industrial settings, and MODBUS and MQTT are common device-to-device communication protocols in IIoT systems. Table 1 shows the testbed components and their roles in the experiments.

### 3.2    Attack Emulation Plan

APT29, also known as 'The Dukes' or 'Cozy Bear', is a sophisticated cyber threat group noted for its advanced cyber espionage tactics and persistent attacks. The group's activities have had significant impacts, leading MITRE to publish an adversary emulation plan for APT29 within the framework of MITRE Caldera [13]. This emulation plan, however, uses tactics and techniques mostly tailored for Windows environments, which are not directly transferable to Linux systems. Therefore, we adapted APT29 emulation plan and the MITRE ATT&CK framework's Tactics, Techniques, and Procedures (TTPs) to design a customized attack emulation plan suitable for the Linux-based testbed. This plan aims to replicate APT29's operational patterns within the unique environment of the testbed. Table 2 shows the different APT tactics and techniques used in the dataset. The developed emulation plan encompasses several stages, each reflecting a typical phase in an APT campaign, including Data Collection and Exfiltration, Deployment of Stealth Toolkits for further activities, Defense and Discov-

**Table 1.** List of the testbed components

| Device | Role |
| --- | --- |
| Ubuntu VM1 | Gateway<br>Local Management<br>MQTT Subscriber |
| Ubuntu VM2 | MQTT Publisher<br>ScadaBR |
| Kali VM1 | Internal Attacker<br>Caldera Server |
| Kali VM2 | External Attacker |
| Raspberry Pi1 | OpenPLC |
| Raspberry Pi2 | WiFi Access Point |
| Litokam Smart Camera | Camera |
| ConnectifyFlood Sensor | Flood Sensor |

ery Evasion, Maintaining Persistence, Accessing System Credentials, and Lateral Movement to other components in the network.

### 3.3 Data Collection and Experiments

The NS3 simulator serves as the primary platform for our testbed, managing network connections and enabling the monitoring and logging of all network packets. It operates in Real-Time mode to facilitate the integration of real and simulated nodes. Along with network logs collected by NS3, system logs are gathered using the Linux Audit Daemon (Auditd), which leverages the Linux Auditing System for efficient log capture. These logs are processed by SPADE [19], a service that generates provenance data, enriching the dataset with an additional layer of information useful in APT detection.

The experiments were conducted in two phases. The first phase, conducted over four days, simulated normal system operations to establish a baseline behavior of the testbed components including VMs, sensors, and Raspberry Pis. The second phase, spanning three days, simulated an APT attack using APT29 tactics executed through Kali VM1 with MITRE Caldera. This phase followed the APT's 'low and slow' approach as attack steps are executed in random time intervals of 45 to 75 min to mimic the stealth and persistence typical of APTs and closely replicate real-world attack dynamics.

### 3.4 Dataset Properties

The dataset is organized into two folders: phase1 data and phase2 data, each containing two types of data—provenance data and network packets. The provenance data files are in CSV format and contain the nodes and edges of the

**Table 2.** APT attack phases and techniques used in the dataset

| Tactic | Technique ID | Attack Type | APT Groups |
| --- | --- | --- | --- |
| Collection | T1074 | Data Staged: Local Data Staging | APT28, APT29, APT39, APT3 |
| | T1005 | Data from Local System | Andariel, APT28, APT29 |
| | T1119 | Automated Collection | APT1, APT28, Chimera |
| | T1113 | Screen Capture | APT28, APT39, Carbanak |
| | T1115 | Clipboard Data | APT29, APT29, APT38 |
| Exfiltration | T1560 | Archive Collected Data: Archive via Utility | APT28, APT29, APT32 |
| | T1041 | Exfiltration Over C2 Channel | Lazarus, APT3, APT32 |
| Command and Control | T1105 | Ingress Tool Transfer | Lazarus, APT29, APT3 |
| Persistence | T1546 | Event Triggered Execution | APT28, APT29, APT3 |
| | T1136 | Create Account: Local Account | Dragonfly, FIN13, APT29 |
| Discovery | T1087 | Account Discovery: Local Account | APT1, APT3, Chimera |
| | T1016 | System Network Configuration Discovery: Internet Connection Discovery | FIN13, Gamaredon, APT29 |
| | | System Network Configuration Discovery: Wi-Fi Discovery | Magic Hound, Wizard Spider |
| | T1033 | System Owner/User Discovery | Chimera, Dragonfly, APT3 |
| | T1518 | Software Discovery | HEXANE, MuddyWater |
| | T1069 | Permission Groups Discovery: Local Groups | Chimera, HEXANE, APT29 |
| | T1082 | System Information Discovery | Chimera, APT3, APT32 |
| | T1083 | File and Directory Discovery | APT28, APT29, APT32 |
| | T1018 | Remote System Discovery | Chimera, APT29, APT32 |
| Credential Access | T1552 | Unsecured Credentials: Credentials In Files | APT3, APT33, FIN13 |
| | | Unsecured Credentials: Bash History | - |
| | T1555 | Credentials from Password Stores: Credentials from Web Browsers | APT33, APT39, HEXANE |
| Lateral Movement | T1021 | Remote Services: SSH | APT29, APT39, Lazarus |
| Defense Evasion | T1036 | Masquerading: Right-to-Left Override | APT28, APT29, Dragonfly |
| | T1485 | Data Destruction | APT38, Gamaredon, Lazarus |

provenance graph. Each node in the provenance data is assigned a unique 32-digit ID, which is utilized by the edge entries to establish connections between nodes in the graph.

**Table 3.** Provenance Data Features

| # | Feature | Description | Provenance Type |
|---|---|---|---|
| 1 | id | Node identifier | All node types |
| 2 | type | Edge or node type | All nodes and edges |
| 3 | from | Source node ID | Edges |
| 4 | to | Destination node ID | Edges |
| 5 | uid | User Id | Process nodes |
| 6 | egid | Effective group ID | Process nodes |
| 7 | exe | Executable path | Process nodes |
| 8 | gid | Group ID | Process nodes |
| 9 | euid | Effective user ID | Process nodes |
| 10 | name | Executable name | Process nodes |
| 11 | pid | Process ID | Process nodes, WDF edges |
| 12 | seen time | Process seen time | Process nodes |
| 13 | source | Data origin | All nodes and edges |
| 14 | ppid | Parent process ID | Process nodes |
| 15 | command line | Full command line used | Process nodes |
| 16 | start time | Process start time | Process nodes |
| 17 | event ID | Unique event ID | All edges |
| 18 | time | Event time | All edges |
| 19 | operation | Type of operation | All edges |
| 20 | path | File path | File,link, directory nodes |
| 21 | subtype | Subtype of nodes | Artifact nodes |
| 22 | permissions | Access permissions | File,link, directory nodes |
| 23 | epoch | Sequence number | Artifact nodes |
| 24 | version | Version number | Artifact nodes |
| 25 | Flag | Resource access mode | Used, WGB edges |
| 26 | remote port | Port number | Network socket nodes |
| 27 | protocol | Used protocol | Network socket nodes |
| 28 | remote address | IP address | Network socket nodes |
| 29 | tgid | Thread group ID | Unknown nodes |
| 30 | fd | File descriptor | Unknown nodes |
| 31 | mode | Permission setting | WGB edges |
| 32 | label | Node label- attack/benign | All nodes |
| 33 | subLabel | Attack category | All nodes |

Besides the IDs, the provenance data files comprise 32 features in total. However, due to the heterogeneous nature of nodes and edges that are all in a single file, not all features apply to every node or edge type, resulting in many fields being populated with NaN values. Table 3 lists all features provided in the provenance data part of the dataset. The provenance data includes two main node types: Process and Artifact. The Artifact node type is further categorized into various subtypes such as file, directory, network socket, link, and unknown, the latter being used for provenance node types that do not fit into the existing subtypes. The other data type in the dataset is the network logs captured using NS3 during the experiments and stored in pcap format. These pcap files can be further processed into CSV format. We generate the CSV format from these pcaps that have the information at the packet level and contain 67 features for each packet. The last file in the dataset is the Attack Information file, which contains all necessary information about the attacks performed during the experiments in phase 2. This information includes attack time, attack PID, and the category of attack. This file helps the researchers to further analyze the dataset behavior during the attacks.

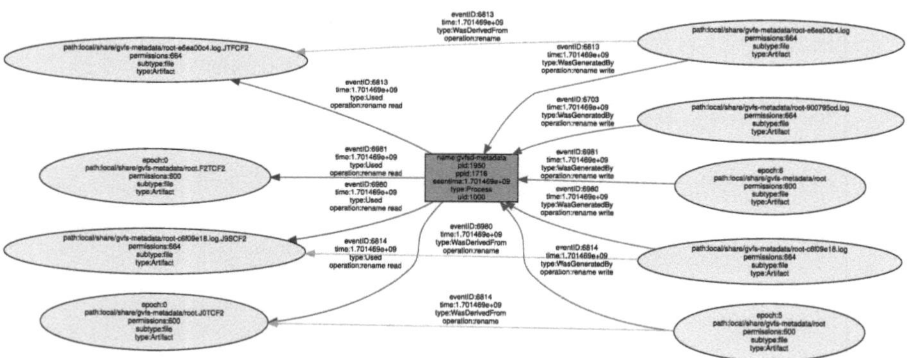

**Fig. 3.** A provenance graph based on a sample of our dataset

Figure 3 displays an example of a provenance graph. This is a subgraph of the complete provenance graph based on the CICAPT-IIoT dataset. This provenance graph shows several rename operations performed on files, resulting in the generation of a new set of files.

## 4    Dataset Assessment

In this section, we provide an assessment of the CICAPT-IIoT dataset, evaluating its structure and utility for advancing research in APT detection within IIoT environments. We begin by presenting general statistics of the dataset to illustrate its composition and scope, followed by a comparative analysis against similar datasets. This evaluation aims to highlight the dataset's attributes and its applicability in developing robust cybersecurity solutions for the IIoT domain

### 4.1  General Statistics of the Dataset

The dataset was generated in two phases: Phase 1, which lasted approximately 96 h, and Phase 2, which lasted about 72 h. It contains of about 10 GB of data. During both phases, network logs and system logs were collected, and provenance logs were generated using the system logs and SPADE. A detailed breakdown of the dataset's segments can be found in Table 4. As shown in the Table 4, the CICAPT-IIoT dataset is notably unbalanced, with approximately 99.5% of the samples representing normal behavior and only a small fraction indicating malicious activities, which is typical in APT scenarios. This significant imbalance is reflective of real-world conditions in IIoT environments, where actual attacks are infrequent relative to regular operations.

In such contexts, using oversampling techniques to artificially balance the dataset by replicating the minority class or generating synthetic samples—can be counterproductive. Although these methods might facilitate algorithmic training in the short term, they distort the reality of how APTs manifest within network systems. By oversampling attack data, the models are trained on scenarios that are not reflective of actual operational conditions. This training approach can lead to models that perform well on balanced or altered datasets in testing environments but fail to detect genuine APT activities when deployed in real-world scenarios.

**Table 4.** Data distribution across different phases and data types

| Attribute | Event type | Provenance Data | Network Data |
|---|---|---|---|
| **Phase 1** | **Benign** | 46773 Nodes | 12103705 Packets |
| **Phase 2** | **Benign** | 52954 Nodes | 9535819 Packets |
| | **Attack** | 330 | 1004 |
| | **Collection** | 100 | 460 |
| | **Exfiltration** | 22 | 42 |
| | **Credential Access** | 82 | 58 |
| | **Defence Evasion** | 45 | 192 |
| | **Discovery** | 36 | 138 |
| | **Persistence** | 19 | 44 |
| | **C&C** | 16 | 56 |
| | **Lateral Movement** | 10 | 14 |

### 4.2  Comparison Against Similar Datasets

The CICAPT-IIoT dataset stands out from other datasets in several ways. First, the inclusion of multiple data sources enhances the analytical capabilities of researchers, and supports the development of new detection methods that utilize both network data and provenance logs. Furthermore, as APT attacks are known for their multi-stage operations, they require a comprehensive coverage of all associated stages, tactics, and techniques to effectively model APT campaigns in a

**Table 5.** Related datasets analysis

| Dataset | [16] | [36] | [2] | [3] | [17] | [34] | CICAPT IIoT (This Work) |
|---|---|---|---|---|---|---|---|
| IoT/IIoT | ✓ | ✓ | ✓ | ✓ | | | ✓ |
| Network Logs | ✓ | ✓ | ✓ | ✓ | | ✓ | ✓ |
| Provenance/Host Logs | | | | | ✓ | | ✓ |
| Duration | N/A | 16(H) | N/A | N/A | 7(D) | 5(D) | 7(D) |
| Establish foothold | ✓ | ✓ | | ✓ | | ✓ | ✓ |
| Collection | | | | | | | ✓ |
| Data exfiltration | | | ✓ | | ✓ | ✓ | ✓ |
| Command & Control | ✓ | ✓ | ✓ | | ✓ | | ✓ |
| Persistence | ✓ | ✓ | | ✓ | ✓ | | ✓ |
| Discovery | ✓ | ✓ | ✓ | ✓ | ✓ | ✓ | ✓ |
| Credential Access | ✓ | ✓ | ✓ | ✓ | ✓ | | ✓ |
| Lateral movement | | | ✓ | | ✓ | ✓ | ✓ |
| Defence Evasion | | | | | ✓ | | ✓ |

cybersecurity dataset. Many existing datasets either do not directly address all APT tactics, as they only map network-based attacks to APT stages, or they fail to cover all the stages necessary to fully represent an APT campaign. In contrast, the CICAPT-IIoT dataset aims to provide a complete and realistic portrayal of an APT attack, encompassing the most relevant and authentic stages and techniques. Table 5 provides an analysis of some of the related datasets. The comparison of these datasets is based on several key factors: the environment in which the data was collected, the types of data included, and the APT tactics they cover.

## 5   Predictive Model for APT Detection

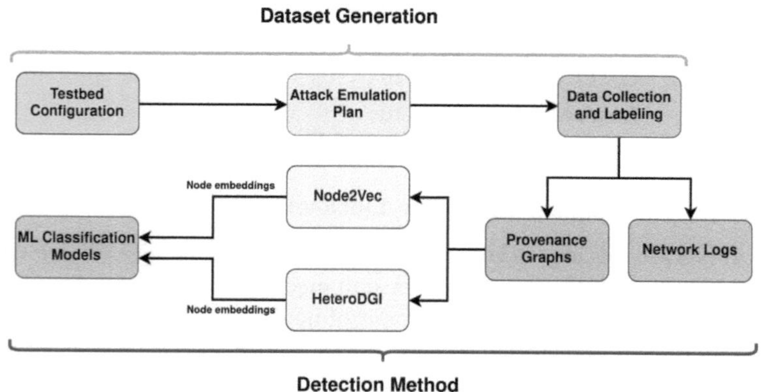


**Fig. 4.** Adopted approach to produce and analyze the dataset

Figure 4 shows the steps taken in this work to generate and analyze this dataset. After data collection and labeling, the provenance and network data are available to use for attack detection tasks. However, given the inherent graph structure of provenance data, the direct application of ML techniques is impractical. Therefore, an embedding method is needed to generate vector embeddings for each node in the graph. These embeddings are then utilized as inputs for various classification models to assess the dataset's effectiveness in machine learning-based APT detection tasks.

## 5.1   Features

Due to the heterogeneous nature of the data, encompassing various types of nodes and edges, each node type is associated with a specific subset of applicable features. The features used for each node and edge type are detailed in the table below (Table 6):

**Table 6.** Selected features for different node and edge types

| Node/Edge Type | Attributes |
| --- | --- |
| Network Socket Nodes | epoch, remote port, remote address |
| Process Nodes | uid, egid, exe, gid, euid, name |
| File Nodes | path, permissions, epoch |
| Directory Nodes | path, permissions |
| Link Nodes | path, permission, epoch |
| Unknown Nodes | version, tgid, fd |
| WTB Edges | type, operation |
| WGB Edges | type, operation |
| USED Edges | type, operation |
| WDF Edges | type, operation |

We select these features based on the values associated with them in the dataset. Specifically, in the feature selection process, we ensure that each feature is relevant to the specific node type it describes. For instance, the "remote port" feature is used exclusively for the Network Socket node type because it is inherently related to network connections and has valid values for these nodes. Conversely, this feature is not applicable to Process nodes and therefore has NaN values for this node type. As a result, the "remote port" feature is excluded from the set of features describing Process nodes to maintain the relevance and accuracy of the feature sets for each node type. This approach ensures that the features chosen are meaningful and contribute to differentiating between nodes within the same category, which enhances the analysis of the provenance graph.

## 5.2   Node2Vec Based Embedding

Node2Vec [20], a popular technique, is an algorithm that generates vector representations of nodes on a graph. Using random walks, Node2Vec efficiently samples diverse neighborhoods that capture each node's essential structural properties and contextual relationships. We employ Node2Vec with a walk length of 10 to generate 64-dimensional vector representations of the nodes in the provenance graph of the dataset.

## 5.3   Self-Supervised Learning Based Embedding

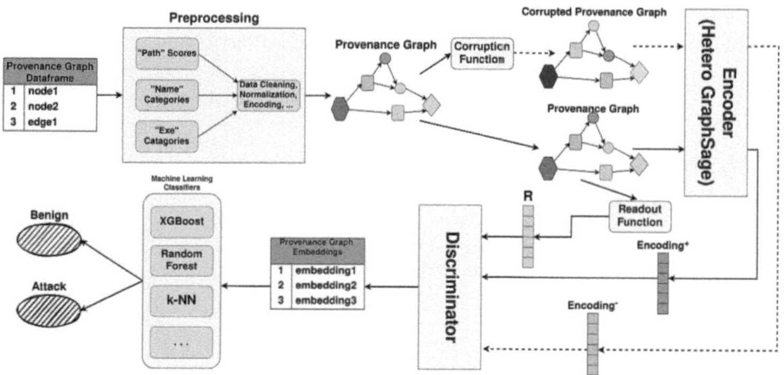


**Fig. 5.** Proposed self-supervised framework

Although Node2Vec embeddings offer a foundational understanding of provenance graphs, this method struggles with provenance graphs and APT detection tasks due to its inherent limitations. For instance, Node2Vec is designed for homogeneous graphs, which means, it cannot effectively handle the heterogeneity and evolving structure of provenance graphs crucial for identifying complex APT activities.

Due to these limitations, we present our Self-Supervised Learning (SSL) based model, which is specifically designed to learn node representations from provenance graphs and is based on Heterogeneous Deep Graph Infomax (HDGI) [41]. We use the Contrastive HDGI method and leverage the HeteroGraphSage as our HDGI encoder. One of the key components of the HDGI model is the encoder that is responsible for processing the graph. While many heterogeneous graph embedding methods utilize MetaPath based approaches, which rely on predefined sequences of edges, this technique is not directly applicable for provenance graphs. The dynamic nature of data interactions in provenance graphs makes it challenging to define relevant paths. Therefore, we utilize a modified Graph-SAGE [21] model that is adjusted to handle heterogeneous graphs effectively. Furthermore, SSL models do not rely on labeled data, making these models suitable to adapt to the nature of APTs. Other crucial aspects of our model's design are the adaptations of the HDGI corruption function, discriminator, and readout function to suit the heterogeneous nodes of provenance graphs.

We use this SSL-based model to generate 64-sized vector embeddings for the nodes in the provenance graph. These embeddings not only reflect the node's own attributes but also embody contextual insights and relational data from its immediate environment, enhancing the overall data representation. Figure 5 presents our proposed framework for using SSL in the APT detection task.

**Encoder Function.** GraphSage (Graph Sample and AggreGatE) [21] is a neural network model designed for graph-based data that generalizes the embedding learning process to graphs that are continuously growing. The key innovation of GraphSage is its ability to generate embeddings by sampling and aggregating features from a node's local neighborhood.

$$\mathbf{h}_{\mathcal{N}(v)}^{(k)} = \text{AGGREGATE}_k \left( \{\mathbf{h}_u^{(k-1)} : u \in \mathcal{N}(v)\} \right) \tag{1}$$

As described in Eq. 1, the features of node $v$'s neighbors are aggregated to compute the node's new feature representation at each layer where:

- $\mathbf{h}_u^{(k-1)}$ are the features of neighbor nodes $u$ of node $v$ at layer $k-1$.
- $\mathcal{N}(v)$ denotes the set of neighbor nodes of $v$.
- $\text{AGGREGATE}_k$ is an aggregation function, such as mean, sum, or max.

Our Heterogeneous GraphSAGE model is designed to work across diverse edge types inherent in heterogeneous graphs. The model leverages SAGEConv layers, each tailored to specific edge types as defined in the graph's metadata. This design enables it to handle the complexities and different types of edge interactions within such graphs. The model structure includes multiple layers of these convolutions, allowing for deeper feature integration across multiple hops in the graph.

**Corruption Function.** The corruption function is crucial in self-supervised learning models like Deep Graph Infomax, primarily for generating negative samples that facilitate contrastive learning. This function alters the graph's structure and node features to create a corrupted version of the original graph, which serves as a negative sample. By differentiating between these negative samples and the original, unaltered graphs, the model learns to develop robust and generalizable node embeddings that capture the essential characteristics of the graph. This process enhances the model's ability to understand and represent the fundamental properties of the graph effectively.

**Readout Function.** The readout function in graph neural networks is crucial for converting node-level information into a graph-level representation, which is vital for understanding the entire graph's structure, especially in applications like contrastive self-supervised learning. Standard readout methods, such as summation, which work well for homogeneous graphs, do not suit heterogeneous graphs

---

**Algorithm 1.** Heterogeneous graphs readout function

---

  **Input:** *embeddings* - Heterogeneous graph embeddings
  **Output:** *graph_summary* - Summarized embeddings
 1: **function** READOUT_FUNCTION(*embeddings*)
 2:     **for** *node_types_embedding* $\in$ *embeddings* **do**
 3:         *types_embedding* $\leftarrow$ mean(*node_types_embedding*)
 4:         *graph_summary.append(types_embedding)*
 5:     **end for**
 6:     **return** *graph_summary*
 7: **end function**

---

like provenance graphs, as they tend to overlook the unique properties of different node types. To overcome this, readout functions need adaptation to handle the complexity of heterogeneous graphs. Our modified readout function processes each node type individually, ensuring that the overall graph representation maintains the distinct characteristics of each node type, thus preserving the structural and semantic integrity of heterogeneous graphs according to Algorithm 1.

## 6  APT Detection Model Evaluation

In this section, we analyze the provenance data component of the CICAPT-IIoT dataset to evaluate its effectiveness for provenance-based APT detection tasks. To assess the effectiveness of the provenance data component of the CICAPT-IIoT dataset in machine learning-based detection, we develop three evaluation methods. Each method utilizes node embeddings generated using the methods described in Sects. 5.2 and 5.3 for machine learning classification tasks. The primary goal of these classification methods is to accurately identify nodes labeled as malicious within the provenance graphs. The methods used to evaluate the dataset are as follows:

1. **Binary Classification:** Initially, the problem is defined as a binary classification task, categorizing all nodes as malicious or benign. This step aims to establish a baseline for detecting harmful entities within the system.
2. **Multi-Class Classification:** Going beyond binary classification, the analysis was expanded to include multi-class classification. This involved not only identifying benign nodes but also classifying the attack types.
3. **Attack Stages Detection:** The final experiment in the classification approach involved defining four distinct stages of attack and correlating specific attack steps to these stages, thereby creating more meaningful classes of attacks. Attack tactics were grouped based on their objectives and functionalities, resulting in this four distinct, commonly observed attack stages. Each attack stage was then treated as a separate binary classification problem.

### 6.1  Results and Discussion

In this section, we present the results obtained from the evaluation methods, described above and then we provide a discussion about the dataset applicability

**Table 7.** Results of the Node2Vec-based binary classification

| Model | Acc | Recall | F1 |
|---|---|---|---|
| XGBoost | 0.9982 | 0.7161 | 0.8270 |
| Extra Trees | 0.9981 | 0.7072 | 0.8218 |
| k-NN | 0.9980 | 0.7161 | 0.8157 |
| Random Forest | 0.9979 | 0.6600 | 0.7881 |
| AdaBoost | 0.9961 | 0.4741 | 0.6001 |
| Decision Tree | 0.9946 | 0.6471 | 0.5997 |
| SVM | 0.9943 | 0.2940 | 0.3900 |
| Naive Bayes | 0.9484 | 0.5482 | 0.1170 |

**Table 8.** Results of the Node2Vec-based multi-class classification

| Model | Acc | Recall | F1 |
|---|---|---|---|
| XGBoost | 0.9964 | 0.3842 | 0.4012 |
| k-NN | 0.9966 | 0.4046 | 0.4182 |
| Random Forest | 0.9967 | 0.3913 | 0.4242 |
| AdaBoost | 0.9934 | 0.1820 | 0.1954 |
| SVM | 0.9969 | 0.3876 | 0.4151 |
| Extra Trees | 0.9967 | 0.3913 | 0.4170 |
| Decision Tree | 0.9935 | 0.3735 | 0.3553 |
| Naive Bayes | 0.8203 | 0.4564 | 0.2546 |

and the effectiveness of employed methods. The accuracy scores were notably high for all ML models in every classification tasks. However, due to the significant class imbalance in the dataset—approximately 99.5% of instances are labeled as benign, the accuracy alone may not be informative enough. As a result, our evaluation puts more weight on criteria like Recall and the F1 score.

Table 7 presents the performance metrics of binary classification models that utilize embeddings generated by the Node2Vec method. While the results display high overall accuracy for all the models, the average recall score is around 70%. The good performance of these models, despite utilizing an embedding method like Node2Vec, underscores the applicability of the CICAPT-IIoT dataset for graph-based APT detection tasks. The overall performance of all models decreases in the attack classification task, as shown in Table 8, due to the increased complexity of this classification challenge. These results suggest that while it is possible to detect malicious nodes in the provenance graph using simpler embedding methods, accurately classifying the attack categories proves more challenging and requires more sophisticated approaches.

The results of the Node2Vec-based attack stage detection are shown in Table 9. All stages are detectable by machine learning models with an average recall score of approximately 60%. This demonstrates that defining distinct attack stages can be effective for detecting APT attacks and providing a holistic view of the APT campaign. However, improvements may be necessary, suggesting the need for more advanced approaches to enhance performance.

These results from Node2Vec embeddings, demonstrate the potential of machine learning methods to classify APTs within IIoT operations. Indeed, this serves as a baseline for any machine learning-based APT detection task.

To employ an embedding method better suited to the features of our dataset, we utilize our proposed SSL model described in Sect. 5.3, applying the same evaluation methods for consistency in our analysis. Table 10 shows the results of the binary classification task using the SSL method. All models show improved performance compared to the Node2Vec model, with recall scores approximately

**Table 9.** Models performance metrics for Node2Vec-based attack stage detection

| Attack Stage | Model | Accuracy | Recall | Precision | F1-Score |
|---|---|---|---|---|---|
| Collection and Exfiltration | XGBoost | 0.9991 | 0.6278 | 0.9732 | 0.7446 |
| | Random Forest | 0.9988 | 0.5069 | 0.9750 | 0.6546 |
| | AdaBoost | 0.9987 | 0.5306 | 0.8714 | 0.6451 |
| Credential Access and C&C | XGBoost | 0.9993 | 0.6405 | 1.0000 | 0.7719 |
| | Random Forest | 0.9993 | 0.6403 | 1.0000 | 0.7698 |
| | AdaBoost | 0.9994 | 0.7143 | 0.9333 | 0.8031 |
| Defense Evasion and Persistence | XGBoost | 0.9993 | 0.4500 | 1.000 | 0.5931 |
| | Random Forest | 0.9990 | 0.1900 | 0.6000 | 0.2800 |
| | AdaBoost | 0.9992 | 0.4100 | 0.8167 | 0.5098 |
| Discovery and Lateral Movement | XGBoost | 0.9995 | 0.4083 | 0.8000 | 0.5406 |
| | Random Forest | 0.9993 | 0.1500 | 0.4000 | 0.2100 |
| | AdaBoost | 0.9994 | 0.4000 | 0.8083 | 0.5357 |

**Table 10.** Results of the SSL-based binary class classification

| Model | Acc | Recall | F1 |
|---|---|---|---|
| Extra Trees | 0.9986 | 0.8444 | 0.8785 |
| Random Forest | 0.9986 | 0.8232 | 0.8760 |
| XGBoost | 0.9984 | 0.8359 | 0.8638 |
| Decision Tree | 0.9983 | 0.8361 | 0.8615 |
| AdaBoost | 0.9980 | 0.7281 | 0.8153 |
| k-NN | 0.9978 | 0.7629 | 0.8097 |
| Naive Bayes | 0.5143 | 0.9699 | 0.0242 |

**Table 11.** Results of the SSL-based multi-class classification

| Model | Acc | Recall | F1 |
|---|---|---|---|
| XGBoost | 0.9975 | 0.5816 | 0.6277 |
| k-NN | 0.9971 | 0.4340 | 0.4724 |
| Random Forest | 0.9975 | 0.5789 | 0.6299 |
| AdaBoost | 0.9934 | 0.1850 | 0.1670 |
| Extra Trees | 0.9973 | 0.5657 | 0.6032 |
| Decision Tree | 0.9967 | 0.5471 | 0.5264 |
| Naive Bayes | 0.4284 | 0.3139 | 0.2338 |

10% higher. These improvements suggest that SSL-based detection methods have a better capability of identifying malicious nodes within the provenance graph. These improvements are also noticeable in Table 12, where we utilized SSL-based embeddings for the attack stage detection task. Here, recall and F1 scores have shown a significant boost, further validating the effectiveness of SSL methods in more complex classification scenarios.

The performance of the SSL model compared to the baseline approach emphasizes that APT detection tasks using provenance graphs require methods tailored to the unique characteristics of such attacks and their data types. Figure 6 shows the F1-score comparison of the Node2Vec and SSL-based approach in the attack stage detection task.

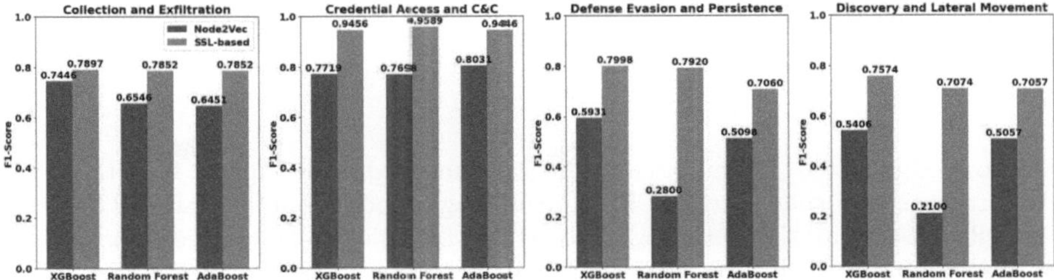

**Fig. 6.** Attack stage detection comparison

**Table 12.** Models performance metrics for SSL-based attack stage detection

| Attack Stage | Model | Accuracy | Recall | Precision | F1-Score |
|---|---|---|---|---|---|
| Collection and Exfiltration | XGBoost | 0.9992 | 0.7294 | 0.8881 | 0.7897 |
| | Random Forest | 0.9991 | 0.7292 | 0.8784 | 0.7852 |
| | AdaBoost | 0.9991 | 0.7292 | 0.8784 | 0.7852 |
| Credential Access and C&C | XGBoost | 0.9999 | 0.9262 | 0.9732 | 0.9456 |
| | Random Forest | 0.9999 | 0.9262 | 1.0000 | 0.9589 |
| | AdaBoost | 0.9998 | 0.9262 | 0.9708 | 0.9446 |
| Defense Evasion and Persistence | XGBoost | 0.9996 | 0.7300 | 0.9300 | 0.7998 |
| | Random Forest | 0.9996 | 0.7100 | 0.9417 | 0.7920 |
| | AdaBoost | 0.9993 | 0.6850 | 0.7693 | 0.7060 |
| Discovery and Lateral Movement | XGBoost | 0.9997 | 0.6833 | 0.9417 | 0.7574 |
| | Random Forest | 0.9997 | 0.6500 | 0.8417 | 0.7074 |
| | AdaBoost | 0.9996 | 0.6833 | 0.7750 | 0.7057 |

# 7   Conclusion

Given the escalating threat of APT attacks on IIoT systems, developing effective
detection solutions is crucial. Datasets are central to these efforts as they enable
the development of defenses against such sophisticated threats. In this paper, we
present CICAPT-IIoT, a dataset designed for IIoT environments, aimed at helping researchers in security analysis and the design of detection techniques against
APTs. The dataset contains over 20 well-known attack techniques, forming 8 different tactics commonly utilized in APT campaigns. The collected data in provenance and network log formats are available in the CIC website[2]. Furthermore,
we provide a thorough analysis of the dataset using well-known machine learning models to aid the researchers in developing more effective methods. Finally,
we use the CICAPT-IIoT dataset to propose a self-supervised learning-based
method for the APT detection task.

Several areas remain open for exploration in our future work. First, our
dataset can be utilized to develop and refine real-time detection algorithms capa-

---

[2] CIC website: https://www.unb.ca/cic/datasets/iiot-dataset-2024.html.

ble of identifying threats as they unfold. Additionally, incorporating more diverse IIoT devices and attack scenarios would further improve the generalizability of detection models.

**Acknowledgments.** The authors graciously acknowledge the support from the Canadian Institute for Cybersecurity (CIC), the funding support from the National Research Council of Canada (NRC) through the AI for Logistics collaborative program, the NSERC Discovery Grant (no. RGPIN 231074), and Tier 1 Canada Research Chair to Dr. Ghorbani.

**Disclosure of Interests.** The authors declare no conflict of interest.

# References


1. Al-Hawawreh, M., Sitnikova, E.: Developing a security testbed for industrial internet of things. IEEE Internet Things J. **8**(7), 5558–5573 (2020)
2. Al-Hawawreh, M., Sitnikova, E., Aboutorab, N.: X-iiotid: a connectivity-agnostic and device-agnostic intrusion data set for industrial internet of things. IEEE Internet Things J. **9**(5), 3962–3977 (2021)
3. Alsaedi, A., Moustafa, N., Tari, Z., Mahmood, A., Anwar, A.: Ton_iot telemetry dataset: a new generation dataset of iot and iiot for data-driven intrusion detection systems. IEEE Access **8**, 165130–165150 (2020)
4. Alshamrani, A., Myneni, S., Chowdhary, A., Huang, D.: A survey on advanced persistent threats: techniques, solutions, challenges, and research opportunities. IEEE Commun. Surv. Tutor. **21**(2), 1851–1877 (2019)
5. Aman, M.N., Basheer, M.H., Sikdar, B.: Data provenance for IoT with light weight authentication and privacy preservation. IEEE Internet Things J. **6**(6), 10441–10457 (2019)
6. Aman, M.N., Chua, K.C., Sikdar, B.: Secure data provenance for the internet of things. In: Proceedings of the 3rd ACM International Workshop on IoT Privacy, Trust, and Security, pp. 11–14 (2017)
7. Anjum, M.M., Iqbal, S., Hamelin, B.: Anubis: a provenance graph-based framework for advanced persistent threat detection. In: Proceedings of the 37th ACM/SIGAPP Symposium on Applied Computing, pp. 1684–1693 (2022)
8. Barre, M., Gehani, A., Yegneswaran, V.: Mining data provenance to detect advanced persistent threats. In: 11th International Workshop on Theory and Practice of Provenance (TaPP 2019) (2019)
9. Bates, A., Tian, D.J., Butler, K.R., Moyer, T.: Trustworthy {Whole-System} provenance for the linux kernel. In: 24th USENIX Security Symposium (USENIX Security 15), pp. 319–334 (2015)
10. Berrada, G., Cheney, J.: Aggregating unsupervised provenance anomaly detectors. In: 11th International Workshop on Theory and Practice of Provenance (TaPP 2019) (2019)
11. Breitenbacher, D., Homoliak, I., Aung, Y.L., Tippenhauer, N.O., Elovici, Y.: Hades-iot: a practical host-based anomaly detection system for iot devices. In: Proceedings of the 2019 ACM Asia conference on computer and communications security. pp. 479–484 (2019)
12. Chen, Z., et al.: Machine learning-enabled iot security: open issues and challenges under advanced persistent threats. ACM Comput. Surv. **55**(5), 1–37 (2022)

13. Corporation, M.: Apt29 (2023). https://attack.mitre.org/groups/G0016/. Accessed Oct 2023
14. Da Xu, L., He, W., Li, S.: Internet of things in industries: a survey. IEEE Trans. Ind. Inf. **10**(4), 2233–2243 (2014)
15. Di Pinto, A., Dragoni, Y., Carcano, A.: Triton: the first ics cyber attack on safety instrument systems. Proc. Black Hat USA **2018**, 1–26 (2018)
16. Ferrag, M.A., Friha, O., Hamouda, D., Maglaras, L., Janicke, H.: Edge-iiotset: a new comprehensive realistic cyber security dataset of iot and iiot applications for centralized and federated learning. IEEE Access **10**, 40281–40306 (2022)
17. Five Directions: Operationally transparent cyber (optc) dataset. https://github.com/FiveDirections/OpTC-data. Accessed 22 Feb 2024
18. Garcia-Teodoro, P., Diaz-Verdejo, J., Maciá-Fernández, G., Vázquez, E.: Anomaly-based network intrusion detection: techniques, systems and challenges. Comput. Secur. **28**(1-2), 18–28 (2009)
19. Gehani, A., Tariq, D.: SPADE: support for provenance auditing in distributed environments. In: Narasimhan, P., Triantafillou, P. (eds.) Middleware 2012. LNCS, vol. 7662, pp. 101–120. Springer, Heidelberg (2012). https://doi.org/10.1007/978-3-642-35170-9_6
20. Grover, A., Leskovec, J.: node2vec: scalable feature learning for networks. In: Proceedings of the 22nd ACM SIGKDD International Conference on Knowledge Discovery and Data Mining, pp. 855–864 (2016)
21. Hamilton, W., Ying, Z., Leskovec, J.: Inductive representation learning on large graphs. Adv. Neural Inf. Process. Syst. **30** (2017)
22. Han, X., Pasquier, T., Bates, A., Mickens, J., Seltzer, M.: Unicorn: run-time provenance-based detector for advanced persistent threats. arXiv preprint arXiv:2001.01525 (2020)
23. Hassan, W.U., Bates, A., Marino, D.: Tactical provenance analysis for endpoint detection and response systems. In: 2020 IEEE Symposium on Security and Privacy (SP), pp. 1172–1189. IEEE (2020)
24. Herschel, M., Diestelkämper, R., Ben Lahmar, H.: A survey on provenance: what for? what form? what from? VLDB J. **26**, 881–906 (2017)
25. Hossain, M.N., et al.: {SLEUTH}: real-time attack scenario reconstruction from {COTS} audit data. In: 26th USENIX Security Symposium (USENIX Security 17), pp. 487–504 (2017)
26. Hu, R., Yan, Z., Ding, W., Yang, L.T.: A survey on data provenance in iot. World Wide Web **23**, 1441–1463 (2020)
27. Jaloudi, S.: Communication protocols of an industrial internet of things environment: a comparative study. Future Internet **11**(3), 66 (2019)
28. Herschel, M., Diestelkamper, R., Ben Lahmar, H.: A survey on provenance: what for? What form? What from? VLDB J. **26**(6), 881–906 (2017)
29. Langner, R.: Stuxnet: dissecting a cyberwarfare weapon. IEEE Secur. Priv. **9**(3), 49–51 (2011)
30. Malik, P.K., et al.: Industrial internet of things and its applications in industry 4.0: state of the art. Comput. Commun. **166**, 125–139 (2021)
31. Michael, Z., Florian, G., Elizabeth, C., Tharam, D.: Provenance-based intrusion detection systems: a survey. ACM Comput. Surv. **55**, 36 (2022)
32. Milajerdi, S.M., Gjomemo, R., Eshete, B., Sekar, R., Venkatakrishnan, V.: Holmes: real-time apt detection through correlation of suspicious information flows. In: 2019 IEEE Symposium on Security and Privacy (SP), pp. 1137–1152. IEEE (2019)
33. MITRE: Group g0016 - APT29. https://attack.mitre.org/groups/G0016/. Accessed Apr 2024

34. Myneni, S., et al.: DAPT 2020 - constructing a benchmark dataset for advanced persistent threats. In: Wang, G., Ciptadi, A., Ahmadzadeh, A. (eds.) MLHat 2020. CCIS, vol. 1271, pp. 138–163. Springer, Cham (2020). https://doi.org/10.1007/978-3-030-59621-7_8

35. Myneni, S., Jha, K., Sabur, A., Agrawal, G., Deng, Y., Chowdhary, A., Huang, D.: Unraveled–a semi-synthetic dataset for advanced persistent threats. Comput. Netw. **227**, 109688 (2023)

36. Neto, E.C.P., Dadkhah, S., Ferreira, R., Zohourian, A., Lu, R., Ghorbani, A.A.: Ciciot 2023: a real-time dataset and benchmark for large-scale attacks in iot environment. Sensors **23**(13), 5941 (2023)

37. NS-3: Ns-3 consortium. https://www.nsnam.org/. Accessed 11 Mar 2024

38. Nwafor, E., Campbell, A., Hill, D., Bloom, G.: Towards a provenance collection framework for internet of things devices. In: 2017 IEEE SmartWorld, Ubiquitous Intelligence & Computing, Advanced & Trusted Computed, Scalable Computing & Communications, Cloud & Big Data Computing, Internet of People and Smart City Innovation (SmartWorld/SCALCOM/UIC/ATC/CBDCom/IOP/SCI), pp. 1–6. IEEE (2017)

39. Pan, B., Stakhanova, N., Ray, S.: Data provenance in security and privacy. ACM Comput. Surv. (2023)

40. Pasquier, T., et al.: Practical whole-system provenance capture. In: Proceedings of the 2017 Symposium on Cloud Computing, pp. 405–418 (2017)

41. Ren, Y., Liu, B., Huang, C., Dai, P., Bo, L., Zhang, J.: Heterogeneous deep graph infomax. arXiv preprint arXiv:1911.08538 (2019)

42. Sadineni, L., Pilli, E.S., Battula, R.B.: Provnet-iot: provenance based network layer forensics in internet of things. Forensic Sci. Int. Digit. Investigat. **43**, 301441 (2022)

43. Sisinni, E., Saifullah, A., Han, S., Jennehag, U., Gidlund, M.: Industrial internet of things: challenges, opportunities, and directions. IEEE Trans. Ind. Inf. **14**(11), 4724–4734 (2018)

44. Stojanović, B., Hofer-Schmitz, K., Kleb, U.: Apt datasets and attack modeling for automated detection methods: A review. Comput. Secur. **92**, 101734 (2020)

45. Whitehead, D.E., Owens, K., Gammel, D., Smith, J.: Ukraine cyber-induced power outage: analysis and practical mitigation strategies. In: 2017 70th Annual Conference for Protective Relay Engineers (CPRE), pp. 1–8. IEEE (2017)

46. Wurm, J., Hoang, K., Arias, O., Sadeghi, A.R., Jin, Y.: Security analysis on consumer and industrial iot devices. In: 2016 21st Asia and South Pacific Design Automation Conference (ASP-DAC), pp. 519–524. IEEE (2016)

47. Xu, K., Tian, K., Yao, D., Ryder, B.G.: A sharper sense of self: probabilistic reasoning of program behaviors for anomaly detection with context sensitivity. In: 2016 46th Annual IEEE/IFIP International Conference on Dependable Systems and Networks (DSN), pp. 467–478. IEEE (2016)

48. Yang, Z., et al.: A systematic literature review of methods and datasets for anomaly-based network intrusion detection. Comput. Secur. **116**, 102675 (2022)

49. Zipperle, M., Gottwalt, F., Chang, E., Dillon, T.: Provenance-based intrusion detection systems: a survey. ACM Comput. Surv. **55**(7), 1–36 (2022)

# Verifying Multi-vendor IoT Deployments Using Conditional Tables

Mubashir Anwar[1]($\boxtimes$)(iD), Matthew Caesar[1](iD), and Anduo Wang[2](iD)

[1] University of Illinois Urbana-Champaign, Urbana, IL 61801, USA
{manwar,caesar}@illinois.edu
[2] Temple University, Philadelphia, PA 19122, USA

**Abstract.** In recent years, IoT devices have seen widespread deployments in critical environments such as healthcare, military, and home security systems. These deployments often involve managing a heterogeneous collection of devices by non-expert users, increasing the risk of errors that could lead to significant monetary and physical damage. Unfortunately, such deployments face unique challenges such as incomplete visibility (e.g., need to interoperate with closed software systems), incompatibility (e.g., need to interact across different protocols and control logic created by different vendors), and management complexity (e.g., need to express complex and diverse intentions in ways that can be understood by inexperienced users). While system verification has been crucial in catching errors early in other domains, these challenges complicate its application in IoT. To perform verification under these conditions, we propose Pyotr, a system based on a mathematical framework from the theory of database systems called *incomplete databases*. Pyotr can integrate data from heterogeneous devices, perform data analysis under failures and uncertain knowledge, verify intended behavior using easy-to-use database-styled queries, and provide a generalized algebraic framework for reasoning about IoT systems in a rigorous and intuitive way. Our experiments on large IoT networks show that Pyotr can scalably answer complex queries on thousands of connected IoT devices within a few milliseconds.

**Keywords:** Formal verification · IoT · Conditional Tables

## 1 Introduction

In recent years, Internet of things (IoT) has experienced a tremendous surge in growth. Today, there are over 15 billion IoT devices in the world, and this figure is expected to double by 2030 [38]. These devices find applications in vital sectors such as healthcare, military, and residential security. These domains involve extremely critical operations such as collection of sensitive data and automation of actuators capable of impacting the physical environment in dangerous ways. Failures and bugs in devices in these domains can have devastating consequences. For instance, a fault in a node in an IoT deployment for healthcare



A. Soylu et al. (Eds.): MobiQuitous 2024, LNICST 634, pp. 145–168, 2026.
https://doi.org/10.1007/978-3-032-10554-7_8

could lead to the leakage of critical patient information to unintended nodes or prevent it from reaching its intended destination (e.g., a doctor), posing risks to privacy and potentially endangering patients' lives. Similarly, incorrect control logic implemented by a home owner for security could result in issues like doors getting unlocked at unintended times or cameras failing to capture events when they should, rendering the house susceptible to intruders. As IoT devices become more integrated into critical domains, their capacity to inflict severe harm in both the digital and physical realms grows.

The awareness of the risks of automation in these critical systems is not new. When computers were first introduced in these domains, the dangers of errors in software were acknowledged. New debugging and verification techniques were introduced to make software more reliable. With the increasing influence of IoT and its capacity to introduce substantial risks, ensuring the safety and reliability of IoT systems has become a crucial imperative. However, IoT systems present unique challenges since they involve system and protocol heterogeneity, inexperienced users, and a lack of complete visibility into the devices:

**System and Protocol Heterogeneity:** IoT devices exhibit significant heterogeneity, making it hard to have a single framework that encompasses all formats. Many deployments involve devices from various vendors, each utilizing its own control language, protocols, management interface, and have differences in the granularity, units, and representation of collected data. Moreover, with high rate of innovation in IoT, the heterogeneity continue to grow, increasing the complexity of deployments. This not only makes it difficult to control IoT devices to work together, but also makes it difficult to manage them and ensure their safety. In a multi-vendor IoT deployment, understanding and reasoning about the collective behavior of devices is difficult, making it hard to guarantee that the devices function as intended.

**Inexperienced Users:** IoT devices are typically configured and administered by non-technical end users. They are used in places like enterprises, home environments, and in field applications such as agriculture where operators may have limited technical expertise. In these settings, users often lack the skills to program and manage the devices correctly, which can lead to errors in device programming and management. The absence of standardization aggravates this issue, as even if a user-friendly interface exists in one device, it may differ or be nonexistent in others. This lack of consistency complicates the user experience, adding another layer of difficulty when interacting with IoT systems. As IoT devices increasingly permeate various domains, they are being utilized by more and more individuals without formal training, making it challenging to guarantee proper configuration and effective troubleshooting. This raises serious concerns regarding safety and security of IoT deployments.

**Lack of Complete Visibility:** IoT deployments often include energy-constrained wireless devices vulnerable to failures and faults. They suffer complex failure modes such as Byzantine faults, communication faults, and timing failures. Moreover, the internal code of these devices is often hidden, making it harder to debug them. Under such challenging conditions, pinpointing the root cause of issues and fixing them is difficult. Unfortunately, we also lack comprehensive information about the faults, which makes it difficult to understand the situation. For instance, some devices in an IoT network may remain operational but are rendered inaccessible due to a variety of reasons (e.g., wireless interference, resource constraints, conserving battery by avoiding information transmission). Assuming the devices have failed would be premature, as they might still be functioning in accordance with our intentions. However, they might be malfunctioning or intentionally attempting to disrupt the system, potentially as a result of malicious user activity. Thus, troubleshooting the problem or ensuring that the system behaves as expected becomes challenging when we lack awareness of a portion of it. Given the critical nature of many IoT domains and the unreliability of methods to access all relevant information, it becomes crucial to model deployments even when certain details are inaccessible. The lack of complete visibility in IoT deployments, compounded by the presence of energy-constrained devices susceptible to various complex failure modes, poses a significant challenge to data accessibility, which is vital for ensuring the safety and reliability of IoT systems.

To tackle the challenges in heterogeneous IoT deployments, we introduce Pyotr, a user-friendly system for reasoning and verification of IoT deployments. Pyotr is based on the theory of *incomplete databases* [22] and uses database-styled semantics to represent the behavior of IoT devices, which allows users to verify policies and ask "what-if" questions using intuitive queries. Database theory has long grappled with the issue of data inconsistencies and offers multiple user-friendly interfaces for inexperienced users. Furthermore, *incomplete databases* [22] have the capability to reason over missing information and integrate data from heterogeneous sources. These inherent qualities position them as excellent candidates to serve as a foundational basis for a reasoning system for IoT devices. At its core, Pyotr uses conditional tables [22] to represent data (e.g., collected from sensors) and rules (e.g., event condition-action (ECA) rules, forwarding rules). These tables effectively store incomplete information through conditions alongside regular data, making them well-suited for representing data and rules in IoT devices. Conditional tables can be queried using traditional relational algebra, allowing users to formulate questions and policies as database queries. A variety of user-friendly visual methods [25,33,37] have been proposed to query over databases, which makes Pyotr easy to use for non-expert users. Moreover, conditional tables can represent missing information and can be used for data integration in heterogeneous environments. Thus, they provide a generalized relational framework for reasoning about various properties of IoT devices, which can simplify development, analysis, and synthesis of other advanced functions for IoT systems. Pyotr is designed to efficiently store, manipulate, and reason over conditional tables. It extends concepts developed in [27] to the domain of IoT. To handle conditional tables, we have developed a query engine, a compiler to parse IoT rules and data, integrated different reasoning engines (e.g., Binary Decision Diagrams (BDD), Satisfiability Modulo Theories (SMT), Difference of Cube (DoC) [30]), and implemented query optimizations such as semi-naive evaluation. We have also modeled diverse use cases for verification in IoT deployments using conditional tables and conducted experiments on three scenarios. The results indicate that Pyotr can verify IoT deployments with minimal overheads. Pyotr also retains desirable scalability properties even in scenarios where portions of devices are inaccessible. Additionally, our evaluation emphasizes the significant impact of the chosen reasoning engine on the performance of conditional tables, illustrated through a comparison of three implemented engines.

The rest of the paper is structured as follows: Sect. 2 presents motivating examples of errors in IoT deployments, outlining their distinct challenges. In Sect. 3, a theoretical exploration of conditional tables is provided, accompanied by examples illustrating their application in modeling and verifying IoT deployments. Section 4 describes the architecture and implementation of Pyotr, including the optimizations that we made. Section 5 presents an evaluation of the performance and scalability of Pyotr for different IoT verification tasks. We discuss related work in Sect. 6 and conclude in Sect. 7.

## 2   Motivating Examples

In this section, we use examples to illustrate the necessity of verification in IoT devices, highlighting the distinctive challenges associated with it. Our examples are drawn from a Fire Suppression System in a factory and IoT networks in health monitoring. The next section shows how conditional tables can model and solve these problems.

### 2.1   Example 1: Configuration Errors

Consider a Fire Suppression System installed in a factory, comprising a smoke sensor equipped with a connected light, linked to both an alarm and water sprinklers. The user configures the smoke sensor using event-condition-action (ECA) rules, as shown in the first half of Fig. 1. The user intends for the light to activate only during nighttime when smoke is detected, aiming to preserve battery life by preventing light activation during daylight hours. An alarm is designed to alert users upon the detection of any type of smoke, while water sprinklers automatically engage when smoke levels are elevated (e.g., at *high* level). However, there is a flaw in the control logic. The user desires the alarm to activate whenever noticeable smoke is detected, irrespective of the time of day. Although rules 3–5 seem to address this, rule 3 is limited to nighttime. This limitation could result in delayed fire response during daylight hours, posing a significant risk to factory employees. Even in this simple example, the bug is not easy to spot manually. Ideally, we want the user to ask a simple query such as "Does the alarm always sound whenever there is any noticeable smoke?".

### 2.2   Example 2: Configuration Errors Across Heterogeneous Devices

Now, let's extend the previous scenario by incorporating an additional smoke sensor from a different vendor into the example. With two sensors now in play, both

```
/* Rules for the first device */
IF smoke=low THEN light=off, alarm=off, sprinkler=off
IF time<20:00 THEN light=off
IF smoke=mid,time>20:00 THEN light=on, alarm=on, sprinkler=off
IF smoke=high,time>20:00 THEN light=on, alarm=on, sprinkler=on
IF smoke=high,time<20:00 THEN light=off, alarm=on, sprinkler=on

/* Rules for the second device */
IF smoke=low THEN lights=off, alarm=off, sprinkler=off
IF time<20:00 THEN light=off
IF smoke=high,time>20:00 THEN light=on, alarm=on, sprinkler=on
IF smoke=high,time<20:00 THEN light=off, alarm=on, sprinkler=on
```

**Fig. 1.** Control rules for a Fire Suppression System

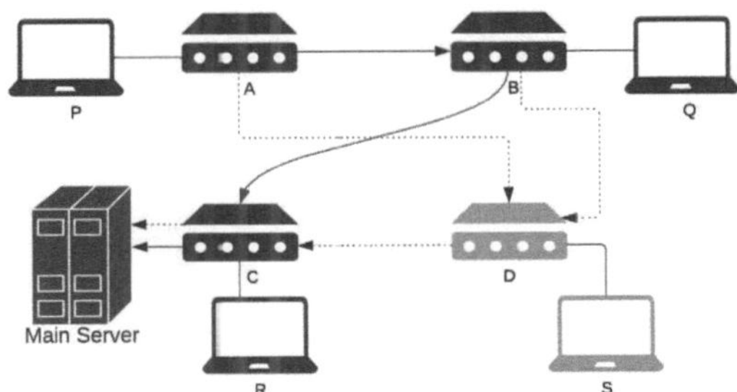


**Fig. 2.** Healthcare IoT network to monitor patients in critical conditions

contribute to the control of the alarm and sprinkler system. The second smoke sensor is less accurate, and can only discern the presence or absence of smoke without distinguishing between *mid* and *high* smoke levels. Figure 1 shows the rules for the second device. To verify the collective behavior of the two devices, establishing a standardized and accurate method for queries becomes important. However, addressing the inconsistency in the accuracy of the devices poses a challenge. For instance, how do we handle queries concerning *mid* levels of smoke when the second device lacks a conception of such a level? One straightforward solution involves encoding into our model that *high* levels of smoke for the second device should encompass both *mid* and *high* levels. However, implementing this requires a method that seamlessly incorporates such information when integrating inconsistent data from multiple devices.

### 2.3   Example 3: Analysis Involving Inaccessible Nodes

While the previous two examples show the potential for bugs in control logic of individual IoT devices, there are further issues that emerge in IoT deployments. Consider a healthcare system that monitors the vitals of all patients in critical conditions, as shown in Fig. 2. Information about the patients is regularly collected by monitoring devices (devices A, B, and C) and then sent to the main server in the hospital, which uses the data to decide if a patient needs attention. The monitoring devices are connected to each other via a reliable wireless connection, forming a mesh network. Relevant doctors are alarmed automatically via the main server if a patient needs urgent attention. Information about the patient is also accessible from a computer inside the room where the patient resides. For privacy, these computers (laptops P, Q, and R) only have access to the local patient's data, and do not have access to the data of other patients. Since this is sensitive data, it should only be allowed to traverse designated nodes. Moreover, since the data is critical to patient's health, the network should be resilient to failures. Thus, the state of the network is regularly verified by a centralized verifier (not shown in the figure) by collecting the data plane state of the network. Consider a scenario where a new bed is added to the hospital. Alongside it, a new monitoring device, D, and a computer, S, are added to the same room. With the new devices added, changes are made to the network. The old path to reach the main server is shown as solid arrows in Fig. 2, while the new path is shown with dotted arrows. The verifier now runs on the new state to make sure that sensitive data never reaches unintended locations and there are no loops or blackholes in the network. However, due to poor wireless signal, the verifier is unable to get the dataplane state of device A. How can the verifier then check for network invariants? If we assume the node has failed, we can proceed to verify the remainder of the network. However, what if the node has not failed but is merely inaccessible to us? This situation could result in sensitive traffic being forwarded to unintended nodes or even cause certain paths to become unreachable from the central server. In the worst-case scenario, we have to assume that the node may forward traffic to any of its connected nodes. Considering the frequent inaccessibility of IoT devices due to issues such as wireless connectivity problems, resource constraints, and battery-saving mechanisms, we need a reasoning method that remains effective even when there is missing information.

## 3    Pyotr: Modeling with Conditional Tables

In this section, we introduce conditional tables [22] and illustrate how they can be employed to model various problems in IoT deployments. We use examples from the preceding section to demonstrate their application.

### 3.1    Conditional Tables

Conditional tables [3, 22] (c-tables for short) provide a strong representation system for incomplete information in relational databases. They support standard operations in relational algebra including projection, selection, union, join, and renaming. They were proposed to process data when some of it is missing, imprecise, or has inconsistencies. C-tables generalize relations by allowing values in relations to be unknown. Each unknown value is represented by a variable, which we call a conditional variable (c-variable for short). Valuation of c-variables (i.e., assigning each c-variable to a concrete constant) in a c-table results in a single instance of a relation. Thus, each c-table represents a set of possible instances that the relation can take. In addition to c-variables, each tuple $t$ in the relation is associated with a *local condition*[1] $\phi(t)$, which is a mathematical formula that defines the set of possible values that the c-variable in that tuple can take. For a given valuation $v$ of c-variables, a tuple appears in the result only if $v(\phi(t))$ is satisfiable.

## 3.2  Querying over Conditional Tables

Since c-tables support standard operations in relational algebra, they can be queried using most relational database query languages. Numerous efforts in the past have focused on enhancing the user-friendliness of database queries. Visual Querying Systems [25,33,37], for instance, have been suggested to enable the construction of queries through visual interfaces, proving to be effective tools for querying and analyzing databases [7]. Techniques such as employing natural language to form database queries [28,39,41], query completion [18], and automatic query recommendation [12] have also been proposed to allow non-technical users to easily use databases. These approaches could potentially be employed to establish a user-friendly interface for conditional tables. As a preliminary step, Pyotr uses Datalog, a rule-based conjunctive query language, as the reasoning language for Pyotr. Datalog has found use in many applications such as declarative networking [2,29], program analysis [20,26,35], network verification [15,30], and big data analysis [34,40]. Its adoption is attributed to its clear and simple syntax, offering a declarative abstraction for querying relational structures. Below, we provide a formal description [3,27] of using a rule-based conjunctive query over incomplete databases:

**Definition 1.** *Let $R$ be a database schema. A rule-based conjunctive query over $R$ is an expression of the form*

$$H(u) :\text{-}\quad B_1(u_1), ..., B_n(u_n) \tag{1}$$

where $n >= 0$, $B_i$'s are relation (predicate) names in **R**, and H is a relation not in **R**; and u and $u_i$'s are free tuples that can either use constants in the attribute domain of **R** (denoted by **dom**) or variables. Let $\mathbf{dom}^C$ be the domain of c-variables, which contains both the constants and the c-variables in the attribute domain of **R**. We use var(q) to denote all variables that appear in the query q. The subexpression $B_1(u_1), ..., B_n(u_n)$ is the body of the rule, and $H(u)$ is the head. A rule generates new facts by valuation of variables—a function (denoted by v) from var(q) to $\mathbf{dom}^C$, whereby constants map to themselves or other c-variables. If one can find values that hold for the body, then one can derive the head. For conjunctive queries, the head is generated by performing a table join of all the tables in the body. Variable valuation finds assignments for the variables in a rule, whereby variables can map to both constants and c-variables. The meaning of a query over c-tables can be defined by *partial* variable valuations. Let q be a conjunctive query given by the foregoing rules, and let **I** be a database instance (i.e., c-table) of **R**, the query result of **I** under q is:

---

[1] C-tables also include global conditions $\Phi_T$ over c-variables, which are just local conditions applied to every tuple in the relation T.

**Table 1.** C-tables representing the control logic of sensors in fire suppression system

**(a) Smoke Sensor 1**

| Time | Smoke | Light | Alarm | Sprink | Condition |
|---|---|---|---|---|---|
| $\hat{t}$ | $\hat{s}$ | 0 | 0 | 0 | $\hat{s} =$ LOW |
| $\hat{t}$ | $\hat{s}$ | 1 | 1 | 0 | $\hat{s} =$ MID$\&\hat{t} > 20:00$ |
| $\hat{t}$ | $\hat{s}$ | 1 | 1 | 1 | $\hat{s} =$ HIGH$\&\hat{t} > 20:00$ |
| $\hat{t}$ | $\hat{s}$ | 0 | 1 | 1 | $\hat{s} =$ HIGH$\&\hat{t} <= 20:00$ |
| $\hat{t}$ | $\hat{s}$ | 0 | 0 | 0 | DEFAULT |

**(b) Smoke Sensor 2**

| Time | Smoke | Light | Alarm | Sprink | Condition |
|---|---|---|---|---|---|
| $\hat{t}$ | $\hat{s}$ | 0 | 0 | 0 | $\hat{s} =$ LOW |
| $\hat{t}$ | $\hat{s}$ | 1 | 1 | 1 | $\hat{s} =$ HIGH$\&\hat{t} > 20:00$ |
| $\hat{t}$ | $\hat{s}$ | 0 | 1 | 1 | $\hat{s} =$ HIGH$\&\hat{t} <= 20:00$ |
| $\hat{t}$ | $\hat{s}$ | 0 | 0 | 0 | DEFAULT |

**(c) Alarm**

| Alarm | Sound Condition |
|---|---|
| 0 | 0 |
| 1 | 1 |

**(d) Sprinkler**

| Sprink | Water Condition |
|---|---|
| 0 | 0 |
| 1 | 1 |

$$q(\mathbf{I}) = \{v(u)|v \text{ is a } partial \text{ valuation and} $$
$$v(u_i) \in \mathbf{I} \text{ for each } i \in [1, n]\}. \tag{2}$$

The *partial* valuation function for c-tables is governed by the following rules:

1. Variables are assigned to constants or c-variables.
2. A constant c is assigned to either itself, or to a c-variable $\hat{x}$ if the constrain $\hat{x} =$ c does not contradict $\hat{x}$'s *local condition*.

The result of a *partial* valuation is another c-table in which the relevant *local conditions* incorporate the restrictions imposed by the *partial* valuation function. Specifically, in the context of a table join, the *local condition* for each tuple in the resulting table is a conjunction of the joining conditions and the *local conditions* of all the corresponding joined tuples.

### 3.3   Models

In this section, we show how problems listed in Sect. 2 can be modeled and solved using conditional tables.

**Example 1: Configuration Errors.** Pyotr expresses rules of IoT devices as conditional tables. Most IoT devices use event condition-action (ECA) rules to configure the control logic. These rules consist of trigger-action pairs, often composed as If-This-Then-That (IFTTT) [21,36] styled rules. Pyotr translates these rules into conditional tables. The triggers and actions become columns in a conditional table, and *local conditions* are used to represent sets of values for each trigger-action pair. Table 1a and 1b show the translation of the program for the smoke sensors in Fig. 1 as c-tables. The first two columns, *Time* and *Smoke* represent the triggers of the device. These triggers are specified after "IF" in IFTTT-styled rules. The next three columns, *Light, Alarm,* and *Sprink(le)* represent the actions of the device. A value of 0 indicates *off*, while a value of 1 indicates *on*. The condition column captures the *local conditions* of rules for both the triggers and the actions. The *DEFAULT* condition in the last row represents the negation of all previous conditions. This can be thought of as an

**Table 2.** C-tables after integrating the two smoke sensors in the fire suppression system

| Time | Smoke | Light | Alarm | Sprink | Condition |
|---|---|---|---|---|---|
| $t$ | $s$ | 0 | 0 | 0 | $s =$ LOW |
| $t$ | $s$ | 1 | 1 | 0 | $s =$ MID$\&t > 20 : 00$ |
| $t$ | $s$ | 1 | 1 | 1 | $s =$ HIGH$\&t > 20 : 00$ |
| $t$ | $s$ | 0 | 1 | 1 | $s =$ HIGH$\&t <= 20 : 00$ |
| $t$ | $s$ | 0 | 0 | 0 | $s =$ LOW |
| $t$ | $s$ | 1 | 1 | 1 | $s =$ HIGH$\&t > 20 : 00$ |
| $t$ | $s$ | 0 | 1 | 1 | $s =$ HIGH$\&t <= 20 : 00$ |
| $t$ | $s$ | 0 | 0 | 0 | DEFAULT |

(a) Incorrect Data Integration

| Time | Smoke | Light | Alarm | Sprink | Condition |
|---|---|---|---|---|---|
| $t$ | $s$ | 0 | 0 | 0 | $s =$ LOW |
| $t$ | $s$ | 1 | 1 | 1 | $s =$ HIGH$\&t > 20 : 00$ |
| $t$ | $s$ | 0 | 1 | 1 | $s =$ HIGH$\&t <= 20 : 00$ |
| $t$ | $s$ | 1 | 1 | 1 | $(s =$ HIGH $\vee$ $s =$ MID$)$ $\&t > 20 : 00$ |
| $t$ | $s$ | 0 | 1 | 1 | $(s =$ HIGH $\vee$ $s =$ MID$)$ $\&t <= 20 : 00$ |
| $t$ | $s$ | 0 | 0 | 0 | DEFAULT |

(b) Correct Data Integration

"else" part, which applies when none of the other triggers apply. In this example, the light is linked to the smoke sensor and is directly governed by it. In contrast, the water sprinklers and alarm function as distinct devices with their individual control logic, stored as c-tables. Table 1c shows the logic of the alarm system: the trigger "alarm" from the smoke sensors control the speakers. The c-table for the sprinkler (Table 1d) is similar.

```
V(t,s,l,a,sp)  :- Smoke(t,s,l,a,sp)[s >= mid], Alarm(a,0)
```

**Listing 1.** Datalog query to verify that alarm always sounds when the smoke levels are at or above *mid*

To verify intentions over this system, the database can be queried. For example, the query "Does the alarm always sound whenever there is any noticeable smoke?" can be translated into the query as shown in Listing 1. The head of this query, $V$ represents a violation of this intention. The query asks whether we can find tuples such that even when the value of the column smoke in the table *Smoke* is higher than *mid* (e.g. either *mid* or *high*) the alarm does not produce a sound (has value $= 0$, as shown as the last attribute of the *Alarm* relation). Additionally, we can extract the tuples that are responsible for this violation. The table violation will contain the last tuple of the smoke sensor, with the *DEFAULT* condition that (after simplification) translates to $s =$ MID$\&t <= 20 : 00$. This tells the user exactly when (for what triggers) the sensor behaves unexpectedly: when the smoke is at level *mid* during day time. In this way, conditional tables allow users to verify expected device behaviors through simple SQL queries, making it straightforward to identify rule violations and unexpected responses in the system.

**Example 2: Configuration Errors Across Heterogeneous Devices.** In this example, remember that there are two smoke sensors with differences in the granularity of smoke levels. This is an example of inconsistency in data. C-tables were originally proposed to deal with interoperability in heterogeneous data sources with inconsistencies by performing data integration. To analyze the behavior of the system with the two sensing devices, a naive method would be to represent the combined behavior as a single conditional table, as shown in Table 2a. However, this is incorrect, as it does not capture the incompatibilities in the accuracy of the two devices. Running the verification query from Listing 1

**Table 3.** C-tables for reachability analysis.

| Node | Destination | Source | Output | condition |
|---|---|---|---|---|
| A | main | $\hat{i_A}$ | $\hat{o_A}$ | $\hat{o_A} \in [B, D, P]$ |
| B | main | A | D | |
| B | main | B | $\hat{o_B}$ | $\hat{o_B} \in [Q, D]$ |
| D | main | $\hat{i_D}$ | C | $\hat{i_D} \in [A, B]$ |
| D | main | D | $\hat{o_D}$ | $\hat{o_D} \in [C, S]$ |
| C | main | $\hat{i_C}$ | main | $\hat{i_C} \in [A, B, D]$ |
| C | main | C | $\hat{o_C}$ | $\hat{o_C} \in [main, R]$ |

(a) Forwarding rules $F$

| Node | Destination | Source | Path | condition |
|---|---|---|---|---|
| A | main | $\hat{i_A}$ | $[\hat{o_A}]$ | $\hat{o_A} \in [B, D, P], \hat{i_A} = A$ |
| B | main | A | $[\hat{o_A}, D]$ | $\hat{o_A} \in [B, D, P], \hat{i_A} = A, \hat{o_A} = B$ |
| D | main | $\hat{i_D}$ | $[\hat{o_A}, C]$ | $\hat{o_A} \in [B, D, P], \hat{i_A} = A, \hat{i_A} = \hat{i_D}, \hat{o_A} = D$ |
| C | main | $\hat{i_C}$ | $[\hat{o_A}, C, main]$ | $\hat{i_C} \in [A, B, D], \hat{o_A} = D, \hat{i_C} = A$ |
| D | main | $\hat{i_D}$ | $[\hat{o_A}, D, C]$ | $\hat{i_D} \in [A, B], \hat{o_A} = B, \hat{i_D} = A, \hat{i_A} = \hat{i_D}$ |
| C | main | $\hat{i_C}$ | $[\hat{o_A}, D, C, main]$ | $\hat{i_C} \in [A, B, D], \hat{o_A} = B, \hat{i_D} = A, \hat{i_C} = A$ |

(b) Partial results of $R$

on this incorrect table would lead to the same output as before: a violation of the alarm policy, which is misleading. The correct way to integrate the data is to capture the fact that a smoke value of *high* for sensor 2 represents a value of either *high* or *mid* in terms of the accuracy of sensor 1. Such incompatibilities are easily fixed using conditional tables, since they can naturally represent incomplete information. A correct integration of control rules is given in Table 2b. The rules from second device denoting $s = $ HIGH are replaced with the condition $s = $ HIGH $\lor$ $s = $ MID, correctly taking care of the incompatibility. The query in Listing 1 does not show any violation, since sensor 2 is correctly programmed and it masks the bug in sensor 1. Conditional tables thus enable accurate integration of inconsistent sensor data, allowing users to capture device-specific variations and ensuring that verification queries reflect correct system behavior.

**Example 3: Analysis Involving Inaccessible Nodes.** The final example demonstrates the ease of modeling uncertainty with conditional tables. Pyotr can reason about devices even when one or more of them are inaccessible. The forwarding table of the example from Sect. 2.3 can be encoded as a c-table as shown in Table 3a. For instance, the third tuple conveys that when *Node* B receives a packet with *Destination* main and *source* B, it sends the packet to the *Output* node D and Q. It's noteworthy that despite being unable to access the forwarding state of node A, we can still incorporate any known information. For example, we know that the only devices in the range of (connected to) A are B, D, P. This is encoded in as conditions in the first tuple of the forwarding table.

```
R(n, "main", A, [o]) :- F(n, "main", A, o)
R(n, "main", A, p || [o2]) :- R(n, "main", A, p)[o2 ∉ p], F(p[-1],
    "main", A, o2)
```

**Listing 2.** Datalog query to perform reachability analysis

A reachability analysis of the network can be done by using the query shown in Listing 2[2]. The forwarding table is stored in relation F. The datalog program calculates paths from all nodes to the destination main, and stores them in table R. Partial results (Table 3b) reveal that for packets with source A and destination main, two possible paths exist: (i) A$->$D$->$C$->$main (fourth tuple) and

---

[2] The operator $||$ is used to concatenate two lists. The attribute $p[-1]$ represents the last value of the list $p$.

(ii) `A-> B-> D-> C-> main` (sixth tuple). From this result, we can see that these packets do not reach any other private computer. With c-tables, we were able to perform this analysis even when node `A` was inaccessible, allowing early verification of the network.

# 4  Pyotr: Architecture and Implementation

In this section, we outline the architecture and implementation of Pyotr, a system developed for the storage, management, manipulation, and querying of conditional tables, specifically tailored for the verification of IoT deployments. Pyotr is engineered to efficiently handle queries over incomplete databases while maintaining the semantics of database query languages that are grounded in relational algebra.

## 4.1  Architecture and Workflow

Figure 3 shows the architecture and workflow of Pyotr. By utilizing a Database Management System (DBMS) for the storage and querying of tables, Pyotr capitalizes on the extensive advantages provided by these systems in the administration of databases, including storage on file systems, managing distributed computing, ensuring security, and performing query planning and optimization. Pyotr can profit from the efficiency and robustness of widely-used and highly optimized DBMSes that already offer support for a diverse range of systems. Pyotr interacts with the DBMS through a *Database Coordinator*, which establishes and maintains a connection to the database. The *Database Coordinator* facilitates communication with the DBMS by using SQL queries to manage and retrieve data. Given that most popular DBMS systems support SQL queries, Pyotr is designed to be agnostic to the underlying DBMS. This flexibility allows Pyotr to seamlessly integrate with various DBMSes, providing versatility and adaptability across different environments.

Figure 3 shows the workflow for both storing and querying conditional tables[3]. The blue squares mark the steps for storing rules and data obtained from IoT devices. The black circles mark the steps for querying conditional tables.

**Workflow for Storing C-Tables:** 1, The rules (e.g., ECA rules, forwarding rules) or data (e.g., collected measurements from sensors) from each IoT device is sent to the *Compiler*, which converts them into c-tables. At this stage, there is a single c-table per device. 2, The c-tables are sent to the *Synthesizer*. The *Synthesizer* uses specified integration rules to integrate the c-tables. This is where inconsistencies between the devices are resolved. Additionally, there is an optional grouping of c-tables based on the provided database schema. This

---

[3] For simplicity, we do not show the interaction between the *Database Coordinator* and the DBMS in the workflow steps.

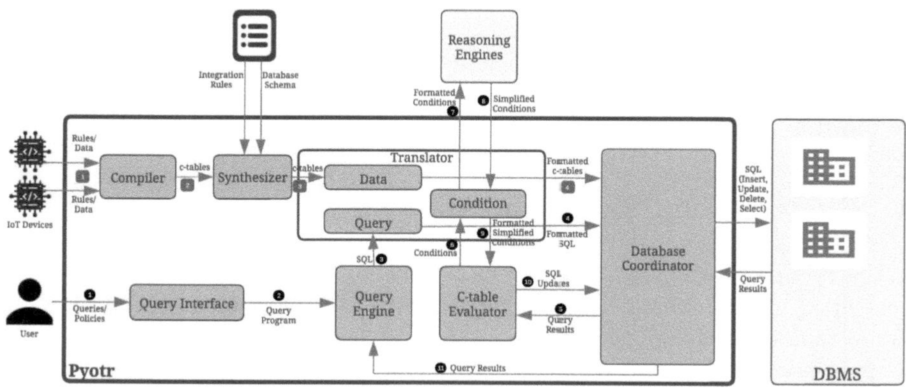



**Fig. 3.** Pyotr architecture and workflow

involves storing same attributes from different devices in a single table to simplify queries. For instance, data from two distinct temperature sensors can be grouped into a single c-table. 3, The *Synthesizer* forwards the integrated c-tables to the *Translator*. In this phase, the translator formats the tables according to the representation of c-variables in use. This step is essential because DBMS lacks the conception of c-variables. The details of various c-variable representations are explored in Sect. 4.2. 4, The *Database Coordinator* stores the formatted c-tables into the DBMS using SQL queries for data insertion.

**Workflow for Querying C-Tables:** 1, User-specified queries and policies are transmitted to the *Query Interface*, where they are processed to generate a program in the specific database query language in use (e.g., datalog). 2, The program is sent to the *Query Engine*, where it is converted into SQL queries. These SQL queries use the selection operation to derive new tables (e.g., facts) and often involve table joins. 3, The SQL queries are sent to the *Translator*, where they are formatted based on the c-variable representation in use. 4, The *Database Coordinator* uses the formatted SQL to run the queries on the database. 5, *Database Coordinator* then sends the generated tables to the *C-table Evaluator*. The job of the *C-table Evaluator* is to handle the conditions in the tables. It extracts the conditions from the results and sends them to the *Translator*. 6, The *Translator* formats conditions based on the employed reasoning engine (e.g., Satisfiability Modulo Theories (SMT) solver) and the c-variable representation in use. This flexibility enables Pyotr to employ various reasoning engines for condition evaluation, with the integration of a new engine requiring modifications solely to the *Condition Translator*. 7, The formatted conditions are then transmitted to the active reasoning engine, which evaluates their satisfiability. In the case of satisfiable conditions, certain reasoning engines can simplify the conditions by identifying parts that constitute a tautology or are unsatisfiable, thereby accelerating future computations on that condition. 8, Simplified conditions undergo translation back into the format understandable by the DBMS through the *Translator*.

However, this step is bypassed for unsatisfiable conditions and reasoning engines that do not perform simplification. In such cases, the determination of satisfiability is directly forwarded to the *C-table Evaluator* (step 9). 9, In the case of simplified conditions, the *C-table Evaluator* constructs SQL updates to modify the conditions within the database. Conversely, for unsatisfiable conditions, the *C-table Evaluator* generates SQL delete queries to remove the corresponding tuples. To enhance performance, all updates to one table are consolidated into a single batched SQL query. 10, The *Database Coordinator* executes the SQL queries received from the *C-table Evaluator* on the DBMS, thereby updating the tables generated in step 4. 11, The revised tables are then returned to the *Query Engine*. If a fixed point is achieved (i.e., when no new tuples are generated) the computation concludes, and the final results are dispatched to the user (not illustrated in the diagram). Alternatively, if a fixed point is not reached, steps 3–11 are iteratively repeated until convergence.

## 4.2   Implementation

In this section, we describe the important implementation details of Pyotr. As outlined in Sect. 3, we adopt datalog as the query language for Pyotr. The practical implementation of conditional tables poses several challenges: (1) effectively storing conditional tables in a database, (2) developing a custom datalog engine capable of executing datalog programs on conditional tables, and (3) incorporating a reasoning engine with the ability to evaluate conditions. While prototypes for conditional tables have been explored in academia [4,16,27], to the best of our knowledge, there is currently no stable implementation for conditional tables within any DBMS.

**Storing Conditional Tables:** Pyotr uses PostgreSQL [17] as the underlying DBMS, since it is an open-source system used by millions of users and is amenable to modifications. To store conditions, we added a *condition* column to every new table created. We implemented the column as a list, where each element represents a condition, and the ultimate condition is a conjunction (logical *and*) of all elements. Given that the conjunction of conditions is frequently computed during c-table evaluation, the use of a list facilitates the rapid addition of new conditions. Global conditions are stored as a shared local condition across all tuples in the table. The type of the condition column is contingent upon the reasoning engine in use. For SMT solvers, we stored conditions as a list of text. For other reasoning engines, we used integer references to represent conditions.

A crucial factor influencing Pyotr's performance and the structure of SQL queries is the representation of c-variables in the database. Unlike constants, which can only take on a single value, c-variables can be valuated (i.e., assigned) to multiple constants. This poses a challenge because conventional database management systems (DBMSes) are designed to support normal constants and lack a built-in conception of c-variables. The manner in which c-variables are implemented directly impacts query performance; inefficient representations can lead to longer query execution times. Moreover, the representation of c-variables affects query translation, as the semantics of c-variables must be encoded into the query structure. This is further described in the next section. We experimented with multiple implementations of c-variables:

**Text:** In this implementation, we made each table column of "text" type. We defined some keywords (e.g., texts that begin with an underscore) to be interpreted as c-variables to distinguish them from regular textual constants. However, this approach meant that we had to use "text" datatype even when the underlying datatype was numeric. We found that querying over numeric columns was faster than "text" columns in PostgreSQL. This is likely to be true in other DBMS too, since integers are generally easier to optimize in databases. It is important to note that, in this solution, the underlying DBMS remained unaware of c-variables, and we managed the semantics of querying over c-variables externally by incorporating user-defined functions into queries for proper translation.

**Modified Datatypes:** To fix the issues with the previous representation scheme, we made modifications to multiple datatypes (e.g. integer, text, and *inet*) in PostgreSQL to incorporate a built-in understanding of c-variables. We introduced defined keywords as c-variables and implemented the logic to handle them within the code for these datatypes in PostgreSQL. The advantage of this approach was the elimination of the need for query translation to handle c-variables, as the logic for their management was integrated into the DBMS itself. Despite our expectation of improved performance, our custom implementation turned out to be slower, especially for larger tables. The key limitation was the inability to support indexing over tables. Indexing in databases organizes information in columns using specialized data structures, leading to accelerated query execution. However, most indexing schemes require defining a partial order on the datatype. As we utilized custom keywords for c-variables, which lack a natural order among them, we were unable to index the tables. Consequently, this limitation resulted in slower query performance.

**Value Partitioning:** In this scheme, we designated specific values (not keywords) within each datatype to represent c-variables. For instance, in the case of integers, we represented c-variables as negative integers. The scheme assumes that the designated values for c-variables never occur in the database as constants. While this approach required the external translation of queries for handling c-variables, it effectively addressed the performance issues associated with indexing and the text datatype. The substantial performance benefits observed led us to adopt this scheme as the default method for Pyotr.

**Executing Queries:** The Datalog Engine is responsible for executing datalog programs on c-tables. To the best of our knowledge, there is no available datalog engine for c-tables. Our datalog engine expects two inputs: (i) a database schema encompassing tables, columns, column types, c-variables used, and the

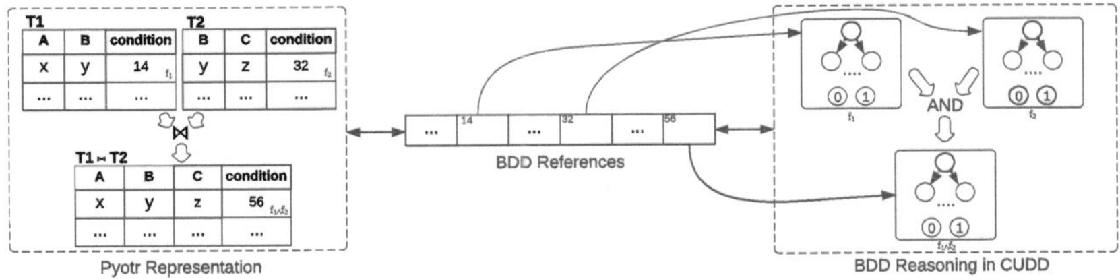


**Fig. 4.** Pyotr stores references to BDDs that represent conditions

domain of columns, and (ii) a datalog program. A datalog program consists of a list of rules, each of which derives new facts for a particular table. The engine transforms each datalog rule into a selection SQL query, typically incorporating table joins. A join occurs for each atom in the body of the rule. For a table join between two tables, we append the conditions of the joining tables along with the corresponding *local conditions* to the *condition* column of the result. The SQL query is modified so that it can append the relevant conditions to the result. The query also needs to be translated to support c-variables. In the *value partitioning* and *text* schemes, we explicitly add conditions to allow multiple constants to be assigned to c-variables. For example, a simple query to select the tuples in the sensor table (Table 2b) where *Alarm* has a value of 1 can be written in SQL as *SELECT * FROM table WHERE Alarm=1*. For the *value partitioning* scheme in which c-variables are represented as negative integers, this query is converted into the query *SELECT * FROM table WHERE (Alarm = 1 or Alarm < 0)*. A key advantage of employing datalog as the query language is its support for recursive queries. The method of executing these recursive queries significantly influences system performance. A naive execution would continuously execute datalog rules until a fixed point is achieved, leading to substantial redundant generation of tuples. To address this, we implemented semi-naive evaluation [6], which avoids recomputing old tuples by utilizing only the generated tuples from the last iteration in each subsequent iteration. The transition to semi-naive evaluation resulted in a noteworthy improvement in performance.

**Reasoning Engine:** The *C-table Evaluator* removes tuples that have unsatisfiable conditions in the generated table. It utilizes a reasoning engine to evaluate conditions. As we will see in Sect. 5, reasoning engines can be the most time consuming part of evaluating queries on conditional tables. Thus, the choice of the reasoning engine can determine the performance of Pyotr. The choice should be based on the problem. We tried three different reasoning engines:

**Satisfiability Modulo Theories (SMT) Solver:** Utilizing an SMT solver is a common approach to evaluate the satisfiability of conditions. SMT solvers generalize the Boolean satisfiability problem for more complex conditions, involving diverse datastructures such as integers, lists, bitvectors etc. We used a well-known SMT solver, Z3 [31], for this purpose. In this scheme, we represent all conditions in a text format that can be understood by Z3 and store these conditions in the condition column. The IP addresses were represented as bitvectors.

**Difference of Cubes (DoC):** While Z3 worked well for general conditions, it performed poorly when dealing with IP addresses. For this purpose, we tried a specialized encoding called Difference of Cube (DoC) from [30]. DoC uses ternary strings to represent IP addresses, and can efficiently represent dependencies using negation. For example, $1**\backslash 10*$ concisely represents all packets that start with "1" excluding those that begin with "10." DoC supports optimizations for simplifying conditions that involve a large number of dependencies, making it efficient for data plane verification. For large verification tasks involving IP addresses, DoC performed better than SMT.

**Binary Decision Diagram[4] (BDD):** BDDs [5] serve as representations for boolean functions in the form of decision DAGs. To use BDDs, we translate conditions from Z3 format into boolean functions by employing a binary encoding of integers and IP addresses [9]. The implementation utilizes the CUDD library [23]. We opted for BDDs because of their efficient support for computing conjunctions, which is a frequent operation in the evaluation of conditional tables. The compact representation of boolean functions in BDDs allow for an optimized computation of *logical and*. Integrating BDDs into Pyotr posed a challenge, particularly in finding a suitable method to store them in a table. Since we cannot easily store the actual DAGs representing BDDs in a database, we opted to store only references to the constructed BDDs in the table. The BDDs themselves were stored in an array using a wrapper written in C for the CUDD library, as depicted in Fig. 4. This approach offered an additional advantage: the conditions were now represented as integers rather than lengthy strings (as in SMT implementation), resulting in faster database operations.

## 5    Evaluation

In this section, we evaluate Pyotr's performance across a range of conditions. First, we assess the benefits and overhead of Pyotr when handling missing information within deployments of heterogeneous devices. Next, we examine Pyotr's efficiency in cases where some nodes are entirely inaccessible. Finally, we showcase the potential of enhancing Pyotr's performance by utilizing different reasoning engines for different problems. We compare three implemented engines, namely SMT, DoC, and BDD. All experiments were conducted using a laptop with an Apple M1 Pro chip and 16GB of memory. For the representation of conditional variables in all experiments, we used the *value partitioning scheme.*

---

[4] Referring to Reduced Ordered Binary Decision Diagram [8] throughout paper.

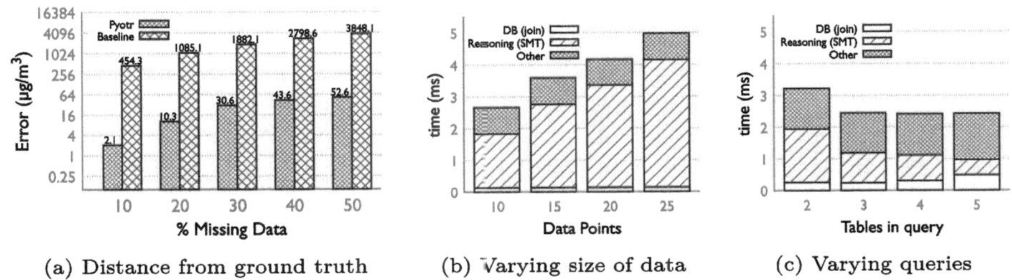

(a) Distance from ground truth        (b) Varying size of data        (c) Varying queries

**Fig. 5.** Error and time taken for data analysis with missing data points.

## 5.1   Verification with Partly Incomplete Information

```
Ans(t, temp, mq4) :- Sensor1(t, temp, humidity, pressure)[temp > 35],
    Sensor2(t, mq4, mq7)[mq4 > 4]
```

**Listing 3.** Datalog query to check for high temperature and high gas leakage

We use a dataset [24] for environmental monitoring through a sensor network, encompassing eight different types of sensors. These sensors measure diverse environmental properties such as temperature, humidity, rainfall, gas leakages, and pollutants. The measurements are transmitted to a central hub at varying frequencies, resulting in instances where specific data may be absent during particular time periods. In our setup, the hub conducts user-defined checks on the received data at regular intervals and notifies the user if any of these checks fail. To address missing data, a basic method involves assuming that values remain the same as the last observation, which we refer to as the baseline approach. However, since environmental properties can change with time, a more refined method would be to account for potential changes since the last observation. Pyotr employs conditional tables to represent a range[5] around the last observed value for missing data. To assess the benefits of this approach, we compared Pyotr's method to the baseline by removing random data points from the dataset and evaluating the difference from the actual values. Such missing data can arise due to various factors, such as unreliable wireless connections and variations in the transmission frequency among different sensors. Figure 5a illustrates the Euclidean error for one of the sensors in the dataset that measures inhalable particulate matter (expressed in $\mu g/m^3$). The error is significantly higher in the baseline approach, and grows with the rise in the percentage of missing points, which is attributed to the increased duration since the last observed value. The utilization of a range by Pyotr, as opposed to a single value, contributes to a significantly reduced error. We noticed a similar trend in all sensed properties in the dataset.

To measure the performance of Pyotr on the dataset, we run a query (Listing 3) that alarms when both the temperature and natural gas leakage levels are

---

[5] We used the standard deviation of the sensed property as the range.

high. We varied the number of data points analyzed in each iteration, adjusting the frequency of data verification. When the verification frequency is lower, a larger batch of data points is analyzed. Figure 5b shows the time taken by different components of Pyotr. Even for larger batches, Pyotr runs the query within ten milliseconds. The DB (join) represents the time taken by the selection query that performs the table joins. The reasoning time is the time taken by the SMT solver (Z3) to detect unsatisfiable conditions. Finally, the time categorized as *other* encompasses tasks related to managing conditional tables (e.g., deleting contradictory tuples, parsing datalog queries, etc.). While the database time remains nearly equal for tables of this size, the reasoning time increases due to the growing number of conditions to evaluate. Finally, we assess the impact of varying queries on performance by experimenting with different queries that involve varying numbers of tables. The evaluation time of databases is influenced by the number of tables involved in a conjunctive query, as more tables necessitate additional table joins. Counterintuitively, the reasoning time decreases when more tables are present in a query. This is because the inclusion of tables in a conjunctive query acts as a filter for results, resulting in fewer conditions to evaluate. Figure 5c shows the time taken when the queries are varied while the number of data points to evaluate are fixed. Notably, while the database time increases, the reasoning time decreases. In general, reasoning time is governed by both the number of conditions to evaluate and the complexity of each condition.

## 5.2   Verification with Inaccessible Nodes

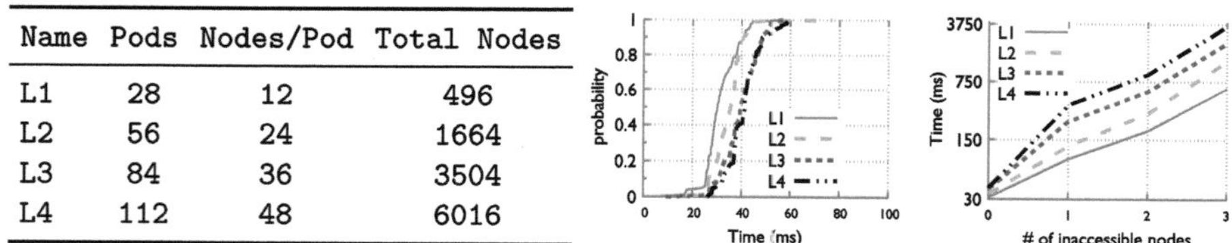

| Name | Pods | Nodes/Pod | Total Nodes |
|------|------|-----------|-------------|
| L1   | 28   | 12        | 496         |
| L2   | 56   | 24        | 1664        |
| L3   | 84   | 36        | 3504        |
| L4   | 112  | 48        | 6016        |

(a) Details of different data center topologies used[8]  (b) Without inaccessible nodes  (c) With inaccessible nodes

**Fig. 6.** Details of datacenter topologies and time taken by Pyotr for reachability analysis on those topologies (All topologies had 4 spines that connect all pods, which adds extra nodes.)

In this section, we evaluate the performance of Pyotr when some nodes in a deployment are completely inaccessible. We consider a deployment of server room monitoring sensors within a data center, utilizing the backhaul network for communication. The network is centrally managed by a controller, and a verifier is integrated with the nodes to verify the reachability policies within the network and ensure that the sensed information is promptly collected and analyzed. Following each update, the devices transmit their forwarding state to the

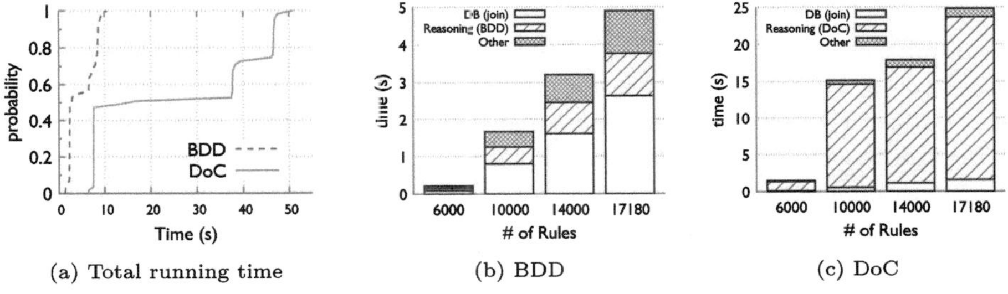

(a) Total running time                (b) BDD                    (c) DoC

**Fig. 7.** Calculation time for all reachable paths from random nodes in a campus network.

verifier. However, delays in sending updates may occur due to various factors, such as network congestion and crashes in the computation of forwarding information bases. A delay in the verification process could potentially result in the disconnection of sensors due to an erroneous update and could lead to a delay in reporting critical server room conditions on time. With conditional tables, we can perform verification even if there are inaccessible nodes in the network. For these nodes, we use any information we already have to model their forwarding behavior. For example, in our experiments we assume that they can forward packets through any of their ports except the ingress port[6].

For our experiments, we use datacenter topologies from [19] and vary the number of nodes. The details of the considered topologies are given in Table 6a. We used a datalog program similar to the one shown in Listing 2 to calculate all paths[7] from random source nodes. Figure 6b shows the time taken to perform reachability analysis on the entire network given a random source node over 100 runs. As the topology size increases, the time taken increases. However, even for the largest topology with more than 6000 nodes, the 90th percentile time is still less than 50ms, which is quick enough to be used in practice. We also did an experiment of an extreme case where we made some nodes completely inaccessible, even though this vastly increases the search space. Figure 6c shows the average time taken for verification with different number of inaccessible nodes. As we increase the number of inaccessible nodes, the search space increases exponentially. However, our results show that even in large networks with 3 simultaneously inaccessible nodes, the reachability analysis still completes within a few seconds. These results show that Pyotr effectively handles real-time verification even with inaccessible nodes, supporting reliable network monitoring and timely issue detection in large networks.

## 5.3  Reasoning Engine Performance

In this experiment, we evaluate the performance of different reasoning engines implemented in Pyotr on large conditional tables. Just like the previous experi-

---

<sup></sup>[6] Most switches do not allow forwarding back to the ingress port to avoid loops.

[7] In practice, we do not always need to compute all paths and can have different queries to catch particular violations (e.g. loops, blackholes, waypointing, firewalls).

ment, we perform a reachability query to calculate all paths in a network from a randomly selected node. However, instead of a datacenter network, we utilize the backbone of a campus network as our testing setup, leveraging a publicly available dataset [1]. Although this is a smaller network with 16 nodes, it is operated using traditional forwarding where all rules are pre-emptively installed. The network encompasses a total of 17,180 rules, which is much more than the number of rules in the previous experiment. Notably, these rules for the network also incorporate packet rewriting, adding an additional layer of complexity to the operational setup. In this experiment, most queries with the SMT engine could not complete. This can be attributed to two main factors: (i) the SMT engine lacks optimization for handling IP addresses, and (ii) string conditions become excessively large during intermediate computations, resulting in a significant increase in database evaluation time. Consequently, we present results solely for the DoC and BDD engines. Figure 7a illustrates the overall time required to execute reachability queries on the network using random source nodes over 100 runs. The BDD engine outperforms the DoC engine significantly, primarily because BDD is faster than DoC at calculating conjunction of conditions—a crucial operation in the evaluation of conditional tables. The running time is dependent on the length and number of reachable paths. The path length dictates the number of iterations of the query, which further dictates the number of database operations and conditions to evaluate. This is why we observe a staircase-like cumulative distribution function, where each step corresponds to different path lengths.

Figures 7b and 7c provide a breakdown of the overhead caused by different components of Pyotr for BDD and DoC, respectively. It is important to note the difference in the y-axis scales between the two graphs. Total time for database operations and conditional table management is similar for both engines, but the BDD engine's total running time is mainly affected by database join operations, while DoC's is influenced by reasoning time. Varying the number of rules results in an increased running time, as more rules affect the length and quantity of reachable paths, impacting overall performance. These results underscore the significant impact of the choice of reasoning engine on Pyotr's performance.

## 6    Related Work

Prior efforts in debugging and verifying IoT devices have proposed the use of model-checking [13,14,32], program analysis [10], and dynamic testing [11] to catch bugs in control programs for IoT devices. Many of these tools borrow techniques directly from Software Engineering which have proven to work well for software systems in the past. While reusing proved-out techniques for verification seems like a natural way forward, IoT deployments pose some unique challenges that require further innovation. Prior verification efforts for IoT devices overlook device heterogeneity, the user-centric nature of IoT, and the missing information due to proneness to various faults in IoT devices. They target specific programming frameworks (e.g. Groove Programming Language) and do not focus on applicability in a heterogeneous deployment with different vendors and device types. Moreover, static-analysis and model checking tools do not provide a user-friendly environment for inexperienced users to articulate and validate their intentions. Lastly, prior tools assume that all relevant information about the deployment is available to them, which is not the case in IoT devices. The scarcity of comprehensive fault information complicates the understanding of IoT deployments, requiring a more nuanced approach to device behavior modeling and troubleshooting.

Pyotr also shares similarities with some of the tools designed for network verification. Notably, Faure [27] employed conditional tables to verify failures in ISP networks. In our case, we use conditional tables for a different purpose (verification of IoT deployments) and have implemented and evaluated a full-fledged system to facilitate querying over and support for conditional tables. Datalog has also found application in some network verification tools [15, 30]. However, none of these tools address all the listed challenges associated with IoT systems.

## 7  Conclusion

The growing prevalence of IoT devices in critical environments has underscored the need for methods that guarantee their safety and reliability. In this paper, we identified three challenges associated with the verification of multi-vendor IoT deployments: system and protocol heterogeneity, usage by inexperienced users, and the presence of incomplete information. Conditional tables offer methods for data integration to resolve incompatibilities, provide an easy-to-use database-styled interface for inexperienced users, and offer a natural approach to handling incomplete information. Through various examples, we demonstrated how problems in IoT deployments can be modeled and reasoned about using conditional tables. Finally, we implemented and evaluated a comprehensive system, Pyotr, designed to support verification in IoT deployments through conditional tables. In the future, we intend to integrate conditional tables into a database management system. This integration would minimize the overhead of external system management and enable optimizations like query planning and incremental evaluation over conditional tables. We envision that conditional tables could find application in reasoning and verification across other domains that face one or more of the identified challenges.

**Acknowledgments.** This work was supported by National Science Foundation Award CNS-1909450, CNS-2145242.

# References


1. Stanford benchmark (2023). https://bitbucket.org/peymank/hassel-public/src/master/hsa-python/examples/stanford/Stanford_backbone/
2. Abiteboul, S., Abrams, Z., Haar, S., Milo, T.: Diagnosis of asynchronous discrete event systems: datalog to the rescue! In: Proceedings of the Twenty-Fourth ACM SIGMOD-SIGACT-SIGART Symposium on Principles of Database Systems, PODS 2005, pp. 358–367. Association for Computing Machinery, New York (2005). https://doi.org/10.1145/1065167.1065214
3. Abiteboul, S., Hull, R., Vianu, V. (eds.): Foundations of Databases: The Logical Level. Pearson, Boston (1995)
4. Abiteboul, S., Kanellakis, P., Grahne, G.: On the representation and querying of sets of possible worlds. ACM SIGMOD Rec. 16(3), 34–48 (1987). https://doi.org/10.1145/38714.38724
5. Akers: Binary decision diagrams (1978). https://doi.org/10.1109/TC.1978.1675141
6. Bancilhon, F.: Naive Evaluation of Recursively Defined Relations, pp. 165–178. Springer, New York (1986). https://doi.org/10.1007/978-1-4612-4980-1_17
7. Bauleo, E., Carnevale, S., Catarci, T., Kimani, S., Leva, M., Mecella, M.: Design, realization and user evaluation of the smartvortex visual query system for accessing data streams in industrial engineering applications. J. Vis. Lang. Comput. 25(5), 577–601 (2014). https://doi.org/10.1016/j.jvlc.2014.08.002. https://www.sciencedirect.com/science/article/pii/S1045926X14000652
8. Bryant: Graph-based algorithms for Boolean function manipulation. IEEE Trans. Comput. C-35(8), 677–691 (1986). https://doi.org/10.1109/TC.1986.1676819
9. Bryant, R.E.: Binary Decision Diagrams, pp. 191–217. Springer, Cham (2018). https://doi.org/10.1007/978-3-319-10575-8_7
10. Celik, Z.B., Fernandes, E., Pauley, E., Tan, G., McDaniel, P.: Program analysis of commodity IoT applications for security and privacy. ACM Comput. Surv. 52(4), 1–30 (2019). https://doi.org/10.1145/3333501
11. Celik, Z.B., Tan, G., McDaniel, P.: Iotguard: dynamic enforcement of security and safety policy in commodity IoT. In: Proceedings 2019 Network and Distributed System Security Symposium (2019). https://doi.org/10.14722/ndss.2019.23326
12. Chatzopoulou, G., Eirinaki, M., Polyzotis, N.: Query recommendations for interactive database exploration (2009)
13. Ding, W., Hu, H., Cheng, L.: Iotsafe: enforcing safety and security policy with real IoT physical interaction discovery. In: Proceedings 2021 Network and Distributed System Security Symposium (2021). https://doi.org/10.14722/ndss.2021.24368
14. Fang, Z., et al.: A model checking-based security analysis framework for IoT systems. High-Confidence Comput. 1(1), 100004 (2021). https://doi.org/10.1016/j.hcc.2021.100004
15. Fogel, A., et al.: A general approach to network configuration analysis. In: 12th USENIX Symposium on Networked Systems Design and Implementation (NSDI 2015), pp. 469–483. USENIX Association, Oakland, CA (2015). https://www.usenix.org/conference/nsdi15/technical-sessions/presentation/fogel
16. Grahne, G., Onet, A., Tartal, N.: Conditional tables in practice. arXiv abs/1304.0959 (2013). https://api.semanticscholar.org/CorpusID:8798537
17. Group, P.G.D.: (2023). https://www.postgresql.org/
18. Guilly, M.L., Petit, J.M., Scuturici, V.M.: SQL query completion for data exploration (2018)

19. Guo, D., Chen, S., Gao, K., Xiang, Q., Zhang, Y., Yang, Y.R.: Flash: fast, consistent data plane verification for large-scale network settings. In: Proceedings of the ACM SIGCOMM 2022 Conference, SIGCOMM 2022, pp. 314–335. Association for Computing Machinery, New York (2022). https://doi.org/10.1145/3544216. 3544246

20. Hajiyev, E., Verbaere, M., de Moor, O.: *codeQuest:* scalable source code queries with datalog. In: Thomas, D. (ed.) ECOOP 2006. LNCS, vol. 4067, pp. 2–27. Springer, Heidelberg (2006). https://doi.org/10.1007/11785477_2

21. IFTTT: automate business and home (2023). https://ifttt.com/

22. Imielnski, T., Lipski, W.: Incomplete information in relational databases. In: Mylopolous, J., Brodie, M. (eds.) Readings in Artificial Intelligence and Databases, pp. 342–360. Morgan Kaufmann, San Francisco (CA) (1989). https://doi.org/10.1016/B978-0-934613-53-8.50027-3. https://www.sciencedirect. com/science/article/pii/B9780934613538500273

23. Ivmai: The cudd package. https://github.com/ivmai/cudd

24. Jayakanth, J.J., Elumalai, P., Ovean, S., Hariharan, N.R., Mohammed Riyas, A.: Lora based wireless sensor network for environmental monitoring - dataset (2021). https://doi.org/10.21227/2g7j-e111

25. Jin, C., Bhowmick, S.S., Choi, B., Zhou, S.: Prague: towards blending practical visual subgraph query formulation and query processing. In: 2012 IEEE 28th International Conference on Data Engineering, pp. 222–233 (2012). https://doi.org/10. 1109/ICDE.2012.49

26. Lam, M.S., et al.: Context-sensitive program analysis as database queries. In: Proceedings of the Twenty-Fourth ACM SIGMOD-SIGACT-SIGART Symposium on Principles of Database Systems, PODS 2005, pp. 1–12. Association for Computing Machinery, New York (2005). https://doi.org/10.1145/1065167.1065169

27. Lan, F., Gui, B., Wang, A.: Fauré: a partial approach to network analysis. In: Proceedings of the Twentieth ACM Workshop on Hot Topics in Networks, Hot-Nets 2021, pp. 123–131. Association for Computing Machinery, New York (2021). https://doi.org/10.1145/3484266.3487391

28. Li, J., et al.: Can LLM already serve as a database interface? A big bench for large-scale database grounded text-to-SQLs (2023)

29. Loo, B.T., et al.: Declarative networking. Commun. ACM **52**(11), 87–95 (2009). https://doi.org/10.1145/1592761.1592785

30. Lopes, N.P., Bjørner, N., Godefroid, P., Jayaraman, K., Varghese, G.: Checking beliefs in dynamic networks. In: 12th USENIX Symposium on Networked Systems Design and Implementation (NSDI 2015), pp. 499–512. USENIX Association, Oakland, CA (2015). https://www.usenix.org/conference/nsdi15/technical-sessions/presentation/lopes

31. Microsoft: (2023). https://microsoft.github.io/z3guide/docs/logic/intro/

32. Nguyen, D.T., Song, C., Qian, Z., Krishnamurthy, S.V., Colbert, E.J., McDaniel, P.: Iotsan. In: Proceedings of the 14th International Conference on emerging Networking EXperiments and Technologies (2018). https://doi.org/10.1145/3281411. 3281440

33. Obaido, G., Ade-Ibijola, A., Vadapalli, H.: Generating SQL queries from visual specifications (2019)

34. Seo, J., Guo, S., Lam, M.S.: Socialite: datalog extensions for efficient social network analysis. In: 2013 IEEE 29th International Conference on Data Engineering (ICDE), pp. 278–289 (2013). https://doi.org/10.1109/ICDE.2013.6544832

35. Smaragdakis, Y., Bravenboer, M.: Using datalog for fast and easy program analysis. In: de Moor, O., Gottlob, G., Furche, T., Sellers, A. (eds.) Datalog Reloaded, pp. 245–251. Springer, Heidelberg (2011)
36. Soares, D., Dias, J.P., Restivo, A., Ferreira, H.S.: Programming IoT-spaces: a user-survey on home automation rules. In: Computational Science – ICCS 2021, pp. 512–525 (2021). https://doi.org/10.1007/978-3-030-77970-2_39
37. Soylu, A., Giese, M., Jimenez-Ruiz, E., Vega-Gorgojo, G., Horrocks, I.: Experiencing optiquevqs: a multi-paradigm and ontology-based visual query system for end users. Univers. Access Inf. Soc. **15**(1), 129–152 (2016). https://doi.org/10.1007/s10209-015-0404-5
38. Vailshery, L.S.: IoT connected devices worldwide 2019–2030 (2023). https://www.statista.com/statistics/1183457/iot-connected-devices-worldwide/
39. Wang, B., Shin, R., Liu, X., Polozov, O., Richardson, M.: Rat-SQL: relation-aware schema encoding and linking for text-to-sql parsers (2021)
40. Wang, J., Balazinska, M., Halperin, D.: Asynchronous and fault-tolerant recursive datalog evaluation in shared-nothing engines. Proc. VLDB Endow. **8**, 1542–1553 (2015). https://api.semanticscholar.org/CorpusID:7191222
41. Yu, T., Li, Z., Zhang, Z., Zhang, R., Radev, D.: Typesql: knowledge-based type-aware neural text-to-sql generation (2018)

# Supporting an Ephemeral Shared Dataspace with a BLE Connectionless Protocol


Mariam Issa[1]([envelope]), Paul Couderc[2], and Jean-Marie Bonnin[3]

[1] Université de Rennes, Rennes, France
`mariam.issa@inria.fr`
[2] Centre INRIA de l'Université de Rennes, Rennes, France
`paul.couderc@inria.fr`
[3] IMT Atlantique/IRISA, Rennes, France
`jean-marie.bonnin@irisa.fr`



**Abstract.** Smart devices would often communicate with other entities in their surroundings, to engage an interaction or get information about the environment. For example, a blind person may want her smartwatch advertising about her disability so that the environment adapts. Short distance wireless communications, such as BLE are a good support for this style of short-lived and immediate communications. However, building applications using these communication interfaces are not so easy as the protocols involved are typically packet level messages, and higher level middleware such as message buses or event based systems are designed in the context of general networking, not "spontaneous" communication system. This paper proposes a higher level protocol to better support ephemeral interactions at the application level, based on a shared data space. The proposed framework allows anonymous communication among nodes, reflects their physical context to the application, while not depending on MAC addressing. It is based on the idea of having the data addressable while it is relevant. We propose a generic packet structure that accommodates different roles and application fields. BLE Connectionless mode is used to transmit data. The system is implemented on ESP32 where multiple application fields are demonstrated to fit under the proposed communication paradigm.

**Keywords:** Ephemeral Interaction · Local Communication · Dataspaces · Association-less Communication · WiFi Beacon Stuffing · BLE Advertisements


## 1 Introduction

A group of friends at a wedding wants to play a game where invitees engage in some Q/A's about the newlyweds. However the venue is at a rural area that doesn't contain neither WiFi nor 4G, and this was overlooked until the




A. Soylu et al. (Eds.): MobiQuitous 2024, LNICST 634, pp. 169–186, 2026.
https://doi.org/10.1007/978-3-032-10554-7_9

game has started, thus rendering it impossible to play. One solution would be to establish a local network and the guests connect to it. Nevertheless, establishing the network, distributing the credentials over the guests who want to play and accepting connections would take more time than the actual game. The existence of a communication paradigm that allows spontaneous interaction among the guests while avoiding the configuration and connection establishment phases would spare the waste in time, battery and ongoing traffic exchange, while delivering the relevant information. The guests merely need to send their vote and the server compiles the results. The data exchanged is relevant while the game is on. There is no need to identify who sent the data. The interactions in this case are said to be local and short-lived or *ephemeral* [1]. This example is just one simple example of many other usecases that fall under local and ephemeral interactions, and that would highly benefit from a spontaneous and direct communication paradigm. Example usecases could generalize to any form of short-lived data exchange that happens among two or more nodes arriving to a common vicinity at the same time. This could be a vehicle to pedestrian (V2P) safety system, or could be a smart museum aisle or a set of sensors broadcasting their readings to mobile gateways.

Characterizing the type of interactions is the starting point to design a spontaneous communication paradigm. Then, in order to implement such a paradigm, one should consider three aspects. The first is at the level of data transmission which is characterized by the wireless communication technology. The second is at the level of the application which is characterized by the interface that the developer and user navigate through. Finally the third is concerned with the mediation layer between the transmission layer and the application layer. Having such a layer would facilitate the seamless integration and interaction between the data transmission layer and the application layer. This mediation layer, often referred to as middleware [2], serves several critical functions: it abstracts the complexities of underlying communication technologies, providing a simpler interface for the application layer, and ensuring interoperability between different systems and devices. Additionally, it manages data collection, processing, and distribution, ensuring the data is in the appropriate format for the application. The mediation layer also handles quality of service parameters like latency, bandwidth, and reliability to meet application requirements. Furthermore, it supports scalability by managing resources efficiently and enabling the addition of new devices or services without significant changes to the existing infrastructure. Lastly, it offers flexibility and adaptability, allowing the system to adjust to changes in network conditions or application requirements dynamically.

We propose in this article a framework that serves as a starting point for implementing the spontaneous communication paradigm considering its three aspects, by following a bottom up approach. We start by defining the wireless communication technology that is needed to support the data transmission. Then we propose a data coordination model to manage the data exchange at the application level, which operates on top of the considered communication technology. We provide in this paper a feasibility study of such system and then we proceed in our future work to finalizing the mediation space that should provide the required abstractions, providing a framework that can support spontaneous communication among heterogenous devices and different technologies.

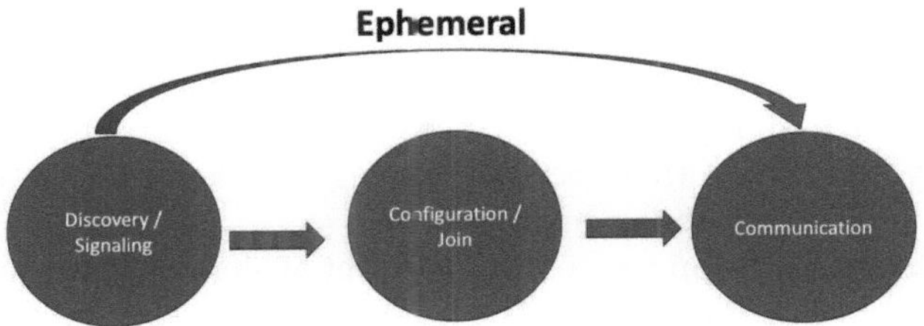


**Fig. 1.** Ephemeral Communication Model.

Motivated by the requirement of eliminating the connection establishment phase at the data transmission level, we consider communication without a prior configuration. This is referred to as "Association-less Communication". It defines the ability for two nodes to communicate directly, without having prior knowledge about each other [3]. Generally, transmission of data from node A to node B is governed by the wireless communication technology. The technology sets the rules of communication and defines physical boundaries including ranges, timing, rates... Examples of wireless communication technologies include and are not limited to WiFi, Bluetooth, BLE, RFID, C-V2X, LoRaWAN ... Each technology incorporates a discovery mechanism among nodes, through exchanging discovery packets before communication. One can find in the literature several works discussing association-less communication in ephemeral interaction contexts [4–6]. This study focuses on the works which rely on abundant and easy to implement technologies, such as WiFi and BLE. Within these, data to be exchanged is embedded in the discovery packets. This is motivated by the fact that these packets are exchanged always before any connection is established, and regardless of the connection state of the nodes. During discovery, nodes broadcast advertisement packets and listening nodes scan for these packets. Thus as illustrated in Fig. 1, applying this technique for the considered ephemeral interactions will serve in unifying the discovery and communication phases, while bypassing the configuration phases.

WiFi Beacon Stuffing [5] and BLE connectionless mode [6] are two techniques that are widely used to realize communication without association, or as termed here association-less communication.

Moving upwards to data management models such as publish/subscribe [7], dataspaces [8] and tuple spaces [9], these models define how information is exchanged among components in a distributed system. These paradigms provide high-level abstractions for communication and coordination among distributed entities [7]. There have been some works that implement some of the mentioned data management schemes on top of association-less communication. For example, publish messages are disseminated over advertisements in [10]. They propose a distributed system where sensor nodes act as distributed brokers and subscribers. These nodes receive notifications from publisher nodes via advertisement beacons. However, they revert to traditional networking in the sense that they form routing tables based on neighbor list discovery.

Another example is [11] where WiFi based advertisements are used to publish alerts for pedestrians subscribed to their alert service. Although this allows to extend the warning ability to pedestrians that are not connected on the 802.11p network, they still rely in their work on having a broker over the internet, that manages the publish/subscribe requests.

This work however proposes a fully distributed shared and ephemeral dataspace which uses association-less communication to transmit data. In particular, BLE advertisements are used to transmit the packets. In the proposed system, nodes can contribute to a shared data space, or read from it. Imagine this dataspace as a whiteboard, where anyone can write or read from it. Advertising a packet that belongs to the proposed format means writing on the whiteboard, and scanning a packet that belongs the proposed format means reading from the whiteboard. Any node who comes to be in range and is interested in the content of the packet, will read the data; and whomever is not interested will discard it. Packets are identified based on their content as will be explained in Sect. 3. This bypasses the need for address based communication.

The whiteboard can be viewed as being the intersection in time and location of an advertiser (provider) and a scanner (Requester) What we propose is that the content and evolution of the shared volatile dataspace will be driven by the proposed advertisement-based protocol. The fact that data is available while two or more nodes intersect in space and time indeed reflects the physical context to the application level.

The contributions of this work can be listed as follows:

- Propose a communication protocol that allows application level data exchange based on association-less communication.
- Propose a volatile shared dataspace that uses BLE connectionless mode to transmit data.
- Propose a generic advertisement packet format that can accommodate several application classes.
- Uniquely identify the packets based on their content.

The rest of this paper is organized as follows: Sect. 2 provides a background about the topic, and discusses some related works. Then in Sect. 3, the proposed framework is provided and discussed. Afterwards implementation and system performance analysis is provided in Sect. 4. Finally, the paper is concluded in Sect. 5.

## 2 Background and Related Works

In this section, some application usecases that fall under the considered interaction scheme are presented. These applications would benefit from the proposed

**Fig. 2.** Example of a smart environment governed by ephemeral interactions. (Image generated by ChatGPT-4 DALL-E)

protocol. Afterwards, a brief overview of association-less communication, in particular (WiFi and BLE based), and dataspaces is presented.

## 2.1 Example Applications Relying on Local Ephemeral Interactions

An application falls under this category when the communication among nodes happen as they come into each others vicinity, and for a short period of time. Examples on such applications are found within applications such as proximity messaging applications, seemless and collaborative data sharing, collision avoidance systems, IoT sensor measurements... The below list presents some of the many example scenarios that fall under this communication scheme. Figure 2 illustrates these examples.

1. A person passes by a shop, and the shop would like to broadcast coupons to people wandering around.
2. A biker is about to hit a pedestrian, so the biker sends a warning to the pedestrian.
3. A group of friends took a bus for a roadtrip. The bakery store would like to reach to them to offer them coupons.
4. A group of strangers joined a game, a judge reads drawings from them and assembles them.
5. A person passes by fountain, and the fountain broadcasts that its water is not potable.

Despite the fact that these examples share the local and ephemeral interaction scheme, each scenario requires a specific design in terms of the timing and reactivity constraints, transmission range, tolerance to power consumption, size of payload that needs to be shared, implementation complexity ... The choice of the communication technology and the data management model determines the performance of each of the examples. Next we elaborate on WiFi Beacon Stuffing and on BLE connectionless mode as two enabling techniques for associationless communication.

## 2.2  Association-Less Communication

A technology that allows devices to communicate without prior configuration, to act in a decentralized manner, to discover and broadcast data to devices in range, while not being affected by node mobility, would be a suitable enabler for association-less communication. WiFi and BLE are two strong candidate technologies for to implement association-less communication. This is motivated by the facts that both of the technologies allow to embed data within packets that are already exchanged among communicating peers. The data to be embedded is small, and usually acts as some state description, some identifier, or even could correspond to some sensor measurements. The other fact is the reliance on existing technologies without the need to deploy and install new equipment or apply major changes to the current infrastructure. For the case of WiFi beacon stuffing, the WiFi is accessible in a highly ubiquitous and dense manner. For the case of BLE beacons, they come at a low cost and are easy to deploy and move.

***WiFi Beacon Stuffing.*** In WiFi infrastructure mode, when an AP wants to announce its existence, it sends periodically beacon frames. Client devices perform active or passive scans to detect these beacons. In default mode of operation, advertisement beacons are broadcasted by APs every 100 ms, at a rate of 1 Mbps. WiFi Beacon Stuffing was first introduced in [5]. This was motivated by the fact that these beacons are exchanged among APs and clients despite of their connection state. Despite the fact that beacon stuffing has been proposed more than 15 years ago (2007), it continues to be a strong candidate for utilization in recent applications. Different implementations of this technique include embedding of the messages within the SSID (Service Set Identifier), BSSID (Basic Service Set Identifier) or the VSIE (Vendor-Specific Information Element) fields of beacon frames, a.k.a management frames.

The following paragraph provides an overview of various applications and implementations of this technique across different domains.

**LoWS** [12] proposed to utilize beacon stuffing to send location based data to mobile users. These information can be location specific such as the nearest emergency exit, or location independent such as the existence of fire. Users perform active scans, and the AP broadcasts codes through the probe responses, using the VSIE field. **SafePath** [13] applied beacon stuffing to transmit collision warnings among vehicles and pedestrians. They embed the data in the SSID fields of the transmitted packets, and devices switch between broadcasting (AP) mode and listening (client). **Wi-LE** [14] proposed that IoT devices (sensors) inject fake beacons carrying their measurements. The receiving end decodes and extracts the messages from the beacons. They state that following this approach consumes energy as low as that of BLE (in connected mode), and they use the VSIE field. The devices act as an AP.

It can be seen how the different parameters are utilized based on the requirements of each application. Each implementation of WiFi beacon stuffing serves different application domains with varying techniques for data embedding, scanning methods, energy efficiency considerations, and user interactions.

Next a brief overview of BLE connectionless mode is provided along with some works implementing it. A more detailed presentation of BLE is provided below as it is the technology adapted to host the proposed framework.

***BLE Connectionless Mode.*** BLE has gained popularity for its energy efficient and short range capabilities. It stands as a promising candidate wireless technology to realize association-less communication. The terms used in literature to describe such mode of communication are "Connectionless communications" or "Legacy advertising". The BLE standard is designed to support ephemeral interactions through its connectionless mode. In this mode, the broadcaster (advertiser) periodically sends advertising packets to any device able to receive them. On the other side, the observer (scanner) continuously scans for these advertisements at periodic intervals [15]. Advertisement packets can take four forms: *Connectable undirected Advertising, Connectable Directed Advertising, Non-connectable Undirected Advertising* or *Scannable Undirected Advertising* [16].

In addition to the frame header, advertisement packets can contain up to 31 bytes of data. At the physical layer, BLE operates at the 2.4GHz ISM band over 40 channels. Channels 37, 38 and 39 are assigned for advertisements. The rest are for data exchange after a connection is established [15]. Moreover, these three advertising channels are not utilized by Wi-Fi, thus avoiding conflict. Each time a device advertises, it transmits the same packet in each of the three advertising channels. This sequence of packets is called an advertising event, and the time between two advertising events is called advertising interval. This interval ranges from as small as 20 ms up to 10.28 s [17]. The transmitter and receiver are not synchronised. Consequently, the packets are received only when they randomly overlap [16]. This means that the scanner might not listen to the advertiser at the right time. Additionally, due to the fact the asynchronous nature of BLE advertising packets, there is a possibility that two or more advertisers would send over the same channel simultaneously. This can occur due to the lack of coordination between advertisers and the random timing of packet transmissions. As a result, receivers may detect overlapping packets, leading to potential interference or collisions. To minimize the probability of such event, a random delay between 0 and 10 ms is induced on the advertising interval [17]; thus, reducing the probability for the two next messages to collide again.

BLE advertising is more mature in the literature than its counterpart WiFi beacon stuffing. **Spachos** [18] discussed the usage of BLE beacons for indoor positioning at an interactive museum. They asses the BLE beacons deployment and efficiency through experimenting on the distance estimation accuracy, localization performance of BLE beacons. **BLEhorn** [19] proposed a vehicle to pedestrian collision warning system. They use data from the GPS in the smartphones, compress and fit them into the payload of the BLE advertisement packet.

**Park** [20] proposed to use the BLE beacons to share safety messages in the context of Bike-to-Pedestrian systems. They fix the bike to be the advertiser and the pedestrian to be the scanner. **OSXE** [21] proposed to advertise the dynamic sensor data using the non-connectable and non-scannable undirected advertising mode of BLE. Moreover, there exists studies to analyse the performance of the connectionless BLE communication mode such as [6,22]. It can be seen that this mode of BLE covers a diverse range of applications, where each one utilizes different type of advertisements based on the specific requirements of the application.

Due to the facts that BLE protocols are well-defined and standardized, making it easy to develop and deploy applications, and to being highly power efficient and being optimized for short range communications, this work adapts BLE connectionless mode as the means of data transmission. In what follows, a brief overview of dataspaces is presented.

### 2.3   Dataspace Systems

A dataspace is generally defined as a conceptual framework for managing and integrating heterogeneous data sources, where the elements indicate a real world entity or data concept [23].

The key characteristics of a dataspace include [24]:

- *Heterogeneous Data Sources:* A dataspace can integrate data from a variety of sources, such as databases, spreadsheets, web services, and enterprise applications, regardless of their format or structure.
- *Loose Coupling:* Dataspaces do not require tight integration or schema alignment between the different data sources. Instead, they use a more loosely coupled approach, allowing data sources to be added or removed without disrupting the overall system.
- *Incremental Integration:* Dataspaces enable incremental integration of data sources, allowing users to start with a subset of data and gradually expand the dataspace as needed, rather than requiring a complete upfront integration.
- *Self-Organizing:* Dataspaces are designed to be self-organizing, meaning that they can automatically discover, index, and manage the data sources without the need for extensive manual configuration or maintenance.
- *Flexible Querying:* Dataspaces provide flexible querying capabilities, allowing users to search and access data across multiple sources using a unified query interface, without needing to know the underlying data structures.

In our system, we utilize the concept of a dataspace however with the view that this dataspace is viable among a group of nodes (providers and requesters) sharing the same interest, and who are in range for a time period $t$. It is to be re-iterated that one of the main rationals of the proposed framework is to offer an application level data exchange. This is already done with BLE however using a client server model (the GATT protocol). A brief overview of this protocol is provided next.

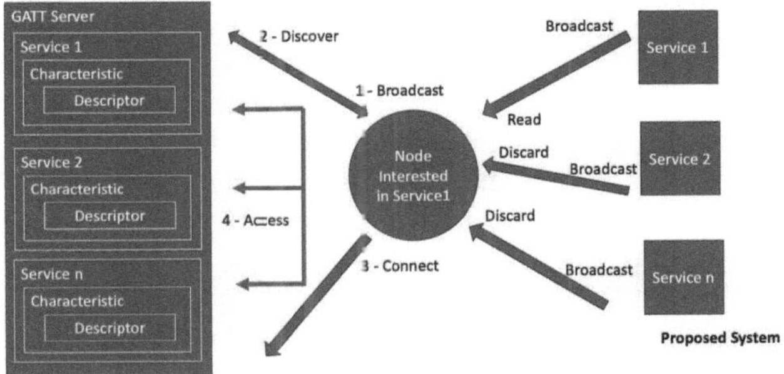


**Fig. 3.** A GATT System vs the Proposed Framework.

## 2.4   Offering Services at the Application Level GATT

The Generic Attribute Profile (GATT) within Bluetooth Low Energy (BLE) technology serves as a cornerstone for application-level data exchange. Embedded within the BLE protocol stack, GATT delineates how devices structure, access, and interact with data. It adheres to a client-server model, delineating central and peripheral roles, which while providing structure, can sometimes impose rigidity in dynamic interactions. GATT's organization of data into services and characteristics enables tailored communication patterns for specific applications [16]. However, this predefined structure may lack the flexibility needed for ephemeral interactions, potentially hindering adaptability in scenarios requiring rapid, transient data exchange. Despite its relatively fixed nature, GATT remains fundamental in enabling standardized communication across BLE devices, ensuring interoperability and seamless data exchange across diverse applications and devices.

We show that for some ephemeral applications, using the framework we designed offers the same functionality at the application with a more flexible communication paradigm. Figure 3 shows a node interested in a certain service "Service1". Following the GATT protocol, the node has to discover available servers offering the service, and then establish a connection in order to access the data specific to the service. On another side, within the proposed protocol, any node offering "Service1" will broadcast it and the node will simply read it as it scans. The next section explains in details how does a node identify the specific service based on the advertised data content, and with a lower cost in power and time.

## 3   Proposed Framework

We propose a custom packet format that allows packets to be identified based on their content. By this, the protocol is agnostic to the type of device issuing the packet and does not depend on the MAC address to identify nodes. This is important since MAC addresses are more and more chosen randomly for privacy concerns. As stated earlier, a piece of information $info_i$ in the dataspace is defined to be the intersection in time and range of an advertiser and a scanner. The proposed packet is composed of the following fields: Role, Application code, Generic Field, Payload and a Hash as can be seen in Fig. 4. Table 1 provides a description of the packet fields and their respective sizes.

| 1 byte | | | 1 byte | 26 bytes | 1 byte | 2 bytes |
|---|---|---|---|---|---|---|
| 2 bits | 2 bits | 4 bits | | | | |
| Role | Application Code | Generic Field | Generic Field | Payload | Generic Field | Hash |

**Fig. 4.** Proposed Generic Packet Format.

The first byte denotes the characteristics of the packet. A node could be a provider of a service that needs a connection to be established such as applications that need authentication, or a service that is self contained in the advertisement such as a warning or a sensor reading or simply the availability of a certain asset. Similarly, the requesting node could request a service that needs a connection or a self contained service such as requesting a warning. This is indicated by the first two bits of the first byte (*Role*).

The proposed framework accommodates 4 application classes. We utilize in this work two application classes (Information providing service and a Vehicle to pedestrian collision warning system). This is indicated in the next 2 bits of the first byte (*Application Code*).

The next 2 bits of the first byte, and the next two following bytes (18 bits) define a generic purpose field *Generic Field)* would possibly accommodate a hop counter or a timing field to indicate the spatio-temporal relevance of the packet. This is not implemented in this work as it requires a deeper study for the trade-offs associated with the inclusion of such fields. For example, the processing and traffic burdens added if packets were to re-broadcast received packets.

The next 26 bytes denote the *payload* related to the specific application indicated in the "Application Code" field. The proposed packet structure can accommodate other applications. For proof of concept, we fit the packet proposed in [19], which serves a V2P warning packet. This will be elaborated in the results section.

Finally, as the packets are advertisement packets that can be viewed and advertised by any BLE device, and in order to avoid falling into false positive cases where any packet could hold the same value for the role and the application code, the hash code appended at the end is used to uniquely identify that the packets contain information that belongs to ephemeral dataspace. In this work, MurmushHash2 is used. MurmurHash2 provides a good balance of speed, distribution, and simplicity, making it a popular choice for non-cryptographic hashing applications where performance and collision resistance are important [25].

An illustration of the proposed system is shown in Fig. 5. Devices $P_1, P_2$ and $P_n$ are three providers of different data $d_1, d_2$ and $d_n$. $R_1$ and $R_m$ are two

**Table 1.** Packet Fields Descriptions and Size

| Field | Size | Description |
|---|---|---|
| Role | 2 bits | To assign one of 4 roles:<br><br>– Provide a service that needs a connection to be established to exchange data.<br>– Provide a Self contained service.<br>– Request a service that needs a connection to be established to exchange data.<br>– Request a Self contained service. |
| Application Code | 2 bits | Identify the application class that the packet belongs to (e.g: warning, sensor reading...) |
| Generic Purpose | 18 bits | Could be for inclusion as additional payload or for the possibility use as a fading parameter in terms of number of hops and time, or as an additional hash byte. |
| Payload | 26 bytes | The payload belonging to the specific application |
| Hash code | 2 bytes | The hash value of the first 29 bytes to identify that the information within the packet belongs to the proposed framework. |

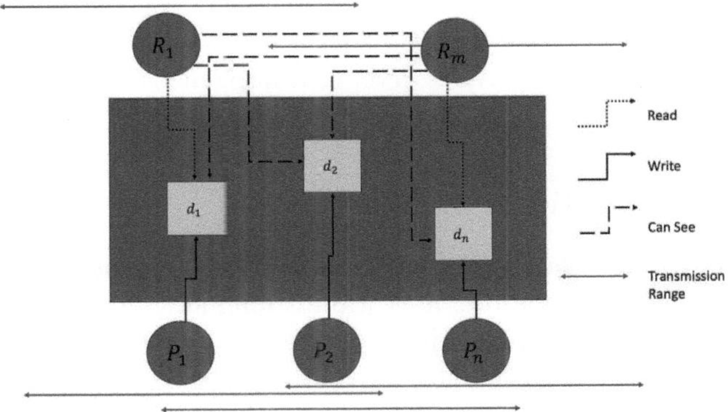


**Fig. 5.** Schematic for the proposed protocol.

devices requesting some services. At the time instant $t_i$, both of them can see $d_1, d_2$ and $d_n$ due to the overlap of transmission ranges at this time instant. After verifying that the hashes of $d_1, d_2$ and $d_n$ match the appended hash, $R_1$ will extract the payload of $d_1$ and $R_m$ will extract that of $d_n$. It can be said that for $t_i$ and $range_m \cap range_n$, there exists a piece of information $info_i$, within the shared ephemeral dataspace. What we propose does not override the standardized BLE packet format. Service UUIDs and other fields can still be fitted into the payload and the generic fields. Dataspace range extension is possible with adding a hop counter that lets nodes to re-broadcast the packets. In regards to the security aspect, the data to be shared within the discovery packets is not considered confidential. As mentioned earlier, it could be a warning that a vehicle or bike is in the way, or could be an ad which is intended to be broadcasted to the public. Complete security is difficult to achieve due to the inherent nature of discovery protocols which are designed to be open and accessible to facilitate device communication. Nevertheless, if confidentiality is required basic encryption schemes could be applied to encrypt the broadcasted data, or the packet could indicate within the role field that the service provided or the requested service needs a connection establishment step as illustrated in Table 1.

In the next section, we implement the system on ESP32 to evaluate its feasibility.

## 4    Implementation and Results

In this article, a feasibility study was conducted to evaluate the practicality and potential of the proposed system. The focus of this study was on assessing the basic functionality, compatibility with existing technologies such as BLE, estimated costs in terms of power consumption, and the overall viability of the system within the intended environment. In the first part of the implementation, we asses for a given hash function length, how many concurrent transmitters could be supported by our system while avoiding false positives. Then we assess the ability of the proposed framework to distinguish data based on the content of the advertised packet. Finally, we compare the current consumed by the proposed framework against that of a GATT server that implements the same functionality of providing a service.

### 4.1    The Hash Function

As mentioned earlier, the murmurhash2 is used as a means to avoid bad identification of the packet type. I.e, as a way to uniquely identify that the packet belongs to the shared dataspace. However, truncating the output of a hash function can lead to a higher probability of collisions due to the loss of information and reduced uniqueness of hash values. This trade-off between collision probability and efficiency should be evaluated in the context of the specific application to determine the most appropriate hash function and output size. In the considered interaction scheme, at any time instant $t$, there would be $b$ neighboring nodes acting as concurrent advertisers. In order to evaluate the probability of collision, i.e., two nodes would share the same hash we use the formula from [26] based on the birthday paradox:

$$P(2^m, b) = 1 - e^{-\frac{(b)(b-1)}{2 \times 2^m}} \qquad (1)$$

where m represents the number of bits considered at the hash output. Figure 6 shows the collision probability $P(2^m, b)$ as a function of the number of neighboring transmitting nodes $b$, for different values of hashed output bits $m$.

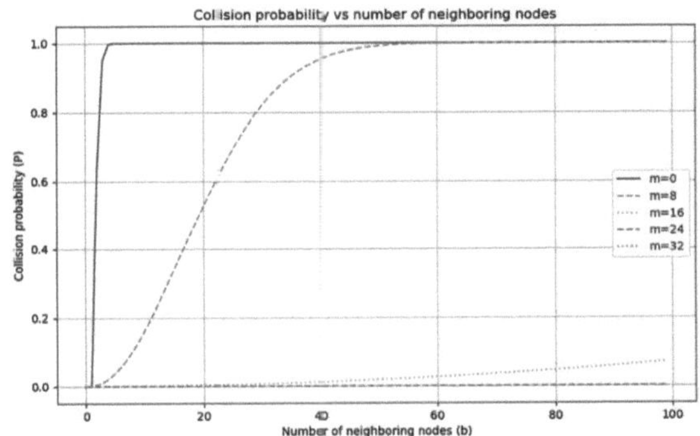


**Fig. 6.** Probability of Collision as a function of number of transmitters.

It can be seen from the figure that considering 2 bytes hash output gives a collision probability less tha 2% for up to 50 neighboring nodes. However, depending on the criticality of the application and the density of the advertisers in a certain proximity at a given instant, considering 3 bytes of hash output gives a 0% collision probability for more than 50 concurrent advertisers. The additional byte for hash output could be allocated from the generic field left. In contemporary settings, having more than 50 potential advertisers is not perceived as a large quantity. For instance, consider a classroom with 25 students. Each student might possess a smartphone, a laptop, a smartwatch, or other electronic devices capable of Bluetooth Low Energy (BLE) advertising. When factoring in these various devices, the number of potential advertisers within the classroom quickly exceeds 50. An interesting direction of this work would be to investigate additional unique identification techniques which do not rely on the hash function, and to asses the resulting trade-offs of such techniques.

### 4.2   Implementation on ESP32

Our scheme and the GATT server/client are implemented on ESP32 WROOM32D. Although ESP32 is not optimized for ultra-low power usage for BLE [14], it is used as a baseline in this work to establish a comparison in the

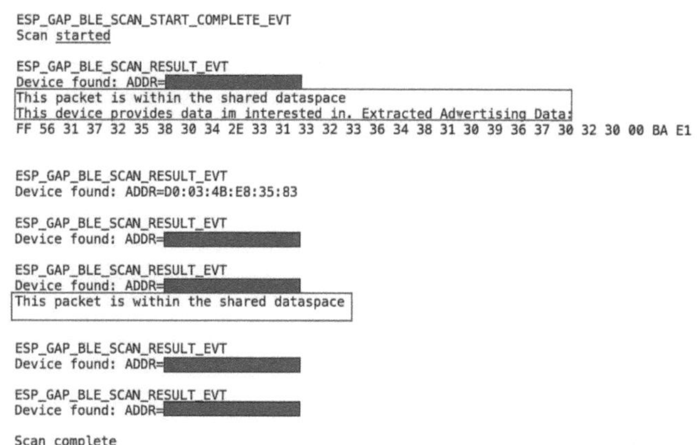

Fig. 7. Sample output of the proposed scheme.

behaviour of the power profiles between the two modes. ESP32 is used within the scope of this project due to its cost-effectiveness, large community, and flexible development environment. On top of that, this study is a part of a running project which establishes a dedicated power study between WiFi Beacon Stuffing and BLE connectionless mode, over the same chip. For the advertiser in both systems (the proposed and the GATT server), the advertising intervals are set to be between 20 ms and 40 ms. Connectable undirected advertising is used as advertisement type. The scanner and the GATT client scan intervals are set to be 50 ms and the scan windows are set to be 30 ms. Finally, the default transmit power of 0 dBm is used for both systems. The current draw is measured using a Joulescope JS220 Precision Energy Analyser[1]. This work build on top of the codes supplied by the esp-idf builtin examples for GAP and GATT.

For proof of concept for the generic nature of the proposed protocol, we implement the following scenario: Consider a Vehicle-to-Pedestrian V2P Collision system, and a service belonging to an application class "X" which broadcasts data. In the V2P system, there is a pedestrian interested in receiving warnings from vehicles passing by. Also, there is the vehicle that provides such warnings. The vehicle data is represented by the proposed packet in **BLEHorn** [19]. It consists of 25 bytes comprising the node type being vehicle or pedestrian, time, speed, bearing, longitude and latitude. For the specific example they provide, a payload of "V1725804.3132364810967020" means there is a vehicle running at a speed of 4.3 m/s around me and its heading is 132. Its longitude and latitude are 116.364810 and 39.967020 respectively. Nevertheless, the structure of the payload is not important in our protocol, which rather acts as a carrier for the payload.

Figure 7 shows the output of the scanner for proposed protocol on ESP32. It can be seen that out of 6 discovered BLE advertisers, two belonging to the

---

[1] https://www.joulescope.com/products/js220-joulescope-precision-energy-analyzer.

proposed framework are successfully detected based on the hash comparison, and that the scanner extracted the data belonging to its application of interest.

Finally, for the considered example usecase, we compare the current draw between our proposed protocol and between GATT server. The GATT server offers two services and the GATT client establishes a connection to the server, to read the data relevant to the service he is looking for.

As shown in Fig. 8, the average current draw for the GATT server for broadcasting a beacon and a connection establishment, and receiving a connection is 108.954mA and over an interval of 200 ms, where as if only the advertisement event were to transfer the same service, the average current draw would be around 50.07mA as in the proposed system. It should be noted that when the GATT connection is established, the average current drops to around 50mA over the period of connection, however spikes of current draw of 70mA are observed when a read request is received, as shown in Fig. 9. For a higher advertising interval, the current draw does not change significantly.

Despite the fact that keeping a connection running brings the system to a low power state, establishing the connection and reading the data from the server consumes energy. Reading data from the server incurs additional energy at the server itself as observed by the spikes. This energy cost is additional to the energy consumed already while scanning. On the other side, with our proposed system, reading the data incurs no cost at the side of the transmitter. The only energy cost is that of the scanner.

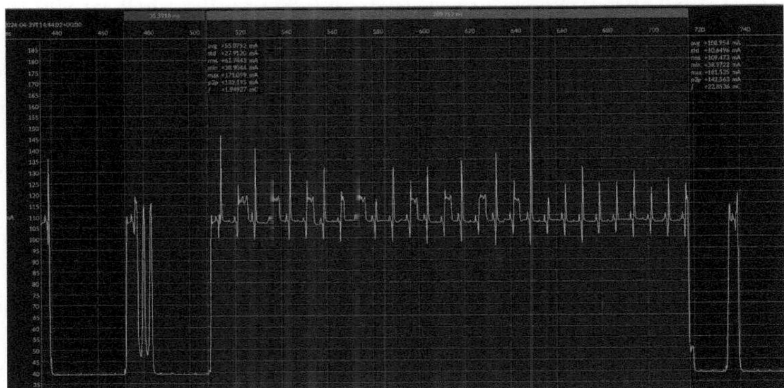

**Fig. 8.** Current Draw of GATT Server and GAP advertisement. Current scale: 35 to 185 mA.

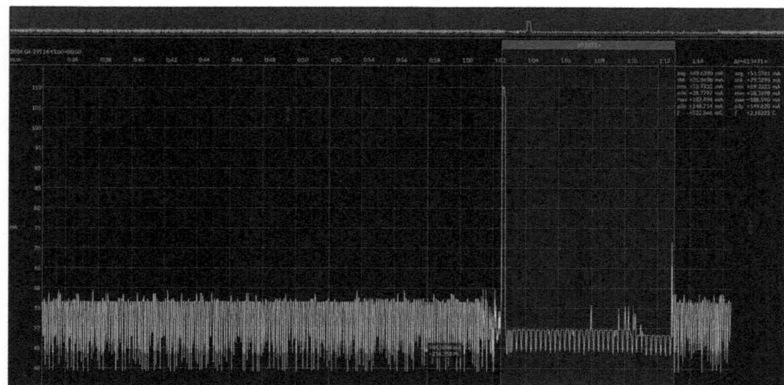

**Fig. 9.** Behavior of the GATT server during advertising, establishing connection, maintaining it, sending data and removing the connection. Current scale: 40 to 110mA.

## 5    Conclusion

To accommodate the special case of ephemeral interaction schemes, where data to be exchanged is no longer relevant after a short period of time or when the interacting devices are no longer in proximity, this paper has proposed an ephemeral dataspace built on top of BLE advertisements. This protocol allows data to be flexibly exchanged among nodes, where it is all about a service provider and a service requester. The provider writes his data to the dataspace and the requesters who deem this data relevant, are able to read it and discard what is irrelevant. The system could be analogous to a whiteboard where everyone can read and write to it. Leveraging BLE advertisements to transmit the data offers the association-less communication feature to the system.

Comparing the proposed protocol to the GATT standard of BLE, where a connection has to be established to access the specific service at the level of the application, it was shown that for this type of ephemeral interactions, the proposed protocol offers the possibility to choose a certain service and discard others, at the application level while being agnostic to MAC addressing and lower networking configurations.

To achieve this goal, a generic packet structure was proposed where any node could be a provider or a requester, four applications could be accommodated and a non-cryptographic hash function is used to identify that the packet belongs to the shared dataspace. This work opens the opportunity for several research directions. The next step of this work is to develop a middleware that provides the necessary abstractions to shield the developer from the complexities of the lower layers concerned with communication, and to allow the protocol to exchange data between different wireless communication technologies, for example WiFi Beacon Stuffing and BLE connectionless mode. Another interesting investigation would be at the level of data identification, where data would be uniquely identified while being encrypted.

# References


1. Frénot, S., Ghorbali, A., Laforest, F., Launay, P., Le Sommer, N., Reimert, D.: Spontaneous and ephemeral social networks: an event-based framework. In: Proceedings of the 9th ACM International Conference on Distributed Event-Based Systems, pp. 364–367 (2015)
2. Chaqfeh, M.A., Mohamed, N.: Challenges in middleware solutions for the internet of things. In: International Conference on Collaboration Technologies and Systems (CTS), pp. 21–26. IEEE (2012)
3. Wirtz, H., Zimmermann, T., Ceriotti, M., Wehrle, K.: CA-Fi: ubiquitous mobile wireless networking without 802.11 overhead and restrictions. In: Proceeding of IEEE International Symposium on a World of Wireless, Mobile and Multimedia Networks 2014, pp. 1–9. IEEE (2014)
4. Couturier, C., Bonnin, J.M.: Local interactions for cooperative ITS: opportunities and constraints. In: Cooperative Intelligent Transport Systems, coordinated. Wiley, p. 30 (to appear in 2024)
5. Chandra, R., Padhye, J., Ravindranath, L., Wolman, A.: Beacon-stuffing: Wi-fi without associations. In: Eighth IEEE Workshop on Mobile Computing Systems and Applications, pp. 53–57. IEEE (2007)
6. Zachariah, T., Jackson, N., Ghena, B., Dutta, P.: ReliaBLE: towards reliable communication via bluetooth low energy advertisement networks. In: Proceedings of 2022 International Conference on Embedded Wireless Systems and Networks, EWSN, vol. 22 (2022)
7. Choi, T., Chon, Y., Cha, H.: Energy-efficient WiFi scanning for localization. Pervasive Mob. Comput. **37**, 124–138 (2017)
8. Couderc, P., Maurel, Y.: Location corroboration using passive observations of IEEE 802.11 Access Points. In: 2019 16th IEEE Annual Consumer Communications & Networking Conference (CCNC), pp. 1–7. IEEE (2019)
9. Rejiba, Z., Masip-Bruin, X., Marín-Tordera, E.: Analyzing the deployment challenges of beacon stuffing as a discovery enabler in fog-to-cloud systems. In: 2018 European Conference on Networks and Communications (EuCNC), pp. 1–276. IEEE (2018)
10. Zehl, S., Karowski, N., Zubow, A., Wolisz, A.: LoWS: a complete Open Source solution for Wi-Fi beacon stuffing based Location-based Services. In: 2016 9th IFIP Wireless and Mobile Networking Conference (WMNC), pp. 25–32. IEEE (2016)
11. Gu, F., Niu, J., Jiang, L., Liu, X., Hancke, G.P.: SafePath: exploiting ubiquitous smartphones to avoid vehicle-pedestrian collision. IEEE Internet Things J. **9**(9), 6763–6777 (2021)
12. Abedi, A., Abari, O., Brecht, T.: Wi-le: can wifi replace bluetooth? In: Proceedings of the 18th ACM Workshop on Hot Topics in Networks, pp. 117–124 (2019)
13. Tosi, J., Taffoni, F., Santacatterina, M., Sannino, R., Formica, D.: Performance evaluation of bluetooth low energy: a systematic review. Sensors **17**(12), 2898 (2017)
14. Townsend, K., Cufí, C., Davidson, R., et al.: Getting started with Bluetooth low energy: tools and techniques for low-power networking. O'Reilly Media, Inc. (2014)
15. Celosia, G., Cunche, M.: Saving private addresses: an analysis of privacy issues in the bluetooth-low-energy advertising mechanism. In: Proceedings of the 16th EAI International Conference on Mobile and Ubiquitous Systems: Computing, Networking and Services, pp. 444–453 (2019)

16. Ortiz, J.C.G., Silvestre-Blanes, J., Sempere-Paya, V., Tortajada, R.P.: Feasability of Bluetooth 5.0 connectionless communications for I2V applications. In: 2020 25th IEEE International Conference on Emerging Technologies and Factory Automation (ETFA), vol. 1, pp. 1119–1122. IEEE (2020)
17. Heydon, R., Hunn, N.: Bluetooth low energy. CSR Presentation, Bluetooth SIG (2012). https://www.bluetooth.org/DocMan/handlers/DownloadDoc.ashx
18. Yang, J., Poellabauer, C., Mitra, P., Neubecker, C.: Beyond beaconing: emerging applications and challenges of BLE. Ad Hoc Netw. **97**, 102015 (2020)
19. Spachos, P., Plataniotis, K.N.: BLE beacons for indoor positioning at an interactive IoT-based smart museum. IEEE Syst. J. **14**(3), 3483–3493 (2020)
20. Wu, M., Ma, B., Liu, Z., Xiu, L., Zhang, L.: BLE-horn: a smartphone-based bluetooth low energy vehicle-to-pedestrian safety system. In: 2017 9th International Conference on Wireless Communications and Signal Processing (WCSP), pp. 1–6. IEEE (2017)
21. Aza, A., Melendi, D., Garcia, R., Paneda, X.G., Pozueco, L., Corcoba, V.: Bluetooth 5 performance analysis for inter-vehicular communications. Wirel. Netw. **28**(1), 137–159 (2022)
22. Tsai, Y.-R., Chen, Y.-C.: Opportunistic connectionless undirected information dissemination based on bluetooth low energy advertising technology on smartphones. IEEE Access **9**, 155851–155860 (2021)
23. Park, H., Lee, S., Moon, E., Ahmed, S.H., Kim, D.: Performance analysis of bicycle-to-pedestrian safety application using bluetooth low energy. In: Proceedings of the International Conference on Research in Adaptive and Convergent Systems, pp. 160–165 (2017)
24. Gautam, S., Verma, R., Kumar, S.: Dynamic data advertising and packet loss analysis using BLE legacy advertising. IEEE Trans. Mob. Comput. (2023)
25. Unold, O., et al.: IoT-based cow health monitoring system. In: International Conference on Computational Science, pp. 344–356. Springer, Cham (2020)
26. Shao, C., Nirjon, S., Frahm, J.-M.: Years-long binary image broadcast using bluetooth low energy beacons. In: 2016 International Conference on Distributed Computing in Sensor Systems (DCOSS), pp. 225–232. IEEE (2016)
27. Siva, J., Yang, J., Poellabauer, C.: Connection-less BLE performance evaluation on smartphones. Procedia Comput. Sci. **155**, 51–58 (2019)
28. Ghena, B.R.: Investigating Low Energy Wireless Networks for the Internet of Things. University of California, Berkeley (2020)
29. Eugster, P.T., Felber, P.A., Guerraoui, R., Kermarrec, A.-M.: The many faces of publish/subscribe. ACM Comput. Surv. (CSUR) **35**(2), 114–131 (2003)
30. Busi, N., Gorrieri, R.: A Survey on Structured Peer-to-Peer Systems for Resource Discovery. Università di Bologna, Dipartimento di Scienze dell'Informazione (2003)
31. Al Maruf, A., Sahin, H., Tak, B.: BLE advertisement flooding for fast content distribution in vehicular networks. IEEE Trans. Mob. Comput. **21**(4), 1554–1568 (2021)

# Adaptive Deployment of Application-Level Sensing and Data Processing Pipelines in a Wireless Network of Embedded Devices

Giorgos Polychronis[1(✉)], Manos Koutsoubelias[1], Foivos Pournaropoulos[1], Spyros Lalis[1], Lefteris Georgiadis[2], Thomas Pazios[2], Stratos Tsatsaronis[2], and Isaias Vrakidis[2]

[1] Electrical and Computer Engineering Department,
University of Thessaly, Volos, Greece
`{gpolychronis,emkouts,spournar,lalis}@uth.gr`
[2] Department of Research and Development, METIS Cybertechnology,
Athens, Greece
`{lefteris.georgiadis,thomas.pazios,stratos.tsatsaronis,`
`isaias.vrakidis}@metis.tech`

**Abstract.** Most IoT devices are nowadays equipped with computing resources so that – besides acting as plain sensor nodes – they can also perform local data processing, aggregation and filtering, before data is forwarded upstream to more powerful servers. In this paper, we present a framework for the flexible and adaptive deployment of application-level sensing and data processing pipelines in a network of such wireless sensor embedded nodes. The system administrator merely provides a high-level, declarative description of the services to be deployed. Based on this input, a helper facility performs a mapping of the specified application services to nodes so as to reduce the wireless network traffic. Furthermore, the service-to-node mapping can be adapted at runtime to handle changes in system configuration. We evaluate our approach for an indicative node topology and different application processing pipeline configurations. Our results show that such an optimized deployment can reduce wireless traffic by up to 51% vs a centralized placement, while the ability to adapt the placement of the data processing pipeline to system configuration changes can achieve up to $3.6x$ savings vs a static deployment that was optimal for a previous system configuration. Also, such adaptations can be performed fast, within a few tens of seconds.

**Keywords:** IoT · Wireless Sensor Networks · In-Network Processing · Edge Computing · Application Service Deployment · Adaptation

## 1 Introduction

The continued advances in embedded computing platforms and short-range wireless communication technologies have enabled the development of wireless

© ICST Institute for Computer Sciences, Social Informatics and Telecommunications Engineering 2026
Published by Springer Nature Switzerland AG 2026. All Rights Reserved
A. Soylu et al. (Eds.): MobiQuitous 2024, LNICST 634, pp. 187–206, 2026.
https://doi.org/10.1007/978-3-032-10554-7_10

devices, which can be flexibly deployed in different kinds of infrastructures and can support a wide range of sensing applications, giving rise to the so-called Internet of Things (IoT). While the main purpose of such devices is typically to collect measurements through a variety of sensors, most of them also have sufficient computing resources to process data locally, in the spirit of edge computing, before forwarding it to more powerful servers or the cloud.

The ability to process data directly on the sensor nodes, becomes even more important when such data is propagated over wireless links. In this case, support for in-network processing to perform aggregation and filtering is crucial to minimize the wireless traffic and increase the robustness of communication over low-bandwidth links. To achieve this, however, one must have a suitable placement of the data processing logic, depending on the location of the nodes that produce the raw data. Moreover, any static placement may turn out to be sub-optimal if the system configuration changes. Therefore, it is also important to be able to adapt the current deployment at runtime.

In this paper, we present support for such a flexible and adaptive deployment for an industrial-strength IoT system targeting the shipping domain. Our work has the following distinctive characteristics. First, it supports the deployment of entire pipelines of application-level data processing tasks on the wireless IoT nodes. Secondly, the placement of the individual data processing tasks can be adapted at runtime. Thirdly, deployment and adaptation can be performed automatically, without manual commands from the system administrator, based on high-level declarative descriptions.

The main contributions of our work are: (i) We present a complete framework for the flexible and adaptive deployment of application-level data processing pipelines in IoT systems. (ii) The desired deployment is captured in a declarative way, through suitable descriptions based on which the necessary actions are performed in an automated way. (iii) We evaluate the benefits of such flexible and adaptive deployment for various system configurations, showing that it can significantly reduce wireless traffic vs fully centralized or static deployments, with only a short downtime for the application due to the adaptation phase.

The rest of the paper is structured as follows. Section 2 provides an overview of the IoT system we target in our work, based on a concrete use-case from the shipping domain, and the available system support for the deployment of application-level sensing and data processing tasks on the wireless embedded nodes. Section 3 presents our approach for the flexible and adaptive deployment of application services in the IoT system, with minimal input from the administrator. Section 4 presents an evaluation of the proposed approach. Section 5 gives an overview of related work. Finally, Sect. 6 concludes the paper.

## 2   System Overview

This section provides an overview of the system we target in our work. We start by describing the physical system infrastructure. Then, we explain how sensing and data processing functionality is achieved by combining smaller application services into more complex data processing pipelines. Finally, we discuss the core underlying system-level support for deploying and interconnecting such application-level services in the system.

## 2.1  Embedded Nodes and Wireless Network

We target IoT systems comprising embedded devices used to collect information from a potentially wide variety of sensors. We assume that these nodes are interconnected via short-range wireless links in a multi-hop network that is deployed on the site of interest. As a concrete case, we consider a wireless sensor network installed on a vessel for monitoring and analyzing its status, including, e.g., engine operation, speed, fuel consumption, sea state, etc. We note that METIS already operates such systems in numerous vessels worldwide.

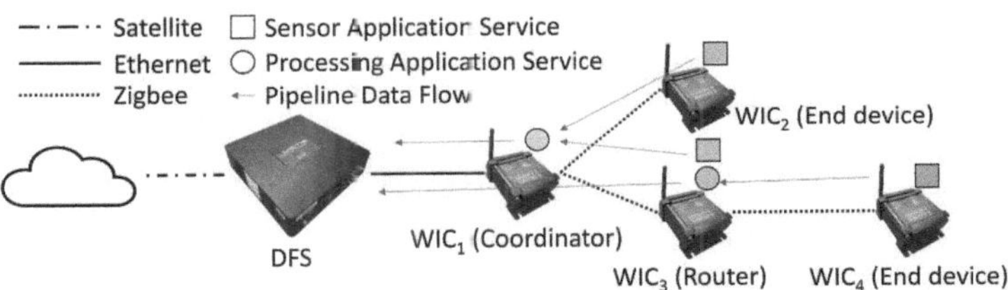


**Fig. 1.** Flexible deployment and execution of application services on the embedded nodes of the IoT system. Rectangles and ovals denote distinct sensor and processing services, respectively. The arrows between the application services indicate the data flow of the respective pipelines.

Figure 1 illustrates an indicative system setup. The basic building block of the system is the wireless intelligent collector (WIC), an industrial-strength device approved for operation on commercial vessels. It has an embedded computing board with different interfaces (such as RS-232, RS-485, CAN, etc.) through which it can be connected to and get data from a wide range of sensors.

In terms of networking, WICs feature an Ethernet and Zigbee interface. Zigbee is used to deploy and interconnect WICs at various locations on the vessel in a fast and flexible way, without the need for any wiring (apart from being costly, this also raises the issue of safety if cables need to cross isolated compartments). The ZigBee network is managed by a coordinator WIC, while the rest act as router nodes or end nodes that do not perform any data forwarding. The coordinator WIC uses its Ethernet interface to connect to the so-called data fusion server (DFS) on the ship via the ship's local area network.

The DFS is where collected data is stored and possibly pre-processed, before forwarding it to the cloud via satellite for further analysis, long-term storage and integration with the ship owner's ERP systems (not shown in the figure). Note that stable Internet connectivity over satellite may not be available all times, thus the DFS may need to store data for longer periods of time until this can be uploaded to the cloud. It is therefore important for the local IoT system to operate autonomously and as efficiently as possible even when being disconnected from the cloud.

## 2.2 Application Services and Data Processing Pipelines

To exploit the processing capacity of the embedded nodes, we depart from the paradigm of monolithic applications and adopt a distributed application approach. More specifically, the application logic is split into smaller components, referred to as services, which can be deployed on the available nodes (WICs), as shown in Fig. 1. We differentiate between two types of application services: sensor and processing services (denoted in the figure as rectangles and ovals), respectively. Sensor services access specific sensors connected to the embedded nodes to collect measurements and forward them upstream, possibly after some filtering. Processing services collect data produced by one or more sensor services or other processing services to produce derivative, more complex information.

This makes it possible to build data processing pipelines that run in a distributed way on top of the IoT infrastructure. Two indicative examples are shown in Fig. 1. One pipeline consists of the green and blue sensor services running on $WIC_2$ and $WIC_3$, and the yellow processing service running on $WIC_1$, which takes as input the values produced by those services to produce a higher-level metric. The other pipeline includes the grey sensor service on $WIC_4$ and the orange processing service running on $WIC_3$. Note that sensor services must run directly on the nodes featuring the respective sensors. In contrast, a processing service can run on any node that has sufficient computing resources to host it, including the DFS. For instance, the orange data processing service could be placed on $WIC_4$ to reduce the amount of data sent over the wireless network.

The formation of data processing pipelines is done indirectly, based on so-called quantity identifiers (QIDs) which uniquely associate data with specific sensor types or metrics produced by the processing services, and additional information that is needed to properly interpret and process the data. More specifically, instead of hard-wiring the components of a pipeline via explicit references or addresses, application services are loosely coupled through producer-consumer relationships captured via the respective QIDs.

For each application service, the information about the QIDs consumed and produced, the logic for parsing and processing data, and any special resources or parameter files required to run the service, is included in a corresponding description. In turn, such descriptions are used to drive the deployment and execution of application services on the embedded nodes.

## 2.3 Basic System-Level Support

The deployment of application services and the data exchange between them based on QIDs is supported via system-level software running on the embedded nodes (WICs) and the DFS. Figure 2 gives a high-level overview of the software architecture, which is discussed in some more detail below.

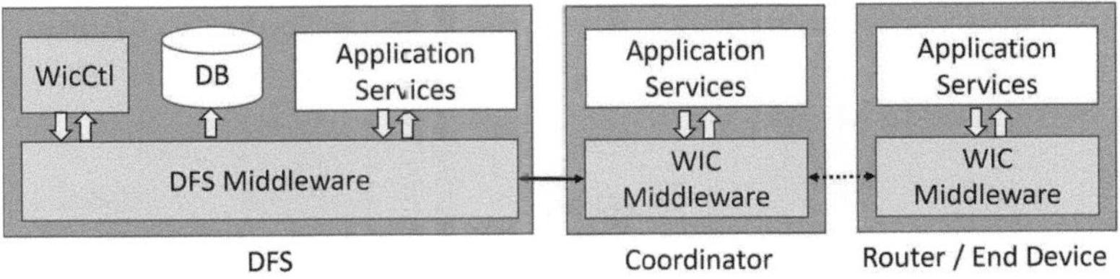


**Fig. 2.** High-level view of the system software architecture.

All interactions that occur in the system are supported via the middleware running on the DFS and the WIC nodes. The middleware implements a pub/sub transport layer, using a combination of ZeroMQ [2] and MQTT/MQTT-sn [1, 15] to support the local interaction between entities running on the same node and the remote interaction between entities running on different nodes over Ethernet/ZigBee, respectively. If a message that is produced by a local entity has remote subscribers, the pub/sub layer will transparently forward it to the respective node(s) and will deliver it to the proper subscriber. Note that the data that is generated by application services flow from the WICs toward the DFS, while requests for system-level operations travel in the reverse direction.

The configuration and control of remote nodes from the DFS is supported by the WIC control tool (WicCtl). This works in a client-server fashion, in the spirit of a simple remote shell, allowing the system administrator to send files and run commands on one or more nodes over ZigBee. Among other things, WicCtl is used to deploy application services on the nodes by sending the service descriptions. The middleware on the WICs is responsible for handling such control/configuration commands, in particular regarding the execution of application services. More concretely, when a command is issued via WicCtl to start a given application service, the middleware on the target node launches a generic service execution process that runs the application logic according to the respective description. Note that the application description must already be available on the node (it can be pre-installed on the node, or sent to it over the wireless network via a WicCtl file transfer command). Conversely, when the runtime layer receives a request to stop an application service, it terminates the corresponding execution process.

Furthermore, the middleware running on the DFS is configured to store the data that is generated from the application services in a local database. From there, it is uploaded to the cloud in an asynchronous way subject to satellite connectivity (a separate system service is used for this, not shown in the figure).

## 3    Flexible and Adaptive Application Service Deployment

### 3.1    Targeted Service Deployment

Using WicCtl, the system administrator can deploy/start or stop/remove arbitrary application services on specific nodes at any point in time. However, this procedure can become quite awkward, especially if one wishes to deploy/remove several services or some commands fail (e.g., due to network instability) and have to be repeated.

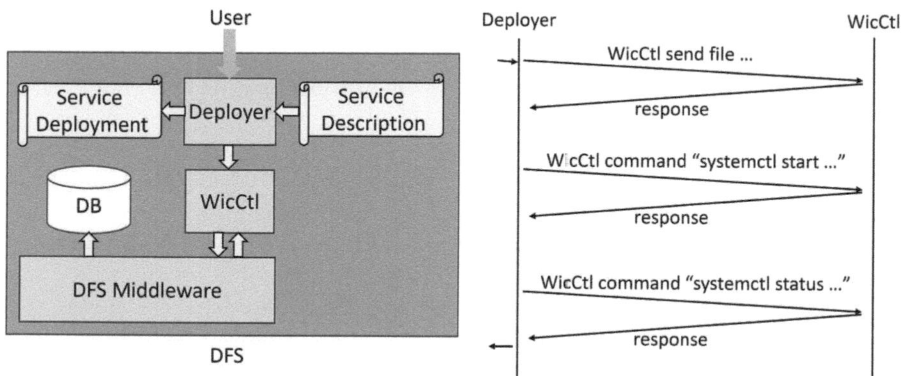


(a) Addition of the Deployer facility on top of the basic system software stack.

(b) Command sequence (via WicCtl) for application service startup.

**Fig. 3.** Service deployment via the Deployer.

To simplify system management, we introduce the Deployer facility, shown in Fig. 3a, which performs the desired application service deployment based on high-level directives/intents from the system administrator. The input is provided in the form of a json file, which contains the description of one or more deployment operations. An indicative example is given in Listing 1, for the deployment of a simple data processing pipeline consisting of a service that calculates the specific fuel oil consumption (SFOC) of the vessel based on engine power and fuel mass flow data produced by respective sensor services; note that the QIDs capturing the producer-consumer relationships are part of the respective service descriptions (not shown for brevity). Each operation consists of the desired action (deploy/start or stop/remove an application service), the service name, the names of the respective description file, and the target node. In some cases, besides the service description, additional files may need to be sent to the node, e.g., describing special input configuration or sensor data parsing parameters for the service in question. The Deployer automatically extracts such information by inspecting the service description and sends the respective files to the node together with the main service description file.

The Deployer executes the specified operations sequentially, by issuing the respective commands via WicCtl, as shown in Fig. 3b. In case the node does not respond, the Deployer retries the command a number of times (the upper bound can be set by the administrator). If the failure persists, the operation is aborted and the Deployer returns a corresponding negative result without proceeding to the next operation in the deployment description. Furthermore, the Deployer

**Listing 1** Input file for deploying an indicative data processing pipeline. SFOC (Specific Fuel Oil Consumption) service using data produced by the EnginePower and FuelMassFlow services.

```
operations: [
    {
        serviceName: "EnginePower_svc"
        serviceDescription: "EnginePower_svc_desc"
        command: "start"
        destination: "WIC-2"
    },
    {
        serviceName: "FuelMassFlow_svc"
        serviceDescription: "FuelMassFlow_svc_desc"
        command: "start"
        destination: "WIC-3"
    },
    {
        serviceName: "SFOC_svc"
        serviceDescription: "SFOC_svc_desc"
        command: "start"
        destination: "WIC-1"
    }
]
```

explicitly confirms the success of the requested operation by retrieving relevant status information from the node, again via WicCtl. Based on the outcome of the operations, the Deployer updates the current service deployment state for the entire system, i.e., the services hosted/running on each of the nodes. In our implementation, this information is kept/updated in a special file using a human-readable format so that it can be easily inspected by the system administrator (as well as by other programs, as will be discussed in the sequel).

## 3.2   Flexible Service Mapping and Deployment

Sensor services must be deployed on the nodes that feature the respective sensors. These nodes are typically installed at very specific locations on the vessel hence are well-known to the system administrator. Therefore, it is straightforward to specify them in the description passed to the Deployer, as done for the EnginePower and FuelMassFlow services in Listing 1.

However, such restrictions do not apply to data processing services, such as the SFOC service in Listing 1, which could be deployed on any node of the system, provided it has sufficient resources. In this case, rather than having the administrator specify a concrete node (as done in Listing 1), it can be desirable to leave the target host open so that it can be selected automatically. Apart from reducing the burden of the system administrator, this makes it possible to optimize service placement in an automated way. Note that this can be hard/awkward to do manually in case multiple application services are arranged in multi-stage data processing pipelines that must be deployed and run concurrently in system configurations with a large number of nodes.

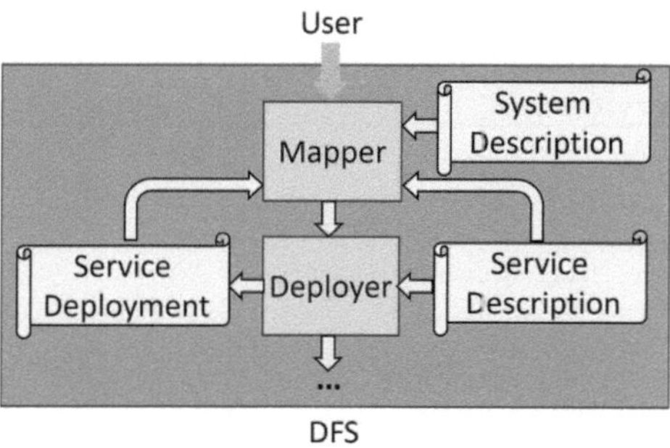



**Fig. 4.** Supporting flexible and adaptive service deployment via the Mapper.

This functionality is implemented through another facility, the Mapper, which operates on top of the Deployer as shown in Fig. 4. Like the Deployer, the Mapper takes as input from the administrator a file describing the application services to be deployed. The difference is that, in this case, the target hosts of certain services can be left unspecified. The Mapper maps such non-anchored services to the available system infrastructure by finding a suitable host for them. Depending on the configuration, it can automatically implement the corresponding deployment plan by invoking the Deployer, or simply return it as a proposal to the system administrator.

### 3.3   Service Mapping Algorithm

The Mapper inspects the system description, service descriptions and current service deployment. It uses this information to populate its internal data structures, which are subsequently used to compute the service-to-node mapping. Table 1 and Table 2 summarize the information that is kept for each node and service, respectively.

The $s.svcProd$ and $s.isProd$ fields are computed by matching the input QIDs of $s$ with the output QIDs of other services to find the respective producer-consumer relationships. Namely, $s.svcProd = \{s' : s.inQIDs \cap s'.outQIDs \neq \emptyset\}$, while $s.isProd = \exists s' : s.outQIDs \cap s'.inQIDS \neq \emptyset$. The $s.inRate$ field is computed by summing-up the output rates of all services that produce data consumed by $s$, taking into account the number of relevant QIDs. More formally, $s.inRate = \sum_{s' \in s.svcProd} s'.outRate \times |s.inQIDs \cap s'.outQIDs|$. Note that for sensor services $s.svcProd = \emptyset$ and $s.inRate = 0$. The $s.host$ field encodes the host where service $s$ is mapped. Note that some services may already have preassigned hosts (recall that the sensor services must be installed on specific nodes). Such anchored services are ignored in the mapping operation, which only tries to map services with $s.host = NULL$. At the end of the mapping operation, the $s.host$ field of each non-anchored service will be assigned a node value. Finally, for each node $n$ of the system, $n.resAvlMap$ is used in the mapping operation to capture the resources that can be used for the hosting of additional services.

**Table 1.** Node information based on the system and service descriptions.

| Notation | Description |
| --- | --- |
| $n$ | Node object |
| $n.id$ | Node identifier |
| $n.resTot$ | Total resource capacity for hosting services |
| $n.resAlloc$ | Resource capacity allocated to hosted services |
| $n.parent$ | Parent in the wireless routing structure |
| $n.hops$ | Number of wireless hops to DFS |
| $n.resAvlMap$ | Available resource capacity for service mapping |

**Table 2.** Service information based on the system and service descriptions.

| Notation | Description |
| --- | --- |
| $s$ | Service object |
| $s.id$ | Service identifier |
| $s.resReq$ | Resource capacity required to host $s$ |
| $s.outQIDs$ | QIDs for which $s$ produces data |
| $s.inQIDs$ | QIDs for which $s$ consumes data |
| $s.outRate$ | Rate at which $s$ outputs data (msgs/sec) |
| $s.svcProd$ | Services that are data producers for $s$ |
| $s.isProd$ | Whether $s$ is a data producer for other services |
| $s.inRate$ | Aggregate input data rate from all producers |
| $s.host$ | Node where $s$ is deployed or mapped |

When the Mapper receives a set of services as input, let $svcInput$, it forms the union of all services that are already deployed, let $svcDeployed$, and the set of non-anchored services in $svcInput$ which have to be mapped to a node ($s \in svcInput \land s.host = NULL$), let $svcToMap$. It then verifies that the requested mapping has no unresolved references. In other words, for each service $s \in svcToMap$ it is checked that all services acting as data producers for it are already deployed or are part of the requested mapping: $s.svcProd \subseteq svcDeployed \cup svcInput$. Then, the Mapper proceeds with the actual mapping operation to find a suitable service-to-node mapping for the non-anchored services in $svcInput$. The optimization objective, subject to resource constraints/requirements, is to minimize the data traffic over the wireless network.

The heuristic for the mapping operation is given in Algorithm 1 in the form of pseudocode. The top-level function is MAP(). As a first step, the mapping information is initialized and the services to be mapped are sorted according to their input data rates (in descending order) via function SORTBYINPUTRATE(). The rationale is to give priority to the services consuming/ingesting the largest amount of data, hoping to map them on a host as close as possible to the respective data sources. Then, the algorithm incrementally maps each service to a node (or the DFS). In each iteration, it invokes function FINDFIRSTSVCCOVERED() which scans the sorted list of unmapped services and returns the first service (with the highest aggregate input rate) whose data producers are already deployed or have been successfully mapped. Then, the best hosting option is found for this service, via function FINDMINTRAFFICCOSTHOST(), and the resource availability of that node is updated accordingly. Note that the DFS is modeled as a node with infinite resources, $n.resAvl = \infty$, so there will always

---

**Algorithm 1** Mapping non-anchored data processing services on nodes.

---

1: **function** MAP($nodes, svcDeployed, svcInput$)
2:     $svcMapped \leftarrow \{s \in svcInput : s.host \neq NULL\}$            $\triangleright$ anchored services
3:     $svcToMap \leftarrow svcInput - svcMapped$       $\triangleright$ non-anchored services, to be mapped
4:     **for each** $n \in nodes$ **do**              $\triangleright$ init service mapping info
5:         $n.resAvlMap \leftarrow n.resTot - n.resAlloc$
6:         **for each** $s \in svcMapped$ **where** $s.host = n$ **do**
7:             $n.resAvlMap \leftarrow n.resAvlMap - s.resReq$
8:         **end for**
9:     **end for**
10:    $dfs.resAvlMap \leftarrow \infty$            $\triangleright$ assume DFS has ample resources
11:    $svcToMapSorted \leftarrow$ SORTBYINPUTRATE($svcToMap$)
12:    **while** $svcToMapSorted \neq \emptyset$ **do**
13:       $s \leftarrow$ FIRSTSVCCOVERED($svcToMapSorted, svcDeployed \cup svcMapped$)
14:       $n \leftarrow$ FINDMINTRAFFICCOSTHOST($nodes + dfs, s$)
15:       $s.host \leftarrow n$
16:       $n.resAvlMap \leftarrow n.resAvlMap - s.resReq$
17:       $svcMapped \leftarrow svcMapped + s$
18:       $svcToMapSorted \leftarrow svcToMapSorted - s$
19:    **end while**
20: **end function**

21: **function** FINDFIRSTSVCCOVERED($svcToMapSorted, svcAvl$)
22:    **for each** $s \in svcToMapSorted$ **do**
23:       **if** $s.svcProd \subseteq s.svcAvl$ **then**
24:          **return** $s$
25:       **end if**
26:    **end for**
27: **end function**

28: **function** FINDMINTRAFFICCOSTHOST($nodes, s$)
29:    $minCost, maxResAvl \leftarrow \infty, 0$
30:    **for each** $n \in nodes$ **where** $n.resAvlMap \geq s.resReq$ **do**
31:       $cost \leftarrow 0$
32:       **for each** $s' \in s.svcProd$ **do**
33:          $cost \leftarrow cost +$ OUTPUTTRAFFICCOST($s, n, s'$)
34:       **end for**
35:       **if** $\neg s.isProd$ **then**            $\triangleright$ add output cost to DFS
36:          $cost \leftarrow cost +$ OUTPUTTRAFFICCOST($s, n, NULL$)
37:       **end if**
38:       $resAvl \leftarrow n.resAvlMap - s.resReq$
39:       **if** $cost < minCost \vee (cost = minCost \wedge resAvl > maxResAvl)$ **then**
40:          $host, minCost, maxResAvl \leftarrow n, cost, resAvl$
41:       **end if**
42:    **end for**
43:    **return** $host$
44: **end function**

45: **function** OUTPUTTRAFFICCOST($s, n, s'$)
46:    **if** $s' \neq NULL$ **then**       $\triangleright$ cost for data produced by $s'$ for $s$ hosted on $n$
47:       **return** $s'.outRate \times |s.inQIDs \cap s'.outQIDs| \times$ hops($n, s'.host$)
48:    **else**          $\triangleright$ cost for data produced by $s$ hosted on $n$ to reach the DFS
49:       **return** $s.outRate \times |s.outQIDs| \times$ hops($n, dfs$)
50:    **end if**
51: **end function**

be at least one available node to host a service (in other words, it is guaranteed that the mapping problem is not infeasible).

Function FINDMINTRAFFICCOSTHOST() finds the node $n$ that has sufficient available resource capacity to host the service in question while incurring the lowest traffic cost over the wireless network. The traffic cost is calculated by summing-up the data traffic caused by each service $s'$ that is a data producer for $s$. In turn, this cost is calculated via OUTPUTTRAFFICCOST() by multiplying the respective output rate $s'.outRate$ by the number of QIDs consumed by $s$ and the number of hops between node $n$ and the host of the data producer $s'.host$. Moreover, if $s$ does not serve as a data producer for another service, its own output data traffic toward the DFS is added to the total cost. This is because this data is not consumed by another service (running on a node in the wireless sensor network) but simply ends-up in the main database on the DFS.

Notably, MAP() returns a *proposed* deployment. To implement the suggested deployment, the Mapper subsequently invokes the Deployer. This can be done incrementally by invoking the Deployer separately for each service, or via a single invocation passing as input the complete deployment plan.

## 3.4   Adapting the Current Service Deployment

In addition to the initial flexible mapping and deployment of application services on the nodes of the system, it can be desirable to adapt the current deployment at runtime. For instance, new nodes may be added in the system that can be used to host application services, the topology/routing structure of the wireless network may change as a side effect of changing the placement of some nodes, or certain services may change their data rates. Such changes may render the current deployment sub-optimal.

The Mapper can be configured to support such adaptation. In this case, after performing the initial deployment, it periodically checks the system description to detect changes or it can be manually invoked by the administrator after such changes occur. If any changes are detected, the Mapper re-computes a new mapping of all processing services using the MAP() function. Then, the total data traffic over the wireless network for the current and new mapping is calculated in the spirit of function OUTPUTTRAFFICCOST() in Algorithm 1, for every producer-consumer service pair of the data processing pipelines.

Finally, the decision whether to actually implement the new mapping is taken based on an improvement threshold that is set as a configuration parameter by the system administrator. If the relative improvement of the new (planned) vs the current service deployment exceeds this threshold, the Mapper proceeds to implement the new mapping by invoking the Deployer. Alternatively, the Mapper can be configured to suggest the adapted deployment to the system administrator, who can examine the proposed mapping to decide whether to adopt the proposal. In this case, the administrator can implement the respective deployment, if desired, by invoking the Deployer manually.

## 4    Evaluation

We evaluate the quality of service-to-node mapping produced by our algorithm for different system configurations with several nodes and indicative data processing pipelines. First, we describe the test configurations and some alternative service mapping approaches which we use as benchmarks for our algorithm. Then, we present and discuss the obtained results.

### 4.1    System Configuration

We perform experiments for a system configuration with eleven embedded IoT nodes, arranged in the topology shown in Fig. 5a. We investigate the case where the system administrator wishes to deploy two data processing pipelines. Both have the same structure, shown in Fig. 5b, but rely on different sensors and corresponding sensor services.

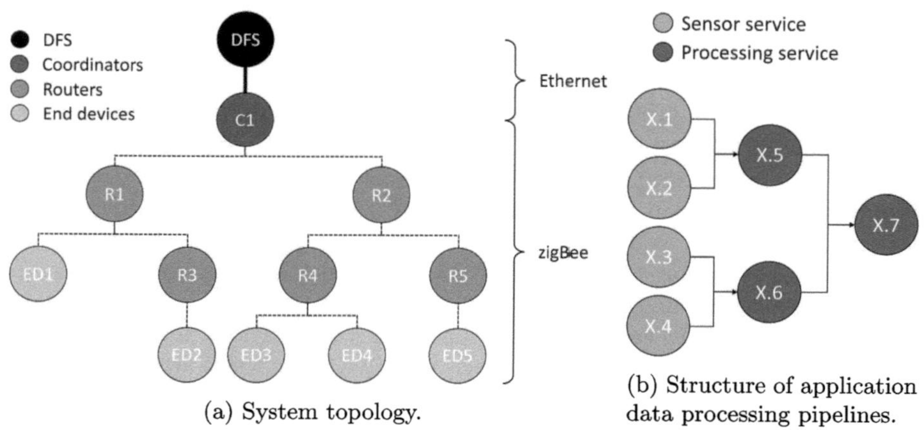


(a) System topology.

(b) Structure of application data processing pipelines.

**Fig. 5.** Experimental setup.

We explore three scenarios regarding the embedded nodes that feature the sensors that are required by the sensor services, given in Table 3. Recall that sensor services must be deployed on the nodes that have the corresponding sensors, thus the location of sensors determines the placement/mapping of the respective sensor services. Also, we investigate three scenarios for the data production rates of the application data processing pipelines, given in Table 4.

Finally, we experiment with three different service hosting capacity scenarios, assuming that each embedded node can host 2, 3 or 4 application services (including the sensor services). As an exception, the DFS can host an unlimited number of application services; for all practical purposes, it is considered to have infinite service hosting capacity.

**Table 3.** Sensor locations.

| Sensors | Nodes 1 | Nodes 2 | Nodes 3 |
| --- | --- | --- | --- |
| 1.1 | R5 | R4 | ED3 |
| 1.2 | ED1 | R3 | ED5 |
| 1.3 | ED2 | ED4 | ED4 |
| 1.4 | ED3 | ED5 | ED2 |
| 2.1 | R3 | ED2 | R4 |
| 2.2 | R4 | R5 | R3 |
| 2.3 | ED4 | ED1 | R4 |
| 2.4 | ED5 | ED3 | R5 |

**Table 4.** Data rates (msg/sec).

| Services | Rates A | Rates B | Rates C |
| --- | --- | --- | --- |
| X.1 | 1 | 0.25 | 1 |
| X.2 | 0.25 | 0.25 | 1 |
| X.3 | 1 | 1 | 1 |
| X.4 | 0.25 | 1 | 1 |
| X.5 | 1 | 0.25 | 0.25 |
| X.6 | 0.25 | 1 | 0.25 |
| X.7 | 0.25 | 0.25 | 0.25 |

## 4.2   Benchmarks

We compare our heuristic with the following benchmarks:

(1) **Proximity:** A data processing service is placed as close as possible to its sources, by selecting hosts based on their average distance with the nodes that run the respective producer services. Ties are broken by picking the host closest to DFS.

(2) **Optimal:** Data processing services are mapped optimally on the nodes by running an exhaustive search algorithm that checks all possible placement options. This always produces the best possible solution.

(3) **DFSonly:** All data processing services are simply placed on the DFS. No data processing takes place on the embedded nodes / in the wireless network. This is used as a baseline for the results obtained via the proposed approach and the rest of the benchmarks.

The metric of comparison is the aggregate data traffic generated over the wireless network when running both processing pipelines concurrently. This is calculated as explained in Sect. 3.4. on the service-to-node mapping produced by each approach. In the following, all results are presented by reporting the relative reduction of wireless message traffic vs DFSonly.

## 4.3   Benchmark Comparison

In a first set of experiments, we compare our algorithm with the above benchmarks for the deployment of the two application processing pipelines on the system, for each of the 27 combinations of the sensor placement, production rate and resource capacity scenarios. The results are shown in Fig. 6. Each row corresponds to a different sensor placement scenario in Table 3, while each column corresponds to a different data rate scenario in Table 4. The code at the top left corner of each plot indicates the specific sensor placement/production rate combination. In each case, the different resource capacity scenarios are shown along the x-axis, while the y-axis shows the reduction of wireless traffic achieved vs the DFSonly approach (higher is better). As it can be seen, the proposed heuristic outperforms the proximity heuristic in most of the scenarios and has

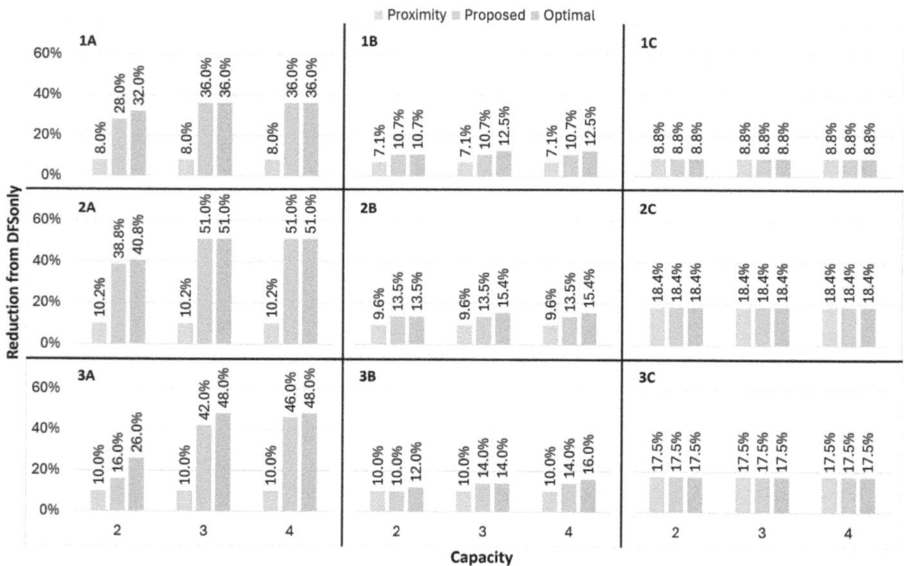

**Fig. 6.** Reduction of wireless message traffic vs DFSonly. Each row (1, 2, 3) corresponds to a different service placement scenario as per Table 3. Each column (A, B, C) corresponds to a different data production rate scenario as per Table 4.

the same performance in all the rest; it is also optimal or close to optimal for sufficient service hosting capacity of the nodes.

The difference between the two heuristics is significant in column A of Fig. 6, where there is greater asymmetry in the production rates of the services that send input data to the same processing service. This is because the proposed heuristic tends to map each processing service on nodes that are closer to the source with the higher rate, while the proximity heuristic picks hosts that are located between the sources ignoring their production rates. An important observation is that the latter does not take advantage of increased resource availability of the nodes. The reason is that if the sources of a processing service are located in different subtrees of the wireless network, the service will be placed on the root node of these subtrees, or (if this does not have sufficient resources) on a node that is even closer to the DFS or on the DFS itself. Apart from achieving only a small wireless traffic reduction vs DFSonly, this fails to exploit the hosting capacity of the subtrees. In contrast, the proposed heuristic achieves consistently better deployments as the node hosting capacity increases. More specifically, the proximity heuristic reduces the wireless traffic merely by 8% - 10.2% vs DFSonly, whereas the proposed heuristic achieves a substantial reduction of 36% - 51%, up to $5x$ more improved deployment vs the simple proximity heuristic. In fact, in scenarios 1A and 2A, the proposed heuristic manages to find the optimal solution already when the nodes have hosting capacity 3, while in scenario 3A it produces a service-to-node mapping that is very close to the optimal, with a difference of just 6% and 2% for capacity 3 and 4, respectively.

In the column B of Fig. 6 showing the results for the Rates B scenarios, data rate asymmetry exists only between services X.5 and X.6 that produce data used as input for X.7. As a consequence, even the optimal heuristic achieves a rather small reduction of wireless traffic vs DFSonly. This indicates that there is only a small improvement opportunity. Therefore, both the proposed heuristic and the proximity heuristic get stuck in local optima, failing to improve the service-to-node mapping when the capacity of the nodes increases. As an exception, in scenario 3B, the proposed heuristic produces an improved deployment plan when capacity increases from 2 to 3. Notably, the proposed heuristic again outperforms the proximity heuristic in all cases (except one where they produce equal service-to-node mappings). In cases where the service hosting capacity is 4, it achieves a traffic reduction of up to 10.7% - 14% vs DFSonly, while the proximity heuristic achieves a reduction of just 7.1% - 10%. These small improvements are justified given the small room for improvement. Nevertheless, the proposed heuristic manages to perform close to optimal in all cases where the capacity is larger than 2, producing deployment plans that are on average about $1.4x$ better than those of the Proximity heuristic.

In column C of Fig. 6, the proposed heuristic but also the simpler proximity heuristic both produce optimal deployment plans in all cases. This is because there is full symmetry in the data rates between the services that produce data for the same processing service, hence there is no benefit in placing a processing service closer to one of its sources. As a result, for all processing services whose sources are hosted on nodes in different subtrees of the routing hierarchy, the best hosting option is to host them on the node that is the root of the these subtrees. In several cases, the best hosting option for such services is the DFS itself, which has infinite hosting capacity. In turn, this relaxes the capacity pressure on all other nodes, which can host the remaining services optimally.

### 4.4   Adaptation

The system configuration may vary during the lifetime of an application processing pipeline, which may be required to run for a very long time. For example, the system administrator may wish to increase the rate at which sensor services sample the respective sensors or the rate at which processing services generate data upstream towards the DFS or other processing services. Such changes may render the current service deployment non-optimal.

In the next set of experiments, we explore the inefficiency of static service placement in case of changes in the system configuration. To this end, we use sensor placement A from Table 3 and a range of different system configurations, given in Table 5, regarding the data rates of each service in the application processing pipelines running in the system.

Figure 7 shows the results for the scenario where the system starts from configuration 1 and successively goes through configurations 2 to 8. The initial

**Table 5.** Different data rate configurations for the two application pipelines.

| Services | Data Rate Configurations (msg/s) | | | | | | | |
|---|---|---|---|---|---|---|---|---|
| | **1** | **2** | **3** | **4** | **5** | **6** | **7** | **8** |
| X.1 | 1 | 1 | 1 | 1 | 0.25 | 0.25 | 0.25 | 0.25 |
| X.2 | 0.25 | 0.25 | 0.25 | 0.25 | 1 | 1 | 1 | 1 |
| X.3 | 1 | 1 | 0.25 | 0.25 | 1 | 1 | 0.25 | 0.25 |
| X.4 | 0.25 | 0.25 | 1 | 1 | 0.25 | 0.25 | 1 | 1 |
| X.5 | 1 | 0.25 | 1 | 0.25 | 1 | 0.25 | 1 | 0.25 |
| X.6 | 0.25 | 1 | 0.25 | 1 | 0.25 | 1 | 0.25 | 1 |
| X.7 | 0.25 | 0.25 | 0.25 | 0.25 | 0.25 | 0.25 | 0.25 | 0.25 |

service deployment plan as produced by the Mapper (using Algorithm 1) is optimal for the first configuration. The red line plots the wireless traffic assuming this deployment remains static throughout all configuration changes. As a reference, the black line shows the wireless traffic for DFSonly; this remains constant because the sum of the service data rates is the same in all configurations and all processing services are placed on the DFS. One can clearly observe that the initial deployment can become significantly inefficient depending on the system configuration changes that occur in the sequel, up to 2.3x worse than DFSonly.

As mentioned in Sect. 3, the Mapper can be configured to adapt service placement by invoking the Deployer if the estimated improvement exceeds a given threshold. Figure 7 shows the resulting wireless traffic for such an adaptive deployment using three different threshold settings 0, 0.3 and 0.5 (green, blue and purple dashed line, respectively). Lower thresholds lead to more frequent adaptations of service deployment. The most aggressive threshold of 0 triggers an adaptation at every configuration change and manages to reduce wireless traffic up to 3.6x vs a static service deployment. Larger thresholds naturally lead to fewer transitions, resulting in higher wireless traffic for certain configurations. Note that the 0.5 threshold is marginally beneficial, as in some cases it does not manage to keep the load of the wireless network traffic below that of DFSonly. Overall, these results illustrate the importance of adapting the placement of application services to the current system configuration.

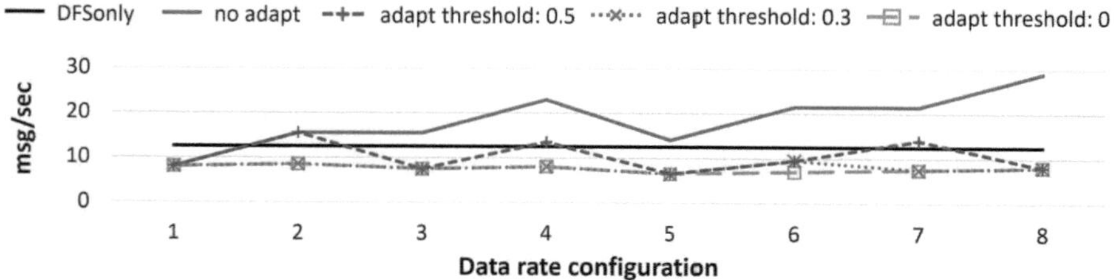


**Fig. 7.** Wireless traffic for the different data rate configurations in Table 5.

## 4.5   Adaptation Delay

Adapting the service placement can reduce the wireless network traffic, but may also lead to application downtime. Namely, the data processing pipeline will remain suspended as long one of its services is being moved to another host. In the worst case, this may extend to the full duration of the adaptation phase. Next, we discuss how to compute a rough estimate of the adaptation delay.

Let $startT(k)$ and $stopT(k)$ be the time needed for the Deployer to perform a service start and stop operation on a node that is $k$ hops away from the DFS (recall that these operations translate to a sequence of file transfer, service start/stop, and check commands to the target node). We have experimentally measured these overheads in our lab setup. For $startT$ we assume a service description file of 400 bytes, which is typical for the services running in practice.

Further, let $P.s.host$ denote the node that hosts service $s$ under placement $P$, function $hops(P, s) = hops(DFS, P.s.host)$ return the number of hops between the DFS and $P.s.host$, and $P1 \otimes P2 = \{s : P1.s.host \neq P2.s.host\}$ denote the set of services that have a different host in two placements $P1$ and $P2$. Then, the total time that is required to perform an adaptation, i.e., to make the transition from service placement $P1$ to a new placement $P2$, can be calculated as

$$adaptT(P1, P2) = \sum_{s \in P1 \otimes P2} stopT(hops(P1, s)) + startT(hops(P2, s))$$

Table 6 gives the estimated adaptation delay for the sequence of configuration changes in Fig. 7 for each of the adaptation thresholds. Recall that thresholds 0.3 and 0.5 do not lead to an adaptation in every configuration change hence in some cases the delay is 0. As it can be seen, the overhead is quite small, in the order of a few tens of seconds. This is perfectly acceptable for systems where major configuration changes are expected to be rather infrequent.

**Table 6.** Adaptation delay for the series of configuration changes in Fig. 7.

| Threshold | Adaptation Delay (sec) | | | | | | |
|---|---|---|---|---|---|---|---|
| | $1 \to 2$ | $2 \to 3$ | $3 \to 4$ | $4 \to 5$ | $5 \to 6$ | $6 \to 7$ | $7 \to 8$ |
| 0.0 | 7.5 | 14.8 | 7.5 | 21.6 | 7.5 | 14.8 | 7.5 |
| 0.3 | 7.5 | 14.8 | 7.5 | 21.6 | 0 | 7.8 | 7.5 |
| 0.5 | 0 | 7.6 | 0 | 21 | 0 | 0 | 15 |

We have verified through experiments in our testbed that the estimated delay produced with the above formula is very close to the time it takes to perform the corresponding adaptation of service placement in reality, with a small inaccuracy of about 5%. Consequently, the formula is a useful tool which can be used by the system administrator to anticipate the delay of a proposed adaptation and the potential downtime of the respective application pipelines.

## 5    Related Work

There is a significant amount of work focusing in the placement of operators (processing tasks) in the fog/edge also combined with or without the cloud. Such applications have the form of directed acyclic graphs, where the nodes are the operators and edges denote the producer-consumer relationships between operators. The authors of [14] study the problem of operator placement for the edge-cloud with the objective to optimize the end-to-end latency and deployment costs. They propose a MILP model with a technique to reduce the search space. Similarly, [13] has the objective to minimize the latency and proposes a heuristic to tackle the problem with two variants for reducing the search space to take faster placement decisions. In [10], different placement heuristics, such as a greedy approach and a local search starting from an initial greedily-built solution, are presented and evaluated for different single or multi objective goals including application response time, application availability and network usage. [7] deals with a similar problem, which is placing operators in the fog but in addition optimizes the placement periodically. There are also works addressing the placement problem with the objective to reduce the amount of data sent over the network. In [11], authors focus on the problem of service placement in the fog while trying to minimize the application delay, network usage and cloud placements. They propose a genetic algorithm to tackle the problem. Another placement problem is studied in [8] where multiple sensors generate data and the goal is to find fog nodes close to the sources to store the data sources, so that the network usage is minimized. The proposed solution considers the generation rate of each data type and picks for each placement the best node given various centrality indexes. Our work also focuses in a placement problem where application-level data processing pipelines are deployed inside a WSN so that the wireless traffic is minimized. Similarly to [13] and [8] we propose a solution that greedily picks the most suitable node for the placement of each processing task, but this is tailored for our particular system/application model and objective.

Another topic well studied in the literature is data aggregation in sensor networks [3]. Aggregators are placed inside the network with most common objectives to reduce the traffic and extend the network's lifetime. A data aggregation approach is studied in [12] for networks arranged in clusters. Authors in [18] consider networks where sensors generate different type of data, while data of the same type can be aggregated. They propose a protocol to route the data which also considers the aggregation of the data. These works aim to extend the lifetime of the network. In [17], the objective is to improve the service latency by reducing the amount of data transferred by applying in-network processing. [6] proposes an in-network outlier detection. Another in-network approach is investigated in [9] with objective to increase transmission opportunities. Our work also supports processing data inside the network to reduce the messages sent over the wireless network, via application-level services that can be dynamically deployed on and moved between nodes.

There is a wide range of work on the dynamic deployment of code in WSNs and IoT devices. In [4] IoT devices execute scripts in a lightweight container on top of RIOT OS. Sensorware [5] provides a runtime environment for flexibly deploying and executing application-level scripts in WSNs. The work in [19] discusses the dynamic deployment of IoT applications composed of tasks while some of them are user-defined. In [16] the application has the form of agents that are dynamically instantiated in a WSN to support in-network processing. In these works, the application logic is given in the form of scripts, while in our case the application services are captured in the form of purely declarative descriptions that are parsed on the node in order to configure a generic service execution engine so that it performs the required sensing and processing operations. Notably, the so-called generic agents in [16] are similar to the data processing services in our work, allowing such application logic to change its location in the WSN so as to reduce wireless network traffic.

## 6    Conclusion

We have presented work on how to automatically deploy and adapt the placement of application-level data processing pipelines in a wireless network of embedded sensor devices so as to minimize the data traffic over the wireless network. Our evaluation shows that optimized deployment can reduce radically wireless traffic up to 51% vs a simple centralized placement at the root of the wireless network, and is close to optimal in most cases. Also, adapting the deployment to system configuration changes can reduce the wireless traffic up to $3.6x$ vs a previously optimal placement that remains static during execution, while such adaptations can be performed fast, within just a few tens of seconds.

Our software architecture is modular, allowing extensions to be introduced in a flexible way. For instance, the service-to-node mapping logic could be changed to balance the services running on the nodes and the amount of data transmitted by each node to achieve an even resource utilization and energy consumption. Another possible optimization objective is to minimize contention on the wireless channel or to reduce the end-to-end latency of data production.

**Acknowledgments.** This work has been co-financed by the European Union-NextGenerationEU and Greek national funds through the Greece 2.0 National Recovery and Resilience Plan, under the call RESEARCH-CREATE-INNOVATE, project VEPIT – Vessel Energy Profiling based on IoT (code: TAEDK-06165).

## References

1. MQTT. https://mqtt.org/
2. ZeroMQ. https://zeromq.org/
3. Abbasian Dehkordi, S., Farajzadeh, K., Rezazadeh, J., Farahbakhsh, R., Sandrasegaran, K., Abbasian Dehkordi, M.: A survey on data aggregation techniques in IoT sensor networks. Wirel. Netw. **26**(2), 1243–1263 (2019). https://doi.org/10.1007/s11276-019-02142-z

4. Baccelli, E., Doerr, J., Kikuchi, S., Padilla, F.A., Schleiser, K., Thomas, I.: Scripting over-the-air: towards containers on low-end devices in the internet of things. In: International Conference on Pervasive Computing and Communications Workshops (PerCom Workshops), pp. 504–507 (2018)

5. Boulis, A., Han, C.C., Shea, R., Srivastava, M.B.: Sensorware: programming sensor networks beyond code update and querying. In: Pervasive and Mobile Computing, vol. 3, pp. 386–412. Elsevier (2007)

6. Branch, J.W., Giannella, C., Szymanski, B., Wolff, R., Kargupta, H.: In-network outlier detection in wireless sensor networks. Knowl. Inf. Syst. **34**, 23–54 (2013)

7. Hiessl, T., Karagiannis, V., Hochreiner, C., Schulte, S., Nardelli, M.: Optimal placement of stream processing operators in the fog. In: 3rd International Conference on Fog and Edge Computing (ICFEC), pp. 1–10 (2019)

8. Lera, I., Guerrero, C., Juiz, C.: Comparing centrality indices for network usage optimization of data placement policies in fog devices. In: 3rd International Conference on Fog and Mobile Edge Computing (FMEC), pp. 115–122 (2018)

9. Lin, S.C., Chen, K.C.: Improving spectrum efficiency via in-network computations in cognitive radio sensor networks. IEEE Trans. Wirel. Commun. **13**, 1222–1234 (2014)

10. Nardelli, M., Cardellini, V., Grassi, V., Presti, F.L.: Efficient operator placement for distributed data stream processing applications. IEEE Trans. Parallel Distrib. Syst. **30**, 1753–1767 (2019)

11. Sarrafzade, N., Entezari-Maleki, R., Sousa, L.: A genetic-based approach for service placement in fog computing. J. Supercomput. **78**, 10854–10875 (2022)

12. Shobana, M., Sabitha, R., Karthik, S.: Cluster-based systematic data aggregation model (CSDAM) for real-time data processing in large-scale WSN. Wirel. Pers. Commun. **117**, 2865–2883 (2021)

13. da Silva Veith, A., de Assuncao, M.D., Lefevre, L.: Latency-aware strategies for deploying data stream processing applications on large cloud-edge infrastructure. IEEE Trans. Cloud Comput. (2021)

14. de Souza, F.R., da Silva Veith, A., Dias de Assurção, M., Caron, E.: Scalable joint optimization of placement and parallelism of data stream processing applications on cloud-edge infrastructure. In: 18th International Conference on Service-Oriented Computing, pp. 149–164 (2020)

15. Stanford-Clark, A., Truong, H.L.: MQTT for sensor networks (MQTT-SN) protocol specification. In: International Business Machines (IBM) Corporation version, vol. 1, pp. 1–28 (2013)

16. Tziritas, N., et al.: Middleware mechanisms for agent mobility in wireless sensor and actuator networks. In: 3rd ICST Conference on Sensor Systems and Software (S-Cube), pp. 30–44 (2012)

17. Wu, H., He, J., Tömösközi, M., Xiang, Z., Fitzek, F.H.: In-network processing for low-latency industrial anomaly detection in softwarized networks. In: Global Communications Conference (GLOBECOM), pp. 01–07 (2021)

18. Yun, W.K., Yoo, S.J.: Q-learning-based data-aggregation-aware energy-efficient routing protocol for wireless sensor networks. IEEE Access **9**, 10737–10750 (2021)

19. Zhang, J., Ma, M., He, W., Wang, P.: On-demand deployment for IoT applications. J. Syst. Archit. **111**, 101794 (2020)

# Exploiting NLOS Links for Energy-Efficient Opportunistic Routing in IoV


Yiming Zhou[1], Xing Tang[1,2(✉)], Pengyu Shi[1], Jing Wang[3], Chunlin Li[1],
Lincheng Jiang[4], Zhen Tan[5], and Fengcai Qiao[4]

[1] School of Computer Science and Artificial Intelligence, Wuhan University of Technology,
Wuhan, China
tangxing@whut.edu.cn
[2] Chongqing Research Institute, Wuhan University of Technology, Chongqing, China
[3] School of Computer Science, Hubei University of Technology, Wuhan, China
[4] College of Advanced Interdisciplinary Studies, National University of Defense Technology,
Changsha, China
[5] Department of Systems Engineering, National University of Defense Technology, Changsha,
China



**Abstract.** As the electric vehicle (EV) market expands, the scarcity of charging stations often leads to extended wait times and difficulties in accessing available charging points. In the context of Internet of Vehicles (IoV) routing, where energy efficiency is paramount, we explore the potential of Non-Line of Sight (NLOS) links in opportunistic routing to enhance communication and energy savings. Specifically, despite the attenuation caused by viaduct surfaces on NLOS links, selecting NLOS links can enhance energy efficiency when options within Line of Sight (LOS) are limited or distant. Traditional energy-efficient routing approaches in IoV typically overlook the utility of NLOS links. This paper introduces a mixed-link algorithm that optimizes throughput and energy consumption by incorporating NLOS links. We develop a hybrid link model that includes both LOS and NLOS transmissions and formulate a problem that is subsequently restructured into a solvable format. Our proposed Hybrid Link Energy-Optimized Routing (HEOR) algorithm leverages the Dinkelbach method to enhance routing efficiency. Simulation results indicate that HEOR surpasses existing energy-efficiency schemes in throughput, packet delivery ratio, and energy efficiency by effectively utilizing NLOS links.

**Keywords:** Opportunistic routing · Internet of Vehicle(IoV) · Dinkelbach
Algorithm · Link connectivity model


## 1 Introduction

As the electric vehicle (EV) market expands, the scarcity of charging stations often leads to extended wait times and difficulties in accessing available charging points. In the context of Internet of Vehicles (IoV) routing, where energy efficiency is paramount,

---

Y. Zhou and P. Shi—Co-first authors.


ⓒ ICST Institute for Computer Sciences, Social Informatics and Telecommunications Engineering 2026
Published by Springer Nature Switzerland AG 2026. All Rights Reserved
A. Soylu et al. (Eds.): MobiQuitous 2024, LNICST 634, pp. 207–221, 2026.
https://doi.org/10.1007/978-3-032-10554-7_11

we explore the potential of the Internet of Vehicles (IoV), which has garnered significant attention for its diverse traffic control and passenger entertainment applications. Nevertheless, the high mobility of vehicles in IoV leads to frequent link interruptions and fluctuations in network topology. Consequently, routing design in such networks is a challenging task.

Energy efficiency is one of the significant concerns in IoV routing design. Recently, the sales of EVs have experienced rapid growth. However, because of the insufficient availability of charging facilities, EVs have to wait a long time to recharge or cannot find an available charging pile. In China, this situation is even worse when extreme weather conditions or holiday traffic congestion occur. In IoV networks equipped with On-Board Units (OBU), EVs consume additional energy for data transmissions. Thus, designing an energy-efficient routing scheme for reaching the green communication target is vital in IoV networks.

Different from traditional energy-efficient routing solutions [1–3] designed for IoV, some studies [4,5] have explored how opportunistic routing (OR) can reduce network overhead by efficiently managing message dissemination and node configuration in vehicular networks. Furthermore, recent studies [6,7] have claimed that OR can reduce the number of transmissions in unreliable and lossy networks and thus can save energy. As for energy optimization in OR within 3D scenarios, the focus has primarily been on the direction of unmanned aerial vehicles [8]. In OR, the source node selects multiple relay nodes and assigns priorities to them. Due to the broadcast transmission nature of the wireless radio in IoV, only one broadcast packet from the source is sufficient to reach all relay nodes. However, existing OR schemes lack utilizing non-line-of-sight (NLOS) links for data transmissions in IoV.

A typical mixed LOS/NLOS transmission scenario is IoV networks considering city viaduct structures, which can alleviate traffic congestion in large cities. This scenario involves vehicles traveling along both upper-level lane and the lower-level lane. Besides, the upper-level lane is above the viaduct, while the lower-level lane is below it. This creates intra-level links and inter-level links. Clearly, intra-level links are LOS links, while inter-level links are NLOS links. Although intra-level links provide better communication quality, inter-level links may bring more communication opportunities. However, whether exploiting NLOS links can improve OR performance needs to be clarified.

To the best of our knowledge, only a few works aim to provide energy-efficiency OR for IoV, and no prior methods focus on exploiting NLOS links for it. Our contributions are as follows: 1) We investigate the potential of NLOS links to enhance communication opportunities for OR in viaduct structure scenarios. 2) We devise an approach to transform the NP-hard problem of multi-hop OR in IoV into a solvable form. 3) We propose a novel routing scheme to maximize energy efficiency specifically tailored for viaduct structure scenarios in IoV.

## 2 System Model and Problem Statement

### 2.1 System Model

This section describes the vehicle-to-vehicle (V2V) scenario, the link model, and the energy consumption model.

We consider an IoV network consisting of a set $V$ of $N$ vehicles, labeled $i = \{1, 2, ..., N\}$. They are driving along a straight road with two levels. On the upper level, vehicles are running on a long expressway viaduct, which goes through the high-traffic sections of a central city. On the other hand, on the lower level, they are traveling below the viaduct and on a straight road segment without intersections. To facilitate the performance analysis of NLOS links, we assume all vehicles move in the same direction. The speeds and distributions of all vehicles follow a *Gaussian distribution*, which has been widely used in many related studies [9, 10].

In our previous work [11, 12], the packet delivery probability $p_{ij}$ of intra-level links and inter-level links is expressed by (1) and (2), respectively.

$$p_{ij}^{intra} = exp\left(-\frac{3d_{ij}}{R_{intra}}\right)\left(1 + 3\left(\frac{d_{ij}}{R_{intra}}\right)^2 + \frac{9}{2}\left(\frac{d_{ij}}{R_{intra}}\right)^4\right) \tag{1}$$

$$p_{ij}^{inter} = \exp\left(-\left(\frac{d_{ij}}{R_{inter}}\right)^4\right) \tag{2}$$

We adopt the energy consumption model proposed in [13], which uses free-space channels. The energy required to transmit $k$ bits of data in a packet to a sensor located $d_{ij}$ meters away is calculated as follows:

$$c_{ij} = k * E_{elec} + k * \varepsilon_{fs}d_{ij}^2 \tag{3}$$

where $E_{elec}$ is the energy consumption required to manipulate each unit, and $\varepsilon_{fs}$ is a transmission parameter for the free-space model.

### 2.2   Contribution Probability Model

We define the vehicle topology graph $G = (\mathbb{V}, \mathbb{E}, \mathbb{S})$. $\mathbb{V} = [v_1', v_2', \ldots, v_N'] \in \mathbb{R}^{1 \times N}$ is sorted by the horizontal distance to the destination node. So $v_1'$ is the source vehicle, and $v_N'$ is the destination vehicle. $\mathbb{E}$ and $\mathbb{S}$ are $N \times N$ matrices. $e_{ij} \in \mathbb{E}$ denotes whether the link is cross-layer, if the link is a cross-layer link, set it to 1, otherwise, set it to 0. Similarly, $s_{ij} \in \mathbb{S}$ denotes whether the link is available; if the link is available, set it to 1; otherwise, set it to 0. Thus we can obtain $s_{ij}$ as follows:

$$s_{ij} = \begin{cases} 1, & d_{ij} \leq R_{intra}, e_{ij} = 0, \\ 1, & d_{ij} \leq R_{inter}, e_{ij} = 1, \\ 0, & d_{ij} > R_{intra}, e_{ij} = 0, \\ 0, & d_{ij} > R_{inter}, e_{ij} = 1. \end{cases} \tag{4}$$

By substituting (1) and (2), we can derive $p_{ij} \in \mathbb{P}$ by:

$$p_{ij} = \begin{cases} \exp\left(-\frac{3d_{ij}}{R_{intra}}\right) \sum\limits_{\gamma=1}^{m=3} \frac{(m(\frac{d_{ij}}{R_{intra}})^2)^{\gamma-1}}{(\gamma-1)!}, & s_{ij} = 1, e_{ij} = 0 \\ \exp\left(-\left(\frac{d_{ij}}{R_{inter}}\right)^4\right), & s_{ij} = 1, e_{ij} = 1 \\ 0, & s_{ij} = 0 \end{cases} \tag{5}$$

In OR, the sender selects from multiple candidates, any of whom may receive and forward the packet. Because only one node can transmit at a time, the highest priority nodes forward packets first. If the highest-priority nodes fail to forward the packet, the lower-priority nodes can take over and continue forwarding the packet. Thus, when the transmission vehicle is $v'_i$, the probability of $v'_j$ $(i < j \leq N)$ being selected as a forwarding vehicle $p^f_{ij}$ is calculated as follows:

$$p^f_{ij} = p_{ij} \prod_{k=i+1}^{j-1} (1 - p_{ik}) \tag{6}$$

$\mathbb{P}$ is a symmetric matrix. For ease of computation, we convert it into the following upper triangular matrix form using (6). Thus, we can get the new probability matrix $\mathbb{P}^f$ as follows:

$$\mathbb{P}^f = \begin{bmatrix} 0 & p^f_{12} & \cdots & p^f_{1N} \\ 0 & 0 & \cdots & p^f_{2N} \\ \vdots & & & \\ 0 & 0 & \cdots & 0 \end{bmatrix} \tag{7}$$

## 3    Problem Formulation and Algorithm Framework

### 3.1    Problem Formulation

We define $\pi_i$ as the forwarding set of $v'_i$, and its size is $k_i$. Since the vehicles are sorted according to their horizontal distance from the destination vehicle, the nonzero elements in the same row are contiguous. This indicates that the $i$th row of $\mathbb{P}^f$ is $[0 \cdots 0 \, p_{i(i+1)} \cdots p_{i(i+k_i)} \, 0 \cdots 0]$.

The advancement of each packet is a crucial optimization objective in OR [14, 15]. By combining our previously proposed contribution probability model, we define a new expected contribution advancement model (ECA). We assume the size of the vehicle's $v'_i$ forwarding set is $k_i$. We can derive the ECA as follows:

$$ECA(\pi_i) = \sum_{j=1}^{k_i} p^f_{i(i+j)} \cdot d_{i(i+j)} \tag{8}$$

Similarly, we can derive the expected energy consumption of the vehicle $v'_i$ as follows:

$$EC(\pi_i) = \sum_{j=1}^{k_i} p^f_{i(i+j)} \cdot c_{i(i+j)} \tag{9}$$

With the packet delivery ratio taken into account, we consider both distance and energy together to analyze the energy-efficient transmission problem in IoV networks, which we formulate as the following optimization problem:

$$\mathcal{P}1 : \max \quad \eta_{EE} = \frac{ECA_{tot}(\boldsymbol{\Omega})}{EC_{tot}(\boldsymbol{\Omega})}$$

$$\text{s.t.} \quad C1 : 0 \leq p_{ij} < 1, \quad \forall i, j,$$

$$C2 : \sum_{j=1}^{k_i} p^f_{i(i-j)}\beta_{i(i+j)} \leq 1, \quad \forall i, j,$$

$$C3 : \sum_{j=1}^{k_i} p^f_{i(i-j)}E_{i(i+j)}\beta_{i(i+j)} \leq E_h, \quad \forall i, j,$$

$$C4 : \beta_{ij} \in \{0, 1\}, \quad \forall i, j \tag{10}$$

where $\beta_{ij} \in \Omega$ is a binary variable (0 or 1) for selecting neighboring vehicles. $\Omega$ is an $N \times N$ matrix representing the forwarding set selection of all vehicles. $E_h$ is the transmission constraint for each vehicle.

In (10), C1 is the packet delivery ratio constraint on each link. C2 represents the expected packet delivery ratio constraints on all neighboring vehicles to the temporary source vehicle. C3 denotes the expected energy constraints among neighboring vehicles at the temporary-source vehicle. We depict the expected energy by the link probability and the binary selection variable because optimizing the expected value is our goal.

Since each node has multiple candidates at each hop in opportunistic routing, the matrix representation of all available paths exhibits exponential growth. In other words, when the size of the forwarding set grows to $n$, the number of all possible subsets is $C_n^1 + \cdots + C_n^n = 2^n - 1$, which exhibits $O(2^n)$ complexity. This complexity is similar to that of classical NP-complete problems, indicating that our problem is also NP-complete. This means that in practical applications, as the number of nodes increases, the computational complexity will grow exponentially, potentially leading to computational infeasibility.

### 3.2   Problem Transformation

The classical Dinkelbach algorithm, designed to solve linear programming problems, cannot be directly used to tackle (10) since its exponential input complexity.

In opportunistic routing, there are various metrics to filter nodes, such as the reliability between links, reputation, and distance, among others [16–18]. In order to solve the problem, we transform it from link selection to path selection. We apply a new metric, referred to as the Communication Efficiency Cost Metric (CECM), to exclude neighboring vehicles that exceed the threshold. The attributes in CECM are the average of the three probability values expressed in Eq. (12). The values are obtained by transmission distance, the expected transmission count, and the required energy.

We only consider vehicles within the transmission range. After the sender vehicle obtains the distances between all the neighboring vehicles and the destination vehicle, it normalizes them between $[0 - 1]$ by Eq. (11). The aim is to set a higher priority on those vehicles that are closer to the destination.

$$\tilde{d_{jd}} = \frac{d_{jd}}{\sum_{j'=1}^{k_i} d_{(i+j')d}} \tag{11}$$

The expected transmission count (ETX) metric is an important indicator for measuring link quality in OR. According to [19], it is given by $ETX_{s'j} = 1/p^f_{s'j}$. The link with lower energy consumption will have a higher priority. The sender vehicle $v'_i$ normalizes $ETX_{ij}$ and $c_{ij}$ in the same way as $d_{jd}$.

Then, the sender vehicle computes the CECM for each neighboring vehicle by Eq. (12):

$$CECM_{ij} = (\tilde{d_{jd}} + \tilde{ETX}_{ij} + \tilde{c_{ij}})/3$$
$$= \frac{d_{jd}}{\sum_{j'=1}^{k_i} d_{(i+j')d}} + \frac{ETX_{ij}}{\sum_{j'=1}^{k_i} ETX_{i(i+j')}} + \frac{c_{ij}}{\sum_{j'=1}^{k_i} c_{i(i+j')}} \tag{12}$$

The higher link quality corresponds to a smaller CECM. The sender vehicle computes the CECM for each neighbor vehicle. Subsequently, it will exclude the neighboring vehicles that do not exceed a specific threshold value, denoted as $CECM_h$. Then, we can obtain all the paths $\psi$ that meet the specified metric.

We denote all the paths that meet the specified criteria as $\Psi = \{\psi_1, \psi_2, ..., \psi_M\}$. $\psi_m \in \Psi$ is a $1 \times N$ binary vector. It represents all the vehicles used for forwarding in the $m$th path. If vehicle $v'_i$ is chosen in path $\psi_m$, we set $\lambda_i \in \psi_m$ to 1. The size of $\Psi$ is $M$. For ease of calculation in the formulas for ECA and EC, we assume $\Phi_m = \{\phi_1, \phi_2, ..., \phi_{k_m}\}$ represents the set of indices in $\psi_m$ where all the values are 1. Thus, the ECA and energy consumption of each path can be calculated by Eq. (13) and Eq. (14).

$$ECA(\psi_m) = \sum_{i=1}^{k_m-1} d_{\phi_{i,i+1}} \prod_{j=1}^{i} p^f_{\phi_{j,j+1}} \tag{13}$$

$$EC(\psi_m) = \sum_{i=1}^{k_m-1} c_{\phi_{i,i+1}} \prod_{j=1}^{i} p^f_{\phi_{j,j+1}} \tag{14}$$

where $\phi_{i,i+1}$ denotes two elements $\phi_i$ and $\phi_{i+1}$.

Thus, we can derive $ECA_{tot}$ and $EC_{tot}$ from the path selection vector $\Omega'$:

$$ECA_{tot}(\Omega') = ECA^t * \Omega'$$
$$= \sum_{m=1}^{M} \beta_m \sum_{i=1}^{k_m-1} d_{\phi_{i,i+1}} \prod_{j=1}^{i} p^f_{\phi_{j,j+1}} \tag{15}$$

$$EC_{tot}(\Omega') = EC_0 + EC^t * \Omega'$$
$$= EC_0 + \sum_{m=1}^{M} \beta_m \sum_{i=1}^{k_m-1} c_{\phi_{i,i+1}} \prod_{j=1}^{i} p^f_{\phi_{j,j+1}} \tag{16}$$

where $EC_0$ denotes the initial energy consumption of the network. $ECA^t$ and $EC^t$ represent $1 \times N$ vectors of the ECA and EC values of all paths, respectively.

The path selection problem is given as follows:

$$\mathcal{P}2 : \max_{\Omega'} \quad \eta_{\text{EE}} = \frac{ECA_{\text{tot}}(\Omega')}{EC_{\text{tot}}(\Omega')} = \frac{ECA^t * \Omega'}{EC_0 + EC^t * \Omega'}$$

$$\text{s.t.} \quad C1 : 0 \leq p_{ij} < 1, \quad \forall i, j,$$
$$C2 : \beta_m EC(\psi_m) \leq (k_m - 1)E_c, \quad \forall m,$$
$$C3 : \beta_m \in \{0, 1\}, \quad \forall m. \tag{17}$$

where $E_c$ is the energy constraint on each link.

**Lemma 1.** *Let $G(\Omega') = \eta_{EE}$, and let $C$ be a convex set such that $EC_{tot} \neq 0$ over $C$. Then $G(\Omega)$ is exhibits both pseudoconvexity and pseudoconcavity on $C$.*

*Proof.* (17) represents a linear fractional function. According to [20], $G(\Omega')$ is both pseudoconvex and pseudoconcave over C.

**Lemma 2.** *$G(\Omega')$ is both strictly pseudoconcave and strictly pseudoconvex within $C$.*

*Proof.* As established by Lemma 1, which indicates that $G(\Omega')$ is both pseudoconvex and pseudoconcave, and as stated in [20], we conclude that $G(\Omega')$ is strictly quasiconcave and strictly quasiconvex on $C$.

**Lemma 3.** *For $G(\Omega')$ over $C$, every local optimum is also its global solution.*

*Proof.* According to [20], Lemma 2 and the characteristics of strictly quasiconvex and strictly quasiconcave functions give rise to Lemma 3.

From Lemma 3, it follows that solving the linear fractional programming (LFP) problem $\mathcal{P}2$ using any nonlinear programming (NLP) solver will yield the global maximum of $\mathcal{P}2$.

**Theorem 1.** *(Optimality). The optimal solution $\Omega^*$ can be obtained if and only if*

$$F(\Omega') = \max\{ECA_{tot}(\Omega') - \eta_{EE}^* EC_{tot}(\Omega')\} = 0 \tag{18}$$

*Proof.* To prove the necessity, let $\Omega^* \in C$ be an optimal solution of (18), then we have:

$$\eta_{EE}^* = \frac{ECA_{tot}(\Omega^*)}{EC_{tot}(\Omega^*)} \tag{19}$$

thus we have:

$$ECA_{tot}(\Omega^*) - \eta_{EE}^* EC_{tot}(\Omega^*) = ECA_{tot}(\Omega^*) - \frac{ECA_{tot}(\Omega^*)}{EC_{tot}(\Omega^*)} \cdot EC_{tot}(\Omega^*)$$
$$= ECA_{tot}(\Omega^*) - ECA_{tot}(\Omega^*) = 0 \tag{20}$$

Therefore, we have shown the necessity of the condition.

214     Y. Zhou et al.

To show the sufficiency, let $\Omega'$ be an optimal solution of (18), then we have:

$$\frac{ECA(\Omega')}{EC(\Omega')} > \frac{ECA(\Omega^*)}{EC(\Omega^*)} = \eta^* \tag{21}$$

Thus, we can deduce that:

$$\frac{ECA(\Omega')}{EC(\Omega')} - \eta^* > \frac{ECA(\Omega^*)}{EC(\Omega^*)} - \eta^* = 0 \tag{22}$$

Since $EC_{tot}(\Omega') > 0$, we have:

$$ECA_{tot}(\Omega') - \eta_{EE}^* EC_{tot}(\Omega') > ECA_{tot}(\Omega^*) - \eta_{EE}^* EC_{tot}(\Omega^*). \tag{23}$$

Therefore, the assumption is not valid, $\eta_{EE}^*$ is the maximum of (18), and $\Omega^*$ is the optimal solution of (17).

**Theorem 2.** *(Convergence). The Dinkelbach algorithm converges superlinearly for problem (17).*

*Proof.* For $ECA(\Omega') - \eta' EC(\Omega') \geq ECA(\Omega'') - \eta' EC(\Omega'')$. Since $EC(\Omega') > 0$, we have:

$$\frac{ECA(\Omega')}{EC(\Omega')} - \eta' \geq \frac{ECA(\Omega'')}{EC(\Omega')} - \eta' \frac{EC(\Omega'')}{EC(\Omega')} \tag{24}$$

we have:

$$
\begin{aligned}
Q(&\Omega'') - Q(\Omega') \\
&= \frac{ECA(\Omega'')}{EC(\Omega'')} - \frac{ECA(\Omega')}{EC(\Omega')} \\
&\leq \frac{ECA(\Omega'')}{EC(\Omega'')} - \left(\frac{ECA(\Omega'')}{EC(\Omega')} - \eta' \frac{EC(\Omega'')}{EC(\Omega')} + \eta'\right) \\
&= -ECA(\Omega'')\left(\frac{1}{EC(\Omega')} - \frac{1}{EC(\Omega'')}\right) + \eta' EC(\Omega'')\left(\frac{1}{EC(\Omega')} - \frac{1}{EC(\Omega'')}\right) \\
&= (-ECA(\Omega'') + \eta' EC(\Omega''))\left(\frac{1}{EC(\Omega')} - \frac{1}{EC(\Omega'')}\right) \\
&= (-F(\Omega'') + (\eta' - \eta'')EC(\Omega''))\left(\frac{1}{EC(\Omega')} - \frac{1}{EC(\Omega'')}\right)
\end{aligned}
\tag{25}
$$

for $\Omega^*$ and $\eta^*$, we have:

$$\eta^* - Q(\Omega') \leq (\eta^* - \eta')\left(1 - \frac{EC(\Omega^*)}{EC(\Omega')}\right) \tag{26}$$

and

$$F(\Omega') = ECA(\Omega') - \eta' EC(\Omega') > 0 = ECA(\Omega') - \eta'' EC(\Omega') \tag{27}$$

where

$$\eta'' = \frac{ECA(\Omega')}{EC(\Omega')} \tag{28}$$

thus, we can derive that:

$$\eta' < \eta'' \tag{29}$$

that is, $\eta$ is increasing.

Moreover, we have:

$$ECA(\Omega') - \eta' EC(\Omega') \geq ECA(\Omega'') - \eta' EC(\Omega'') \tag{30}$$

and

$$ECA(\Omega'') - \eta'' EC(\Omega'') \geq ECA(\Omega') - \eta'' EC(\Omega') \tag{31}$$

Adding (30) and (31), we can obtain:

$$(\eta'' - \eta') EC(\Omega') \geq (\eta'' - \eta')EC(\Omega'') \tag{32}$$

From (29) and (32), we can derive $EC(\Omega'') \leq EC(\Omega')$.

That is, $1 - \frac{EC(\Omega^*)}{EC(\Omega')}$ is monotonically non-increasing.

Due to the fact that $\eta^* > \eta^i$, as $i$ approaches infinity, we have $\eta^i = \eta^*$. Thus $\Omega^i$ is the optimal solution, hence we derive that:

$$\lim_{i \to \infty} \frac{|\eta^* - \eta^{(i+1)}|}{|\eta^* - \eta^{(i)}|} \leq \lim_{i \to \infty} 1 - \frac{EC(\Omega^*)}{EC(\Omega^i)} = 0 \tag{33}$$

Furthermore, due to $\lim_{i \to \infty} \frac{|\eta^* - \eta^{(i+1)}|}{|\eta^* - \eta^{(i)}|} \geq 0$ and according to the Squeeze Theorem, we have:

$$\lim_{i \to \infty} \frac{|\eta^* - \eta^{(i+1)}|}{|\eta^* - \eta^{(i)}|} = 0 \tag{34}$$

In summary, the Dinkelbach algorithm converges superlinearly for the problem (17).

## 3.3  Algorithm Framework

In this section, we develop a new Dinkelbach algorithm for energy efficiency.

According to Theorem. 1, our problems can be transformed into a parametric subtractive form as:

$$\mathcal{P}2.1 : \max \quad ECA_{\text{tot}}(\Omega_k^*) - \eta_{EE}^k EC_{\text{tot}}(\Omega_k^*)$$
$$\text{s.t.} \quad C1, C2, \text{ and } C3 \tag{35}$$

where $\Omega_k^*$ represents the optimal solution of the $k$th iteration and $\eta_{EE}^k$ is the ratio of $ECA_{\text{tot}}$ to $EC_{\text{tot}}$ at the $k$th iteration.

By substituting (15) and (16) into (35), we have:

$$\mathcal{P}2.2 : \max \quad \sum_{m=1}^{M} \beta_m^k \sum_{i=1}^{k_m-1} \left( d_{\phi_{i,i+1}} - \eta_{EE}^k c_{\phi_{i,i+1}} \right) \prod_{j=1}^{i} p_{\phi_{j,j+1}}^f$$

$$\text{s.t.} \quad \text{C1, C2, and C3} \tag{36}$$

For the notational simplicity, we let

$$\varphi_m = \sum_{i=1}^{k_m-1} (d_{\phi_{i,i+1}} - \eta_{EE}^k c_{\phi_{i,i+1}}) \prod_{j=1}^{i} p_{\phi_{j,j+1}}^f \tag{37}$$

We proceed by presenting the following theorem.

**Theorem 3.** *For any given path $\psi_i$, the optimal path selection $\beta_i^k$ is given by:*

$$\beta_m^k = \begin{cases} 0, & \text{if } \varphi_m \leq 0 \\ 1, & \text{if } \varphi_m > 0 \text{ and } \psi_m^k \in \Omega_\phi \\ 0, & \text{if } \varphi_m > 0 \text{ and } \psi_m^k \notin \Omega_\phi \end{cases} \tag{38}$$

*where $\psi_m^k \in \Omega_\phi$ represents the path $\psi_m^k$ that satisfies the constraints in the kth iteration.*

*Proof.* To demonstrate the subsequent claims in Theorem 2, we first reformulate (36) equivalently as

$$\mathcal{P}2.3 : \max \quad \sum_{m=1}^{M} \beta_m^k \varphi_m$$

$$\text{s.t.} \quad \text{C1, C2, and C3} \tag{39}$$

We need to set $\beta_m^k = 0$ for paths with $\varphi_m \leq 0$ to maximize the objective function. For $\varphi_m > 0$, we choose paths that satisfy the given conditions.

Jointly considering (17) and (39), we develop Efficient Network Opportunistic Routing with Dinkelbach Optimization (HEOR) algorithm to determine path selection optimally.

---

**Algorithm 1.** HEOR

---

1: **Input:** The selected path $\Psi$; The distance matrix $D$ ; The probability matrix $P$; The energy matrix $E$; Tolerance $\epsilon$;
2: **Output:** the 0-1 vector for path selection $\Omega'$;
3: $\eta_{EE}^0 = 0$; $i = 0$; $F(\eta_{EE}^0) = 1$;
4: **while** $F(\eta_{EE}^i) > \epsilon$ **do**
5:    **for all** $\psi_m \in \Psi$ *that satisfies constraints* **do**
6:       Obtain $\beta_m^i$ by Theorem 3
7:    **end for**
8:    Combine $\beta_m^i$ to get $\Omega_i^*$
9:    Calculating $ECA_{tot}(\Omega_i^*)$ and $EC_{tot}(\Omega_i^*)$ based on (15) and (16), respectively;
10:    $F(\eta_{EE}^i) \leftarrow ECA_{tot}(\Omega_i^*) - \eta_{EE}^i EC_{tot}(\Omega_i^*)$;
11:    $\eta_{EE}^{i+1} \leftarrow \frac{ECA_{tot}(\Omega_i^*)}{EC_{tot}(\Omega_i^*)}$;
12:    $i \leftarrow i + 1$;
13: **end while**
14: $\Omega' \leftarrow \Omega_i^*$
15: **return** $\Omega'$

---

## 4 Performance Evaluation

In this section, we compare our algorithm against the Thompson Sampling-Based Opportunistic Routing (TSOR) algorithm [19] and the SDN-based opportunistic routing for asynchronous duty-cycled WSNs (SDORP) algorithm [13] in terms of throughput, packet delivery ratio, and energy efficiency $\eta_{EE}$. Specifically, TSOR is a recently published OR protocol designed for IoV networks; it can effectively minimize the routing cost. SDORP is an energy-efficiency routing protocol designed for wireless sensor networks.

### 4.1 Experimental Setup

The experiments were conducted using MATLAB R2019B in conjunction with the traffic simulator SUMO. The simulation was run on a 3500 m $\times$ 5000 m $\times$ 25 m three-dimensional urban viaduct scenario. The height of the viaduct is 15 m. All vehicles move in the same direction. Vehicles travel at 60–80 km/h on the viaduct, while speeds are reduced to 40–60 km/h on ground-level roads. The transmission ranges for inter-links $R_{inter}$ and intralinks $R_{intra}$ are 250 m and 200 m, respectively. Both the upper and lower levels of the edge have three lanes each. The number of vehicles per lane follows an exponential distribution with parameter $\lambda$. We fix $\lambda$ of the upper layer of the viaduct at 0.15 and change $\lambda$ of the lower layer to detect the impact of cross-layer link traffic. Fewer vehicles are on the upper level and more on the lower level, facilitating the study of communication probabilities brought about by NLOS links. The data rate is set at 2 Mbps, and the packet size is configured to 512 bytes. Three performance parameters (the throughput, the packet delivery ratio, and the energy efficiency $\eta_{EE}$)

are considered for comparisons. We set $\lambda$ between 0.15 and 0.25 to understand the performance variation of HEOR as the vehicle density transitions from sparse to dense. The end-to-end distance is fixed at 850 m. In the second set of simulations, we vary the end-to-end distance from 600 m to 900 m to assess the performance of HEOR as the hop count increases. Each experiment runs for 200 s and is repeated 500 times with different seeds to report the average value.

Specifically, the throughput is defined as the number of bits successfully transmitted per second in the network. The packet delivery ratio is the ratio of the number of packets successfully received by the destination to the total number of packets generated by the source.

## 4.2  Impact of Traffic Density on Performance

In the first set of simulations, we investigate the impact of varying traffic densities in the lower layer of the viaduct on routing performance.

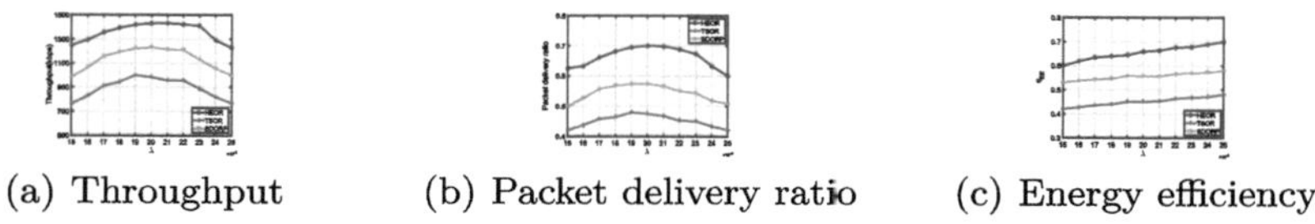

(a) Throughput          (b) Packet delivery ratio          (c) Energy efficiency

**Fig. 1.** Impact of traffic density on performance.

As $\lambda$ of the lower layer of the viaduct increases from 0.15 to 0.25, the number of vehicles in the lower layer changes from sparse to dense. The throughput changes with $\lambda$, as shown in Fig. 1(a). When $\lambda$ increases from 0.15 to about 0.21, the throughput increases with the density of vehicles. This is because OR can enhance throughput by utilizing more feasible links brought by more neighbor nodes. When $\lambda$ increases from 0.21 to 0.25, frequent exchanges of information between neighboring vehicles might occupy the bandwidth available for data transmission, thereby reducing throughput under high load conditions. HEOR's throughput increases faster than that of TSOR and SDORP, and decreases slower than theirs. This is because HEOR optimizes network traffic distribution through multipath selection, iteratively identifying the path with the highest throughput and quickly alleviating congestion on heavily congested links.

As $\lambda$ of the lower layer of the viaduct increases from 0.15 to 0.25, the number of vehicles in the lower layer changes from sparse to dense. The throughput changes with $\lambda$, as shown in Fig. 1(a). When $\lambda$ increases from 0.15 to about 0.21, the throughput increases with the density of vehicles. This is because OR can enhance throughput by utilizing more feasible links brought by more neighbor nodes. When $\lambda$ increases from 0.21 to 0.25, frequent exchanges of information between neighboring vehicles might occupy the bandwidth available for data transmission, thereby reducing throughput under high load conditions. HEOR's throughput increases faster than that of TSOR and SDORP and decreases slower than theirs. This is because HEOR optimizes the network traffic distribution through multi-path selection to find the path with the higher throughput through iteration and quickly release the congested links in the highly congested network.

Figure 1(c) shows that the energy efficiency $\eta_{EE}$ increases as the number of vehicles increases. This is attributed to the fact that the three protocols are all designed for energy efficiency. While the TSOR algorithm is specifically designed for highly dynamic networks where link metrics are unknown and change frequently, in our scenario, when the traffic in the lower level becomes heavy, the speed of vehicles decreases quickly due to the topology of vehicles becoming more stable, and its advantages cannot be fully realized. For SDORP, it introduces additional control overhead by centralizing decision-making. While this can improve coordination and routing efficiency, it also creates a single point of failure and potentially increases latency due to the centralized control decisions needing to propagate back to the nodes. Together with the results in Fig. 1(b), we can conclude that HEOR achieves a higher $\eta_{EE}$ by dropping more packets when no path is available upon packet arrival, compared to TSOR and SDORP.

## 4.3   Impact of End-to-End Distance on Performance

We set $\lambda$ of the lower layer of the viaduct to 0.2 and the end-to-end distance to range from 600 m to 900 m to examine the impact of distance on routing performance as the number of hops changes.

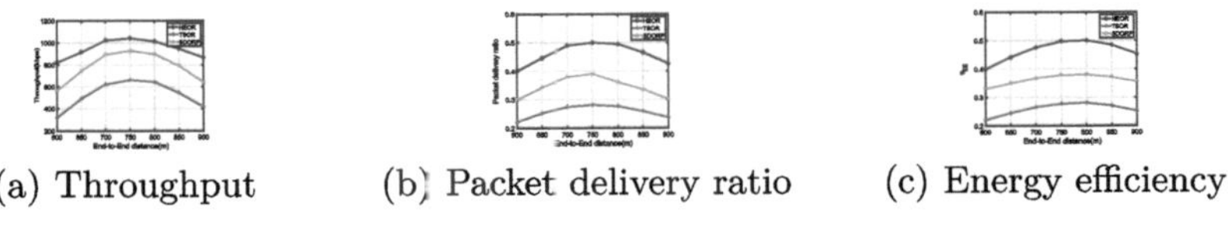

(a) Throughput          (b) Packet delivery ratio          (c) Energy efficiency

**Fig. 2.** Impact of end-to-end distance on performance.

As shown in Fig. 2(a), when end-to-end distance increases from 600 m to about 750 m, the throughput increases accordingly. This is because more vehicles are between the source and destination vehicles, which can bring more available links and paths. When the end-to-end distance increases from 750 m to 900 m, the expected hop count also increases from 3 to 4. Accumulated delays and error rates can lead to increased retransmissions, reducing effective throughput. A notable observation is that HEOR consistently achieves the highest throughput. The reason is that, by using a Dinkelbach algorithm, the path selected by HEOR is more stable. However, other protocols struggle to perform effectively in viaduct scenarios, leading to more frequent link disconnections.

It is shown in Fig. 2(b) that the PDR of the three protocols increases as end-to-end distance increases, but after the distance increase grows to about 750 m, it begins to decrease. The data packets have more opportunities to pass through different relay vehicles to reach the destination. Adding such relay vehicles can improve the data delivery probability to a certain extent, especially in scenarios where each node is likely to forward data packets successfully. However, as paths become longer, the costs of managing them increase. Long paths may result in higher latency and more packet timeouts, which can decrease PDR. HEOR can adjust the path selection strategy through iterative optimization to adapt to these changes, thereby improving or maintaining PDR.

From Fig. 2(c), we can see that the value of $\eta_{EE}$ continues to increase until the end-to-end distance reaches about 800 m. The $\eta_{EE}$ of HEOR increases faster than SDORP and TSOR. The reason for this is that the Dinkelbach algorithm aims to find the global optimal solution, which can ensure maximum energy efficiency throughout the transmission process, not just the efficiency of a single link. As $\eta_{EE}$ decreases with end-to-end distance when it reaches 800 m, HEOR still maintains the highest $\eta_{EE}$. The reason is that HEOR can accurately evaluate the performance of each link and make optimal choices accordingly. This granular link evaluation capability helps the algorithm avoid choosing paths that may appear efficient in the short term but have higher energy consumption in the long term, thereby maintaining lower energy consumption over increased end-to-end distances.

## 5   Conclusion

This paper proposes an Efficient Network Opportunistic Routing with Dinkelbach Optimization (HEOR) algorithm for IOV networks by accounting for the specific structure of urban viaducts. In OR multi-hop environments, complexity grows exponentially. To transform the issue into a solvable problem, we converted neighbor node selection into path selection. Additionally, we introduced new metrics to filter neighboring vehicles. Simulation results indicate that HEOR performs better in throughput, packet delivery ratio, and energy efficiency. Furthermore, the results affirm that utilizing inter-level links enhances the performance of OR.

**Acknowledgments.** This work was supported in part by the National Natural Science Foundation of China under Grant 62272356, Grant 62302155, and Grant 62372344, in part by the Natural Science Foundation of Chongqing under Grant CSTB2022NSCQ-MSX1414, and in part by the Hubei Key Research and Development Program in China under Grant 2023BAB075.

## References

1. Wang, X., Weng, Y., Gao, H.: A low-latency and energy-efficient multimetric routing protocol based on network connectivity in vanet communication. IEEE Trans. Green Commun. Network. **5**(4), 1761–1776 (2021)
2. Wang, J., Zhu, K., Hossain, E.: Green internet of vehicles (iov) in the 6g era: toward sustainable vehicular communications and networking. IEEE Trans. Green Commun. Network. **6**(1), 391–423 (2022)
3. Garcia, A.G., Tria, L.A.R., Talampas, M.C.R.: Development of an energy-efficient routing algorithm for electric vehicles. In: 2019 IEEE Transportation Electrification Conference and Expo (ITEC), pp. 1–5 (2019)
4. Tirumalasetti, R., Singh, S.K.: Automatic dynamic user allocation with opportunistic routing over vehicles network for intelligent transport system. Sustainable Energy Technol. Assess. **57**, 103195 (2023)

5. Wang, J., Zhang, H., Tang, X., Li, Z.: Delay-tolerant routing and message scheduling for cr-vanets. Futur. Gener. Comput. Syst. **110**, 291–309 (2020)
6. Zhou, X., Yang, X., Ma, J., Wang, K.I.-K.: Energy-efficient smart routing based on link correlation mining for wireless edge computing in iot. IEEE Internet Things J. **9**(16), 14988–14997 (2022)
7. Zhu, R., Jiang, Q., Huang, X., Li, D., Yang, Q.: A reinforcement-learning-based opportunistic routing protocol for energy-efficient and void-avoided uasns. IEEE Sens. J. **22**(13), 13589–13601 (2022)
8. Polychronis, G., Lalis, S.: Joint edge resource allocation and path planning for drones with energy constraints. In: Longfei, S., Bodhi, P. (eds.) Mobile and Ubiquitous Systems: Computing, Networking and Services, pp. 378–399. Springer, Cham (2023). https://doi.org/10.1007/978-3-031-34776-4_20
9. Bar-Shalom, Y., Li, X.R., Kirubarajan, T.: Estimation with Applications to Tracking and Navigation: Theory Algorithms and Software. John Wiley & Sons, Hoboken (2004)
10. Duan, W., Gu, X., Zhang, G., Wen, M., Ding, Z., Ho, P.-H.: Sum-rate maximization for ris-iov: from instantaneous to statistical CSI. IEEE Trans. Wirel. Commun. **23**(7), 8071–8084 (2024)
11. Tang, X., Tao, Y., Liu, W., Shi, B., Wang, J.: A hybrid link connectivity model for opportunistic routing in iov networks under viaduct scenarios. In: 2022 18th International Conference on Mobility, Sensing and Networking (MSN), pp. 786–790 (2022)
12. Wang, J., Mei, A., Tang, X., Shi, B.: Social-based link reliability prediction model for CR-VANETs. In: Liu, Z., Wu, F., Das, S.K. (eds.) WASA 2021. LNCS, vol. 12937, pp. 376–388. Springer, Cham (2021). https://doi.org/10.1007/978-3-030-85928-2_30
13. Farooq, M.U., Wang, X., Hawbani, A., Zhao, L., Al-Dubai, A., Busaileh, O.: SDORP: SDN based opportunistic routing for asynchronous wireless sensor networks. IEEE Trans. Mob. Comput. **22**(8), 4912–4929 (2023)
14. Jiang, J., Yan, Q., Han, G., Wang, H.: An opportunistic routing based on directional transmission in the internet of underwater things. IEEE Internet Things J. **10**(18), 16392–16403 (2023)
15. Tang, X., Zhou, J., Xiong, S., Wang, J., Zhou, K.: Geographic segmented opportunistic routing in cognitive radio ad hoc networks using network coding. IEEE Access **6**, 62766–62783 (2018)
16. Xu, C., Xiong, Z., Han, Z., Zhao, G., Yu, S.: Link reliability-based adaptive routing for multilevel vehicular networks. IEEE Trans. Veh. Technol. **69**(10), 11771–11785 (2020)
17. Wang, X., Zhou, W., Hawbani, A., Liu, P., Zhao, L., Alsamhi, S.H.: A dynamic opportunistic routing protocol for asynchronous duty-cycled WSNS. IEEE Trans. Sustain. Comput. **8**(3), 314–327 (2023)
18. Agate, V., De Paola, A., Lo Re. G., Virga, A.: Reputation-based dissemination of trustworthy information in vanets. In: Zaslavsky, A., Ning, Z., Kalogeraki, V., Georgakopoulos, D., Chrysanthis, P.K. (eds.) Mobile and Ubiquitous Systems: Computing, Networking and Services, pp. 445–463. Springer, Cham (2024). https://doi.org/10.1007/978-3-031-63989-0_23
19. Huang, Z., Xu, Y., Pan, J.: TSOR: thompson sampling-based opportunistic routing. IEEE Trans. Wirel. Commun. **20**(11), 7272–7285 (2021)
20. Bazaraa, M.S., Sherali, H.D., Shetty, C.M.: Nonlinear Programming: Theory and Algorithms. John wiley and sons, Hoboken (2013)

# Spatio-Temporal Analysis of Concurrent Networks

Heinz Schmidt[1]([✉])[iD], Peter Herrmann[2][iD], Maria Spichkova[1][iD],
James Harland[1][iD], Ian Peake[1][iD], and Ergys Puka[2][iD]

[1] RMIT University, Melbourne, Australia
{heinz.schmidt,maria.spichkova,james.harland,ian.peake}@rmit.edu.au
[2] Norwegian University of Science and Technology (NTNU), Trondheim, Norway
{peter.herrmann,ergys.puka}@ntnu.no

**Abstract.** Many very large-scale systems are networks of cyber-physical systems in which humans and autonomous software agents cooperate. To make the cooperation safe for the humans involved, the systems have to follow protocols with rigid real-time and real-space properties, but they also need to be capable of making competitive and collaborative decisions with varying rewards and penalties. Due to these tough requirements, the construction of system control software is often very difficult. This calls for applying a model-based engineering approach, which allows one to formally express the time and space properties and use them as guidance for the whole engineering process from requirement definition via system design to software development. Moreover, it is beneficial, if one can verify with acceptable effort, that the time and space requirements are preserved throughout the development steps. This paper focuses on modelling spatio-temporal properties and their model-checking and simulation using different analysis tools in combination with the methods and tool extensions proposed here. To this end, we provide an informal overview of CASTeL, our Concurrent Alliances Spatio-Temporal Logic. CASTeL is stochastic and includes real-time concurrency and real-space distribution.

**Keywords:** Communication Protocols · Concurrent Systems · Coordination · Cyber-Physical Systems · Distributed Systems · Internet of Things · Model Checking · Probabilistic Reasoning · Real-Time Systems · Reward Structures · Simulation · Spatio-Temporal Logic

## 1 Introduction

Very Large Scale Collaborative (VLSC) systems comprise defence, logistics, healthcare, and transport systems (including networked and autonomous vehicles) as well as widely distributed cloud computing and social networks, which may include millions of customers. Many of these VLSC systems are *cyber-physical systems* (CPS) [8], others are *cyber-social systems* (CSS), and some


A. Soylu et al. (Eds.): MobiQuitous 2024, LNICST 634, pp. 222–237, 2026.
https://doi.org/10.1007/978-3-032-10554-7_12

are both [1]. A CPS operates, monitors and controls physical infrastructure such as power and transport networks or manufacturing sites. A CSS involves humans with mobile devices and many configurations and preferences. Cooperative intelligent transport systems are examples of uniting CPS and CSS, which include vehicle-to-vehicle and vehicle-to-infrastructure communication and wearable mobile devices that combine automated agents with human decision-making. An increasing portion of VLSC software is generated using rapid development tools and, more recently, generative Artificial Intelligence. Such systems often exhibit a significant number of program errors, which require automatic detection, reporting, correction and other responses in the large, that have been well studied in the literature, see, e.g., [5].

Our approach is based on abstract concurrent behaviour modelling with Petri Nets (PNs) and their use for model-checking stochastic logic specifications in Computation Tree Logic (CTL) variants [14]. These logics include notions of abstract players (agents), with and without reward/penalty and other utility cost structures. They have a long history of model-checking over diverse PN model classes. PNs are a versatile form of state-transition systems that are suited to model system behaviour on very different levels of abstraction. For instance, one can use them to specify limited synchronisation capabilities provided by integer semaphores, train rail segments, or car traffic crossings with limited capacity.

The relationship between different classes of PNs and various temporal logics is well known, which means that PNs can be considered as abstract, logical, operational, and executable specifications. In particular, via model-checking one can formally carry out various analyses such as verifying structural properties of the nets, proving purely logical inference on the level of specified formulae, or simulating dynamic behaviour by executing the net either exhaustively or stochastically, in search of counter-examples that violate a logical formula.

This paper builds on our prior work for model-based and architecture-aware analysis of cyber-physical systems using a combination of *dependent finite state machine* interface descriptions, based on state-machine decomposable Petri Nets [32]. Further, this work is based on core aspects of readability that we introduced in [31].

**Contributions:** This paper proposes a model-driven approach called *CASTeL*, which is short for *Concurrent Alliances Spatio-Temporal Logic*. CASTeL makes the modelling of decisions, tactics and strategies in *competitive and cooperative systems* possible. Moreover, we show how one can use model-checking to verify, whether CASTeL-formulae are realized by Coloured Stochastic Petri Nets (CSPNs). Besides the traditional strengths of modularity and temporal concurrency of CSPNs, the approach includes *spatial* reasoning about the *enforceability of properties*.

**Outline:** The rest of the paper is organised as follows. Section 2 introduces a motivating scenario for the proposed approach, while Sect. 3 informally highlights features of our CASTeL specifications and PN models. Section 4 provides an overview of related approaches. Finally, Sect. 5 summarises the paper and suggests future work.

## 2  Motivating Scenario

In this section, we introduce our motivating scenario, which is about context-aware communication protocols for cellular dead spot mitigation. Vehicles cooperating with each other and their infrastructure to realize Intelligent Transportation Systems (ITS), often suffer from the presence of dead spots, i.e., areas with no mobile network coverage. Dead spots are quite common on large land masses such as Australia and Canada, where very few people live outside larger population centres. One example in Australia is a 300+km portion of the Silver Highway in New South Wales (NSW) between Mildura and Broken Hill.

To alleviate this problem, we created special communication protocols which use opportunistic mobile ad hoc networks between nearby vehicles in a dead spot to alleviate transmission delays, see [26,27,29]. If the vehicles have reasonable estimates of their dead spot exit times, the ad hoc networks make the transfer of messages to those vehicles possible, that are anticipated to regain connectivity fastest. The protocols were simulated using the versatile traffic simulator SUMO [24]. The simulations have shown that using the context-aware protocols and the ad hoc networks may reduce the average waiting times in a dead spot by more than 40% [28].

While various vehicular network technologies can be used to realise ad hoc networks between vehicles, we prefer the popular WiFi Direct protocol [35], available on most state-of-the-art mobile phones. It allows us to communicate over a distance of up to 200 m, which is sufficient in most cases, see [28]. In this paper, we *assume* that the WiFi Direct protocol is correctly implemented, and focus instead on the *emerging properties* across large numbers of vehicles participating in *message exchanges*.

While the SUMO-based simulations revealed interesting results [28], they lack formal proofs of important spatiotemporal properties. These formal verification tasks will be outlined below. We ignore the possibility of messages getting lost in transit, such as a car not meeting the predicted exit time due to a driver changing the route or taking a break. We leave this to more refined ad hoc network protocols of our future work. For simplicity, we also abstain from modelling our more advanced Context-Aware Message Flooding Protocol (CAMFLooP), which uses copies of the same message in multiple vehicles to guarantee an optimal reduction of the delivery time [28,29]. Instead, we restrict ourselves to a prior version in which only one copy of a message is kept in the system at a time. In ad hoc networks, this message is transmitted to the network peer predicted to leave the dead spot first [26,27].

Figure 1 depicts a simple schematic dead spot, where $A$ and $B$ are two entry/exit points of the main road. The points are at the coordinates $(0,0)$ and $(100,0)$, respectively. Further, the dead spot contains a T-intersection at point $T$ located at $(60,0)$, in which a side road from point $C$ at $(60,20)$ joins the main road. In this scenario, we assume the car's destination is known to the protocol in advance, like when we use Google or Apple Maps' "Directions" features. In the following, we consider through traffic on the routes $ATB$, $ATC$, $BTA$, $BTC$, $CTA$ and $CTB$. The blue, red, and green circles in Fig. 1 outline

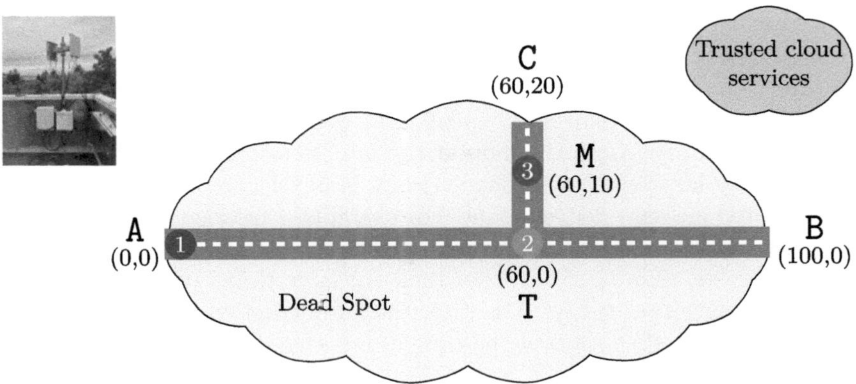


**Fig. 1.** Simple Dead Spot Road Network with a T-intersection.

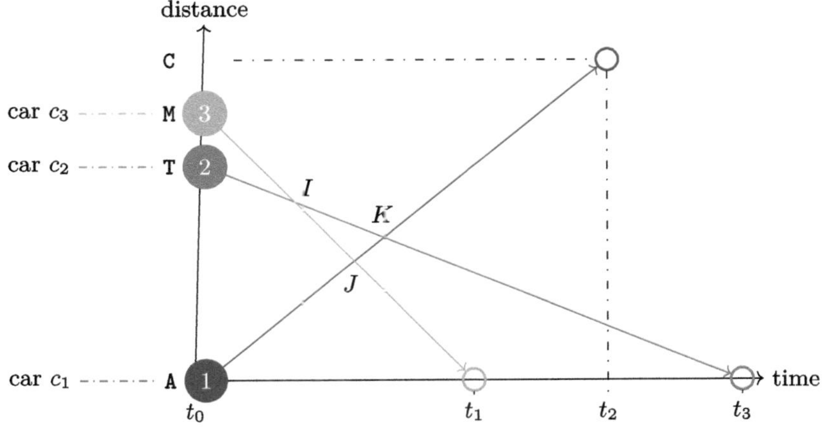


**Fig. 2.** Simple scenario for the three cars shown in Fig. 1.

the positions of three cars $c_1$, $c_2$, and $c_3$, that are all cut off from cellular network access in the depicted situation.

The trajectories of the three cars in our scenario are shown in Fig. 2. Here, car positions in the current situation (time $t_0 = 0$), i.e., the ones highlighted in Fig. 1, are described by filled circles. With hollow circles, we further designate the events in which vehicles leave the dead spot. We calculate the average speed through the dead spot from the time and relative distance, resulting in idealised linear car trajectories. Car $c_1$ travels from $A$ to $C$ in time $t_2$. Car $c_2$ travels in the opposite direction from $T$ to $A$ in time $t_3$. Car $c_3$ entered at $C$ and travels to $A$ from its current point $M$ in the centre between $C$ and $T$, see Fig. 1. The cars operate at different average speeds, represented by the gradients of the lines.

For instance, $c_3$ travels at a higher speed than $c_2$, which is overtaken at point $I$ between $T$ and $A$. At point $J$, $c_3$ is passing $c_1$, that runs in the opposite direction.

As described above, the dissemination protocol uses ad hoc networks to transmit messages between vehicles to speed their delivery [27]. When two cars are in relative proximity (approximately at the intersection of their respective lines on Fig. 2), they may form an ad hoc network and exchange messages to improve the anticipated message delivery time. For example, a message jumping from the blue car $c_1$ to the green car $c_3$ at about $J$ (between $A$ and $T$) can be delivered at the earlier exit time $t_1$ of $c_3$ rather than the later time $t_2$ of $c_1$. The message takes the effective route $AJA$. Likewise, the ad-hoc networks created at points $I$ and $K$ can be used to shorten the time of message deliveries.

## 3    Highlights of CASTeL Models and Logical Definitions

### 3.1    Petri Net Model Variations for the Dead Spot Scenario

**Discrete and Continuous Dynamic Models.** The actual continuous trajectories of the cars $c_1$, $c_2$ and $c_3$ may deviate from the idealised linear trajectories depicted in Fig. 2. We can imagine the accurate trajectories winding around the idealised average speed lines. If the changing speeds are known or stochastically generated in simulations, such a varying trajectory can be linearly approximated by a piecewise linear polygon.

Each segment of this polygon represents the average speed of the given car on the corresponding road section. We envisage this by an equidistant segmentation of the $y$-axis of Fig. 2, i.e., the *spatial* division, rather than an equidistant division on the $x$-axis (time). This keeps with the interpretation of a Coloured Stochastic Petri Net (CSPN) as a compact discrete and continuous process generator. If the CSPN ignores the stochastic rates assigned to its transitions, one can analyse the abstract synchronization of its transitions by utilizing their net-induced partial order. The rates allow mapping any such partially ordered process onto a continuous timeline. If the specified rates are parameters in exponential distributions, the CSPN behaviour graph is equivalent to a continuous Markov chain or Markov decision process (if the CSPN is associated with reward structures), see [7]. Note that the behaviour graph of a Petri Net represents branching order or time. It forgets the spatial distribution and, therefore, the concurrency of transition firings.

Figure 3 shows parts of a CSPN for the dead spot net in Fig. 1. To describe segments of the roads in our scenario, it uses the concept of *zones*. For simplicity, we apply the distance of a road segment to the central point $T$, see Fig. 1, to denominate a zone. For example, car $c_1$ which is at the coordinate $(1, 0)$, is 59 units away from $T$ (coordinate $(60, 0)$) and therefore in zone 59. The zones allow us to describe spatial properties, e.g., where on the road a car is or if two cars are nearby such that they can build up an ad hoc network.

Like in most PN descriptions, circles represent places and rectangles transitions. The places K and L are marked by regular tokens (colour type *Dot*). K is used to bound the number of cars allowed in the dead spot, while L restricts the

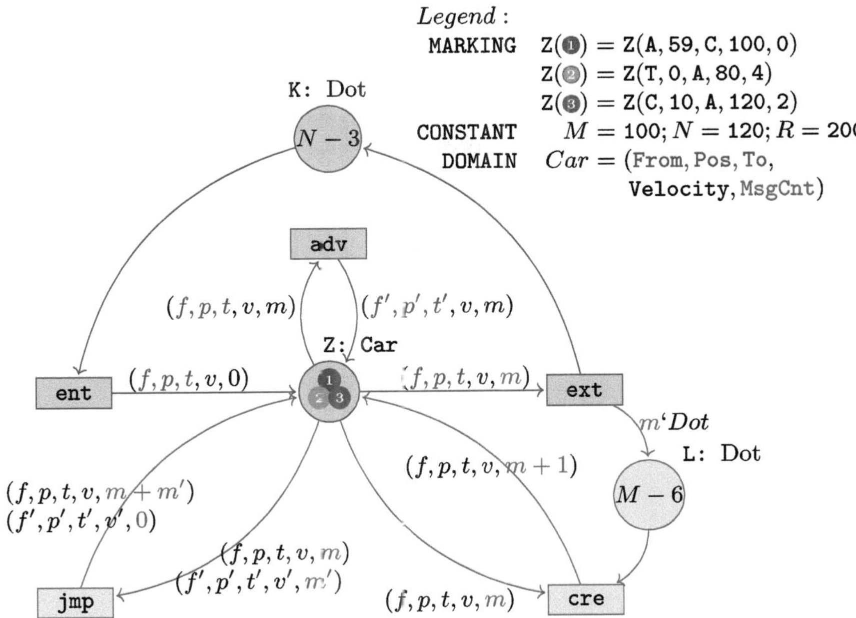


**Fig. 3.** Coloured Stochastic Petri Net for concurrent car interactions in the simple dead spot network of Fig. 1.

number of messages, the cars in the dead spot may carry at maximum. In this way, it is guaranteed that our CSPN specifies only a finite number of different system states. Place Z contains coloured tokens representing the cars currently in the dead spot. Its tokens are marked by tuples from type $Car$, that have the form $(f, p, t, v, m)$ and include the following elements:

- The entrance point $f \in \{A, B, C, T\}$, i.e. the point a car is coming from.
- $p \in \mathbb{N}$ is an integer denoting the zone, the vehicle is currently in.
- The exit point $t \in \{A, B, C\}$, i.e., the point it is heading to.
- $v \in \mathbb{N}$ is the velocity of the car.
- $m \in \mathbb{N}$ lists the number of messages, the car carries.

In the marking shown in Fig. 3, place L has $M - 6$ tokens. $M$ is a constant model parameter describing the maximum number of messages possible in the system. Thus, the tuple element $m$ of a token in place Z cannot exceed the value $M$, i.e., $0 \leq m \leq M$. Another constant model parameter is $N$, that bounds the number of cars in the dead spot, i.e., the number of tokens in place Z. In the marking depicted in Fig. 3, Z has three colour tokens of type $Car$. In accordance with that, place K has $N - 3$ tokens. More precisely, the current marking $Mrk$ (during this hypothetical simulated run) includes $Mrk(L) = M - 6$ and $Mrk(K) = N - 3$, while $Mrk(Z) = \{(A, 59, C, 100, 0), (T, 0, A, 80, 4), (C, 10, A, 120, 2)\}$ contains three colour tokens of type $Car$. This marking is reached after the three cars $c_1$ (blue), $c_2$ (red) and $c_3$ (green) entered the dead spot by executing transition ent and then advanced approximately to the situation depicted in Fig. 2 (transition adv). Moreover, cars $c_2$ and $c_3$ created some message payload (transition cre). For each car entering the dead spot, the car capacity K shrinks by 1. Likewise, the message capacity L shrinks by 1 for each message created in the dead spot. As a car exits the dead spot (transition ext), these capacities grow accordingly.

**Table 1.** Guards and rates for the transitions in Fig. 3.

| Transition | Guard | Rate |
|---|---|---|
| ent | $IsRoute(f,t) \wedge f \neq T \wedge p = START(f)$ | 1 |
| ext | $IsRoute(f,t) \wedge f = T \wedge p = START(t)$ | 1 |
| adv | $IsRoute(f,t) \wedge$ <br> $((f \neq T \wedge$ <br> $((p \neq 0 \Rightarrow p' = p - 1 \wedge f' = f) \vee$ <br> $(p = 0 \Rightarrow p' = 0 \wedge f' = T))) \vee$ <br> $(f = T \wedge p \neq START(t) \wedge$ <br> $f' = f \wedge p' = p + 1 \wedge t' = t))$ | $0.04 \cdot v$ |
| cre | $true$ | 3 |
| jmp | $IsClose(f,p,t,f',p',t') \wedge$ <br> $ETA(f,p,t,v) < ETA(f',p',t',v')$ | 5 |

**Logical Constraints and Stochastic Rates:** Table 1 shows the guards and rates of the transitions used for the transitions in Fig. 3. In CSPNs, guards can be interpreted dynamically as transition firing conditions or statically as conditions for unfolding the coloured net into a basic uncoloured net. A fundamental transition exists only for colour value combinations that satisfy the transition guard in the basic net. In the coloured net, the higher-level transition fires only if the required input tokens are available and their values satisfy the guard, i.e., they generate an identical reachability graph on the same reachable markings.

Moreover, we use some additional predicates and functions: $IsRoute(f,t)$ is a predicate that holds if $f$ and $t$ are different points and $t$ is an exit point of the dead spot. The function $START(f)$ indicates the initial zone position at a point $f$. The predicate $IsClose(f,p,t,f',p',t')$ is $true$ if and only if the positions of the car with the tuple colours $f$, $p$, and $t$ and of the one characterised by $f'$, $p'$, and $t'$ are nearby. This accounts for cars driving in different directions, currently at different positions $p \neq p'$ but still in direct wifi range, and so on. Finally, we use the function $ETA$ to express the expected time of arrival of a vehicle.

Rates of CSPNs are either probabilistic or they are real-valued parameters in probability density functions, for example, negative exponential functions $E(c,r,t) = c \cdot r \cdot e^{-r \cdot t}$ over time $t$ and rate $r$, with a scaling factor $c$. The rate function of the transition adv depends on the velocity $v$ of a car.

**Parameterized Component-Based Architecture of Models:** In the initial marking (not shown in the figure), only place K is marked with $N$ tokens and place L with $M$ tokens. The current marking, depicted in the figure, is reachable from the above initial net marking. The constants $M$ and $N$ bounding the numbers of messages and the vehicles in the dead spot, respectively, are definable model parameters. Likewise, we use a constant $R$, that expresses the number of zones into which the roads in our scenario is segmented in. Thus, our models are parameterised and give rise to a combinatorial family of nets over the possible range of these parameters. Parallel parameter sweeps [36] may result in different simulation runs with a series of stochastic plots of various model performance measurements, such as statistical frequencies of combinations of states, transitions or formulae.

CSPNs are compositional. Linear algebra methods, including products, sums, scaling, and various other operations, have been proven to underpin their composition. These operations on CSPNs can be visualized as merging the corresponding component nets by identifying some places or transitions. In Fig. 3, we illustrate this by highlighting two net components:

- The blue subnet includes transitions for entry (**ent**) to and exit (**ext**) from the dead spot, respectively, or advancing (**adv**) within a zone and between adjacent zones.
- The magenta subnet is an extension adding messaging transitions, allowing the creation (**cre**) of messages incrementing the message number of a car in transit; the jumping (**jmp**) of messages between cars in proximity transfers all messages of one car to another vehicle if that car can reach its exit faster.

As mentioned above, the properties of the dead spot mitigations protocols have already been modelled and simulated in SUMO [22] in long runs, sometimes running on several workstations or virtual machines for weeks [28]. The protocols may be extended by further features like considering the reputation of drivers (agent) with respect to keeping their planned routes and speeds or their reliability in delivering the messages after having left the dead spot. This reputation can then be used to decide which vehicle is the most reliable target for a given message. Furthermore, one can assume that some communication subscriptions support micro-payments, data entitlements, or other gratifications for drivers, so that trustworthy behaviour will also be rewarded financially. Thus, the modelling and simulation may include game-theoretic elements, where agents make ad hoc decisions regarding speed or destination with rewards in mind. Another variation provides modelling cyberattacks, where cars are hacked and behave maliciously, e.g., by offering their peers fake improvements in the message delivery when, in fact, they are discarding messages. Protocol variations offering increased fault tolerance in the presence of such attacks are of growing interest.

This raises the question of how CASTeL can feature component and product-line variation. In addition to parameters like $M$ and $N$, colour variations are an essential means of parametrisation. For example, the combinatorial complexity of a CSPN may be managed by starting from simple models with a very limited enumeration or range type. The model can then be step-wise refined by increasing the cardinality of the colour domain, i.e., by values that change the outcome of guard evaluations. Likewise, a colour product domain may be restricted using some formulae. Conversely, conservative extensions correspond to injections. They permit some simulation between a component model and the corresponding subnet or partial composition of the system as a whole. These colour restrictions and extensions correspond to projections and injections regarding nets and their runs. Parameter variations may change a component's qualitative and quantitative interface or execution behaviour characteristics. These may result in the inclusion or exclusion of modules in the incremental or full integration of the system.

**Gaps:** As mentioned above, CSPN modelling and simulation have been studied in the literature, and several education and industry-strengths tools exist. However, our spatial interpretation in the CASTeL context requires extensions, explicitly identifying spatial dimensions in these nets. For example, the highlighted blue colour variables $f$, $p$, and $t$ (see Fig. 3) represent abstract coordinates in terms of distances and zone points. Thus, they are *spatial variables* modelling the spatial aspects in the model of the dead spot mitigation protocol.

In Petri Nets, conflicts are branches in places where sufficient tokens enable multiple transitions, which can fire mutually exclusively. In coloured nets, conflicts are resolved in one of two ways. Either the information is already contained in the marking of the net, for example, the colour values of tokens. Or conflicts are non-deterministic since information enters the system from outside, for instance, by player choices, when we use the variant with alliances sketched above. In CASTeL, player labels are particular colours, which may occur in tokens. According to the rules of the game, these are then assigned to the conflicts. A conflict between transitions must only be resolved by the players assigned to it.

### 3.2   Model Design and Logical Requirement Elicitation in CASTeL

The CSPN shown in Fig. 3 is a simplified discrete and abstract model for a variant of previously studied protocols [26,27]. We assume that each car $c_i$ enters with a random speed $v_i$ chosen from a few discrete values (e.g., 80–120 km/h). It is easy to extend this variant to include variable speeds if desired. This can be easily realized by assuming, that the speed $v$ of a given car is constant in a zone, but that the transition **adv** may change $v$ according to simulated choices of drivers or probabilistic events abstracting from traffic uncertainties. In consequence, the vehicle may have varying speeds in the different zones, it passes.

Based on this simple formal model, that includes the creation of messages by car passengers, by IoT components for machine-to-machine (M2M) communication, or logistic tracking, we may wish to express its benefit by a precise specification, such as:

> *At least p percent of the messages created in the dead spot arrive in less than half the time, it would take the generating car to reach the planned*

*exit of the dead spot. Suppose furthermore $1 \leq n < 10$ cars out of 10 have satellite connection and offer forwarding of messages from other cars. This improves the average time to delivery by a factor $A \cdot n + B$, where $A$ and $B$ are constants determined by simulation runs.*

Our logic CASTeL permits us to express claims like this one, including necessary spatial and temporal constraints, in an unambiguous and precise formalism. CASTeL draws elements of its syntax from different CTL-based logics and extends and reconciles them through its use of extended Generalised Stochastic Petri Nets (GSPNs) as model generators for both state-transition models and their interpretations. The use of GSPNs allow us to combine probabilistic chance with non-deterministic agent choice and reward. They are more general than models underlying, for example, ATL (Alternating-Time Temporal Logic, see [3]) and rPATL (Probabilistic Alternating-time Temporal Logic with Rewards, see [11]). In particular, stochastic rates may be real-valued time and space distributions (typically parameters in exponential distributions), for which Markovian probabilistic constraints may hold only under further constraints and normalisation. At the same time, non-Markovian PNs can be simulated statistically. PN models are not limited to alternating agent choice but can be truly concurrent. This differs from interleaving models, where concurrency is specified by allowing two agents to operate in arbitrary order but not in parallel. That is an important differentiator, especially in widely distributed systems and their performance analysis, simulation and estimation.

While the work here aims at model-checking and simulation modulo theory, our goal is also to lift necessary spatial abstractions onto an equal footing with real-time abstractions in logic based on PCTL. Such logics use bounded path formulae, in particular a logical *until* and *unless* operator with temporal bounds [16]. Such a bound limits the number of clock ticks for which a model checker checks whether safe conditions from states that might lead to hazards can be reached. In CASTeL we therefore also permit spatial bounds, which count discrete spatial steps, i.e. routes that allow mobile actors to reach spatial goals, including a safe spatial region, and reap corresponding rewards. This can be realized by bounding firing sequences $t^n$ of a dangling stochastic transition $t$ stochastically by the rate of $t$, while in the underlying place-transition nets (ignoring the rates), they will be unbounded. An equivalent completion (closure) is possible by adding a place $p_t$ initialised with $n$ tokens. For example, we use the place K representing the maximal number $M$ of cars in the dead spot for this purpose. In this way, we guarantee a hard bound in the underlying net beside the soft bound by rates of the stochastic net.

Specifications like the one listed above make assumptions such as the following:

*With a high probability (say 99%), vehicles passing each other communicate reliably while in a range of 200 meters.*

Constraints are relevant for model realism, on the one hand, as we may need to exclude degenerate cases of dead spot models or car behaviour. On the other hand, constraints can avoid combinatorial explosions and unnecessary simulations of borderline cases, such as times of the day or week, when all cars travel in total isolation, times of major construction work or other hurdles, for which the protocol is not designed, or for which historical traffic data is not available. Principally, there are two kinds of constraints:

1. *Qualitative* constraints using different premises. For these, our improvement formulae become conclusions. Thus, the models and theories effectively become qualitative scenarios with different or varying surrounding conditions.
2. *Quantitative* constraints. Here, we use stochastic model parameters. These vary stochastic rates in CASTeL formulae. We may be able to plot behavioural observations or secondary stochastic observations as functions of varying parameter values; the variations may be discrete or continuous. We can also plug these varying parameters into the Petri Net simulation and look at the resulting variation of Petri Net properties and its provable or observed quantitative behaviour across various simulation runs.

Let us make this a little more concrete by looking at the example of *"coverage bubbles"*—groups of at least two collaborating cars temporarily forming an ad hoc network. In the terminology of game-theoretic logic like the Alternating Temporal Logic (ATL) [3], such collections are called *alliances of players*, i.e., mutually independent decision makers. To deal with mobility, CASTeL alliances are ad hoc. They form dynamically in space depending on the distance between the cars. Moreover, the vehicles operate independently, i.e., their messaging process is automated, and they move concurrently. For example, multiple pairs of cars in one or more bubbles may exchange messages while moving in and out of proximity. Likewise, players in CASTeL can make concurrent choices, such as changing their speed, adapting to traffic situations dynamically, etc. Regarding bubble formation, CASTeL assumptions may include the following:

*With a significant minimal probability, say 20%, the spatial density of cars allows for the formation of bubbles of at least 3 cars somewhere in the space of the dead spot.*

On the one hand, considering such assumptions in CSPN simulations limits the scenarios to be analysed by simulation runs, exploring possible processes and their stochastic properties. On the other hand, the assumptions simplify model-checking of logical guarantees required as part of requirements definitions.

Stochastic rates of car arrivals at entry points can set time intervals at the same space point, i.e., bounds for the average space-time density across a dead spot. Following the concept of Multi-hop Cellular Network (MCN) [23], in which a mobile unit communicates with a fixed base station utilizing others as relay stations, the proximity relation between cars may define a connected graph for a crowded dead spot. This graph is the *support* of the coverage bubble. Messages inside a coverage bubble can exit by a sequence of hops at a speed limited by communication speed and the number of hops required. An example scenario is depicted in Fig. 4. Here, the ad hoc network connections between the five vehicles

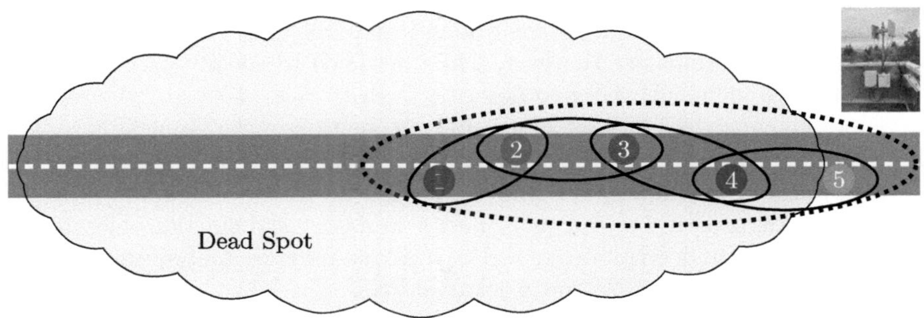


**Fig. 4.** Scenario with a coverage bubble formed from ad hoc networks between vehicles.

$c_1$ to $c_5$ (solid ellipses) form a coverage bubble, which is visualized as a dotted ellipse. This makes it possible that, e.g., messages stored in $c_1$ can be forwarded via some other vehicles acting as relay stations to $c_5$, which is outside the dead spot and can forward the messages via the cellular network.

The time of a single hop is dominated by the time it takes to establish a connection or switch from one to another. Furthermore, it depends on message lengths. Since the density of cars may vary, coverage bubbles may not connect directly to the dead spot exit. Moreover, a bubble may disintegrate fast when its support cars travel in opposing directions, e.g., in Fig. 4 cars $c_2$ and $c_3$ move in the opposite direction of all the other cars and will soon be out of range. Then, $c_1$ cannot form a bubble with $c_4$ and $c_5$ anymore. However, a group of vehicles travelling in the same direction at similar speeds may maintain a coverage bubble for an extended period, e.g., $c_2$ and $c_3$.

**Gaps.** Like for models, the CASTeL logical specification requires extensions to the logics it builds upon. Firstly, our PCTL-like formulae use a bounded *until* operator. While this is sufficient for iterative time bounds, CASTeL also needs spatial bounds for iterating over space. For example, when reasoning inductively about vehicle routes, one may specify that cars will reach their planned destination based entirely on the road network's structure and spatial decisions. Secondly, players in alliances may resolve conflicts concurrently, and reward structures may be associated with alliances or individual players. Thirdly, alliances may be ad hoc. For example, bubbles of vehicles in proximity form such alliances. To this end, ATL-like formulae using the enforceability operator must be allowed to range over ad hoc alliances. To this end, we use player sets constrained by predicates like the *IsClose* predicate used in Table 1.

## 4   Related Work

Stochastic reward PNs have been used prior in the work of Chiola et al. [12] and Marsan et al. [2]. Their main objective was modelling close to the domain-specific informal models of practitioners, their quantitative reliability estimates, and risk management requirements. However, while methods to specify external events and risks were included, those to describe security risks such as cyber-attacks were not. The approach formed a basis for the creation of the GreatSPN tool for the stochastic analysis of systems modelled as (stochastic) PNs, see [6,13]. Heiner et al. introduced a comparative study of stochastic analysis techniques in [18]. Part of their approach was the tool *Snoopy* to model and simulate hierarchical graph-based system descriptions, see [17]. It allows users to analyse several kinds of PNs, including timed PNs and stochastic PNs.

The probabilistic model checker *Storm* was introduced in [15,19]. Storm supports the analysis of discrete- and continuous-time variants of both Markov chains and Markov decision processes (MDPs). Open-source Storm methods and tools are used in the backend of GreatSPN and PRISM.

Spatio-temporal models for formal analysis and property-based testing were presented in [4,33]. These works focus on supporting software engineers in understanding temporal models (making formal representations more accessible to the industrial application). Moreover, they provide a schematic translation of time-based constructs to the spatial analyser BeSpaceD [10]. Another approach to model spatial aspects of safety-critical systems was presented in [33]. That work applies the formal language Focus$^{ST}$ and presents an example system based on interacting autonomous vehicles.

In our previous work on BSpaceD [20,21], we have used theorem-proving modulo theory based on the Microsoft SMT prover Z3 [9] applied to industrial robotics and autonomous vehicles, such as collision avoidance in a primarily automated fulfilment centre. Space-time-related algorithms were written in Scala and check the satisfiability of speed-dependent safe spatiotemporal separation of any pair of mobile autonomous objects in proximity, including robot-to-robot movement or mobile robots in safe separation from human staff and movement.

## 5   Conclusion and Future Work

This paper presented an overview of CASTeL, a Concurrent Alliances Spatio-Temporal Logic. We illustrated it by a motivating scenario, in which we model an opportunistic mobile ad-hoc network formed by the cars or trucks crossing a communication dead spot and analyse possible variations.

The CASTeL approach builds on the marriage of elements from PCTL and ATL with reward structures and model-checked using concurrent Petri Nets, particularly Coloured Generalised Stochastic Petri Nets (GSPN). CASTeL stands apart from other temporal logics by providing extensions for spatial abstractions and spatially stochastic distributions. The concurrent interpretation of players (decision makers) enables reasoning and analyses about the collaboration within alliances and competition between them. Furthermore, the modelling focuses on system-level properties, which emerge from the interaction of the system components in the context of many concurrent individual failures, misbehaviours or malicious actions. We motivated these novel extensions with a mobile ad hoc network example and showed how dynamic alliance formation can be modelled. Moreover, we outlined how emergent safety and security properties can be guaranteed by model-checking within stochastic bounds using existing tools or suggested extensions. Our work uses backend tools with well-documented scalability limitations, in particular stochastic model-checkers and Petri net tools.

**Future Work:** Our future work will focus on detailed presentation of the CASTeL semantics and performance evaluations to help prioritise backend extensions aiming to relax limitations. One of the directions to evolve CASTeL is to cover scenarios where speeds vary arbitrarily by player choices, potentially due to road or traffic conditions. We already modelled the spatio-temporal resolution using model parameters (constants) and can therefore generate a sequence of models of finer granularity and plot the increasingly refined approximations of continuous models. Another direction is to consider the behaviour of drivers in an ad hoc alliance, and to classify them into categories such as cooperative, uncommitted or adversarial, corresponding to their willingness to deliver messages when exiting dead spots. This may include consideration of the relative rates of each type, such as in say 20 vehicles, there are expected to be 12 cooperative drivers, 7 uncommitted and 1 adversarial. In addition, one could consider the relative probabilities of cooperative, uncommitted and adversarial behaviour across sparse versus dense areas, or according to the number of vehicles in a given area.

In a future refined model, (i) the average speed may vary during a simulation run, for example, by the hour of the day and the day of the year, and (ii) the speed at a location may be varied for different cars, by adding additional token colours to a car (such as some proxy for speed: slow, moderate, fast or speeding).

Recent research has used machine learning to determine or fine-tune the rates in stochastic Petri Nets. About CASTeL and its underlying CSPN models, there are two promising approaches. Firstly, machine learning may assist in reducing the complexity of the reachability problem [30], permitting relatively fast simulation and model-checking by trading off accuracy about rare events. Secondly, AI learning of Markov processes has been applied to stochastic Petri Nets based on their reachability graphs when these are Markovian [25,34]. Then, machine-learning methods for Markov models and decision processes can be applied directly. However, non-Markovian reachability graphs reflect some history sensitivity. Large language models may capture sufficient history in the current state, i.e. via additional states and weights of their outgoing transitions.

# References


1. Ahmed, K., Blech, J.O., Gregory, M.A., Schmidt, H.: Software defined networking for communication and control of cyber-physical systems. In: 2015 IEEE 21st International Conference on Parallel and Distributed Systems (ICPADS), pp. 803–808. IEEE (2015)
2. Ajmone Marsan, M., Balbo, G., Bobbio, A., Chiola, G., Conte, G., Cumani, A., et al.: On Petri nets with stochastic timing. In: Timed Petri Nets, pp. 80–87. IEEE Computer Society Press (1985)

3. Alur, R., Henzinger, T.A., Kupferman, O.: Alternating-time temporal logic. J. ACM (JACM) **49**(5), 672–713 (2002)
4. Alzahrani, N., Spichkova, M., Blech, J.O.: Spatio-temporal models for formal analysis and property-based testing. In: Milazzo, P., Varró, D., Wimmer, M. (eds.) STAF 2016. LNCS, vol. 9946, pp. 196–206. Springer, Cham (2016). https://doi.org/10.1007/978-3-319-50230-4_14
5. Amanullah, M.A., Loke, S.W., Baruwal Chhetri, M., Doss, R.: A taxonomy and analysis of misbehaviour detection in cooperative intelligent transport systems: A systematic review. ACM Comput. Surv. **56**(1) (2023)
6. Amparore, E.G., Balbo, G., Beccuti, M., Donatelli, S., Franceschinis, G.: 30 years of GreatSPN. Principles of Performance and Reliability Modeling and Evaluation: Essays in Honor of Kishor Trivedi on his 70th Birthday, pp. 227–254 (2016)
7. Baarir, S., Beccuti, M., Cerotti, D., De Pierro, M., Donatelli, S., Franceschinis, G.: The GreatSPN tool: recent enhancements. ACM SIGMETRICS Performance Evaluation Review **36**(4), 4–9 (2009)
8. Bennaceur, A., et al.: Modelling and Analysing resilient cyber-physical systems. In: 2019 IEEE/ACM 14th International Symposium on Software Engineering for Adaptive and Self-Managing Systems (SEAMS), pp. 70–76 (2019)
9. Bjørner, N., Eisenhofer, C., Kovács, L.: Satisfiability modulo custom theories in Z3. In: Dragoi, C., Emmi, M., Wang, J. (eds.) Verification, Model Checking, and Abstract Interpretation, pp. 91–105. Springer Nature Switzerland, Cham (2023)
10. Blech, J.O., Schmidt, H.: BeSpaceD: Towards a Tool Framework and Methodology for the Specification and Verification of Spatial Behavior of Distributed Software Component Systems. Technical Report 1404.3537, arXiv.org (2014)
11. Chen, T., Forejt, V., Kwiatkowska, M., Parker, D., Simaitis, A.: Automatic verification of competitive stochastic systems. Formal Methods Syst. Design **43**, 61–92 (2013)
12. Chiola, G.: A software package for the analysis of generalized stochastic Petri net models. In: International Workshop on Timed Petri Nets, pp. 136–143. IEEE Computer Society, USA (1985)
13. Chiola, G., Franceschinis, G., Gaeta, R., Ribaudo, M.: Greatspn 1.7: Graphical editor and analyzer for timed and stochastic Petri nets. Perf. Eval. **24**(1-2), 47–68 (1995)
14. Clarke, E.M., Emerson, E.A.: Design and Synthesis of Synchronisation Skeletons using Branching Time Temporal Logic. In: Workshop on the Logic of Programs, pp. 52–71. No. 131 in LNCS, Springer-Verlag, Berlin (1981)
15. Dehnert, C., Junges, S., Katoen, J.P., Volk, M.: A storm is coming: A modern probabilistic model checker. In: Computer Aided Verification: 29th International Conference (CAV), pp. 592–600. Springer (2017)
16. Hansson, H., Jonsson, B.: A logic for reasoning about time and reliability. Formal Aspects Comput. **6**(5), 512–535 (1994)
17. Heiner, M., Richter, R., Schwarick, M.: Snoopy: a tool to design and animate/simulate graph-based formalisms. In: Proceedings of the 1st International Conference on Simulation Tools and Techniques for Communications, Networks and Systems & Workshops, pp. 1–10 (2008)
18. Heiner, M., Rohr, C., Schwarick, M., Streif, S.: A comparative study of stochastic analysis techniques. In: Proceedings of the 8th International Conference on Computational Methods in Systems Biology, pp. 96–106 (2010)
19. Hensel, C., Junges, S., Katoen, J.P., Quatmann, T., Volk, M.: The probabilistic model checker Storm. Int. J. Softw. Tools Technol. Transfer, pp. 1–22 (2022)

20. Herrmann, P., Blech, J.O.: Formal analysis of control software for cyber-physical systems. In: 2017 IEEE International Conference on Software Quality, Reliability and Security Companion (QRS-c), pp. 563–564 (2017)
21. Herrmann, P., Blech, J.O., Han, F., Schmidt, H.: Model-based development and spatiotemporal behavior of cyber-physical systems. In: Innovative Solutions and Applications of Web Services Technology, pp. 69–93. IGI Global (2019)
22. Krajzewicz, D.: Traffic simulation with SUMO simulation of urban mobility. In: Fundamentals of Traffic Simulation. International Series in Operations Research & Management Science, vol. 145, pp. 269–293. Springer, United States (2010)
23. Lin, Y.D., Hsu, Y.C.: Multihop Cellular: A New Architecture for Wireless Communications. In: IEEE INFOCCM, Conference on Computer Communications, vol. 3, pp. 1273–1282 (2000)
24. Lopez, P.A., et al.: Microscopic Traffic Simulation using SUMO. In: IEEE Intelligent Transportation Systems Conference (ITSC), pp. 2575–2582. IEEE (2018)
25. Mao, H., Liu, Z., Qiu, C.: Adaptive disassembly sequence planning for VR maintenance training via deep reinforcement learning. Int. J. Adv. Manuf. Technol. **124**(9), 3039–3048 (2023)
26. Meyer, J.A.E., Puka, E., Herrmann, P.: Utilizing Connectivity Maps to Accelerate V2I Communication in Cellular Network Dead Spots. In: 6th International Conference on Internet of Vehicles (IOV), pp. 76–87. No. 11894 in LNCS, Springer-Verlag, Kaohsiung, Taiwan (2019)
27. Puka, E., Herrmann, P.: Data dissemination for vehicles in temporary Cellular network dead spots. Int. J. Cyber-Phys. Syst. (IJCPS) **1**(2), 38–55 (2019)
28. Puka, E., Herrmann, P.: Simulating a Context-Aware Message Flooding Protocol to Mitigate Cellular Dead Spots with Realistic Drivers' Behavior. In: 24th IEEE International Conference on Intelligent Transportation (ITSC), pp. 1041–1048. IEEE, Indianapolis, IN, USA (2021)
29. Puka, E., Herrmann, P., Taherkordi, A.: Hybrid Context-aware Message Flooding for Dead Spot Mitigation in V2I Communication. In: 92nd IEEE Vehicular Technology Conference (VTC-Fall) pp. 1–7. IEEE VTS, Victoria, BC, Canada (2020)
30. Qi, H., Guang, M., Wang, J., Yan, C., Jiang, C.: Probabilistic reachability prediction of unbounded Petri nets: A machine learning method. IEEE Trans. Autom. Sci. Eng. pp. 1–13 (2023)
31. Schmidt, H., Spichkova, M.: Towards readability aspects of probabilistic mode automata. In: Proceedings of the 14th International Conference on Evaluation of Novel Approaches to Software Engineering, pp. 555–562 (2019)
32. Schmidt, H.W., Peake, I., Aysan, H.A., Punnekkat, S., Dobrin, R.: Towards probabilistic mode automata for adaptable resource-aware component-based systems design. In: Proceedings of the International Improoving Systems and Software Engineering Conference (2012)
33. Spichkova, M., Blech, J.O., Herrmann, P., Schmidt, H.: Modeling spatial aspects of safety-critical systems with focus-st. In: MoDeVVa'14, pp. 49–58. Springer (2014)
34. Vanson, G., Marangé, P., Levrat, E.: End-of-Life Decision making in circular economy using generalized colored stochastic Petri nets. Auton. Intell. Syst. **2**(1), 1–18 (2022)
35. Wi-Fi Alliance, P2P Technical Group: Wi-Fi Peer-to-Peer (P2P) Technical Specification v1.7 (2016)
36. Yusuf, I.I., et al.: Chiminey: Reliable computing and data management platform in the cloud. In: 37th IEEE International Conference on Software Engineering, vol. 2, pp. 677–680. IEEE (2015)

# VF-RL: A Reinforcement Learning-Based Coverage Improvement in Mobile IoT Networks Using Virtual Force


Raheleh Samadi[1]([✉]) [iD], Amin Nazari[1,2] [iD], and Jochen Seitz[1] [iD]

[1] Communication Networks Group, Technische Universität Ilmenau, Ilmenau, Germany
{samadi.raheleh,jochen.seitz}@tu-ilmenau.de
[2] Artificial Intelligence Group, Bu-Ali Sina University, Hamedan, Iran
a.nazari@eng.basu.ac.ir



**Abstract.** In low-power networks, sensors are typically deployed randomly or in a predetermined pattern to monitor an area for various applications such as environmental monitoring, surveillance, and disaster management. Efficient coverage strategies can significantly affect the energy consumption and operational lifetime of WSNs. By optimizing sensor deployment and coverage patterns, WSNs can minimize redundant sensing, communication overhead, and energy waste. This results in longer network lifetimes, reduced maintenance costs, and improved stability, especially in applications deployed in remote or harsh environments. In this paper, we aim to create a trade-off between balancing mobile sensors in IoT networks and achieving environmental coverage by presenting an approach based on the Q-learning reinforcement algorithm (VF-RL). This approach allows us to manage the mobility of the nodes in order to increase energy consumption and improve network coverage. For this purpose, the virtual force approach is used to calculate the distance of neighbors and their orientation. Simulation results with different scenarios show that the proposed approach performs well compared to VFA [18], VFPSO [16], ALO [1] and VF-IALO [17] algorithms in three different scenarios.

**Keywords:** Mobile Internet of Things · Q-Learning · Coverage


## 1 Introduction

In recent years, low-power sensor networks have emerged as a leading technology in wireless communication and the Internet, for a wide variety of applications, from environmental monitoring to healthcare and industrial automation. Sensor networks consist of small, resource-constrained sensor nodes equipped with sensing, processing, and communication capabilities that are designed to operate efficiently with minimal energy consumption. These networks play a pivotal role



A. Soylu et al. (Eds.): MobiQuitous 2024, LNICST 634, pp. 238–255, 2026.
https://doi.org/10.1007/978-3-032-10554-7_13

in collecting and transmitting environmental data from remote or inaccessible locations and facilitate real-time monitoring and analysis for various purposes.

One of the most important challenges faced in the field of low-power Internet of Things networks is the issue of environmental coverage. The challenge is to ensure that sensor nodes are strategically deployed to adequately cover the target area, thereby enabling monitoring and data collection. The importance of achieving effective environmental coverage cannot be ignored, as it directly affects the reliability, accuracy, and usefulness of the data collected by the sensor network [9].

The effect of coverage on energy consumption in mobile and static sensor nodes in environmental monitoring systems is significant. In most applications, more nodes are deployed to cover the environment better, and this increase in density leads to more energy consumption. These nodes often need to transmit data frequently to ensure event coverage, which increases communication costs and energy consumption. On the other hand, in environments where nodes are deployed in a dispersed manner, they need to transmit data over longer distances, which leads to higher transmission power and, as a result, more energy consumption. Also, in mobile sensor networks, energy consumption is affected by frequency and movement patterns. Nodes may need to spend additional energy to adjust their position or maintain connectivity while moving, which affects overall energy consumption.

Sensor nodes are deployed in the environment in two ways: random and deterministic. In *random* distribution, sensor nodes are randomly placed in the environment, without considering a particular pattern or structure of the environment. This method is usually used for environments that are unknown or dynamic because it has the ability to adapt to environmental changes. In *deterministic* distribution, sensor nodes are placed deterministically and according to certain patterns and structures of the environment. This method often requires detailed knowledge and analysis of the environment and is usually used for environments with a specific and stable structure [3].

Various approaches and techniques have been proposed to deal with the environmental coverage challenge in low power sensor networks. In [2], the authors divide the coverage algorithms into three groups: centralized, distributed and local. In the process of deploying nodes in a local and distributed manner, since the topology is dynamic in nature, neighborhood information is used in each node, and in the centralized method, the decision-making process is centralized. However, due to the limitations of low-power sensors and the diverse environments in which they may be used, creating algorithms that both guarantee the coverage of the environment and are optimal creates many challenges.

The main contribution of this article is as follows:

- Using reinforcement learning for intelligent node movement without the need for comprehensive network information.
- Improving coverage rate and algorithm convergence speed by learning the displacement rate.

- Switching off nodes whose coverage area is fully covered by other nodes reduces energy consumption and network traffic and prevents redundant packets from transferring in the network.

Section 2 delves into recent research that has focused on coverage in sensor and low-power networks as its main research theme. Section 3 discusses system modeling and the definition of this study's main mechanisms. Section 4 addresses the simulation parameters and the evaluation of the results. Finally, Sect. 5 presents the conclusion.

## 2   Related Work

Coverage in sensor networks is a quality of service metric. Its purpose is the balanced distribution of nodes in the defined environment so that area events can be sensed at the lowest cost. In general, the coverage problem is solved in two ways: full and partial coverage. In large-scale networks with randomly distributed nodes, probabilistic coverage is inefficient, and node density in a specific area leads to energy wastage and reduced network reliability. Many researches and studies have investigated coverage protocols, and different classifications have been created based on the techniques used. They classified coverage problems according to the frequency of the network field monitor, the area to be monitored, and connection-aware and non-connection-aware protocols. On the other hand, coverage protocols are implemented in two ways: distributed or centralized [2,5, 8,13].

In [17], the authors define the coverage problem as an NP-hard problem. They utilize an improved Ant Lion optimization algorithm to optimize node movement and enhance coverage in both local and global forms in wireless sensor networks. For this purpose, the node positions in the network are updated using the Virtual Forces algorithm.

In the study [7], the authors designed a distributed approach for activating a number of relay nodes needed for data transmission in IoT networks. For this purpose, each relay node individually considers a trade-off between network throughput and individual transmission power consumption. Furthermore, the authors consider the cumulative future reward system for large-scale state-action pairs using a deep neural network.

Authors in [10] propose a Delaunay-based coordinate-free mechanism (DECM) for full coverage in wireless sensor networks (WSNs). In this work, Delaunay triangulation is executed based on a mathematical model, and the desired environment is divided into triangles. Then, by meeting the defined conditions, the holes are identified, and the search for the shortest path to cover the holes is accomplished.

Study [15] proposes an approach to solving the coverage optimization problem by combining two metaheuristic algorithms: the Artificial Bee Colony (ABC) algorithm and the Simulated Annealing (SA) algorithm. By considering various strategies, this work enhances the possibility of escaping from a local optimum and improving global search.

A game-theoretic approach based on reinforcement learning designed for a harsh and hostile environment is presented in [6]. In this study, each node only communicates with its neighboring nodes and utilizes node mobility and transmission power adjustment to cover existing holes in the defined environment in a decentralized way.

Another notable work on efficient coverage is the study [12]. In this work, the authors present a scheduling approach that uses Nash Q-learning reinforcement learning for connection coverage and maintenance. Furthermore, a threshold is considered for the deployment of nodes, and the learning ability is placed inside each sensor to minimize the total number of active nodes in each scheduling cycle.

In the work [4], the authors consider a network with mobile sensor nodes and introduce a new approach by integrating the Voronoi cell structure and the K-means algorithm. In the proposed mechanism, the cluster centers are determined by the K-means algorithm. Then, the problem of covering the desired environment by the Voronoi cell structure is considered with the help of the Glowworm Swarm Optimization (GSO) algorithm to find the optimal positions of the sensor nodes.

In recent years, the importance of the coverage issue in sensor networks has been paid more attention and significant work has been done in this field. Most recent studies have used meta-heuristic algorithms for coverage optimization. These algorithms need information such as coordinates of nodes, neighbors, etc. to solve the problem. First, this data is collected in a central node or sink and then distributed among the nodes, which causes traffic overhead and energy consumption. Since the proposed method uses the reinforcement learning algorithm, it does not need the coordinates of the nodes and operates based on the strength of the signal received from the neighbors and the orientation algorithm. On the other hand, due to the mobility of nodes, the network is highly dynamic and a node may be removed or fail at any moment. This problem is investigated locally in the proposed method without involving the whole network and the simulation results also show the fast convergence of the network.

## 3   System Model

### 3.1   Q-Learning Algorithm

Q-learning algorithm is one of the most important reinforcement learning algorithms used in the field of artificial intelligence and machine learning. This algorithm, using the Markov bounded decision process (MDP), allows the agent to gain experience through interaction with the environment and learn an optimal behavior or strategy by trying to obtain the maximum reward. One of the important features of Q-learning is that it uses offline learning. In the sense that the agent collects the required information through interaction with the environment and gradually learns an optimal solution without the need for contextual communication with an external trainer. According to Eq. (1), the goal of Q-learning is to approximate the value-action function $NewQ(s, a)$, which represents the expected cumulative reward of performing action $a$ in state $s$ and the reward that will be received in the future.

$$NewQ(s,a) = Q(s,a) + \alpha \cdot [R(s,a) + \gamma \cdot max_{a'}Q(s',a') - Q(s,a)] \tag{1}$$

where

- $Q(s,a)$ is the Q-value for taking action $a$ in state $s$.
- $\alpha$ is the learning rate ($0 < \alpha \leq 1$), which determines how quickly the Q-values are updated based on new experiences. A rate of 0 means the agent doesn't learn anything new and sticks to old data, while a rate of 1 means it completely ignores old data and only learns from new information.
- $R(s,a)$ is the immediate reward received after taking action $a$ in state $s$.
- $\gamma$ is the discount factor ($0 < \gamma \leq 1$) which determines the importance of future rewards. By prioritizing immediate rewards over future rewards, it ensures convergence and avoids infinite loops. So a value of 0 forces the agent to seek immediate rewards, while a rate of 1 forces it to strive for long-term rewards.
- $max_{a'}Q(s',a')$ represents the maximum Q-value over all possible actions $a'$ in the next state $s'$ reached after taking action $a$ in state $s$.

One of the key challenges in reinforcement learning is the trade-off between exploration and exploitation. Q-learning typically uses the parameter $\varepsilon$, where with probability $\varepsilon$, a random action is chosen to encourage exploration, and with probability $1-\varepsilon$, the action with the highest Q-value is chosen to exploit current knowledge.

### 3.2    Computation of Virtual Force

Since the considered environment is highly dynamic due to the movement of sensor nodes, the goal of learning is to reach an equilibrium state in the network and fully cover the environment. Therefore, we use the Virtual Force Algorithm (VFA) to calculate the balance of the distribution of nodes in the network.

In wireless sensor networks (WSN), "virtual forces" is a concept used to model and analyze the behavior of sensor nodes in a distributed manner. VFA is inspired by disk packing theory and the virtual force field concept from robotics and applies them metaphorically to the movements and interactions of sensor nodes in the network [18].

Virtual forces in WSNs provide a decentralized approach to node coordination and optimization, allowing sensor nodes to self-organize and adapt to changing network conditions without centralized control. By mimicking natural phenomena such as attraction and repulsion, Virtual Forces algorithms provide a scalable and robust framework to improve coverage, connectivity, and energy efficiency. Each sensor acts as a "power source" for other sensors. This force can be positive (attractive) or negative (repulsive). The repulsive force pushes the nodes away from each other to maintain the minimum distance based on the threshold. Each node calculates the force applied to itself based on the Euclidean distance of Eq. (2) by calculating the distance of its neighbors and their orientation. The amount of movement is calculated as follows in the Eqs. (3) to (7):

$$d(x_i, P) = \sqrt{(x_i - x)^2 + (y_i - y)^2} \tag{2}$$

$$f_i^x = \sum_{j \in N_i} \frac{1}{x_i - x_j} \tag{3}$$

$$f_i^y = \sum_{j \in N_i} \frac{1}{y_i - y_j} \tag{4}$$

$$\overrightarrow{F} = \sum_{dir \in \text{Top,Right,Bottom,Left}} f_{dir} \tag{5}$$

$$dx = \frac{\text{MaxIter} - \text{iter}}{\text{MaxIter}} \times \overrightarrow{F} \tag{6}$$

$$X^{new} = X + \alpha \cdot dx \tag{7}$$

First, $f_i^x$ and $f_i^y$ calculate the forces in the x and y directions for all neighbors within the node's coverage range. Then, the resultant forces are determined by $\overrightarrow{F}$ based on the directions of the neighboring nodes. Initially, the amount of movement is more and decreases over time. $dx$ represents the effect of the applied force over time. $MaxIter$ and $iter$ mention the maximum number of iterations and current iteration, respectively. Also, $\alpha$ is the coefficient.

When the node reaches equilibrium, the result of the forces becomes zero ($\overrightarrow{F} = 0$). Therefore, the reward received from the environment is equal to the result of forces. For node movement, we have considered a Markov model. At the beginning, the node is in the state $s_0$, and the result of the forces is computed. Unlike previous works that choose only one action among all possible operations, we choose two actions simultaneously. First, the up and down force is calculated, and the direction with the highest q-value is considered. Then, we choose the movement with the highest q-value between moving to the left or right. Figure (1) shows the sequence of these two actions.

The future reward is based on the amount of coverage that the node can achieve in the entire network. For this purpose, the hole areas are detected locally first, and the nearest node is moved to the hole by the gravitational movement mechanism, and then force reinforcement is considered to increase the maximum coverage. The description of the functioning of these mechanisms is discussed in the following sections.

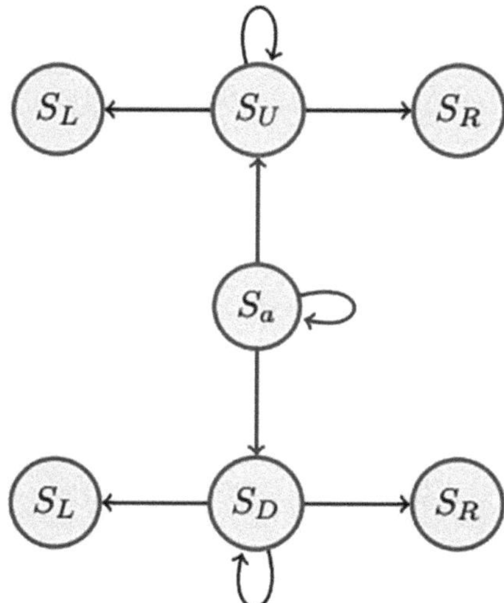

**Fig. 1.** The sequence of node movement: First, node $S_a$ chooses to move up or down according to the highest q-value, and then considers the direction of its movement to the left or right by calculating the highest q-value.

### 3.3   Hole Detection

This study used the Delaunay triangulation algorithm to identify the hole [14]. The Delaunay triangulation algorithm is used in computational geometry to create triangles from a set of points in a plane. It is commonly employed in various fields, including computer graphics, geographic information systems, and wireless sensor networks (WSNs). In this work, each node performs triangulation according to Fig. (2), considering the information of its one-step neighbors. Afterward, if the length of one of the sides is equal to or greater than two times the coverage range for each triangle, that triangle has a hole. By looking at the triangles formed by the Delaunay triangulation, it is possible to see where the sensors are densely packed (many triangles) and where there may be gaps (fewer or no triangles). If the node detects a hole around itself, it moves towards the hole to get the future reward. This movement is considered a type of gravitational movement.

In addition, when no force enters the node from one side, it means that it is probably a hole. Therefore, the force on the opposite side is strengthened by the alpha factor. The next location of the node will be determined from the combination of these forces.

### 3.4   Switching Off Overlapping Nodes

After applying Delaunay triangulation and identifying holes, the nodes create a triangulation among their neighbors, considering their distances but ignoring their own position. If the neighbors can cover the area completely without

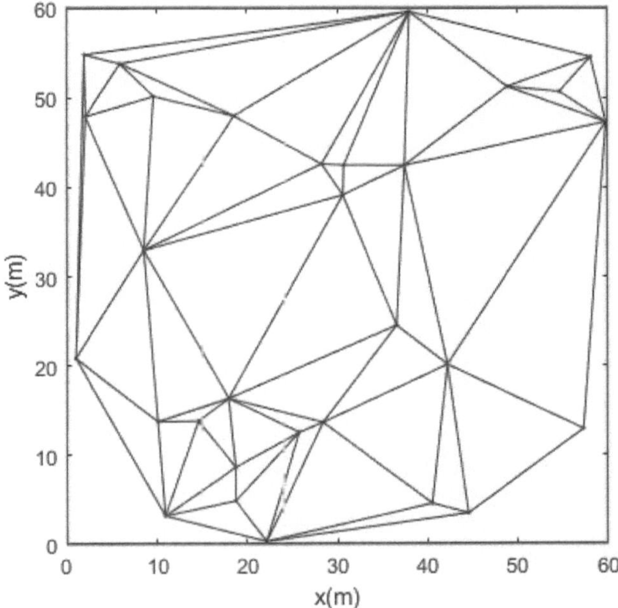

**Fig. 2.** Delaunay triangulation.

creating holes, the node goes into sleep mode. This means the node becomes temporarily inactive until it is needed again. In this way, complete coverage of the area is ensured, and excessive energy consumption is prevented since nodes are only active when there is a real need for their presence. Additionally, by deactivating nodes during non-essential times, no redundant data is generated, and the transmission of duplicate packets is avoided. Figure (3) shows an overview of the process.

Consequently, network traffic is reduced, and the overall efficiency of the network improves. This method not only leads to energy savings but also extends the networks lifespan, as optimal energy consumption reduces the depreciation of nodes and network equipment. Overall, this smart management strategy increases efficiency, reduces costs, and improves network performance in the long term.

## 4   Simulation and Results

This section analyzes and evaluates the effectiveness and performance of the proposed protocol in different scenarios. The Delaunay triangle is implemented to find the holes using MATLAB, and afterward the mobile sensor nodes choose the optimal position for coverage in the network using the Q-learning algorithm based on Virtual Forces and move to that direction. Figure (4) show how to triangulate and detect holes, respectively.

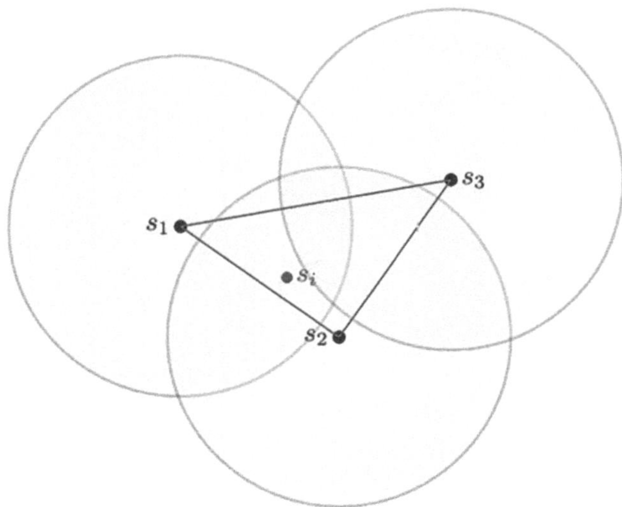



**Fig. 3.** Creating a triangulation among the neighbors $s_1$, $s_2$ and $s_3$ of node $s_i$.

The proposed approach (VF-RL) is compared with VFA [18], VFPSO [16], ALO [1] and VF-IALO [17] algorithms in three different scenarios and the results are evaluated based on the defined criteria. The simulation parameters are shown in Table 1, and the scenarios are defined in Table 2.

**Coverage Criteria:** Assume that $N$ sensor nodes are randomly deployed in the monitoring area $A$ with an area of $L \times L (m^2)$ and all nodes have the ability to move in the environment. All sensor nodes have the same sensing radius $R_s$. $S = s_1, s_2, ..., s_N$ represents the set of sensor nodes and the node $s_i$ is located at the point $(x_i, y_j)$. We can divide the monitored environment into $m \times n$ points. If the Euclidean distance between the position of node $i$ and point $k$ is less than the coverage range of the node, that point is covered by the node. Our goal is to calculate only the points that are covered by at least one node. Figure (5) shows the random deployment of sensor nodes in the first stage and then the final coverage affected by the implementation of the VF-RL.

Therefore, the coverage rate can be calculated according to the Eqs. 9 and 8:

$$R_{cov} = \frac{\sum_{k=1}^{m \times n} C(s_i, P_k)}{m \times n} \tag{8}$$

$$C(s_i, P_k) = \begin{cases} 1, & \text{if } d(s_i, P_k) \leq R_s \\ 0, & \text{if } d(s_i, P_k) > R_s \end{cases} \tag{9}$$

where $d(s_i, P_k)$ represents the distance of the $ith$ sensor to the point that needs to be covered. If this distance from any of the sensors to the point in

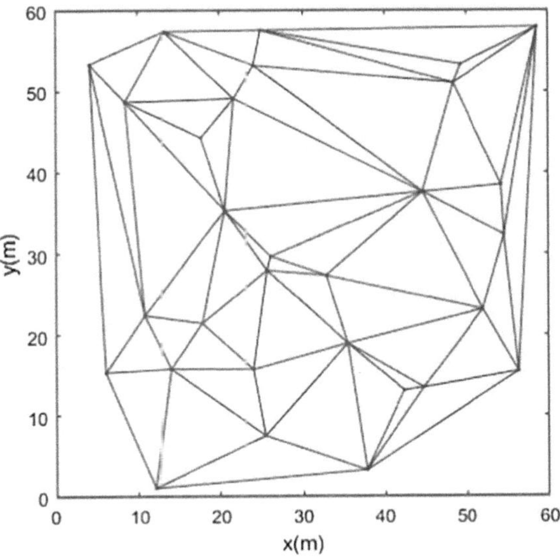

(a) Initial Delaunay triangle.

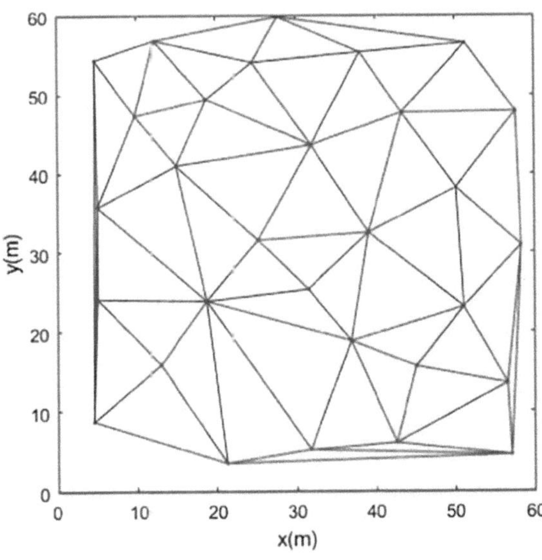

(b) Final Delaunay triangle.

**Fig. 4.** The Delaunay triangulation in VF-RL approach for monitoring area 60x60.

question is less than the sensor's coverage range $R_s$, coverage is achieved; otherwise, that point is not covered. Furthermore $C$ indicates the coverage rate, which represents the number of points that are covered.

**Table 1.** Simulation Parameters.

| Parameters | Values |
| --- | --- |
| | $60m \times 60m$ |
| Monitoring Area Size | $120m \times 120m$ |
| | $210m \times 210m$ |
| Maximum Number of Repetitions | 30 |
| Coverage Range $(R_s)$ | $10m$ |
| Data Packet size | $4000 Bits$ |
| Hello Packet size | $256 Bits$ |
| $E_{fs}$ | $10pJ/bit/m^2$ |
| $E_{mp}$ | $0.0013pJ/bit/m^4$ |
| $E_{DA}$ | $5nJ/bit$ |
| $ETx/ERx$ | $50nJ/bit$ |
| Learning rate | $\alpha = 0.1$ |
| Discount rate | $\gamma = 0.9$ |

**Table 2.** Scenarios

| Scenario | Network Size | Number of Nodes |
| --- | --- | --- |
| 1 | $60m \times 60m$ | 30 |
| 2 | $120m \times 120m$ | 120 |
| 3 | $200m \times 200m$ | 340 |

The evaluation results in Figs. (6), (7) and (8) show that in the first scenario, the proposed approach outperforms VFA by 14.94%, VF-ALO by 14.5%, VF-PSO by 5.3%, and VF-IALO by 2.04%. Additionally, as the size of the area and the number of sensor nodes increase, in the second scenario, VF-RL demonstrates an average improvement of 10.74%. In the final scenario, VF-RL proves its optimal performance with an average improvement of 14.19% compared to the aforementioned methods.

Additionally, the speed of convergence in VF-RL is very high, achieving over 95% coverage in just 5 rounds, while other methods require more time for complete coverage. This rapid convergence is due to the proposed approach's ability to adapt to existing conditions. This means that the speed and displacement of the nodes are selected intelligently, and node reinforcement with gravitational force results in quicker coverage of holes.

**Node Movement:** The energy consumption for node movement is much more than the communication energy consumption. Since the energy consumption for node movement is determined by distance, node movement is an important measure of the algorithm's efficiency, which is calculated as the Eq. 10:

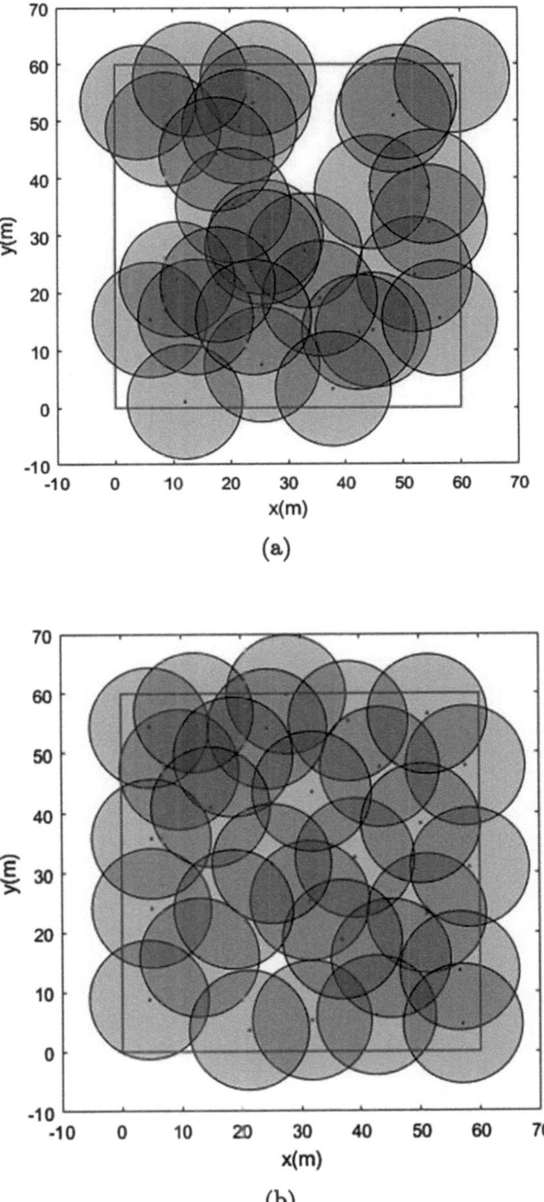

**Fig. 5.** Random deployment of sensor nodes and the final coverage affected by the VF-RL for monitoring area 60x60. (a) Random deployment of sensor nodes. (b) Final coverage.

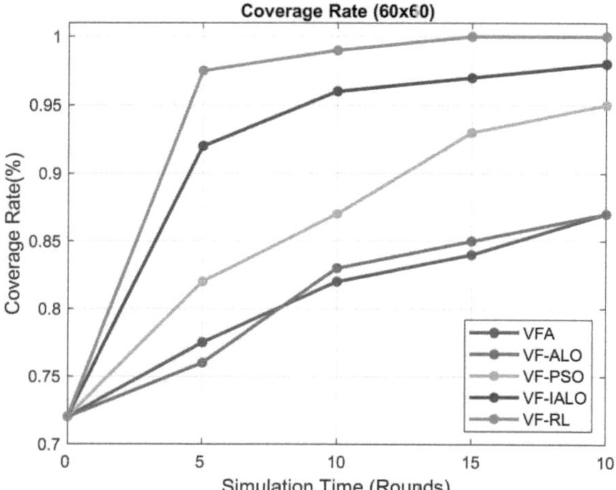

**Fig. 6.** Coverage rate in the first scenario.

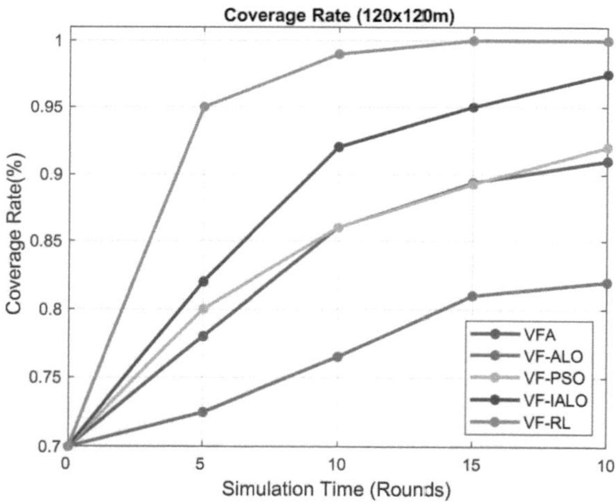

**Fig. 7.** Coverage rate in the second scenario.

$$d = \frac{1}{S} \sum_{i=1}^{S} d_i \tag{10}$$

As Fig. (9) shows, in the first scenario, the proposed approach significantly improves the average movement distance compared to VF-ALO and VF-PSO algorithms by 26.73% and 33.71%, respectively. However, with a slight differ-

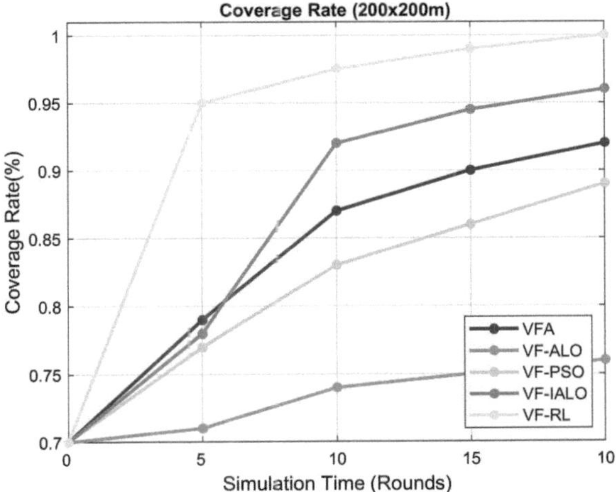



**Fig. 8.** Coverage rate in the third scenario.

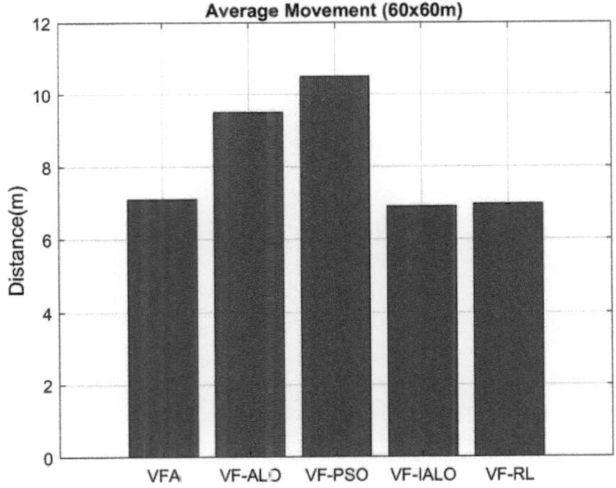



**Fig. 9.** The average moving distance in the first scenario.

ence, VF-RL works better than VFA and VF-IALO algorithms. As the network expands, VF-RL in Fig. (10) demonstrates increasingly acceptable performance in managing mobility and conserving energy. In the second scenario, the proposed approach shows improvements of 15.26%, 19.5%, and 46.33% compared to the VFA, VF-ALO, and VF-PSO approaches, respectively. According to Figure (11), in the third scenario, VF-RL achieves improvements of 13.66%, 23.37%, and 44.27% over the same approaches. The simulation results reveal nearly identical performance for the VF-RL and the VF-IALO approach, highlighting the optimal effectiveness of these methods.

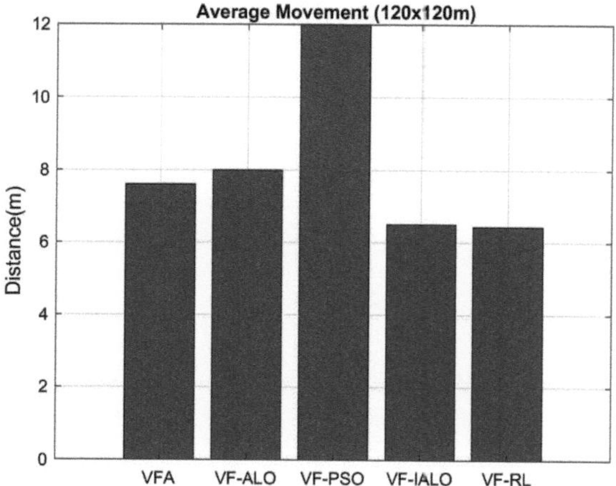

**Fig. 10.** The average moving distance in the second scenario.

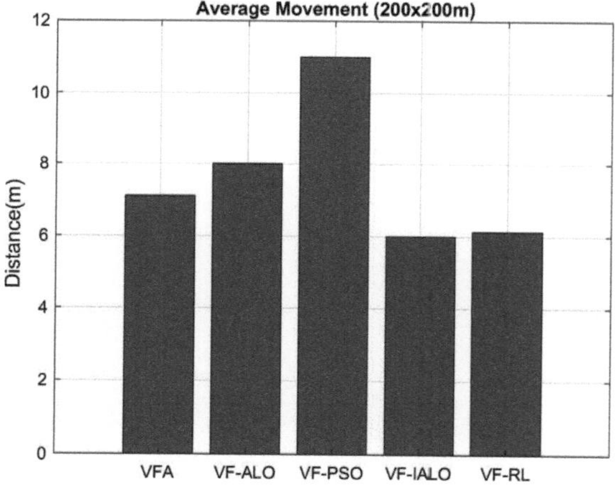

**Fig. 11.** The average moving distance in the third scenario.

**Reducing Energy Consumption:** Sleeping overlapping nodes is essential because nodes located in the same coverage area produce similar data, which causes data redundancy. Figures (12) and (13) indicate the number of sleeping nodes and the amount of energy saved in different scenarios, respectively. This amount of energy is measured for one round and in seconds.

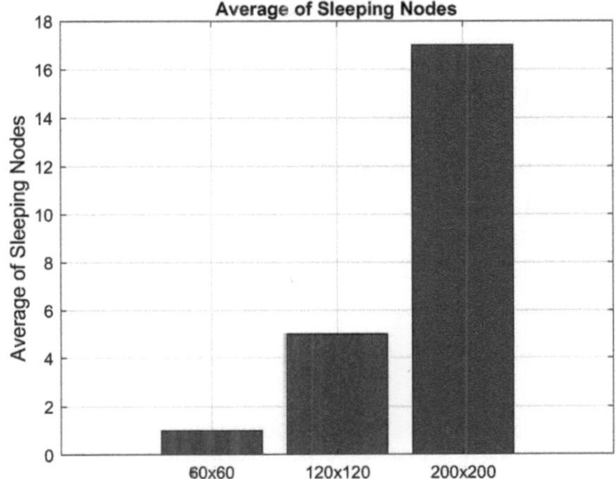

**Fig. 12.** The number of sleeping nodes in each scenario.

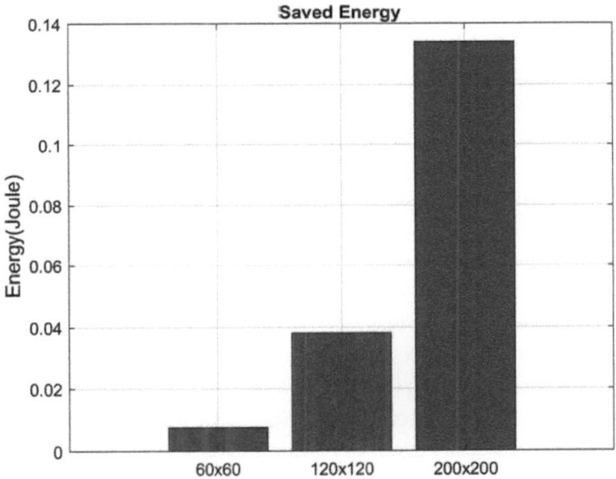

**Fig. 13.** The amount of energy saved in each scenario.

# 5   Conclusion

In this paper, we have introduced the VF-RL approach, which achieves environmental coverage by using the Q-Learning algorithm while balancing the mobile sensor nodes. For this purpose, the Delaunay algorithm was used to identify network holes and virtual force was used to calculate the distance and orientation of neighbors. Also, to save the energy of the sensor nodes and reduce the network traffic, the overlapping nodes in this study temporarily go to sleep mode. This method increases the network's efficiency and lifetime.

In the last step, various criteria have been used to evaluate this study. The simulation results show that the proposed approach can reach convergence quickly and cover the network well.

In our future work, we aim to enhance the average movement of mobile nodes within the network and increase the number of nodes entering sleep mode. We plan to treat coverage as a task for the controller in the software-defined networking (SDN) in our previous paper [11] and assess its performance in SDN-based mobile low-power sensor networks.

# References


1. Ammari, H.M., Das, S.K.: Coverage, connectivity, and fault tolerance measures of wireless sensor networks. In: Datta, A.K., Gradinariu, M. (eds.) SSS 2006. LNCS, vol. 4280, pp. 35–49. Springer, Heidelberg (2006). https://doi.org/10.1007/978-3-540-49823-0_3
2. Amutha, J., Sharma, S., Nagar, J.: WSN strategies based on sensors, deployment, sensing models, coverage and energy efficiency: review, approaches and open issues. Wireless Pers. Commun. **111**(2), 1089–1115 (2020)
3. Cheng, C.F., Hsu, C.C.: The deterministic sensor deployment problem for barrier coverage in WSNs with irregular shape areas. IEEE Sens. J. **22**(3), 2899–2911 (2021)
4. Chowdhury, A., De, D.: Energy-efficient coverage optimization in wireless sensor networks based on voronoi-glowworm swarm optimization-k-means algorithm. Ad. Hoc. Netw. **122**, 102660 (2021)
5. Elhabyan, R., Shi, W., St-Hilaire, M.: Coverage protocols for wireless sensor networks: review and future directions. J. Commun. Netw. **21**(1), 45–60 (2019)
6. Hajjej, F., Hamdi, M., Ejbali, R., Zaied, M.: A distributed coverage hole recovery approach based on reinforcement learning for wireless sensor networks. Ad. Hoc. Netw. **101**, 102082 (2020)
7. Kwon, M., Lee, J., Park, H.: Intelligent IoT connectivity: deep reinforcement learning approach. IEEE Sens. J. **20**(5), 2782–2791 (2019)
8. Osamy, W., Khedr, A.M., Salim, A., Al Ali, A.I., El-Sawy, A.A.: Coverage, deployment and localization challenges in wireless sensor networks based on artificial intelligence techniques: a review. IEEE Access **10**, 30232–30257 (2022)
9. Priyadarshi, R., Gupta, B., Anurag, A.: Wireless sensor networks deployment: a result oriented analysis. Wireless Pers. Commun. **113**(2), 843–866 (2020). https://doi.org/10.1007/s11277-020-07255-9
10. Qiu, C., Shen, H.: A delaunay-based coordinate-free mechanism for full coverage in wireless sensor networks. IEEE Trans. Parallel Distrib. Syst. **25**(4), 828–839 (2013)
11. Samadi, R., Nazari, A., Seitz, J.: Intelligent energy-aware routing protocol in mobile IoT networks based on SDN. IEEE Trans. Green Commun. Netw. (2023)
12. Sharma, A., Chauhan, S.: A distributed reinforcement learning based sensor node scheduling algorithm for coverage and connectivity maintenance in wireless sensor network. Wireless Netw. **26**(6), 4411–4429 (2020)
13. Singh, M.K., Amin, S.I., Choudhary, A.: A survey on the characterization parameters and lifetime improvement techniques of wireless sensor network. Frequenz **75**(9–10), 431–448 (2021)

14. Soundarya, A., Santhi, V.: An efficient algorithm for coverage hole detection and healing in wireless sensor networks. In: 1st International Conference on Electronics, Materials Engineering and Nano-Technology (IEMENTech), pp. 1–5. IEEE (2017)
15. Wang, J., Liu, Y., Rao, S., Zhou, X., Hu, J.: A novel self-adaptive multi-strategy artificial bee colony algorithm for coverage optimization in wireless sensor networks. Ad Hoc Netw. **150**, 103284 (2023)
16. Wang, X., Wang, S., Bi, D.: Virtual force-directed particle swarm optimization for dynamic deployment in wireless sensor networks. In: Huang, D.-S., Heutte, L., Loog, M. (eds.) ICIC 2007. LNCS, vol. 4681, pp. 292–303. Springer, Heidelberg (2007). https://doi.org/10.1007/978-3-540-74171-8_29
17. Yao, Y., Li, Y., Xie, D., Hu, S., Wang, C., Li, Y.: Coverage enhancement strategy for wsns based on virtual force-directed ant lion optimization algorithm. IEEE Sens. J. **21**(17), 19611–19622 (2021)
18. Zou, Y., Chakrabarty, K.: Sensor deployment and target localization based on virtual forces. In: IEEE INFOCOM 2003. Twenty-second Annual Joint Conference of the IEEE Computer and Communications Societies (IEEE Cat. No. 03CH37428). vol. 2, pp. 1293–1303. IEEE (2003)

# Machine Learning, AI, and Smart Systems

# A Service-Based Real-Time Anomaly Detection Method for Sensor Stream Data


Zhongmei Zhang[1(✉)] and Shuai Zhang[2]

[1] School of Management Engineering, Shandong Jianzhu University, Jinan 250101, Shandong, China
zhangzhongmei20@sdjzu.edu.cn

[2] Jinan Branch of China Unicom Software Research Institute, Jinan 250100, Shandong, China
zhangs837@chinaunicom.cn



**Abstract.** Amounts of sensor stream data are collected in industrial area, diverse modes and dynamic working condition, and puts forward higher requirements for efficient and effective anomaly detection. The interplay and mutual influence among sensor streams suggest that underlying correlation can be used to identify and explain abnormal problems. This paper introduces an innovative service-based anomaly detection method that leverages lag-correlation analysis of stream data. It first constructs correlation graph model based on lag-correlation analysis of history data, and divides sensor stream data groups based on correlation degree. Then sensor stream groups are encapsulated as corresponding stream data services, and realize the real-time anomaly detection within and out of stream groups in a discrete way based on service collaboration. Experimental results on a real industrial sensor dataset demonstrate the effectiveness of the proposed method in detecting anomalies across multiple sensor streams.

**Keywords:** Stream Data Service · Anomaly Detection · Lag-correlation Analysis · Service Collaboration


## 1 Introduction

With the rapid development of digitalization in the manufacturing industry, amounts of sensors, controllers, and intelligent products are employed to record and percept the operational status and operating environment [1, 2], and accumulated and generated a large amount of industrial sensor stream data. By analyzing and mining multi-dimensional stream data, it is possible to diagnose and warn monitored and predicted anomaly problems. It is an important task for lean production and smart manufacturing, as well as an important research question in industrial big data analysis [3].

Currently, complex anomaly in high-dimensional sensor streams is gradually receiving attention. The anomaly of one sensor stream often involves the interaction and effects of other streams, making it more difficult to detect and identify these abnormal patterns. And sensor streams have characteristics such as large volume, heterogeneity, continuously, low value density, and strong dynamics, which brings difficulties and challenges to anomaly detection.




A. Soylu et al. (Eds.): MobiQuitous 2024, LNICST 634, pp. 259–274, 2026.
https://doi.org/10.1007/978-3-032-10554-7_14

Most existing anomaly detection methods focus on addressing anomalies in single-dimensional sensor stream with periodicity or simple patterns, making it difficult to effectively model and differentiate between abnormal and normal patterns. They cannot meet the requirements of anomaly detection in industrial sensor streams with diverse patterns and variable operating conditions. Although there are some machine learning-based models for handling high-dimensional time series data, their computations often lack interpretability, and the reliability of their results is insufficient for industrial sensor streams anomaly detection needs.

Leveraging the reusability and interoperability of services, numerous researchers [4–6] have incorporated Service-Oriented Architecture (SOA) technologies into IoT systems to decouple low-level streaming data from upper-layer applications. The servitization of industrial sensor streams enables developers to process sensor data more effectively through the flexible management of software components. In studies [7, 8], a service abstraction known as proactive data service was introduced, designed to facilitate flexible service collaboration for dynamic stream data.

The correlation among sensor streams can enhance the discriminative accuracy of anomaly detection tasks. While in industrial production environments, there may exist a certain latency in the correlation between sensor stream data. For instance, in the primary fan equipment of a thermal power plant, the inlet pressure impacts the outlet pressure after a few seconds. This lag-correlation can also be indicative of the anomaly propagation path. In this paper, we focus on developing sensor stream services that leverages lag-correlation analysis combined with proactive data service model to effectively and efficiently detect anomalies in real time. The key contributions can be summarized as follows:

- For discovering the correlation among sensor streams more accuracy, we used Dynamic Time Warping (DTW) based algorithm to analyze the lag-correlation between sensor stream data, and constructs a correlation graph model to record the correlation information.
- We proposed a stream data service-based method to realize the anomaly detection more efficiency in a discrete way. We partitioned sensor streams into different groups based on correlation graph model, and encapsulated each group's streams into services based on proactive data service model. And correlation pruning is adopted to further improve the efficiency.
- Through experiments conducted on real datasets, this paper validated the effectiveness and efficiency of our method. By comparing with machine learning-based and ordinary correlation analysis methods, the proposed method outperforms baseline algorithms in terms of precision and recall, and can effectively saving computation time.

The organization of this paper is as follows: Sect. 2 introduces related work. Section 3 details the main methods of this paper. Section 4 presents the experiment and analysis. Section 5 gives the conclusion.

## 2  Related Work

### 2.1  Anomaly Detection Methods

Anomaly detection is a widely researched problem across various disciplines and applications, which aims to identify unusual data values or patterns that do not conform to normalcy, constraints, rules, or a given model [9]. With the growing emphasis on temporal and time-sensitive data, researchers have focused on anomaly detection in temporal data, such as on time series, data streams, spatiotemporal data, and temporal network data [10]. Current anomaly detection methods can generally be categorized into three types: constraint rule-based methods [11, 12], traditional machine learning-based methods [13–17], and deep learning-based methods [18–20].

Constraint rule-based anomaly detection methods are mostly specific to certain fields, detecting anomalies in time series data based on predefined rules. Although this approach is simple and easy to implement, it cannot handle situations where anomaly patterns are complex and variable. Anomaly detection methods based on traditional machine learning models can be effectively applied to various detection tasks, including those based on statistical models [13, 14] (such as ARIMA and FP-Growth), clustering-based methods [15] (such as K-Means), and classification models [16, 17] (such as SVM, Random Forest, and Neural Networks). In addition, some work [18, 19] have leveraged RNNs and other deep learning models to achieve anomaly detection in time series data. In recent years, researchers [20] have also explored the use of transformer models for this purpose, demonstrating significant improvements and achieving commendable results.

Existing machine learning-based models are capable of handling high-dimensional temporal data, but their computations often lack interpretability, and the reliability of their results may not meet the requirements of industrial time series data anomaly detection. Some works have explored the mechanism of data correlations and utilized the information of correlations for anomaly detection. For example, Ding et al. [21] proposed a latent sequence correlation calculation model for anomaly detection in industrial data sequences. Zhang et al. [14] proposed an improved FP-growth algorithm to discover status co-occurrence patterns in power plant data for anomaly detection. Additionally, Ding et al. [22] proposed a multidimensional time series anomaly detection method based on sequence correlation analysis, but they did not consider the possibility of correlation offsets between data. Building upon existing work, this paper aims to address the offset of data correlations for more accurate anomaly detection.

### 2.2  Stream Data Services

With the rapid development of stream data research, the fusion between service computing and IoT has garnered significant interest from both academic and industrial circles. Researchers have investigated the integration of Service-Oriented Architecture (SOA) technology into stream data applications [4–6], resulting in two distinct approaches based on the fundamental concept of service models.

The first approach emphasizes "resource" as the central concept [23–26], viewing sensors and their data streams as shareable assets accessible to external systems. Several studies [25, 26] have investigated the use of lightweight Web service protocols to enable the servitization of sensor data, effectively transforming the Internet of Things (IoT) into the Web of Things (WoT). This approach leverages open Web standards to facilitate the sharing and interoperability of sensor data. The second approach [27–29] revolves around "function" as the core concept, focusing on a service model tailored to stream data processing. This research encapsulates stream processing functionalities within services, allowing applications to seamlessly access general or advanced stream data processing capabilities through service invocation.

Existing research on stream data servitization has significantly enhanced the sharing and reusability of stream data across diverse user scenarios. Encapsulating stream data processing functionalities simplifies the development of complex applications by enabling efficient service composition and collaboration. Furthermore, several studies [30–32] have addressed the adaptation of service composition to dynamic operational environments and evolving data requirements, aiming to reduce user workload and proactively manage the challenges posed by dynamic and complex data processing.

In this paper, we aim to encapsulate the anomaly detection functionality into stream data services, leveraging the service's characteristics such as shareability and reusability, and achieve real-time anomaly detection in a discrete manner based on service collaboration.

## 3   Method Overview

This paper is based on real data from coal-fired power plants for anomaly detection analysis. Each sensor deployed on equipment in the coal-fired power plants is responsible for monitoring specific indicators, such as outlet pressure, outlet temperature, outlet flow rate, etc. We first provide the definition of sensor data stream.

**Definition 1. Sensor Stream Data.**  One sensor stream data is a set of continuous data records which can be represent as $S = \{r_1, r_2, ..., r_k, ...\}$, in which data record $r_k = <a_k, t_k >$ is a two-tuples, where $a_k$ is attribute of certain indicator, and $t_k$ is the timestamp.

The sensor stream data set comprises sensor stream data generated by all sensors deployed on the equipment. Sensor data often exhibit stable and consistent correlations. We employ a sliding window to analyze these data, dividing sensor data into multiple subsequences. These subsequences within the window serve as the basic observation units for analysis. After computing the correlation between subsequences, we can utilize this correlation information to identify hidden anomalous data. Figure 1 illustrates an example of the research problem addressed in this paper.

Figure 1 illustrates four sensor stream data that exhibit correlations. In the dashed box, stream$_3$ presents an anomaly despite its data values appearing within the normal range. However, its correlation with other data streams has significantly changed.

During the correlation analysis of sensor data in coal-fired power plants conducted in this paper, the correlation between sensor data usually shifts over time, which can be regarded as lag-correlation [33]. Figure 1 also shows some examples of lag-correlation between different streams. The definition of lag-correlation is as followed.

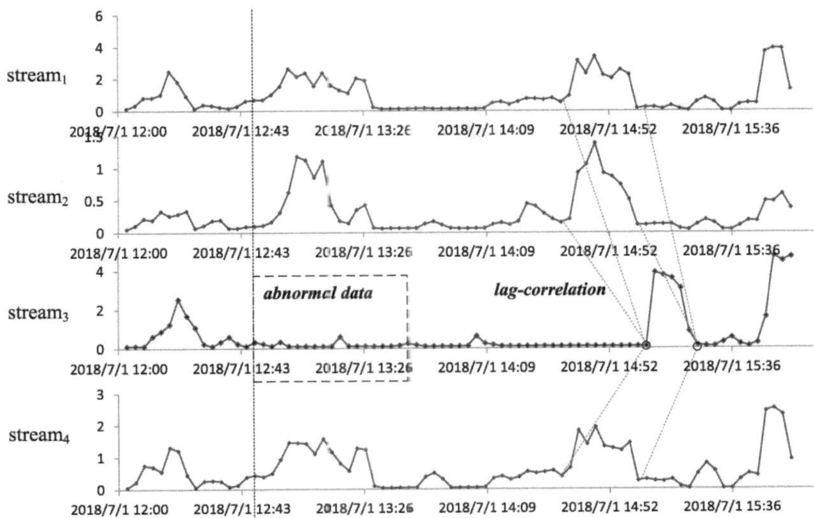



**Fig. 1.** Examples of abnormal data and lag-correlation

**Definition 2. Lag-correlation.** Given two sensor stream data $S_i$ and $S_j$, suppose $S_{ik} = \{r_{i1}, r_{i2}, \ldots, r_{in}\}$ and $S_{ik} = \{r_{j1}, r_{j2}, \ldots, r_{jn}\}$ are two corresponding fragments in a slide window, if there exists a time lag vector $\Delta = \{t'_1, t'_2, \ldots, t'_n\}$ makes

$$cor_{(S_{ik},S_{jk},\Delta)} = \frac{\sum_1^n \left(r_{i(t)} - \overline{r_i}\right)\left(r_{j(t+tk')} - \overline{r_j}\right)}{\sqrt{\sum_1^n \left(r_{i(t)} - \overline{r_i}\right)^2} \times \sqrt{\left(r_{j(t+tk')} - \overline{r_j}\right)^2}} \geq \delta_{cor}$$

in which $\delta_{cor}$ is a given correlation threshold. we regard these two fragments $S_{ik}$ and $S_{jk}$ are correlated.

If we ignore the time shift between the correlation of sensor stream data, it may affect the accuracy of correlation analysis, thus further impacting the accuracy of anomaly detection. Hence, we summarized the problem definition of this paper in Definition 3.

**Definition 3. Problem Definition about Anomaly Detection.** Given a set of sensor stream data $S = \{S_1, S_2, \ldots, S_n\}$, implement following tasks:

(1) for any two sensor stream data in $S$, Quantify and calculate the lag-correlation based on historical data.

(2) Based on the correlation information calculated in (1), perform anomaly detection on real-time data from $S$, and identify all anomalous patterns $< T[l,e], S' >$, in which $T[l,e]$ is the time fragment from $l$ to $e$ when the anomaly happened, and $S'$ is the set of sensor stream data where the anomaly happened.

Given $n$ sensor stream data, analyzing the lag-correlation between each pair involves a substantial workload, requiring the analysis of n! pairs of data. This significantly impacts the efficiency of data analysis, particularly for real-time analysis needs. To improve data processing efficiency, this paper proposes a method based on proactive data service model, utilizing service collaboration to discretely analyze sensor stream data.

The anomaly detection method proposed in this paper is illustrated in Fig. 2. According to the data processing procedure, this method is divided into training and testing phases.

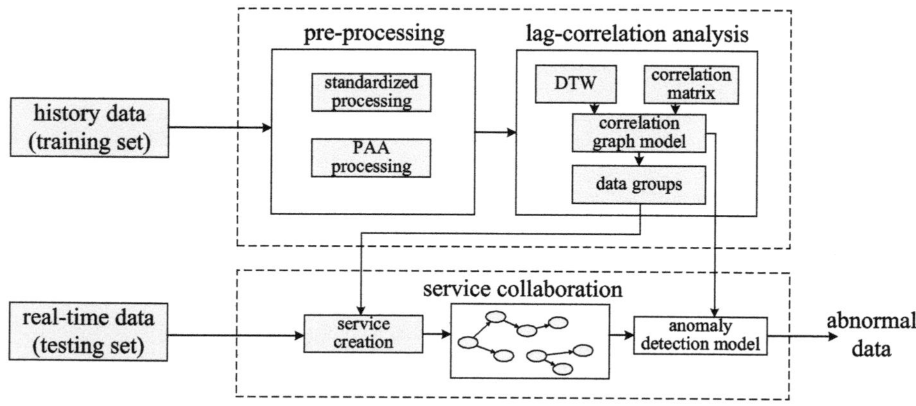


**Fig. 2.** Method framework overview.

In the training phase, historical data of each sensor streams is used as the training set. All data undergo preprocessing and lag-correlation analysis to establish a stream data correlation graph model, which records the correlation information between each stream data. And all sensor stream data can be divided into different groups based on the graph model.

During the testing phase, we encapsulate each divided sensor stream data group into corresponding service. Based on the correlation information obtained during the training phase, each service internally implements anomaly pattern detection within each sensor stream data group in parallel. Simultaneously, through service collaboration, anomaly pattern detection between sensor stream data groups is achieved to complete the anomaly detection process.

## 4 Anomaly Detection Service Based on Lag-Correlation

### 4.1 Lag-Correlation Analysiss

Due to the data quality issues in the collected raw data, we need to preprocess the data first, including time stamp alignment to ensure that data points from different sensors are synchronized in time, and filling in missing values to maintain the integrity and continuity of the dataset. Then, we divide the historical data into several data segments using a sliding window.

Once preprocessing is completed, we use a sliding window approach to divide the historical data into several smaller and more manageable segments. The sliding window technique allows for continuous analysis of the entire dataset by moving the window across the time series data, ensuring that each segment overlaps with the previous one to capture all relevant information.

Since sensor data exhibit characteristics of continuous value changes within short time intervals with a relatively small range, it is necessary to standardize the data to normalize the different measurement scales. After standardization, we apply Piecewise Aggregate Approximation (PAA) to each data segment. PAA reduces the dimensionality of the data by averaging values within predefined intervals, effectively capturing the essential trends and patterns while significantly reducing the data volume. The combination of standardization and PAA processing helps to retain the floating features of the data, which are the subtle variations and trends necessary for accurate analysis. By reducing the data volume through PAA, subsequent calculations become more convenient, efficient, and accurate. The streamlined data not only improves processing speed but also enhances the accuracy of analytical models, thereby increasing the overall effectiveness of the data analysis pipeline.

For the preprocessed data segment sets, we need to measure the lag-correlation of data segments. Dynamic Time Warping (DTW) algorithm can find the optimal alignment between two time series, even if there are misalignments on their time axes. This makes DTW particularly useful for handling data with time inconsistencies. Hence, we preliminarily calculate the lag-correlation $cor$ for each pair of data segments using the DTW algorithm, and obtain a correlation matrix as shown in Eq. (1). This matrix represents the correlation of $n$ data segments within the $l$th time interval on the sensor data set.

$$CM^l = \begin{pmatrix} cor^l_{11} & \cdots & cor^l_{1n} \\ \vdots & \ddots & \vdots \\ cor^l_{n1} & \cdots & cor^l_{nn} \end{pmatrix} \tag{1}$$

During the training process, we consider the results of lag-correlation calculations for all $L$ time intervals in the historical data to obtain the final correlation parameter values. Equation (2) shows the calculation method for the final correlation coefficient matrix.

$$CM = \begin{pmatrix} cor_{11} & \cdots & cor_{1n} \\ \vdots & \ddots & \vdots \\ cor_{n1} & \cdots & cor_{nn} \end{pmatrix},$$

$$cor_{ij} = \begin{cases} \dfrac{\sum_1^L cor^l_{ij}}{L}, & i \neq j \\ 0, & i = j \end{cases} \tag{2}$$

After obtaining the correlation coefficient matrix $CM$ for $n$ sensor data, in order to more effectively represent the relationships between the data, we construct a correlation graph based on the values of the matrix elements. We establish an undirected correlation graph $G_r(S) = (V, E)$, where the vertex set $V$ records all sensor stream data, and the edge set $E$ records the correlation information between the data. Figure 3 illustrates an example of a sensor data correlation graph. Vertexes that have a correlation, meaning their correlation coefficient is greater than a given threshold, are connected by undirected edges.

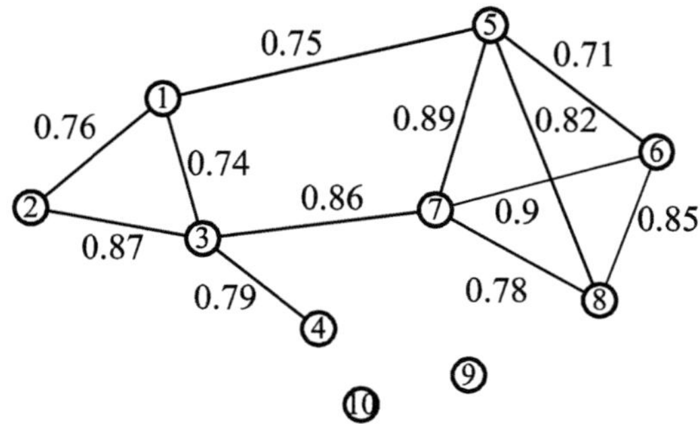



**Fig. 3.** An example of sensor stream data's correlation graph

### 4.2  Anomaly Detection Services Realization

To efficiently conduct anomaly detection, we propose leveraging our previously established proactive data service model [7, 8] and utilizing service collaboration in a discretized manner to achieve real-time anomaly detection.

By observing Fig. 3, we can notice that in the graph, stream data with strong correlations tend to form local data groups where each vertex is connected to every other vertex within the group, such as $\{v_1, v_2, v_3\}$ and $\{v_5, v_6, v_7, v_8\}$. There are also a few edges connecting data groups with weaker correlations, such as $v_3$ and $v_7$. Additionally, there are relatively independent vertices, such as $v_9$ and $v_{10}$. Based on the concept of graph models, we define the fully connected graph.

**Definition 4. Full Connected Graph.** Giving one correlation graph $G_r$, for any two vertex $v_i$ and $v_j$ in $G_r.V$, there is an edge $e_{ij}$ between them in $G_r.E$, it can be called $v_i$ and $v_j$ are connected and graph $G_r$ is a full connected graph.

To further analyze the data groups with different levels of correlation strength on the correlation graph, we partition the sensor stream data based on the connectivity between vertexes in the graph. Then, we create corresponding stream data services for the partitioned sensor stream data groups. Through this partitioning approach, each fully connected graph can be associated with a stream data service, where the any two data inside the service are correlated. Additionally, we gather all isolated points together to create one stream data service. Algorithm 1 demonstrates the pseudocode for partitioning the stream data sets based on correlation graph.

Algorithm 1: Stream Data Partition.

Input: $G_r$, the correlation graph.

Output: $G_r' = (\boldsymbol{P}=\{P_1, P_2,\ldots P_k\}, \boldsymbol{PE} = \{<P_i, P_j, E_{ij}>| P_{i,j}\in P \})$, the partition of $G_r$, in which $\boldsymbol{P}$ is the set of stream data groups, and $\boldsymbol{E}$ records the correlations of stream data in different groups.

1. define visited vertexes $visted\_v =\{\}$ and visited edges $visted\_e = \{\}$;
2. for each $v$ in $G_r.V$ - $visted\_v$
3.     $P_i$.add($v$);
4.     $visted\_v$.add($v$);
5.     for $v_j$ in $v_$neighbors
6.         if $v_j$ is neighbor of all vertexes $v_k$ in $P_i$
7.             $P_i$.add($v_j$);
8.             $P_i$.add($E_{jk}$);
9.             $visted\_e$.add($E_{jk}$);
10.        end if
11.    end for
12.    $\boldsymbol{P}$.add($P_i$);
13. end for
14. $\boldsymbol{P}$.add($G_r.V$ - $visted\_v$);
15. for each edge $e_k$ in $G_r.E$- $visted\_e$
16.    find $P_i$ and $P_j$ in $\boldsymbol{P}$ that include vertexes in $e_k$;
17.    $PE' = < P_i, P_j, e_k >$;
18. end for
19. reduce all $PE'$ by $P_i$ and $P_j$ and generate $\boldsymbol{PE} = \{<P_i, P_j, E_{ij}>$;
20. return $\boldsymbol{P}$ and $\boldsymbol{PE}$;

In algorithm 1, we first define two list $visted\_v$ and $visted\_e$ to store visited vertexes and edges from $G_r$ (line 1). Then we find all full connected sub graph from $G_r$ (line 2–13). For each vertex $v$ in the unvisited vertex set (line 2), we generate a new set $P_i$ to store a full connected sub graph, and find all $v$'s neighbors and add vertexes in the neighbor set into $P_i$ which are neighbor of all vertexes that are already in $P_i$ (line 5–11). All the remaining isolated vertexes will be uniformly partitioned into a single partition (line 14). Then we generated the relationships between different partitions (line 15–19). For each edge that is unvisited, we find the partitions that include its two vertexes (line 16) and generate a tripe $< P_i, P_j, e_k >$ (line 17). We aggregate the relationships between the same partition pair into one set $\boldsymbol{E}$, and obtain all relationships between each pair of partitions (line 19).

For example, the correlation graph in Fig. 3 can be divided into three groups shown in Fig. 4. There are two full connected sub graph and the remaining vertexes constitute partition $P_3$ as $\{v_4, v_9, v_{10}\}$. And there are also relationships between different partitions, such as $< P_1, P_3, \{ <v_3, v_4, 0.79 >\} >$ and $< P_1, P_2, \{ <v_1, v_5, 0.75 >, < v_3, v_7, 0.86 >\} >$.

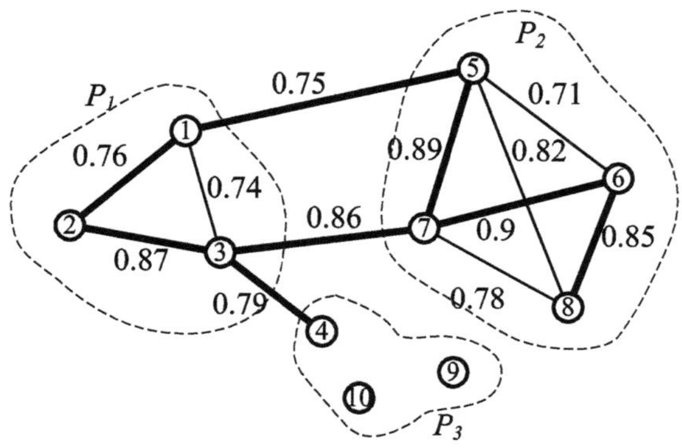



**Fig. 4.** An example of sensor streams partition and correlation pruning

After partitioning the sensor data, we can create corresponding sensor stream data services based on proactive data service model. Within each service, we similarly apply standardization and PAA processing to the input stream data using a sliding window. And we then analyze the lag-correlation for each pair of sensor stream data. Additionally, within each service, we can perform anomaly pattern detection such as point anomalies and subsequence anomalies on individual sensor stream data.

Between services, we map the relationships between partitions to hyperlinks and declarative rules within the services. Through hyperlinks, preprocessed stream data is sent to specified services, and the declarative rules within the specified services are used to trigger the analysis of correlation between stream data in different partitions. Previous work on hyperlinks and declarative rules can be referenced for further details [7, 8]. For example, for the three partitions in Fig. 3, we create three services as $service_1$, $service_2$, and $service_3$ respectively. For the relationship $< P_1, P_3, \{ <v_3, v_4, 0.79 > \} >$, we generate a service hyperlink as $< service_1.stream_3, service_3 >$ within service $service_1$, and a declarative rule $< service_1, stream_3, stream_4, 0.79 >$ within $service_3$. Thus, preprocessed $stream_3$ will be sent to $service_3$, where the correlation between $stream_3$ and $stream_4$ is analyzed to detect any changes in their correlation.

For a fully connected graph, if the relationship between any two vertexes changes, we assume that the relationship between other vertexes related to these two vertexes will also change. For example, in Fig. 1, if the correlation between $stream_3$ and $stream_1$ changes, the correlations between $stream_3$ and $stream_2$, as well as between $stream_3$ and $stream_4$, will also change. Therefore, we believe that it is unnecessary to conduct correlation analysis for all pairs of data streams within a service.

To further enhance the efficiency of anomaly detection within services, we performed pruning based on the correlation between sensor data, and reducing the amount of data for analysis. Within each service, we look for a path that includes all vertexes and maximizes the sum of correlations on each edge. The bold lines in Fig. 4 represent the data pairs for which we need to analyze correlations. For example, for $service_1$ corresponding to $P_1$, we only need to analyze the correlation between $stream_1$ and $stream_2$, and correlation between $stream_2$ and $stream_3$. Through the correlation pruning, we can reduce the complexity of analysis within the service from $O(n!)$ to $O(n)$.

# 5 Experiments

## 5.1 Experiment Setup

**Dataset.** The dataset utilized in our experiment comprises real sensor data and artificial maintenance records from a coal-fired power plant. Each sensor recorded one value every 30 s, spanning from 2018-01-31 00:00:00 to 2019-01-31 23:59:59. Detailed information about the dataset is provided in Table 1. To evaluate the effectiveness of our anomaly detection method, we selected sensor data from five primary systems. The dataset includes data from 1751 sensors and records 466 equipment anomalies.

**Table 1.** Detailed Information of Dataset in Our Experiment

| System Name | Equipment Number | Sensor Number | Anomaly Number |
| --- | --- | --- | --- |
| Air and Gas System (AGS) | 32 | 344 | 44 |
| Environmental Protection System (EPS) | 10 | 49 | 119 |
| Coal Mill System (GMS) | 36 | 334 | 141 |
| Turbonator System (TS) | 50 | 299 | 101 |
| Water Supply System (WSS) | 69 | 725 | 61 |
| **Total** | 197 | 1751 | 466 |

**Comparison Methods.** In the experiments, we implemented our method, called Improved Anomaly Detection Service based on Lag-correlation (LC-IADS) method. To objectively evaluate the effectiveness and performance of our method, we implemented three other anomaly detection methods as baseline algorithms for comparison.

(1) LCAD algorithm [21]: an anomaly detection algorithm based on machine learning models. It utilizes the Expectation-Maximization (EM) algorithm to classify data into normal or abnormal probabilities.
(2) CGAD algorithm [22]: an anomaly detection algorithm based on Pearson correlation and graph model-based anomaly detection, which didn't consider the time shift of sensor stream data.
(3) LC-ADS method: our method excluding correlation pruning operations.

**Evaluation Criterion.** To evaluate the effectiveness of proposed method, we establish the following criteria:

(1) Precision: the precision can be calculated as the following formula:

$$precision = \frac{|L \cap T|}{|L|} \times 100\% \tag{3}$$

(2) Recall: the recall can be calculated as the following formula:

$$recall = \frac{|L \cap T|}{|T|} \times 100\% \tag{4}$$

Here, $L = \{l_1, l_2, ..., l_m\}$ represents the list of anomalies detected by our method, and $T = \{t_1, t_2, ..., t_n\}$ denotes the actual anomalies that occurred in practice.

And we also use *runtime* to verify the performance of our method.

## 5.2  Effectiveness

We first evaluate the effectiveness of different methods under various correlation thresholds. We randomly selected 1000 sensor data from all available data and simulated stream data based on the actual timestamps of the data records. The data generation rate was adjusted to one data point per second. Then, we set the correlation thresholds to 0.5, 0.6, 0.7, 0.8, and 0.9 respectively, and calculated the precision and recall of different methods. Figure 5 illustrates the precision and recall of different methods under various correlation thresholds.

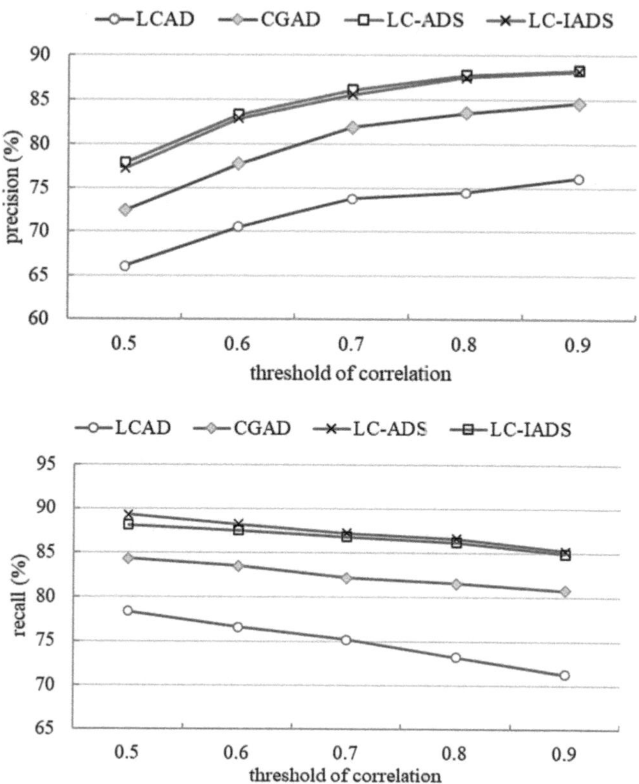

Fig. 5. Effectiveness of anomaly detection with different correlation threshold

As shown in Fig. 5, it can be observed that our method (including LC-ADS and LC-IADS) exhibits higher precision and recall compared to the LCAD and CGAD method under different correlation thresholds. This is because our method further considers the possibility of time offsets in analyzing correlations, allowing for a more accurate determination of the correlation between stream data. Additionally, compared to the LC-ADS method, our method prunes the analysis of correlations within services to enhance performance, resulting in a slight decrease in precision and recall. However, the average decrease in precision and recall is within 1%, indicating that the overall effectiveness of the method is small affected.

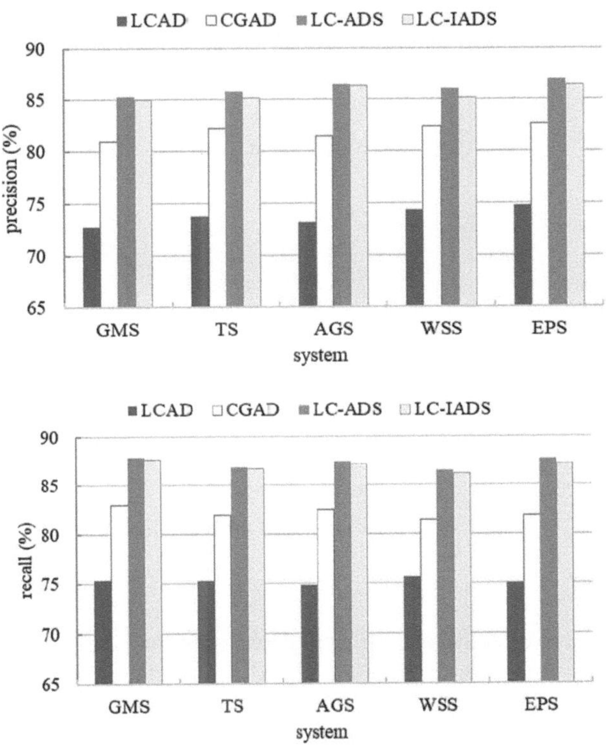


**Fig. 6.** Comparison of anomaly detection effectiveness across different methods

We also evaluated the effectiveness of different methods on different systems separately. We randomly selected 5 sets of sensor stream data from 5 different systems and fixed the correlation threshold as 0.7. We then calculated the precision and recall of different methods for each system. Figure 6 illustrates the effectiveness of different methods on different systems.

As shown in Fig. 6, our method consistently exhibits higher precision and recall compared to other methods, indicating that our method has a certain degree of universality and can adapt to different industrial equipment.

## 5.3  Performance

This section presents comparative experiments on the computational runtime of different methods for anomaly detection. We set the correlation threshold as 0.7 and randomly selected 600, 800, 1000, 1200, 1400, and 1600 sensor data from all available data. We recorded the average computational runtime for anomaly detection using different methods. Figure 7 illustrates the efficiency of different methods.

As shown in Fig. 7, our method requires the least amount of runtime for anomaly detection compared to other methods, and the increase in runtime is the slowest as the dataset size increases. This is because we prune data correlations during the detection process, significantly reducing the amount of data processing.

The experimental results demonstrate that our method has higher and more stable efficiency, achieving a balance between method efficiency and effectiveness.

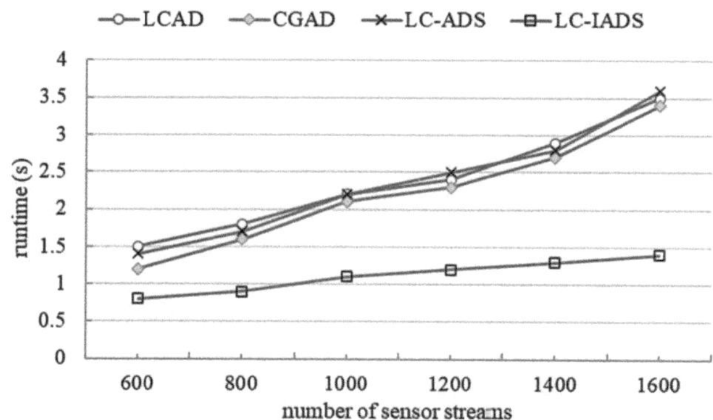


**Fig. 7.** The performance of different methods

## 6   Conclusion

In this paper, to more effective and efficient detect abnormal data in industrial area, we proposed anomaly detection services based on lag-correlation analysis and proactive data service model. Specifically, we partition historical sensor data into multiple data fragments using a sliding window, and implement lag-correlation analysis based on Dynamic Time Warping (DTW) to construct a correlation graph model. Subsequently, by partitioning the sensor stream data based on graph model, we create corresponding stream data services, and further enhance anomaly detection efficiency through correlation pruning within service. Through service collaboration, we achieve anomaly detection in a discrete way. Through extensive experiments on a real-world dataset from a power plant, this paper validates that the proposed method outperforms existing basic methods in terms of both accuracy and efficiency in solving the problem of anomaly detection in stream data.

**Acknowledgment.** This work was supported by Youth Foundation of Shandong Natural Science Foundation (No. ZR2021QF099).

## References

1. Lin, L., Pan, L., Liu, S.: A cost-effective framework for running industrial big data analysis applications in public clouds. IEEE Internet Things J. **9**(13), 10554–10562 (2022)

2. Zhang, J., Cui, H., Yang, A.L., Gu, F., Shi, C., Zhang, W., et al.: An intelligent digital twin system for paper manufacturing in the paper industry. Expert Syst. Appl. **230**, 120614 (2023)
3. Wang, J.M.: Summary of industrial big data technology. Big Data Res. **6**, 3–14 (2017)
4. Showail, A., Tahir, R., Zaffar, M.F.: An internet of secure and private things: A service-oriented architecture. Comput. Secur. **120**, 102776 (2021)
5. Mishra, S., Sarkar, A.: Service-oriented architecture for internet of things: a semantic approach. J. King Saud Univ. Comput. Inf. Sci. **34**, 8765–8776 (2021)
6. Huang, B., Zhang, B., Sheng, Q. Z. et al.: A Multi-task learning approach for predicting intentions using smart home IoT services. Service-Oriented Computing-ICSOC, pp. 413–421 (2022)
7. Zhang, Z., Liu, C., Su, S., Zhang, S., Han, Y.: SDaaS: a method for encapsulating sensor stream data as services. China J. Comput. **40**(2), 445–463 (2017)
8. Zhang, Z., Yu, J., Li, X., Liu, C., Han, Y., Ma, Y.: A data-driven service creation approach for effectively capturing events from multiple sensor streams. In: 2019 IEEE International Conference on Web Services (ICWS), pp. 346–354 (2019)
9. Toledano, M., Cohen, I., Ben, Y. Real-time anomaly detection system for time series at scale. In: Proceedings of Machine Learning Research, SIGKDD Workshop, vol. 71, pp. 56–65 (2017)
10. Gupta, M., Gao, J., Aggarwal, C., Han, J. W.: Outlier detection for temporal data. IEEE Trans. Knowl. Data Eng. **26**(9), 2250–2267. Morgan & Claypool Publishers (2014)
11. Heinrich, M., Gölz, A., Arul, T.A., Katzenbeisser, S.: Rule-based anomaly detection for railway signaling networks. Int. J. Crit. Infrastruct. Prot. **42**, 100603 (2023)
12. Song, S., Zhang, A., Wang, J. et al.: SCREEN: stream data cleaning under speed constraints. In: Proceedings of the 2015 ACM SIGMOD International Conference on Management of Data, ACM, pp. 827-841 (2015)
13. Zhu, M.L., Liu, C., Han, Y.: An event correlation based approach to predictive maintenance. APWeb/WAIM **2**, 232–247 (2018)
14. Zhang, Z.M., Liu, C., Li, X., Han, Y., Lv, C., Ding, W.: A declarative service-based method for adaptive aggregation of sensor streams. IEEE Access **7**, 89–98 (2019)
15. Ma, J., Ma, J., Perkins, S.: Time-series novelty detection using one-class support vector machines. In: Proceedings of the International Joint Conference on Neural Networks, IEEE, vol. 3, pp. 1741–1745 (2003). https://doi.org/10.1109/IJCNN.2003.1223670
16. Jain, M., Kaur, G., Saxena, V.: A K-Means clustering and SVM-based hybrid concept drift detection technique for network anomaly detection. Expert Syst. Appl. **193**, 116510 (2022)
17. Guo, X., An, H., Du, X., Wang, Y., Lu, Z., Weng, Y.: Improved random forest based anomaly detection for urban rail transits. SmartCloud, pp. 148–153 (2023)
18. Leroux, S., Simoens, P.: Sparse random neural networks for online anomaly detection on sensor nodes. Future Gener. Comput. Syst. **144**, 327–343 (2023)
19. Li, G., Jung, J.J.: Deep learning for anomaly detection in multivariate time series: approaches, applications, and challenges. Inf. Fusion **91**, 93–102 (2023)
20. Xiao, T. et al.: Loader: A log anomaly detector based on transformer. IEEE Trans. Serv. Comput. **16**(5), 3479–3492 (2023)
21. Ding, J., Liu, Y., Zhang, L. et al. An anomaly detection approach for multiple monitoring data series based on latent correlation probabilistic model. Appl. Intell. **44**(2), 340–361 (2016)
22. Ding, X.O., Yu, S.J., Wang, M.X., Wang, H.Z., Gao, H., Yang, D.H.: Anomaly detection on industrial time series based on correlation analysis. Ruan Jian Xue Bao/J. Softw. **31**(3), 726–747 (2020)
23. Ali, Z.H., Ali, H.A., Badawy, M.M.: A new proposed the Internet of Things (IoT) virtualization framework based on sensor-as-a-service concept. Wirel. Pers. Commun. **97**(1), 1419–1443 (2017)

24. Mondal, A., Misra, S., Das, G., Chakraborty, A.: QoS-aware resource allocation for green sensor-as-a-service provisioning in vehicular multi-sensor-cloud. IEEE Trans. Green Commun. Netw. **7**(1), 224–233 (2023)
25. Silva, B.N., Khan, M., Han, K.: Integration of big data analytics embedded smart city architecture with restful web of things for efficient service provision and energy management. Future Gener. Comput. Syst. **107**, 975–987 (2018)
26. Belhadi, A., Djenouri, Y., Srivastava, G., Lin, J. C.: Fast and accurate framework for ontology matching in web of things. ACM Trans. Asian Low Resour. Lang. Inf. Process. **22**(5), 147:1–147:19 (2023)
27. Aguilar, J., Sanchez, M., Cordero, J.: Learning analytics tasks as services in smart classrooms. Univ. Access Inf. Soc. **17**(4), 693–709 (2019)
28. Yang, X., Wang, G., Gao, J.: MaritimeDS: a data service framework for unsupervised maritime traffic monitoring based on trajectory big data. J. Reliab. Intell. Environ. **8**(1), 3–19 (2022)
29. Lu, Y., Misra, A., Wu, H.: Smartphone sensing meets transport data: a collaborative framework for transportation service analytics. IEEE Trans. Mob. Comput. **17**(4), 945–960 (2018)
30. Zatout, S., Boufaida, M., Benabdelhafid, M.S., Berkane, M.L.: A model-driven approach for the verification of an adaptive service composition. Int. J. Web Eng. Technol. **15**(1), 18–26 (2021)
31. Zhang, Z., Zhang, S.: A stream data service framework for real-time vehicle companion discovery. In Mobile and Ubiquitous Systems: Computing, Networking and Services. MobiQuitous 2023, vol. 593, pp. 281–296 (2024). https://doi.org/10.1007/978-3-031-63989-0_14
32. Wang, Y., Wang, S., Yang, B. et al.: An effective adaptive adjustment method for service composition exception handling in cloud manufacturing. J. Intell. Manuf. **33**, 735–751 (2022)
33. Lin, Y., Liang, W., Zhang, L., Yu, X., Qiu, J.: A time lag-based correlation analysis model for index selection in state evaluation of centrifugal compressor unit. J. Intell. Fuzzy Syst. **35**(4), 4685–4699 (2018)

# AI Robust Anomaly Localization for DC Microgrid Using Adversarial Autoencoder


Jieqi Rong[1], Weirong Liu[1(✉)], Fu Jiang[2], Heng Li[2], Lisen Yan[2], Jun Peng[2], and Zhiwu Huang[3]

[1] School of Computer Science and Engineering, Central South University, Changsha 410083, China
{rongjieqi,frat}@csu.edu.cn
[2] School of Electronic Information, Central South University, Changsha 410083, China
{jiangfu,liheng,yanlisen,pengj}@csu.edu.cn
[3] School of Automation, Central South University, Changsha 410083, China
hzw@csu.edu.cn



**Abstract.** Accurate anomaly localization can ensure the continuity and reliability of power supply in DC microgrid. However, it is still a challenge to improve the robustness of anomaly localization methods under the complexity and dynamics of DC microgrids. To address this issue, an adversarial autoencoder method is proposed to improve the generalization of anomaly localization and sensitivity for anomaly data. Firstly, the physical-cyber model of microgrid system is established, and the attack model under false data injection attack is analyzed. Then, an adversarial autoencoder is proposed to accurately locate anomalies, enhancing its robustness through noise and reducing false positives with a discriminator. Consequently, the DC microgrid anomaly localization simulation platform was constructed to obtain the dataset for training the localization model. Extensive experiments are conducted to validate the proposed method, which can improve the recall rate by up to 33.3% and reduce the false positive rate by 8.2%.

**Keywords:** DC microgrid · Anomaly localization · Generative adversarial network · Auto-encoder


## 1 Introduction

Distributed generators (DGs) of microgrid rely on wireless communication for efficient data transmission, which is beneficial for coordinating the power distribution across the microgrid [1]. However, the reliance on wireless communication in distributed generators presents a risk for false data injection attacks, which


This work was supported in part by the National Natural Science Foundation of China under Grant 62172448 and Hunan Provincial Natural Science Foundation 2021JJ30868.




A. Soylu et al. (Eds.): MobiQuitous 2024, LNICST 634, pp. 275–289, 2026.
https://doi.org/10.1007/978-3-032-10554-7_15

can disrupt power operation [2]. Anomaly localization in DC microgrid is essential for maintaining system stability and preventing the attack risk in power supply [3].

Extensive studies have been carried out to achieve the detection and localization of anomalies within microgrid. These studies can be divided into three categories: signal processing-based [4], model-based [5], and machine learning-based methods [11–15]. Signal processing-based methods focus on analyzing signals collected from sensors and other data sources to identify data anomalies [6], such as ensemble empirical mode decomposition (EEMD) [7] and local outlier factor (LOF) [8]. Model-based methods are adapted to distributed DC microgrids [9]. These methods rely on local information and communication with neighboring agents to detect attacks, although the unpredictable nature of attack vectors presents a challenge for creating a robust and accurate detection system [10]. However, there is still a lack of means to detect some anomalies whose mechanisms are unclear.

Machine learning-based methods for anomaly localization can be divided into supervised learning and unsupervised learning methods. Supervised anomaly localization methods [11] usually need to label data as normal or abnormal, such as SVM [12] and deep neural networks [13]. However, the challenge is how to obtain sufficient training data that accurately represents both benign and abnormal conditions. Unsupervised anomaly localization usually handle anomaly localization problem as a one-class problem [14], which can be trained just on normal operation data. As a typical unsupervised learning method, autoencoder uses neural networks to model normal behavior and detect outliers based on reconstruction errors [15]. The methods do not require rare abnormal data for training, and these methods can find unknown anomalies and help capture the sophisticated patterns of the data [16].

Existing autoencoder methods have the problem of overfitting [17], and it is difficult to directly apply to anomaly location in the actual complex and dynamic microgrid environment. Some methods combine adversarial training with networks to accurately reconstruct normal data and score novelties for effective outlier detection [18,19]. In [20,21], GANs generate data similar to the training set to define normalcy and assign novelty scores to detect anomalies. To realize anomaly location in complex microgrid, an adversarial autoencoder model is proposed. The training data came from the built simulation environment of the microgrid. The overall architecture of the proposed method is shown in Fig. 1.

The main contributions of this paper can be summarized as follows:

- The physical-cyber and attack model of microgrid are constructed, which can help define benign and abnormal data characteristics, allowing for more accurate training of anomaly localization algorithm.
- An adversarial autoencoder is proposed for anomaly location, which incorporates noise to learn a robust hidden vector to resist interference and realize the generalization of the location algorithm. The discriminator is introduced to improve the sensitivity to abnormal data and reduce the false positive rate of anomaly location.

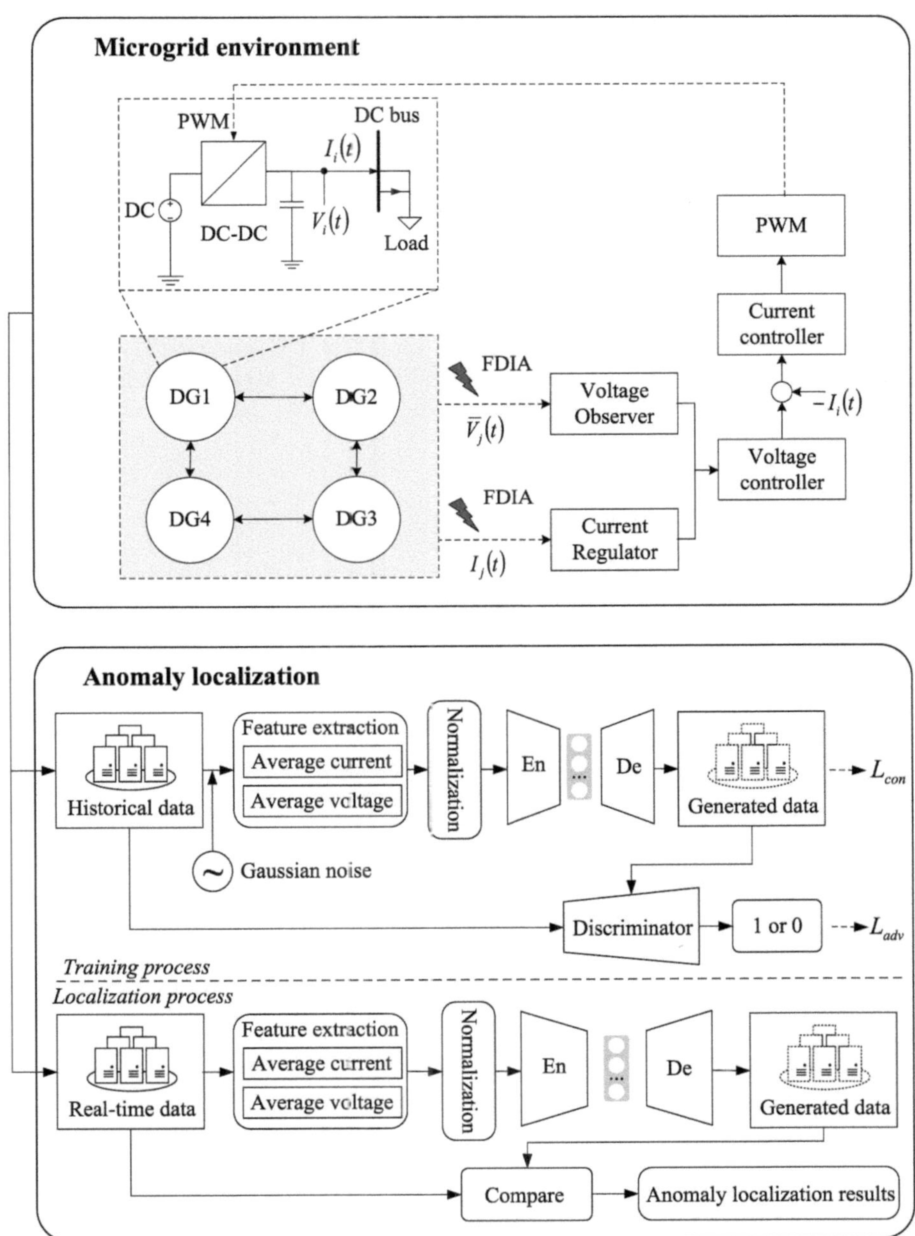


**Fig. 1.** The architecture of proposed AAE algorithm for anomaly localization in DC microgrid. The data generated by the microgrid environment is used for the training of the proposed adversarial auto-encoder algorithm and real-time anomaly localization.

– A simulation platform is constructed to generate the training dataset. The experiment results show that the proposed AAE method has higher recall rate and lower false positive rate than the existing methods.

This paper is organized as follows. The system description for microgrid is constructed in Sect. 2. The proposed adversarial auto-encoder localization method is designed in Sect. 3. The performance evaluation of FDIA localization is conducted in Sect. 4, and conclusions are presented in Sect. 5.

## 2   System Description

This section describes the physical-cyber model of DC microgrid system and the attack model under FDIA. The physical-cyber and attack models provide a baseline for simulation environments and define normal data characteristics for unsupervised anomaly location algorithms.

### 2.1   Physical Model

In the microgrid secondary control model, the controller of each distributed generator sends and receives a set of measured values $\{e_{i,V}(t), e_{i,I}(t)\}$ directly via wireless communication. By adjusting its own voltage to attain average voltage regulation and proportionate current sharing.

$$e_{i,V}(t) = a_{ij}(\bar{V}_j(t) - \bar{V}_i(t)) \tag{1}$$

$$e_{i,I}(t) = a_{ij}(\bar{I}_j(t) - \bar{I}_i(t)) \tag{2}$$

where $e_{i,V}(t)$ is the voltage deviation between distributed generator $i$ and the neighboring distributed generators, $e_{i,I}(t)$ is the current deviation between distributed generator $i$ and the neighboring distributed generators. $\bar{V}_j(t)$ is the estimated value of the neighbor voltage. $a_{ij} = 1$ indicates that distributed generator $i$ can receive information from distributed generator $j$, and $a_{ij} = 0$ indicates that it cannot.

### 2.2   Cyber Model

The cyber model is used to characterize the interconnections between distributed generators. The cyber model of the microgrid is constructed as a digraph. The communication topology of this system can be represented as a graph $\mathbf{G} = \{\mathbf{V}, \mathbf{E}\}$ with DGs as nodes and the communication links between them as edges. The node set is denoted as $\mathbf{V} = \{1, 2, \ldots, n\}$. The properties of the graph $\mathbf{G}$ can be simplified by using the adjacency matrix $\mathbf{A}$, degree matrix $\mathbf{D}$ and Laplace matrix $\mathbf{L}$ as follow.

The adjacency matrix $\mathbf{A}$ represents the connections between distributed generators, where $a_{ij} = 1$ indicates that distributed generator $i$ can receive information from distributed generator $j$, and $a_{ij} = 0$ indicates that it cannot. The adjacency matrix $\mathbf{A}$ is set by

$$\mathbf{A} = [a_{ij}]_{n \times n}. \tag{3}$$

The in-degree matrix $\mathbf{D}_{in}$ is set by

$$\mathbf{D}_{in} = \mathrm{diag}\left\{d_i^{in}\right\}, \tag{4}$$

$$d_i^{in} = \sum_{j \in N_i} a_{ij}, \tag{5}$$

where $d_i^{in}$ is the neighbor set of DG $i$ that transmit information to it.

The out-degree matrix $\mathbf{D}_{out}$ is set by

$$\mathbf{D}_{out} = \mathrm{diag}\left\{d_i^{out}\right\}, \tag{6}$$

$$d_i^{out} = \sum_{i \in N_j} a_{ji}, \tag{7}$$

where $d_i^{out}$ is the neighbor set of DG $i$ that receive information from it.

The Laplacian matrix is balanced if the in-degree matrix $\mathbf{D}_{in}$ equals to the out-degree matix $\mathbf{D}_{out}$. The matrix $\mathbf{L}$ is calculated from the adjacency matrix $\mathbf{A}$ and the degree matrix $\mathbf{D}$. The Laplacian matrix $\mathbf{L}$ for the communication topology as

$$\mathbf{L} = \mathbf{D}_{in} - \mathbf{A}, \tag{8}$$

where $\mathbf{A}$ and $\mathbf{D}$ represent the adjacency matrix and degree matrix for the graph.

### 2.3   Attack Model

The false data injection attack occurred on a communication link transmitted between four DGs, the FDIA model is defined as

$$\bar{V}_{j,\mathrm{att}}(t) = \bar{V}_j(t) + \alpha C_{\mathrm{att}}, \alpha \in \{0,1\} \tag{9}$$

$$\bar{I}_{j,\mathrm{att}}(t) = \bar{I}_j(t) + \alpha C_{\mathrm{att}}, \alpha \in \{0,1\} \tag{10}$$

where $\bar{V}_{j,\mathrm{att}}(t)$ and $\bar{I}_{j,\mathrm{att}}(t)$ are the actual voltage and current value received by the neighbors. $\alpha{=}0$ represents no attack and $\alpha =1$ indicates an attack. $C_{\mathrm{att}}$ is the attack magnitude of FDIA.

## 3    Adversarial Auto-Encoder for Anomaly Localization

This section describes the training and online localization process of the proposed anomaly localization method. The proposed adversarial auto-encoder (AAE) method consists of two parts: a denoising auto-encoder and a discriminator. The detailed procedure is shown in Algorithm 1.

---

**Algorithm 1.** Anomaly localization based on AAE

---

**Input:** DG data $x$, noise factor $nf$, iteration $I$, learning rate $lr$, epoch $E$, Encoder network $\omega_{En}$, Decoder network $\omega_{De}$, Discriminator network $\omega_D$;
**Output:** Anomaly localization results;
**Training process:**
1: **Initialize** $\omega_{En}$, $\omega_{De}$ and $\omega_D$;
3: **for** iteration $= 1 : I$ **do**
4:     **for** epoch $= 1 : E$ **do**
5:        Add noise to the source data $x + s$;
6:        The reconstructed samples $x' = De(En(x + s))$;
7:        The discriminator loss is calculated by (12);
8:        Back-propagate discriminator loss $L_D$;
9:        Update $\omega_D$;
10:        The DAE loss is calculated by (11);
11:        Back-propagate DAE loss $L_{DAE}$;
12:        Update $\omega_{En}$ and $\omega_{De}$;
13:    **end for**
14: **end for**
**Localization process:**
1: **Initialize** Real-time DG data;
2: Input real-time data to trained AAE ;
3: Calculate the reconstruction error $e'_i$;
4: Calculate the reconstruction error threshold $t_h$;
5: **if** $e'_i < t_h$
6:    The DG is normal;
7: **else**
8:    The DG is abnormal;
9: **end if**

---

### 3.1    Training of Proposed AAE

Compared with the traditional autoencoder method, the proposed anomaly localization method based on AAE introduces a discriminator to better learn the latent representation of the data, and adds noise to the input data to avoid overfitting and enhance the generalization of the model. The autoencoder acts as the generator $G$ in the GAN network.

Noise is added to the training data and make the autoencoder learn to remove this noise to obtain a realistic input that is not contaminated by noise. As a result, this forces the encoder to learn to extract the most important features and learn a more robust representation of the input data, improving its generalization ability. By introducing adversarial training, the discriminative ability of the model is strengthened and the sensitivity to abnormal data is improved, so as to enhance the performance of the model in the anomaly localization.

The loss function of AAE is formulated by combining two parts, each of which optimizes a different part of the whole architecture.

The loss function of DAE:

$$L_{\text{DAE}} = |x - De(En(x + s))|^2, \tag{11}$$

where $x$ is the true data and $s$ is the added noise. $En(\bullet)$ is the output of encoder and $De(\bullet)$ is the output of decoder. In our work, anomaly localization is achieved by comparing the deviation between input data and reconstructed data after network training. $L_{\text{DAE}}$ is ultimately used to locate the anomaly.

The loss function of GAN:

$$\min_G \max_D L(D, G) = \mathbb{E}_{x \sim p(x)}[\log D(x + s)] \\ + \mathbb{E}_{x \sim p(x)}[\log(1 - D(G(x + s)))], \tag{12}$$

where $p(x)$ is the true sample distribution. $G$ is the generator, which is equivalent to $DE(En(\bullet))$. $D$ is the discriminator used to distinguish whether the data is reconstructed data or true data.

In (12), $G$ optimizes the generated data, and makes its distribution as far as possible the same as the real data distribution, which let $D$ cannot distinguish data authenticity. $D$ optimizes the discriminant ability to distinguish between true and reconstructed data as much as possible. The goals of the two models $G$ and $D$ are opposite, which forms a confrontation. Model training is terminated when the generated model $G$ generates a sample exactly like the real data.

During the training process, one of $G$ and $D$ is fixed, the parameters of the other network are updated, and the error of the other network is maximized alternately. In the end, $G$ can estimate the distribution of sample data, which means that the generated sample is more real. The $G$ generates the forged data distribution to make the forged distribution $G(x + s)$ can fool the discriminator $D$. The goal of the $G$ is to make $D(G(x+s))$ as big as possible, and the bigger the $D(G(x + s))$ can fool the $D$ network, that is, the smaller the loss of generator $G$ as small as possible. The discriminator $D$ has two training objectives, distinguish between real data and reconstructed data, that is, the larger the $D(x + s)$ of the real data and the smaller $D(G(x + s))$.

### 3.2   Anomaly Localization Based on AAE

By (12), the reconstruction error $e$ is obtained for anomaly localization. We set the set of reconstruction errors $\mathbf{e} = \{e_i, i \in N\}$, and then apply feature scaling to have the reconstruction error within the probabilistic range of $[0, 1]$.

$$e_i' = \frac{e_i - \min(\mathbf{e})}{\max(\mathbf{e}) - \min(\mathbf{e})} \tag{13}$$

where $e_i' \in [0, 1]$, $\max(\mathbf{e})$ and $\min(\mathbf{e})$ are the maximum and minimum of the reconstruction error in the set, respectively.

The reconstruction error threshold $t_h$ is introduced to identify specific abnormal points. If $e_i' < t_h$, the DG is normal. If $e_i' > t_h$, the DG is abnormal. The thresholds $t_h$ are calculated based on $3\sigma$ rules as follows:

$$t_h = \bar{e}' + 2 * \sigma \tag{14}$$

$$\bar{e}' = \frac{1}{N} \sum_{i=1}^{N} e_i' \tag{15}$$

$$\sigma = \sqrt{\frac{1}{N} \sum_{i=1}^{N} (e_i' - \bar{e}')^2} \tag{16}$$

where $\bar{e}'$ is the average of the reconstruction errors for all samples, and the standard deviation $\sigma$ measures the dispersion of these error values.

By utilizing the real-time operation data of the microgrid and the generated data by the generator, the proposed AAE can identify anomaly DGs. If the reconstruction error is higher than the anomaly threshold, it signifies the occurrence of an anomaly at that specific DG. The introduction of GAN makes the anomaly data more obvious and can detect the anomaly more precisely.

## 4    Performance Evaluation

A simulation platform was created in Matlab/Simulink (version: 2022b) with 79 DGs to obtain the operation data of the microgrid. Anomaly location simulation verification is performed in Python 3.8, leveraging the TensorFlow framework to model and train our neural network. The software was installed on a desktop computer equipped with a 12th Intel(R) Core(TM) i7-12700H CPU @2.30GHz. The dataset and simulation parameter settings, performance metrics and simulation result comparison are given in this section.

### 4.1    Dataset and Parameter Setup

**Dataset Setting.** A DC microgrid simulation platform is developed in Matlab/Simulink environment to obtain benign training data and abnormal test data. The size of the training data set is $10000 \times 2$, and the size of the test set is $79 \times 2$. The data set includes two characteristics: voltage and current. Normal voltage is maintained at bus voltage 315V.

To verify the superiority of the proposed anomaly location method, the microgrid simulation platform generates test data under voltage attack and current attack, respectively. In the voltage attack scenario, DG 8 and 33 are attacked by false data injection of +3V; DG 38 and 58 are attacked by +2V; DG 63 and 65 are attacked by -2V. In the current attack scenario, DG 8 and 33 are attacked by +4A; DG 38 and 58 are attacked by +2A; DG 63 and 65 are attacked by -2A.

**Parameter Setup.** Both encoder and decoder use LSTM network, and discriminator network uses fully connected neural network. For encoder, the first LSTM layer is configured with 128 memory cells, and the second LSTM layer is configured with 64 memory cells. The structure of discriminator network is $256 \times 512 \times 1$. Dropout layer is set to 0.3. The initial learning rate is set to 0.0001, the minimum learning rate is set to 1e-20, and the early stop mechanism is introduced. The batch size is 28. The noise factor of denoising autoencoder is set to 0.5.

## 4.2  Performance Metrics

The recall rate $Recall$ and false positive rate $FPR$ is used to assess the anomaly localization performance of different methods. In this paper, the benign samples are labeled as 0 and abnormal samples are labeled as 1.

The anomaly localization success rate $Recall$ is calculated as follow, which indicates the proportion of abnormal samples that are correctly identified as anomaly.

$$Recall = TP/(TP + FN), \tag{17}$$

where $TP$ represents abnormal sample that is correctly detected as abnormal by the localization method, and $FN$ represents abnormal sample that is incorrectly identified as benign.

The false positive rate $FPR$ is calculated as follow, which indicates the proportion of benign samples that are incorrectly identified as anomaly.

$$FPR = FP/(FP + TN), \tag{18}$$

where $TN$ represents benign sample that is correctly detected as benign, and $FP$ represents benign sample that is incorrectly identified as abnormal.

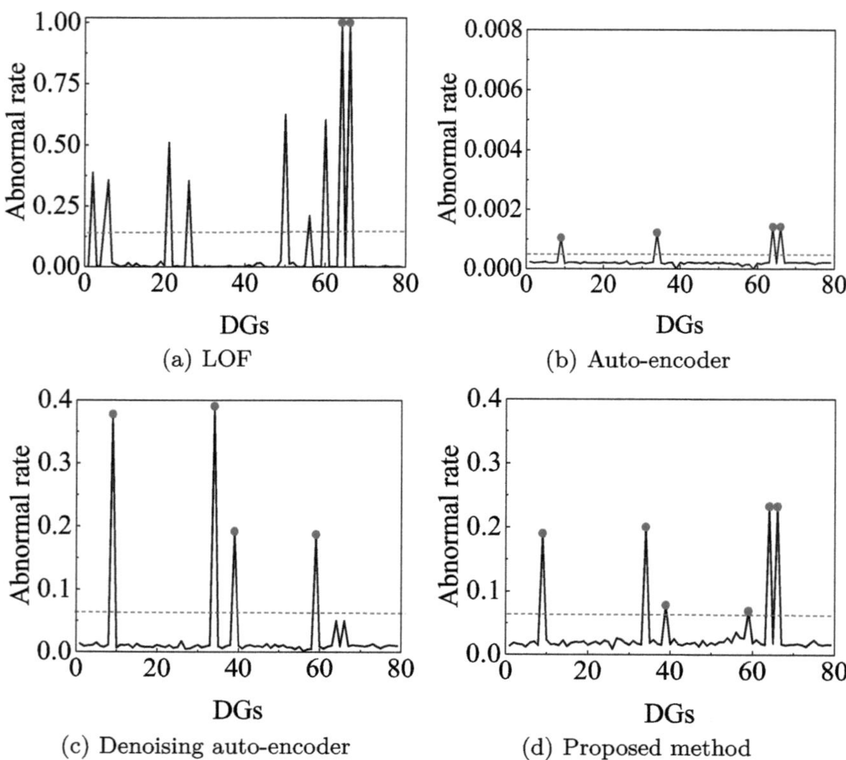

(a) LOF

(b) Auto-encoder

(c) Denoising auto-encoder

(d) Proposed method

**Fig. 2.** Comparison of anomaly localization results of LOF, auto-encoder, denoising auto-encoder and proposed AAE method under voltage attack scenario. The red dots indicate the anomalies correctly identified by the method. The red dotted line indicates the threshold for anomaly localization. (Color figure online)

### 4.3   Simulation and Result Analysis

In this subsection, to verify the superiority of the proposed anomaly localization method, two scenarios of voltage attack and current attack are set up. And the anomaly location performance of Local Outlier Factor (LOF) method, auto-encoder (AE), denoising auto-encoder (DAE) and proposed AAE are compared respectively.

**Voltage Attack Scenario.** In this scenario, the voltage value of the DG is attacked by false data injection. The anomaly localization results of LOF, auto-encoder, denoising auto-encoder and proposed AAE method under voltage attack scenario are shown in Fig. 2, Fig. 3 and Table 1.

In Fig. 2, the anomaly localization result under different methods is shown. The red dots indicate the anomalies correctly identified by the method. The red dotted line indicates the threshold for anomaly localization. The larger the

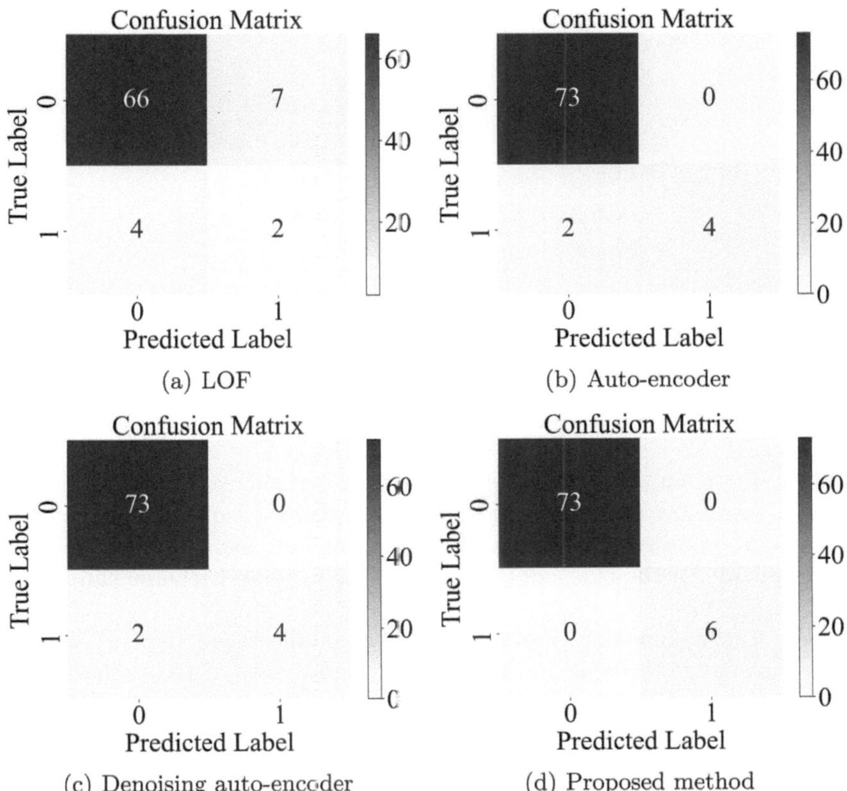



**Fig. 3.** Comparison of confusion matrix of LOF, auto-encoder, denoising auto-encoder and proposed AAE method under voltage attack scenario.

anomaly rate, the better the scheme can locate the anomaly. It can be seen that LOF has many false positives for normal DGs. Auto-encoder has fewer false positives, but are less capable of locating abnormal DGs. The DAE method and the proposed method have stronger anomaly location ability and fewer false positive samples. Under the same threshold, the proposed scheme has better anomaly locating ability than DAE method.

In Fig. 3, the confusion matrix of different methods are shown. The results showed that the LOF identifies 2 anomalies, and 7 normal DGs are incorrectly identified as anomalies. Both AE and DAE methods detect 4 anomalies, and no normal DG was incorrectly located as anomaly. The proposed method locates all 6 anomalies.

In Table 1, compared with LOF, auto-encoder and denoising auto-encoder, the proposed method has larger recall rate. Compared with the LOF, there are lower false positive rate in the other three methods.

**Table 1.** Comparison of Performance Metrics for Different Anomaly Localization Methods Under Voltage Attack.

|                                    | Recall | FPR   |
| ---------------------------------- | ------ | ----- |
| LOF [8]                            | 0.333  | 0.096 |
| Auto-encoder [16]                  | 0.667  | 0     |
| Denoising auto-encoder [17]        | 0.667  | 0     |
| Proposed method                    | 1      | 0     |

**Current Attack Scenario.** In this scenario, the current value of the DG is attacked by false data injection. The anomaly localization results of LOF, auto-encoder, denoising auto-encoder and proposed AAE method under current attack scenario are shown in Fig. 4, Fig. 5 and Table 2.

In Fig. 4, the anomaly localization result under different methods is shown. It can be seen that LOF, AE and DAE have some false positives for normal DGs. The proposed method has no false positive samples. All schemes have the same recall rate. If the threshold is lowered, the proposed scheme can locate all anomalies.

In Fig. 5, the confusion matrix of different methods are shown. The results showed that the LOF identifies 4 anomalies, and 3 normal DGs are incorrectly identified as anomalies. Both AE and DAE methods detect 4 anomalies. In AE, 6 normal DG was incorrectly identified as anomaly. In DAE, 5 normal DG was incorrectly identified as anomaly. The proposed method locates 4 anomalies, and no normal DG was incorrectly identified as anomaly.

**Table 2.** Comparison of Performance Metrics for Different Anomaly Localization Methods Under Current Attack.

|                                    | Recall | FPR   |
| ---------------------------------- | ------ | ----- |
| LOF [8]                            | 0.667  | 0.041 |
| Auto-encoder [16]                  | 0.667  | 0.082 |
| Denoising auto-encoder [17]        | 0.667  | 0.069 |
| Proposed method                    | 0.667  | 0     |

In Table 2, LOF, auto-encoder, denoising auto-encoder and the proposed method have the same recall rate. Compared with the other three methods, the proposed method has lower false positive rate.

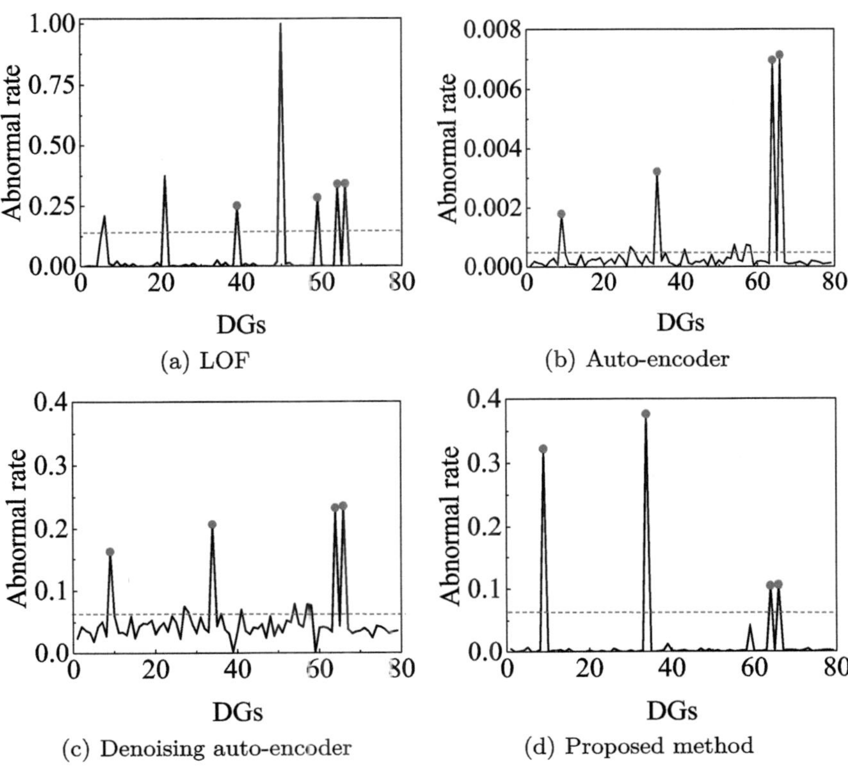

(a) LOF        (b) Auto-encoder

(c) Denoising auto-encoder        (d) Proposed method

**Fig. 4.** Comparison of anomaly localization results of LOF, auto-encoder, denoising auto-encoder and proposed AAE method under current attack scenario.

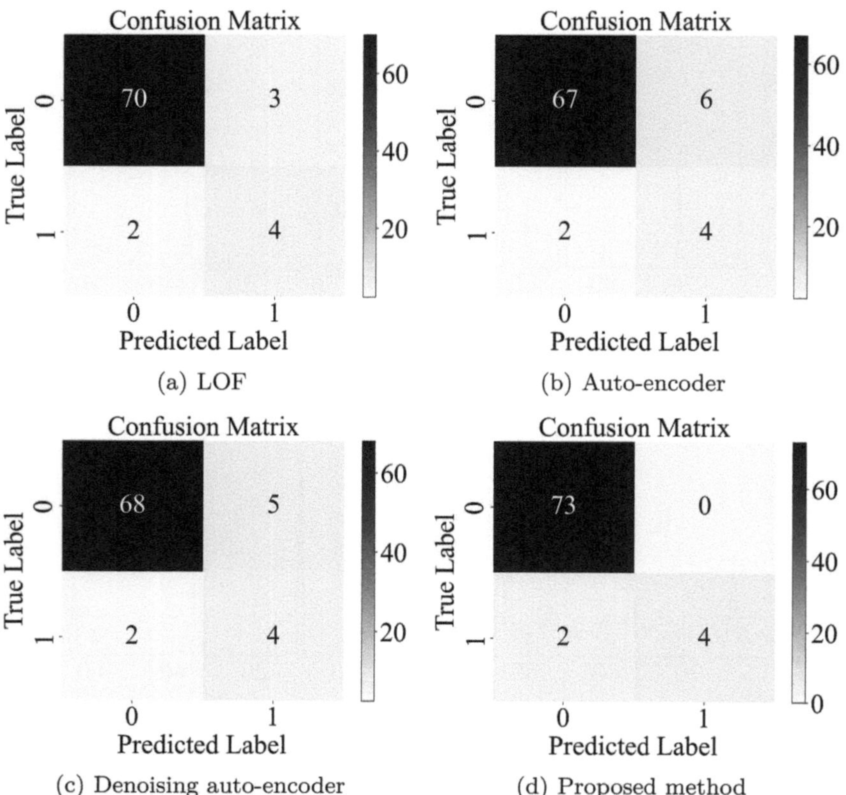



**Fig. 5.** Comparison of confusion matrix of LOF, auto-encoder, denoising auto-encoder and proposed AAE method under current attack scenario.

## 5    Conclusion

This paper proposes an adversarial autoencoder for microgrid anomaly location. Noise is leveraged to make the model accustomed to dealing with more actual anomalies, which enhances the generalization of the model. And the discriminator is introduced to reduce the false positive rate. The Matlab/Simulink microgrid simulation platform is built to obtain data, and the simulation results show that the proposed method can improve the recall rate by up to 33.3% and reduce the false positive rate by 8.2%.

## References

1. Alam, M.N., Chakrabarti, S., Ghosh, A.: Networked microgrids: state-of-the-art and future perspectives. IEEE Trans. Industr. Inf. **15**(3), 1238–1250 (2019)
2. Sahoo, S., Peng, J.C.-H., Mishra, S., Dragicevic, T.: Distributed screening of hijacking attacks in DC microgrids. IEEE Trans. Power Electron. **35**(7), 7574–7582 (2020)

3. Liu, R., Vellaithurai, C., Biswas, S.S., Gamage, T.T., Srivastava, A.K.: Analyzing the cyber-physical impact of cyber events on the power grid. IEEE Trans. Smart Grid **6**(5), 2444–2453 (2015)

4. Doroudi, R., Lavassani, S. H. H., Shahrouzi, M.: Optimal tuning of three deep learning methods with signal processing and anomaly detection for multi-class damage detection of a large-scale bridge. Structural Health Monitoring, no. 14759217231216694 (2024)

5. Cheng, P., et al.: An event-based stealthy attack on remote state estimation. IEEE Trans. Autom. Control **65**(10), 4348–4355 (2019)

6. Kromanis, R., Kripakaran, P.: Performance of signal processing techniques for anomaly detection using a temperature-based measurement interpretation approach. J. Civ. Struct. Heal. Monit. **11**, 15–34 (2021)

7. Zhang, J., et al.: Mitigating concurrent false data injection attacks in cooperative DC microgrids. IEEE Trans. Power Electron. **36**(8), 9637–9647 (2021)

8. Tirulo, A., Chauhan, S., Issac, B.: Ensemble LOF-based detection of false data injection in smart grid demand response system. Comput. Electr. Eng. vol. 116, no. 109188 (2024)

9. Gallo, A. J., et al.: Distributed cyber-attack detection in the secondary control of DC microgrids. In: 2018 European Control Conference (ECC), IEEE, pp. 344-349 (2018)

10. Mavikumbure, H. S., et al.: Cy-Phy ADS: cyber physical anomaly detection framework for EV charging systems. IEEE Trans. Transp. Electr. (2024)

11. Guan. Q., et al.: Exploiting the potential anomaly detection in automobile safety data with multi-type neural network. International Conference on Mobile and Ubiquitous Systems: Computing, Networking, and Services. Cham: Springer Nature Switzerland: 489-501 (2023)

12. Lafleni, S. P., Sumbwanyambe, M., Hlalel, T. S.: Multi-class fault analysis using quadratic svm classifier fault detection technique for micro-grid. In: 2024 32nd Southern African Universities Power Engineering Conference (SAUPEC), IEEE, pp. 1-6 (2024)

13. Huang, B., Cohen, K., Zhao, Q.: Active anomaly detection in heterogeneous processes. IEEE Trans. Inf. Theory **65**(4), 2284–2301 (2019)

14. Huang, B., Salgia, S., Zhao, Q.: Disagreement-based active learning in online settings. IEEE Trans. Signal Process. **70**, 1947–1958 (2022)

15. Takiddin, A., et al.: Data-driven detection of stealth cyber-attacks in DC microgrids. IEEE Syst. J. **16**(4), 6097–6106 (2022)

16. Takiddin, A., et al.: Deep autoencoder-based anomaly detection of electricity theft cyberattacks in smart grids. IEEE Syst. J. **16**(3), 4106–4117 (2022)

17. Creswell, A., Bharath, A.A.: Denoising adversarial autoencoders. IEEE Trans. Neural Netw. Learn. Syst. **30**(4), 968–984 (2018)

18. Ghojogh. B., et al.: Generative adversarial networks and adversarial autoencoders: tutorial and survey[J]. arXiv preprint arXiv:2111.13282 (2021)

19. Pidhorskyi, S., Almohsen, R., Doretto, G.: Generative probabilistic novelty detection with adversarial autoencoders. Adv. Neural Inf. Proc. Syst. vol. 31 (2018)

20. Di Mattia. F., et al.: A survey on GANs for anomaly detection[J]. arXiv preprint arXiv:1906.11632 (2019)

21. Yu. Z., et al.: RADEAN: a resource allocation model based on deep reinforcement learning and generative adversarial networks in edge computing. International Conference on Mobile and Ubiquitous Systems: Computing, Networking, and Services. Cham: Springer Nature Switzerland, 2023: 257-277

# DERGB: An Android Malware Adversarial Attack Technique Based on RGB Images

Zhiqiang Wang[1,2]([email]) (ORCID), Sicheng Yuan[1], Qiulong Yu[1], Ying Chen[1], and Yuheng Lin[1]

[1] Department of Cyberspace Security, Beijing Electronic Science and Technology Institute, Beijing 102627, China
wangzq@besti.edu.cn
[2] State Information Center Postdoctoral Research Station, Beijing 100045, China

**Abstract.** Android is a popular target for malware attacks due to its open-source and open nature. However, machine learning-based malware detection systems are vulnerable to adversarial sample attacks. The generation of adversarial sample primarily focuses on methods such as adding API perturbations, redundant code, and permissions. Nevertheless, these attack methods suffer from improper execution and corruption of the original malicious functions. In this paper, we investigate malware adversarial techniques, design an algorithm (DERGB algorithm) for generating adversarial samples targeting Android malware, based on RGB images, and utilize the Differential Evolution (DE) algorithm to identify the pixels in the image that impact the classification results for perturbation. Our algorithm aims to minimize the number of pixels requiring perturbations. Additionally, we leverage the header information class.dex file features, which contain the data area offsets, to constrain the range of pixel modifications in the algorithm for adversarial sample generation. This ensures that the malicious functionality and executability of the adversarial sample software remain uncompromised. The Experimental results demonstrate that our algorithm incurs a decrease in the accuracy of the detection model by approximately 34.8% when subjected to an attack by a single pixel point, and about 77.14% when subjected to five-pixel point attacks. These findings demonstrate that our algorithm achieves a comparable attack effect to other anti-sample attack algorithms, even with minimal perturbations.

**Keywords:** Android malware · adversarial attack technique · RGB

---

This research was supported by the Fundamental Research Funds for the Central Universities (Grant No. 3282024021, 3282024050, 20230045Z0114, 3282023013), First-class Discipline Construction Project of Beijing Electronic Science and Technology Institute (Grant No. 3201012).


A. Soylu et al. (Eds.): MobiQuitous 2024, LNICST 634, pp. 290–308, 2026.
https://doi.org/10.1007/978-3-032-10554-7_16

# 1   Introduction

The cyber arms race between malicious attackers and security researchers is cyclical, with malicious adversaries developing new means of countering attacks as soon as malware detection methods become more accurate [23,24].

There are many kinds of research on malware adversarial techniques, mainly based on algorithms such as adding API perturbation, adding redundant code, and adding permissions. Still, there are problems, such as the adversarial samples not being executed properly and the original malicious functions being destroyed.

Many researchers have confirmed the apparent vulnerability of machine learning-based detection models in dealing with adversarial attacks by adding some perturbations that make the malware unrecognizable by the detection model while ensuring the regular operation of the Android software. Therefore, constructing the adversarial samples used to attack different detection models is essential for the robustness and stability of the detection models.

Szegedy et al. [21] were the first to introduce the concept of adversarial samples, They point out that with full knowledge of the network parameters, for multiple neural network models with different structures and any image that the model can correctly classify, It is always possible to generate samples that are hard for a human to see the difference but are misclassified by the model, and the Limited-memory BroydenFletcherGoldfarbShanno (L-BFGS) algorithm is proposed. Papernot et al. [14] proposed the Jacobian-based Saliency Map Attack (JSMA) algorithm that can minimize the number of features of a sample that are altered without imposing a constraint on the size of the alteration, based on finding pairs of anti-significant map features to select pixels for alteration.

The main research objects of malware adversarial techniques include Android malware, IoT malware [11] [19], and Windows PE malware [18] [1]. In this paper, we focus on the adversarial sample generation method for Android malware.

Gross et al. [6] used the Fast Gradient Signed Method (FGSM) and JSMA algorithms for attacks against neural networks that classify functional features based on Android, using the idea that adding a small feature module may not affect the functionality of the malware, and for binary a feature, changing it to present when this feature is not present, but their study was limited to the feature level only, and did not result in actual malware. Khormali et al. [10] used Cleverhans to generate adversarial perturbations spliced at the tail of the grayscale image. They converted the synthesized grayscale image into binary to generate malicious code adversarial samples. Since the method uses splicing to generate adversarial samples, i.e., the generation of perturbations is not linked to the original grayscale image, there is no guarantee that the spliced samples are still adversarial. This directly affects the attack performance of the generated adversarial samples and also leads to less efficient generation of adversarial samples. Grosse et al. [7] perform minimal modifications that preserve semantics and modify only a single line of code in the manifest; however, these modifications can be detected using a static analysis tool, and it is not verified that the adversarial samples can be executed correctly.

Rosenberg et al. [17] proposed an adversarial attack based on API calls and static features, and this evasive strategy is also applicable to similar Android classifiers, which are attacked by both adding no-op(no operation) commands and patching the imported address table. Yang et al. [25] proposed an adversarial Android malware generation method for malware obfuscation attacks by reusing existing reality instead of randomly mutated or synthesized code, transforming malware features from raw feature values to feature values that are indistinguishable for malware detection, and modifying feature values that can be shared by malware samples and benign applications to obfuscate the malware detector. Demontis et al. [4] perform feature mutation and obfuscation to evade malware detection. However, their computed feature mutations may be infeasible attacks.

Xiaolei Liu et al. [12] realized the interference of Android applications by adding the request permission code in the AndroidManifest.xml file, which analyzed and limited the types and number of permissions that can be added accordingly. Without knowing the internal parameters, such as the gradient and structure of the target network, it is sufficient to know the probability of each type of label output by the model. However, there is no guarantee that the malware will execute properly after modification or that the malicious functionality has not been corrupted. Bao et al. [22] proposed a method to add adversarial noise to resource parts to generate adversarial malware samples at the raw byte level. They convert the given file into an image, add perturbations to the image using the FGSM algorithm, thereby generating an adversarial image, and finally convert the adversarial sample image into bytes.

Fabrizio et al. [2] implement an injection strategy that circumvents the required calls while preserving the overall functionality of the application. Pierazzi et al. [15] proposed a new formalization for adversarial machine learning evasion attacks in problem spaces, which includes the definition of a comprehensive set of constraints on available transformations, preserved semantics, preprocessing robustness, and rationality. Use automated software porting to extract bytecode fragments (i.e., gadgets) from benign donor applications and inject them into malicious hosts to mimic the appearance of benign applications and induce learning algorithms to misclassify malicious hosts as benign. Rosenberg et al. [16] generate adversarial samples by modifying the malware's API call sequences and non-sequential features, adding API calls that have no or irrelevant impact on the malware's functionality, and generating adversarial sequences while minimizing the number of queries to the target classifier. Song et al. [20] proposed an MAB(multi-armed bandit)-based reinforcement learning framework to generate ineffective actions by inferring the attributes of an action and dynamically adding new machine-generated adversarial samples with unseen successful content, replacing the original action with minimal feature changes. Shangyu Gu et al. [8] proposed a grayscale image-based method for generating malware adversarial samples against Android malware classifiers, where the generated image adversarial samples capable of deceiving the classifiers are converted into corresponding .dex files and repackaged to make them executable files. In 2021, L. Demetrio [3] and others proposed a new series of black-box attacks, injecting benign content that never executes at the end of a binary file or in some newly created section, taking advantage of the ambiguity of the file format in which the program is stored on disk to inject the content into a malicious program without altering its execution trajectory. In 2022, J. Yuste et al. [26] proposed a fraction-based black-box attack, which is based on dynamically introducing unused blocks or section caves in malware binaries. In 2023, Gibert [5] et al. proposed a GAN-based attack for generating adversarial malware that looks similar to executables of benign software in the feature space.

The above is part of the current research status on malware adversarial samples. As a whole, domestic and international research on malware adversarial sample generation mainly focuses on adding, changing, or deleting the extracted features, which makes the detection accuracy of malware detection models lower than the original detection accuracy.

However, malware adversarial techniques have been less studied in the field of RGB images. In 2019, Since the byte code and the RGB color code in class.dex are both in hexadecimal, Huang et al. [9] convert the bytecode of classes.dex from Android archive file to RGB color code and store it as a color image with fixed size, and then the color image is input to the convolutional neural network for automatic feature extraction and training. In 2023, Although Ouahab et al. [13] did not mention the reason for using RGB images for their experiments, the results of their experiments show that using RGB images for Android malware detection is a very good way to have advanced and effective. Therefore, in this paper, based on the RGB image transformed from the Android malware dex file, a single-pixel attack algorithm is used to modify a certain pixel point of the image so that the malware detection model makes errors in its detection. Unlike prior approaches that either focus on feature manipulation or lack verification of malware integrity, our method modifies the data section of the dex file, ensuring that essential malicious capabilities remain intact despite adversarial perturbations. This approach addresses a key gap by generating adversarial malware samples that both evade detection and retain operational functionality. It is verified through experiments that the malware adversarial samples proposed in this paper can achieve an attack effect similar to that of other adversarial sample algorithms. The main contributions and innovations of this paper are as follows:

- The modified APK retains its original functionality and remains executable.
- This black-box attack does not require knowledge of the malware detection model's internals; it operates solely based on probabilistic label outputs, enhancing its applicability.
- The algorithm perturbs only a single pixel, thereby generating effective adversarial samples while minimally interfering with the original data, enhancing its stealthiness.
- The DERGB algorithm in this paper reduces the correctness of the malware detection model from 96.80% to 57.50% when perturbing one pixel point, and reduces the correctness to 19.66% when perturbing five pixel points.

## 2    Towards Generating Adversarial Malware Examples with RGB Images

The DERGB algorithm for generating malware adversarial samples is shown in Fig. 1, it includes three key components: information extraction, malware to RGB conversion, and generation of malware adversarial samples. After the information extraction module extracts information from the APK of the software to be attacked, the data area offset value of the classes.dex file is obtained, and the Android malware-to-image algorithm is utilized to convert the malware binary file into an RGB image. Finally, the RGB image is inputted into the malware adversarial sample generator module for perturbation.

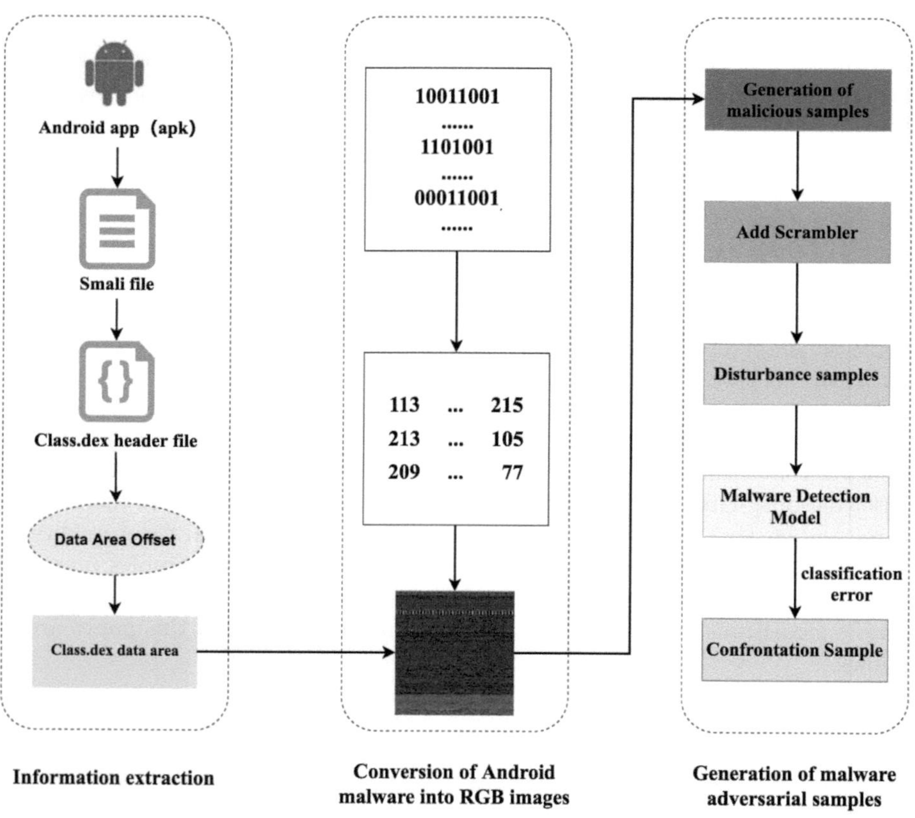


**Fig. 1.** Generating Adversarial Malware Examples with RGB images.

## 2.1   Information Extraction

This module needs to extract the header file offset value of the classes.dex file of the APK to be attacked, decompile the APK of the software to be detected, and obtain the corresponding Smali file.

Instead of using class files directly, Android aggregates and packages all class files into dex files that can be executed directly under the Android Runtime. Android platform source code files are compiled, refactored, rearranged, compressed, and obfuscated to form bytecode files named dex. Dex file consists of several data blocks, the structure of which is shown in Fig. 2 and consists of the dex file header, string_ids, type_ids, proto_ids, field_ids, method_ids, class_def, data area data, and static link data area link_data. From the header to the data stored between are equipped with an array of offsets, not stored in the dex file, which contains the actual data, the file all the data are placed in the data area and need to be used according to the file offset for the calculation of the search.

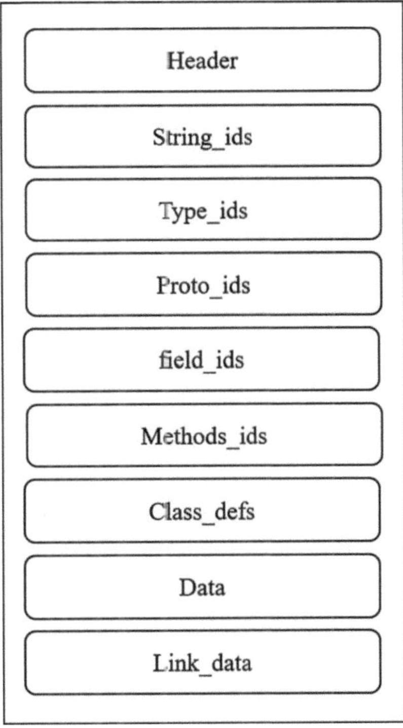


**Fig. 2.** Malware adversarial technology general design.

The functions of the various parts of the Dex file structure are shown in Table 1. The dex header is the first part of the file that specifies the attributes and holds the physical offset addresses of the remaining six data blocks. The string_ids, type_ids, proto_ids, field_ids, method_ids, and class_def are the index structure area, which mainly contains the indexes of strings, types, method prototypes, fields, methods, data to store the valid data, link_data is the link data area, which mainly stores the static link library.

**Table 1.** Symbols and their descriptions

| Dex file structure | Function |
| --- | --- |
| header | The dex file header records the relevant properties of the entire dex file, and the dex file contains some basic information to memorize the general distribution of data |
| string_ids | The string data index records the offset of each string in the data area |
| type_ids | A data-like index that records a string index for each type, which must be sorted by string_id index and must not contain any duplicate entries |
| proto_ids | The prototype data index, records the method declaration string, return type string, and parameter list |
| field_ids | Index of field data, recording class, type, and method name |
| method_ids | The class method index records the class name, method declaration, and method name of the method |
| class_defs | Class Definition Data Index, which records all types of information about the specified class, including interfaces, superclasses, and class data offsets |
| data | The data area, holds the real data of each class, different items by different alignment requirements, if necessary, insert padding bytes before each item to achieve the alignment effect |
| link_data | Link data area, data used by statically linked files, empty when not linked, may be used at runtime where appropriate |

The "Header" belongs to the header of the dex file, including the offset address and length information of the checksum and other structures, the length of the header is fixed at $0 \times 70$, in which each piece of information also occupies a fixed amount of memory space as well, the header of the various fields of information as shown in Table 2.

The classes.dex header file is available from the Smali file, based on the header file you can get the data area offset value of the file and thus calculate where the data area is located in the classes.dex file.

**Table 2.** Dex file header information

| Field name | Offset value | Lengths | Description |
| --- | --- | --- | --- |
| magic | 0 × 0 | 8 | The dex file header records the relevant prop erties of the entire dex file, and the dex file of some basic information to memorize the gen eral distribution of data. |
| checksum | 0 × 8 | 4 | The check digit of the entire header is used to verify that the header is not corrupted. |
| signature | 0 × c | 20 | Sha-1 signature. |
| file_size | 0 × 20 | 4 | The total length of the dex file is used to cal culate offsets and facilitate positioning. |
| header_size | 0 × 24 | 4 | File header length, used to calculate the start ing position of the next block in the file, ver sion 009=0 × 5c, version 035=0 × 70. |
| endian_tag | 0 × 28 | 4 | A constant that identifies the byte order, ac cording to which you can determine whether a file has swapped byte order. |
| link_size | 0 × 2c | 4 | If the size of the link segment is 0, then it is a static link. |
| link_off | 0 × 30 | 4 | Start position of the link segment. |
| map_off | 0 × 34 | 4 | Map database address. |
| string_ids_size | 0 × 38 | 4 | Number of strings in the string list. |
| string_ids_off | 0 × 3c | 4 | String list base address. |
| type_ids_size | 0 × 40 | 4 | Number of types in the class list. |
| type_ids_off | 0 × 44 | 4 | Class list base address. |
| proto_ids_size | 0 × 48 | 4 | Number of prototypes in the prototype list. |
| proto_ids_off | 0 × 4c | 4 | Prototype list base address. |
| field_ids_size | 0 × 50 | 4 | Number of fields in the field list. |
| field_ids_off | 0 × 54 | 4 | Field list base address. |
| method_ids_size | 0 × 58 | 4 | Number of methods in the method list. |
| method_ids_off | 0 × 5c | 4 | Method list base address. |
| class_defs_size | 0 × 60 | 4 | Number of classes in the class definition label. |
| class_defs_off | 0 × 64 | 4 | Class Definition List Base Address. |
| data_size | 0 × 68 | 4 | The size of the data segment must be aligned in 4 bytes. |
| data_off | 0 × 6c | 4 | Data segment base address. |

## 2.2   Malware to RGB Conversion

In this paper, we opt to extract features to form a binary file, which is then converted into an RGB image. Specifically, the binary file obtained during the process of file and feature extraction is converted to an RGB image. After loading the data from the binary file into an array, the data are sequentially loaded into the R, G, and B arrays. Finally, the data in these three arrays are processed and transformed into an RGB image. The detailed conversion process is illustrated in Fig. 3 below.

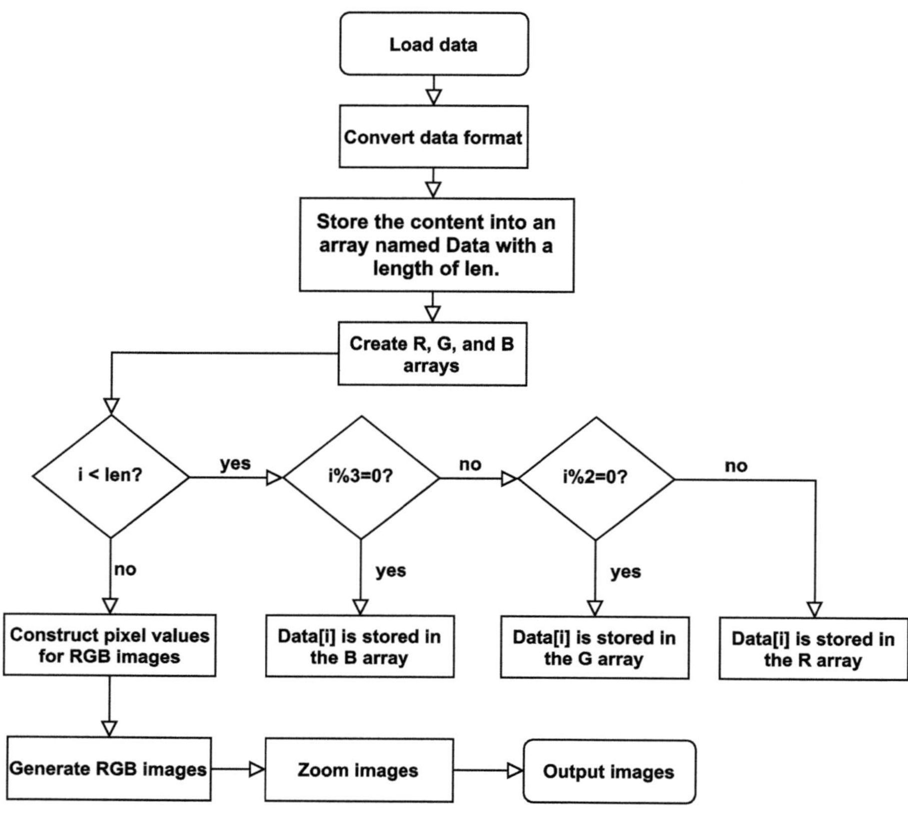


**Fig. 3.** The process of converting a binary file to an RGB image.

## 2.3   Generation of Malware Adversarial Samples

The Malware Adversarial Sample Generation Module uses the Single Pixel Attack algorithm as an adversarial sample generation method, which is a black-box attack that will only perturb a single pixel, with the only available information being the probability labels, which allows for the generation of effective adversarial samples while minimizing interference with the original data. Many data points may be located in the vicinity of the image classification decision boundary, so by moving along a few dimensions to find the points that let the category labels change, the detection model can be allowed to make classification errors.

The single-pixel attack uses an algorithm called differential evolution (DE) to generate an antagonistic book that attempts to minimize the confidence in the classification of the neural network model. Differential evolution was proposed in 1997 by Rainer Storn and Kenneth Price based on evolutionary ideas such as genetic algorithms, which simulate hybridization, mutation, and replication in genetics to design genetic operators. Like the genetic algorithm, the DE algorithm's process also randomly generates an initial population to set the fitness value of each individual in the population as a selection criterion. Unlike genetic algorithms, where the probability of the resulting offspring being selected after the parent's hybridization and mutation needs to be controlled based on the fitness value, differential evolutionary algorithms generate a vector of variants from the parent's vector of differences and the vector of offspring individuals will cross with the parent's vector of individuals to generate a new vector of individuals. Another set of candidate solutions (children) is generated during each iteration based on the current solution (parent). Compare the child with the corresponding parent, and if the child is fitter (has a higher value) than the parent, keep it. Increasing value while achieving the goal of maintaining diversity by comparing parents and offspring.

## 3   Implementation of Adversarial Techniques

The Android malware Adversarial technique pseudo-code is shown in Algorithm 1, where $f(x)$ denotes classifying the image $x$, Get_dex$(x)$ denotes extracting the dex file from the APK file $x$, File_to_RGB$(x)$ denotes converting the binary file $x$ to an RGB image, and Modify$(x)$ denotes performing an adversarial sample attack on the image $x$, the epoch denotes the number of modifications performed.

The dex file of the malware targeted to be attacked is converted into an RGB image, the index structure area and the data area of the file are distinguished according to the offset of the dex file header, and the modification area is restricted to the data area. The converted image is modified in the limited rounds. The attack is successful if it succeeds in misdirecting the malware detection model, the adversarial samples are returned, and they are used to replace the original file in the APK file. If the attack does not succeed in the specified rounds, the program returns False to show that the attack has failed.

### 3.1   Implementation of Information Extraction

As can be seen from the structure of the dex file, the offset of each block in the dex file can be obtained from the header, and the data location of each block can be calculated from the offset. By reading the data offset in the dex file, calculating the location of the data segment, and restricting the area to be modified to the data segment of the dex file to counter the sample attack, it is possible to make the malware detection error without affecting the malicious function of the malware.

---

**Algorithm 1.** Conjugate Gradient Algorithm with Dynamic Step-Size Control

---

**Input:** APK, epoch
**Output:** Adversarial sample $x'$
1: $File = \text{Get\_dex}(APK)$
2: $x = \text{File\_to\_RGB}(File)$
3: **for** $i = 1$ to epoch **do**
4:     $x' = \text{Modify}(x)$
5:     **if** $f(x')$ is misclassified **then**
6:         return $x'$
7:     **end if**
8:     $i = i + 1$
9: **end for**
10: **if** $i = $ epoch  **then**
11:     return False
12: **end if**

---

The specific implementation algorithm is shown in Algorithm 2. Among them, Apktool_decode_apk() function is the Apk decompile function, which is used to decompile Apk to get smali files, and the Find() function is the data area offset value finding function, which is used to find the data area offset value in the file.

---

**Algorithm 2.** Offset Calculation Algorithm

---

**Input:** APK file address APK_file
**Output:** classes.dex File data area offset value
1: **for** apk in APK_list **do**
2:     Smali $\leftarrow$ Apktool_decode_apk(apk)
3:     **for** file in Smali **do**
4:         **for** i in file **do**
5:             data = Find(file)
6:         **end for**
7:         Save data
8:     **end for**
9: **end for**

---

## 3.2 Implementation of Adversarial Sample Generation

The specific algorithm for the DE algorithm is shown in Algorithm 3, where the population size is typically between five and ten times the vector dimension. First, initialize the population and set the parameters of the algorithm; calculate the adaptation value of each individual in the population; if the adaptation value can meet the set termination conditions, output the optimal result; if the final conditions are not met, carry out the variation, crossover and selection operations, and then calculate the adaptation value of each individual until the termination conditions are met, and stop the cycle. The mutation is realized by using two different vectors in the population to interfere with an existing vector by performing a difference operation, crossover operation as a crossover between each individual and the offspring variant vector it generates, and selecting offspring variant vectors with a certain probability for each component thus generating test individuals. The selection operation uses a greedy algorithm to select the individual that meets the objective as the next generation based on the value of the fitness function.

---

**Algorithm 3.** Differential Evolution Algorithm for Single Pixel Attack

---

**Input:** Population size $M$, vector dimension $D$, maximum number of evolutionary generations $T$

**Output:** optimal vector $\Delta$

1: $t = 1$
2: **for** $i = 1$ to $M$ **do**
3:     **for** $j = 1$ to $D$ **do**
4:         $x_{i,t}^{j} = x_{\min}^{j} + \text{rand}(0,1) \cdot \left(x_{\max}^{j} - x_{\min}^{j}\right)$
5:     **end for**
6: **end for**
7: **while** $(|f(\Delta)| \geq \varepsilon)$ or $(t \leq T)$ **do**
8:     **for** $i = 1$ to $M$ **do**
9:         **for** $j = 1$ to $D$ **do**
10:            $v_{i,t}^{j} = \text{Mutation}\left(x_{i,t}^{j}\right)$
11:            $u_{i,t}^{j} = \text{Crossover}\left(x_{i,t}^{j}, v_{i,t}^{j}\right)$
12:         **end for**
13:         **if** $f(u_{i,t}) < f(x_{i,t})$ **then**
14:            $x_{i,t} = u_{i,t}$
15:            **if** $f(x_{i,t}) < f(\Delta)$ **then**
16:                $\Delta = x_{i,t}$
17:            **end if**
18:         **else**
19:            $x_{i,t} = x_{i,t}$
20:         **end if**
21:     **end for**
22:     $t = t + 1$
23: **end while**
24: **return** $\Delta$

---

The single-pixel attack algorithm modifies an entire image by selecting a single pixel in the range of the whole image, in this research paper, the range of modification of the single-pixel attack is limited to allow it to modify only the content of the dex file data area to preserve the malicious functionality of the malware samples and their executability, the specific algorithms are shown in Algorithm 4. The Get_disturbance() function is used to generate a tuple of perturbations, the disturbance() function adds perturbations to the image, choose()

selects the perturbations that are most likely to improve the target label, and Add_disturbance() is used to add the perturbations to the original image.

---

**Algorithm 4.** Algorithm for adversarial sample attack in this paper

---

**Input:** RGB image and type label to be transformed by the attacking software, classification model Detection()
**Output:** The software produces adversarial samples
 1: offset = offset_dex
 2: rgb = Get_disturbance()
 3: disturbance(rgb)
 4: **for** $i = 1$ in epoch **do**
 5:     RGB_new = choose(rgb)
 6:     disturbance(RGB_new)
 7:     **if** detection(RGB_new) != lable **then**
 8:         $S$ = RGB_new
 9:     **end if**
10: **end for**
11: return Add_disturbance(RGB, rgb)

---

After inputting the image to be perturbed, a pixel of the original image is randomly modified to generate a different image and detected using the malware detection model. The modified image combines the previous pixel position and color to generate more modified images. It is the best modification solution if this new image causes the malware detection model to make a detection error. The last step is repeated until the model detection error occurs or the number of pixel modifications reaches the set number. Finally, if the modification is successful, the generated adversarial sample is returned, and if the modification fails, False is returned.

## 4    Experiments

### 4.1    Experimental Setup

The dataset used in the image-based Android malware adversarial sample generation algorithm consists of 5,676 malicious samples and 4,039 benign samples, where the malicious samples are from DREBIN and CICDataset, and the benign samples are from CICDataset and samples sourced from Google's official app store and detected by scanning.

The experimental environment uses Ubuntu 16.04.7 LTS system, GPU, and CUDA 11.2 to accelerate the speed of neural network training, the use of Python language to implement the various parts of the model, with the help of Tensorflow to implement the deep learning model, the use of NVIDIA GPU GeForce RTX 2070 to accelerate the model training and running.

## 4.2   Evaluation Indicators

Regarding the adversarial sample attack, the degree of decline in the detection accuracy of the Android malware detection model can be used as an evaluation index, and the percentage of the number of adversarial samples in the dataset that successfully generate samples that can allow the malware detection model to be misled can be used as an evaluation index, so the following two evaluation indexes are introduced, and the calculations are shown as follows. The meaning of the symbols is shown in Table 3 below.

**Table 3.** Symbol Meanings

| Symbols | Descriptions |
| --- | --- |
| TN | true negative |
| TP | true positive |
| FN | false negative |
| FP | false positive |

- Accuracy: The proportion of all correctly predicted samples to the total sample can represent the overall prediction accuracy, as shown in Equation (1).

$$ACC = \frac{TP + TN}{TP + FP + TN + FN} \tag{1}$$

- Degree of decline in model detection accuracy (DMDA): The correct rate of the original dataset detected in the malware detection model is subtracted from the correct rate of the malicious sample dataset detected in the malware detection model, as shown in Equation (2), where $ACC_{ori}$ denotes the detection accuracy of the original dataset, and $ACC_{adv}$ denotes the detection accuracy of the adversarial sample dataset.

$$DMDA = ACC_{ori} - ACC_{adv} \tag{2}$$

## 4.3   Experimental Results and Analysis

The Android malware adversarial sample is implemented using Python language, based on the DE algorithm to select the pixels of the image to be modified, and the attack is carried out by perturbing a pixel point in the data area of the corresponding RGB image of the software to be attacked, the accuracy of the model detection rate decreases from 96.8% to 57.5% when one-pixel point is perturbed. Although the decrease in accuracy is not large enough, the algorithm only perturbs one pixel at this point, which does not affect the executability of the malware while ensuring a small amount of perturbation.

The DERGB algorithm can perturb more than one-pixel point in addition to perturbing one-pixel point, when more pixel points are perturbed, the accuracy decreases more and more, when five-pixel points are perturbed, the accuracy decreases to 19.66%, as shown in Table 4, with the bar chart depicting the results displayed in Fig. 4. Since the model being attacked remains consistent (ViT, Vision Transformer), the Pre-attack ACC is the same.

**Table 4.** Attack results of the DERGB algorithm

| Attack algorithm | Pre-attack ACC | Post-attack ACC | DMDA |
| --- | --- | --- | --- |
| DERGB(one pixel) | 0.9680 | **0.5750** | 0.3930 |
| DERGB(three pixels) | 0.9680 | **0.3510** | 0.6170 |
| DERGB(five pixels) | 0.9680 | **0.1966** | 0.7714 |

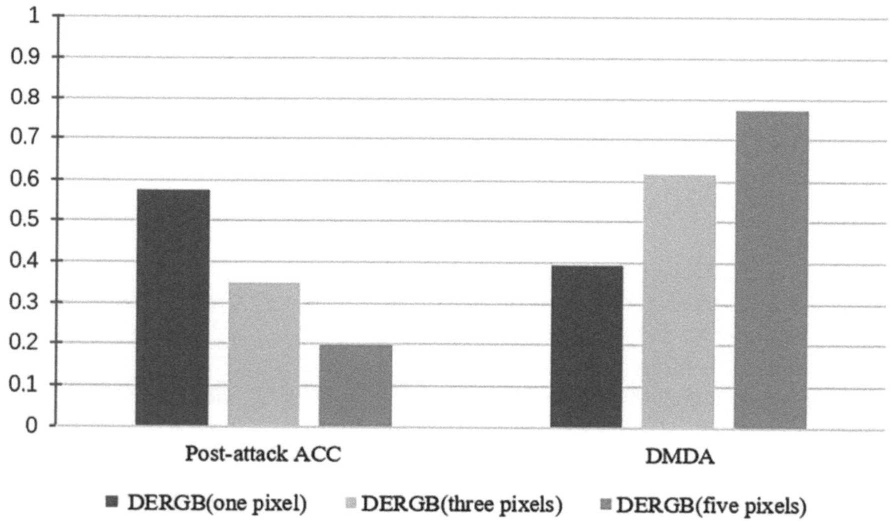


**Fig. 4.** Attack results of the DERGB algorithm.

This paper selects the FGSM algorithm, Deepfool algorithm, random modification algorithm, and this paper's DERGB algorithm perturbation of five pixels when the attack results are compared, the attacked model is also the ViT, and the attack results are as shown in Table 5, with the bar chart depicting the results displayed in Fig. 5, the DERGB algorithm attack effect is the same as other attack algorithms effect, although not as good as the FGSM algorithm, but achieves a similar result. Moreover, the DERGB algorithm in this paper is not only simple in principle, but also has a lot of improvement space, and thus has a strong research forward, which is difficult for the FGSM algorithm to have.

**Table 5.** Comparison of results of different adversarial sample attack algorithms

| Attack algorithm | Pre-attack ACC | Post-attack ACC | DMDA |
| --- | --- | --- | --- |
| **DERGB** | **0.9680** | **0.1966** | **0.7714** |
| FGSM | 0.9680 | 0.1667 | 0.8013 |
| DeepFool | 0.9680 | 0.5833 | 0.3847 |
| Randomization | 0.9680 | 0.8720 | 0.0960 |

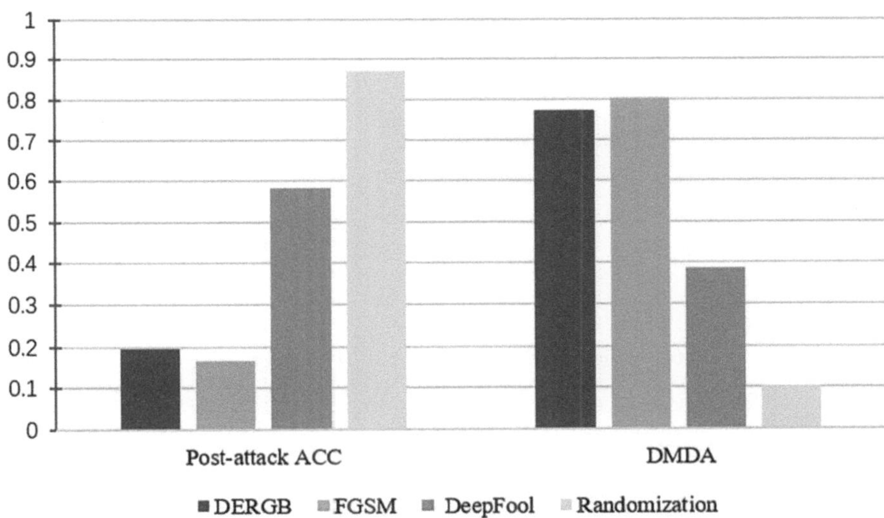


**Fig. 5.** Comparison of results of different adversarial sample attack algorithms.

The DERGB algorithm can be used to attack not only the ViT model but also other models as well. In this paper, DERGB algorithm is used to attack CNN, VGG, and other models by perturbing only one-pixel point, and the results of the attack are shown in Table 6, with the bar chart depicting the results displayed in Fig. 6, which shows that there is a substantial decrease in the accuracy of each model, with the VGG model's accuracy is the most affected by a reduction of 0.5760. This proves that the DERGB algorithm in this paper can achieve the attack effect on different models. It is precisely because the attacked models are different and consist of four distinct models that the Pre-attack ACC varies.

**Table 6.** Comparison of Attacks with Different Models

| Attack model | Pre-attack ACC | Post-attack ACC | DMDA |
|---|---|---|---|
| **ViT** | **0.9680** | **0.5000** | **0.4680** |
| CNN | 0.9260 | 0.4007 | 0.5153 |
| VGG | 0.8440 | 0.2680 | 0.5760 |
| MLP | 0.9280 | 0.4683 | 0.4597 |

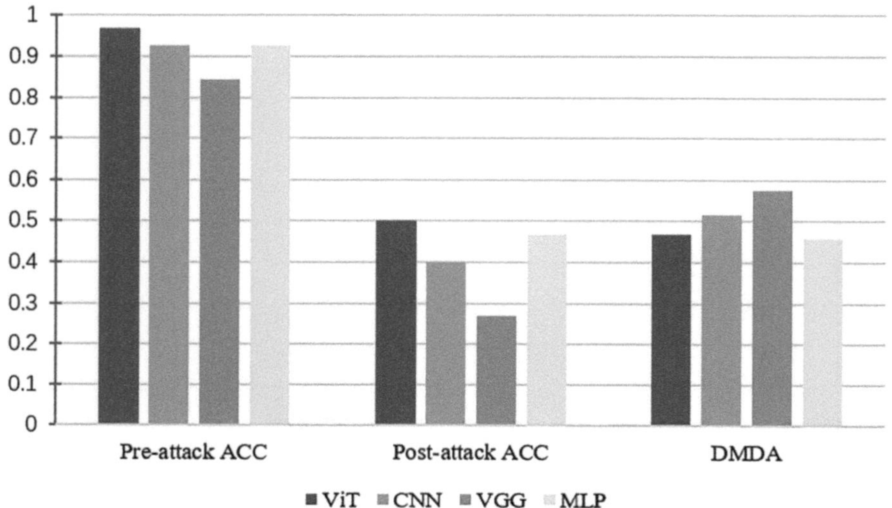


**Fig. 6.** Comparison of Attacks with Different Models.

## 5    Conclusion and Future Work

This paper mainly introduces the overall structure of DERGB, an RGB image-based Android malware adversarial sample generation algorithm, and the specific implementation of the algorithm, to the attack algorithm and provides a detailed description of it, i.e., the main use of differential evolutionary algorithm iteratively generates the adversarial sample image, the use of a combination of the parent generation and the offspring generation to generate the required malware adversarial samples, and the minimization of the malware detection confidence calculated during the model classification process. This paper mainly compares with three classical attack algorithms, and the experimental results prove that the DERGB algorithm in this paper achieves the effect of the attack, and the effect of the attack is similar to the other algorithms when the number of modifications is smaller than that of the other algorithms, and at the same time, this paper also compares the effect of the attack of the DERGB algorithm on different models, and proves that the attack algorithm of this paper achieves the effect of the attack on all different models.

Due to the use of the Differential Evolution algorithm for searching modified pixel points, the attack effectiveness decreases as image size increases, requiring a higher number of iterations to achieve an optimal solution. This approach, however, leads to an increase in computational resources. In future work, we aim to improve the search methodology to develop a more efficient algorithm with enhanced performance.

# References


1. Anderson, H.S., Kharkar, A., Filar, B., Evans, D., Roth, P.: Learning to evade static PE machine learning malware models via reinforcement learning (2018)
2. Cara, F., Scalas, M., Giacinto, G., Maiorca, D.: On the feasibility of adversarial sample creation using the android system API. Information **11**(9) (2020). https://doi.org/10.3390/info11090433, https://www.mdpi.com/2078-2489/11/9/433
3. Demetrio, L., Biggio, B., Lagorio, G., Roli, F., Armando, A.: Functionality-preserving black-box optimization of adversarial windows malware. IEEE Trans. Inf. Forensics Secur. **16**, 3469–3478 (2021). https://doi.org/10.1109/TIFS.2021.3082330
4. Demontis, A., et al.: Yes, machine learning can be more secure! a case study on android malware detection. IEEE Trans. Dependable Secure Comput. **16**(4), 711–724 (2019). https://doi.org/10.1109/TDSC.2017.2700270
5. Gibert, D., Planes, J., Le, Q., Zizzo, G.: A wolf in sheep's clothing: query-free evasion attacks against machine learning-based malware detectors with generative adversarial networks. In: 2023 IEEE European Symposium on Security and Privacy Workshops (EuroS&PW), pp. 415–426 (2023). https://doi.org/10.1109/EuroSPW59978.2023.00052
6. Grosse, K., Papernot, N., Manoharan, P., Backes, M., McDaniel, P.: Adversarial perturbations against deep neural networks for malware classification (2016)
7. Grosse, K., Papernot, N., Manoharan, P., Backes, M., McDaniel, P.: Adversarial Examples for Malware Detection. In: Foley, S.N., Gollmann, D., Snekkenes, E. (eds.) ESORICS 2017. LNCS, vol. 10493, pp. 62–79. Springer, Cham (2017). https://doi.org/10.1007/978-3-319-66399-9_4
8. Gu, S., Cheng, S., Zhang, W.: From image to code: executable adversarial examples of android applications. In: Proceedings of the 2020 6th International Conference on Computing and Artificial Intelligence, pp. 261–268. ICCAI '20, Association for Computing Machinery, New York, NY, USA (2020). https://doi.org/10.1145/3404555.3404574, https://doi.org/10.1145/3404555.3404574
9. Huang, T.H.D., Kao, H.Y.: R2-d2: Color-inspired convolutional neural network (CNN)-based android malware detections. In: 2018 IEEE International Conference on Big Data (Big Data), pp. 2633–2642 (2018). https://doi.org/10.1109/BigData.2018.8622324
10. Khormali, A., Abusnaina, A., Chen, S., Nyang, D., Mohaisen, A.: Copycat: practical adversarial attacks on visualization-based malware detection (2019)
11. Liu, Q., Wang, J., Yin, J., Chen, Y., Liu, J.: Application of adversarial machine learning in network intrusion detection. J. Commun. **42**(11), 1 (2021). https://doi.org/10.11959/j.issn.1000-436x.2021193
12. Liu, X., Du, X., Zhang, X., Zhu, Q., Wang, H., Guizani, M.: Adversarial samples on android malware detection systems for IOT systems. Sensors **19**(4) (2019). https://doi.org/10.3390/s19040974, https://www.mdpi.com/1424-8220/19/4/974

13. Ouahab, I.B.A., Alluhaidan, Y., Elaachak, L., Bouhorma, M.: Malware detection using RGB images and CNN model subclassing. In: Abd El-Latif, A.A., Maleh, Y., Mazurczyk, W., ELAffendi, M., I. Alkanhal, M. (eds.) Advances in Cybersecurity, Cybercrimes, and Smart Emerging Technologies, pp. 3–13. Springer International Publishing, Cham (2023)

14. Papernot, N., et al.:cleverhans v2. 0.0: an adversarial machine learning library. arXiv preprint arXiv:1610.00768 **10** (2016)

15. Pierazzi, F., Pendlebury, F., Cortellazzi, J., Cavallaro, L.: Intriguing properties of adversarial ml attacks in the problem space. In: 2020 IEEE Symposium on Security and Privacy (SP). pp. 1332–1349 (2020). https://doi.org/10.1109/SP40000.2020.00073

16. Rosenberg, I., Shabtai, A., Elovici, Y., Rokach, L.: Query-efficient black-box attack against sequence-based malware classifiers. In: Proceedings of the 36th Annual Computer Security Applications Conference. pp. 611–626. ACSAC '20, Association for Computing Machinery, New York, NY, USA (2020). https://doi.org/10.1145/3427228.3427230, https://doi.org/10.1145/3427228.3427230

17. Rosenberg, I., Shabtai, A., Rokach, L., Elovici, Y.: Generic black-box end-to-end attack against state of the art API call based malware classifiers. In: Bailey, M., Holz, T., Stamatogiannakis, M., Ioannidis, S. (eds.) Research in Attacks, Intrusions, and Defenses, pp. 490–510. Springer International Publishing, Cham (2018)

18. Rui, Z., Qiuyun, W., Jianming, F., Zhengwei, J., Riguga, S., Shuwei, W.: A novel malware classification model based on deep learning. J. Cyber Secur. **5**(1), 1–9 (2020)

19. Singh, A., Sikdar, B.: Adversarial attack and defence strategies for deep-learning-based IOT device classification techniques. IEEE Internet Things J. **9**(4), 2602–2613 (2022). https://doi.org/10.1109/JIOT.2021.3138541

20. Song, W., Li, X., Afroz, S., Garg, D., Kuznetsov, D., Yin, H.: Mab-malware: a reinforcement learning framework for attacking static malware classifiers (2021)

21. Szegedy, C., et al.: Intriguing properties of neural networks (2014)

22. Vi, B.N., Noi Nguyen, H., Nguyen, N.T., Truong Tran, C.: Adversarial examples against image-based malware classification systems. In: 2019 11th International Conference on Knowledge and Systems Engineering (KSE), pp. 1–5 (2019). https://doi.org/10.1109/KSE.2019.8919481

23. Wang, Z., et al.: A deep learning method for android application classification using semantic features. Secur. Commun. Netw. **2022** (2022)

24. Wang, Z., Liu, Q., Chi, Y.: Review of android malware detection based on deep learning. IEEE Access **8**, 181102–181126 (2020). https://doi.org/10.1109/ACCESS.2020.3028370

25. Yang, W., Kong, D., Xie, T., Gunter, C.A.: Malware detection in adversarial settings: exploiting feature evolutions and confusions in android apps. In: Proceedings of the 33rd Annual Computer Security Applications Conference, pp. 288–302. ACSAC '17, Association for Computing Machinery, New York, NY, USA (2017). https://doi.org/10.1145/3134600.3134642, https://doi.org/10.1145/3134600.3134642

26. Yuste, J., Pardo, E.G., Tapiador, J.: Optimization of code caves in malware binaries to evade machine learning detectors. Comput. Secur. **116**, 102643 (2022). https://doi.org/10.1016/j.cose.2022.102643, https://www.sciencedirect.com/science/article/pii/S0167404822000426

# Deep Generative Domain Adaptation with Temporal Relation Knowledge for Cross-User Activity Recognition

Xiaozhou Ye[✉] and Kevin I-Kai Wang

Department of Electrical, Computer, and Software Engineering, The University of Auckland, Auckland, New Zealand
xye685@aucklanduni.ac.nz, kevin.wang@auckland.ac.nz

**Abstract.** In human activity recognition (HAR), the assumption that training and testing data are independent and identically distributed (i.i.d.) often fails, particularly in cross-user scenarios where data distributions vary significantly. This discrepancy highlights the limitations of conventional domain adaptation methods in HAR, which typically overlook the inherent temporal relations in time-series data. To bridge this gap, our study introduces a Conditional Variational Autoencoder with Universal Sequence Mapping (CVAE-USM) approach, that addresses the unique challenges of time-series domain adaptation in HAR by relaxing the i.i.d. assumption and leveraging temporal relations to align data distributions effectively across different users. This method combines the strengths of the Variational Autoencoder (VAE) and Universal Sequence Mapping (USM) to capture and utilize common temporal patterns between users for improved activity recognition. Our results, evaluated on two public HAR datasets (OPPT and PAMAP2), demonstrate that CVAE-USM outperforms existing state-of-the-art methods, offering a more accurate and generalizable solution for cross-user activity recognition.

**Keywords:** Human Activity Recognition · Domain Adaptation · Conditional Variational Autoencoder · Universal Sequence Mapping · Temporal Relations · Time-Series Classification

## 1  Introduction

Human Activity Recognition (HAR) is an essential field within Human-Computer Interaction, ubiquitous computing [16], and the Internet of Things [1]. It involves identifying human activities using sensor data and contextual information [19]. HAR finds applications in diverse areas like medical treatment, assisted living, fitness, security, and home automation. Current HAR methods, especially those processing time-series sensor data, operate under the assumption that training and testing data are drawn from the same distribution, meaning they are independent and identically distributed (i.i.d.) [31]. This approach


A. Soylu et al. (Eds.): MobiQuitous 2024, LNICST 634, pp. 309–326, 2026.
https://doi.org/10.1007/978-3-032-10554-7_17

assumes that a model trained on source data will perform similarly on target data, as long as both sets of data are from the same domain with consistent features and distribution characteristics. However, this is often not the case in real-world scenarios, where training and testing datasets may have different distributions due to data heterogeneity, also known as the out-of-distribution (o.o.d.) problem. This discrepancy can lead to reduced model performance when applied to new, unseen data [18].

Transfer learning, specifically domain adaptation [17], is a method that addresses the out-of-distribution (o.o.d.) problem by mitigating data heterogeneity. Its core principle is to identify and transfer common knowledge between different domains to minimize the distribution differences between the source and target datasets. While domain adaptation methods have shown success in handling static data, such as images, where each sample is treated as independent and identically distributed (i.i.d.) within its domain [18], their application to time-series data presents additional challenges. In the context of time-series data, particularly in HAR, this assumption of independence does not hold [34]. Human activities are inherently sequential, where consecutive data segments exhibit temporal dependencies. For example, an activity like walking consists of a series of interconnected movements (e.g., lifting the leg, moving it forward, placing it down), each depending on the previous step. Therefore, treating time-series data as i.i.d. fails to capture these vital temporal relations. This oversight limits the effectiveness of current domain adaptation approaches, as they miss the temporal dynamics crucial for accurately recognizing human activities. As a result, models often struggle with performance, particularly in cross-user scenarios, where the common temporal patterns of activities across different users are not effectively captured.

This paper introduces a novel approach called Conditional Variational Autoencoder with Universal Sequence Mapping (CVAE-USM) for time series domain adaptation in HAR. This method focuses on capturing temporal relations in activity data through USM encoding, enabling better adaptation between different users' data. By preserving these temporal relations, our approach effectively regularizes the adaptation process, enhancing the alignment of sub-activity distributions across users. This results in improved performance in domain adaptation tasks. Moreover, We propose a new generative model of variational autoencoder (VAE) based architecture that captures temporal relation knowledge for cross-user HAR, which enhances the generalized capability of VAE generative model. Our extensive testing on two public HAR datasets shows that this method outperforms existing approaches in time series domain adaptation, particularly in cross-user scenarios.

The paper is organized as follows: Section 2 reviews related work in HAR, transfer learning, and domain adaptation. Section 3 details our proposed CVAE-USM method, focusing on capturing and aligning temporal relations. Section 4 outlines our experimental setup and compares our method against existing approaches. Finally, Sect. 5 concludes the paper and suggests directions for future research.

# 2   Related Work

## 2.1   Human Activity Recognition Out-of-Distribution Challenges

Human Activity Recognition (HAR) is a fundamental aspect of ubiquitous computing, playing a vital role in enhancing daily human activities. Its primary goal is to recognize and analyze human behaviors by interpreting high-level knowledge derived from multi-modal sensor data and contextual information. Based on sensor modalities, HAR can be categorized into five distinct types: Smartphones/wearable sensors-based HAR, ambient sensors-based HAR, device-free sensors-based HAR, vision-based sensors-based HAR, and other modality sensors-based HAR [7,12]. This paper specifically delves into HAR using wearable sensors.

Within machine learning research, sensor-based HAR is often approached as a time series classification problem [4]. Various classification models, including ensemble learning [25], SVM [5], and HMM [3], have been proposed to solve HAR challenges. With advancements in deep learning, numerous state-of-the-art results have been achieved for a wide range of tasks. Deep learning-based HAR techniques excel in learning high-level features and autonomously extracting features from extensive data sets [19]. However, these approaches predominantly rely on the assumption that the training and testing data are drawn from the same distribution, meaning the data is considered independent and identically distributed (i.i.d.) [31]. This assumption often fails in real-world applications, where the collected training and testing datasets are out-of-distribution (o.o.d.). Our focus in this paper is on addressing the challenges associated with sensor-based HAR in the context of o.o.d. data.

There are several categories of sensor-based HAR o.o.d. challenges: First, differences in data may result from the use of various sensor types, platforms, manufacturers, and modalities, leading to diverse data formats and distributions [33]. Second, the data pattern might change over time, a phenomenon known as concept drift [14]. For example, a person's walking pattern could be influenced by changes in health status. Third, behavioral differences between individuals can be significant [35]; for instance, walking pace may vary from person to person. Fourth, the positioning of physical sensors on the body [21] or the layout of environmental sensors in smart homes [27] can also lead to different data distributions. Our research specifically targets sensor-based HAR o.o.d. problems stemming from behavioral differences among individuals.

## 2.2   Transfer Learning and Domain Adaptation

Transfer learning enables models to learn from one or more source domains and then apply this knowledge to related target domains lacking labelled data. This process is crucial to address the out-of-distribution (o.o.d.) problem by minimizing distribution differences between the source and target domains. Domain adaptation, a subset of transfer learning, specifically tackles the o.o.d. issue while maintaining the same task across source and target domains. This approach typically involves leveraging labelled data from the source domain and unlabeled data from the target domain [31].

Domain adaptation has experienced significant growth, particularly in the area of feature-based transfer learning [17]. Techniques like Subspace Alignment (SA) [8] focus on finding similarities between the feature subspaces of the source and target domains, using principal component analysis and linear transformations. Optimal Transport for Domain Adaptation (OTDA) [9], is grounded in optimal transport theory, aiming to establish a cost-effective correspondence between different domains. Deep domain adaptation has also seen advancements with approaches like the Domain Adversarial Neural Network (DANN) [10], which employs adversarial learning to train a model so that its features cannot be used to distinguish between source and target domains. This promotes the generation of domain-invariant features. FedMAT [26] works by treating each individual's data as a distinct task within a federated learning system. It uniquely combines a central shared feature representation network with individual-specific networks equipped with attention modules in decentralized nodes, enabling the learning of both shared and individual-specific features from multi-modal sensor data.

These feature-based methods primarily target static data like images, often applying the same framework to time series data [13,15]. However, this approach may be less effective for time series data, where temporal relationships are crucial. Current domain adaptation strategies often overlook these temporal relations, leading to models that may not perform reliably, especially in cross-user HAR applications where models trained on data from one user are applied to others. Incorporating temporal relation knowledge could enhance the identification of commonalities between users, improving domain adaptation in sensor-based HAR. This paper focuses on exploring and integrating temporal relation knowledge to enhance domain adaptation effectiveness in cross-user HAR.

## 3   Method

### 3.1   Problem Formulation

In a cross-user HAR problem, a labelled source user $S^{Source} = \left\{ \left( x_i^{Source}, y_i^{Source} \right) \right\}_{i=1}^{n^{Source}}$ drawn from a joint probability distribution $P^{Source}$ and a target user $S^{Target} = \left\{ \left( x_i^{Target}, y_i^{Target} \right) \right\}_{i=1}^{n^{Target}}$ drawn from a joint probability distribution $P^{Target}$, where $n^{Source}$ and $n^{Target}$ are the number of source and target samples respectively. $S^{Source}$ and $S^{Target}$ have the same feature spaces (i.e. the set of features that describes the data from sensor readings) and label spaces (i.e. the set of activity classes). The source and target users have different distributions, i.e., $P^{Source} \neq P^{Target}$, which means that even for the same activity, the sensor readings look different between the two users. Given the labelled source user data and unlabelled target user data, the goal is to obtain the labels $\left\{ \left( y_i^{Target} \right) \right\}_{i=1}^{n^{Target}}$ for the target user activities.

## 3.2 Conditional Variational Autoencoder with Universal Sequence Mapping

In this study, we present the Conditional Variational Autoencoder with Universal Sequence Mapping (CVAE-USM), a novel approach for cross-user HAR. The foundation of this method is the understanding that human physical movements are influenced by preceding actions, and these temporal dependencies are generally consistent across different individuals. By capturing these shared temporal patterns in human activity time series data, our model aims to enhance its performance and generalizability for cross-user HAR tasks.

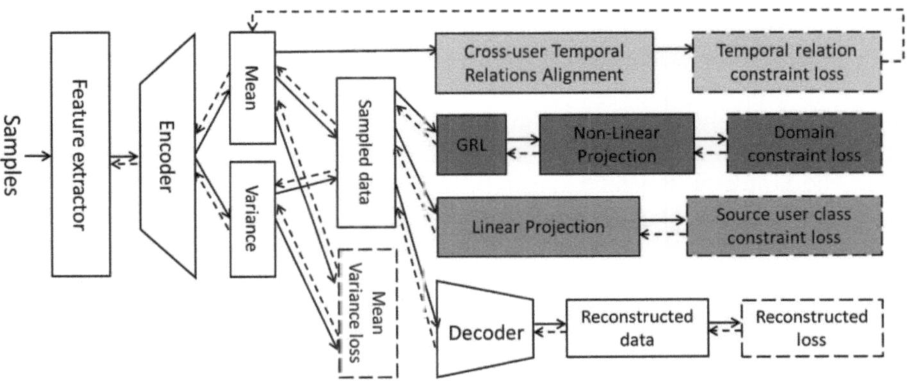


**Fig. 1.** CVAE-USM Learning Process.

**3.2.1 Generative Model Architecture.** Our approach utilizes a generative model framework, as depicted in the CVAE-USM Learning Process shown in Fig. 1, to achieve effective model generalization. Generative models are advantageous in that they can produce new data samples that are similar to the training data, aiding in data augmentation and improving generalization capabilities. Even in scenarios where some class labels are missing during training, generative models focus on modelling the data distribution itself, which is more effective in uncovering the underlying data patterns and structures [23]. For cross-user HAR, where labels for target users are not available (or only partially available), generative models are particularly useful as they are capable of modelling user-invariant activity data distributions. They achieve this by encoding data into a compact latent space, capturing the underlying factors or patterns in the data [29].

In implementing our method, we employ the Variational Autoencoder (VAE) architecture [11] as the foundational generative model. The VAE aims to learn a structured latent space where similar data samples are closely aligned, such as patterns found in time series data, typically following a Gaussian distribution. In the VAE structure, input data (like sensor features in HAR) is compressed into a lower-dimensional latent space via an encoder. This latent space is represented probabilistically with mean and variance parameters, encapsulating intrinsic characteristics of human activities. The VAE employs the reparameterization trick for differentiability during training, sampling from the latent space based on Gaussian distributions and then using a decoder to reconstruct the original input. This method enables the capturing of complex temporal activity patterns, making the VAE an ideal model for cross-user HAR tasks.

The VAE's sampling process offers several benefits for generalization and domain adaptation. The randomness introduced through sampling acts as a regularization form, preventing overfitting and enhancing generalization. By encoding data into a distribution instead of a deterministic decision boundry and encouraging the latent variables to approximate a Gaussian distribution (via the KullbackLeibler divergence), the latent space becomes more structured and continuous [24]. In such a structured latent space, alignment techniques like Gradient Reversal Layer (GRL) adversarial learning, which we will discuss later, can be more effectively applied for domain adaptation in HAR.

Moreover, we implement an adversarial learning strategy, specifically utilizing the Gradient Reversal Layer (GRL) technique [10] as the blue parts in Fig. 1. This strategy is integral to modifying the model's loss functions related to domain constraints (i.e. confusing the data distributions between source and target users). The GRL adversarial learning operates by reversing the gradients during the training phase. The primary goal of this technique is to ensure that the features learned by the model are not solely tied to the specific user but also lean towards a generalized model. Through this approach, our model can generate user-invariant representations. Therefore, this strategy is integrated as a constraint condition to the original CVAE for model learning.

Furthermore, after acquiring the sampled features, they are input into a process focusing on the source user's activity class constraint as the grey parts in Fig. 1. This involves using a linear transformation to shape how the data distribution is generated. Specifically, this step takes into consideration the activity class labels associated with the source user. This means that the transformation is guided by the types of activities the source user performed, helping to tailor the model's understanding of the data based on these specific activities. Therefore, this source user class constraint is integrated as another constraint condition to the original CVAE for model learning.

**3.2.2 Cross-User Temporal Relations Alignment.** The key element of the CVAE-USM method is the cross-user temporal relations alignment. This CVAE constraint condition is shown in the yellow parts in Fig. 1. In this component, Gaussian Mixture Model (GMM), Universal Sequence Mapping (USM), and Wasserstein Distance techniques are included. Each component plays a pivotal role in capturing and adapting temporal relation knowledge for domain adaptation. The overall process of cross-user temporal relations alignment is described in Algorithm 1.

---

**Algorithm 1.** Cross-user Temporal Relations Alignment

---

**Input:** Mean values from CVAE encoder for source ($\mu_s$) and target ($\mu_t$) users, number of components ($K$) in GMM.

**Output:** Aligned temporal relation features, Wasserstein distance ($W$) temporal relation loss.

**Begin Algorithm**

**1. Sub-Activity Identification with GMM:**

- Apply GMM to sensor data for source and target users: $GMM_{init}(\{\mu_s, \mu_t\}, K)$.
- This step is to identify and decompose complex activities into simpler sub-activities.

**2. Temporal Relations Encoding with USM:**

- Transform sub-activities into feature space using USM: $F_s = \mathcal{U}(Seq_s)$, $F_t = \mathcal{U}(Seq_t)$.
- This step aims to capture and encode temporal relation for activities. Here, $\mathcal{U}$ denotes the USM function, and $Seq_s$, $Seq_t$ are sequences of encoded sub-activities for source and target, respectively, with each value in the sequences encoded into the set $\{0, K - 1\}$.

**3. User-Specific Temporal Feature Analysis:**

- Perform separate GMM clustering on the USM-encoded features for source ($F_s$) and target ($F_t$) users: $GMM_s(F_s, K)$ and $GMM_t(F_t, K)$.
- This step is to analyze the variations and similarities between the sub-activities' data distributions across users. Let $P_s$ and $P_t$ denote the resulting distributions from $GMM_s$ and $GMM_t$ respectively, capturing distinct temporal patterns of each user group.

**4. Data Distribution Alignment with Wasserstein Distance:**

- Minimize the Wasserstein distance between source and target distributions: $W(P_s, P_t) = \inf_{\gamma \in \Pi(P_s, P_t)} \mathbb{E}(x, y) \sim \gamma[\|x - y\|]$.
- This step aims to adjust model parameters to align $Ps$ and $P_t$, focusing on common temporal relations.

**End Algorithm**

---

The first step is the Gaussian Mixture Model (GMM) for sub-activity identification. GMM [36] is a probabilistic model for representing normally distributed subpopulations within an overall population. It is defined as:

$$p(x) = \sum_{k=1}^{K} \pi_k \mathcal{N}(x|\mu_k, \Sigma_k) \tag{1}$$

where $x$ is the data point. $K$ is the number of Gaussian distributions in the mixture. $\pi_k$ are the mixture weights, with $\sum_{k=1}^{K} \pi_k = 1$ and $\pi_k \geq 0$. $\mathcal{N}(x|\mu_k, \Sigma_k)$ denotes the Gaussian distributions with mean $\mu_k$ and covariance $\Sigma_k$.

GMM identifies sub-activities hidden in the sensor data, effectively decomposing complex activities into simpler sub-activities which represent common knowledge across different users. This model identifies inherent sub-structures within the dataset, irrespective of their originating domain (source or target). This decomposition is vital for two reasons: firstly, it simplifies the complex temporal patterns into more manageable segments, and secondly, the common sub-activities are used for subsequent temporal relation capture and analysis between the source and target domains.

Following the identification of sub-activities, the next step is using USM for temporal feature encoding. This step is crucial for transforming the identified sub-activities into a feature space that encapsulates both their spatial structural and temporal characteristics. USM [2] is a technique for encoding sequences to capture their inherent structure and temporal relations. It can be mathematically represented as:

$$F = \mathcal{U}(Seq) \tag{2}$$

where $F$ represents the feature space encoding the sequence. $\mathcal{U}$ is the USM function. $Seq$ is the sequence of sub-activities.

USM plays a pivotal role in maintaining the integrity of temporal relations within the activity sequences. This encoding not only represents the sequence of sub-activities but also preserves the temporal dynamics associated with each activity  that is, the temporal order and sequence of sub-activities, particularly when analyzing complex human behaviours, thus offering a more precise representation of human activities. This encoding respects the chronological order of events, ensuring that the temporal dynamics—such as the duration, sequence, and intervals between sub-activities—are accurately captured and reflected in the feature vectors. This is particularly important for understanding how sub-activities unfold over time.

By effectively encoding the temporal order, USM enables the identification of recurrent temporal patterns and relationships within the data. This can include regular sequences of activities, the typical duration of certain activities, or the common intervals between sub-activities. Moreover, USM-encoded features facilitate the comparison of temporal sequences across different users. By providing a uniform method of encoding, USM allows for the direct comparison of temporal features, supporting the data distribution alignment of temporal relations across users. This step paves the way for the following temporal relation alignment across users.

The next step is user-specific feature analysis. The USM-encoded features, now rich with temporal relational information, undergo separate GMM clustering for the source and target domains. This bifurcation is key to understanding how temporal patterns manifest uniquely in each domain. By analyzing these user-specific GMMs, the approach gains insights into the variations and similarities in activity patterns across users. This comparative analysis is essential for identifying user-specific differences in temporal activity structures.

Finally, Wasserstein Distance is applied for data distribution alignment across users with the above-learned temporal relation knowledge. The Wasserstein Distance [32], also known as the Earth Mover's Distance, measures the distance between two probability distributions. It is defined as:

$$W(P_s, P_t) = \inf_{\gamma \in \Pi(P_s, P_t)} \mathbb{E}_{(x,y)\sim\gamma}[\|x - y\|] \tag{3}$$

where $W(P_s, P_t)$ is the Wasserstein Distance between two distributions. $P_s$ and $P_t$ are the probability distributions of source and target users being compared. $\gamma$ represents a joint distribution with marginals $P_s$ and $P_t$. $\Pi(P_s, P_t)$ denotes the set of all possible joint distributions $\gamma(x, y)$ with marginals $P_s$ and $P_t$. $\mathbb{E}_{(x,y)\sim\gamma}[\|x-y\|]$ is the expected value of the Euclidean distance between sampled points $x$ and $y$ from $\gamma$.

Wasserstein distance is computed using the means of the GMMs from the source and target users. This distance metric quantifies the disparity in the temporal feature distributions between the two domains. Minimizing the Wasserstein distance is used to align the source and target user distributions in the temporal relation view based on the idea that source and target users should have common temporal relation sub-activities. This alignment is central to the model's ability to generalize and accurately recognize activities across users.

## 4   Experiments

### 4.1   Datasets and Experimental Setup

To validate our cross-user domain adaptation method in sensor-based HAR, we employed two widely recognized public datasets as outlined in Table 1. Our focus was on the practical application scenario involving a smartwatch. To this end, we only utilized sensor data from accelerometers and gyroscopes positioned on the right lower arm. Below, we provide a brief overview of each dataset, highlighting their key aspects.

**Table 1.** Two sensor-based HAR datasets information.

| Dataset | Subjects | #Activities | Common Activities |
|---|---|---|---|
| OPPT | S1, S2, S3 | 4 | 1 standing, 2 walking, 3 sitting, 4 lying |
| PAMAP2 | 1, 5, 6 | 11 | 1 lying, 2 sitting, 3 standing, 4 walking, 5 running, 6 cycling, 7 Nordic walking, 8 ascending stairs, 9 descending stairs, 10 vacuum cleaning, 11 ironing |

The OPPORTUNITY (OPPT) dataset [6] contains recordings of people doing morning activities in a natural way, without strict guidance, recorded at 30 Hz. The Physical Activity Monitoring (PAMAP2) dataset [20] features over 10 h of data recorded at 100 Hz, with subjects performing specific, pre-defined activities.

In the experimental setup for cross-user HAR, the sliding window technique is employed for data segmentation. This widely-used approach in sensor-based HAR involves creating fixed time intervals of 3 s with a 50% overlap between windows, in line with standard practices in HAR tasks [30]. The study compares four methods, divided into traditional domain adaptation and deep domain adaptation categories. Notably, the TrC method requires a few target domain labels for fine-tuning, unlike other methods which do not require any labelling in the target domain.

**Traditional Domain Adaptation Methods:**

**CORAL** (Covariance Alignment) [28]: Aims to align the covariance of feature layers across domains, fostering domain-agnostic features.

**SOT** (Substructure Optimal Transport) [15]: Focuses on underlying domain structures to facilitate detailed substructure mapping, balancing broad and specific mapping.

**Deep Domain Adaptation Methods:**

**DANN** (Domain-Adversarial Neural Network) [10]: A deep learning approach using adversarial training to produce features indistinguishable between domains by a discriminator.

**TrC** (Temporal Regularized CNNs) [22]: Employs CNNs for discerning temporal features, trained on source domain data and fine-tuned on the target domain.

Hyper-parameters tuning is implemented on these methods with the methodology suggested by Flamary et al. [9], specifically to prevent overfitting during testing. We divide the target user's data into two parts: a validation subset and a test subset. The validation subset is utilized to fine-tune the hyper-parameters to achieve the highest accuracy. After optimizing these hyper-parameters, we evaluate the performance of the model on the test subset. The key metric we use for evaluation is the classification accuracy specific to the target user.

### 4.2    Cross-User HAR Performance Results

We evaluate the performance of various methods on the OPPT and PAMAP2 datasets. Each method is tested for its ability to transition between individual users. Within each dataset, three users are selected randomly, and a one-to-one cross-user HAR task is conducted for every possible user pair.

In the results of the OPPT dataset as shown in Fig. 2, CVAE-USM stands out by achieving almost 100% accuracy in all testing scenarios. This exceptional performance underscores CVAE-USM's adaptability and effectiveness in various conditions specific to the OPPT dataset. One of the primary reasons for this performance is the way CVAE-USM leverages temporal information. By effectively capturing the temporal dependencies inherent in the dataset, CVAE-USM is able to model the sequential relationships between the time points more precisely. The use of CVAE allows the model to learn a richer latent representation that includes both cross-user variations and temporal patterns, enabling it to generalize well across users. The added mechanism of USM further enhances the model's adaptability by allowing it to align latent features between users, thus reducing discrepancies during transitions. TrC also achieves a reasonably good performance, consistently reaching accuracy levels in the low to mid-80% range. This indicates its competence in the OPPT dataset, though it doesn't

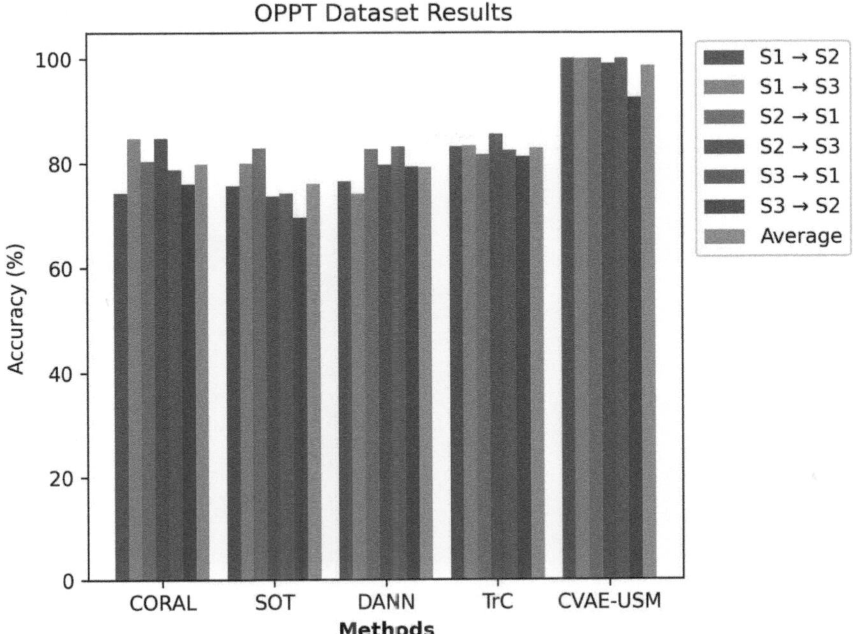


**Fig. 2.** OPPT dataset classification results.

match the superior performance of CVAE-USM. The TrC model captures temporal features to some extent, but lacks the full capability of explicitly modeling the latent space interactions across users as CVAE-USM does. The absence of a robust user adaptation mechanism like USM means that TrC is less effective in bridging the variations between users, leading to slightly reduced accuracy compared to CVAE-USM.

Another method, DANN, demonstrates moderate performance, with accuracy generally fluctuating between the mid-70% and mid-80% range. The DANN aims to reduce the domain shift between different users by aligning feature distributions. However, the method relies primarily on adversarial training without explicitly leveraging temporal data. This limited use of temporal context prevents DANN from capturing the finer temporal dynamics present in the OPPT dataset, resulting in a somewhat limited performance compared to CVAE-USM.

SOT and CORAL exhibit slightly lower performance levels compared to the others. One notable distinction contributing to these performance discrepancies is the utilization of temporal information. SOT and CORAL do not effectively utilize temporal features within the datasets, focusing instead on static feature alignment or transfer learning techniques that are less capable of capturing the dynamic evolution of activities. Consequently, they are not able to adapt to the sequential patterns that are crucial for understanding HAR tasks. This further highlights the strength of CVAE-USM, which leverages both temporal features and user similarity to achieve superior results.

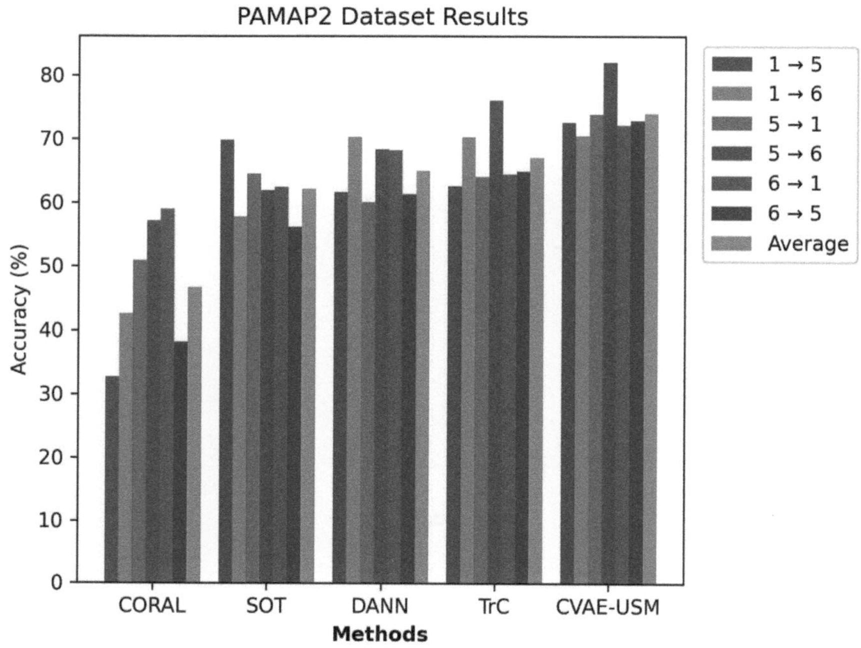


**Fig. 3.** PAMAP2 dataset classification results.

In the results of the PAMAP2 dataset as shown in Fig. 3, CVAE-USM again dominates, with accuracy consistently above 70% and peaking at 82.12% in certain scenarios. This dominance further demonstrates CVAE-USM's strong adaptability and learning capabilities across different conditions. A critical factor contributing to this success is the ability of CVAE-USM to capture intricate temporal dependencies and encode them in a latent space that facilitates cross-user adaptability. The CVAE framework, by utilizing a stochastic latent representation, allows for an effective synthesis of data that captures underlying activity patterns while maintaining robustness to user-specific differences. This enables the model to generalize exceptionally well across users.

In contrast, TrC, SOT, and DANN show respectable performances in specific scenarios, suggesting that they may be better adapted to situations with minimal variance between training and testing data or where data patterns are more consistent and less complex. Specifically, TrC benefits from temporal feature extraction but lacks the stochastic latent representation and user-matching mechanism that make CVAE-USM more adaptable. DANN and SOT, on the other hand, are primarily focused on domain adaptation, which is less effective when temporal features play a significant role in understanding the data.

DANN, for example, struggles with aligning user-specific features when temporal patterns are not explicitly modeled, leading to less robust performance.

CORAL struggles significantly, with accuracies mainly ranging between 30%-40%. This poor performance can be attributed to its inability to handle complex temporal relationships and significant cross-user variance. Unlike CVAE-USM, CORAL does not incorporate mechanisms to align user similarities at a feature level that captures temporal dynamics, which is crucial for accurately modeling activities in the PAMAP2 dataset. Without the capability to extract and exploit temporal features, CORAL falls short when dealing with the dynamic nature of human activities, especially in cross-user scenarios.

**Table 2.** Average Accuracies and Standard Deviations for Methods Across Datasets.

| Dataset | Metrics | Methods | | | | |
|---------|---------|-------|------|------|------|----------|
|         |         | CORAL | SOT  | DANN | TrC  | CVAE-USM |
| OPPT    | AA      | 79.77 | 75.92 | 79.16 | 82.78 | 98.56 |
|         | SD      | 4.02  | 4.33 | 3.17 | 1.41 | 2.78 |
| PAMAP2  | AA      | 46.78 | 62.12 | 64.98 | 67.08 | 74.05 |
|         | SD      | 9.69  | 4.47 | 4.06 | 4.68 | 3.75 |

Table 2 illustrates the average classification accuracy and standard deviation achieved by five methods across two datasets. As we can observe, CVAE-USM stands out, achieving the highest average accuracy, followed by TrC, which also performs relatively well but at a lower accuracy level. In contrast, the remaining methods (CORAL, SOT, and DANN) exhibit notably lower and more varied results. This discrepancy in results suggests that certain methods are more capable of handling the inherent challenges of cross-user classification, particularly those related to user variability and the temporal dynamic nature of human activity data. In terms of standard deviation (SD), which measures the consistency of each method, we observe a few important trends. CORAL shows relatively high SD values, which suggests that the performance fluctuates more between different instances. This variability could indicate that the method is less stable when applied across different samples or users. SOT and DANN show moderate SD values, suggesting a more consistent performance compared to CORAL, though still with some variability. TrC demonstrates lower SD in the OPPT dataset, indicating highly stable and consistent performance, making it a more reliable method overall. CVAE-USM, while achieving the highest average accuracy, also has relatively low SD values, meaning that its performance is both accurate and consistent across trials.

Overall, across both the OPPT and PAMAP2 datasets, CVAE-USM consistently achieves the highest accuracy, proving its adaptability, robustness, and effectiveness in handling cross-user HAR tasks. The underlying factors for CVAE-USM's superior performance lie in its use of a conditional variational framework to generate rich latent representations, its explicit modeling of temporal dynamics, and its USM mechanism, which facilitates better cross-user adaptation. TrC shows a reasonable performance across both datasets, indicating its potential adaptability to different scenarios, albeit not at the level of CVAE-USM due to the absence of an explicit user alignment strategy. CORAL, SOT, and DANN exhibit varied and mixed results, suggesting that their effectiveness and adaptability are conditional based on specific dataset characteristics and scenarios. Some methods, particularly CORAL, show significant struggles in adapting to these datasets, highlighting the need for further development to enhance their effectiveness in time series data that involves temporal relation knowledge.

### 4.3   Effect of Temporal Information

In this section, we analyze the impact of integrating temporal relation knowledge into cross-user HAR, concentrating on the OPPT and PAMAP2 datasets. The comparison involves SOT, a traditional domain adaptation method; DANN, known for its deep domain adaptation approach; and our CVAE-USM, which is specifically designed for time series domain adaptation.

Figure 4 displays the confusion matrices for CVAE-USM, SOT, and DANN, reflecting their average performance across the OPPT and PAMAP2 datasets. The matrices use color gradients, with warmer colors (closer to yellow) indicating higher values. The x-axis represents predicted activities, while the y-axis corresponds to the actual activities. The diagonal line from the top left to the bottom right of these matrices signifies correct predictions, where the predicted activity aligns with the true activity.

In these analyses, all methods exhibit pronounced values along their diagonals, indicating accurate recognition of most activities and underscoring their effectiveness in cross-user scenarios. Common activities such as 'lying', 'walking', 'standing' and 'cycling' are efficiently identified by all methods. The reason could be attributed to their distinct movement patterns, making them easily distinguishable from other activities. However, confusion arises in differentiating activities with inherent similarities, such as activities like 'ascending stairs' and 'descending stairs'. The key difference between these two activities lies in the direction of motion (up vs. down). These differences are often too subtle for traditional domain adaptation methods like SOT and DANN to fully exploit. CVAE-USM, while strong in handling complex temporal relations, might struggle with these small variations due to the fact that both activities share a similar rhythm and sequence of movements, despite the directional change.

CVAE-USM, in particular, excels in identifying activities with complex temporal relations like 'Nordic walking' and 'vacuum cleaning' as the yellow squares shown in Fig. 4, with higher accuracy compared to SOT and DANN. Additionally, while SOT and DANN show dispersed classification outcomes, CVAE-USM exhibits a more focused and clear classification pattern due to its effective handling of temporal states and extraction of sub-activities as the red squares shown in Fig. 4. CVAE-USM demonstrates a superior ability to distinguish activities like 'standing', 'sitting', and 'walking' as the green squares shown in Fig. 4, possibly due to its nuanced capture of temporal relation context and subtle sensor data

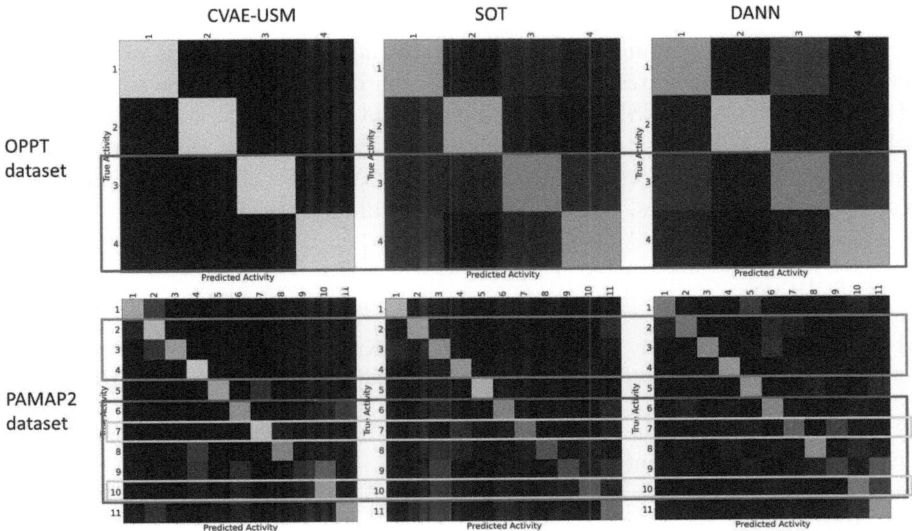


**Fig. 4.** Confusion matrices of CVAE-USM, SOT, and DANN methods for the average performance of tasks in the OPPT and PAMAP2 datasets.

variations. Moreover, transitional movements within activities, often overlooked by SOT and DANN, are effectively captured by CVAE-USM. For example, repositioning a vacuum cleaner during 'vacuum cleaning' is better understood and classified by CVAE-USM, thanks to its comprehension of temporal relations.

In conclusion, the use of temporal relation knowledge in CVAE-USM effectively reduces the variance in activity patterns between different users, especially in dynamic activities with complex temporal relations. Extracting temporal relation knowledge from time series data enhances the robustness and accuracy of activity recognition. This approach is especially beneficial for activities with rhythmic or sequential traits, allowing for a more nuanced understanding of various activities and highlighting the importance of temporal knowledge in improving cross-user activity recognition capabilities.

## 5 Conclusion

In this study, we present a new approach called CVAE-USM for cross-user HAR tasks from time series data. This method is particularly effective in adapting to different users' data by focusing on the temporal relation knowledge of activities. CVAE-USM uses VAE generative model and adversarial learning techniques to align different users' data distributions, leading to more accurate activity recognition.

The validation is implemented on two public datasets show that CVAE-USM outperforms existing methods in recognizing activities across various users. This success demonstrates CVAE-USM's potential to analyse time series data in HAR. Overall, CVAE-USM represents its advantages in understanding temporal relations and adapting to the complex activity data from different users. In future, we aim to explore the application of CVAE-USM to more complex or less structured activities, to evaluate its adaptability and robustness.

# References


1. Abdallah, Z.S., Gaber, M.M., Srinivasan, B., Krishnaswamy, S.: Activity recognition with evolving data streams: a review. ACM Comput. Surv. (CSUR) **51**(4), 1–36 (2018)
2. Almeida, J.S., Vinga, S.: Universal sequence map (USM) of arbitrary discrete sequences. BMC Bioinform. **3**, 1–11 (2002)
3. Amft, O., Junker, H., Troster, G.: Detection of eating and drinking arm gestures using inertial body-worn sensors. In: Ninth IEEE International Symposium on Wearable Computers (ISWC 2005), pp. 160–163. IEEE (2005)
4. Andreas, B., Blanke, U., Schiele, B.: A tutorial on human activity recognition using body-worn inertial sensors. ACM Comput. Surv. (CSUR) **46**(3), 33 (2014)
5. Bulling, A., Ward, J.A., Gellersen, H.: Multimodal recognition of reading activity in transit using body-worn sensors. ACM Trans. Appl. Percept. (TAP) **9**(1), 1–21 (2012)
6. Chavarriaga, R., et al.: The opportunity challenge: a benchmark database for on-body sensor-based activity recognition. Pattern Recogn. Lett. **34**(15), 2033–2042 (2013)
7. Chen, K., Zhang, D., Yao, L., Guo, B., Yu, Z., Liu, Y.: Deep learning for sensor-based human activity recognition: overview, challenges, and opportunities. ACM Comput. Surv. (CSUR) **54**(4), 1–40 (2021)
8. Fernando, B., Habrard, A., Sebban, M., Tuytelaars, T.: Unsupervised visual domain adaptation using subspace alignment. In: Proceedings of the IEEE International Conference on Computer Vision, pp. 2960–2967 (2013)
9. Flamary, R., Courty, N., Tuia, D., Rakotomamonjy, A.: Optimal transport for domain adaptation. IEEE Trans. Pattern Anal. Mach. Intell. **1**, 1–40 (2016)
10. Ganin, Y., et al.: Domain-adversarial training of neural networks. J. Mach. Learn. Res. **17**(1), 2096–2030 (2016)
11. Kingma, D.P., Welling, M.: Auto-encoding variational bayes. In: 2nd International Conference on Learning Representations, ICLR 2014, Banff, AB, Canada, April 14–16, 2014, Conference Track Proceedings (2014)
12. Lentzas, A., Vrakas, D.: Non-intrusive human activity recognition and abnormal behavior detection on elderly people: a review. Artif. Intell. Rev. **53**(3), 1975–2021 (2020)
13. Li, S., Xie, B., Wu, J., Zhao, Y., Liu, C.H., Ding, Z.: Simultaneous semantic alignment network for heterogeneous domain adaptation. In: Proceedings of the 28th ACM International Conference on Multimedia, pp. 3866–3874 (2020)
14. Lu, J., Liu, A., Dong, F., Gu, F., Gama, J., Zhang, G.: Learning under concept drift: a review. IEEE Trans. Knowl. Data Eng. **31**(12), 2346–2363 (2018)
15. Lu, W., Chen, Y., Wang, J., Qin, X.: Cross-domain activity recognition via substructural optimal transport. Neurocomputing **454**, 65–75 (2021)

16. Ma, H., Li, W., Zhang, X., Gao, S., Lu, S.: Attnsense: multi-level attention mechanism for multimodal human activity recognition. In: IJCAI, pp. 3109–3115 (2019)
17. Pan, S.J., Yang, Q.: A survey on transfer learning. IEEE Trans. Knowl. Data Eng. **22**(10), 1345–1359 (2009)
18. Patel, V.M., Gopalan, R., Li, R., Chellappa, R.: Visual domain adaptation: a survey of recent advances. IEEE Signal Process. Mag. **32**(3), 53–69 (2015)
19. Qian, H., Pan, S.J., Da, B., Miao, C.: A novel distribution-embedded neural network for sensor-based activity recognition. In: IJCAI, vol. 2019, pp. 5614–5620 (2019)
20. Reiss, A., Stricker, D.: Introducing a new benchmarked dataset for activity monitoring. In: 2012 16th International Symposium on Wearable Computers, pp. 108–109. IEEE (2012)
21. Rokni, S.A., Ghasemzadeh, H.: Autonomous training of activity recognition algorithms in mobile sensors: a transfer learning approach in context-invariant views. IEEE Trans. Mob. Comput. **17**(8), 1764–1777 (2018)
22. Rokni, S.A., Nourollahi, M., Ghasemzadeh, H.: Personalized human activity recognition using convolutional neural networks. In: Proceedings of the AAAI Conference on Artificial Intelligence, vol. 32 (2018)
23. Ruthotto, L., Haber, E.: An introduction to deep generative modeling. GAMM-Mitteilungen **44**(2), e202100008 (2021)
24. Rybkin, O., Daniilidis, K., Levine, S.: Simple and effective VAE training with calibrated decoders. In: International Conference on Machine Learning, pp. 9179–9189. PMLR (2021)
25. Sekiguchi, R., Abe, K., Yokoyama, T., Kumano, M., Kawakatsu, M.: Ensemble learning for human activity recognition. In: Adjunct proceedings of the 2020 ACM International Joint Conference on Pervasive and Ubiquitous Computing and Proceedings of the 2020 ACM International Symposium on Wearable Computers, pp. 335–339 (2020)
26. Shen, Q., Feng, H., Song, R., Teso, S., Giunchiglia, F., Xu, H., et al.: Federated multi-task attention for cross-individual human activity recognition. In: IJCAI, pp. 3423–3429. IJCAI (2022)
27. Sukhija, S., Krishnan, N.C.: Supervised heterogeneous feature transfer via random forests. Artif. Intell. **268**, 30–53 (2019)
28. Sun, B., Feng, J., Saenko, K.: Return of frustratingly easy domain adaptation. In: Proceedings of the AAAI Conference on Artificial Intelligence, vol. 30 (2016)
29. Van Kasteren, T., Englebienne, G., Kröse, B.J.: An activity monitoring system for elderly care using generative and discriminative models. Pers. Ubiquit. Comput. **14**, 489–498 (2010)
30. Wang, G., Li, Q., Wang, L., Wang, W., Wu, M., Liu, T.: Impact of sliding window length in indoor human motion modes and pose pattern recognition based on smartphone sensors. Sensors **18**(6), 1965 (2018)
31. Wilson, G., Cook, D.J.: A survey of unsupervised deep domain adaptation. ACM Trans. Intell. Syst. Technol. (TIST) **11**(5), 1–46 (2020)
32. Wu, H., Yan, Y., Ng, M.K., Wu, Q.: Domain-attention conditional wasserstein distance for multi-source domain adaptation. ACM Trans. Intell. Syst. Technol. (TIST) **11**(4), 1–19 (2020)
33. Xing, T., Sandha, S.S., Balaji, B., Chakraborty, S., Srivastava, M.: Enabling edge devices that learn from each other: cross modal training for activity recognition. In: Proceedings of the 1st International Workshop on Edge Systems, Analytics and Networking, pp. 37–42 (2018)

34. Ye, X., Kevin, I., Wang, K.: Deep generative domain adaptation with temporal relation attention mechanism for cross-user activity recognition. Pattern Recogn. **156**, 110811 (2024)
35. Ye, X., Wang, K.I.K.: Cross-user activity recognition via temporal relation optimal transport. In: International Conference on Mobile and Ubiquitous Systems: Computing, Networking, and Services (2023)
36. Zhang, Y., et al.: Gaussian mixture model clustering with incomplete data. ACM Trans. Multimedia Comput. Commun. Appl. (TOMM) **17**(1s), 1–14 (2021)

# Genetic Algorithm Optimization for Mobile Crowd-Sensing of On-Street Parking


Yaxuan Li[1], Wenjun Zheng[2], and Ruizhi Liao[3,4(✉)]

[1] School of Management and Economics, The Chinese University of Hong Kong, Shenzhen, China
yaxuanli1@link.cuhk.edu.cn
[2] School of Data Science, The Chinese University of Hong Kong, Shenzhen, China
wenjunzheng@link.cuhk.edu.cn
[3] Guangdong Provincial Key Laboratory of Mathematical Foundations for Artificial Intelligence, Shenzhen, China
[4] School of Humanities and Social Science, The Chinese University of Hong Kong, Shenzhen, China
rzliao@cuhk.edu.cn



**Abstract.** This paper addresses the challenge of minimizing the number of sensors needed to detect available on-street parking spaces while maintaining high accuracy. By utilizing a natural-selection inspired genetic algorithm, we aim to optimize sensor deployment on moving vehicles, such as buses and taxis, to effectively monitor parking availability. Traditional fixed sensor systems are labor-intensive and vulnerable to environmental damage. Our approach leverages mobile sensors, which provide cost-effective and accurate parking information. The findings highlight the efficiency of the proposed genetic algorithm in solving complex optimization problems related to parking sensor allocation in urban environments.

**Keywords:** On-street parking · Sensor allocation · Mobile crowd-sensing · Genetic algorithm · Optimization


## 1 Introduction

Finding an available parking space on the street is a time-consuming task that frustrates many drivers [1]. Occupancy previews can directly guide drivers to open parking spaces. However, traditional methods for providing these previews face issues like neglecting the gap between reported parking availability and actual driver arrival times [2] and relying on fixed sensor systems, which require extensive labor and are susceptible to environmental damage [3].

Mathur et al. proposed a novel method that uses sensors on moving buses and taxis to detect parking availability [4]. Since a single sensor can detect



A. Soylu et al. (Eds.): MobiQuitous 2024, LNICST 634, pp. 327–340, 2026.
https://doi.org/10.1007/978-3-032-10554-7_18

multiple parking spaces while in motion, this system can provide accurate on-street parking information at a lower cost than fixed sensing solutions. However, not all buses (or taxis) should be equipped with sensors due to the high costs involved. Additionally, detecting parking availability during certain times, such as midnight hours, is unnecessary [5]. Therefore, an allocation model is required to determine which buses, and at what times, should be equipped with sensors.

The goal of this work is to accurately detect roadside parking spaces with the most efficient use of sensors while maintaining a consistently high level of performance, thereby enhancing the reliability and effectiveness of parking management systems. We introduce a penalty term in the evaluation function to balance detection accuracy with the number of sensors deployed. We also modify the crossover pattern and mutation rate to simulate traffic jam conditions and implement a program to simulate parking behavior. The contribution of this paper lies in the implementation and improvement of a genetic algorithm that utilizes past parking data over an extended period to develop a robust sensor allocation model for efficient urban roadside parking detection.

## 2   Problem Refinement

In our study, we assume that the routes of the moving vehicles, buses in this case, are predetermined. Therefore, the focus of the study is on optimizing sensor allocation along these fixed routes.

The working scenario is illustrated in Fig. 1. The routes of the buses (route 1 and route 2) are fixed, the distances between buses are constant, and only some buses are equipped with ultrasonic sensors. For example, the first blue bus on route 1 is equipped with an ultrasonic sensor to detect changes in parking

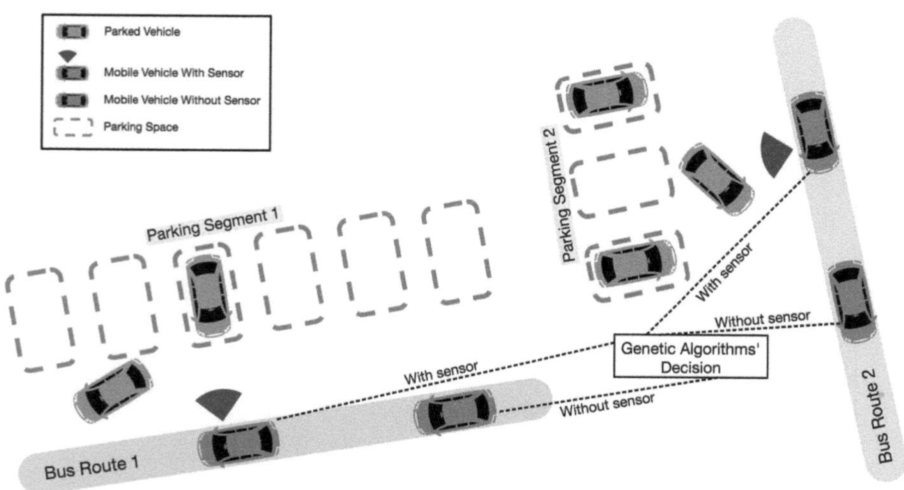


**Fig. 1.** Working scenario of mobile sensing system

availability, while the second blue bus on the same route does not have a sensor since there is no change to detect. The same scenario applies to bus route 2. Despite not all buses being equipped with sensors, the detection accuracy remains the same as all vehicles were equipped with detection sensors, resulting in cost reduction.

Unlike fixed sensors that can directly indicate parking availability upon request, a moving sensor detection system requires a different method to provide parking information to drivers: monitoring the "change in occupied parking spaces" can provide parking availability information at any given time.

To further demonstrate the concept of "change in occupied parking spaces" with genetic algorithms, we transformed the parking space data into a binary matrix by introducing the definitions of "Minimum Detection Period" and "Final Change".

**Definition 1 "Minimum Detection Period"**: Given that buses leave the starting point at regular intervals and that there is no traffic to disrupt the distance between them, the "Minimum Detection Period" is the time interval between the two consecutive buses passing the same parking space.

**Definition 2 "Final Change"**: The "Final Change" represents the highest observed change, converted into binary form, during a "Minimum Detection Period" that sensors on buses can achieve, representing the theoretical limit of the system's accuracy. The "Final Change" $\Delta P(t)$ can be expressed mathematically as follows.

$$\Delta P(t) = \begin{cases} 0, & \text{if } |P(t+T) - P(t)| = 0 \\ 1, & \text{if } |P(t+T) - P(t)| \neq 0 \end{cases} \tag{1}$$

In Eq.(1), $T$ denotes the "Minimum Detection Period", and $P(t)$ denotes the number of available parking spaces at time $t$. The reason for converting the changes into 1 s and 0 s is to use the change in parking spots as a signal. If there is a change, it indicates that a detector is needed. Although the digit 1 does not indicate the specific change, placing a detector on bus at the position marked by 1 allows the detector to identify the specific changes.

To carry out the conversion, we combined all minimum detection periods from Definition 1 throughout a day and represented each period as either 1 or 0 in a list. The value of 1 or 0 in the list corresponded to the value of the "Final Change" $\Delta P(t)$ (as defined in Definition 2). This process was then repeated for each day in the historical data, generating a matrix known as the "RealVector". In the matrix, RealVector$_j$ represents the data (list) for the j-th day.

Figure 2 depicts the hourly average change in parking spaces across 420 streets in San Francisco from June 13, 2013, to July 24, 2013 [6]. The horizontal axis represents the hour of the day, while the vertical axis indicates the average change in parking availability across all parking segments. It shows that the peak parking activity occurs between 6:00 and 22:00. To address this, we adjusted the 'RealVector' from a 24-hour format to a 6:00–22:00 format.

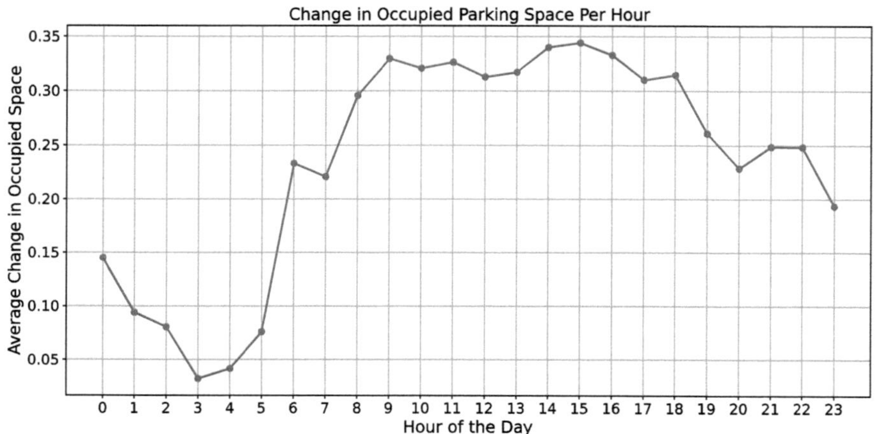


**Fig. 2.** Change in occupied parking spaces

Additionally, we set up the 'GenerationVector', which represents the sensor allocation model generated by our genetic algorithm. It is worth noting that the 'RealVector' is an $n \times m$ matrix (where $n$ is the number of days and $m$ is the number of minimum detection periods in a day from 6:00 to 22:00) that describes the "change in occupied parking spaces" behavior in the historical data. In contrast, the 'GenerationVector' is a $1 \times m$ vector representing a sensor allocation model across various days. Ultimately, the problem can be refined as follows.

**Problem Definition**

**Objective:**

Minimize the error of failed sensor allocation and the cost of sensors.

$$\text{Minimize} \quad \text{Error} + \text{Cost}$$

where:

$$\text{Error} = \frac{1}{N} \sum_{j=1}^{N} |\text{GenerationVector} - \text{RealVector}_j| \tag{2}$$

$$\text{Cost} = \alpha \times \text{num\_sensors} \tag{3}$$

**Constraints**

1. Fixed bus departure times.
2. Fixed bus routes.
3. Fixed number of buses.
4. Binary decision variable for sensor deployment on buses $(x_i)$, where $x_i = 1$ if the bus is equipped with a sensor, and $x_i = 0$ otherwise.

**Model Formulation**

Let $m$ be the number of minimum detection periods in a day, and $n$ be the number of days in the dataset.

**Variables:**

- RealVector$_j$: Binary matrix representing the actual change in occupied parking spaces for the $j$-th day.
- GenerationVector: Binary vector representing the sensor allocation model.
- $x_i$: Binary decision variable for sensor deployment on the $i$-th bus, $x_i \in \{0, 1\}$.

**Objective Function**

$$\text{Minimize} \quad \frac{1}{n} \left\| R - \mathbf{1}_n G^T \right\|_1 + \alpha \mathbf{1}_m^T \mathbf{x}$$

$$= \frac{1}{n} \sum_{j=1}^{n} \sum_{i=1}^{m} \left| \text{GenerationVector}_i - \text{RealVector}_{j,i} \right| + \alpha \sum_{i=1}^{m} x_i \quad (4)$$

where:

- The first term, $\frac{1}{n} \sum_{j=1}^{n} \sum_{i=1}^{m} \left| \text{GenerationVector}_i - \text{RealVector}_{j,i} \right|$, represents the average discrepancy between the predicted sensor allocation (GenerationVector) and the actual changes in parking occupancy (RealVector) over all $n$ days and $m$ detection periods. This term measures the error or mismatch between the predicted and real data.
- The second term, $\alpha \sum_{i=1}^{m} x_i$, is a penalty term proportional to the number of sensors deployed. The penalty factor $\alpha$ balances the trade-off between minimizing sensor deployment and improving accuracy.

**Constraints:**

1. $\sum_{i=1}^{m} x_i \leq B$ (Total number of buses with sensors should not exceed the number of fixed sensors $B$).
2. $x_i \in \{0, 1\}$ for all $i$.

## 3  Genetic Algorithm and Modifications

Genetic Algorithms (GAs) are a class of optimization techniques inspired by the principles of natural selection and genetics. Developed by John Holland, GAs are used to solve complex optimization problems by iteratively evolving a population of candidate solutions [7]. Each candidate, often referred to as a "chromosome," is evaluated based on a fitness function, and the most fit individuals are selected for reproduction. Through processes akin to crossover (recombination) and mutation, new generations of solutions are created, with the aim of converging towards an optimal or near-optimal solution over successive generations [8].

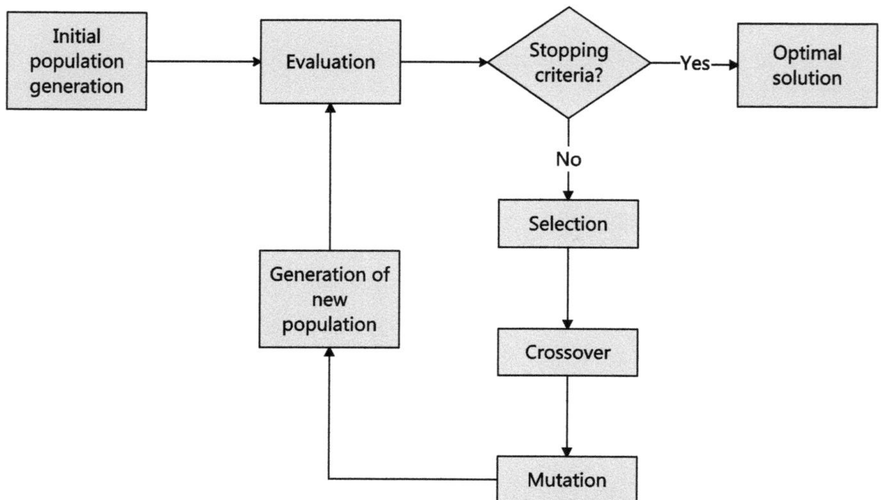


**Fig. 3.** Flowchart of the Genetic Algorithm

As shown in Fig. 3, the main components of a genetic algorithm are initialization, selection, crossover, mutation, and evaluation. Detailed explanations for minimizing sensor allocation costs are presented in sub-sections A, B, C, D, and E, respectively.

## A. Initialization

Initialization is the first step in our algorithm, where an initial sequence of 0 s and 1 s, representing sensor allocation patterns on moving buses, is generated. Each chromosome in the population signifies a potential sensor allocation pattern, providing a solution to the problem.

Key factors considered in initializing the sensor allocation-based genetic population include:

- **Chromosome Representation**: We represent each chromosome as a binary string of 0 s and 1 s, indicating sensor assignments to buses at the end of each minimum detection period. This binary representation enables efficient manipulation and evaluation of sensor allocation patterns.
- **Population Size**: To increase the likelihood of finding the optimal sensor allocation, we use a population size of 500. This size balances computational feasibility with the need for genetic diversity.
- **Diverse Initial Population**: To ensure diverse allocation patterns, the initial population is generated randomly. Each bit in the chromosome is assigned a 0 or 1 with equal probability, providing a broad search space for the algorithm.

This initialization approach lays a solid foundation for the genetic algorithm by ensuring a diverse and representative search space. Table 1 presents the initialization result, showcasing a 500*96 matrix representing the initial population.

In Table 1, the 96 columns represent the scheduled buses from 6:00 to 22:00, while the 500 rows correspond to the individual chromosomes generated during initialization.

**Table 1.** Initialization Result (500*96)

| 0 | 1 | 1 | 0 | 0 | ... | 1 | 1 | 1 | 0 | 1 |
|---|---|---|---|---|-----|---|---|---|---|---|
| 1 | 1 | 1 | 0 | 1 | ... | 1 | 0 | 0 | 1 | 1 |

...

| 0 | 0 | 1 | 1 | 0 | ... | 1 | 1 | 0 | 1 | 1 |
|---|---|---|---|---|-----|---|---|---|---|---|
| 1 | 0 | 1 | 1 | 0 | ... | 1 | 0 | 1 | 0 | 1 |

## B. Selection

Selection is the process of choosing the fittest chromosome from the current population to create offspring for the next generation [9]. The fitness of each chromosome is evaluated using a fitness function that measures how well the solution aligns with the real occupancy changing pattern, as shown in Fig. 2.

For sensor allocation:

- **Fitness Function**: The fitness function evaluates each chromosome based on the total number of changes detected and the cost associated with the number of sensors deployed. Solutions that detect more changes while using fewer sensors receive higher fitness scores.
- **Tournament Selection**: To select the best chromosome for the sensor allocation pattern, we employed a selection model called Tournament [10]. In this method, we first randomly selected $k$ chromosomes and then ranked them based on their relative fitness. Ultimately, the fittest chromosome is chosen for reproduction. This entire process is repeated $n$ times across the entire population. Consequently, the probability of each individual being selected is given below.

$$p(i) = \begin{cases} \frac{C_{n-1}^{k-1}}{C_n^k} & \text{if } i \in [1, n-k-1] \\ 0 & \text{if } i \in [n-k, n] \end{cases} \tag{5}$$

The implementation of Tournament Selection ensures that the best-matched chromosomes have a higher chance of passing their allocation pattern to the next generation, guiding the population toward optimal solutions.

## C. Crossover

Crossover (or recombination) is a genetic operator used to combine the genetic information of two parent chromosomes to produce offspring [11]. This process mimics biological reproduction and introduces variability into the population.

For sensor allocation, we first implemented the Single-Point Crossover method for non-peak hours. In this method, a single crossover point is chosen, and the segments of the parent chromosomes beyond this point are swapped [12].

This maintains the integrity of the sensor allocation patterns during non-peak hours, as shown in Fig. 4.

Then, we implemented the Multi-Point Crossover method for peak hours. Multiple crossover points are selected to create more complex recombination patterns [12]. This captures various allocation patterns arising during peak hours, as illustrated in Fig. 5.

## D. Mutation

The mutation is a genetic operator that introduces random changes to individual genes (bits) in a chromosome [13]. It is essential for maintaining sensor allocation pattern diversity within the population and preventing premature convergence to sub-optimal solutions.

The mutation rate is a vital parameter in the sensor allocation problem, as it determines the frequency of mutations [14]. In our study, we adopt a problem-specific approach to guide the mutation process, rather than relying solely on random mutations. During peak hours, we apply a higher mutation rate to the bits that represent those times to explore more diverse solutions. This targeted approach effectively addresses the varying demands and complexities associated with different traffic patterns and parking needs.

The mutation process in our algorithm enables it to escape local optima by exploring new solutions that may not be achievable through crossover alone. By utilizing problem-specific mutations, this process can be further improved by focusing the exploration on critical aspects of the traffic conditions.

## E. Evaluation

Directly, the original evaluation function computes the absolute difference between the generated solution and the real solution. The smaller the difference, the better the fit. The original fitness function is defined as:

$$\text{Fitness}_{\text{original}}(i) = \frac{1}{N} \sum_{j=1}^{N} |\text{GenerationVector}_i - \text{RealVector}_j|, \tag{6}$$

where $\text{GenerationVector}_i$ and $\text{RealVector}_j$ are the $i$-th elements of the generated vectors and real vectors in the problem definition in Sect. 2, respectively, and $N$ is the number of evaluation periods.

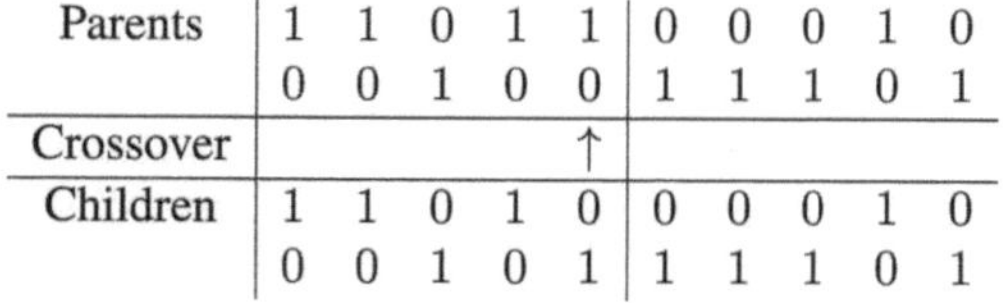
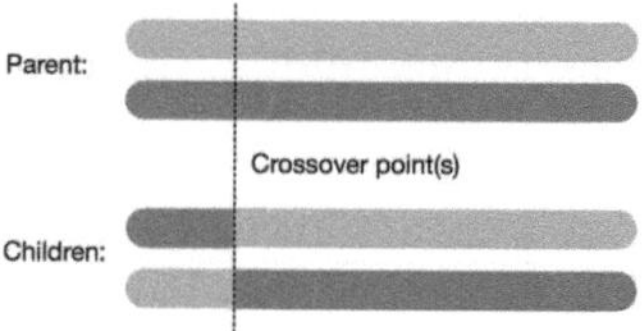

**Fig. 4.** Single-Point Crossover

| Parents | 1 1 0 1 1 | 0 0 0 1 0 |
|---|---|---|
|  | 0 0 1 0 0 | 1 1 1 0 1 |
| Crossover | ↑ | ↑ ↑ |
| Children | 1 1 0 1 0 | 0 1 1 1 0 |
|  | 0 0 1 0 1 | 1 0 0 0 1 |

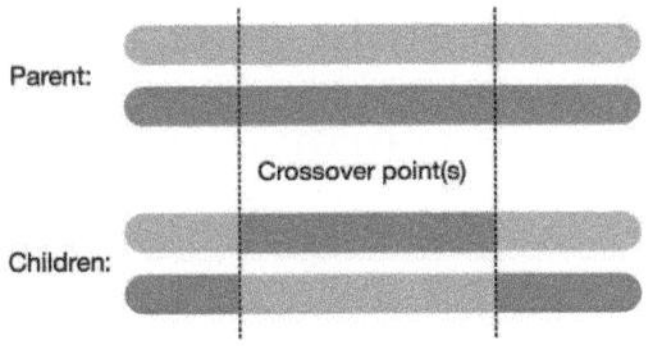

**Fig. 5.** Multi-Point Crossover

We introduced a modified evaluation function to enhance performance and resource efficiency by balancing the accuracy of parking detection with the number of sensors deployed. This new function includes a penalty term that is based on the number of sensors used.

Let $\text{error}(i)$ represent the detection error for individual $i$, calculated as the norm of the difference between the generated and real vectors. Let $\text{num\_sensors}(i)$ denote the number of sensors used by individual $i$, represented as the sum of 1 s in the individual's binary string. The modified fitness function $\text{Fitness}_{\text{modified}}(i)$ is defined as:

$$\text{Fitness}_{\text{modified}}(i) = \frac{1}{N} \sum_{j=1}^{N} \left| \text{GenerationVector}_i - \text{RealVector}_j \right| \tag{7}$$
$$+ \alpha \times \text{num\_sensors}(i),$$

where $\alpha$ is a penalty factor that determines the weight of the penalty term relative to the error term. This formulation ensures that the genetic algorithm seeks to minimize both the detection error and the number of sensors used, leading to more efficient and cost-effective solutions.

In our implementation, we conducted a sensitivity analysis to examine the impact of varying the penalty factor $\alpha$ on the genetic algorithm's performance. The penalty factor $\alpha$ directly influences the balance between detection accuracy and the number of sensors used. A higher $\alpha$ prioritizes minimizing sensor deployment, potentially at the cost of detection accuracy, while a lower $\alpha$ focuses more on achieving accurate detection, even if it requires more sensors. By testing different values of $\alpha$, we found that $\alpha = 0.005$ offered the most practical balance, effectively reducing sensor usage while maintaining a high level of detection accuracy.

The results of the sensitivity analysis indicate that small deviations in $\alpha$ can significantly affect the number of sensors required, but the detection accuracy remains relatively stable within a certain range of $\alpha$. This robustness suggests that the algorithm is adaptable to various operational conditions with minor adjustments. However, in scenarios where operational constraints fluctuate, dynamically adjusting $\alpha$ based on real-time conditions could further enhance performance and resource efficiency. Future work may explore this dynamic adaptation as a way to optimize the system under diverse urban conditions.

## 4    Results and Evaluation

### 4.1    Performance Comparison

**Performance Comparison of Before and After Modifications:** Figure 6 illustrates the sensor distribution over the 96 minimum detection periods (Definition 1), showing how sensors are allocated differently before and after the improvement. The improved algorithm allocates sensors more efficiently, especially during peak hours. As shown in Fig. 6, the orange line (representing the post-improvement data) demonstrates a greater concentration of sensor allocation in the 0–20 and 50–70 minimum detection periods, corresponding to the morning and evening peaks. This reflects a more balanced and resource-efficient approach.

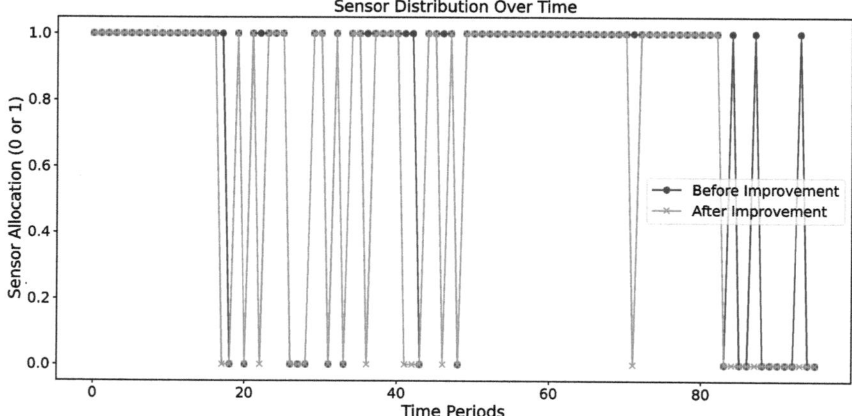


**Fig. 6.** Sensor distribution over 96-time periods

Figure 7 visually compares the performance metrics before and after modifications. The bar chart uses normalized values to highlight the relative changes in incorrect estimations (detection error) and the number of sensors (cost). This visualization effectively demonstrates the trade-off between accuracy and sensor usage. The improved algorithm achieves a substantial reduction in the number of sensors required while maintaining the same level of accuracy, indicating its practicality for real-world applications.

- The Fitness value without penalty term of the algorithm before improvement resulted in a value of 6.06, indicating approximately 6 incorrect estimations per day per parking segment. This corresponds to an accuracy of about 94%. The best individual in this version had 77 ones in its binary representation, reflecting a high number of sensors used to achieve this accuracy.
- After introducing the penalty for the number of sensors in the evaluation function and modifications in crossover and mutation, the Fitness value slightly

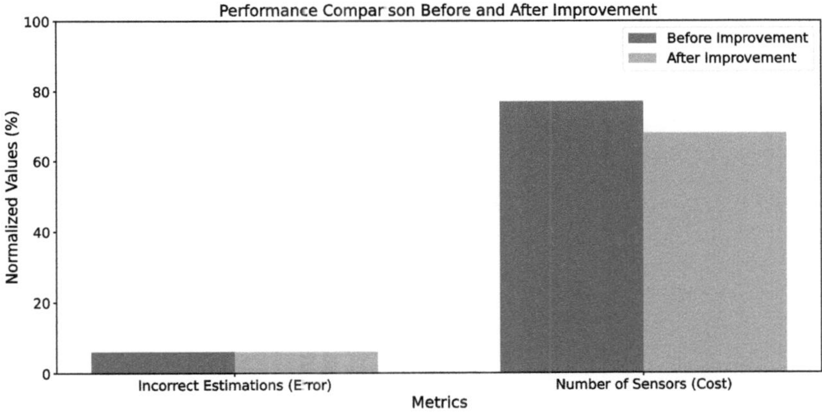


**Fig. 7.** Performance comparison before and after modifications

increased to 6.08, indicating a marginal decrease in accuracy but still maintaining a high level of performance. The system now has an average of approximately 6 incorrect estimations per day per parking segment, corresponding to an accuracy rate of about 94%. The best individual in this version had 68 ones in its binary representation. This reduction in the number of sensors represents a significant improvement in terms of resource efficiency.

**Performance Comparison for Different Departure Frequencies:** We examined how different departure frequencies influence the algorithm's performance by considering various bus departure times from bus stations. Specifically, we selected departure frequencies of 5, 10, 15, and 20 min. As shown in Fig. 8, the blue line represents the incorrect estimations per day, indicating the error rate increases as the departure frequency grows. The orange curve illustrates the number of sensors needed, showing how sensor requirements vary with different bus frequencies. Additionally, the green line, labeled "Weighted Cost", represents the combined cost after applying appropriate weights to different departure frequencies.

The relatively constant incorrect estimations (blue line) indicate that our algorithm maintains a stable error rate regardless of changes in departure times. The orange curve shows that the number of sensors required increases with longer departure intervals, whereas the cost for 5-minute intervals is extremely low. This is likely because buses depart at very short intervals, but the actual occupancy changes in daily parking do not vary significantly. Therefore, the need for detection remains constant, but the number of available spaces for sensors—the denominator—increases significantly, leading to a low normalized value. As a result, this line does not accurately reflect the real cost of practical implementation.

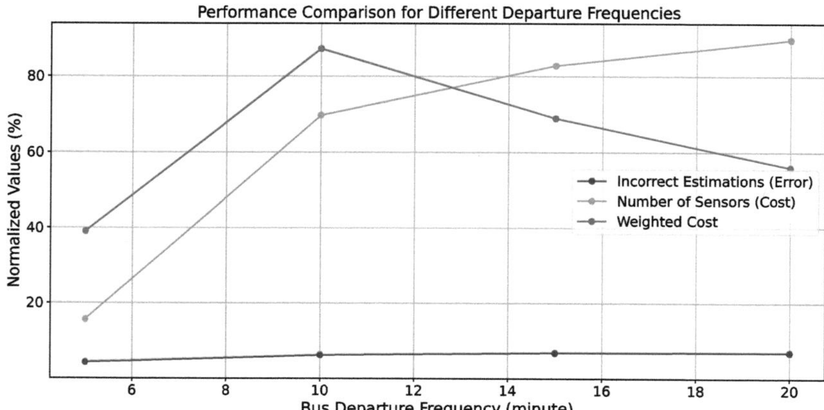


**Fig. 8.** Performance comparison with different departure frequencies

To address the problem, we weighted the departure times based on the orange curve and subsequently generated the green curve. As shown in Fig. 8, the normalized cost value is approximately 65%, indicating that the cost of sensors after implementing our system is 65% of the cost before the mobile sensing system was in place. Additionally, the error rate remains low at approximately 7%.

## 4.2  Trade-Off Analysis

To further investigate the relationship between the detection error and the number of required sensors, a scatter plot (Fig. 9) was generated to visualize this trade-off. The scatter plot depicts a discernible trend, where fewer sensors generally lead to higher detection error, while more sensors reduce error. The improved algorithm has effectively struck a balance between this trade-off by identifying configurations that use fewer sensors without significantly increasing the detection error.

## 4.3  Parking Behavior Simulations

We developed a simulation program that utilizes Genetic Algorithms (GA) to solve the sensor allocation problem, allowing for data customization. This approach permits testing on the simulation platform and avoids data-specific results. The provided data consists of binary matrices of the "RealVector" mentioned in Sect. 3. The accuracy of our algorithm was tested using the simulation program, as shown in Fig. 10.

In Fig. 10, errors ranging from approximately 4.14 to 6.09 are displayed, with the mean error rate represented by the vertical red dashed line at around 5.11. The low variation in error rates indicates consistent performance and stability across different simulations. Additionally, most error values are in close proximity to the mean, which reinforces the system's stability.

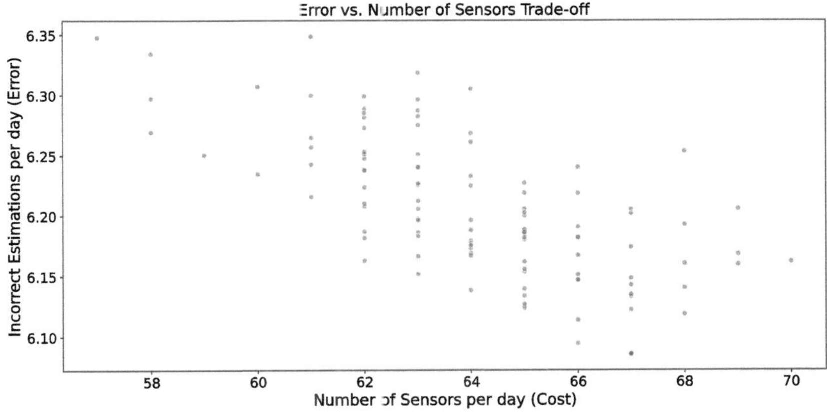



**Fig. 9.** Scatter plot of detection error vs. number of sensors

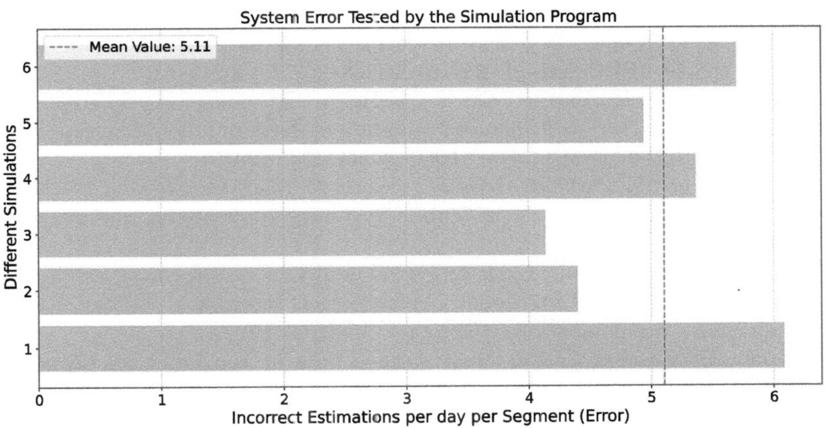



**Fig. 10.** System Error Tested by the Simulation Program

## 5   Conclusions

In this paper, we adopt an innovative genetic algorithm to minimize sensor allocation for on-street parking detection. The key contributions include the development of a distributed genetic algorithm that optimizes sensor deployment on moving vehicles for cost-effective and accurate roadside parking detection. Additionally, we introduced a penalty term in the evaluation function to balance detection accuracy with the number of sensors. The results show a significant reduction in sensor usage while maintaining high detection accuracy, indicating a balanced trade-off between detection error and resource usage.

To further enhance the practical applicability and resilience of the system for urban parking management, future improvements could focus on exploring the dynamic adjustment of the penalty factor $\alpha$ to maintain optimal performance under varying conditions. Additionally, incorporating models that account for traffic variability could ensure robust sensor allocation despite operational fluctuations, making mobile crowd-sensing a practical tool for urban parking management.

**Acknowledgement.** This work was supported in part by the Shenzhen Science and Technology Program (JCYJ20241202124021028), Shenzhen Stability Science Program (20231130170021001), Guangdong Provincial Science and Technology Department (2025A0505000083), Guangdong Provincial Key Laboratory of Mathematical Foundations for Artificial Intelligence (2023B1212010001), and SRIBD Doctoral Scholarship Program.

# References


1. Liao, R., Chen, L.: An evolutionary note on smart city development in China. Front. Inf. Technol. Electron. Eng. **23**(6), 966–974 (2022)
2. Shi, Z., Ou, Q., Zheng, W., Liao, R.: A driver-side parking evaluation model for roadside spaces. IEEE Sens. J. **24**(16), 26248–26257 (2024)
3. Roman, C., Liao, R., Ball, P., Ou, S., de Heaver, M.: Detecting on-street parking spaces in smart cities: performance evaluation of fixed and mobile sensing systems. IEEE Trans. Intell. Transp. Syst. **19**(7), 2234–2245 (2018)
4. Mathur, S., et al.: Parknet: drive-by sensing of road-side parking statistics. In: 8th International Conference on Mobile Systems, Applications, and Services, pp. 123–136 (2010)
5. Zheng, W., Liao, R., Zeng, J. An analytical model for crowdsensing on-street parking spaces. In: 2019 International Conference on Internet of Things, Embedded Systems and Communications, IEEE, pp. 56-61 (2019)
6. Bock, F., Di Martino, S.: On-street parking data in San Francisco-Sfpark sensor data and simulated crowd-sensing data. Harvard Dataverse (2018)
7. Sourabh, K., Singh, C.S., Vijay, K.: A review on genetic algorithm: past, present, and future. Multimedia Tools Appl. **80**, 8091–8126 (2021)
8. Lambora, A., Gupta, K., Chopra, K.: Genetic algorithm- a literature review. In: 2019 International Conference on Machine Learning, Big Data, Cloud and Parallel Computing (COMITCon), pp. 380–384 (2019)
9. Jian, Z., Zhongsheng, H.: A correlation guided genetic algorithm and its application to feature selection. Appl. Soft Comput. **123** (2022)
10. Santi, P., Ainul, H., Erna, N.S.S.: Analysis effect of tournament selection on genetic algorithm performance in traveling salesman problem (TSP). J. Phys. Conf. Ser. **1566**(1) (2020)
11. Bushra, A., Awajan, A.: Genetic algorithms: theory, genetic operators, solutions, and applications. Evol. Intel. **17**(7), 1245–1256 (2024)
12. Umbarkar, A.J., Sheth, P.D.: Crossover operators in genetic algorithms: a review. ICTACT J. Soft Comput. **6**(1), 1083–1092 (2015)
13. Shifen, H., Xiao, L.: An improved adaptive genetic algorithm. SHS Web Conf. **140** (2022)
14. Nishtha, J., Suri, B.: Particle swarm and genetic algorithm applied to mutation testing for test data generation: a comparative evaluation. J. King Saud Univ. Comput. Inf. Sci. **32**(4), 514–521 (2020)

# GNN-XAR: A Graph Neural Network for Explainable Activity Recognition in Smart Homes

Michele Fiori[✉], Davide Mor, Gabriele Civitarese, and Claudio Bettini

University of Milan, Milan, Italy
{michele.fiori,gabriele.civitarese,claudio.bettini}@unimi.it,
d.mor1@campus.unimib.it

**Abstract.** Sensor-based Human Activity Recognition (HAR) in smart home environments is crucial for several applications, especially in the healthcare domain. The majority of the existing approaches leverage deep learning models. While these approaches are effective, the rationale behind their outputs is opaque. Recently, eXplainable Artificial Intelligence (XAI) approaches emerged to provide intuitive explanations to the output of HAR models. To the best of our knowledge, these approaches leverage classic deep models like CNNs or RNNs. Recently, Graph Neural Networks (GNNs) proved to be effective for sensor-based HAR. However, existing approaches are not designed with explainability in mind. In this work, we propose the first explainable Graph Neural Network explicitly designed for smart home HAR. Our results on two public datasets show that this approach provides better explanations than state-of-the-art methods while also slightly improving the recognition rate.

**Keywords:** Human Activity Recognition · Graph Neural Networks · Smart Homes · eXplainable AI

## 1 Introduction

The recognition of Activities of Daily Living (ADLs) in Smart Home environments is a widely studied research topic in the pervasive computing community [7]. Recognizing the daily activities that humans do in their daily life at home (e.g., cooking, watering plants, taking medicines) has several important healthcare applications, including the early detection of cognitive decline [25].

The majority of the approaches in the literature are based on deep learning models, mainly due to their effectiveness in reaching high recognition rates [14]. The most common architectures used for ADLs recognition are Convolutional [4] and Recurrent [19] neural networks. However, these approaches may not fully capture the spatiotemporal properties of sensor data. In the literature, Graph Neural Networks (GNNs) have emerged as a promising approach for time series classification [12]. In GNNs, sensor data time windows are encoded as graphs capturing both spatial and temporal relationships between sensors. While


A. Soylu et al. (Eds.): MobiQuitous 2024, LNICST 634, pp. 341–360, 2026.
https://doi.org/10.1007/978-3-032-10554-7_19

the majority of existing studies focused on human activity recognition with mobile/wearable devices [22], only a few GNN-based approaches have been proposed for ADLs recognition in smart home environments [27,30].

In general, deep learning models are often considered as *"black boxes"* mapping windows of sensor data into activities, and it is challenging to understand the rationale behind their decisions. The field of eXplainable Artificial Intelligence (XAI) has the goal of mitigating this problem by providing human-understandable explanations to the output of machine learning models [3].

Since important decisions in ambient assisted living applications may rely on the output of ADLs recognition, inferring *why* a specific ADL was predicted by the classifier is crucial to provide understandable, trusted, and transparent solutions [29]. For instance, XAI would allow clinicians to increase their trust in decision support systems that rely on ADLs recognition (e.g., supporting early detection of cognitive decline). Data scientists may also benefit from explanations to refine the recognition system, the sensing infrastructure, or the training set.

A few works proposed explainable ADLs recognition in smart homes environments [4,10]. However, to the best of our knowledge, eXplainable GNN approaches for sensor-based ADLs recognition in smart homes have not been explored yet. Therefore, in this paper we present GNN-XAR, the first explainable GNN-based system for ADLs recognition. Specifically, GNN-XAR dynamically constructs a graph starting from windows of environmental sensor data taking into account spatial and temporal aspects. Each graph is processed by a Graph Convolutional Network (GCN) for ADLs classification. An adapted state-of-the-art XAI method specifically designed for GNNs is in charge of determining the most important nodes and arcs of the input for activity classification. This information is finally used to generate an explanation in natural language.

To sum up, the contributions of this paper are the following:

- We propose GNN-XAR: the first Explainable Graph Neural Network system for Smart Home HAR.
- Starting from windows of raw sensor data, GNN-XAR dynamically constructs a graph that a GNN processes to classify the most likely activity.
- For each prediction, GNN-XAR leverages an eXplainable AI approach to produce explanations in natural language.
- Our results show that GNN-XAR generates superior explanations with respect to state-of-the-art explainable HAR methods, while slightly improving the recognition rate.

## 2   Related Work

### 2.1   GNN-Based Methods for HAR

GNNs have been widely adopted in IoT scenarios, in applications including multi-agent interaction, Human State-dynamic, sensor interconnection, and autonomous vehicles [11]. Considering sensor-based human activity recognition,

GNNs have been mainly proposed tc recognize activities from mobile/wearable devices [28].

The differences between existing work lies in how the graph is constructed from sensor data. For instance, a common solution is to consider each time window as a node with the goal of performing node classification [21,23,26]. Other works consider a node for each sensor, considering a graph classification task [18].

Only a few works applied GNNs to ADLs recognition in smart home environments. For example, [27] uses graphs to model sensor dependencies. In that work, a graph is built such that each node represents an environmental sensor, while a directed arc represents the influence of the behavior of one sensor to another one. The arcs of the graph structure and their weights are learned using an attention mechanism. The graph classification task is then considered to perform ADLs classification. The work in [30] is closely related to GNN-XAR since it dynamically constructs each graph from the time window of sensor data, where each node is a sensor event. Differently from our work, the arcs are automatically learned from the network considering spatial and temporal properties at the same time.

While it may be possible to apply XAI techniques on such methods, it would be challenging to obtain meaningful explanations. For instance, considering the work in [27], it may be possible to obtain explanations only about the sensors triggered consecutively, without considering longer temporal relationships. On the other hand, since in [30] the arcs are automatically learned, they are not associated with a specific semantic and hence it would be challenging to explain them.

### 2.2  XAI Methods for Human Activity Recognition

The first attempts for explainable sensor-based activity recognition considered simple inherently interpretable models [5,6,15,17]. However, such models usually underperform deep learning models that, on the contrary, are more complex to explain.

A few works proposed XAI methods for deep learning for sensor-based activity recognition [16,20]. However, only a few of them focused on ADLs recognition in smart homes. For instance, DeXAR [4] leverages CNN models and explores the use of various XAI methods for computer vision by converting sensor data into semantic images. Similarly, the work in [10] applies several XAI methods to LSTM-based neural networks. Both works generate explanations in natural language for non-expert users.

While eXplainable Graph Neural Networks have been studied in the general machine learning community [1], this is the first work exploring this combination for sensor-based ADLs recognition in smart homes.

## 3   GNN-XAR Under the Hood

In this work, we consider a smart home environment equipped with binary environmental sensors (e.g., motion sensors, magnetic sensors, pressure sensors). We assume that the smart-home is inhabited only by a single resident, and that sensor events are the result of the interaction of the subject with the environment. We also assume that the same timestamp will never be assigned to two distinct sensor events, hence we consider a total order in the sensor event sequence[1]. The goal of GNN-XAR is to provide the most likely activity from time windows of sensor events and, at the same time, to provide an explanation in natural language about the aspects of the input that mostly contributed to the prediction.

### 3.1   Overall Architecture

Fig. 1 depicts the architecture of GNN-XAR.

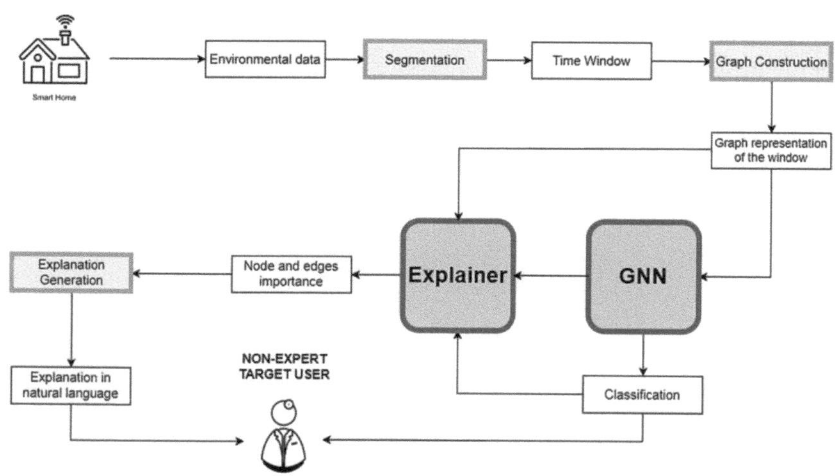


Fig. 1: Overall architecture of GNN-XAR.

First, the stream of environmental sensor data is segmented into fixed size overlapping time windows. Each time window is then processed by the GRAPH CONSTRUCTION module to obtain a graph representation of the window, encoding both spatial and temporal properties with an heuristic-based approach. Each graph is processed by the GNN module for ADLs classification. Then, the EXPLAINER module leverages posthoc XAI methods to obtain the nodes and arcs that were the most important in the input to obtain the classified activity.

---

[1] Note that this is a realistic assumption, since typically events are queued by a single process on the gateway that assigns different timestamps even if the events occurred at the same time, without any impact on our results.

Posthoc XAI approaches consider the model as a black box and generate explanations by analyzing the relationships between inputs and outputs. Finally, the EXPLANATION GENERATION module uses this information to generate an explanation in natural language for non-expert users.

## 3.2   Graph Construction

The GRAPH CONSTRUCTION module dynamically constructs a graph $G_w$ starting from a temporal window $w$ of sensor events. GNN-XAR leverages a heuristic-based strategy for graph construction, taking into account spatial and temporal properties (that will be leveraged to generate meaningful explanations).

Let $w = \langle E_1, E_2, \ldots, E_n \rangle$ be a temporal window including $n$ sequential sensor events. An event $E_i$ is associated with the following information:

- An identifier of the sensor that produced it ($E_i^{id}$), that encodes the sensor type (magnetic, motion ...) and the position (fridge, sofa...).
- The event type ON or OFF ($E_i^{type}$).
- The timestamp of the event ($E_i^{ts}$).

In our framework, we consider the events differently based on the type of sensor that generated them:

- The first type of sensor includes sensors whose both activation and deactivation require explicit actions by the user (e.g. opening or closing a cabinet). In this case, we are interested in both the activation and deactivation (i.e. ON and OFF) events.
- The second type includes sensors that are automatically deactivated after some time, for instance, motion sensors. In this case, we are interested in the ON event and in the duration of the *active state* of the sensor, computed as the time from the ON event to the OFF event.[2]

Given a window $w$, we denote the corresponding graph with $G_w = (V, A)$, where $V$ is the set of nodes and $A$ is the set of arcs. In GNN-XAR, the set $V$ is created as follows:

- We add a node $v$ for each event in $w$ (activation or deactivation) generated by the first type of sensor. These are **event nodes**.
- We add a node $v$ for every *active* state of a sensor of the second type. These are **state nodes**.

In our system, each node has the sensor identifier as a feature. As common in deep learning, a (trainable) embedding layer computes an embedding vector representing this feature. State nodes have the duration of the corresponding *active state* as an additional feature.

The set of arcs $A$ is created as follows: For each pair of node $v_i, v_j \in V$ such that $i \neq j$, there is an oriented arc $(v_i, v_j) \in A$ in the following two cases:

---

[2] In the case of motion sensors if there are multiple subsequent detections of movements, a single active state is considered. This is also how the events are reported in the public datasets we considered.

1. $v_i$ and $v_j$ are event nodes derived from consecutive events generated by the same sensor $S$ (i.e., there are no other events from $S$ between them). This is shown in Fig. 2.

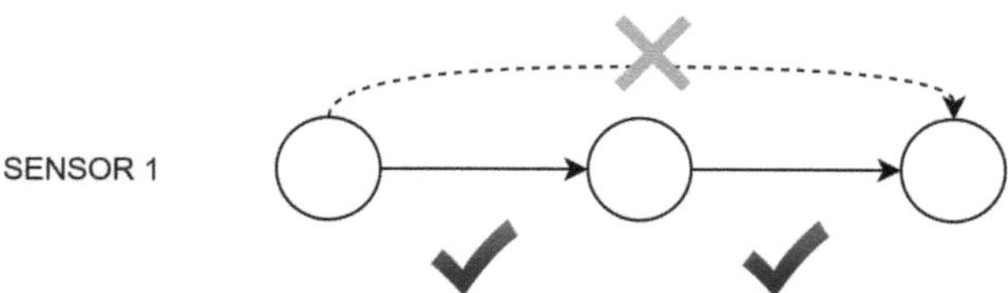


Fig. 2: Arcs between event or state nodes generated by different sensors.

2. $v_i$ and $v_j$ are state nodes derived from consecutive active states of the same sensor $S$.
3. $v_i$ and $v_j$ are derived from events/states generated by different sensors $S_a$ and $S_b$ and there are no other events/states generated by $S_a$ or $S_b$ between them. This temporal relationship is computed considering as timestamp of an active state the timestamp of the activation (ON) event. This is shown in Fig. 3.

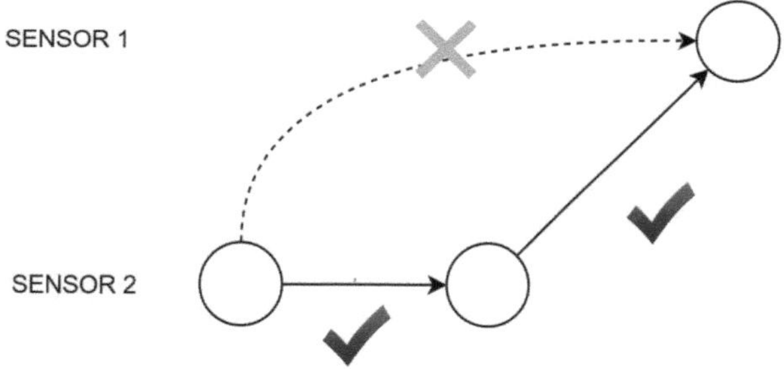


Fig. 3: Arcs between event nodes generated by the same sensor.

Each arc $(v_i, v_j) \in A$ has as associated feature the time difference between the timestamp of the event/state corresponding to $v_j$ and the timestamp of the event/state corresponding to $v_i$, considering as timestamp of an active state the timestamp of the activation (ON) event.

This method for building the graph has also the advantage of maintaining a sparse structure, avoiding the graph degeneration into a fully connected graph.

Our graph construction strategy makes it possible to consider spatiotemporal relationships between sensor events. Considering temporal aspects, a directed arc from a node $v_i$ to a node $v_j$ models the fact that the event/state corresponding to $v_i$ occurred before the event/state corresponding to $v_j$. This temporal relationship is also quantitative since the arc feature encodes the time distance between them. Moreover, when $v_i$ and $v_j$ are generated by different sensors $S_a$ and $S_b$, the directed arc also implicitly encodes spatial relationships about the resident interacting with sensors in different home positions.

A challenge with graphs with a variable number of nodes is that it complicates the graph pooling process (i.e., creating an embedding for the whole graph). For instance, pooling by concatenation would lead to graph embeddings of different shapes. GNN-XAR solves this problem by augmenting $V$ with a fixed number of *super-nodes*: fictitious nodes not corresponding to real sensor events or states. Specifically, we add a super node $SN_S$ to $V$ for each sensor $S$. We also add an arc $(v_i, SN_S) \in \mathbf{A}$ if $v_i$ corresponds to an event/state generated by the sensor $S$. Note that, if a window $w$ does not contain events/states generated by a sensor $S_a$, $V$ would include the super node $SN_{S_a}$ without associated arcs. Hence, all the nodes corresponding to an event/state generated by a sensor are connected to its super-node. Super-nodes have the role of summarizing all the graph information into a fixed number of nodes. Thanks to this approach, it is possible to concatenate the information of the whole graph only by performing pooling on super-nodes.

In the following, we show a simple example of how to build a graph $G_w$ starting from a window $w$ including active states from three sensors. The window $w$ and its states are depicted in Fig. 4.

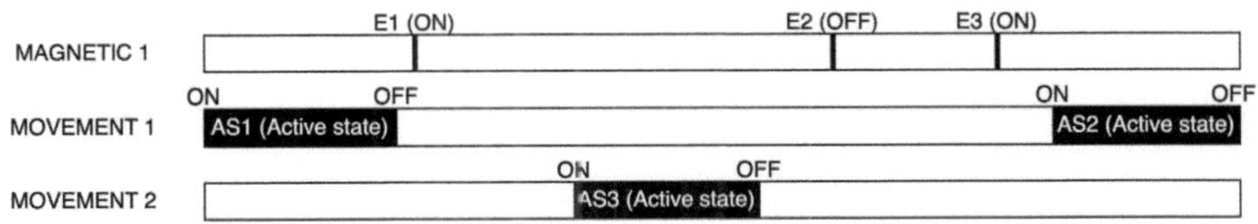


Fig. 4: Example of a time window. For the magnetic sensor, the black lines represent the events. For the movement sensors, the black regions represent the active states

Figure 5 shows the resulting graph $G_w$, that is constructed with the following steps:

- For each sensor $S$, a super-node is created (represented as squares in the figure).
- For each event/state a node $v_i$ is generated (represented as circles in the figure).
- Each event/state generated by $S$ is connected to the respective super-node associated with $S$ (the dashed arrows).
- We include arcs based on the rules defined above (the solid arrows).

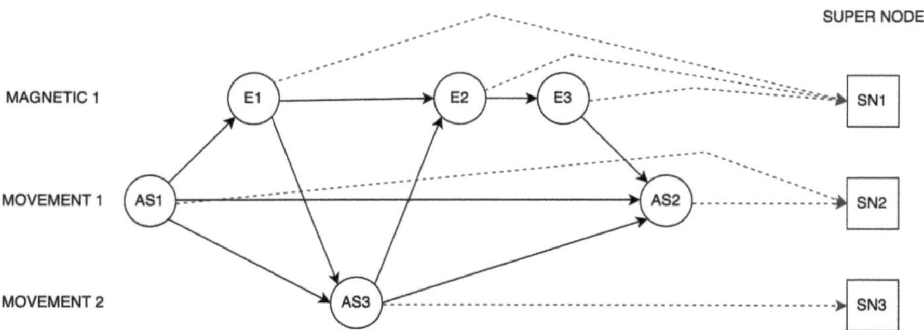


Fig. 5: The directed graph computed from the sensor window in Fig. 4.

## 3.3   Graph Neural Network

In the following, we describe the steps for graph classification.

**Message Passing.** Message passing is a crucial step in GNNs for transmitting information between nodes in a graph. This technique allows nodes to share and update their features based on the features of their neighbors, facilitating the extraction of meaningful patterns and relationships in graph-structured data.

Information propagates through the graph in two distinct steps. The first step aggregates and processes all the known information, including event duration and distances between events, to compute the new node features, while the second step has the goal of further spreading this information into the graph. The second step is particularly useful for spreading information to the super nodes.

More specifically, in the first iteration, for each node, a message is computed by applying a linear layer to the concatenation of the node embeddings and the arc features. This linear layer reduces the message's dimension to match the original node feature dimension. Subsequently, the aggregate message for each node is computed using a sum aggregation function, and the new node feature is obtained by summing the previous embedding with the aggregated message.

The second phase involves a simplified propagation in which only the new node embeddings are considered. Given that less information is processed in this phase, no linear layer is applied. Instead, a sum aggregation function is used directly. The same update function from the first phase is then applied, summing the previous node feature with the aggregated messages to compute the new node feature.

Although this propagation process can be iterated multiple times, the high connectivity of the graphs generated by GNN-XAR makes it possible to leverage a small number of iterations to allow information to travel throughout the entire graph.

**Graph Pooling and Classification.** Figure 6 shows the GNN model architecture of GNN-XAR. Graph Pooling consists in generating an embedding that is representative of the whole graph. As we previously mentioned, since the number of nodes is different for each instance, we leverage super-nodes. Thus, the pooling strategy proposed for this model consists of considering only the embeddings of super nodes and concatenating them to obtain a vector of length equal to the embedding dimension multiplied by the number of sensors.

The classification is carried out using linear layers: the flattened embedding encoding the graph is passed through two linear layers, each one followed by a LeakyReLU function. Finally, the output of the network is the probability distribution over the possible ADLs, obtained thanks to a softmax layer.

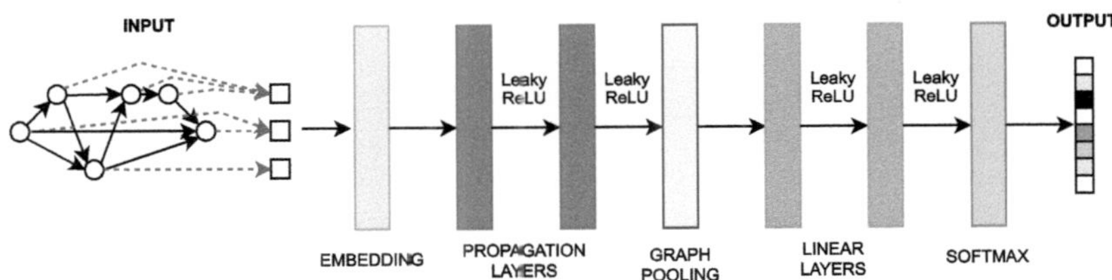


Fig. 6: The model architecture of GNN-XAR.

## 3.4 Explainer

XAI methods applied on GNNs aim to find the subset of nodes and arc that mostly contributed to a specific prediction. In GNN-XAR, a node is selected for the explanation if the corresponding sensor event/state was important for classifying the activity; an arc is selected if the specific order of sensor events/states was important for classifying the activity.

GNN-XAR leverages the GNNexplainer [31] method for explanations. Through an optimization method, GNNexplainer derives a subgraph maximizing the mutual information between the GNN's prediction and the prediction that would have been obtained by the GNN based only on this subgraph. This is achieved by perturbing the graph and its features, and observing the effect of these perturbations on the GNN's predictions. Given the most likely ADL predicted by the GNN, the input graph and the GNN model, GNNexplainer computes importance values for nodes and arcs. The algorithm leverages gradient descent to derive node and arc masks that modulate the information spread in the graph during the message-passing procedure.

In its original version, the GNNexplainer algorithm includes the multiplication of each node feature by a value in the range $[0, 1]$ to generate the node mask. However, this approach cannot be adopted in GNN-XAR since the sensor id node feature represents a categorical value, the perturbation of that value would not convey the intended meaning. For this reason, we apply the original GNNExplainer but extract only the arc mask. We then compute the importance of each node as the importance of the arc connecting it to its corresponding super node. The intuition behind this strategy is that there is only one arc through which the information from the node is propagated to the super node. Since it is the super node that is used for the classification, the importance of this arc is a good indicator of the importance of the information conveyed by the node.

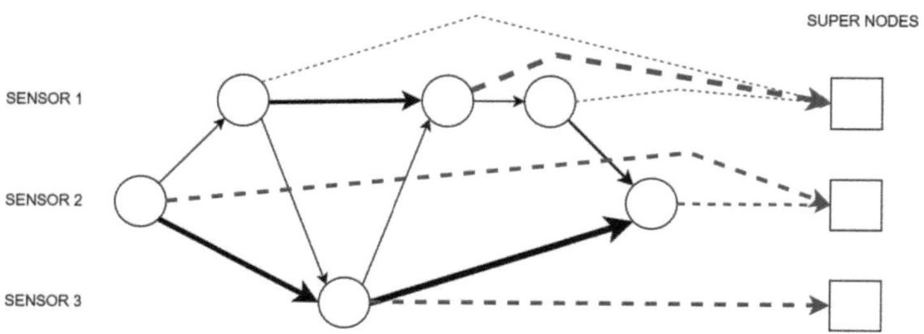


Fig. 7: Output of the original GNNExplainer limited to arcs importance. The thickness of each arrow represents the importance values on the arcs.

Figure 7 represents the arcs importance as computed by the original GNNExplainer on an example in our domain. Note that the dashed lines, connecting nodes with super nodes, also have different thicknesses representing different importance.

As stated above, our adapted version of GNNexplainer assigns as importance of each node the importance of the arc connecting it with its super node. Figure 8 shows the output of our adapted version of GNNexplainer on the same example of Fig. 7. Note that super nodes are not part of the output and that an importance value is associated with each node, denoted in the figure by the thickness.

GNNexplainer is a non-deterministic algorithm. For this reason, it requires multiple executions, and only the average of the masks obtained at each execution is considered for the explanations. A major challenge of using GNNexplainer is that the importance values obtained for nodes and arcs are not directly comparable, since they range in different intervals. Since we observed that arcs scorers are usually associated with lower importance values, we rescale them by a multiplicative factor such that the importance values of the nodes and the ones for the arcs have the same mean.

Finally, GNN-XAR aims at extracting a supgraph $G_w^\star = (V^\star, A^\star)$ where $V^\star$ is the set of the most important nodes, while $A^\star$ is the set of the most important arcs. A straightforward approach to achieve this task would be using a threshold on the importance value. However, we observed that different predictions

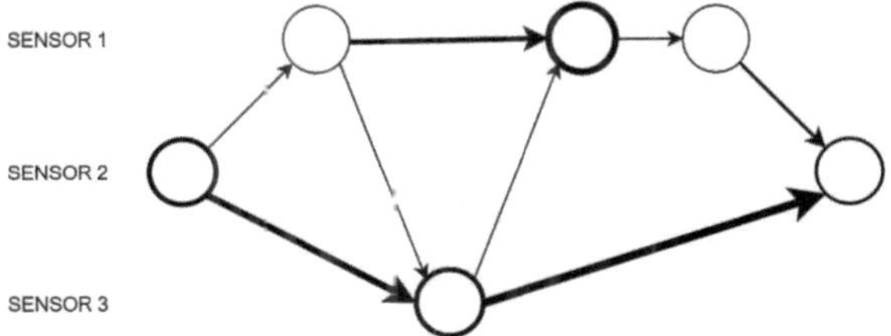


Fig. 8: Output of our adapted version of GNNExplainer on the same input example of Fig. 7.

are usually associated with importance values in completely different ranges. Hence, defining a robust threshold is challenging. We mitigated this problem by adopting a clustering approach. Indeed, we cluster arcs and nodes based on their importance values. We consider as the most important arcs and nodes the ones in the cluster associated with the highest importance values.

### 3.5   Generating Explanations in Natural Language

As a final step, GNN-XAR converts $G^*$ into a natural language explanation for non-expert users.

Given the set of most important arcs $A^*$, we compute the longest path. We then use a heuristic-based approach similar to the one proposed in [4] to generate from this path a natural language explanation. For instance, the continuous activation of certain sensors implies that the resident has moved toward the sensor multiple times: in this case, in the path explanation, the expression "*multiple times*" is added:

"*I predicted preparing a meal mainly due to the following observations: Bob was near the fridge, then he opened the fridge multiple times*"

## 4   Experimental Evaluation

### 4.1   Datasets

Two datasets have been used to evaluate the model proposed in this work. They are *CASAS Milan* [9] and *CASAS Aruba* [8].

**CASAS Milan.** CASAS Milan consists of data gathered from the home of a female adult volunteer living with a pet and where the woman's children visited periodically. The dataset contains about three months of recording and includes the following classes: Bed-to-Toilet, Chores, Desk Activity, Dining room Activity, Evening Medications, Guest Bathroom, Kitchen Activity, Leave Home, Master Bathroom, Meditate, Watch TV, Sleep, Read, Morning Medications, Master

Bedroom Activity. Some of these activities are very under-represented in the dataset; for this reason, following what has been done in [4], the less represented classes, that are Bed to Toilet, Chores, Meditation, Evening Medications and Morning Medications, are not taken into consideration. Moreover, Master Bathroom and Guest Bathroom have been fused obtaining a new class that contains similar activities in a number comparable with the other classes.

**CASAS Aruba.** CASAS Aruba is a dataset collected in the home of a woman whose children and grandchildren visited regularly. The dataset contains Meal Preparation, Relax, Eating, Work, Sleeping, Wash Dishes, Bed to Toilet, Enter Home, Leave Home, Housekeeping and Resperate. Resperate and Bed To toilet classes have been dropped according to what has been done in [19].

### 4.2   Implementation Details

We implemented GNN-XAR using Python 3.10.5, using Pytorch and Pytorch Geometrics for the models and the explainer. Other libraries used include Scikit-learn for the evaluation, Networkx for graph visualization, and Pandas and Numpy for data processing.

### 4.3   Evaluation

**Baseline.** We decided to focus our comparison of GNN-XAR only with state-of-the-art explainable ADL recognition methods, selecting the one that demonstrated the highest recognition accuracy in the literature. For this reason, we chose DeXAR [4] as a baseline, since it is the method that meets these criteria. DeXAR converts sensor data into semantic images, leveraging XAI methods for computer vision to generate natural language explanations. Since GNN-XAR uses a posthoc explanation method, we compare DeXAR when used with LIME [24].

The original DeXAR implementation also considered previously predicted ADLs as input, while this aspect is not captured by GNN-XAR. Hence, we implemented a version of DeXAR not considering past activities.

**Experimental Setup.** We consider a standard 70%-20%-10% split to partition the datasets into training, test and validation sets.The models have been trained using the early stopping strategy with a patience of 50 epochs, the Adam optimizer with a learning rate of 0.0001, and a CrossEntropy loss function.

For segmentation, we used the same hyper-parameters suggested in [4] for the CASAS datasets, where the window size is 360 seconds with an overlap factor of 80%. We discarded all the windows not corresponding to an activity label (i.e., transitions or other activities) as well as temporal windows without sensor events.

## 4.4  Evaluation Metrics

We use the standard metrics for precision, recall, and F1 score to assess the recognition rate of GNN-XAR. These metrics provide a comprehensive understanding of the model's performance from different perspectives.

However, evaluating the effectiveness of explanations is more challenging. A standard way adopted in the literature involves user surveys [4,10,16]. However, such method is time and money-consuming. We leverage a recent work proposing LLMs to automatically compare alternative XAI methods, since it proved to be aligned with user surveys [13]. Specifically, we provide to an LLM the explanations generated by GNN-XAR and DeXAR on the same window, asking the LLM to choose the best one (using the prompt proposed in [13]).

## 4.5  Results

**Classification Results.** Tables 1 and  2 compare GNN-XAR and DeXAR considering the F1 score for each class.We observe that our approach achieves slightly better recognition rates in the overall F1 score for both datasets.By observing the confusion matrices in Fig. 9 and 10, both models struggle to distinguish activities taking place in the same room, like Bathroom and Dress Undress.

Considering the CASAS Milan dataset, this is likely due to the fact that the wardrobe is located in the master bedroom near the bathroom entrance. To distinguish between these two activities, it is probably necessary to consider additional context information, such as past activities and time. Another remarkable difference between the two models is the higher f1 score of GNN-XAR on Leave Home (see table 1). In fact, this ADL strongly depends the temporal order of sensor events, that is better captured by our GNN model.

Considering the CASAS Aruba dataset, the GNN model performs better than DeXAR for almost all the activities. The main difference with respect to the results obtained in CASAS Milan is that two activities are completely misclassified by both GNN-XAR and DeXAR: washing dishes and housekeeping. These two activities are the least represented in the dataset. Wash dishes is always confused with meal preparation. Similarly to CASAS Milan, the activities that benefit more from the GNN model are entering home and leaving home.

**Explainability Results.** As we previously mentioned, we leverage an LLM-based approach to compare GNN-XAR and DeXAR. However, due to the costs of LLM-based APIs requests, we sampled 30 random windows for each activity. Similarly to [4], we only evaluate the quality of explanations associated to correct predictions, since evaluating explanations of wrong predictions is still an open problem and we will consider it for future work. For each window, we provide the LLM with the explanations generated by the two models and we obtain as output the explanation preferred by the LLM. Table 3 shows an example of how the LLM compares the explanations.

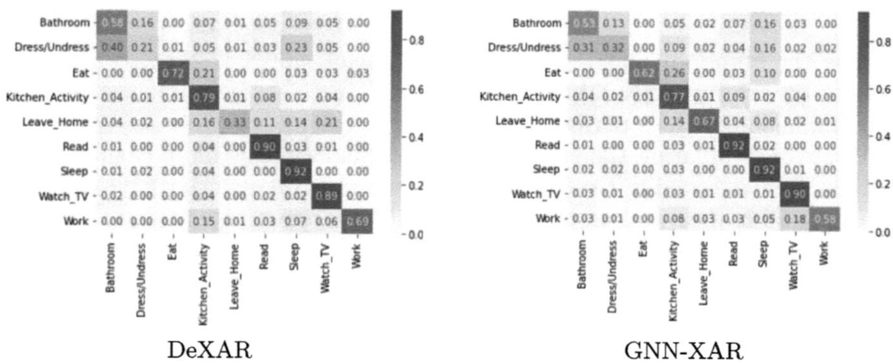

DeXAR          GNN-XAR

Fig. 9: Confusion Matrices for CASAS Milan.

Table 1: CASAS Milan: Classification results (F1 score).

|                  | DeXAR [4] | GNN-XAR |
|------------------|-----------|---------|
| Bathroom         | **0.55**  | 0.53    |
| Dress/Undress    | 0.26      | **0.37**|
| Eat              | **0.67**  | 0.61    |
| Kitchen activity | **0.77**  | **0.77**|
| Leave Home       | 0.46      | **0.74**|
| Read             | 0.90      | **0.91**|
| Sleep            | 0.85      | **0.87**|
| Watch TV         | 0.84      | **0.89**|
| Work             | **0.80**  | 0.70    |
| weighted avg.    | 0.77      | **0.81**|

Table 2: CASAS Aruba: Classification results (F1 score).

|                  | DeXAR [4] | GNN-XAR |
|------------------|-----------|---------|
| Eating           | 0.69      | **0.75**|
| Enter Home       | 0.53      | **0.76**|
| Housekeeping     | 0.09      | **0.14**|
| Leave Home       | 0.71      | **0.82**|
| Meal Preparation | 0.80      | **0.81**|
| Relax            | 0.94      | **0.96**|
| Sleeping         | 0.93      | **0.96**|
| Wash Dishes      | **0.06**  | 0.00    |
| Work             | 0.79      | **0.87**|
| weighted avg.    | 0.90      | **0.92**|

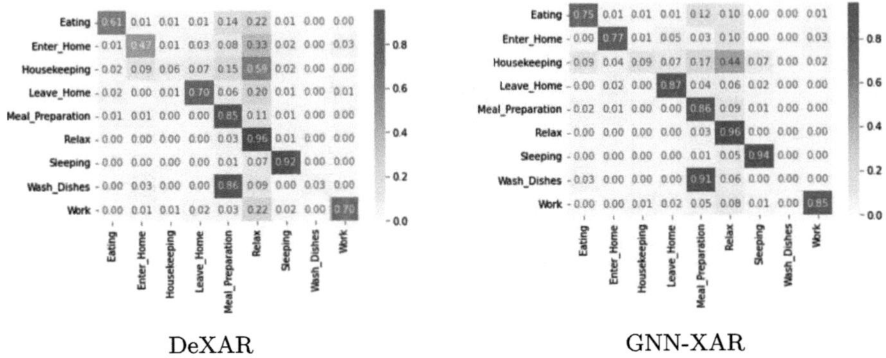

DeXAR          GNN-XAR

Fig. 10: Confusion Matrices for CASAS Aruba.

Figure 11 shows, for both datasets, the percentage of times where the LLM preferred explanations from GNN-XAR compared to the ones generated by DeXAR. We observe that the explanations generated by GNN-XAR were preferred by the LLM in 80% of the times for the CASAS Milan dataset and 69% of the times for the CASAS Aruba dataset.

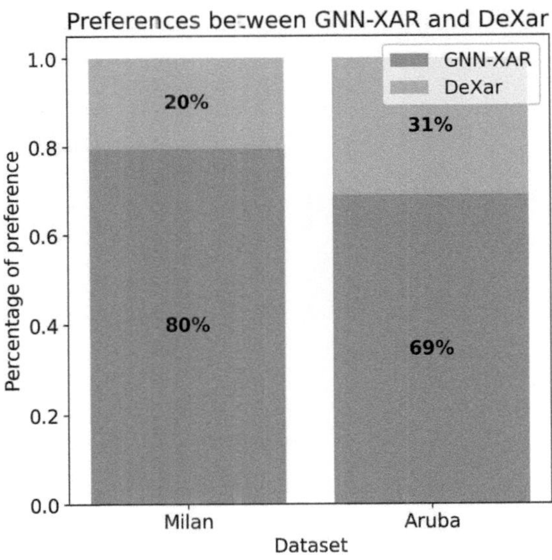


Fig. 11: Overall percentage of preferences given by the LLM to explanations given by GNN-XAR and DeXar.

It is important to note that this preference is not uniform over all the classes classes. Indeed, Figs. 12 and 13 shows that more dynamic activities, like entering and leaving home, eating, and preparing a meal achieve a higher score with

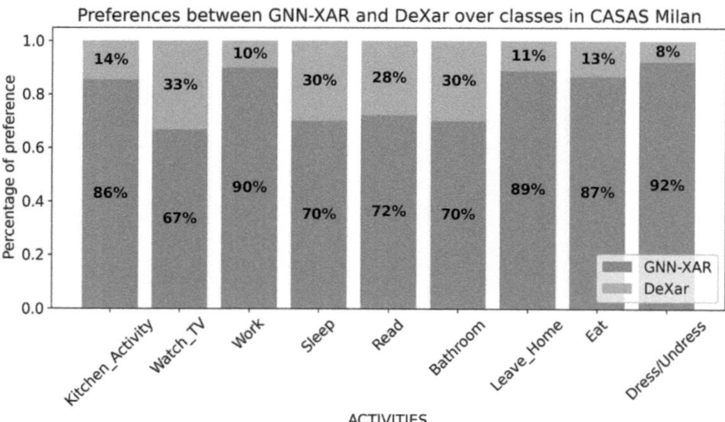

Fig. 12: Percentage of preferences (for each activity class) given by the LLM to explanations given by GNN-XAR and DeXar for CASAS Milan.

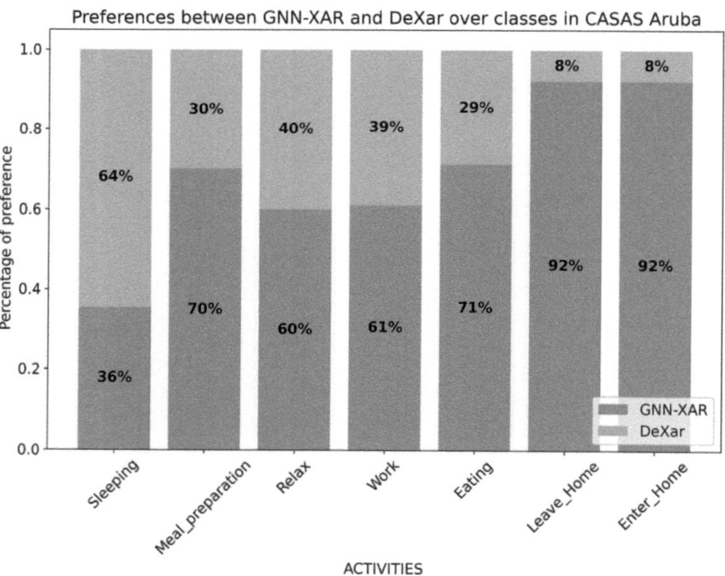

Fig. 13: Percentage of preferences (for each activity class) given by the LLM to explanations given by GNN-XAR and DeXar for CASAS Aruba.

respect to static activities like sleeping, reading, relaxing and watching TV. This is reasonable since our graph encoding is better at capturing temporal relations in dynamic activities. The only time where DeXAR explanations "wins" over the ones of GNN-XAR is on the Sleep activity for the CASAS Aruba dataset. This is probably due to the fact that in this dataset there is a higher number of sensors in the bedroom, and a slight movement during sleep may trigger more sensors at

Table 3: Example of LLM-based explaination evaluation.

| GNNExplainer | I predicted leaving home mainly due to the following observations: Bob approached the area between the dining room and the hall multiple times, and then the front door. |
|---|---|
| DeXAR | I predicted leaving home mainly because Bob has been near the front door and between the dining room and the hall. |
| LLM answer | Let's break down each explanation:<br>1) The first explanation mentions specific observations of Bob approaching the area between the dining room and the hall multiple times before heading to the front door. This sequence of movements aligns with the common behavior of someone preparing to leave home, such as gathering belongings or checking for keys before exiting. Therefore, this explanation provides a clear and logical connection between Bob's movements and the prediction of leaving home.<br>2) The second explanation is similar to the first one but lacks the detail of multiple approaches to the specific areas. While it still mentions Bob being near the front door and between the dining room and the hall, the repetition of movements in the first explanation adds more weight to the prediction of leaving home.<br>Considering the clarity and specificity of the observations provided in the first explanation, it offers a more detailed and plausible rationale for predicting leaving home based on Bob's movements.<br>CHOICE=1. |

once. Thus, the GNN may tend to explain the sequence of actions transmitting a false sense of movement from one sensor to the other. This probably can be fixed in future work by adding further heuristics to refine the explanations.

## 5   Conclusion and Future Work

In this paper we presented GNN-XAR, an explainable Graph Neural Network framework for ADLs recognition in smart home environments. Our results suggest that GNN-XAR generates effective explanations by leveraging the structural properties of the graph representation. While the results are promising, this work still has limitations, and we plan to extend it following several research directions.

Currently, GNN-XAR only considers binary environmental sensors. We will investigate how to also integrate continuous sensor data from mobile/wearable devices, information about past activities, and other context information.

Another limitation of GNN-XAR is that it assigns an importance score to a node or arc within a graph structure, but it does not consider nodes or arcs features in the explanations. Therefore, another possible development might consist in improving the explainer algorithm to also provide such details.

Regarding the segmentation, in this work we considered fixed time sliding windows, that is the standard approach. In future work, we will investigate the impact of dynamic segmentation [2] on GNN-XAR.

Finally, while we used LLMs to evaluate the explanations, we will investigate where it is possible to leverage them also to automatically generate explanations starting from the most important nodes and arcs obtained by GNNexplainer.

**Acknowledgements.** This work was supported in part by MUSA, SERICS, and FAIR projects under the NRRP MUR program funded by the EU-NGEU. Views and opinions expressed are those of the authors only and do not necessarily reflect those of the European Union or the Italian MUR. Neither the European Union nor the Italian MUR can be held responsible for them.

**Disclosure of Interests.** The authors have no competing interests to declare that are relevant to the content of this article.

# References


1. Agarwal, C., Queen, O., Lakkaraju, H., Zitnik, M.: Evaluating explainability for graph neural networks. Scientific Data **10**(1), 144 (2023)
2. Aminikhanghahi, S., Cook, D.J.: Using change point detection to automate daily activity segmentation. In: 2017 IEEE International Conference on Pervasive Computing and Communications Workshops (PerCom Workshops), pp. 262–267. IEEE (2017)
3. Arrieta, A.B., et al.: Explainable artificial intelligence (XAI): Concepts, taxonomies, opportunities and challenges toward responsible AI. Inform. Fusion **58**, 82–115 (2020)
4. Arrotta, L., Civitarese, G., Bettini, C.: Dexar: Deep explainable sensor-based activity recognition in smart-home environments. Proc. ACM Interact. Mobile, Wearable Ubiquitous Tech. **6**(1), 1–30 (2022)
5. Atzmueller, M., Hayat, N., Trojahn, M., Kroll, D.: Explicative human activity recognition using adaptive association rule-based classification. In: 2018 IEEE International Conference on Future IoT Technologies (Future IoT), pp. 1–6. IEEE (2018)
6. Bettini, C., Civitarese, G., Fiori, M.: Explainable activity recognition over interpretable models. In: 2021 IEEE International Conference on Pervasive Computing and Communications Workshops, pp. 32–37. IEEE (2021)
7. Bouchabou, D., Nguyen, S.M., Lohr, C., LeDuc, B., Kanellos, I.: A survey of human activity recognition in smart homes based on IOT sensors algorithms: Taxonomies, challenges, and opportunities with deep learning. Sensors **21**(18), 6037 (2021)
8. Cook, D.J.: Learning setting-generalized activity models for smart spaces. IEEE Intell. Syst. **2010**(99), 1 (2010)
9. Cook, D.J., Schmitter-Edgecombe, M.: Assessing the quality of activities in a smart environment. Methods Inf. Med. **48**(05), 480–485 (2009)
10. Das, D., et al.: Explainable activity recognition for smart home systems. ACM Trans. Int. Intell. Syst. **13**(2), 1–39 (2023)

11. Dong, G., et al.: Graph neural networks in IOT: a survey. ACM Trans. Sen. Netw. **19**(2) (2023)
12. Duan, Z., et al.: Multivariate time-series classification with hierarchical variational graph pooling. Neural Netw. **154**, 481–490 (2022)
13. Fiori, M., Civitarese, G., Bettini, C.: Using large language models to compare explainable models for smart home human activity recognition. In: Companion of the 2024 on ACM International Joint Conference on Pervasive and Ubiquitous Computing, pp. 881–884 (2024)
14. Gu, F., Chung, M.H., Chignell, M., Valaee, S., Zhou, B., Liu, X.: A survey on deep learning for human activity recognition. ACM Comput. Surv. (CSUR) **54**(8), 1–34 (2021)
15. Guesgen, H.W.: Using rough sets to improve activity recognition based on sensor data. Sensors **20**(6), 1779 (2020)
16. Jeyakumar, J.V., Sarker, A. Garcia, L.A., Srivastava, M.: X-char: a concept-based explainable complex human activity recognition model. Proc. ACM on int. mobile, wearable ubiquitous tech. **7**(1), 1–28 (2023)
17. Khodabandehloo, E., Riboni, D., Alimohammadi, A.: Healthxai: collaborative and explainable AI for supporting early diagnosis of cognitive decline. Futur. Gener. Comput. Syst. **116**, 168–189 (2021)
18. Liao, T., Zhao, J., Liu, Y., Ivanov, K., Xiong, J., Yan, Y.: Deep transfer learning with graph neural network for sensor-based human activity recognition. In: 2022 IEEE International Conference on Bioinformatics and Biomedicine (BIBM), pp. 2445–2452 (2022)
19. Liciotti, D., Bernardini, M., Romeo, L., Frontoni, E.: A sequential deep learning application for recognising human activities in smart homes. Neurocomputing **396**, 501–513 (2020)
20. Meena, T., Sarawadekar, K.: An explainable self attention based spatial-temporal analysis for human activity recognition. IEEE Sensors J. (2023)
21. Mohamed, A., Lejarza, F., Cahail, S., Claudel, C., Thomaz, E.: HAR-GCNN: Deep graph CNNs for human activity recognition from highly unlabeled mobile sensor data. In: 2022 IEEE International Conference on Pervasive Computing and Communications Workshops and other Affiliated Events (PerCom Workshops), pp. 335–340 (2022)
22. Mondal, R., Mukherjee, D., Singh, P.K., Bhateja, V., Sarkar, R.: A new framework for smartphone sensor-based human activity recognition using graph neural network. IEEE Sens. J. **21**(10), 11461–11468 (2020)
23. Nian, A., Zhu, X., Xu, X., Huang, X., Wang, F., Zhao, Y.: HGCNN: deep graph convolutional network for sensor-based human activity recognition. In: 2022 8th International Conference on Big Data and Information Analytics (BigDIA), pp. 422–427 (2022)
24. Ribeiro, M.T., Singh, S., Guestrin, C.: why should i trust you? explaining the predictions of any classifier. In: Proceedings of the 22nd ACM SIGKDD international conference on knowledge discovery and data mining, pp. 1135–1144 (2016)
25. Riboni, D., Bettini, C., Civitarese, G., Janjua, Z.H., Helaoui, R.: Smartfaber: recognizing fine-grained abnormal behaviors for early detection of mild cognitive impairment. Artif. Intell. Med. **67**, 57–74 (2016)
26. Sarkar, A., Sen, T., Roy, A.K.: Grafehty: Graph neural network using federated learning for human activity recognition. In: 2021 20th IEEE International Conference on Machine Learning and Applications (ICMLA), pp. 1124–1129 (2021)
27. Srivatsa, P., Plötz, T.: Using graphs to perform effective sensor-based human activity recognition in smart homes. Sensors **24**(12) (2024)

28. Wieland, C., Pankratius, V.: Tinygraphhar: enhancing human activity recognition with graph neural networks. In: 2023 IEEE World AI IoT Congress (AIIoT), pp. 0047–0054 (2023)
29. Wolf, C.T.: Explainability scenarios: towards scenario-based XAI design. In: Proceedings of the 24th International Conference on Intelligent User Interfaces, pp. 252–257 (2019)
30. Ye, J., Jiang, H., Zhong, J.: A graph-attention-based method for single-resident daily activity recognition in smart homes. Sensors **23**(3), 1626 (2023)
31. Ying, Z., Bourgeois, D., You, J., Zitnik, M., Leskovec, J.: Gnnexplainer: generating explanations for graph neural networks. Adv. Neural Inf. Proc. Syst. **32** (2019)

# Resource-Aware Mixed-Precision Quantization for Enhancing Deployability of Transformers for Time-Series Forecasting on Embedded FPGAs


Tianheng Ling[✉], Chao Qian, and Gregor Schiele

Intelligent Embedded Systems Lab, University of Duisburg-Essen,
47057 Duisburg, Germany
{tianheng.ling,chao.qian,gregor.schiele}@uni-due.de



**Abstract.** This study addresses the deployment challenges of integer-only quantized Transformers on resource-constrained embedded FPGAs (Xilinx Spartan-7 XC7S15). We enhanced the flexibility of our VHDL template by introducing a selectable resource type for storing intermediate results across model layers, thereby breaking the deployment bottleneck by utilizing BRAM efficiently. Moreover, we developed a resource-aware mixed-precision quantization approach that enables researchers to explore hardware-level quantization strategies without requiring extensive expertise in Neural Architecture Search. This method provides accurate resource utilization estimates with a precision discrepancy as low as 3%, compared to actual deployment metrics. Compared to previous work, our approach has successfully facilitated the deployment of model configurations utilizing mixed-precision quantization, thus overcoming the limitations inherent in five previously non-deployable configurations with uniform quantization bitwidths. Consequently, this research enhances the applicability of Transformers in embedded systems, facilitating a broader range of Transformer-powered applications on edge devices.

**Keywords:** Time-series Forecasting · Transformers · Mixed-precision Quantization · Embedded FPGAs · On-device Inference · Deployability


## 1 Introduction

The integration of Artificial Intelligence (AI) into the Internet of Things (IoT) is significantly reshaping interactions among devices, humans, and environments, enhancing decision-making capabilities and responsiveness [1]. Deploying Deep Learning (DL) models directly on edge devices, termed Edge Intelligence, leverages data proximity to improve the timeliness and relevance of computational tasks [2]. Local data processing under this paradigm can considerably reduce the need for continuous data transmission to the Cloud, thus minimizing latency, conserving bandwidth, and bolstering data privacy and security [3].


© ICST Institute for Computer Sciences, Social Informatics and Telecommunications Engineering 2026
Published by Springer Nature Switzerland AG 2026. All Rights Reserved
A. Soylu et al. (Eds.): MobiQuitous 2024, LNICST 634, pp. 361–381, 2026.
https://doi.org/10.1007/978-3-032-10554-7_20

Despite these advantages, implementing sophisticated DL models, such as Transformers, which are renowned for their efficacy in sequence modeling tasks, including time-series forecasting, encounters significant challenges on IoT devices [4]. These challenges primarily stem from the limited computational power and memory capacities of such platforms [5], which are critical for the widespread adoption of autonomous and efficient ubiquitous computing technologies [6]. A notable research gap exists in time-series forecasting with integer-only quantized Transformers on platforms like embedded Field-Programmable Gate Arrays (FPGAs). These FPGAs have been widely used to accelerate DL models but have yet to be thoroughly explored for this specific task [7].

Our previous work [8] investigated the implementation of integer-only quantized Transformers for time-series forecasting on Spartan-7 XC7S15 FPGA from Xilinx. The results demonstrated that our 4-bit quantized models achieved precision comparable to 6-bit quantized counterparts on a traffic flow dataset [9] and even outperformed 8-bit quantized counterparts on an air quality (AirU) dataset [10] by 2.83%. Additionally, we explored the feasibility of deploying models with various configurations on this embedded FPGA, examining their resource utilization, inference time, and power and energy consumption. Our findings indicated that while smaller models could be easily supported, larger models exceeded the resource capacities of the XC7S15 FPGA, thus highlighting a significant scalability issue.

This scalability challenge underpins our current research, which focuses on exploring and enhancing the deployability of Transformers on embedded FPGAs. The primary contributions of this paper are as follows:

- We enhanced the configurability of our solution by introducing selectable resource types for storing intermediate results across model layers. This enhancement enables the deployment of two previously infeasible model configurations by mitigating inefficient BRAM utilization.
- We extended our quantization framework to support mixed-precision quantization for Transformer models, incorporating resource awareness to streamline the selection process for deployable model configurations. By utilizing a knowledge database that catalogs the resource utilization of each model component, we can estimate the resource utilization for each configuration. This predictive capability allows us to pre-select potential candidate models based on threshold and score-based filtering for training and deployment.
- Our method efficiently navigates the extensive search space without requiring in-depth Neural Architecture Search expertise. The resource estimation based on our knowledge database shows only a 3% difference compared to Vivado's estimation, validating the reliability of our database as a robust foundation for advanced techniques, enabling their future integration.
- We systematically evaluated our approach against two baseline methods and performed further validation using Vivado's synthesis and actual hardware measurements.

The remainder of this paper is organized as follows: Sect. 2 describes the FPGA-friendly Transformer architecture tailored for time-series forecasting. Section 3 details the deployment challenges of complex Transformer models on resource-constrained FPGAs. Section 4 describes our strategic approaches to overcome these challenges. Section 5 presents the experimental results validating the effectiveness of our approaches. Section 6 reviews the relevant literature. Finally, Sect. 7 concludes the paper and suggests avenues for future research.

## 2   Transformers for Time-Series Forecasting

This section revisits the architecture of the FPGA-friendly Transformer tailored for single-step ahead time-series forecasting, as initially proposed in our prior work [8]. Figure 1 depicts the model, composed of three primary components: an input module, an encoder layer, and an output module. This modular structure allows the model to handle univariate and multivariate time-series.

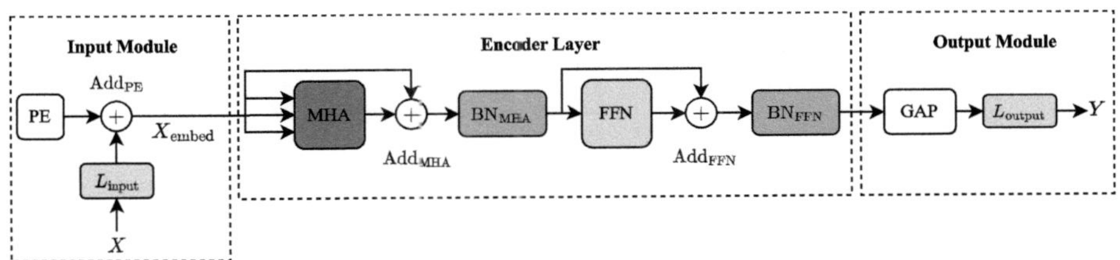



**Fig. 1.** The Architecture of the Transformer Model

The input module begins by processing the input sequence $X$, consisting of $n$ data points, each with $m$ dimensions. This process is facilitated by a linear layer (denoted $L_{input}$), which projects the input data into a higher-dimensional feature space ($d_{model}$). Positional Encoding (PE) is applied after that to incorporate positional information into the transformed data, resulting in $X_{embed}$ with dimensions $(n, d_{model})$. This embedding is then fed into the encoder layer. The encoder layer is structured around a Multi-head Self-attention (MHA) module coupled with a Feedforward Network (FFN) module. Each module is followed by Residual Connection (Add) and Batch Normalization (BN), enhancing stability and learning efficacy. The output module then consolidates the encoder layer's outputs using Global Average Pooling (GAP) and a final linear transformation (denoted $L_{output}$) to produce the forecast output $Y$.

We standardized several key dimensions to streamline the architecture and mitigate training complexity. Specifically, the dimensions of the query, key, value, and output vectors within the MHA module were unified at $d_{model}$, and the dimension of the FFN was expanded to $4 \times d_{model}$. Furthermore, the number of heads $h$ in the MHA was minimized to 1 for simplicity, as increasing $h$ does not obviously improve model precision on our target datasets.

In subsequent sections, we will applying mixed-precision quantization on this model by targeting specific key components: $L_{input}$, $Add_{PE}$, MHA, $Add_{MHA}$, $BN_{MHA}$, FFN, $Add_{FFN}$, $BN_{FFN}$, GAP, and $L_{output}$. These components are selected due to their crucial role in balancing model precision and deployment efficiency. Our design also allows researchers and developers to adapt the granularity by grouping or separating our key components to meet the specific needs of their applications. For example, the FFN module can be dissected into two linear layers with an intervening ReLU activation function.

## 3   Problem Statement

Our previous work [8] evaluated the deployment of Transformer models with various configurations on the XC7S15 FPGA, focusing on different input sequence lengths $(n)$, embedding dimensions $(d_{\mathrm{model}})$, and quantization bitwidths $(b)$. It highlighted that configurations with smaller dimensions often incurred significant losses in model precision while adhering to hardware constraints. In contrast, bigger configurations had better model precision but frequently exceeded the resource capacities of FPGAs even with low quantization bitwidth.

**Table 1.** Resource Utilization of Transformers on XC7S15 FPGA [8]

| $n$ | $d_{\mathrm{model}}$ | $b$ | | | | | | | | |
|---|---|---|---|---|---|---|---|---|---|---|
| | | 4 | | | 6 | | | 8 | | |
| | | LUTs | BRAM | DSPs | LUTs | BRAM | DSPs | LUTs | BRAM | DSPs |
| 6 | 8 | 34.2 | 10.0 | 65.0 | 42.0 | 10.0 | 90.0 | 55.6 | 10.0 | 100.0 |
| | 16 | 37.3 | 30.0 | 65.0 | 47.0 | 30.0 | 95.0 | 57.1 | 40.0 | 100.0 |
| | 32 | 41.1 | 40.0 | 65.0 | 50.5 | 55.0 | 95.0 | 62.7 | 55.0 | 100.0 |
| | 64 | 47.4 | 75.0 | 60.0 | 57.2 | 100.0 | 90.0 | 89.5 | 100.0 | 100.0 |
| 12 | 8 | 36.5 | 10.0 | 65.0 | 46.0 | 10.0 | 95.0 | 58.0 | 20.0 | 100.0 |
| | 16 | 42.7 | 35.0 | 60.0 | 51.5 | 35.0 | 95.0 | 65.1 | 45.0 | 100.0 |
| | 32 | 46.8 | 40.0 | 65.0 | 58.9 | 55.0 | 95.0 | 74.3 | 60.0 | 100.0 |
| | 64 | 58.2 | 75.0 | 65.0 | 75.3 | 100.0 | 95.0 | **115.0** | **100.0** | **100.0** |
| 18 | 8 | 40.8 | 15.0 | 55.0 | 49.9 | 15.0 | 95.0 | 63.4 | 20.0 | 100.0 |
| | 16 | 45.8 | 35.0 | 65.0 | 55.8 | 35.0 | 95.0 | 71.0 | 45.0 | 100.0 |
| | 32 | 53.0 | 40.0 | 65.0 | 67.0 | 55.0 | 95.0 | 85.3 | 60.0 | 100.0 |
| | 64 | **72.8** | **75.0** | **60.0** | **93.6†** | **100.0** | **90.0** | **136.5** | **100.0** | **100.0** |
| 24 | 8 | 39.2 | 15.0 | 50.0 | 52.7 | 20.0 | 90.0 | 67.8 | 20.0 | 100.0 |
| | 16 | 48.7 | 40.0 | 65.0 | 60.7 | 40.0 | 95.0 | 77.4 | 45.0 | 100.0 |
| | 32 | 58.3 | 45.0 | 65.0 | 73.7 | 60.0 | 95.0 | **99.5*** | **60.0** | **100.0** |
| | 64 | **82.4**** | **80.0** | **65.0** | **107.8** | **100.0** | **90.0** | **157.6** | **100.0** | **100.0** |

† The utilization of DRAM is 105.5%.
⋆ The utilization of DRAM is 112.5%.
⋆⋆ The utilization of DRAM is 104.4%.

To gain a detailed understanding of the specific resource bottlenecks that prevented these model configurations from being deployed, we executed multiple Vivdao syntheses for these eight configurations, whose resource utilization ware highlighted in the Table 1. The 4-bit quantized model with configuration $n = 18$ and $d_{\mathrm{model}} = 64$ was previously considered too resource-intensive to be deployed. As colored in green in Table 1, this model now meets FPGA constraints with additional synthesis iterations. This discrepancy indicates that local minima might have affected initial synthesis, highlighting the need for multiple synthesis iterations to verify deployability accurately.

Further investigation revealed that two configurations (colored in yellow in Table 1) maxed out LUTs as memory (DRAM) but left significant portions of Block RAM (BRAM) underutilized. For instance, the 8-bit quantized model with $n = 24$ and $d_{\text{model}} = 32$ displayed near-maximal utilization of Look-Up Tables (LUTs) at 99.5% and DRAM at 112.5%, yet 40% of BRAM remained unused. Similarly, the 4-bit model with $n = 24$ and $d_{\text{model}} = 64$ utilized 82.4% of LUTs and 104.42% of DRAM, with 20% of BRAM still available. These findings indicate that prior implementations may over-allocate DRAM resources while leaving a significant portion of BRAM underutilized. Thus, an in-depth investigation into optimizing resource allocation is warranted to enhance efficiency.

Moreover, as colored in pink in Table 1, the remaining five configurations were non-deployable as they exhausted all FPGA resources. For example, the 8-bit quantized model with $n = 12$ and $d_{\text{model}} = 64$ exceeded the FPGA's LUT capacity and fully utilized the available BRAM, rendering deployment infeasible. Similarly, while the LUT utilization for the 6-bit quantized model with $n = 18$ and $d_{\text{model}} = 64$ remained within acceptable limits, its DRAM was over-utilized at 105.5%.

We believe that quantization with uniform bitwidth across all model layers may be contributing to excessive resource consumption and unacceptable drops in precision. To address these issues, recent studies [11–13] advocate for mixed-precision quantization, which assigns varied bitwidths to different layers or components. However, this approach necessitates the efficient selection of optimal combinations of layer-specific bitwidths. The entire workflow—from selecting quantization bitwidths and conducting quantization-aware training (QAT) to model convergence, synthesizing hardware accelerators, and reviewing Vivado reports—often results in substantial time and effort. This issue is particularly pronounced when, after extensive efforts, the final model fails to fit the FPGA [14]. Thus, integrating resource awareness early in the workflow is crucial to streamline the deployment process and mitigate potential inefficiencies.

## 4 Proposed Solutions

This section delineates our proposed solutions for embedded FPGAs. Building on the challenges identified in Sect. 3, we focus on two principal approaches: 1) adaptive resource allocation and 2) resource-aware mixed-precision quantization.

### 4.1 Adaptive Resource Allocation

In our prior designs of the Transformer accelerator [8], memory allocation was predominantly designated for two purposes: 1) storing model parameters (including weights, biases, and positional encoding information) in BRAM, and 2) accommodating intermediate computational results in DRAM. Initially, it was presumed that model parameters would necessitate more memory than intermediate results, leading to the prioritization of DRAM for intermediate results to maximize the availability of BRAM for model parameters. However, subsequent analysis of accelerator implementations from our earlier work [8] indicated that this approach could lead to underutilization of BRAM resources and overutilization of DRAM, as mentioned in Sect. 3. This issue becomes more pronounced with increasing input sequence lengths in the Transformer model, where the volume of intermediate computation results can surpass that of the model parameters.

To rectify this misalignment, we introduce a configurable parameter within the VHDL template that explicitly specifies the type of resource: 1) BRAM, 2) DRAM, or 3) automatic allocation (BRAM or DRAM) by Vivado for storing intermediate results. This enhancement introduces flexibility in resource allocation for intermediate results, allowing adaptations based on each model's specific condition. For instance, intermediate results can be organized by size at the model level, prioritizing the storage of larger intermediate results in BRAM wherever feasible, thereby optimizing resource efficiency. In this work, we prefer to apply option 3 to rely on Vivado's algorithm to find feasible solutions. Manual intervention remains possible, enabling users to adjust settings if automatic allocation does not yield the desired outcomes. With option 3, we successfully deployed two models previously deemed non-deployable, highlighted in yellow in Table 1, on the XC7S15 FPGA. Detailed results of these deployments are thoroughly discussed in Sect. 5.2.

### 4.2   Mixed-Precision Quantized Transformer

Building upon the optimized resource allocation, we further explore the resource-aware mixed-precision quantization. This exploration unfolds in two steps: 1) transitioning from uniform to mixed-precision quantization and 2) introducing resource awareness within the mixed-precision quantization.

**Transition to Mixed-Precision Quantization.** In our preceding study [8], quantization with uniform bitwidths was applied across all layers. As detailed on the left side in Fig. 2, in a typical linear layer under uniform 8-bit quantization, inputs ($X_q$), outputs ($Y_q$), and weights ($W_q$) were processed using an 8-bit asymmetric scheme. To reduce computational overhead, biases ($B_q$) adopted a symmetric quantization scheme using a quantization scale factor determined by $X_q$ and $W_q$. The quantization bitwidth for $B_q$ was set to 18 bits, a value derived from the bitwidth of the multiply-accumulator unit in this linear layer.

The current work expands on these foundations and introduces a mixed-precision quantization, permitting individual layers to operate with distinct bitwidths. In our case, the quantization bitwidth of the layer's inputs is dictated by the quantization bitwidth of the preceding layer's outputs to avoid additional rescaling caused by bitwidth mismatches. Hence, it is not specified independently within our naming conventions. Illustratively, as depicted on the right side of Fig. 2, using mixed 8-bit quantization as example, where $W_q$ and $Y_q$ within a linear layer are quantized at 8 bits, while the $X_q$ can vary between 4, 6, or 8 bits depending on the preceding layer's $Y_q$. This cascading effect also influences the quantization bitwidth of $B_q$, which varies from 14 to 18 bits.

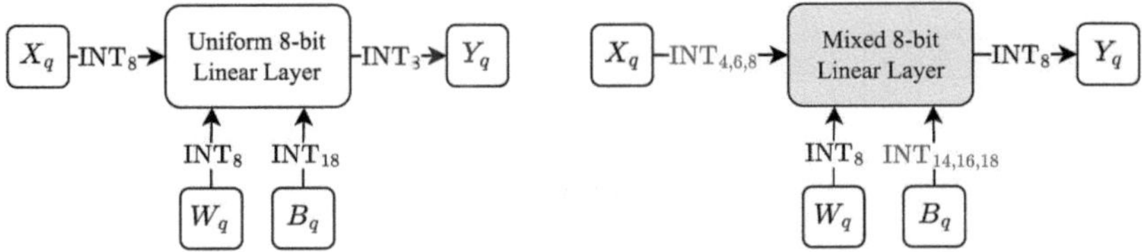

**Fig. 2.** Uniform (left) vs Mixed (right) 8-bit Linear Layer

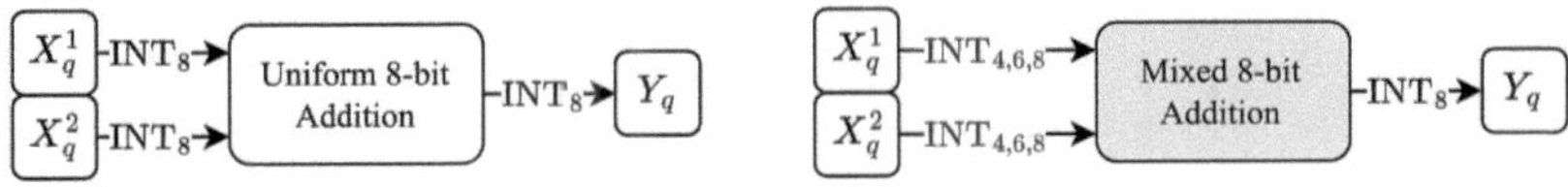

**Fig. 3.** Uniform (left) vs Mixed (right) 8-bit Addition Operation

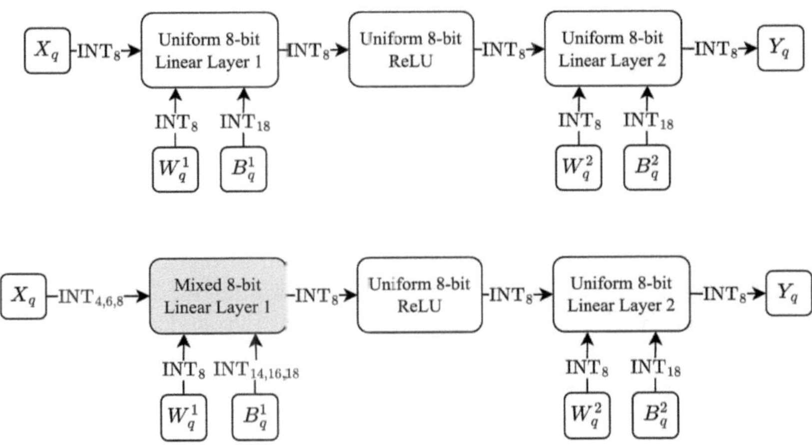

**Fig. 4.** Uniform (up) vs Mixed (down) 8-bit FFN Module

This principle of mixed-precision quantization are also applied to other operations and modules in the Transformer model. For instance, Fig. 3 illustrates a mixed 8-bit quantized addition operation where the bitwidths of its Inputs1 ($X_q^1$) and Inputs2 ($X_q^2$) are determined by the previous layers' outputs, but its outputs ($Y_q$) remains at 8 bits. For mixed-precision quantized modules such as the FFN, depicted in Fig. 4, only the initial linear layer utilizes mixed 8-bit quantization. Subsequent operations within this module consistently maintain uniform 8-bit quantization.

**Resource-Aware Mixed-Precision Quantization.** As illustrated in Fig. 5, we proposed an extended workflow of implementing our resource-aware approach to the mixed-precision quantized Transformers. This workflow is segmented into four phases: 1) Preparation, 2) Estimation, 3) Filtering, and 4) Validation. Each

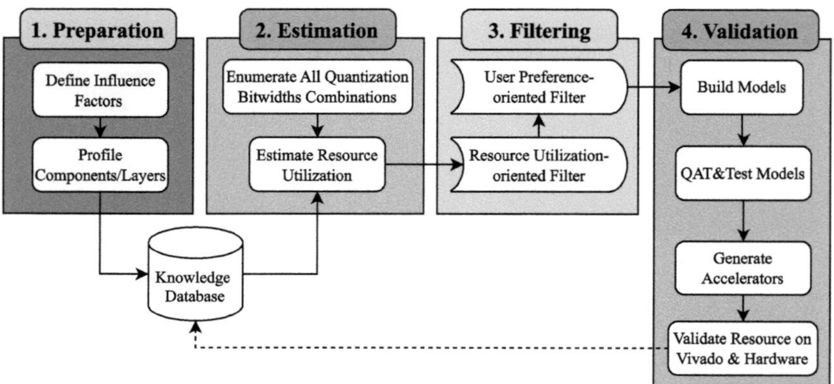



**Fig. 5.** Workflow of Resource-aware Mixed-precision Quantization

phase plays a crucial role in ensuring that the models are optimized for the resource constraints of embedded FPGAs.

*Phase 1: Preparation.* The initial phase involves developing a comprehensive knowledge database for subsequent phases. Initially, we identify key factors influencing model precision and resource utilization. We then select the key components of the model for profiling. Following this, variations in these factors are systematically explored. This process involves training models under varying conditions, generating accelerators, and synthesizing detailed resource utilization reports. Each report details the resource breakdown for individual components, culminating in a comprehensive lookup table called the knowledge database. The preparation of this database will be detailed in Sect. 4.3.

*Phase 2: Estimation.* Utilizing the knowledge database, this phase predicts the resource utilization of mixed-precision quantized models with various quantization bitwidth combinations. The estimation process entails consulting the knowledge database for each key component to assess its resource consumption. These individual estimations are then aggregated to ascertain the total resource consumption of a model. Users can enumerate all quantization bitwidth combinations or specify a subset based on their domain knowledge and specific requirements. In Sect. 4.4, we will further introduce the resource estimation process executed in our study.

*Phase 3: Filtering.* The filtering phase strategically selects a limited number of model candidates for further training and accelerator generation. Initially, this phase employs a threshold-based filter for each resource type, which excludes models whose estimated resource consumption exceeds predefined limits. It can be supplemented by additional user-defined criteria that refine the selection process to meet specific deployment requirements. Section 4.4 will explain the filters implemented in our study.

*Phase 4: Validation.* The final phase validates models with the chosen bitwidth combinations through a rigorous process involving model construction, QAT, and performance testing. Each model's resource utilization and operational efficiency are evaluated using Vivado and actual FPGA hardware. In addition, while not yet implemented, reports generated during the validation phase hold the potential to enrich the knowledge database, thereby enhancing its predictive accuracy and robustness.

### 4.3   Preparation of Knowledge Database

To address the deployability challenges identified in prior research [8], this study defines three influence factors for constructing a knowledge database: 1) input sequence length $(n)$, 2) embedding dimension $(d_{\mathrm{model}})$, and 3) quantization bitwidth $(b)$. Expressly, $d_{\mathrm{model}}$ is uniformly set to 64, while sequence lengths are selected as 12, 18, and 24, paired with uniform quantization bitwidths of 4, 6, and 8 bits. This setup creates a total of 9 different model configurations.

As mentioned in Sect. 2, our study mainly profiles model components: $L_{\mathrm{input}}$, $\mathrm{Add}_{\mathrm{PE}}$, MHA, $\mathrm{Add}_{\mathrm{MHA}}$, $\mathrm{BN}_{\mathrm{MHA}}$, FFN, $\mathrm{Add}_{\mathrm{FFN}}$, $\mathrm{BN}_{\mathrm{FFN}}$, GAP, and $L_{\mathrm{output}}$. Furthermore, our study also incorporates the resource overhead from $O_{\mathrm{model}}$, $O_{\mathrm{encoder\ layer}}$, and $O_{\mathrm{middleware}}$, attributable to LUTs required for component interconnections and data buffering.

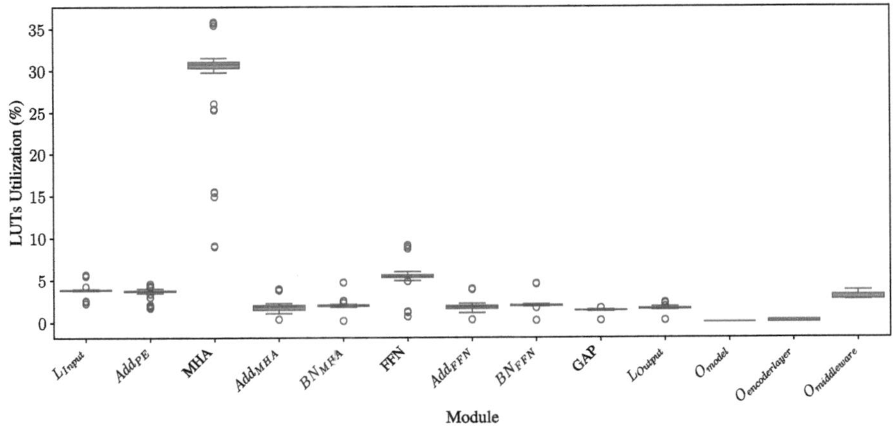

**Fig. 6.** LUTs Utilization Cross Key Components for $n=12$, $d_{\mathrm{model}} = 64$ and $b=4$

For each model configuration, 50 training sessions are conducted, generating 450 distinct accelerators. Each accelerator undergoes five separate synthesis iterations to aggregate the knowledge database, primarily focusing on LUTs, DRAM, BRAM, and DSPs. Derived from 250 resource utilization reports, Fig. 6 demonstrates the distribution of LUTs utilization across key components, focusing on the configuration where $n = 12$ and $b = 4$. The analysis reveals that the

LUTs utilization of each component has a slight variation. However, the presence of outliers, likely due to the optimization algorithms utilized by Vivado, suggests variability in synthesis outcomes.

To mitigate the impact of such variability, median values are employed to provide a more stable representation of resource utilization. Through an extensive analysis of 2250 utilization reports, we constructed a knowledge database, as cataloged in Table 2. This database has been systematically validated for accuracy and dependability on quantized models with uniform quantization bitwidths. For instance, the median LUT utilization for the model configuration with $n = 12$ at a 4-bit quantization is predicted to be 57.2%, aligning closely with previous measurements of 58.1% on actual FPGA hardware (as detailed in Table 1), confirming the reliability of the database.

### 4.4 Resource Estimation and Filtering

In this study, we introduce an algorithm designed to perform resource estimation and filtering efficiently. Algorithm 1 supports the systematic selection of mixed-precision quantization bitwidth combinations. This algorithm commences with selecting input sequence lengths $(n)$, correlated with the entries in the knowledge database $K_n$. Furthermore, upper limit thresholds for each resource type, including $T_{\mathrm{LUTs}}$, $T_{\mathrm{DRAM}}$, $T_{\mathrm{BRAM}}$, and $T_{\mathrm{DSPs}}$, are established to define the maximum permissible resource usage. A set of quantization bitwidth combinations $(C_{\mathrm{all}})$ that the user wants to explore should also be input.

---

**Algorithm 1.** The Process of Selecting Mixed-precision Combination

---

1: **Input:** Knowledge database $K_n$, thresholds $T_{\mathrm{LUTs}}$, $T_{\mathrm{DRAM}}$, $T_{\mathrm{BRAM}}$, $T_{\mathrm{DSPs}}$, quantization combinations $C_{\mathrm{all}}$

2: **Output:** Selected quantization combinations $C_{\mathrm{selected}}$

3: **Procedure:**

4: Initialize an empty list $C_{\mathrm{filtered}}$

5: **for** each combination $c$ in $C_{\mathrm{all}}$ **do**

6:     Estimate $\mathrm{Util}_{\mathrm{LUTs}}$, $\mathrm{Util}_{\mathrm{DRAM}}$, $\mathrm{Util}_{\mathrm{BRAM}}$, $\mathrm{Util}_{\mathrm{DSPs}}$ for $c$ using $K_n$

7:     **if** $\mathrm{Util}_{\mathrm{LUTs}} \leq T_{\mathrm{LUTs}}$ **and** $\mathrm{Util}_{\mathrm{DRAM}} \leq T_{\mathrm{DRAM}}$ **and** $\mathrm{Util}_{\mathrm{BRAM}} \leq T_{\mathrm{BRAM}}$ **and** $\mathrm{Util}_{\mathrm{DSPs}} \leq T_{\mathrm{DSPs}}$ **then**

8:         Compute $sum(c) = \sum_{i=1}^{10} c_i$

9:         Append $[c, sum(c)]$ to $C_{\mathrm{filtered}}$

10:     **end if**

11: **end for**

12: Sort $C_{\mathrm{filtered}}$ by $sum(c)$ in descending order

13: $C_{\mathrm{selected}} \leftarrow$ Select the top 5 combinations from $C_{\mathrm{filtered}}$

14: **Output:** $C_{\mathrm{selected}}$

---

Initially, the resource utilization for each combination is estimated and compared against these thresholds, as detailed in steps 5–11 of Algorithm 1. Combinations that adhere to these criteria are then included in $C_{\mathrm{filtered}}$. Applying a

**Table 2.** Knowledge Database of Resource Utilization

| $n$ | Components | LUTs | | | DRAM | | | BRAM | | | DSPs | | |
|---|---|---|---|---|---|---|---|---|---|---|---|---|---|
| | | 4-bit | 6-bit | 8-bit | 4-bit | 6-bit | 8-bit | 4-bit | 6-bit | 8-bit | 4-bit | 6-bit | 8-bit |
| 12 | $L_{\text{input}}$ | 3.9 | 5.6 | 7.1 | 4.0 | 5.3 | 8.0 | 5.0 | 0.0 | 0.0 | 5.0 | 5.0 | 5.0 |
| | $\text{Add}_{\text{PE}}$ | 3.8 | 4.4 | 5.7 | 4.0 | 5.3 | 8.0 | 5.0 | 0.0 | 0.0 | 0.0 | 10.0 | 10.0 |
| | MHA | 30.8 | 35.6 | 61.3 | 14.3 | 29.8 | 44.7 | 15.0 | 30.0 | 10.0 | 30.0 | 30.0 | 30.0 |
| | $\text{Add}_{\text{MHA}}$ | 1.8 | 3.9 | 5.1 | 0.0 | 5.3 | 8.0 | 5.0 | 0.0 | 0.0 | 0.0 | 10.0 | 10.0 |
| | $\text{BN}_{\text{MHA}}$ | 1.9 | 4.7 | 5.3 | 0.0 | 5.3 | 8.0 | 5.0 | 0.0 | 0.0 | 5.0 | 5.0 | 10.0 |
| | FFN | 5.4 | 8.9 | 11.4 | 0.0 | 5.3 | 8.0 | 55.0 | 70.0 | 90.0 | 10.0 | 10.0 | 10.0 |
| | $\text{Add}_{\text{FFN}}$ | 1.8 | 3.9 | 5.0 | 0.0 | 5.3 | 8.0 | 5.0 | 0.0 | 0.0 | 0.0 | 10.0 | 10.0 |
| | $\text{BN}_{\text{FFN}}$ | 2.0 | 4.5 | 5.0 | 0.0 | 5.3 | 8.0 | 5.0 | 0.0 | 0.0 | 5.0 | 5.0 | 10.0 |
| | GAP | 1.4 | 1.6 | 1.9 | 0.3 | 0.3 | 0.5 | 0.0 | 0.0 | 0.0 | 5.0 | 5.0 | 5.0 |
| | $L_{\text{output}}$ | 1.8 | 2.2 | 2.4 | 0.2 | 0.2 | 0.3 | 0.0 | 0.0 | 0.0 | 5.0 | 5.0 | 5.0 |
| | $O_{\text{model}}$ | 0.0 | 0.0 | 0.0 | 0.0 | 0.0 | 0.0 | 0.0 | 0.0 | 0.0 | 0.0 | 0.0 | 0.0 |
| | $O_{\text{encoder layer}}$ | 0.0 | 0.3 | 0.3 | 0.0 | 0.0 | 0.0 | 0.0 | 0.0 | 0.0 | 0.0 | 0.0 | 0.0 |
| | $O_{\text{middleware}}$ | 2.7 | 3.2 | 3.7 | 0.5 | 0.7 | 0.0 | 0.0 | 0.0 | 1.0 | 0.0 | 0.0 | 0.0 |
| 18 | $L_{\text{input}}$ | 5.6 | 8.1 | 10.4 | 8.0 | 10.7 | 16.0 | 5.0 | 0.0 | 0.0 | 5.0 | 5.0 | 5.0 |
| | $\text{Add}_{\text{PE}}$ | 5.4 | 6.7 | 8.9 | 8.0 | 10.7 | 16.0 | 5.0 | 0.0 | 0.0 | 0.0 | 10.0 | 10.0 |
| | MHA | 40.1 | 53.4 | 86.1 | 36.3 | 59.2 | 88.7 | 10.0 | 20.0 | 0.0 | 0.0 | 30.0 | 30.0 |
| | $\text{Add}_{\text{MHA}}$ | 1.8 | 6.2 | 8.4 | 0.0 | 10.7 | 16.0 | 5.0 | 0.0 | 0.0 | 0.0 | 10.0 | 10.0 |
| | $\text{BN}_{\text{MHA}}$ | 1.9 | 6.9 | 8.3 | 0.0 | 10.7 | 16.0 | 5.0 | 0.0 | 0.0 | 5.0 | 5.0 | 10.0 |
| | FFN | 5.6 | 11.4 | 14.6 | 0.0 | 10.7 | 16.0 | 60.0 | 75.0 | 100.0 | 10.0 | 10.0 | 10.0 |
| | $\text{Add}_{\text{FFN}}$ | 1.8 | 6.2 | 8.4 | 0.0 | 10.7 | 16.0 | 5.0 | 0.0 | 0.0 | 0.0 | 10.0 | 10.0 |
| | $\text{BN}_{\text{FFN}}$ | 1.9 | 6.7 | 8.2 | 0.0 | 10.7 | 16.0 | 5.0 | 0.0 | 0.0 | 5.0 | 5.0 | 10.0 |
| | GAP | 1.4 | 1.8 | 2.0 | 0.3 | 0.3 | 0.5 | 0.0 | 0.0 | 0.0 | 5.0 | 5.0 | 5.0 |
| | $L_{\text{output}}$ | 1.6 | 2.2 | 2.4 | 0.2 | 0.2 | 0.3 | 0.0 | 0.0 | 0.0 | 5.0 | 5.0 | 5.0 |
| | $O_{\text{model}}$ | 0.0 | 0.0 | 0.0 | 0.0 | 0.0 | 0.0 | 0.0 | 0.0 | 0.0 | 0.0 | 0.0 | 0.0 |
| | $O_{\text{encoder layer}}$ | 0.3 | 0.4 | 0.6 | 0.0 | 0.0 | 0.0 | 0.0 | 0.0 | 0.0 | 0.0 | 0.0 | 0.0 |
| | $O_{\text{middleware}}$ | 3.0 | 3.4 | 3.7 | 0.5 | 0.7 | 1.0 | 0.0 | 0.0 | 0.0 | 0.0 | 0.0 | 0.0 |
| 24 | $L_{\text{input}}$ | 5.5 | 7.8 | 10.4 | 8.0 | 10.7 | 16.0 | 5.0 | 0.0 | 0.0 | 5.0 | 5.0 | 5.0 |
| | $\text{Add}_{\text{PE}}$ | 5.4 | 6.7 | 8.9 | 8.0 | 10.7 | 16.0 | 5.0 | 0.0 | 0.0 | 0.0 | 10.0 | 10.0 |
| | MHA | 45.2 | 55.6 | 89.2 | 48.3 | 64.5 | 96.7 | 5.0 | 20.0 | 0.0 | 30.0 | 30.0 | 30.0 |
| | $\text{Add}_{\text{MHA}}$ | 2.0 | 6.2 | 8.4 | 0.0 | 10.7 | 16.0 | 5.0 | 0.0 | 0.0 | 0.0 | 10.0 | 10.0 |
| | $\text{BN}_{\text{MHA}}$ | 2.0 | 6.9 | 8.3 | 0.0 | 10.7 | 16.0 | 5.0 | 0.0 | 0.0 | 5.0 | 5.0 | 10.0 |
| | FFN | 5.6 | 11.3 | 14.6 | 0.0 | 10.7 | 16.0 | 60.0 | 75.0 | 100.0 | 10.0 | 10.0 | 10.0 |
| | $\text{Add}_{\text{FFN}}$ | 1.8 | 6.2 | 8.3 | 0.0 | 10.7 | 16.0 | 5.0 | 0.0 | 0.0 | 0.0 | 10.0 | 10.0 |
| | $\text{BN}_{\text{FFN}}$ | 1.9 | 6.8 | 8.2 | 0.0 | 10.7 | 16.0 | 5.0 | 0.0 | 0.0 | 5.0 | 5.0 | 10.0 |
| | GAP | 1.4 | 1.7 | 2.0 | 0.3 | 0.3 | 0.5 | 0.0 | 0.0 | 0.0 | 5.0 | 5.0 | 5.0 |
| | $L_{\text{output}}$ | 1.6 | 2.3 | 2.4 | 0.2 | 0.2 | 0.3 | 0.0 | 0.0 | 0.0 | 5.0 | 5.0 | 5.0 |
| | $O_{\text{model}}$ | 0.0 | 0.0 | 0.0 | 0.0 | 0.0 | 0.0 | 0.0 | 0.0 | 0.0 | 0.0 | 0.0 | 0.0 |
| | $O_{\text{encoder layer}}$ | 0.0 | 0.4 | 0.6 | 0.0 | 0.0 | 0.0 | 0.0 | 0.0 | 0.0 | 0.0 | 0.0 | 0.0 |
| | $O_{\text{middleware}}$ | 2.7 | 3.3 | 3.9 | 0.0 | 1.0 | 1.5 | 5.0 | 0.0 | 0.0 | 0.0 | 0.0 | 0.0 |

higher threshold will potentially lead to the remaining combinations having more components quantized to higher bitwidth. Decreasing these thresholds allows us to spare resources for other logic, such as data preprocessing when necessary.

Despite resource constraint filtering, the number of feasible combinations can remain extensive. To manage this effectively, we applied sorting on them, outlined in lines 8, 9, and 12 of the algorithm, where combinations $C_{\text{filtered}}$ are evaluated based on the cumulative sum of their layers' quantization bitwidths. These scores are subsequently used to rank the combinations, selecting the top five $C_{\text{selected}}$ for further development into mixed-precision quantized models. This scoring mechanism, although fundamental, lays the groundwork for more advanced filtering techniques in future enhancements. Notably, our algorithm identifies five viable candidates of 59,049 combinations within 10 s for each $n$, whereas in previous work, synthesizing a single accelerator with Vivado required over one minute.

## 5    Experiments and Evaluation

This section describes the experimental setup and subsequent analyses conducted to validate the efficacy of the proposed adaptive resource allocation and our resource-aware mixed-precision quantization.

### 5.1    Experiments Setup

Out experiments utilize the *AirU* dataset[1], which comprises multivariate air quality measurements with 19,380 data entries. After rectifying discontinuities, the dataset was narrowed to 15,258 feature-target pairs, allocated into 14,427 for training and 831 for testing, aligning with the test period configuration reported in [10]. Data normalization was uniformly applied using MinMax scaling to ensure consistency of input features.

Each model configuration underwent 50 training sessions, with each session comprising 100 epochs. An early stopping mechanism with 10 patience epochs was employed to mitigate overfitting. The training was executed using batches of 256 samples, with the Adam optimizer (with $\beta_1 = 0.9$, $\beta_2 = 0.98$, $\epsilon = 10^{-9}$). The learning rate was set at 0.001 and was adjusted through a decay scheduler, which halved the rate every three epochs. These training sessions were conducted on an NVIDIA GeForce RTX 2080 SUPER GPU, utilizing CUDA 11.0 and PyTorch 3.11 within the Ubuntu operating system. The objective metric for training was the minimization of the Mean Squared Error. In evaluation, model outputs and targets were inverse transformed from their normalized states, and the Root Mean Square Error (RMSE) was computed to assess model performance.

The quantized models were converted into their hardware equivalents through Python scripts that translated model and quantization parameters into VHDL code using predefined templates. The VHDL files were synthesized in Vivado to evaluate resource utilization, timing, and power metrics. The performance and efficiency of the synthesized FPGA accelerators were validated on the ElasticNode V5 hardware platform [15], equipped with an XC7S15 FPGA.

---

[1] https://dx.doi.org/10.21227/aeh2-a413.

## 5.2   Experiment 1: Adaptive Resource Allocation

This experiment was designed to assess the efficacy of the adaptive resource allocation approach on XC7S15 FPGA. By employing optimized VHDL templates and configuring the storage of intermediate results with the automatic allocation option, we allowed Vivado to optimize resource allocation within the FPGA constraints autonomously. Expressly, the synthesis strategy was set to maximize BRAM utilization, anticipating full utilization prior to the saturation of DRAM.

**Table 3.** Optimized Resource Utilization of Two Model Configurations

| Configs. $(n,d_{\mathrm{model}},b)$ | | Resource Utilization (%) | | | |
|---|---|---|---|---|---|
| | | LUTs | DRAM | BRAM | DSPs |
| (24, 32, 8) | in [8] | 99.5 | 112.5 | 60.0 | 100 |
| | this work | 73.3 | 41.3 | 100.0 | 100.0 |
| (24, 64, 4) | in [8] | 82.4 | 104.4 | 80.0 | 65.0 |
| | this work | 74.6 | 56.8 | 100.0 | 65.0 |

Table 3 shows the current resource utilization for model configurations that previously exceeded FPGA constraints (highlighted in yellow in Table 1). These configurations now conform to fit the XC7S15 FPGA. Notably, BRAM utilization reached 100%, affirming our synthesis strategy's efficacy.

## 5.3   Experiment 2: Resource-Aware Mixed-Precision Quantization

Based on the optimization in Experiment 1, this experiment assesses the feasibility of our resource-aware mixed-precision quantization. Focusing on the ten key components identified in Sect. 2, each component has the option of being quantized at 4, 6, or 8 bits. This setup generates a total of $3^{10} = 59,049$ potential combinations for each input sequence length $(n)$. Notably, components such as $O_{\mathrm{model}}$, $O_{\mathrm{encoder\ layer}}$, and $O_{\mathrm{middleware}}$ are automatically adjusted based on the key components' settings to streamline the deployment process. Moreover, to verify the effectiveness of our approach, we compare it against two baselines.

**Baseline 1: Random Combination.** We randomly selected five quantization bitwidth combinations from 59,049 potential mixed-precision configurations to establish Baseline 1 and constructed models for three distinct input sequence lengths $(n)$, totaling 15 configurations. Table 4 describes the experimental outcomes, showcasing the minimum RMSE and the median resource utilization for each configuration across FPGA resources. The "combinations" column specifies the bitwidth combination for each component: $L_{\mathrm{input}}$, $\mathrm{Add_{PE}}$, MHA, $\mathrm{Add_{MHA}}$, $\mathrm{BN}_{MHA}$, FFN, $\mathrm{Add_{FFN}}$, $\mathrm{BN}_{FFN}$, GAP, and $L_{\mathrm{output}}$.

As highlighted in pink in Table 4, we found that 10 of the 15 configurations failed to meet FPGA resource constraints. We assume that the high failure rate in model deployment is primarily attributed to assigning 4-bit quantization to components with fewer parameters and lower computational overhead, while more complex components are quantized at 6 or 8 bits. This outcome illustrates the inherent inefficiencies and deployment challenges associated with random quantization bitwidth assignments, underscoring the need for a more targeted approach in the selection process.

**Table 4.** Resource Utilization of Baseline 1

| $n$ | Combination | Measured Utilization (%) | | | | RMSE |
|---|---|---|---|---|---|---|
| | | LUT | DRAM | BRAM | DSP | |
| 12 | | 95.0 | 92.3 | 100.0 | 100.0 | 4.46 |
| 18 | 4, 8, 8, 6, 8, 6, 8, 8, 4, 6 | 140.0 | 183.0 | 95.0 | 100.0 | 4.30 |
| 24 | | 143.4 | 191.3 | 95.0 | 100.0 | 4.20 |
| 12 | | 93.3 | 87.5 | 100.0 | 95.0 | 5.22 |
| 18 | 8, 8, 8, 4, 8, 6, 4, 4, 4, 4 | 136.5 | 172.8 | 95.0 | 95.0 | 4.95 |
| 24 | | 139.3 | 181.3 | 95.0 | 100.0 | 5.24 |
| 12 | | 86.2 | 90.0 | 100.0 | 95.0 | 4.50 |
| 18 | 4, 8, 8, 4, 8, 4, 8, 8, 8, 8 | 115.9 | 162.0 | 100.0 | 95.0 | 4.26 |
| 24 | | 124.8 | 185.5 | 100.0 | 95.0 | 4.33 |
| 12 | | 72.9 | 73.7 | 100.0 | 85.0 | 4.49 |
| 18 | 6, 4, 6, 8, 6, 4, 4, 8, 6, 6 | 94.51 | 121.7 | 100.0 | 87.5 | 4.59 |
| 24 | | 102.5 | 142.3 | 100.0 | 85.0 | 4.84 |
| 12 | | 79.1 | 70.2 | 100.0 | 80.0 | 4.93 |
| 18 | 8, 4, 6, 6, 4, 6, 4, 8, 4, 8 | 113.4 | 138.2 | 95.0 | 82.5 | 4.67 |
| 24 | | 116.0 | 144.0 | 95.0 | 80.0 | 4.35 |

**Baseline 2: Experience-Based Combination.** Building upon insights garnered from Baseline 1, Baseline 2 refined the quantization by specifically assigning a 4-bit quantization to the MHA and FFN modules, which are characterized by higher parameter counts and compuational overhead. Subsequently, these revised configurations underwent synthesis and were appraised using the identical evaluative benchmarks established in Baseline 1. Table 5 presents the outcomes of Baseline 2, illustrating the successful FPGA deployment of all revised model configurations, thereby validating the efficacy of targeted bitwidth assignments.

Additionally, the latter two columns of Table 5 detail the models' precision in terms of RMSE, alongside comparisons to Baseline 1. We found that while 7 out of the 15 models demonstrated a decrease in RMSE, the remaining 8 models experienced an increase in RMSE. Among these 7 models, 4 models had already implemented a 4-bit quantized FFN during Baseline 1, necessitating only the quantization of MHA to 4-bit in Baseline 2. It is posited that the imposition of a 4-bit constraint on the FFN module may act as a computational bottleneck. However, the concurrent reduction of MHA's bitwidth did not substantially exacerbate RMSE outcomes. Conversely, the additional reduction in bitwidths for FFN and MHA for the remaining three models potentially alleviated overfitting, thereby enhancing the models' generalization capability.

**Our Approach.** Baseline 1 demonstrated the pitfalls of relying solely on random configuration selections, often culminating in inefficient and unsuccessful deployments. Moreover, Baseline 2 incorporated empirical insights to enhance deployment success rates. However, this approach did not stabilize model accuracy, as evidenced by unpredictable fluctuations in RMSE.

**Table 5.** Resource Utilization of Baseline 2

| $n$ | Combination | Measured Utilization (%) | | | | RMSE | |
|---|---|---|---|---|---|---|---|
| | | LUT | DRAM | BRAM | DSP | Value | Change |
| 12 | 4, 8, <u>4</u>, 6, 8, <u>4</u>, 8, 8, 4, 6 | 62.2 | 27.3 | 100.0 | 90.0 | 4.78 | ↑7.17% |
| 18 | | 76.8 | 61.3 | 100.0 | 85.0 | 4.71 | ↑9.53% |
| 24 | | 81.2 | 72.8 | 100.0 | 90.0 | 4.29 | ↑2.14% |
| 12 | 8, 8, <u>4</u>, 4, 8, <u>4</u>, 4, 4, 4, 4 | 66.0 | 38.8 | 100.0 | 87.5 | 5.24 | ↑0.38% |
| 18 | | 80.5 | 68.8 | 100.0 | 85.0 | 4.87 | ↓1.62% |
| 24 | | 81.9 | 72.8 | 100.0 | 85.0 | 4.98 | ↓4.96% |
| 12 | 4, 8, <u>4</u>, 4, 8, <u>4</u>*, 8, 8, 8, 8 | 63.3 | 26.7 | 100.0 | 85.0 | 4.47 | ↓0.67% |
| 18 | | 75.1 | 53.7 | 100.0 | 85.0 | 4.47 | ↑4.93% |
| 24 | | 80.5 | 65.2 | 100.0 | 85.0 | 4.30 | ↓0.69% |
| 12 | 6, 4, <u>4</u>, 8, 6, <u>4</u>*, 4, 8, 6, 6 | 59.7 | 24.8 | 100.0 | 80.0 | 4.72 | ↑5.12% |
| 18 | | 71.7 | 48.2 | 100.0 | 77.5 | 4.48 | ↓2.40% |
| 24 | | 76.2 | 59.5 | 100.0 | 82.5 | 4.44 | ↓8.26% |
| 12 | 8, 4, <u>4</u>, 6, 4, <u>4</u>, 4, 8, 4, 8 | 62.9 | 27.0 | 100.0 | 70.0 | 4.97 | ↑0.81% |
| 18 | | 77.4 | 61.0 | 100.0 | 70.0 | 4.65 | ↓0.43% |
| 24 | | 79.3 | 65.0 | 100.0 | 70.0 | 4.46 | ↑2.53% |

* FFN was already quantized to 4-bit in Baseline 1.

In response, our study implemented the Algorithm 1 detailed in Sect. 4.4. We applied it across three distinct input sequence lengths ($n$), each exploring a comprehensive range of 59,049 possible quantization combinations, referred to as $C_{all}$. To streamline this vast array, specific resource utilization thresholds were set: $T_{LUTs} = 80\%$, $T_{DRAM} = 100\%$, $T_{BRAM} = 100\%$, and $T_{DSPs} = 100\%$.

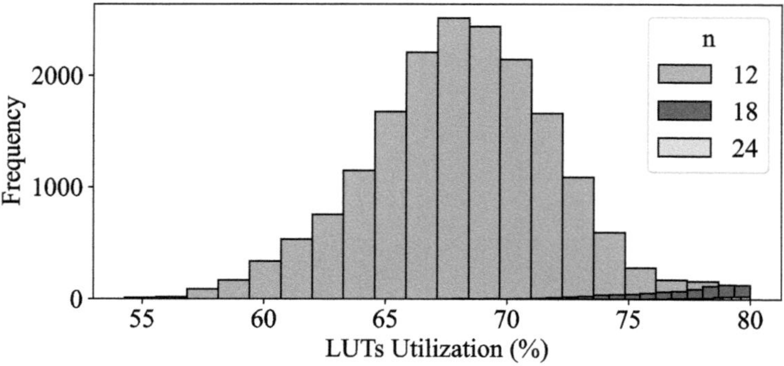

**Fig. 7.** Distribution of Candidate Mixed-Precision Bitwidth Combinations

These thresholds effectively narrowed the feasible combinations by 69.3% for $n = 12$, 98.5% for $n = 18$, and 99.7% for $n = 24$. The histogram in Fig. 7 illustrates the distribution of remaining quantization combinations across different input sequence lengths after applying the specified resource utilization thresholds. Notably, the majority of combinations for $n = 12$ fall within the middle range of LUT utilization, while the distributions for $n = 18$ and $n = 24$ are significantly narrower, reflecting the stringent filtering process that effectively reduces the number of viable configurations, especially for higher sequence lengths.

**Table 6.** Resource Utilization of Our Approach

| $n$ | Combination | Estimated Utilization (%)* | | | | Measured Utilization (%) | | | | RMSE |
|---|---|---|---|---|---|---|---|---|---|---|
| | | LUT | DRAM | BRAM | DSP | LUT | DRAM | BRAM | DSP | |
| 12 | 6, 8, 6, 8, 6, 6, 8, 8, 8, 8 | 80.0 | 78.7 | 100.0 | 100.0 | 85.7 | 79.3 | 100.0 | 100.0 | 3.81 |
| | 8, 8, 6, 8, 8, 4, 8, 6, 8, 8 | 78.1 | 76.0 | 85.0 | 100.0 | 80.9 | 82.7 | 100.0 | 100.0 | 3.89 |
| | 8, 8, 6, 8, 6, 4, 8, 8, 8, 8 | 78.0 | 76.0 | 85.0 | 100.0 | 80.3 | 80.0 | 100.0 | 100.0 | 3.77 |
| | 8, 8, 4, 8, 8, 6, 8, 6, 8, 8 | 76.7 | 65.8 | 85.0 | 100.0 | 80.3 | 55.2 | 100.0 | 100.0 | 4.14 |
| | 8, 8, 4, 8, 6, 6, 8, 8, 8, 8 | 76.6 | 65.8 | 85.0 | 100.0 | 79.2 | 52.5 | 100.0 | 100.0 | 4.07 |
| 18 | 8, 4, 4, 4, 4, 4, 8, 4, 8, 8 | 80.0 | 77.2 | 90.0 | 75.0 | 77.2 | 61.2 | 100.0 | 75.0 | 4.65 |
| | 8, 4, 4, 4, 8, 4, 4, 4, 8, 8 | 79.8 | 77.2 | 90.0 | 70.0 | 77.8 | 61.2 | 100.0 | 75.0 | 5.16 |
| | 8, 4, 4, 4, 4, 4, 4, 8, 8, 8 | 79.7 | 77.2 | 90.0 | 70.0 | 77.8 | 61.2 | 100.0 | 65.0 | 4.55 |
| | 8, 6, 4, 4, 6, 4, 4, 4, 8, 8 | 79.7 | 74.5 | 85.0 | 75.0 | 76.3 | 56.5 | 100.0 | 80.0 | 4.19 |
| | 6, 8, 4, 4, 6, 4, 4, 4, 8, 8 | 79.6 | 74.5 | 85.0 | 75.0 | 76.3 | 56.5 | 100.0 | 80.0 | 4.53 |
| 24 | 6, 8, 4, 4, 4, 4, 4, 4, 8, 8 | 79.7 | 75.8 | 85.0 | 75.0 | 80.7 | 67.8 | 100.0 | 80.0 | 4.10 |
| | 8, 6, 4, 4, 4, 4, 4, 4, 8, 6 | 79.9 | 75.7 | 85.0 | 75.0 | 80.4 | 67.7 | 100.0 | 80.0 | 4.49 |
| | 8, 6, 4, 4, 4, 4, 4, 4, 6, 8 | 79.8 | 75.7 | 85.0 | 75.0 | 80.0 | 67.7 | 100.0 | 80.0 | 4.65 |
| | 4, 6, 4, 4, 4, 4, 6, 4, 8, 8 | 79.6 | 78.5 | 85.0 | 85.0 | 77.7 | 67.8 | 100.0 | 75.0 | 4.23 |
| | 6, 8, 4, 4, 4, 4, 4, 4, 8, 6 | 79.5 | 75.7 | 85.0 | 75.0 | 80.2 | 67.7 | 100.0 | 80.0 | 4.37 |

* The overhead from $O_{model}$, $O_{encoder\ layer}$, and $O_{middleware}$ is excluded.

After score-based filtering, 5 candidates for each input sequence length were subjected to training and evaluation, with their performance and resource utilization detailed in Table 6. This table presents "Estimated Utilization (%)" derived from our knowledge database and "Measured Utilization (%)" obtained from Vivado synthesis, affirming the precision and reliability of our database. For example, when $n = 12$, the estimated LUT utilization of 80.0% closely mirrored the measured value of 85.7%. It is noteworthy that the overhead from $O_{\mathrm{model}}$, $O_{\mathrm{encoder\ layer}}$, and $O_{\mathrm{middleware}}$, typically accounting for 2.7% to 4.0% of LUT utilization, were excluded from these estimates. Including this overhead will bring the estimated results closer to the actual measurements.

Table 6 also elucidates the impact of our method on test RMSE. Across different input sequence lengths, our approach consistently resulted in lower average RMSEs compared to Baseline 2. However, for an input sequence length of 18, while Baseline 1 showed a lower average RMSE than our approach, the models it produced were not deployable due to exceeding FPGA resource constraints. Notably, our approach often utilized 4-bit quantization for model components at $n = 18$ and $n = 24$, constrained by stringent resource thresholds. In contrast, Baseline 2 configurations typically used fewer than four components quantized at 4 bits. This observation suggests that refining our score-based filter to reduce reliance on 4-bit quantization could further improve RMSE, enhancing model performance across different sequence lengths while maintaining deployability.

## 5.4   Experiment 3: Model Performance on Hardware

Following the results of Experiment 2, accelerators associated with the lowest RMS for each input sequence length $(n)$ underwent further performance evaluations using Vivado's synthesis and actual hardware validation. Table 7 details the RMSE, inference time, power and energy consumption for each configuration.

**Table 7.** Performance Comparison on Spartan-7 XC7S15 FPGA

| n | Combinations | RMSE | Time(ms)[†] | Power(mW)[†] | | | Energy(mJ) |
|---|---|---|---|---|---|---|---|
| | | | | Static | Dynamic | Total | |
| 12 | 8, 8, 6, 8, 6, 4, 8, 8, 8, 8 | 3.77 | 5.78 | 31 | 39 | 70 | 0.405 |
| 18 | 8, 6, 4, 4, 6, 4, 4, 4, 8, 8 | 4.19 | 8.79 | 31 | 37 | 68 | 0.598 |
| 24 | 6, 8, 4, 4, 4, 4, 4, 4, 8, 8 | 4.10 | 11.92 | 31 | 37 | 68 | 0.811 |

† The estimates obtained from GHDL and Vivado exhibit 2% variance in time, and 5% variance in power when compared to the actual hardware measurements.

For an input sequence length of 12, deploying an accelerator configured with uniform 6-bit quantization was successfully implemented on the XC7S15 FPGA, as previously discussed in [8]. This configuration achieved an RMSE of 3.76. In comparison, our mixed-precision quantized accelerator, as detailed in the first row of Table 7, registered a slightly higher RMSE of 3.77. The inclusion of 8-bit quantized components restricted the maximum clock frequency to 100 MHz, compared to 125 MHz for the uniform 6-bit configuration. This contributed to a bottleneck that increased the inference time for our mixed-precision quantized accelerator by 25%, resulting in a duration of 5.78 ms. Although there was a 12.85% reduction in power consumption, the extended inference time led to an increase in energy consumption to 0.405 mJ, illustrating that our mixed-precision quantized accelerator underperformed relative to the uniform 6-bit quantized accelerator. However, we believe that optimizing the score-based filter to limit mixed-precision combinations to 4 and 6-bit could potentially alleviate the maximum clock frequency constraints imposed by 8-bit components, potentially reducing inference time and decreasing energy consumption.

For $n = 18$, prior implementations were limited to uniform 4-bit quantization, resulting in poor model precision with an RMSE of 5.286. Our mixed-precision quantized accelerator significantly enhanced model precision, reducing the RMSE to 4.19—an improvement of 20.73%, as detailed in the second row of Table 7. Moreover, compared to the floating-point counterpart, our mixed-precision quantized accelerator recorded only a 3.33% higher RMSE. For an input sequence length of 24, previous efforts could not deploy any accelerators even with uniform 4-bit quantization due to excessive resource demands. In this study, however, adaptive memory allocation enabled the deployment of a uniform 4-bit quantized accelerator, as outlined in Sect. 5.2. Our mixed-precision quantized accelerator further improved upon this, reducing the RMSE by 24.85%. Relative to the floating-point counterpart, our mixed-precision quantized accelerator showed only a 2.80% higher RMSE.

However, increasing the input sequence length from 12 to 24 nearly doubled the inference time. Notably, dynamic power consumption was reduced by 2 mW, attributable to a 20% decrease in DSPs utilization, as detailed in Table 6. Despite this reduction in power consumption, the prolonged inference duration led to a doubling of the energy required per inference. Furthermore, extending the input sequence length did not reduce RMSE for the *AirU* dataset, indicating that the configuration detailed in the first row of Table 7 is the most effective for this particular dataset. This outcome underscores the complex interplay between model architecture, quantization strategy, and dataset characteristics. Despite these nuances, our primary contribution is the enhanced deployability of sophisticated Transformer models on resource-constrained devices. We anticipate that further validation across different datasets will substantiate the broader applicability and benefits of our approach.

## 6    Related Work

Recent research has increasingly focused on optimizing Transformers through quantization to balance computational efficiency with model precision [16]. Zhang et al. [17] reviewed vector quantization and K-Means-based methods applied to large language models for time-series analysis. In addition, Zhao et al. [18] proposed an innovative Transformer architecture that replaces the traditional FFN module with vector quantization to enhance efficiency and precision in multivariate time-series forecasting. However, the substantial computational resources required for their implementations, as evidenced by their use of the NVIDIA A100 80GB GPU, highlight the challenges of deploying such models on IoT devices.

In the realm of FPGA-targeted deployment, accelerating quantized Transformers presents specific challenges due to the stringent resource limitations of these platforms. Okubo et al. [19] developed a compact Transformer model that incorporates Neural Ordinary Differential Equations, significantly reducing both parameter count and resource utilization. This model has shown considerable gains in inference speed and energy efficiency on a modest-sized ZCU104 FPGA. Furthermore, the application of mixed-precision quantization, which assigns different quantization bitwidths to various model components, is increasingly acknowledged as essential for optimizing FPGA deployment [12]. For example, Chang et al. [20] demonstrated that their mixed-precision quantization approach, which assigns multiple precision levels within the weight matrix at the row level, enhances the efficiency of quantized BERT models on System-on-Chip-based FPGAs (ZYNQ XC7Z020 and XC7Z045). Additionally, Li et al. [21] have implemented mixed-precision quantized Vision Transformer accelerators on the ZCU102 FPGA, utilizing distinct bitwidths for model weights and activations.

However, it is critical to recognize that the FPGAs used in these studies are relatively large, and the FPGA resource capacities often exceed those required for typical applications. This underscores a gap in research for deploying Transformer-based models on embedded FPGAs, where resource constraints are more pronounced. Our study addresses this gap by proposing adaptive resource allocation and resource-aware mixed-precision quantization to enhance the deployability of Transformer models on FPGAs with limited resources. Additionally, this research offers a detailed analysis of the Transformer accelerators, specifically tailored for time-series forecasting, thereby advancing practical understanding of efficient model deployment on resource-constrained platforms.

## 7  Conclusion and Future Work

This study has demonstrated the efficacy of adaptive resource allocation and mixed-precision quantization for deploying Transformer models for time-series forecasting on embedded FPGAs. Our approach, underpinned by a comprehensive knowledge database for precise resource estimation, facilitates the effective implementation of mixed-precision quantization. By integrating resource awareness into our workflow, we have streamlined the deployment process on resource-constrained devices, ensuring both deployability and maintaining competitive model precision. This study sets a benchmark for future optimizations in similar applications in ubiquitous computing.

In the future, we plan to refine our score-based filter to enhance the precision and deployment efficiency of the quantized Transformer model. Additionally, we aim to validate our approach across other datasets, verifying its advantages and applicability in diverse scenarios. Furthermore, we intend to explore the potential of mixed-scheme quantization strategies, which combine different quantization techniques within a single model architecture, aiming to further optimize computational efficiency.

**Acknowledgments.** The authors gratefully acknowledge the financial support provided by the Federal Ministry for Economic Affairs and Climate Action of Germany for the RIWWER project (01MD22007C).

# References


1. Chander, B., Pal, S., De, D., Buyya, R.: Artificial intelligence-based internet of things for industry 5.0. In: Artificial Intelligence-Based-Based Internet of Things Systems, pp. 3–45 (2022)
2. Zhou, Z., Chen, X., Li, E., Zeng, L., Luo, K., Zhang, J.: Edge intelligence: paving the last mile of Artificial Intelligence with edge computing. Proc. IEEE **107**(8), 1738–1762 (2019)
3. Dave, R., Seliya, N., Siddiqui, N., Mao, S.: The benefits of edge computing in healthcare, smart cities, and IoT. J. Comput. Sci. Appl. **9**(1), 23–34 (2021)
4. Wen, Q., et al.: Transformers in time series: a survey. In: Proceedings of the Thirty-Second International Joint Conference on Artificial Intelligence. IJCAI 2023 (2023)
5. Chen, C., et al.: Deep Learning on computational-resource-limited platforms: a survey. Mob. Inf. Syst. **2020**, 1–19 (2020)
6. Gill, S.S., et al.: AI for next generation computing: emerging trends and future directions. Internet Things **19**, 100514 (2022)
7. Seng, K.P., Lee, P.J., Ang, L.M.: Embedded intelligence on FPGA: survey, applications and challenges. Electronics **10**(8), 895 (2021)
8. Ling, T., Qian, C., Schiele, G.: Integer-only quantized Transformers for embedded FPGA-based time-series forecasting in AIoT. In: 2024 IEEE Annual Congress on Artificial Intelligence of Things (AIoT), pp. 38–44. IEEE (2024)
9. Qian, C., Ling, T., Schiele, G.: Enhancing energy-efficiency by solving the throughput bottleneck of LSTM cells for embedded FPGAs. In: Joint European Conference on Machine Learning and Knowledge Discovery in Databases, pp. 594–605. Springer (2022)
10. Becnel, T., Kelly, K., Gaillardon, P.E.: Tiny time-series transformers: realtime multi-target sensor inference at the edge. In: 2022 IEEE International Conference on Omni-Layer Intelligent Systems (COINS), pp. 1–6. IEEE (2022)
11. Nagel, M., Fournarakis, M., Amjad, R.A., Bondarenko, Y., Van Baalen, M., Blankevoort, T.: A white paper on Neural Network quantization. arXiv preprint arXiv:2106.08295 (2021)
12. Rakka, M., Fouda, M.E., Khargonekar, P., Kurdahi, F.: A review of state-of-the-art mixed-precision neural network frameworks. IEEE Trans. Pattern Anal. Mach. Intell. (2024)
13. Ding, S., Meadowlark, P., He, Y., Lew, L., Agrawal, S., Rybakov, O.: 4-bit Conformer with native quantization aware training for speech recognition. arXiv preprint arXiv:2203.15952 (2022)

14. Dong, Z., Yao, Z., Arfeen, D., Gholami, A., Mahoney, M.W., Keutzer, K.: HAWQ-V2: hessian aware trace-weighted quantization of deep neural networks. Adv. Neural. Inf. Process. Syst. **33**, 18518–18529 (2020)
15. Qian, C., Ling, T., Schiele, G.: ElasticAI: creating and deploying energy-efficient deep learning accelerator for pervasive computing. In: 2023 IEEE International Conference on Pervasive Computing and Communications Workshops and other Affiliated Events (PerCom Workshops), pp. 297–299. IEEE (2023)
16. Chitty-Venkata, K.T., Mittal, S., Emani, M., Vishwanath, V., Somani, A.K.: A survey of techniques for optimizing transformer inference. J. Syst. Archit. 102990 (2023)
17. Zhang, X., Chowdhury, R.R., Gupta, R.K., Shang, J.: Large language models for time series: a survey. In: Proceedings of the Thirty-Third International Joint Conference on Artificial Intelligence. IJCAI 2024 (2024)
18. Zhao, Y., Zhou, T., Chen, C., Sun, L., Qian, Y., Jin, R.: Sparse-VQ Transformer: an FFN-free framework with vector quantization for enhanced time series forecasting. arXiv preprint arXiv:2402.05830 (2024)
19. Okubo, I., Sugiura, K., Matsutani, H.: A cost-efficient FPGA implementation of tiny Transformer model using neural ODE. arXiv preprint arXiv:2401.02721 (2024)
20. Chang, S.E., et al.: RMSMP: a novel deep neural networks quantization framework with row-wise mixed schemes and multiple precisions. In: Proceedings of the IEEE/CVF International Conference on Computer Vision, pp. 5251–5260 (2021)
21. Li, Z., et al.: Auto-VIT-ACC: an FPGA-aware automatic acceleration framework for vision Transformer with mixed-scheme quantization. In: 2022 32nd International Conference on Field-Programmable Logic and Applications (FPL), pp. 109–116. IEEE (2022)

# Scene Graph Driven Context Query Generation: A Focus on Diversity and Situation-Specific Queries

Ravindi de Silva[1]($\boxtimes$), Arkady Zaslavsky[1], Seng W. Loke[1], and Prem Prakash Jayaraman[2]

[1] Deakin University, Melbourne, Australia
{ardesilva,arkady.zaslavsky,seng.loke}@deakin.edu.au
[2] Swinburne University of Technology, Melbourne, Australia
pjayaraman@swin.edu.au

**Abstract.** The rapid growth of IoT has produced vast data, but isolated systems limit comprehensive analysis and interoperability, hindering intelligent applications. To address this challenge, Context Management Platforms (CMPs) have emerged. However, current CMP performance evaluations often emphasize data ingestion, overlooking data digestion. This study introduces a novel scenario-based context query generation approach to evaluate data digestion performance of CMPs. Real-world scenes are modeled as context-aware scene graphs using ontology-based knowledge. This approach integrates ontological knowledge, sensor data, and real-world images to comprehensively represent urban road situations. We infer dynamic situations from the scene graph, forming the basis for generating diverse queries. A template-based query generation method ensures a range of queries with varying complexity. We evaluated the proposed approach using real-world datasets, demonstrating the query generation effectiveness and practicality. The findings show the correlation between the volume of queries and the scene complexity. We also analyzed computation time for query generation against scene complexity and assessed query relevance through weighted attribute coverage, demonstrating that our method effectively tailors queries to each scene's dynamics. The proposed query generation approach lays a strong foundation for automating the evaluation of CMPs' data retrieval/digestion capabilities.

**Keywords:** Context Management Platforms · Context Queries · Situation · Context-aware Scene Graphs

## 1 Introduction

The rapid evolution of Internet of Things (IoT) technology is transforming industries by providing innovative solutions to complex problems. In sectors such as healthcare, manufacturing, smart cities, and environmental monitoring, IoT devices are generating vast amounts of data, driving efficiency, and enabling new capabilities. However, this


A. Soylu et al. (Eds.): MobiQuitous 2024, LNICST 634, pp. 382–401, 2026.
https://doi.org/10.1007/978-3-032-10554-7_21

explosion of data comes with its own set of challenges, particularly in terms of data integration, interoperability, and effective utilization [1]. Despite the advancements in IoT hardware and the proliferation of smart devices, a significant hurdle remains: the seamless exchange of data across different IoT systems. Currently, many IoT deployments operate in silos, limiting the potential for comprehensive data analysis and cross-system communication. This fragmentation hinders the development of truly intelligent applications that can leverage data from diverse sources to provide meaningful insights. To address this challenge, there is a growing emphasis on developing sophisticated middleware solutions known as Context Management Platforms (CMPs) [2]. CMPs are designed to facilitate the aggregation, processing, and dissemination of contextual data from various IoT sources. These platforms aim to break down the barriers between isolated IoT systems, enabling a more holistic approach to data utilization. Evaluating the CMPs is crucial for ensuring their effectiveness in handling both data ingestion and retrieval, which are essential for real-time context-aware applications. For developers, robust performance evaluation helps in optimizing CMPs to meet stringent latency requirements and ensures that they can handle diverse and complex context queries efficiently. This leads to the development of more reliable and responsive applications. For product consumers, high-performing CMPs guarantee timely and accurate context information, enhancing user experience and satisfaction in applications ranging from smart cities to autonomous vehicles.

Standardization efforts in the realm of CMPs and context query languages are currently spearheaded by the ETSI CIM [3] working group. They are basing their proposed standard on the NGSI-LD [4] language and the FIWARE [5] platform. However, currently there are no appropriate and accepted benchmarking methodology and/or tests for evaluating CMPs. Despite the importance, the current approaches for performance testing of CMPs often emphasize data ingestion while overlooking data retrieval. Therefore, there is a significant need to develop a mechanism that simplifies and automates the generation of context queries. To overcome the above limitations, we propose a scenario-based context query generation approach to evaluate the performance of CMPs, with a particular focus on data digestion performance. This method involves creating realistic, context-rich scenarios that mimic real-world conditions. These scenarios are deconstructed into sequences of scenes that mirror actual images from the real world. These images are then translated into context-aware scene graphs. By integrating contextual frameworks and state-based models we model situation transitions in scenes. Rule-based reasoning helps to define the rules related to these transitions. These situations, involving different entities in the scene, serve as the foundation for query generation, enhancing its precision and robustness. This approach is highly effective in presenting query loads for evaluating CMP performance. By simulating real-world scenarios and generating context-aware queries, our framework offers a thorough evaluation of the CMP's ability to handle diverse and complex queries. This approach ensures a precise assessment of the CMP's data digestion capabilities, leading to optimized platform performance. The proposed approach aims to close the gap between traditional benchmarking methods and the evolving requirements of modern IoT ecosystems. It not only identifies strengths and weaknesses in current CMPs but also paves the way for future advancements in the field.

In summary, this paper makes the following contributions:

- proposing an automated context query generation approach to generate situation-specific queries
- introducing a novel approach that integrates contextual frameworks and state-based models to represent situation transitions in scenes, triggering the query generation process.
- evaluating the proposed query generation approach using real-world scenes and analysing the query distribution, computation efficiency across diverse scene complexities, assessing query relevance through weighted attribute coverage and comparing the queries against existing IoT application/middleware benchmarking test suites

The rest of this paper is organized as follows. Section 2 presents the related work in the field of query generation approaches in evaluating IoT middleware platforms. Section 3 highlights the concepts of Scene, Scenario and Situation which lays the basis for proposed query generation approach and then presents the multi-stage context query generation methodology in detail. Section 4 presents the experiment settings including the list of scenes, IoT datasets and method followed. Section 5 discusses the results of the conducted experiments, in terms of number of queries, computation times, completeness and query coverage. Finally, Sect. 6 concludes the paper.

## 2 Related Work

Designing IoT queries for performance evaluations necessitates a deep understanding of the relationships between data, which is crucial for creating meaningful and efficient benchmarks. In recent years, there has been a notable increase in research focusing on evaluating IoT platforms [7–11]. However, most of these studies concentrate on measuring IoT platforms' performance regarding data ingestion, with less emphasis on data retrieval performance. From a cloud middleware performance evaluation perspective, IoTAbench [6] is specifically designed for smart meter scenarios and focuses on simple analytical queries that support basic aggregation operations. Its performance measurement is sequential, and this approach is limited in scope, as it addresses only one use-case and models a single sensor data type, restricting its applicability to more diverse IoT scenarios. On the other hand, TPCx-IoT [7] simulates simple time-series queries, which are prevalent in IoT data analysis, but it does not include support for aggregation queries. TPCx-IoT is capable of handling concurrent query operations, making it more suitable for scenarios requiring high throughput and real-time processing. However, its lack of support for more complex query types, such as those involving aggregation, limits its comprehensiveness. Another limitation is the benchmark's inability to compare systems under varying load conditions that differ from the specific queries used in TPCx-IoT [8]. Furthermore, the benchmark does not account for the querying aspect in its IoTps (performance metric) metric, even though querying is just as important as data ingestion for CMPs. Despite these issues, TPCx-IoT serves as a valuable starting point for IoT Gateways benchmarking discussions.

Another research in [9] investigated the data ingestion and storage performance of IoT platforms, using OpenIoT as a case study. This study measured the platform's efficiency in handling large volumes of incoming data and its ability to store and retrieve data, focusing on performance metrics such as ingestion rate and storage latency. However, most of the aforementioned research has concentrated on the data ingestion performance of IoT platforms, neglecting the performance of data digestion. Recent efforts [12] have proposed and validated a benchmarking approach for Context Management Platforms (CMPs) by developing a framework for generating context query loads. However, the queries used in these efforts only varied the number of entities, limiting the diversity of queries involving different filtering conditions, logical or comparison operators, date-time queries, or functions that accurately reflect real-world user requirements. An approach to generate situation-based queries tailored for cloud-managed IoT applications is proposed in [13]. The framework is exhibited based on two smart city use cases to highlight how the framework can be used to generate queries. One major limitation is the absence of empirical results or performance metrics for the queries generated. The ability to generate queries that can dynamically adjust to new situations is essential, but the paper does not address this aspect thoroughly. Based on the existing work, it is evident that there is a clear need for high-level and complex queries that address the unique characteristics of IoT applications. CMPs require more advanced benchmarks that address analytical queries, subscriptions, and continuous data stream monitoring. These aspects are essential for accurately evaluating CMP performance and ensuring comprehensive functionality assessment. Developing such advanced query sets will better capture the dynamic and multifaceted nature of IoT environments, ultimately leading to more accurate and effective performance evaluations. The proposed approach models scenes representing a wide range of real-world situations, serving as the foundation for query generation. This ensures a more representative and accurate evaluation of a CMP's data retrieval strategy.

## 3   Methodology

This section provides an overview of the methodology for Scenario-based Context-Query Generation. We propose a novel notion of the dynamic context-aware scene graph, incorporating concepts of scene, scenario, situation, and spatio-temporal elements to provide the basis for context query generation. In our approach, a scenario is like a story unfolding over time, showing how things change in an environment. A scene represents a specific moment in that scenario, with all the elements and context at that time. Each scene can have different situations. The formal definitions for the above terms and further details are found in [14] and [15]. The study's use cases revolve around urban road scenarios, particularly those related to bicycle riding. These scenarios include potential hazards such as dooring accidents, collisions, approaching potholes, puddles, and navigating heavy traffic near intersections. For example, in a bicycle dooring scenario, a cyclist riding along a street with parked cars faces the hazard of a car door suddenly opening into their path. The real-world scenarios highlight how situations evolve and how context-specific queries can be dynamically generated to enhance safety and provide actionable insights for cyclists in urban environments.

### 3.1  Context Query Generation Approach -ACOCA-G

In this section, we provide the high-level architecture of the context query generator (ACOCA-G) that assists in evaluating the data digestion mechanism of a given CMP. The context query generation is a multi-stage process as shown in Fig. 1.

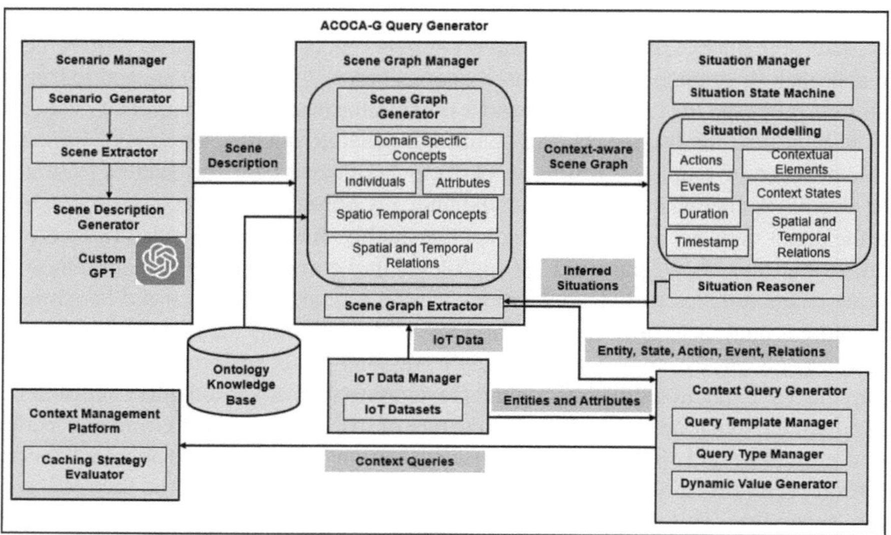


**Fig. 1.** High-Level Architecture for Context Query Generation

### *IoT Data Manager and Scenario Manager*

IoT Data Manager integrates multi-modal data, including IoT data, real-world images, and ontology, to enhance scene understanding and context-aware scene graph generation. We refer to the RSIF Bicycle Riding dataset that includes locations and speeds of cyclists in specific bicycle routes in Melbourne. Also, we leveraged a collection of real-world publicly available datasets [19] to enrich our analysis. We combine real-world images with corresponding sensor data by aligning timestamps and locations to create an integrated and coherent analysis. The real-world images are then presented Scenario Manager, which uses a custom modified Generative Pre-training Transformer (GPT) [20] that is pre-loaded with the developed ontology, with specific instructions to generate a scene description in the form of triples.

### *Scene Graph Manager*

We use an ontology-based approach to model knowledge related to urban road scenes, providing a structured framework for capturing complexities and constructing a scene graph. The ontology comprises five layers: Road Network, Road Infrastructure, Participant, Environment, and Sensor. The sensor layer utilizes the Semantic Sensor Network Ontology (SSN) [16] to represent sensors and their properties related to vehicles, smart phones, bicycles, and environment. These layers represent different aspects such as road topology, physical elements, entities, environmental factors, and sensors. Our ontology extends the Core SAW Ontology [17] by integrating sensors as smart objects, embedding context, and focusing on spatial, temporal, and contextual elements crucial for understanding urban road scenes. We also enhanced relations defined in the GeoSPARQL by integrating with direction-based relations to define spatial arrangements. We used Allen's Interval Algebra [18] to establish the order of events as temporal relationships, enhancing it with contextual information to qualify these relationships. The Scene Graph Generation Application (SGGA), a Python application, processes triples to build the context-aware scene graph (CSG) based on the ontology. It identifies unique subjects and objects, mapping them to nodes linked by relations. SGGA prompts users to align or create concepts as needed for novel elements. It automates the process of generating sensor instances for vehicles, bicycles, cyclists, and pedestrians. Functions handle these tasks, and the initial Resource Description Framework (RDF) version of the scene graph is refined in Protégé [21] for precise alignment with the ontology's concepts.

### *Situation Manager*

Situation Manager models situations using Context Spaces Theory (CST) [22] as the foundational framework. CST model situations by representing contexts as multidimensional spaces, with each dimension corresponding to a specific contextual attribute. In our ontology, distinct context spaces are mapped to the contextual element's superclass, with their states represented as subclasses. For example, weather condition context space is modeled with states such as "Sunny," "Rainy," and "Cloudy," and transitions between these states can capture the dynamic nature of the environment. This multidimensional representation is crucial for understanding how different contextual elements interact and influence each other. Additionally, we use Situation State Machines (SSM) as a conceptual framework to understand how situation transitions of an entity occur. For instance, the transition of context states of weather (Sunny to Rainy) could trigger a transition in the rider's state from Riding to Stopping, reflecting the impact of contextual changes on entity behavior. SSM further refines this by adding a temporal and logical dimension to the context modeling. It enables us to track and predict how entities transition between different states based on contextual changes. This holistic approach allows for more nuanced and precise reasoning about complex real-world situations. By integrating CST and SSM, our ontology not only captures static contextual information but also dynamically models how entities and contexts evolve over time, providing a robust foundation for generating context-aware scene graphs and queries. To perform reasoning on the context information as to infer the situations, multiple SWRL (Semantic Web Rule Language) [23] rules are defined. Table 1 illustrates the types of reasoning conducted using SWRL rules in the proposed ontology. This comprehensive approach allows us to infer implicit situations which are not directly observable but derived from available data, consider inferring the presence of slippery road conditions based on the observation of rain and the absence of explicit mentions of slippery roads. Also, we infer explicit situations, which are directly observed in the scene. Furthermore, we infer co-existing situations belonging to different entities, and causal relationships where one situation leads to another, such as a collision results in heavy traffic congestion situation. We extract the information including entities, their states, spatial relations, and actions and pass them to query generation application.

**Table 1.**  Different types SWRL Reasoning.

| Reasoning Basis | SWRL Rule |
| --- | --- |
| Spatial Reasoning | Bicycle(?b) ^ Intersection(?i) ^ ahead(?b, ?i) - > Approaching Intersection(?b) |
| Temporal Reasoning | Bicycle(?b) ^ Weather(?w) ^ has Weather Condition(?w, "Rainy") ^ during(?b, ?w) - > Riding In Rain(?b) |
| Reasoning on Actions | Bicycle(?b) ^ Car(?c) ^ is Ahead Of(?c, ?b) ^ Driver(?d) ^ is Opening Door(?d, ?c) - > Dooring Hazard(?b) |
| Event Reasoning | Bicycle(?b) ^ Pedestrian(?p) ^ crossing Road(?p) ^ near(?b, ?p) - > Potential Collision(?b, ?p) |
| Contextual Reasoning | Bicycle(?b) ^ Traffic Condition(?t) ^ heavy Traffic(?t) - > Increased Accident Risk(?b) |

***Context Query Generator.***
We can classify Context Query Languages (CQL) into two distinct groups: basic and high-level CQLs. Basic CQLs are limited to supporting queries that involve a single entity type. In contrast, high-level CQLs are more advanced and can handle queries that retrieve multiple entities simultaneously. We adhere to the Context Description Query Language (CDQL) [24] syntax, a high-level CQL which is used on the CoaaS platform [24] and the NGSI queries, a basic CQL that can interact with the FIWARE Orion Context Broker [5]. In our research, we utilize a template-based query generation approach to create context queries. These templates provide a predefined structure (static) while allowing for the dynamic assignment of attribute values at runtime. The query templates are of different query types as in Table 2.

**Table 2.**  Query Types based on different criteria.

| Type | Number of entities | Number of WHERE clauses | Logical operators | Number of Joins | Number of functions |
| --- | --- | --- | --- | --- | --- |
| 01 | 1 | 1 | 0 | 0 | 0 |
| 02 | 1 | 1 | > = 1 | 0 | 0 |
| 03 | 2 | < = 2 | > = 3 | 1 | 0 |
| 04 | > 3 | < = 3 | > = 3 | > = 2 | 0 |
| 05 | > 2 | < = 3 | > = 2 | > = 1 | > = 1 |

Queries of varying complexity are generated, ensuring credibility through expert intervention in the query generation process. The entities and their attributes needed for WHERE clauses are determined by the entities available in the real-world scenes, as included in the IoT datasets. The extracted information of the scene graph is stored as a list in query generation application, where each element contains the subject of interest (e.g., "Bicycle", "Car"), its current state (e.g., "Riding", "Parking"), a list of relationships with other objects, including spatial relations (e.g., "ahead", "behind"), the entity with which the subject has a relationship (e.g., "Car" for the bicycle, "Bicycle" for the car), and the perception of the scene graph (e.g., "First Person", "Third Person"). Query templates are maintained for entities, with various conditional statements evaluating the object, subject, states, and their relationships. Based on the outcomes of these evaluations, the appropriate query templates are selected. A sample CDQL query template (Type 03) that selects bicycles near a vehicle traveling at a specific speed, with conditions adjustable based on operand values, ensuring flexibility for different scenarios is shown below.

```
string query1 = @$" prefix mv:http://mobivoc.org
pull (bicycle.*)
define
entity bicycle is FROM mv:Bicycle where bicycle.proximityToVehicle {operandValue}
{GenerateRandomNumericValue(1, 40)} and bicycle.speed {operandValue} {GenerateR-
andomNumericValue(1, 6)},
entity car is FROM mv:Car where car.presenceOfPersonInside = ""true"" and car.clusterId
= bicycle.clusterId";
```

Type 05 queries include aggregation functions or situations functions. The aggregation functions comprise of MIN, MX AVG, Count etc. Situation functions are predefined functions that play a crucial role in context-aware systems, enabling them to define and detect specific scenarios or situations of interest. These functions adhere to a specific format, following the CST concept as the underlying principle. Situations are defined by parameters, each with a weight and divided into ranges. These ranges represent values, with beliefs applied based on the input value. The weights and beliefs of each parameter contribute to the final probability value of the situation. The function returns this probability, which can then be compared to a threshold to determine if the situation is hazardous. We have defined situation functions for determining dooring hazards, hazard of a moving vehicle from behind, hazard of riding in rainy weather, hazard of riding in high pedestrian density area. These situation function-related query templates are activated when the inferred situation of an entity matches one of the conditions defined by the situation functions, such as "dooring" or "moving Vehicle Behind". An example illustrating a situation function, and its corresponding query is depicted in Fig. 2. These queries are supported in the CDQL (Context Definition Query Language) in CoaaS.

The NGSI query template of Type 02 as shown below allows dynamic generation of the queries based on the speed and proximity to vehicles. The NGSI relies on query output, which is the result of previous queries, to construct subsequent queries. This dynamic nature of NGSI queries makes it challenging to predefine templates for generating queries compared to CDQL [24]. Hence, we cannot maintain NGSI query templates except for Type 01and Type 02. Due to this limitation, we are referring to CDQL for conducting experiments and evaluation.

```
Situation Function for detecting Dooring hazard

prefix schema:http://schema.org
create sFunction dooringHazardousSituation is on
schema:Car as car
schema:MotorizedBicycle as bike
{
    "doorHazardous":{
        bike.speed: {
            ranges: [
                {value:(0;8),belief:50},
                {value:(8;20),belief:80}
            ],
            weight:8
        },
        bike.proximityToCar: {
            ranges: [
                {value:(0;10],belief:80},
                {value:(10;25],belief:60},
    {value:(25;50],belief:40},
    {value:(50;75],belief:30},
    {value:(75;100],belief:30}
            ],
            weight: 15
        }
    }
}
```

```
Type 05 Query

select (bicycle.id, car.vin)

when

bicycle.proximityToVehicle

<= {GenerateRandomNumericValue(1, 40)}

define

entity car is from schema:car where car.
doorOpenStatus = 'true'

entity bicycle is from schema:bicycle where
bicycle.speed = {GenerateRandomNumericValue (4,8)}

    and dooringHazardousSituation

(bicycle, car) >= 0.6;
```

**Fig. 2.** Situation Function and Sample of a Type 05 Query

```
string ngsiQuery = $@"
    {{ ""entities"": [
        {{ ""type"": ""Bicycle"",
         ""isPattern"": ""true"",
        "options": "keyValues",
        "attrs": [""id"", ""speed"", ""proximityToVehicle""]
        ""q"": ""speed> '{speedValue}';proximityToVehicle<{proximityValue}"" }}
        ] }}";
```

## 4  Experiment Settings

The goal of our experiment is to investigate how our approach can automatically generate context queries based on real-world scenarios, focusing on query richness, diversity (simple to complex queries) among the query elements, and quality of the queries.

We are presenting ten different scenes belonging to different scenarios related to cyclists as shown in Table 3.

The selected scenes demonstrate a dynamic range of situations that bicycle riders may encounter in real-world scenarios, each posing unique hazards and challenges. These scenes are part of larger scenarios involving multiple interactions and events; for instance, a scenario could start with a cyclist riding on a lane, encountering a parked car ahead, passing it safely, then reaching an intersection where they need to navigate through moving vehicles and pedestrians. By presenting these scenes, we aim to highlight the diversity and complexity of situations that our approach can handle, showcasing its ability to automatically generate context queries that capture the richness and variety of real-world scenarios. We use RSIF bicycle riding dataset and publicly available IoT

**Table 3.** List of Scenes and potential hazard.

| ID | Scene overview | Potential Hazard |
|---|---|---|
| 1 | Cyclist riding a bicycle on road | Hazards from weather, road conditions and traffic |
| 2 | Bicycle rider approaching a parked car with a person inside and door closed. | Moderate Hazard of possible Dooring |
| 3 | Bicycle rider approaching a parked car where car door is opening | High risk of Dooring accident |
| 4 | Bicycler riders ahead of a moving car | Hazard of having a moving car behind and maintaining safe distance |
| 5 | Bicycles and Cars on Motor Lane | Hazard from vehicles on Motor Lane |
| 6 | Bicycle Riders riding side by side on road | Maintaining safe distance from vehicles on road |
| 7 | Bicycle Rider approaching a puddle | Hazard of loss of traction and splash from vehicles passing |
| 8 | Bicycle Rider approaching an intersection/ Crossing | Hazard of collision with vehicles and pedestrians |
| 9 | Bicycle Riding in Rainy Weather | Hazard of slippery and wet road |
| 10 | Bicycle Rider meeting with Dooring Accident and Fallen on Road | Possible injuries and emergency situation |

datasets [19] related to on-street car parking sensor data, pedestrian counting system, on-street parking space sensor data, micro-climate dataset and have augmented them further to include additional attributes that we need to generate situation specific query templates, such as proximity to vehicle/road obstacle, road surface condition, heart rate of the rider etc. that help generate queries to determine hazards for cyclists.

### 4.1 Methodology

First, we take each real-world image and present it to the customized GPT [20] to generate a scene description. GPT is loaded with the pre-developed domain ontology and instructions are given to generate scene description as triples using the concepts and relations in the existing ontology. The scene description is then sent to the SGGA, which constructs the initial scene graph. The flow of basic scene graph generation, situation reasoning, and visualization is shown in Fig. 3.

SGGA identifies unique subjects and objects in the scene description and creates corresponding nodes in the scene graph. It then adds relations as edges connecting the relevant subjects and objects. If new classes or relations are detected, the user is prompted to either add a new class/relation or use an existing one. The entire scene graph is saved to an RDF file. The generated scene graph is further refined in Protégé to address any missing data or object properties. Once the situation graph is comprehensive, situation

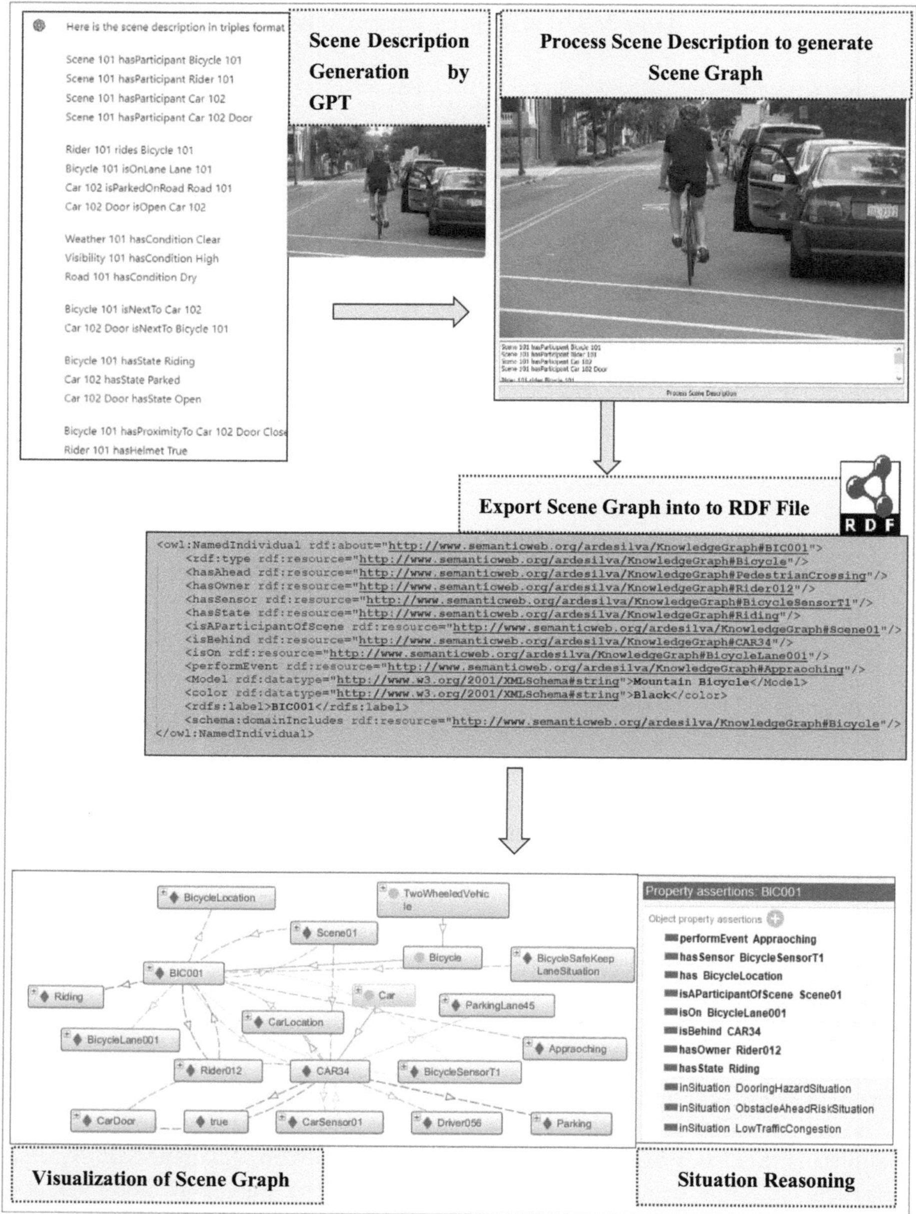



**Fig. 3.** Overall process of Scene Graph Generation and Situation Reasoning

reasoning is performed using pre-defined SWRL rules. The inferred axioms are then exported to an RDF file to be utilized in the query generation process.

After saving the inferred ontology file, upload it to the Query Generation Application (QGA). In the QGA, we extract the necessary information from the inferred ontology, including entities, actions, events, situations, and spatial relations, to generate context-aware queries. The QGA maintains query templates of different types to generate context queries related to a specific situation of an entity. Here's an overview of the query generation process. In this process, a list of tuples is defined, each containing information about an entity, its state, relations, and related objects. This list is then serialized into a JSON string for storage or transmission and deserialized back into a list of tuples. A String Builder object is initialized to build queries. The tuples are iterated over in parallel, extracting entity, state, and related object information to generate queries using the Generate Queries function, which are then appended to String Builder object after locking to ensure thread safety. If the tuple contains relations, another parallel iteration is done to generate queries for each relation using the Generate Queries For Relations function, which are appended to String Builder object after locking. Finally, the content of String Builder object is displayed, and if the list of tuples is empty, an error is returned. Figure 4 represents the sequence flow related to query generation process.

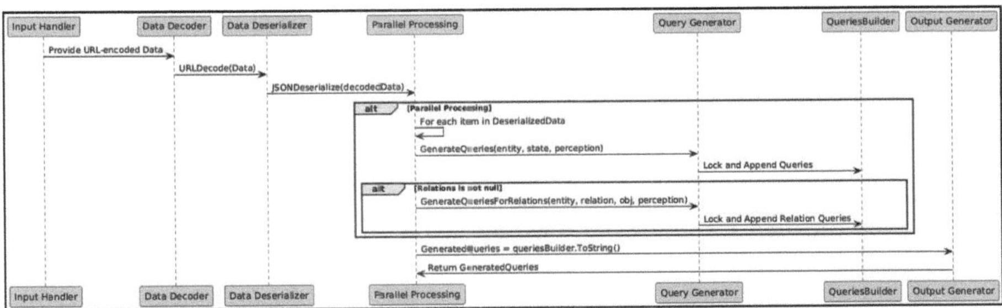

**Fig. 4.** Sequence flow for the Query Generation Algorithm

Some of the generated queries are as follows. These queries are then presented to the CMP, which is CoaaS for our study to evaluate the data digestion performance.

Type 03 – Retrieve distinct bicycle IDs that have a speed greater than 0 and are within 30m of a stationary car at a specific timestamp:

*prefix mv:http://mobivoc.org*
*pull (distinct(bicycle.id))*
*define*
*entity car is FROM mv:Car where car.speed = 0 AND car.timestamp = '13/05/2023 5:16:00 PM',*
*entity bicycle is FROM mv:Bicycle where bicycle.speed> 0 and bicycle.proximityToVehicle <= 30*
*and bicycle.clusterId = car.clusterId;*

Type 04 - This query looks for bicycles with low tire wear and close proximity to vehicles, cars with closed doors and stationary status, and riders over 30 years old:

*prefix mv:http://mobivoc.org*
*pull (distinct(bicycle.id, car.vin, bicycle.location))*
*define*
*entity bicycle is FROM mv:Bicycle where bicycle.wearingOfTyres = "Low" and bicycle.proximityToVehicle <= 30,*
*entity car is FROM mv:Car where car.vehicleDoorStatus = "Closed" and car.speed = 0 and car.clusterId = bicycle.clusterId,*
*entity rider is FROM mv:Person where rider.physicalAge > 30 and rider.riderId = bicycle.riderId;*

Type 05 - Selects the ID of bicycles and the VIN of cars when the proximity of bicycles to vehicles is less than 50 m, considering only bicycles and cars with a door hazard score of at least 0.7:

*select (bicycle.Id, car.vin)*
*when bicycle.proximityToVehicle<{"value":50,"unit":"m"}*
*define*
*entity car is from schema:car*
*entity bicycle is from schema:bicycle and doorHazardous (bicycle, car)>= 0.7;*

Figure 5 illustrates the web application interface for generating queries after uploading the inferred RDF file.

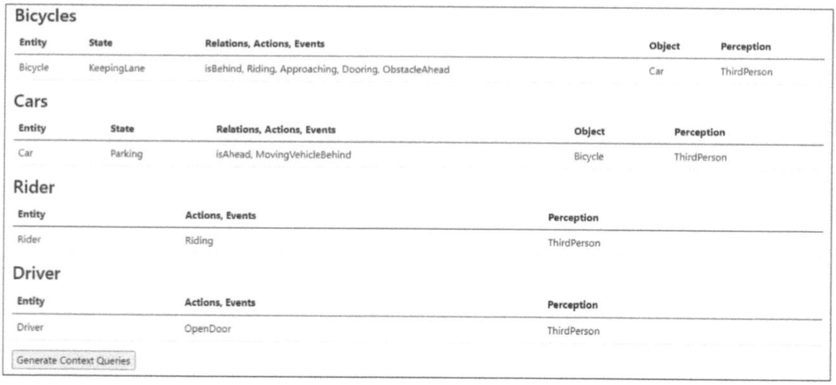

**Bicycles**

| Entity | State | Relations, Actions, Events | Object | Perception |
|---|---|---|---|---|
| Bicycle | KeepingLane | isBehind, Riding, Approaching, Dooring, ObstacleAhead | Car | ThirdPerson |

**Cars**

| Entity | State | Relations, Actions, Events | Object | Perception |
|---|---|---|---|---|
| Car | Parking | isAhead, MovingVehicleBehind | Bicycle | ThirdPerson |

**Rider**

| Entity | Actions, Events | Perception |
|---|---|---|
| Rider | Riding | ThirdPerson |

**Driver**

| Entity | Actions, Events | Perception |
|---|---|---|
| Driver | OpenDoor | ThirdPerson |

Generate Context Queries

**Fig. 5.** Web Interface of the Query Generation Application

## 5   Evaluation

Scene complexity is defined by the number of interacting entities, dynamic interactions, potential hazards, and spatial relationships. We calculated it by assigning points based on the presence and intensity of these factors. More entities, higher interaction levels, greater hazards, and complex spatial arrangements all contribute to a higher scene complexity score. This point-based system provides a comprehensive measure of the intricacy and dynamics of each scene. The analysis in Fig. 6 reveals how varying levels of complexity affect the diversity and frequency of queries across different scenes. Scene complexity affects the type and nature of queries generated in different ways. Simple scenes like Scene1, featuring a cyclist riding a bicycle on the road, and Scene7, involving a bicycle rider approaching a puddle, are less complex as they involve fewer interactions and entities tend to generate more Type01 and Type02 queries, which focus on single entities and their specific attributes without involving joins. As scenes become more complex such as Scene3, Scene4, and Scene, there is a shift towards generating Type03, Type04, and Type05 queries. These more advanced query types often include joins to capture interactions between multiple entities, aggregation functions, and situational evaluations. However, the volume of queries generated does not necessarily increase linearly with scene complexity. In complex scenes, the need for joins and aggregation can restrict the inclusion of certain attributes, leading to fewer but more comprehensive queries.

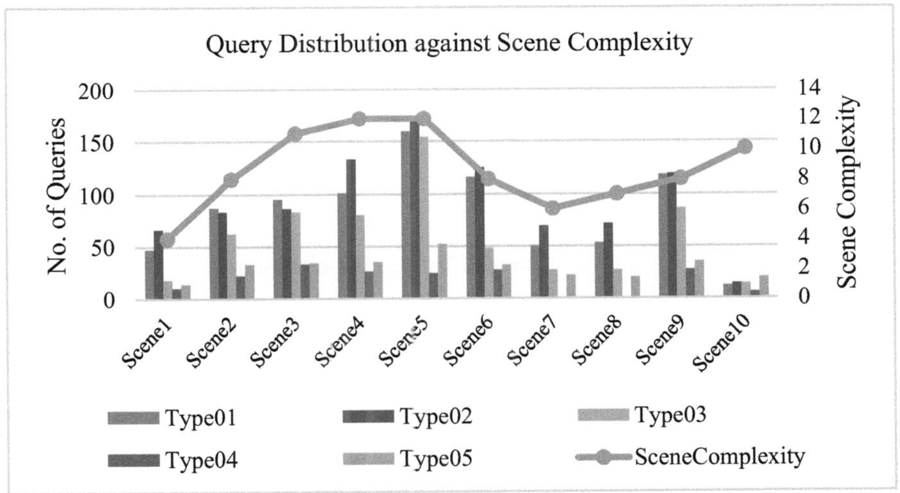


**Fig. 6.** Number of queries against different scene complexities

Sometimes, specific attributes may be eliminated based on the situation to focus on the most critical interactions and conditions. Scene10 presents a unique case where, despite the inherent complexity of an accident scene, few queries are generated. The streamlined query generation process addresses only the key entities and immediate conditions relevant to the accident, leading to a lower overall number of queries compared to scenes with a broader range of attributes and interactions. This selective query generation means that although the complexity of the queries increases, their overall volume might not. Instead, complex scenes generate a smaller number of more detailed and multifaceted queries, reflecting the intricate nature of the scenario and the necessity to analyze multiple entities and their interactions within a single query. Type05 queries, which involve aggregation and situation functions, are generally moderately frequent across all scenes. They are more common in scenes requiring data summarization or specific situational evaluations. For example, Scene9, depicting bicycle riding in rainy weather, has a notable number of Type05 queries due to the need to aggregate weather-related data and its impact on the scene. These queries are less frequent in other scenes as they evaluate multiple attributes in a single function, making them less common in scenes that do not require comprehensive data summarization. Type04 queries are not generated for Scene7, and Scene8, as they do not involve more than three entities. We also assessed the quality of the queries based on the queried data items. Some queries focus on querying fresh data, which is vital for attributes like speed and, location as these frequently change and need to be returned with minimal response time. Moreover, some queries retrieve static values of an entity, such as a person's age or bicycle id. Although these static data items may not be frequently queried, they are useful for evaluating the adaptability and performance of the caching mechanism. Also, some queries handle aggregation operations, while others process streams of data over a period, particularly for situation monitoring. This variety ensures that the system can handle diverse types of data requests efficiently. As for the second experiment we evaluated the computation time for query generation as shown in Fig. 7. Table 4 illustrates the hardware and software specifications for the conducted experiment.

**Table 4.** Hardware and Software Specifications.

| Processor | RAM | Operating System | Windows Version |
|---|---|---|---|
| Intel (R) Core (TM)i510310U-CPU@1.70GHz | 16.0GB | 64-bit Processor | Windows 10 Enterprise |
| **Visual Studio Version** | **. NET Framework Version** | **Compiler Option** | **Execution Mode** |
| Microsoft Visual Studio Community 2022 (64-bit) -Version 17.0.5 | Version - 4.8.04084 | Optimization enabled, Debug mode | IIS Express |

Scene complexity influences query types and computation time in a detailed manner. For example, Scene1, with a complexity of 4, generates a high number of Type01 and Type02 queries and this results in a higher total query count and relatively shorter computation time because these queries are less complex and processed more quickly. In contrast, Scene5, with a high complexity, showcases a more intricate scene with Type01 and Type02 queries, but also significant numbers of Type03, Type04, and Type05 queries. While Scene 5 generates fewer Type03 to Type05 queries compared to Type01 and Type02, each of these queries is more computationally demanding. Consequently, even though the total number of queries is not as high as in simpler scenes, the computation time is substantially greater due to the complexity of joins and aggregations. Despite having fewer Type03 and Type04 queries compared to Scene5, Scene 4's total computation time is high due to the extensive involvement of Type03 and Type04 queries, which are complex and require significant processing power for joins and complex relationships. Despite the lower number of queries, Scene 10 has lower computation times compared to Scene4 and Scene5. This is because Scene10, although generating Type03 to Type05 queries, has fewer aggregation or situational functions compared to the other scenes.

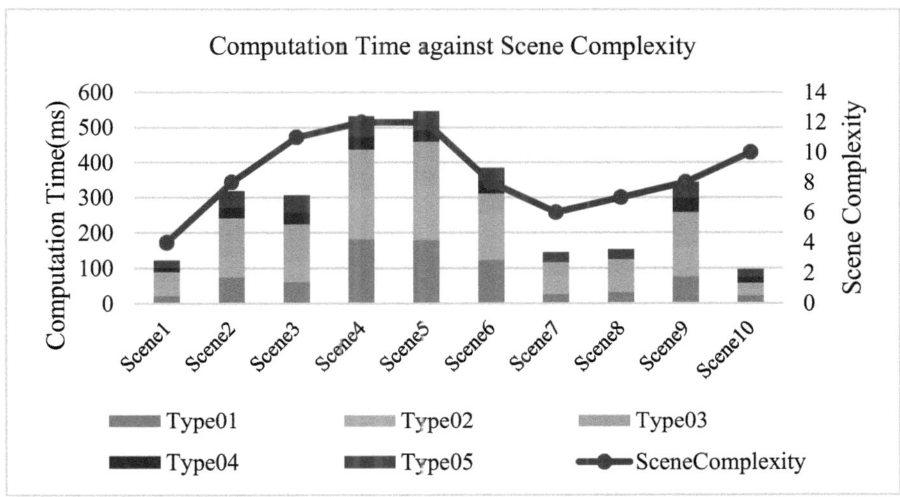


**Fig. 7.** Computation time for query types against scene complexity

The computation time for queries is influenced by several factors beyond scene complexity, including the number of templates based on situation, and query complexity. Type01 and Type02 queries, which are more numerous due to the higher number of templates, generally take longer to process because they involve straightforward conditions but a large volume of queries. In contrast, Type03 and Type04 queries, though fewer in number, involve joins and multiple entities, making them more complex and time consuming. Type05 queries, which involve aggregation and situational functions, are also computationally intensive. Despite their limited number of templates, these queries are complex because they require summarizing and evaluating data over different situations, which increases processing time. As for the third experiment, we evaluated the query relevance based on the attribute coverage across scenes. For each scene, the relevance of the generated queries is evaluated using a weighted average of the metric scores. The objective of evaluating query relevance using a weighted average approach is to determine how effectively the generated queries capture the necessary context for cyclist safety in various scenes. The considered metrics and the assigned weights for each scene are shown in Table 5.

**Table 5.** Metric Weights per Scene

| Scene Id | Speed | Location | Weather | Proximity To Vehicle/ Obstacle | Traffic Condition |
| --- | --- | --- | --- | --- | --- |
| 1 | 0.25 | 0.25 | 0.15 | 0.15 | 0.2 |
| 2 | 0.2 | 0.2 | 0.1 | 0.3 | 0.2 |

(continued)

**Table 5.** (*continued*)

| Scene Id | Speed | Location | Weather | Proximity To Vehicle/ Obstacle | Traffic Condition |
|---|---|---|---|---|---|
| 3 | 0.2 | 0.2 | 0.1 | 0.4 | 0.1 |
| 4 | 0.3 | 0.2 | 0.15 | 0.2 | 0.15 |
| 5 | 0.15 | 0.25 | 0.15 | 0.2 | 0.25 |
| 6 | 0.2 | 0.25 | 0.1 | 0.2 | 0.25 |
| 7 | 0.3 | 0.25 | 0.25 | 0.1 | 0.1 |
| 8 | 0.2 | 0.3 | 0.15 | 0.2 | 0.15 |
| 9 | 0.15 | 0.25 | 0.4 | 0.1 | 0.1 |
| 10 | 0.2 | 0.2 | 0.15 | 0.3 | 0.15 |

These weights were determined based on the importance of each metric in contributing to the overall safety and context of the scene. By assigning appropriate weights to each metric for different scenes, we ensure that the evaluation reflects the critical aspects of each scenario, thereby providing a robust measure of query relevance. Figure 8 demonstrates the relevance score for queries across different scenes.

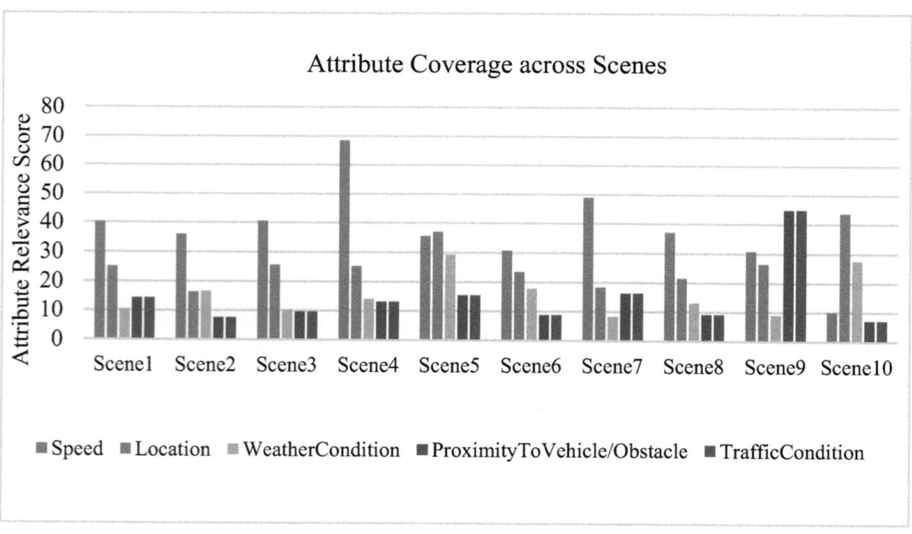


**Fig. 8.** Attribute Coverage and Weight Analysis

In scenes like Scene9, where the cyclist is riding in rainy weather, weather conditions emerge as the most significant factor. The high attribute coverage for weather conditions underscores the critical role that environmental factors play in assessing cycling risks, especially when combined with proximity to vehicle/obstacle. Rainy weather dramatically increases the risk of accidents, making it imperative to include detailed weather data in safety assessments. Scenes involving dynamic elements, such as Scene3 (approaching a parked car with an open door) and Scene10 (meeting with a dooring accident), reveal the importance of speed and location. In these scenes, tracking the cyclist's speed and position relative to obstacles or moving vehicles is crucial for predicting and preventing accidents. These attributes are vital for understanding how changes in the environment impact safety, especially in high-risk situations. In mixed-traffic scenes like Scene5 (bicycles and cars on a motor lane), both traffic condition and proximity to vehicle/obstacle are highlighted as significant. This indicates the need for comprehensive monitoring of traffic conditions and how close cyclists are to vehicles. Effective management in high-traffic environments requires integrating both traffic data and proximity measures to assess risks accurately. Scenes involving environmental hazards, such as Scene7 (approaching a puddle) and Scene8 (approaching an intersection), show the relevance of weather conditions and location. Monitoring how weather impacts road conditions and the cyclist's location relative to potential hazards is essential for ensuring safe navigation and minimizing accident risks. The analysis highlights the critical importance of dynamic interactions and environmental factors in cycling safety, emphasizing the need for queries that prioritize weather conditions, speed, and proximity to obstacles to effectively assess and mitigate risks.

We also evaluated the queries generated by our approach against existing IoT applications and middleware benchmarking test suites against query diversity and richness. The TPCx-IoT [7] queries are primarily designed for simple tasks like real-time monitoring and basic data comparisons, using single-entity queries with minimal WHERE clauses, no joins, and basic aggregation functions. They are scalable for straightforward queries but struggle with complex relationships or large datasets. IoTAbench [6] queries, on the other hand, handle a wider range of complexities, involving 1 to multiple entities, basic to moderate aggregation functions, and 0 to 1 join, making them suitable for applications like smart metering, consumption tracking, and building administration. They scale well across various levels of complexity. The proposed approach takes complexity and flexibility a step further. It supports both simple and complex queries, ranging from single-entity queries to multi-entity queries with multiple joins and custom aggregation and situation functions. With high query richness, it allows advanced analytical tasks, context-aware queries, and situational awareness. It covers a broader range of use cases and offers more scalability and flexibility in query generation. Compared to [12], where query richness was validated based solely on entities, our approach handles varying levels of query richness. A key innovation of our approach is the introduction of random query generation based on scenarios. This avoids the limitations of a static query suite, which can lead to overfitting or fine-tuning to specific benchmarks. By generating diverse queries dynamically, we ensure more robust and realistic evaluations, enhancing scalability and adaptability in real-world applications.

## 6  Conclusion

In conclusion, this study presents a novel scenario-based context query generation approach to evaluate the data digestion performance of CMPs. The proposed method leverages, knowledge modelling, data integration, scene graph generation, situation inferencing and knowledge extraction techniques to automatically generate context queries.

The dynamic nature of situations existing within the scenes, serves as the basis for query generation. We evaluated the proposed approach using real-world scenes and IoT datasets demonstrating its practical applicability and effectiveness. We used a template-based query generation method, where five different query types are maintained with varying degrees of query richness. Also, we evaluated the diversity of queries in terms of data retrieval options and query attributes, that help in assessing the CMP's ability to handle a wide range of query types and requirements. The computation times related to the query generation process suggest that the proposed approach can generate a significant number of queries in minimum time with the use of parallelism. Moreover, the evaluation of query relevance using weighted coverage metrics such as speed, weather, location, traffic, and proximity underscores the effectiveness of our approach in generating contextually comprehensive queries for cyclist safety in various scenes. This approach forms the foundation for creating a comprehensive framework to evaluate the data digestion/retrieval performance of CMPs by generating queries with diverse complexity, efficiency, relevance, and comprehensive entity coverage, which ultimately enhances the efficiency of IoT middleware platforms.

**Acknowledgment.** Support for this publication from the Australian Research Council (ARC) Discovery Project Grant DP200102299 and Road Safety Innovation Fund (RSIF) – Round 2 [RSIF2-27] is thankfully acknowledged.

# References


1. An, J. et al.: Toward global IoT-enabled smart cities interworking using adaptive semantic adapter. IEEE Internet Things J. **6**(3), 5753–5765 (2019). https://doi.org/10.1109/JIOT.2019.2905275
2. Li, X., Eckert, M., Martinez, J.F., Rubio, G.: Context aware middleware architectures: survey and challenges. Sensors (Switzerland) **15**(8), 20570–20607 (2015)
3. ETSI - ETSI ISG CIM group releases first specification for context exchange in smart cities: https://www.etsi.org/newsroom/news/1300-2018-04-news-etsi-isg-cim-group-releases-first-specification-for-context-exchange-in-smart-cities. Accessed 24 Sept 2023
4. NGSI-LD: https://en.wikipedia.org/wiki/NGSI-LD. Accessed 18 Feb 2023
5. FIWARE: https://www.fiware.org/. Accessed 16 May 2023
6. Arlitt, M., Marwah, M., Bellala, G., Shah, A., Healey, J., Vandiver, B.: IoTAbench: an Internet of Things Analytics Benchmark. In ICPE 15: Proceedings of the 6th ACM/SPEC International Conference on Performance Engineering, New York, NY, USA: Association for Computing Machinery, Jan 2015, pp. 133–144 (2015)
7. TPCx-IoT: http://www.tpc.org/tpcxiot/default.asp. Accessed 02 Apr 2023
8. Poess, M., Nambiar, R., Kulkarni, K, Narasimhadevara, C., Rabl, T., Jacobsen, H.-A.: Analysis of TPCx-IoT: the first industry standard benchmark for iot gateway systems. In: 2018 IEEE 34th International Conference on Data Engineering (ICDE), Apr 2018, pp. 1519–1530, iSSN: 2375-026X (2018)
9. Medvedev, A. et al.: Data ingestion and storage performance of IoT platforms: study of OpenIoT. In: Lecture Notes in Computer Science (including subseries Lecture Notes in Artificial Intelligence and Lecture Notes in Bioinformatics), vol. 10218, pp. 141–157. LNCS (2017)
10. da Cruz, M.A.A., Rodrigues, J.J.P.C., Sangaiah, A.K., Al-Muhtadi, J., Korotaev, V.: Performance evaluation of IoT middleware. J. Netw. Comput. Appl. **109**, 53–65 (2018)

11. Salhofer, P., Joanneum, F.H.: Evaluating the FIWARE platform: a case-study on implementing smart application with FIWARE. In: Proceedings of the 51st Hawaii International Conference on System Sciences, pp. 5797–5805 (2018)

12. Medvedev, A., Hassani, A., Zaslavsky, A., Haghighi, P.D., Ling, S., Jayaraman, P.P.: Benchmarking IoT context management platforms: high-level queries matter. In: 2019 Global IoT Summit (GIoTS), Aarhus, Denmark, pp. 1-6 (2019). https://doi.org/10.1109/GIOTS.2019.8766395.

13. Mondal, S., Jayaraman, P.P., Hassani, A., Haghighi, P.D., Georgakopoulos, D.: Situation-based query generation for performance evaluation of cloud managed IoT applications. In: 2023 24th IEEE International Conference on Mobile Data Management (MDM), Singapore, Singapore, pp. 352–357 (2023). https://doi.org/10.1109/MDM58254.2023.00064

14. Ulbrich, S., Menzel, T., Reschka, A., Schuldt, F., Maurer, M.: Defining and substantiating the terms scene, situation, and scenario for automated driving. In: 2015 IEEE 18th International Conference on Intelligent Transportation Systems, pp. 982–988 (2015). https://doi.org/10.1109/ITSC.2015.164

15. Ye, J., Dobson, S., McKeever, S : Situation identification techniques in pervasive computing: a review. Pervasive Mob. Comput. 8(1), 36–66 (2012)

16. Semantic Sensor Network (SSN): https://www.w3.org/TR/vocab-ssn/. Accessed 18 Jun 2022

17. GeoSPARQL: https://www.ogc.org/standard/geosparql/. Accessed 29 May 2023

18. Allen's Interval Algebra: https://en.wikipedia.org/wiki/Allen%27s_interval_algebra. Accessed 14 Mar 2023

19. Melbourne Open Data Website: https://data.melbourne.vic.gov.au/pages/home/. Accessed 28 Aug 2023

20. OpenAI: ChatGPT (Mar 14 version) [Large language model] (2023). https://chat.openai.com/chat. Accessed: 2023/10/26

21. Protégé: https://protege.stanford.edu/. Accessed 06 Aug 2023

22. Padovitz, A., Loke, S.W., Zaslavsky, A.: Towards a theory of context spaces. In: IEEE Annual Conference on Pervasive Computing and Communications Workshops. Proceedings of the Second, Orlando, FL, USA, pp. 38–42 (2004). https://doi.org/10.1109/PERCOMW.2004.1276902

23. Semantic Web Rule Language: https://en.wikipedia.org/wiki/Semantic_Web_Rule_Language. Accessed 18 Sept 2023

24. Hassani, A. et al.: Context definition and query language: conceptual specification, implementation, and evaluation. Sensors 19(6), 1478 (2019)

# Robotics and Autonomous Systems

# A Framework for Devising, Evaluating and Fine-Tuning Indoor Tracking Algorithms


Alpha Diallo[(⊠)] [iD] and Benoît Garbinato [iD]

University of Lausanne, Lausanne, Switzerland
{alpha.diallo,benoit.garbinato}@unil.ch



**Abstract.** In recent years, we have observed a growing interest in Indoor Tracking Systems (ITS) for providing location-based services indoors. This is due to the limitations of Global Navigation and Satellite Systems, which do not operate in non-line-of-sight environments. Depending on their architecture, ITS can rely on expensive infrastructure, accumulate errors, or be challenging to evaluate in real-life environments. Building an ITS is a complex process that involves devising, evaluating and fine-tuning tracking algorithms. This process is not yet standard as researchers use different types of equipment, deployment environments, and evaluation metrics. Therefore, it is challenging for researchers to build novel tracking algorithms and for the research community to reproduce the experiments.

To address these challenges, we propose *MobiXIM*, a framework that provides a set of tools for devising, evaluating and fine-tuning tracking algorithms in a structured manner. For devising tracking algorithms, *MobiXIM* introduces a novel plugin architecture, allowing researchers to collaborate and extend existing algorithms. We assess our framework by building an ITS encompassing the key elements of wireless, inertial, and collaborative ITS. The proposed ITS achieves a positioning accuracy of 4 m, which is an improvement of up to 33% compared to a baseline Pedestrian Dead Reckoning algorithm.

**Keywords:** Indoor Tracking · Collaborative Systems · Peer-to-Peer Communication · Networking · Signal Processing


## 1 Introduction

*Indoor Tracking* refers to solutions that overcome the limitations of Global Navigation and Satellite Systems (GNSS), such as the Global Positioning System (GPS) and Galileo, in non-line-of-sight environments. It is becoming a trendy topic in the industry and the research community because of its potential impact on people's lives.

To track mobile devices indoors, researchers propose solutions built with technologies whose primary goals were not specifically designed for indoor tracking. These solutions can be classified into three categories described hereafter.


© ICST Institute for Computer Sciences, Social Informatics and Telecommunications Engineering 2026
Published by Springer Nature Switzerland AG 2026. All Rights Reserved
A. Soylu et al. (Eds.): MobiQuitous 2024, LNICST 634, pp. 405–427, 2026.
https://doi.org/10.1007/978-3-032-10554-7_22

**Infrastructure-based ITS**, defined as *wireless-based*, rely on existing or dedicated communication infrastructure mainly using a centralized architecture by offloading computationally extensive tasks to a remote server. In this approach, the tracking is done by measuring a Received Signal Strength Indication (RSSI) between an emitter and a receiver to either estimate distance or capture signal fingerprints. RSSI is sensitive to signal variation caused by multipath, fading, reflection or signal scattering. To improve the accuracy of wireless-based ITS, researchers use multiple techniques such as trilateration [3], multilateration [1], map matching [29] or fingerprinting [25]. These techniques leverage signals from nearby devices or use landmarks to track mobile devices [12]. For instance, fingerprinting, popular across the literature, requires researchers to collect signals at predefined locations and compare them to signals received by a mobile device to estimate its location. This approach is challenging to implement as it requires regular data collection and a high cost for deploying and maintaining the infrastructure.

**Infrastructure-less ITS**, defined as *inertial—and magnetic-based* ITS, rely on inertial and magnetic sensors embedded in recent mobile devices. These sensors measure physical activity or the magnetic field. The accelerometer measures a linear acceleration, usually on three axes, the gyroscope measures an angular velocity, and the magnetometer measures the strength and direction of the Earth's magnetic field [16]. This approach is commonly used in decentralized ITS as mobile devices can compute their location without relying on a central server [8]. However, these ITS suffer from an accumulation of errors due to noisy sensors affecting their tracking estimates.

**Collaborative ITS** is a novel approach to overcome the limitations of the above-listed type of ITS. It consists of leveraging the communication capability of mobile devices to sense their environment and exchange information with nearby mobile devices [8]. In some configurations, this approach can be combined with a limited number of fixed infrastructures to improve accuracy.

## 1.1   Scope and Methodology

This paper focuses on the three types of ITS, specifically those deployed on *digital consumer electronics* such as smartphones, tablets, microcontroller units (MCUs), etc. Therefore, we exclude industrial or military tracking systems requiring expensive infrastructure.

ITS within our scope of interest are built using principles centred around devising, evaluating, and fine-tuning the tracking algorithms. Given the lack of standards for devising tracking algorithms, it is difficult for researchers to collaborate and reuse existing algorithms. Additionally, most of these algorithms are evaluated on data collected by the researchers. Collecting data is a time-consuming task that requires multiple devices, well-planned coordination between participants, and an infrastructure for storing and analysing the data.

We also observe that ITS are evaluated using different metrics, making comparisons between them challenging. Additionally, the lack of a framework hinders the reuse of existing tracking algorithms and complicates the reproduction of experiments. Regarding reproducibility, a survey shows that more than 70% of researchers have tried and failed to reproduce another scientist's experiments, and even more than half have failed to reproduce their own experiments [2]. Reproducibility is a major concern in ITS as experiments are conducted in specific environments, use costly infrastructure, and require timely interactions between mobile devices and meticulous coordination between participants. Indeed, once the experiments are done, it is difficult for other researchers to reproduce because of the absence of data and the difficulty of replicating the environment in which the experiments were achieved.

## 1.2   Problem Statement

This paper addresses the problem of standardizing the process of devising, evaluating, and fine-tuning tracking algorithms. Setting up a clear methodology and providing tools are key to accelerating the process of building ITS and facilitating the reproducibility of experiments.

To achieve these objectives, we propose a novel framework that defines a standard set of processes for collecting data, devising, evaluating and fine-tuning tracking algorithms. Our framework integrates an orchestrator platform for preparing the data collection, processing the data and replaying the movement of participants. A mobile companion app is also proposed, allowing participants to follow instructions to collect data along selected paths defined using the orchestrator platform. At its core, *MobiXIM* uses an extensible plugin architecture, allowing researchers to devise specific parts of their tracking algorithm and implement them on top of existing state-of-the-art algorithms. This methodology, commonly used in software engineering, accelerates the development of prototypes by removing the complexity of non-core components of a system.

To the best of our knowledge, we are the first to propose a complete framework for devising and evaluating the three types of ITS.

## 1.3   Roadmap

The remainder of this paper is organized as follows. In the next section, we present the related work and explain the need for a framework encompassing most ITS. In Sect. 3, we place the context and define some key terms. We present the methodology used in the literature in Sect. 4. Section 5 introduces *MobiXIM* and describes each component. In Sect. 6, we run experiments by building an ITS. We evaluate this ITS built using *MobiXIM* in Sect. 7. In Sect. 8, we discuss the strengths and limitations of *MobiXIM* and conclude the paper in Sect. 9.

## 2   Related Work

This section presents recent frameworks for devising indoor tracking algorithms. We introduce these frameworks, discuss their main contributions and show how they compare to *MobiXIM*. We summarise our findings in Table 1.

**Table 1.** Comparing the features of MobiXIM and other frameworks

| | MobiXIM | Ko and Wu [15] | Chen et al. [5] | De Wynckel and Signer [27] |
|---|---|---|---|---|
| Wireless-based | Yes | Yes | Yes | Yes |
| Inertial-based | Yes | No | No | Yes |
| Collaborative | Yes | No | No | Yes |
| Execution replay | Yes | No | No | No |
| Evaluation metrics | Trajectories similarity and Positioning Accuracy | Classification accuracy and Positioning error (MSE) | Positioning Accuracy | Positioning Accuracy |
| Type of data | Simulated and Real-life | Simulated and Real-life | Real-life | Real-life |
| Wireless Protocol | BLE | Wi-Fi | BLE | Wi-Fi, BLE, RFID, LTE |
| Multi-user Platform | Yes | No | No | No |
| Type of trackees | Smartphones and tablets | Laptops | Microcontrollers | Smartphone, tablets, MCUs, laptops, etc. |
| Floorplan representation | GeoJSON | Local coordinate frame with image overlay | Local coordinate frame with image overlay | Not specified |

In the literature, most researchers focus on wireless-based ITS and propose frameworks for improving the processes for devising ITS based on fingerprinting [4,15,24]. One such framework, proposed by Ko and Wu, incorporates channel modelling, position estimation, and error analysis methods for wireless-based ITS using RSSI collected from Wi-Fi Access Points (AP) [15]. Their framework uses two positioning methods to achieve coarse positioning and fine positioning. For coarse positioning, RSSI are partitioned into clusters by their source spaces. Then, they use a Support Vector Machine (SVM) to classify the RSSI and find the corresponding room where a mobile device is located. They use a Bayesian estimation technique for fine positioning to pinpoint a mobile device's location based on its previously estimated coarse location. They achieve a 99.1% accuracy for estimating a coarse location and about 3 m of positioning accuracy for fine positioning in a $608\,\text{m}^2$ environment and a density of 2.1 Wi-Fi AP every $100\,\text{m}^2$. Their framework's main limitation is its limited scope, focusing solely on devising tracking algorithms using fingerprinting. ITS based on fingerprinting are challenging to deploy in real-life environments because they require time-consuming data collection, and their performance depends strongly on environmental changes. In addition, the framework proposed by Ko and Wu uses a classification model based on SVM coupled with Bayesian estimation methods, which requires significant computational resources. Therefore, their proposed techniques are unsuitable for real-time applications.

Chen et al. propose a framework for devising ITS using Machine Learning (ML) algorithms [5]. They collect Bluetooth signals at predefined locations and pass them to neural networks to estimate the location of mobile devices. Then, they compare the performance of a Multilayer Perceptron (MLP) with a Recurrent Neural Network (RNN) on a dense dataset of collected signals. They demonstrate that the MLP outperforms the RNN and offers an accuracy of up to 98% with six receivers (a density of 8.3 receivers per $100\,\mathrm{m}^2$). Their proposed framework addresses the challenges of finding an optimal algorithm to solve the environmental factors affecting indoor positioning. However, as this approach requires a lot of data, it is important to consider the challenges of collecting data in a large environment. Furthermore, their framework does not include aspects related to the representation of deployment environments and does not provide guidelines for reproducing the experiments. The latter limitation is common in the literature, as most authors do not provide enough information to reproduce their experiments. Even if they detail their methodology for devising their algorithms, researchers expect a thorough discussion, code, and datasets to facilitate the reproducibility of the experiments.

De Wynckel and Signer propose OpenHPS, an open-source hybrid positioning system using a modular framework that supports multiple technologies and positioning methods [27]. It is designed to be flexible by fusing data from multiple sources, thus integrating wireless and inertial measurements. The collected data can be stored in databases or locally on a mobile device. Their proposed framework is built in TypeScript, a cross-platform superset of JavaScript, ensuring deployment on mobile, client, and server-side applications. Their framework is primarily aimed at a community of developers, enabling them to design a hybrid, multi-platform system encompassing indoor and outdoor positioning. Therefore, they do not address the challenges of evaluating ITS and reproducing experiments.

Other frameworks proposed in the literature come with powerful tools and structured processes to orient and speed up research. An example of a framework for a specific use case is proposed by Kitras et al. [14]. They focus on integrating location modules into air quality measurement systems. By proposing a Location and Movement Detection of the Application layer (LaMDA) framework, they challenge researchers to check the reliability of location information provided by low-cost devices for analysing Air Quality.

In the literature, researchers have not yet provided a complete framework that considers all the significant aspects of an ITS, from devising the tracking algorithms to evaluation, emphasising reproducibility. Our proposed framework addresses this, providing guidelines and tools for devising tracking algorithms in a structured manner.

## 3   System Model

We consider environments where an ITS is needed such as undergrounds, buildings with multiple rooms, facilities, corridors, etc. We aim to track mobile devices with embedded computational and communication capabilities. These mobile devices, typically smartphones and tablets, can sense their environment, collect inertial and magnetic measurements and wireless signals, run some tracking algorithms, and communicate with nearby devices wirelessly.

We also consider Bluetooth Low-Energy (BLE) beacons with fixed positions to correct mobile device estimates. In this setting, mobile devices detect nearby beacons and estimate their location according to the beacon with the strongest signal or compare the signal fingerprints with priorly collected signals. Beacons can be physical or virtual. Physical beacons are commercial devices running on batteries and broadcasting advertisements following the Eddystone or iBeacon standards. Virtual beacons are simulated devices used to facilitate the execution of scenarios under several configurations without installing and maintaining physical beacons. They emit signals propagating using a path loss model that models the relationship between RSSI and distance.

The goal of an ITS is to estimate single locations or trajectories by using measurements from mobile devices. A trajectory $T$ consists of a set of $n$ tuples $L_{i \in \{1..n\}} = (\lambda_i, \phi_i, t_i)$, where $\lambda_i$ is a latitude, $\phi_i$ is a longitude and $t_i$ is a timestamp. In this paper, we distinguish three types of trajectories:

- **Groundtruth trajectory** is a sequence of points representing the real locations of users at a given time.
- **Estimated trajectory** represents locations as computed by a tracking algorithm associated with a baseline tracking algorithm.
- **Corrected trajectory** is the trajectory resulting from improving the estimated trajectory.

To obtain the estimated and corrected trajectories, researchers devise tracking algorithms that can fit into one of the following categories.

- **Filtering algorithm** is used to remove the noise from collected data or to smooth a signal. One such algorithm is a low-pass filter used to smooth rapid fluctuation of RSSI in wireless-based ITS or to smooth inertial measurements that go beyond a given threshold [8,20].
- **Positioning algorithm** estimates the location of a device using the data processed by the filtering algorithm. For inertial-based ITS, the baseline positioning algorithm is the Pedestrian Dead Reckoning (PDR), which estimates a new location based on the previous location coupled with the orientation of a user and its step length. For wireless-based ITS, k-nearest neighbors (k-NN) is a well-known technique for detecting the closest priorly collected signal to a newly detected RSSI in a fingerprinting approach.
- **Collaborative algorithm** is used to further improve the location estimates of a positioning algorithm by leveraging the proximity between users.

# 4   Methodology

This section presents the common steps researchers take to build new ITS. These steps are part of a methodology that *MobiXIM* aims to simplify and standardise.

## 4.1   Devising Tracking Algorithms

Most tracking algorithms proposed in the literature are enhancements of existing algorithms, such as the PDR commonly used for inertial-based ITS or k-NN for finding nearest neighbours in wireless-based ITS. These algorithms are popular and have been implemented multiple times. Rewriting them requires a lot of time and can even introduce errors due to a wrong implementation, thus impacting the performance of the tracking algorithms. Researchers must reuse existing algorithms and assemble them easily to reduce the hassle of devising new tracking algorithms.

## 4.2   Evaluating Tracking Algorithms

After devising and implementing tracking algorithms, researchers must evaluate their performance and compare them with existing algorithms. In the literature, ITS are evaluated regarding positioning accuracy, coverage, complexity, robustness, scalability, cost, privacy and power consumption [21]. However, positioning accuracy remains by far the most used evaluation criterion. Rainer Mautz defines positioning accuracy as the degree of conformance of an estimated or measured position at a given time to the true value [19]. Therefore, researchers assess the performance of the tracking algorithms by comparing the corrected trajectories with the corresponding groundtruth and estimated trajectories. They use multiple metrics, such as the Mean Squared Error (MSE), the Mean Absolute Error (MAE), or the Root Mean Squared Error (RMSE). However, these metrics are sensitive to outliers and do not measure the similarity between the groundtruth and the corresponding estimated and corrected trajectories. It is important to define evaluation metrics that would be used as standards in the literature to compare ITS better. After selecting the metrics for measuring the performance of their tracking algorithms, researchers evaluate them using one of the approaches described hereafter.

**Evaluating Tracking Algorithms on Existing Data.** Some researchers use existing or synthetic datasets to evaluate their tracking algorithms. Existing data are public mobility datasets or datasets initially collected in previous experiments. Synthetic datasets are generated during a simulation to mimic the real movements of users in an indoor environment [11,17]. Such datasets accelerate the evaluation of the proposed tracking algorithms. However, in real-life environments, the performance of the tracking algorithms may diverge as environments have different layouts, which affect the raw measurements and the resulting estimated and corrected trajectories. On the other hand, synthetic datasets can be biased or unrealistic, thus failing to capture the real movements of people in indoor environments [7].

**Evaluating Tracking Algorithms on Collected Data.** Another method for evaluating an ITS involves collecting data. While this approach provides greater flexibility for the researcher, it requires completing the following steps before evaluating the tracking algorithms.

- **Planning the data collection.** Before collecting the data, researchers need to understand their targeted deployment environment. This involves knowing the dimensions of the environment, its occupancy rate, constraints related to the architecture of the building, and the layout of the furniture. These parameters can impact the technology choice and the performance of the tracking algorithms.
- **Building a data collection app.** In the literature, most authors use ad-hoc software tools to collect data. For instance, Jimenez et al. propose *GetSensor-Data*, an Android app for collecting data from wireless, inertial and magnetic sensors [13]. However, the code source is no longer maintained to consider the updates from the Android Operating System. Using a standard mobile application to collect raw measurements will reduce the time and effort needed to evaluate ITS. To fully benefit from this mobile application, it must be fully integrated into an ecosystem to better coordinate the data collection.
- **Collecting the data.** Data collection is a tedious task usually done by a small group of participants. In the literature, most ITS are evaluated in small deployment environments, generally less than $500\,\mathrm{m}^2$, and with a small number of trajectories. This is mainly due to the difficulties of coordinating teams for large-scale data collection. For example, in collaborative ITS, researchers must capture participants' interactions during the data collection. Since collaborative ITS perform better with a high number of interactions between participants, the data collection process must involve multiple participants moving simultaneously [8].

Once the evaluation metrics are set and the data are ready, researchers proceed with the optional steps outlined below.

**Designing the Floor Plans.** After selecting an indoor environment, the next step is to model it to facilitate the data collection and visually display the trajectories. In the literature, most researchers use georeferenced images to model their indoor environment [5,15,26]. This approach is tedious to implement and difficult to update when the building changes. It also requires integrating properties of the environment, such as rooms, walls, or doors.

To facilitate the widespread adoption of an ITS, researchers should integrate dynamic maps that consider the specific features of the environment. Additionally, the map should use a geographic coordinate system to facilitate its integration into existing outdoor positioning systems.

**Cleaning the Data.** Raw measurements collected by digital consumer electronics are noisy and can contain outliers impacting ITS performance. Some authors use filtering algorithms to smooth the raw measurement, attenuating the noise or removing outliers by eliminating anomalous signals [28]. Multiple tools exist for data cleaning. One such tool is the SciPy library, available in Python for processing signals.[1] Instead of devising the filtering algorithms from the ground, researchers can use existing libraries and plug them into their positioning algorithms.

**Adjusting Parameters.** After cleaning the data, researchers may need to adjust the parameters associated with each participant or mobile device. These parameters include the sampling rate, the step length, the initial orientation, the transmission power, and the error correction threshold. It would be helpful to have tools to adjust these parameters and observe how they impact the performance of the tracking algorithms.

The methodology presented in this section demonstrates the numerous challenges researchers face when devising and evaluating their tracking algorithms. The complexity of the processes, coupled with the absence of standards, makes it even more challenging to compare ITS and reproduce the experiments. Therefore, it is crucial to have a framework that guides researchers and offers functionalities such as pre-loaded datasets to accelerate devising and evaluating new tracking algorithms. Therefore, such a framework would provide a common baseline for comparing tracking algorithms.

## 5   *MobiXIM* Architecture

This section describes the components and the process flow of *MobiXIM*, associated with the characteristics of ITS listed in Sect. 4. Figure 1 highlights these components and indicates how they interact.

### 5.1   Mobile Companion App

As discussed in Sect. 4, some researchers evaluate their tracking algorithms with collected data that best fits their needs. This task is time-consuming and does not follow any standard protocol. *MobiXIM* facilitates the data collection with a mobile companion app that integrates seamlessly with other framework components. Built for iOS and Android, it is intended to be used by participants to collect raw measurements along predefined groundtruths. These raw measurements are made of the following fields stored in CSV files.

- **AccX**. It measures the acceleration on the X-axis, corresponding to the left and right horizontal movements.
- **AccY**. It measures the acceleration on the Y-axis, corresponding to the horizontal forward and backward movements.
- **AccZ**. It measures the acceleration on the Z-axis corresponding to the vertical movements up and down.

---

[1] https://scipy.org/.

- **Gyroscope.** It measures the orientation relative to the body frame.
- **Azimuth.** It measures the rotation angle between the device's Y-axis and the magnetic north pole.
- **Pitch.** It measures the rotation angle on the X-axis, the angle between a plane parallel to the device's screen and a plane parallel to the ground.
- **Roll.** It measures the tilt of the device on the Y-axis.
- **RSSI.** It measures the signal strength in decibel-milliwatts (dBm) emitted by physical BLE beacons at a short distance, estimated using the inverse relationship between distance and RSSI. A strong RSSI indicates a short distance between a mobile device and a beacon. A weak RSSI indicates a larger distance. We set a default value of -100 dBm to indicate a beacon that is not within the detection range of a mobile device.

### 5.2  Orchestrator Platform

The orchestrator platform is a web application built in Python using the Django Framework and hosted on a remote server. It is intended to prepare the data collection, set up the experiments, and run the evaluation. The user interface, mainly built in HTML/CSS and JavaScript, is intended for use on a desktop browser. Figure 2 shows the user interfaces of the mobile companion app and the orchestrator platform. The role of the orchestrator platform and its interaction with the mobile companion app are detailed hereafter.

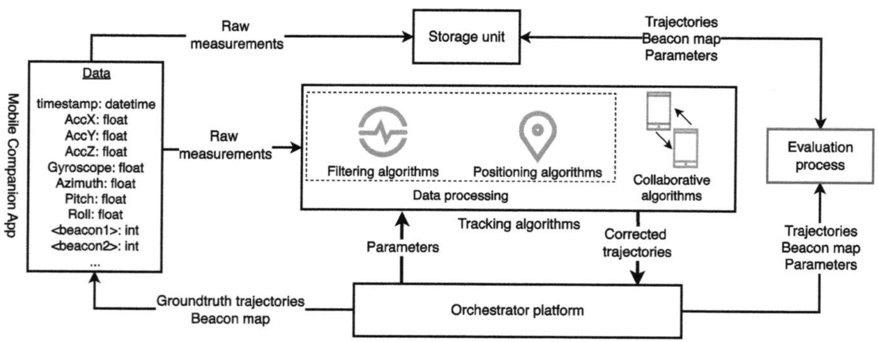


**Fig. 1.** Architecture and process flow of *MobiXIM*

**Planning Scenarios.** Prior to the data collection, as shown in Fig. 1, researchers plan the execution scenario by designing the groundtruth trajectories on the orchestrator platform. These trajectories are then sent to the mobile companion app via a QR code scanned by participants to receive the groundtruths along which they collect data. During the data collection, participants regularly signal when they reach checkpoints using the Mobile Companion App.

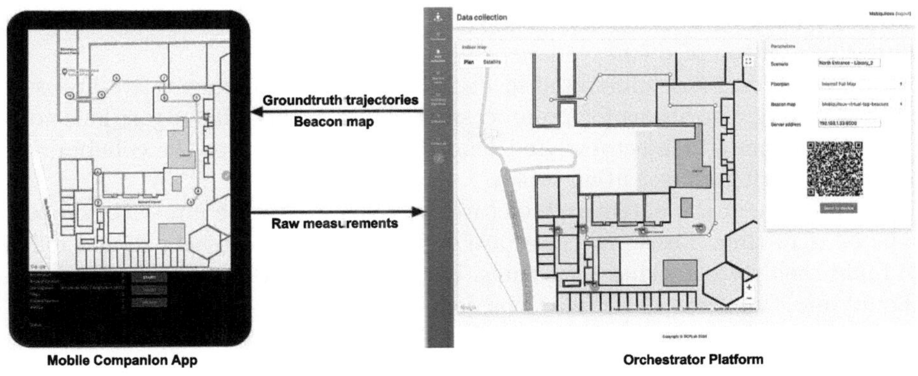


**Fig. 2.** User interfaces of the Mobile Companion App and the Orchestrator Platform

**Floorplan Representation.** To facilitate the construction of floorplans, we use the GeoJSON format for encoding geographic features. This format is particularly useful for running spatial queries such as detecting rooms, corridors or intersecting walls. In the literature, most authors represent their deployment environment with an image layer in a 2D cartesian representation system [18,22]. However, this representation is static and difficult to scale and manipulate. Representing an indoor space with a GeoJSON format facilitates interoperability with existing outdoor tracking systems due to its scalability.

**Execution Replay.** Another function of the orchestrator platform is to aggregate the raw measurements and groundtruth trajectories into a single environment to reproduce the movement of participants simultaneously. We define this approach as *execution replay*, allowing researchers to replay the real displacement of participants. This approach helps researchers to visualize the performance of their tracking algorithms better. It also allows them to create environments that foster collaboration using real-life data collected by participants. This approach addresses the challenges of synchronizing participants in real environments where many people exchange data simultaneously. Additionally, it significantly reduces the time and cost of running experiments while relying on real-life data reflecting the real movements of people indoors.

### 5.3  Tracking Algorithms

The role of a tracking algorithm is to process raw measurements and estimate locations. As *MobiXIM* aims to facilitate reusability, we structure the tracking algorithms with a plugin architecture. A plugin architecture is a design pattern used in software engineering to build modular components that are independent of each other. These components can be placed together without altering the core codebase. This novel approach for indoor tracking allows us to separate the main steps for devising an ITS, such as cleaning the data, computing the location estimates, and simulating data exchanges. With this approach, researchers can reuse existing filtering and positioning algorithms and build their tracking algorithms on top of them.

In the process flow illustrated in Fig. 1, the raw measurements are first sent to the filtering algorithms for preprocessing. Then, positioning algorithms compute the estimated trajectories and send these trajectories to the collaborative algorithm during an execution replay.

To implement the plugin architecture, we specify software interfaces for each type of algorithm. These interfaces are skeletons that researchers should follow to build their own tracking algorithms. For instance, all the tracking algorithms should implement the basic functions defined below.

- *get_plugin_name*: returns the full name of a plugin.
- *get_plugin_slug*: returns a slug, an abbreviated form of the full name used as a unique plugin identifier.
- *get_plugin_display_name*: returns the name displayed on the orchestrator platform.
- *get_plugin_category*: returns one of the three types of algorithms implemented by the plugin, namely, filtering, positioning and collaborative.

In addition to these functions, each algorithm possesses a predefined function for data processing. For filtering algorithms, this function is called *get_filtered_data* and takes as inputs raw measurements and returns smoothed data. For positioning algorithms, the function is called *get_positioning_data*. It takes as inputs the groundtruths, filtered or raw measurements, the initial location of the device and optional parameters such as the estimated step length, and it returns an estimated trajectory. Collaborative algorithms are executed only when at least two devices are within a detection range set by the researcher.

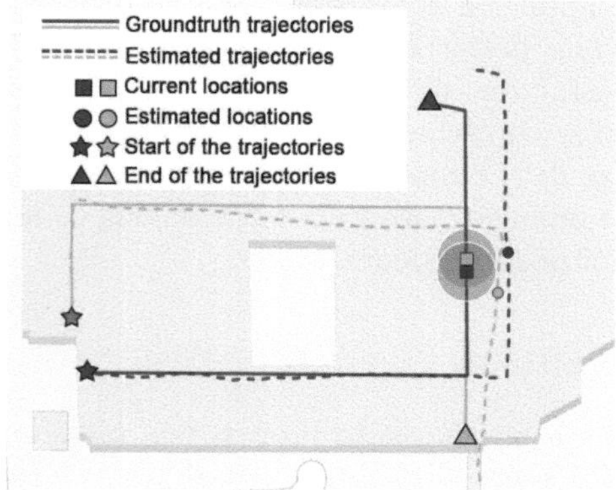


**Fig. 3.** Devices within a collaboration range

Therefore, their main function, called *handle_matches*, receives as parameters a list of devices as objects, a timestamp representing the moment when the devices started collaborating, and two additional values representing the lower threshold of errors. The lower threshold indicates the error above which a device considers its estimates divergent enough from the groundtruth and can, therefore, collaborate to improve them. Figure 3, extracted from the orchestrator platform, illustrates two devices within a collaboration range with their groundtruth and estimated trajectories. We can see that the error on the estimated trajectories accumulates over time, thus leading to location estimates that diverge over time.

### 5.4   Storage Unit

The storage unit stores raw measurements, trajectories, beacon maps, and parameters used for the experiments. It consists of disk storage and a relational database. The disk storage stores large files such as raw measurements, trajectories, and beacon maps. The relational database offers a structured data organization to store and fetch information about the experiments. It connects the user via the orchestrator platform to the data stored on the disk. It also manages the users' privileges to the orchestrator platform, enabling the framework to be multi-user and multi-task.

### 5.5   Evaluation Process

The evaluation process aims to compare the corrected trajectories with their corresponding estimated and groundtruth trajectories. Unlike other components listed in Fig. 1, we consider the evaluation as a process that can be carried out independently of the framework. After the execution replay, the orchestrator platform provides data on trajectories, beacon locations and execution parameters in structured files (JSON, CSV) that researchers can use to evaluate their algorithms.

## 6   Experiments and Execution Replay

This section describes the tracking algorithms built using *MobiXIM*. It also shows how we collect raw measurements and replay participants' movements.

### 6.1   Tracking Algorithms

We devise an inertial-based ITS incorporating an opportunistic error correction mechanism using nearby mobile devices' location estimates and locations of fixed BLE beacons. To achieve this, we start by filtering the inertial data to remove outliers associated with noise. Then, we run a state-of-the-art positioning algorithm to obtain the estimated trajectories. With the execution replay, we simulate peer-to-peer data exchanges and execute a collaborative algorithm. The tracking algorithms are described hereafter.

**Filtering Algorithm.** As inertial sensors are prone to noise and generate outliers, we filter the data using a low-pass filter. This filter is designed to attenuate high-frequency signals above a cutoff frequency. We apply it to smooth the magnitude of acceleration computed using the following equation.

$$mag = \sqrt{x^2 + y^2 + z^2} \tag{1}$$

where $mag$ is the magnitude of acceleration, $x$, $y$ and $z$ are the acceleration of a device on each of the corresponding three-axis.

We implement the algorithm in Python using the signal module of the SciPy library. Then, we integrate the code as a plugin into the framework.

**Positioning Algorithm.** After filtering the raw measurements, we use the PDR algorithm to estimate the participants' locations. First, we start by detecting steps in the magnitude of acceleration with a peak detection technique. We consider peaks in the acceleration amplitude as steps and trigger the PDR to detect the next location of a participant whenever a step is detected. The peak detection technique is also implemented using the SciPy library by analysing the acceleration magnitude as signals.

The PDR algorithm used at the core of the positioning algorithm is defined as follows.

$$\begin{aligned} X_k &= X_{k-1} + L * \cos(\theta) \\ Y_k &= Y_{k-1} + L * \sin(\theta) \end{aligned} \tag{2}$$

where the couple $(X_k, Y_k)$ represents the Cartesian coordinates of the next location computed using the previous coordinates $(X_{k-1}, Y_{k-1})$. $L$ is the step length of a user. We assume that users are aware of their step length, which they estimate by counting steps over a given distance. $\theta$ is the orientation obtained by the gyroscope. The step length and the initial orientation of a device are parameters that can be adjusted on the orchestrator platform. The resulting location is then converted to the WGS84 geographic coordinate system to construct an estimated trajectory.

**Collaborative Algorithm.** In our experiments, we use an enhanced version of a collaborative algorithm proposed in our previous research to correct the estimates of the PDR [8]. The algorithm, defined in Algorithm 1, uses the inter-ranging distance between mobile devices as well as signals from nearby beacons to correct the estimated trajectories. When two mobile devices are close to each other in real life, they exchange their estimated errors and locations. We estimate the error using an incremental value initially set to 0, which linearly increases over time. We decrease the error if the mobile device becomes stationary and starts collaborating with a peer or when it encounters a beacon, as depicted in Lines 10 and 16 of Algorithm 1. We estimate that two devices are close to each other when they are below a distance of 4 m. This distance respects social norms as it remains outside the area that individuals consider their personal space. Indeed, the *theory of Proxemics* estimates the public space of individuals to be a circle of radius ranging between 3.6 and 7.6 m [10].

When two mobile devices are within a collaboration distance, they draw a straight line between their two location estimates and position themselves at a distance on the straight line corresponding to the ratio of errors of each of the devices. Using a ratio of errors, we ensure that diverging devices, i.e. those with a large accumulated error, marginally affect devices with better estimates.

In addition to peer-to-peer collaboration, we also correct the estimates of mobile devices whenever they encounter fixed beacons. We estimate the distance between a mobile device and a beacon using the path loss model commonly used in the literature to model the relationship between RSSI and distance [6]. The location of a mobile device is corrected to match the known location of a beacon only when the estimated distance between the mobile device and the beacon is below 2 m. Our previous research shows that distance estimates are more reliable on short distances using BLE beacons [8,9].

---

**Algorithm 1.** Drift correction with a mobile device or a beacon

---

1: **Input:** devices: $A$ and $B$, lower-threshold $l$
2: **Output:** $A$
3: **if** $B.type$ is *"mobile"* and $A.errors > l$ **then**
4:       $sumErrors \leftarrow A.errors + B.errors$
5:       **if** $sumErrors \neq 0$ **then**
6:           $ratio \leftarrow A.errors/sumErrors$
7:           $intermediatePoint \leftarrow intermediatePoint(A.location, B.location, ratio)$
8:           $A.location \leftarrow intermediatePoint$
9:           **if** $A.location_{(t-1)} = A.location_t$ **then**
10:                $A.errors \leftarrow A.errors - 1$
11:           **end if**
12:       **end if**
13: **end if**
14: **if** $B.type$ is *"beacon"* and $l < A.errors$ **then**
15:       $A.location \leftarrow B.location$
16:       $A.errors \leftarrow 0$
17: **end if**
18: **return** $A$

---

## 6.2   Data Collection

To evaluate our proposed framework, participants collected raw measurements along representative groundtruths, i.e. based on the usual displacement of users. Our deployment environment is a single floorplan of a university building covering an area of up to $8400\,m^2$ made of multiple rooms, corridors and facilities such as a restaurant, toilets and a library. The data collection resulted in 45 trajectories spanning a cumulative distance of 5257 m.

Participants collected data using six mobile devices: an iPhone 15 Pro, an iPhone 12 Pro, an iPhone 12, a Samsung Galaxy Tab S7, a Samsung Galaxy

Tab A8, and a One-Plus Nord 2. These devices have different sensors, functionality, and prices. For this experiment, we only need the inertial measurements to run the PDR algorithm. However, some mobile devices also collected signal measurements from physical beacons, creating a dense dataset that researchers could reuse to propose other tracking algorithms. We position five virtual beacons, i.e. a density of 0.05 beacon per $100\,m^2$, located at the most visited areas of the building. We use a hotspot detection algorithm to identify the ideal locations for positioning the beacons to maximize the chances of encountering mobile devices [9].

### 6.3  Execution Replay

A major strength of *MobiXIM* is the possibility for researchers to replay the movement of participants under multiple scenarios. For our experiments, we use the execution replay to combine all the collected trajectories into the same deployment environment before reproducing the movement of participants simultaneously to simulate a collaborative environment with data collected at different periods. We also used the execution replay to adjust the number and location of beacons and observe how they affect the ITS's performance. Finally, we executed movements associated with 45 trajectories collected using only six devices.

## 7  Evaluation

In this section, we measure the performance of the tracking algorithms. We introduce the evaluation metrics and then present our results before sharing the resources for reproducing the results and the experiments.

### 7.1  Evaluation Metrics

To evaluate the tracking algorithms, we compare each groundtruth trajectory with its corresponding estimated and corrected trajectories regarding similarity and positioning accuracy as described hereafter.

**Discrete Frechet Distance (DFD).** The DFD, defined in Eq. 3, is a measure of similarity used to compare two trajectories by considering the order and the location of each of their points.

$$dfd(i,j) = \begin{cases} d(P_i, Q_j) & \text{if } i = j = 1 \\ max \begin{cases} d(P_i, Q_j) \\ min \begin{cases} dfd(i-1, j) \\ dfd(i, j-1) \\ dfd(i-1, j-1) \end{cases} \end{cases} & \text{otherwise} \end{cases} \quad (3)$$

where $P$ and $Q$ represent trajectories such as $P = \langle p_1, ..., p_m \rangle$ and $Q = \langle q_1, ..., q_n \rangle$, with $p_i$ and $q_i$ representing points on each of the trajectories.

$d(P_i, Q_j)$ is the ground distance $d$ between points pertaining to their respective trajectories $P$ and $Q$. The ground distance between two points $p_l = (\phi_l, \lambda_l)$ and $q_k = (\phi_k, \lambda_k)$ is computed with the Haversine formula defined in Eq. 4.

$$d = 2R \arcsin \sqrt{\sin^2\left(\frac{\varphi_l - \varphi_k}{2}\right) + \cos(\varphi_k)\cos(\varphi_l)\sin^2\left(\frac{\lambda_l - \lambda_k}{2}\right)} \qquad (4)$$

where $R$ is a constant representing the radius of Earth.

**Third Quartile of Localization Errors.** Also defined as *positioning accuracy*, the third quartile of localization errors measures the 75th percentile of pairwise ground distances, defined in Eq. 4, between each point in two given trajectories. Compared to other metrics, such as the MSE or the MAE, the third quartile of localization errors is robust to outliers [23].

## 7.2   Results

As we observe in Fig. 4, our proposed algorithms significantly improve the positioning accuracy of 29 trajectories out of 45. In this figure, the red bars show the third quartile of localization errors of the positioning algorithm, and the green bars represent the results of the corrected algorithm. As expected, combining a collaborative algorithm with the PDR improves the estimates of trajectories that significantly deviate from their groundtruth. It is worth noting that some estimated trajectories with a high accuracy may experience minor degradation. However, in our experiments, the mean deviation observed was only 1.32 m for the affected trajectories. This degradation is negligible compared to the significant positive impact they have on the remaining trajectories.

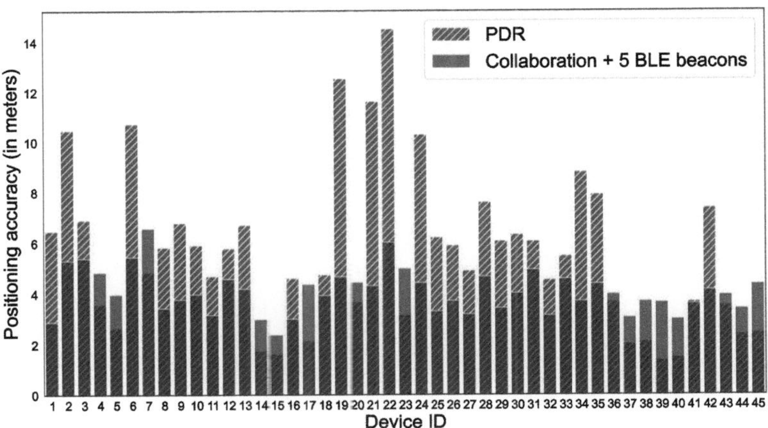


**Fig. 4.** Third quartile of localization errors of all the devices

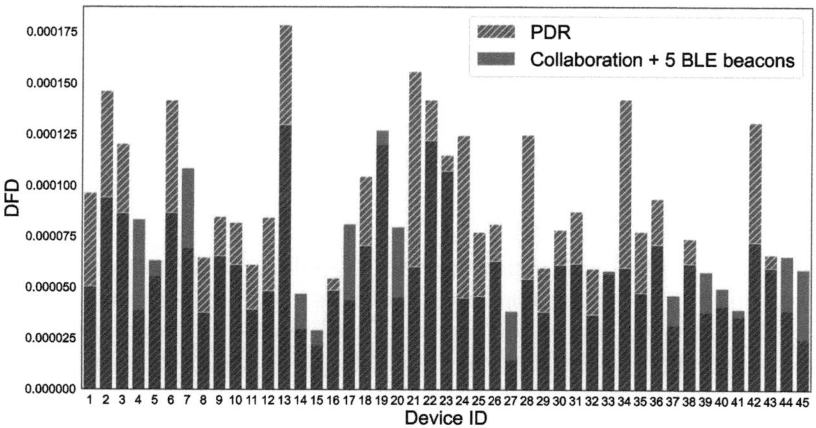


**Fig. 5.** DFD score for all the devices

Our proposed algorithms also improve the similarity score of 29 trajectories out of 45. Figure 5 shows the similarity score between the estimated and the corrected trajectories. A low score indicates a closer similarity with the groundtruth whereas a high score indicates divergence from the groundtruth.

Figure 6 shows the Cumulative Distribution Function (CDF) of the localization errors for all the trajectories. The square dots are the third quartile of localization errors. With only five beacons coupled with peer-to-peer collaboration in a large deployment environment, we obtain an accuracy increase of up to 30% with a mean positioning accuracy of 5.98 m for the estimated trajectories and 4 m for the corrected trajectories.

### 7.3   Code and Dataset

A demo of the orchestrator platform is available on the following link: https:// doplab.unil.ch/mobixim. We preloaded the data used in the experiments to facilitate their reproducibility. Readers can access the dataset containing the raw measurements, the location of the beacons, the floorplan and the trajectories on the following link: https://github.com/doplab/mobixim-evaluation.

## 8   Discussion and Future Work

In this section, we highlight the importance of incorporating collaborative ITS into *MobiXIM*, we detail the impact of collaboration on the performance of the proposed tracking algorithms, and we conclude by presenting the limitations of the framework and the direction of our future research.

### 8.1   Interest in Collaborative ITS

One of the significant contributions of *MobiXIM* over other frameworks is the integration of collaborative algorithms. Collaborative ITS have recently emerged after the massive interest in mobile contact tracing apps during the COVID-19 pandemic. By building an ITS that integrates a collaborative aspect, we emphasize the challenges of devising and evaluating collaborative tracking algorithms in a real-world environment. Therefore, we introduce execution replay to reproduce the real movements of participants in a controlled environment to facilitate interactions with nearby mobile devices. Additionally, *MobiXIM* facilitates collaboration with nearby virtual and physical beacons to increase the accuracy of the ITS using RSSI. Integrating beacons is essential to enabling researchers to devise wireless-based ITS or to leverage the RSSI from beacons to further improve the accuracy of a collaborative ITS. Indeed, as presented in Fig. 6, combining collaboration with a fixed beacon significantly improves the accuracy of a baseline positioning algorithm.

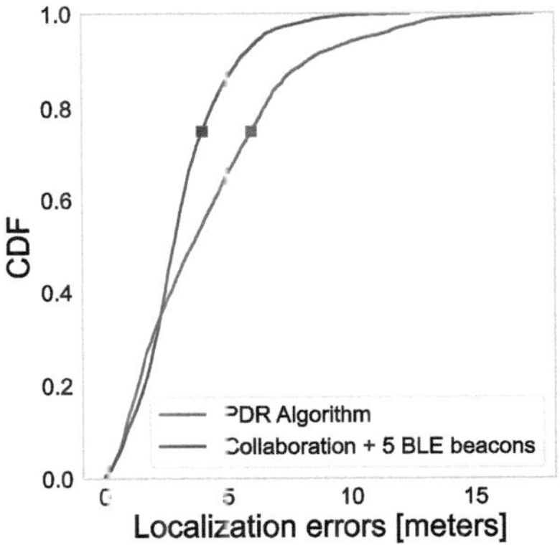


**Fig. 6.** Cumulative Distribution Function (CDF) of the localization errors

### 8.2   Performance of the Tracking Algorithms

Figure 7 shows groundtruth, estimated and corrected trajectories of three devices. Device 27 made 91 collaborations with peers and never encountered any beacon. It improves its localization accuracy by 35% compared to the PDR. However, achieving multiple collaborations negatively impacts its similarity score, as it frequently uses nearby mobile devices' estimates to correct its location estimates. Indeed, due to many collaborations, some devices frequently update their estimates, and their corrected trajectories follow irregular paths diverging from the groundtruth.

Device 15 collaborates only 36 times with peers and corrects its location estimates with three beacons. Due to the small number of collaborations, we observe

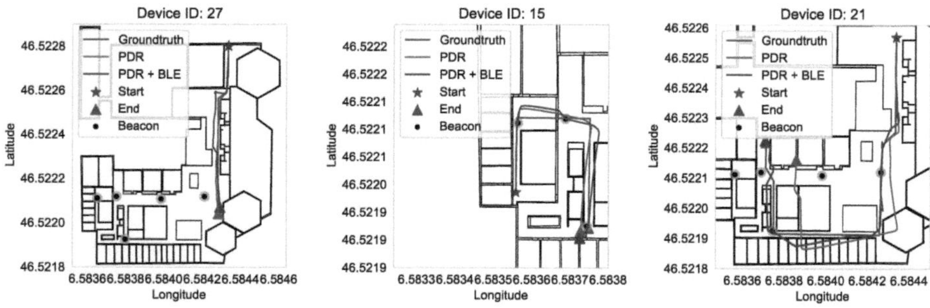

**Fig. 7.** Sample of groundtruth, estimated and corrected trajectories in a single floor plans with virtual beacons

a slight decrease in positioning accuracy and similarity score. For instance, collaborating with other devices slightly degrades its positioning accuracy from 1.62 m to 2.39 m, thus causing it to lose only 77 cm of positioning accuracy while improving peers' estimates. Device 21 made 224 collaborations with peers and two corrections with beacons. By efficiently balancing the number of collaborations and corrections, it improved its similarity score by up to 61% and its positioning accuracy by up to 63%, from 11.6 m to 4.3 m. Devices 15 and 21 correct their positions when they enter a beacon detection range. They position themselves at the beacon's position because we cannot reliably estimate the location of a mobile device solely based on the RSSI from a single beacon.

## 8.3   Limitations and Future Work

To facilitate the data collection, we designed a mobile application that could be easily integrated into an ecosystem. We opted for a data collection process that requires participants to place markers on the ground to guide them along the groundtruth drawn on the orchestrator platform. However, we are aware that this approach can lead to errors in the order of a few centimetres or even a metre. This choice enables data to be obtained quickly to evaluate a tracking algorithm. For researchers looking for centimetre-level accuracy, Mobixim allows uploading their own data using the same format as the mobile companion app.

Some ITS are starting to incorporate techniques such as Angle-of-Arrival, which measures the slight phase differences of the Bluetooth signals across the anchor's multi-antenna array. However, this is not yet ubiquitous because of a lack of hardware implementing this new Bluetooth 5.1 standard feature, as it requires specialized hardware embedding antenna array technology. In the future, we aim to integrate such hardware by extending the capabilities of the beacons as currently designed in *MobiXIM*.

## 9   Conclusion

We propose *MobiXIM*, a framework for devising, evaluating and fine-tuning indoor tracking algorithms. We integrate a novel plugin architecture to ensure its extensibility, allowing researchers to reuse existing tracking algorithms. We evaluate it by designing an ITS that incorporates the three main types of ITS: inertial-based, wireless-based and collaborative. Using real-life inertial measurements, we substantially increase the accuracy of a baseline PDR algorithm. *MobiXIM* helps collect data, set up a deployment environment, and replay movements, allowing researchers to visualize the real and estimated locations of participants and facilitate collaboration. Additionally, we emphasize reproducibility by allowing researchers to exchange their data, tracking algorithms and parameters. In future versions of *MobiXIM*, we aim to incorporate new indoor tracking algorithms based on the Angle-of-Arrival, as defined in recent specifications of the Bluetooth protocol.

## References


1. Adhikari, B., Fernando, X.N.: A neural network based recursive least square multilateration technique for indoor positioning. In: 2021 IEEE 26th International Workshop on Computer Aided Modeling and Design of Communication Links and Networks (CAMAD), pp. 1–6 (2021). https://doi.org/10.1109/CAMAD52502.2021.9617769. https://ieeexplore.ieee.org/abstract/document/9617769. ISSN: 2378-4873

2. Baker, M.: 1,500 scientists lift the lid on reproducibility. Nature **533**(7604), 452–454 (2016). https://doi.org/10.1038/533452a. https://www.nature.com/articles/533452a

3. Bembenik, R., Falcman, K.: BLE indoor positioning system using RSSI-based trilateration. J. Wirel. Mob. Networks Ubiquitous Comput. Dependable Appl. **11**(3), 50–69 (2020)

4. Brunello, A., Montanari, A., Saccomanno, N.: A framework for indoor positioning including building topology. IEEE Access (2022). https://doi.org/10.1109/ACCESS.2022.3218301

5. Chen, M.C., Cheng, Y.T., Chen, R.W.: A novel indoor positioning framework. Comput. Model. Eng. Sci. **130**, 1459–1477 (2021). https://doi.org/10.32604/cmes.2022.015636

6. Debus, W., Axonn, L.: RF path loss & transmission distance calculations. Axonn, LLC, pp. 1–5 (2006)

7. Diallo, A., Garbinato, B.: Mobixim: A Framework for Devising Collaborative Algorithms (2023)

8. Diallo, A., Garbinato, B.: Decentralized collaborative inertial tracking. In: Zaslavsky, A., Ning, Z., Kalogeraki, V., Georgakopoulos, D., Chrysanthis, P.K. (eds.) Mobile and Ubiquitous Systems: Computing, Networking and Services, pp. 26–45. Springer, Cham (2024). https://doi.org/10.1007/978-3-031-63989-0_2

9. Diallo, A., Konstantinidis, S., Garbinato, B.: A pragmatic trade-off between deployment cost and location accuracy for indoor tracking in real-life environments. In: 2024 International Conference on Localization and GNSS (ICL-GNSS), pp. 1–7 (2024). https://doi.org/10.1109/ICL-GNSS60721.2024.10578486. https://ieeexplore.ieee.org/abstract/document/10578486. ISSN: 2325-0771

10. Hall, E.T., et al.: Proxemics [and comments and replies]. Curr. Anthropol. **9**(2/3), 83–108 (1968)
11. Huang, C., Jin, P., Wang, H., Wang, N., Wan, S., Yue, L.: IndoorSTG: a flexible tool to generate trajectory data for indoor moving objects. In: 2013 IEEE 14th International Conference on Mobile Data Management, vol. 1, pp. 341–343. IEEE (2013)
12. Jang, B., Kim, H., Kim, J.W.: Survey of landmark-based indoor positioning technologies. Inf. Fusion **89**, 166–188 (2023). https://doi.org/10.1016/j.inffus.2022.08.013. https://www.sciencedirect.com/science/article/pii/S1566253522001051
13. Jiménez, A.R., Seco, F., Torres-Sospedra, J.: Tools for smartphone multi-sensor data registration and GT mapping for positioning applications. In: 2019 International Conference on Indoor Positioning and Indoor Navigation (IPIN), pp. 1–8. IEEE (2019)
14. Kitras, C., Pollan, C., Myers, K., Tischner, C.W., Lundrigan, P.: Location verification of crowd-sourced sensors. In: 2023 32nd International Conference on Computer Communications and Networks (ICCCN), pp. 1–7 (2023). https://doi.org/10.1109/ICCCN58024.2023.10230111. https://ieeexplore.ieee.org/abstract/document/10230111. ISSN: 2637-9430
15. Ko, C.H., Wu, S.H.: A framework for proactive indoor positioning in densely deployed WiFi networks. IEEE Trans. Mob. Comput. **21**(1), 1–15 (2022). https://doi.org/10.1109/TMC.2020.3001127. https://ieeexplore.ieee.org/document/9112662
16. Kunze, K., Bahle, G., Lukowicz, P., Partridge, K.: Can magnetic field sensors replace gyroscopes in wearable sensing applications? In: International Symposium on Wearable Computers (ISWC) 2010, pp. 1–4. IEEE, Seoul, Korea (South) (2010). https://doi.org/10.1109/ISWC.2010.5665859. http://ieeexplore.ieee.org/document/5665859/
17. Li, H., Lu, H., Chen, X., Chen, G., Chen, K., Shou, L.: Vita: a versatile toolkit for generating indoor mobility data for real-world buildings. Proc. VLDB Endow. **9**(13), 1453–1456 (2016)
18. Mansour, A., Chen, W., Luo, H., Weng, D.: The Power of Many: Multi-User Collaborative Indoor Localization for Boosting Standalone User-Based Systems in Different Scenarios, p. 3161 (2023). https://doi.org/10.33012/2023.19439
19. Mautz, R.: Indoor positioning technologies, p. 1 Band (2012). https://doi.org/10.3929/ETHZ-A-007313554. http://hdl.handle.net/20.500.11850/54888. Artwork Size: 1 Band Medium: application/pdf Publisher: ETH Zurich
20. Mehrabian, H., Ravanmehr, R.: Sensor fusion for indoor positioning system through improved RSSI and PDR methods. Future Gener. Comput. Syst. **138**, 254–269 (2023). https://doi.org/10.1016/j.future.2022.09.003. https://www.sciencedirect.com/science/article/pii/S0167739X22002874
21. Mendoza-Silva, G.M., Torres-Sospedra, J., Huerta, J.: A meta-review of indoor positioning systems. Sensors **19**(20), 4507 (2019). https://doi.org/10.3390/s19204507. https://www.mdpi.com/1424-8220/19/20/4507
22. Pascacio, P., Torres-Sospedra, J., Casteleyn, S., Lohan, E.S.: A Collaborative Approach Using Neural Networks for BLE-RSS Lateration-Based Indoor Positioning (2022). http://arxiv.org/abs/2205.10559. arXiv:2205.10559
23. Potortì, F., et al.: Comparing the performance of indoor localization systems through the EvAAL framework. Sensors **17**(10), 2327 (2017). https://doi.org/10.3390/s17102327. https://www.mdpi.com/1424-8220/17/10/2327
24. Song, X., et al.: A novel convolutional neural network based indoor localization framework with WiFi fingerprinting. IEEE Access **7**, 110698–110709 (2019)

25. Torres-Sospedra, J., Gaibor, D.P.Q., Nurmi, J., Koucheryavy, Y., Lohan, E.S., Huerta, J.: Scalable and efficient clustering for fingerprint-based positioning. IEEE Internet Things J. **10**(4), 3484–3499 (2022)
26. Werner, M.: Efficiently Using Bitmap Floorplans for Indoor Navigation on Mobile Phones (2011)
27. de Wynckel, M.V., Signer, B.: Indoor positioning using the OpenHPS framework. In: 2021 International Conference on Indoor Positioning and Indoor Navigation (IPIN), pp. 1–8 (2021). https://doi.org/10.1109/IPIN51156.2021.9662569. https://ieeexplore.ieee.org/abstract/document/9662569. ISSN: 2471-917X
28. Ye, F., Chen, R., Guo, G., Peng, X., Liu, Z., Huang, L.: A low-cost single-anchor solution for indoor positioning using BLE and inertial sensor data. IEEE Access **7**, 162439–162453 (2019)
29. Zhang, L., Cheng, M., Xiao, Z., Zhou, L., Zhou, J.: Adaptable map matching using PF-net for pedestrian indoor localization. IEEE Commun. Lett. **24**(7), 1437–1440 (2020). https://doi.org/10.1109/LCOMM.2020.2984036. https://ieeexplore.ieee.org/abstract/document/9057598 Communications Letters

# CSI Phase Fingerprinting for Indoor Positioning Services Using Deep Reinforcement Learning

Wiem Fekih Hassen[(⊠)] and Haifa Ben Salem

Chair of Distributed Information Systems, University of Passau, Innstraße 41, 94032 Passau, Germany
{wiem.fekihhassen,haifa.bensalem}@uni-passau.de

**Abstract.** In response to the escalating demand for Indoor Positioning Services (IPS) everywhere, this study explores techniques to enhance accuracy and adaptability in a dynamic environment. Leveraging the WiFi fingerprinting and the Channel State Information (CSI) phase of a dataset collected inside the University of Passau in Germany, this research introduces a groundbreaking approach by integrating Dueling Q-Network (Dueling QN) within Deep Reinforcement Learning (DRL). The trained agent achieves precise localization within a remarkable *0 cm* distance error, even without prior knowledge of the floor plan. Experimental results compare the position predicted using CSI phase and CSI amplitude, providing insights into their respective contributions. The promising findings emphasize the potential of DRL as a robust solution, opening new avenues for exploration and application in 3D WiFi datasets.

**Keywords:** IPS · CSI phase · fingerprinting · dueling Q-Network · dynamic environment

## 1 Introduction

In the realm of navigation, the ubiquity of outdoor positioning systems like GPS has revolutionized how we navigate our world. However, when we step indoors, the limitations of GPS become apparent, with signals obstructed by buildings and tunnels. This is where Indoor Positioning Systems (IPS) step in, addressing the challenges faced by GPS in environments such as hospitals, malls, and underground spaces [3].

Unlike GPS, IPS utilizes wireless technologies such as WiFi, Bluetooth, and Zigbee for accurate indoor localization [5,11]. Among these, WiFi emerges as a particularly attractive solution, with fingerprinting playing a pivotal role in indoor positioning [5]. Fingerprinting involves an Offline Phase, where a database is created by analyzing signal parameters at various Reference Points (RPs) throughout the indoor space, focusing significantly on WiFi signals. The Online


A. Soylu et al. (Eds.): MobiQuitous 2024, LNICST 634, pp. 428–446, 2026.
https://doi.org/10.1007/978-3-032-10554-7_23

Phase then compares signal measurements of a mobile user to the fingerprint database, with Machine Learning (ML) algorithms enhancing accuracy [18]. WiFi fingerprinting, a subset of fingerprinting, has gained popularity due to its cost-effectiveness and scalability, offering high accuracy when properly calibrated.

In the context of fingerprinting, Channel State Information (CSI) and Received Signal Strength Indicator (RSSI) are essential metrics [15,17,20]. RSSI represents the power level of received radio signals, while CSI provides detailed information about the channel conditions, including amplitude and phase. RSSI has traditionally been a common choice, but recent advancements have seen a shift towards exploiting the stability of CSI amplitude despite its phase being less stable. Both signals play crucial roles in enhancing the precision of WiFi-based indoor positioning systems.

As the demand for precise and scalable indoor localization solutions rises, ML algorithms, such as Deep Neural Networks (DNN), Convolutional neural networks (CNN), and Long short-term memory (LSTM), emerge as tools to overcome the limitations of conventional techniques [1,13]. Traditional methods often struggle with scalability issues, particularly in expansive environments like airports and shopping malls, where large training datasets are essential. Moreover, these methods lack adaptability in dynamic settings with multi-dimensional and heterogeneous data applications. These techniques try to solve the challenge of fluctuating RSSI and CSI signals, a major concern impacting location accuracy in IPS, but never demonstrated favorable results in practice. Meanwhile, Reinforcement Learning (RL), transfer learning, and deep learning techniques further contribute to addressing such challenges [7,22]. RL is a powerful paradigm for optimal control in IPS, allowing agents to autonomously learn and optimize actions for effective navigation in complex environments. Introducing Dueling-Q-Networks (Dueling QN), a subtype of Q-Networks, enhances RL's effectiveness in IPSs by leveraging deep neural networks to approximate the Quality function [19].

The optimization of ML models heavily relies on the quality and quantity of the dataset. Recognizing the significance of data augmentation in enhancing model performance, Generative Adversarial Networks (GANs) emerged as a powerful tool for data augmentation, offering the ability to generate synthetic data that closely mimic real-world scenarios [10].

Several methods are reported in the literature to address the issue of indoor positioning. A notable exploration in paper [13] integrated RSSI and CSI amplitude metrics, employing CNNs as the positioning algorithm. The outcomes showcased an accuracy of a Root Mean Squared Error (RMSE) of 54 cm.

Moving to the findings of paper [9], the focus shifted toward the effectiveness of a combination involving a CNN and LSTM network. Intriguingly, this study leveraged only RSSI information, achieving a good improvement in accuracy. However, it's essential to note that this enhancement came at the cost of extended testing times. The delicate balance between accuracy and efficiency in indoor positioning algorithms, particularly when relying on specific information sources, is a critical aspect that necessitates consideration.

Shifting the spotlight to the advancements in paper [8], the study opted for a cutting-edge approach by incorporating Deep Reinforcement Learning (DRL) as a positioning algorithm. The reported results were noteworthy, with positioning errors around 24 cm. It's crucial to highlight that this investigation exclusively relied on RSSI signals sourced from three public datasets. Additionally, the study introduced data generation through Gaussian noise, a technique that, while effective, is considered somewhat outdated in the contemporary landscape of data augmentation.

Most prior studies have concentrated on using RSSI and CSI Amplitude as primary signal metrics [6,8,9]. Notably, the use of CSI phase is less common, due to its perceived instability compared to CSI Amplitude, which is more commonly used in IPS [21]. This disparity in usage pushes the need to explore and understand the untapped potential of CSI Phase in enhancing indoor localization accuracy.

In synthesizing these findings, the dynamic landscape of indoor positioning algorithms reveals a nuanced trade-off between the choice of metrics and algorithm and the computational efficiency demanded in real-world applications. Each approach contributes to our evolving understanding of navigating these intricate trade-offs for optimal performance in diverse indoor environments. This leads us to the primary exploration of this paper, where we delve into the application of RL, addressing challenges in dynamic indoor environments, as well as focusing on the fluctuation of wireless signals, particularly in CSI phase signals. The presented approach eliminates the need for prior knowledge of the floor plan and facilitates real-time precise localization. The contributions of this paper can be outlined as follows:

1. Exploiting CSI phase information, an unstable and rarely exploited metric, by designing a specialized environment for IPS. In pursuit of this goal, we integrated a Dueling Q-Network (Dueling QN) model into the environment and training the agent exclusively on CSI phase information. This nuanced metric is a focal point in our research that aims to enhance its use for precise target localization within the constructed IPS environment.
2. Implementing Generative Adversarial Networks (GANs) as an advanced data augmentation technique and surpassing traditional methods to enhance the robustness and generalization of indoor positioning systems.
3. Optimizing the agent's decision-making process for more efficient and rapid convergence and evaluating the impact of our approach on the precision and adaptability of WiFi based IPS in dynamic indoor environments.


The paper outlines a well-structured framework, beginning in Sect. 2 by introducing the proposed model, encapsulating the used dataset, data preprocessing, and data augmentation. Subsequently, Sect. 3 delves into the reinforcement learning approach, presenting the creation of the environment as well as the model implementation for agent training. Following that, Sect. 4 presents the results of the trained agent. The paper concludes with a comprehensive summary and outlines directions for future work.

## 2    Proposed Model

This section details our proposed solution for IPS, outlined in Fig. 1. Our model operates in two distinct phases. The initial offline phase involves the meticulous processing of the CSI fingerprinting dataset, followed by a crucial data augmentation step to enhance training effectiveness. Subsequently, real and synthetic data are explored to test the environment, aligning with our indoor positioning case. The next step encompasses training a Dueling QN model, which is then saved for subsequent use. Transitioning to the online phase, data collection from mobile devices, specifically capturing CSI phase information, is executed. This collected data is utilized to predict positions in real-time by applying the pre-trained Dueling QN model. The two-phase model provides a comprehensive solution tailored to overcome challenges in indoor positioning.

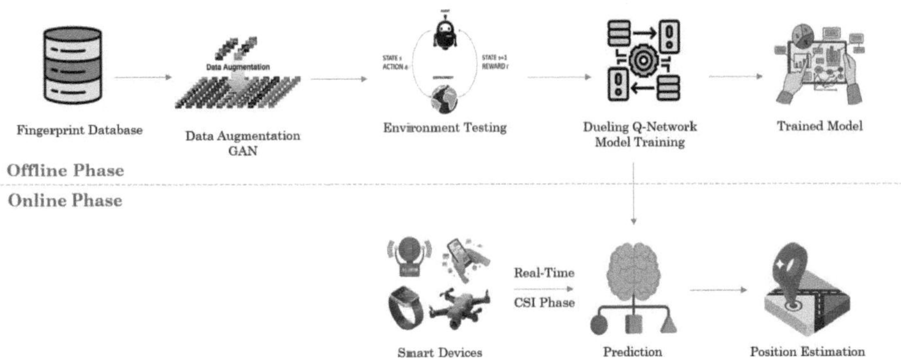


**Fig. 1.** Proposed Approach Architecture.

### 2.1    Used CSI Dataset

The used CSI dataset was collected inside a conference room situated in the ITZ Building at the University of Passau in Germany [4,13]. Details regarding the collection of CSI data are given in [4,13]. This room, characterized by a pentagon shape, covers an approximate area of $45\,\mathrm{m}^2$, as illustrated in Fig. 2. The resulting dataset includes X and Y coordinates, accompanied by 256 subcarriers of both CSI phase and amplitude. Initially, the dataset consists of 17,999 entries.

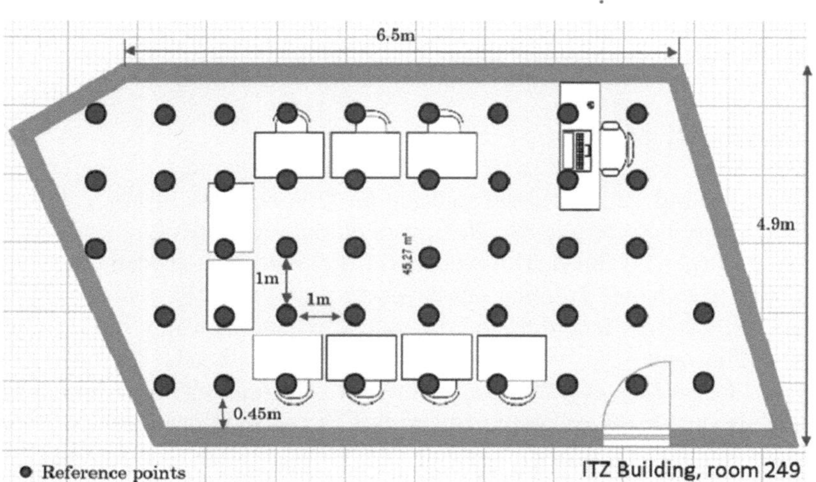


**Fig. 2.** Floor Plan [4].

## 2.2  Data Preprocessing

Dataset preprocessing plays a crucial role in shaping the input data for machine learning models, ensuring their efficiency and robustness. In this section, we discuss the steps taken to preprocess the indoor positioning dataset, preparing it for subsequent model training.

- Exclusion of RSSI Values: The original dataset included x and y coordinates along with RSSI values and 256 subcarriers of CSI phase and amplitude. Recognizing that RSSI values are widely exploited and no longer necessary for exploration, we excluded them from the dataset. This simplification reduces noise and streamlines the data for our specific use case.
- Removal of Redundant Columns: A further analysis revealed the presence of columns with identical values. These redundant columns act as noise and can potentially hinder the performance of the proposed model. Consequently, we excluded these columns to enhance the dataset's clarity and eliminate irrelevant information.
- Handling Null Values: Null values in the dataset pose a challenge for machine learning models. To address this, we replaced the null values with the median of their respective columns. This step is crucial for maintaining data integrity and preventing the introduction of unwanted biases during model training. Null values can significantly impact data generation processes such as GANs, and by addressing them, we ensure the robustness of subsequent data augmentation steps.
- Normalization of CSI Values: The final preprocessing step involved the normalization of CSI phase and amplitude values expressed by the following Equation:

$$CSI_{NV} = \frac{CSI_{values} - \min(CSI_{values})}{\max(CSI_{values}) - \min(CSI_{values})} \tag{1}$$

This formula scales the values to the range between *0* and *1*, facilitating effective learning within the neural network.

Null values can disrupt the training process, especially when employing techniques like GANs for data augmentation. The absence of values can hinder the GAN's ability to learn and generate meaningful synthetic data, potentially introducing artifacts or biases. Besides, normalization is particularly beneficial for DNN models as it enables them to converge faster during training. It enhances the model's stability by preventing numerical instability and ensuring that all features contribute proportionately to the learning process.

### 2.3  Data Augmentation

To address the challenges posed by traditional data augmentation methods, we recognized that merely cleaning the dataset and normalizing values might not suffice for training a stable model, particularly given the constraints of our small private dataset.

Understanding the limitations imposed by the dataset size, we sought innovative solutions to enhance our model's performance. Acknowledging the significance of data augmentation, we turned to Tabular Generative Adversarial Networks (GANs), a cutting-edge deep learning technique. GANs operate through a generator, which synthesizes data resembling the original dataset distribution, and a discriminator, which distinguishes between real and synthetic data. This advanced approach proved pivotal in mitigating data limitations and significantly improving the robustness of our model for training and evaluation [2]. Figure 3 depicts an explanation of GANs. In this architecture, a label **y** is incorporated into the generator's input, aiming to generate the corresponding data point. The discriminator receives both the sample **x** and its associated label **y**.

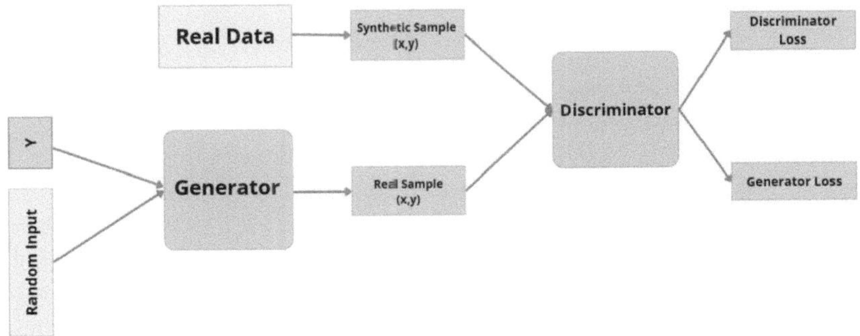


**Fig. 3.** Simplified GANs explanation.

The models engage in a two-player minimax game, wherein optimizing the objective function of the discriminator adversely affects the objective function of the generator and vice versa. Our initial step involved the definition of the generator model, a neural network designed to transform random noise into synthetic data mirroring the characteristics of the original dataset. This was realized through the specification of the generator model architecture, involving two dense layers with ReLU activation functions. On the other hand, the discriminator model, another integral part of the GAN architecture, was established to distinguish between real and generated data. It consisted of two dense layers with ReLU activation, followed by a single dense layer with a sigmoid activation function.

To train the GAN effectively, we needed a unified approach connecting both the generator and discriminator. During the training iterations, the generator was connected to the discriminator, with the latter set to non-trainable. This configuration facilitated the generator's learning to produce synthetic data challenging for the discriminator to differentiate from real data. Our actual dataset, essential for preserving the authenticity of the synthetic samples, was integrated into the system and converted into a Numpy array for efficient processing.

Training the GAN involved alternating between training the discriminator and the generator. Batches of real and generated data were utilized to train the discriminator, while the generator was trained using the combined model. This adversarial training process aimed to iteratively refine the generator's ability to generate synthetic data of high fidelity. After completing GAN training, we utilized the trained generator to generate synthetic data by feeding it random noise.

## 3   Reinforcement Learning (RL) Approach

In this section, we provide a detailed explanation of the RL paradigm employed in our approach and outline the procedures involved in crafting the environment using the OpenAI Gym framework.

### 3.1   OpenAI Gym

OpenAI Gym is a widely used toolkit in the field of reinforcement learning (RL), offering a diverse collection of environments for developing and testing RL algorithms [16]. OpenAI Gym allows users to create custom environments tailored to specific research needs, fostering innovation and adaptability in RL research. It integrates smoothly with Stable Baselines, a set of high-quality RL algorithm implementations, simplifying the training and evaluation of RL agents within Gym environments. On the other hand, training RL agents is easier with Stable baseline models, enabling users to focus on algorithmic development rather than intricate implementation details.

Motivated by the effectiveness of this toolkit, we opted to construct an environment compatible with IPS. This choice facilitates the training of agents using Stable Baselines' predefined models, presenting an optimal solution for our research objectives.

## 3.2  Environment Creation for Indoor Positioning Services

The proposed method introduces a precise and efficient searching approach for indoor localization, devoid of prior knowledge of the floor plan. Leveraging its hierarchical structure, the method offers real-time localization resolution based on computational preferences. The process of the environment creation involves formulating indoor localization as a Markov Decision Process (MDP), where an agent continuously interacts with the environment, making decisions based on a predefined action space [14]. At each step, the agent dynamically interacts with the environment, selecting sequential actions to progressively localize the target by transforming a bounding square window, as depicted in Fig. 4. Then, positive rewards are received whenever the agent gets closer to the target, motivating it to continue its pursuit until reaching the final position. The MDP model uses the following key components: actions, states, and rewards.

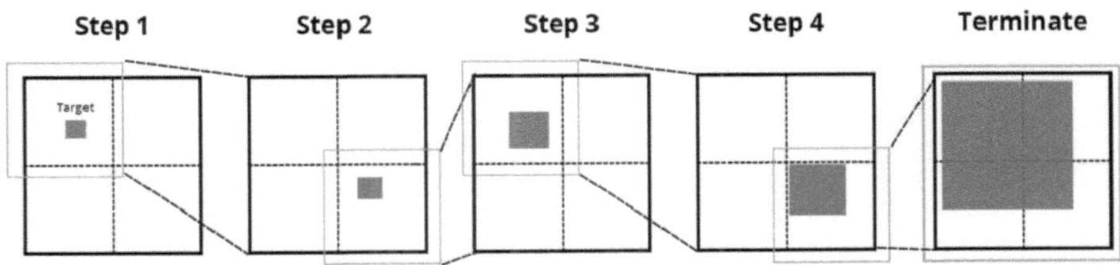


**Fig. 4.** Illustration of the Process.

**Actions:** In DRL, actions represent the decisions made by an agent in an environment to maximize its cumulative reward. These actions are typically chosen from a predefined set, determined by the agent's current state and its learned policy. This selection influences the agent's interaction with the environment and its goal achievement capabilities.

Upon the entry of the target object into the environment, the agent assumes its initial position, and the environment initializes its first state by considering the initial coordinates of the agent and the set of CSI phase measurements, with further explanation of the state in the next subsection. The primary objective is for the agent to efficiently localize the target based on a series of CSI phase measurements by taking a sequence of predefined actions.

In our scenario, the agent can access five discrete actions, as presented in Fig. 5. Each action is defined as a dictionary in the implementation:

```
#Possible actions
actions = {
    0:  (-1, 1),    % "UP-LEFT"
    1:  (1, 1),     % "UP-RIGHT"
    2:  (-1, -1),   % "DOWN-LEFT"
    3:  (1, -1),    % "DOWN-RIGHT"
    4:  (0, 0)      % "CENTER"
}
```

It is noteworthy that the agent can either stay in the center window or change to another window to inspect it during its search for the target. If the window changes, the agent considers it as the new floor plan to investigate. The agent continues this procedure until the position of the user is reached.

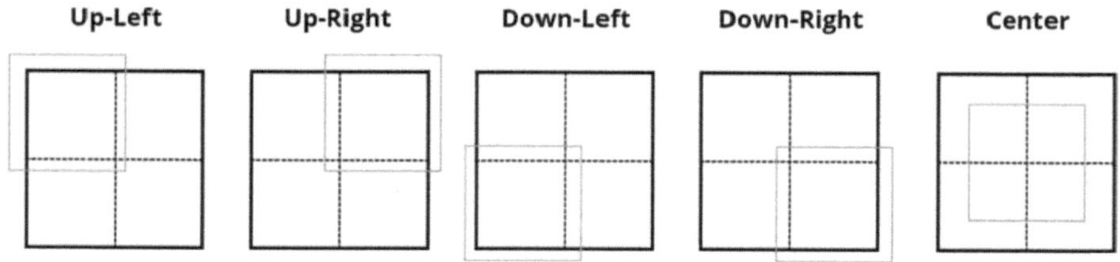


**Fig. 5.** Set of Actions.

**State:** At the initial time instant $t = 0$, the agent's spatial position is defined as $(x = 5, y = 5)$, representing the central coordinates of the conference room. The initial state, denoted as $S_0 = [\text{CSI\_Values}, (x_0, y_0)]$, encompasses the CSI Amplitude/Phase values and the agent's starting coordinates. In this state, the agent commences the search for target coordinates by executing a series of actions that shift and transform a bounding square window. After completing a specific action in the current state, the agent progresses to the subsequent state.

For instance, if the agent executes the "UP-LEFT" action denoted by $(-1, 1)$, the subsequent state $S_{t+1} = [\text{CSI\_Values}, (x_{t+1}, y_{t+1})]$ is determined. Here, $x_{t+1}$ and $y_{t+1}$ represent the new agent coordinates leading to the target, computed as follows:

$$\begin{cases} x_{t+1} = x_t + \text{actions}[a_t] \\ y_{t+1} = y_t + \text{actions}[a_t] \end{cases} \tag{2}$$

The agent's observation at each step involves assessing whether the center remains unchanged or relocates to an arbitrary center within the four quarters of the preceding window. Guided by the obtained rewards, the agent fine-tunes its parameters iteratively to approach the target until eventually achieving an accurate localization. Figure 6 provides an illustrative depiction of the approach.

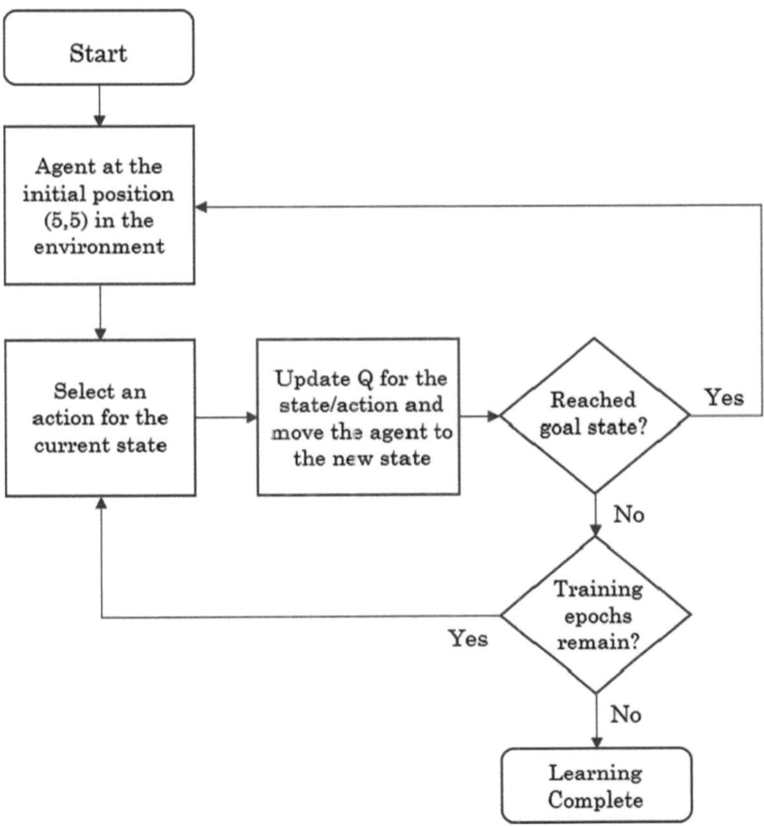


**Fig. 6.** Approach Flowchart.

In this manner, the agent dynamically navigates through the environment, iteratively updating its state based on the executed actions, with the ultimate goal of reaching the target coordinates.

**Reward Function:** After each step, rewards or penalties are computed to guide the agent in refining its subsequent actions. The reward function $r$ serves as an indicator of the agent's progress in locating the target position. This function quantifies the improvement between the current state and its subsequent state. Specifically, the reward is determined by calculating the Euclidean distance between the agent and the target, with the negative value of the distance serving as the reward. The reward function is defined as follows:

$$r_{a_t} = \begin{cases} -d & \text{if } d \neq 0 \\ +3 & \text{if } d = 0 \end{cases} \tag{3}$$

where, $r_{a_t}$ represents the reward for action $t$, and $d$ denotes the distance between the agent and the target. As the agent gets closer to the target, the reward gradually decreases until it hits zero. At this point, a positive reward of *+3* is given, signifying that the agent has reached the target destination ($s_t = [\text{CSI\_Values}, (x_{\text{target}}, y_{\text{target}})]$). The decision to use *+3* as the reward value was based on previous research using DRL [8]. This iterative reward system helps the agent learn adaptively, refining its precision in reaching the target location.

### 3.3   Dueling Q-Network for Indoor Localization

Stable Baselines offers a diverse set of reinforcement learning algorithms, each tailored to specific scenarios and types of problems. The selection of the most suitable algorithm depends on the nature of the environment, the action space, and the characteristics of the problem at hand.

In the case of our indoor localization environment, we observe that the action space is discrete, comprising five possible actions. Additionally, the nature of the problem involves an unlimited number of steps for the agent to localize the target accurately.

Considering the discrete action space and the requirement for handling unlimited steps, Dueling QN emerges as the most fitting choice for training the agent in our environment. Dueling QN's effectiveness in handling discrete actions aligns seamlessly with the characteristics of our problem.

The foundational principles of Dueling Q are rooted in Tesauro's TD-Gammon architecture, which updates network parameters estimating the value function using on-policy samples of experiences [12]. Its architecture features two streams within the neural network, one dedicated to estimating the state value and the other to estimating action advantages. This separation enables a more nuanced understanding of the Q-values, with the state value representing the intrinsic value of a given state and the action advantages capturing the additional value associated with each action.

Experience replay remains a vital component in Dueling Q, where the agent's experiences are stored in a replay memory. Q-learning updates are then applied to random samples from this memory, enhancing the stability and efficiency of the learning process [12]. This approach addresses concerns about the inefficiency of learning from consecutive samples and reduces the variance of updates by breaking correlations.

For practical implementations, reinforcement learning libraries like Stable Baselines extend support for Dueling Q, allowing agents to train in custom environments, such as those relevant to Indoor Positioning Systems. These libraries streamline the integration of Dueling Q with the environment, manage experience replay, and optimize Q-learning updates effectively.

Algorithm 1 represents a simplified pseudocode outlining the operation of Dueling QN in indoor localization.

Algorithm 1 represents the following components:

1. Dueling Q-Network ($Q$): it is the neural network used by the agent to approximate the quality (Q) function, which estimates the expected future rewards

---

**Algorithm 1.** Dueling QN for Indoor Localization

---

Initialize replay memory $D$ to capacity $N$ #Store Transitions
Initialize dueling Q-network $Q$ with random weights for value and advantage streams
**for** *episode* $= 1$ to $M$ **do**
    Initialize sequence $s_1 = \{(x_0, y_0), CSI\_PhaseValues\}$ and preprocess sequence $\phi_1 = \phi(s_1)$
    **for** $t = 1$ to $T$ **do**
        With probability $\varepsilon$, select a random action $a_t$
        Otherwise,
        select $a_t = \arg\max_a \left(Q_V^*(\phi(s_t); \theta) + Q_A^*(\phi(s_t), a; \theta)\right)$
        Execute action $a_t$ in emulator and observe reward $r_t$ and image $x_{t+1}$
        Set $s_{t+1} = s_t, a_t, x_{t+1}$ and preprocess $\phi_{t+1} = \phi(s_{t+1})$
        Store transition $(\phi_t, a_t, r_t, \phi_{t+1})$ in $D$
        Sample random minibatch of transitions $(\phi_j, a_j, r_j, \phi_{j+1})$ from $D$
        Set $y_j = r_j$ for terminal $\phi_{j+1}$
        $y_j = r_j + \gamma(Q_V(\phi_{j+1}; \theta)$
            $+ Q_A(\phi_{j+1}, \arg\max_{a'} Q_A(\phi_{j+1}, a'; \theta); \theta))$ for non-terminal $\phi_{j+1}$
        Perform a gradient descent step on $(y_j - (Q_V(\phi_j; \theta) + Q_A(\phi_j, a_j; \theta)))^2$ according to Equation 4
    **end for**
**end for**

---

for taking an action in a given state. It consists of two streams: the value stream ($Q_V$) and the advantage stream ($Q_A$), which separately estimate the state value and the advantage of each action over others.

2. State Representation ($\phi$): The state of the environment, denoted as $\phi$, represents the current situation the agent is in. In this algorithm, the state includes the agent's position (coordinates) and the CSI phase values obtained from the environment.

3. Exploration and Exploitation ($\epsilon$-greedy policy): The agent balances exploration and exploitation by following an $\epsilon$-greedy policy. With probability $\epsilon$, it explores the environment by taking random actions to discover potential strategies. With probability $1 - \epsilon$, it exploits its learned knowledge by selecting actions based on the current state to maximize cumulative rewards.

4. Gradient Calculation (Eq. 4):
The gradient calculation represents the process of updating the Q-network's weights during training. It involves computing the gradient of a loss function concerning the Q-network's parameters ($\theta_i$). This equation incorporates the Bellman equation, which expresses the relationship between the current state, action, reward, and the next state's value, presented as follows:

$$
\begin{aligned}
\nabla_{\theta_i} L_{i,t}(\theta_i) = \mathbb{E}_{s_t, a_t, s_{t+1}} [ & (r_t + \gamma(Q_V(s_{t+1}; \theta_{-i}) \\
& + Q_A(s_{t+1}, \arg\max_{a'} Q_A(s_{t+1}, a'; \theta_{-i}); \theta_{-i})) \\
& - (Q_V(s_t; \theta_i) + Q_A(s_t, a_t; \theta_i))) \nabla_{\theta_i} (Q_V(s_t; \theta_i) \\
& + Q_A(s_t, a_t; \theta_i))]
\end{aligned}
\tag{4}
$$

The agent iteratively interacts with the environment over a series of episodes. In each episode, it follows a sequence of actions based on the current state and updates its Q-network using a variant of the Q-learning algorithm. The weights of the Q-network are adjusted using gradient descent to minimize the difference between the predicted Q-values and the target Q-values, which are calculated based on the observed rewards and the estimated future rewards.

## 4    Results and Discussions

In this section, we explore the evaluation of the proposed Dueling QN approach, assessing the agent's performance through distinct metrics. The comprehensive analysis is divided into two key aspects, each shedding light on crucial facets of the model's efficacy.

1. In the initial step of our evaluation, we focus on appraising the agent's performance by scrutinizing the number of steps taken in each episode. To enhance the RL environment, a strategic modification was implemented to significantly reduce the number of steps. This adjustment aimed to optimize the learning process and streamline the agent's decision-making, ultimately contributing to more efficient and effective outcomes.
2. The subsequent subsection centers on a multifaceted evaluation, considering both the running time and variations in the number of steps. This assessment is conducted by providing the agent with two distinct sets of measurements: CSI phase measurements and CSI amplitude measurements. This comparison enables us to recognize the significance of CSI phase measurements, given that it imparts more informative details compared to amplitude measurements. However, the primary challenge lies in the inherent instability of the phase, prone to noise interference, making it challenging to measure accurately.

### 4.1    Performance Evaluation Based on Episode Steps

To assess the performance of our trained model, we generated new data using GANs to ensure fresh testing scenarios. We then input this data into the model to observe how well the trained agent could locate the target position. The process involved visualizing the steps taken by the agent during prediction, as shown in Fig. 7a. We repeated this process 500 times to collect these results. The first and most important conclusion from these findings is that our model achieved a distance error of **0 cm**. Our model showed excellent results, outperforming the state-of-the-art [8, 13].

During prediction, the agent randomly selects actions from a predefined set of possible actions. The reward system is designed to penalize the agent based on the negative Euclidean distance between its current position and the target. However, when the agent accurately reaches the target position, it receives a positive reward of +3. This reward system stimulates the agent to progressively approach the target position while penalizing deviations from the target.

As depicted in Fig. 7b, the agent initially required approximately $10^3$ steps to successfully locate the target. This extended number of steps indicates suboptimal decision-making, prompting us to explore optimizations to expedite the agent's learning process.

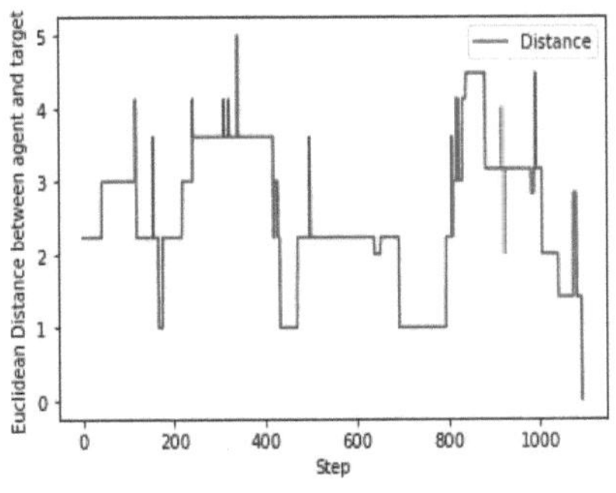

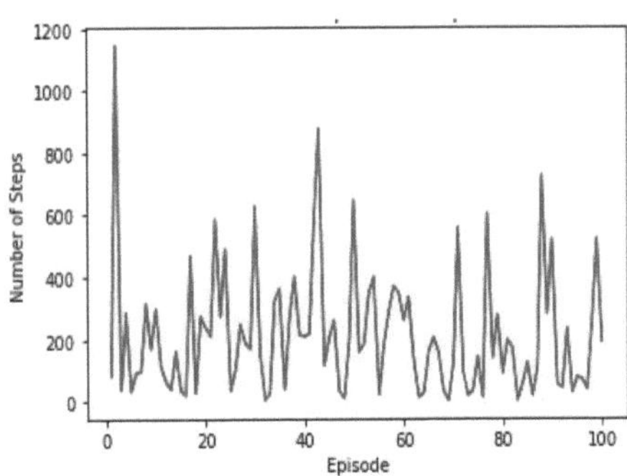

(a) Variation of Euclidean Distance               (b) Number of Steps per Episode

**Fig. 7.** Trivial Solution.

Observing the fluctuating Euclidean distance during prediction (Fig. 7a), an optimization approach was implemented. The agent now refrains from taking the next action unless it contributes to a closer proximity to the target. If an action doesn't lead the agent closer to the target, an alternative action is sought to optimize the decision-making process. The new reward function $r$ that yields an optimized solution for the proposed approach, with a significantly reduced number of steps, is defined as follows:

$$r_{a_t}(s_t, s_{t+1}) = \begin{cases} -d_{s_t} & \text{if } d_{s_{t+1}} \leq d_{s_t} \\ +3 & \text{if } d_{s_{t+1}} = 0 \\ \text{Otherwise generate} \\ \text{another action} \end{cases} \tag{5}$$

where, $r_{a_t}$ is the reward for action $a_t$, $d_{s_t}$ is the distance between the target and the agent for the state $t$, and $d_{s_{t+1}}$ is the distance for the state $t+1$.

The optimization strategy resulted in a significant reduction in the number of steps required for successful target prediction, as outlined in Fig. 8a. The refined approach ensures that the agent consistently moves towards the target, minimizing unnecessary steps. Consequently, the running time of the optimized solution for predicting the target's position is significantly lower compared to the trivial solution within the same batch, as illustrated in Table 1. It's worth noting that the table shows low running time due to the powerful server we are utilizing, equipped with excellent computational capabilities. Running the model on such a server facilitates efficient processing and faster execution.

**Table 1.** Comparative Table of Running Time

| Solution | Running time in Seconds |
|---|---|
| Trivial | 3.0392 |
| Optimized | 0.7410 |

Figure 8b showcases the effectiveness of this optimization, highlighting a maximum of 20 steps in the tested batch, affirming the success of our approach in enhancing the efficiency of the agent's decision-making.

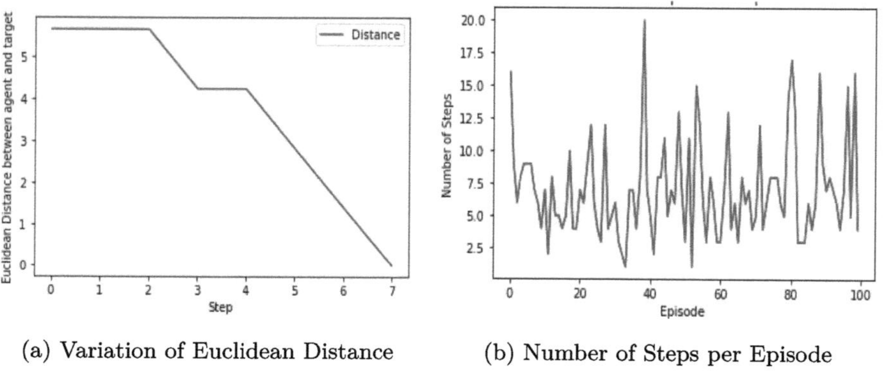

(a) Variation of Euclidean Distance    (b) Number of Steps per Episode

**Fig. 8.** Optimized Solution.

## 4.2 Performance Evaluation Based on CSI Measurements

In this subsection, we explore assessing the agent's performance based on the CSI measurements, specifically focusing on CSI phase and CSI amplitude. The primary objective is to determine whether training the agent on either CSI phase or CSI amplitude improves performance, allowing for a detailed comparison between agents trained on each aspect. Conducting two distinct training sessions, we dedicated the first session to training an agent solely on CSI amplitude, while the second session exclusively focused on the CSI phase. Subsequent evaluations of both agents took place on the same batch, facilitating a comprehensive comparative analysis. The first agent, trained exclusively on CSI amplitude, showcased exceptional proficiency in locating the target within the conference room. Achieving precise positioning based on amplitude measurements, this agent required a mere 9 steps for accurate predictions. Figure 9a visually depicts the agent's efficiency, providing insights into the number of steps per episode for a batch of 100. In contrast, the second agent, trained solely on CSI phase, exhibited an even more rapid convergence. Remarkably, this agent determined the target's position within the conference room in 6 steps, as illustrated in Fig. 9b.

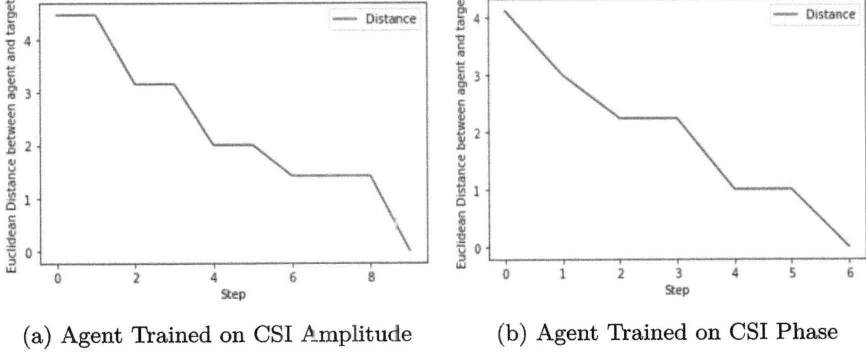

(a) Agent Trained on CSI Amplitude          (b) Agent Trained on CSI Phase

**Fig. 9.** Variation of Agent's Performance.

A comparative analysis between the two trained agents, conducted over approximately 1000 runs, yielded a noteworthy observation: despite the distinct focus on either CSI phase or amplitude, there wasn't a substantial difference in the number of steps required to predict the target's coordinates. Both agents achieved precise predictions within a maximum of 25 (Fig. 10) and 20 steps (Fig. 8b), respectively, indicating a comparable running time for predicting the target's position.

Moreover, it was evident that the agent trained solely on CSI phase outperformed its counterpart trained on CSI amplitude. Specifically, the agent utilizing CSI phase consistently achieved precise predictions with fewer steps compared to the agent trained on CSI amplitude.

In conclusion, the experiments suggest that training the agent solely on CSI phase or amplitude doesn't significantly impact the efficiency of predicting the target's coordinates. As illustrated in Table 2, the mean number of steps for both approaches is remarkably close. However, it's crucial to highlight that the agent trained on CSI phase demonstrated superior performance, achieving precise results within a shorter range of steps on average. This finding emphasizes the effectiveness of utilizing CSI phase measurements for indoor localization tasks, showcasing its superiority over CSI amplitude and highlighting its potential for enhanced accuracy and efficiency in real-world applications.

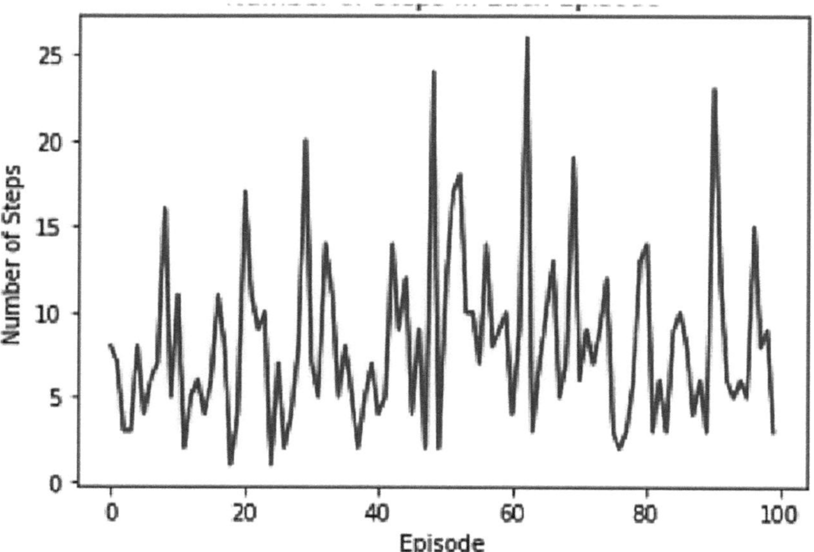

**Fig. 10.** Steps Number per Episode of CSI Amplitude.

**Table 2.** Comparative Table of Number of Steps

| Agent | Mean Steps |
| --- | --- |
| Trained on CSI Amplitude Values | 9.23 |
| Trained on CSI Phase Values | 6.56 |

## 5   Conclusions

In this paper, we proposed a novel Dueling QN approach tailored for WiFi CSI phase fingerprinting in indoor localization, focusing on real-time positioning. The proposed solution adeptly manages the dynamic variations in CSI phase, eliminating the need for prior knowledge of the floor plan. Utilizing a Dueling QN model, we trained the agent to precisely localize the target using only CSI phase measurements. In the initial implementation, the agent exhibited successful target localization but required an elevated number of steps. Recognizing the need for optimization in the decision-making process, we refined the approach, significantly reducing the number of steps and enhancing the agent's efficiency. Furthermore, we conducted experiments comparing the use of CSI phase and CSI amplitude for target localization. Remarkably, both approaches yielded precise results within a similar range of steps. This observation emphasizes the flexibility in selecting CSI measurements based on availability or specific system considerations. Our study is compelling evidence for the efficacy of Deep Reinforcement Learning, showcasing its superiority in addressing challenges in various domains, particularly in real-time positioning applications. As future work, we aim to extend our model's applicability by testing it on 3D datasets with $(x,y,z)$ coordinates. This expansion will enable us to assess the performance of our approach in more complex environments, offering valuable insights into its adaptability and effectiveness in three-dimensional space.

# References


1. Al-Ammar, M.A., et al.: Comparative survey of indoor positioning technologies, techniques, and algorithms. In: 2014 International Conference on Cyberworlds, pp. 245–252. IEEE (2014)
2. Ashrapov, I.: Tabular GANs for uneven distribution. arXiv preprint arXiv:2010.00638 (2020)
3. Basiri, A., et al.: Indoor location based services challenges, requirements and usability of current solutions. Comput. Sci. Rev. **24**, 1–12 (2017)
4. Elaoud, M.A., Hassen, W.F.: Wi-Fi CSI/RSSI fingerprints positioning based on data augmentation technique. In: The Seventeenth International Conference on Mobile Ubiquitous Computing, Systems, Services and Technologies (UBICOMM) (2023)
5. Hassen, W.F., Najjar, F., Brunie, L., Kosch, H., Slimani, Y.: Smart PDR integration for ubiquitous pedestrian navigation service. In: 2017 13th International Wireless Communications and Mobile Computing Conference (IWCMC), pp. 1558–1563 (2017). https://doi.org/10.1109/IWCMC.2017.7986516
6. Hsieh, C.H., Chen, J.Y., Nien, B.H.: Deep learning-based indoor localization using received signal strength and channel state information. IEEE Access **7**, 33256–33267 (2019)
7. Li, Y., Hu, X., Zhuang, Y., Gao, Z., Zhang, P., El-Sheimy, N.: Deep reinforcement learning (DRL): another perspective for unsupervised wireless localization. IEEE Internet Things J. **7**(7), 6279–6287 (2019)
8. Liu, W., Chen, H., Deng, Z., Zheng, X., Fu, X., Cheng, Q.: LC-DNN: local connection based deep neural network for indoor localization with CSI. IEEE Access **8**, 108720–108730 (2020)
9. Mahdavi, F., Zayyani, H., Rajabi, R.: RSS localization using an optimized fusion of two deep neural networks. IEEE Sens. Lett. **5**(12), 1–4 (2021)
10. Mao, X., Li, Q.: Generative Adversarial Networks for Image Generation. Springer (2021)
11. Mendoza Silva, G.M., et al.: Received signal strength-based indoor positioning: integrative outlooks and solutions. Ph.D. thesis, Universitat Jaume I (2020)
12. Mnih, V., et al.: Human-level control through deep reinforcement learning. Nature **518**(7540), 529–533 (2015)
13. Mühl, M., Hassen, W.F.: Deep learning based indoor positioning approach using Wi-Fi CSI/RSSI fingerprints technique. In: The Seventeenth International Conference on Mobile Ubiquitous Computing, Systems, Services and Technologies (UBICOMM) (2023)
14. Romac, C., Béraud, V.: Deep recurrent Q-learning vs Deep Q-learning on a simple partially observable Markov decision process with minecraft. arXiv preprint arXiv:1903.04311 (2019)
15. Samadh, S.A., Liu, Q., Liu, X., Ghourchian, N., Allegue, M.: Indoor localization based on channel state information. In: 2019 IEEE Topical Conference on Wireless Sensors and Sensor Networks (WiSNet), pp. 1–4. IEEE (2019)

16. Stable Baselines Authors: Stable baselines documentation (2022). https://stable-baselines.readthedocs.io/en/master/guide/rl.html
17. Stahlke, M., Yammine, G., Feigl, T., Eskofier, B.M., Mutschler, C.: Indoor localization with robust global channel charting: a time-distance-based approach. IEEE Trans. Mach. Learn. Commun. Network. 1, 3–17 (2023)
18. Tian, X., Zhu, S., Xiong, S., Jiang, B., Yang, Y., Wang, X.: Performance analysis of Wi-Fi indoor localization with channel state information. IEEE Trans. Mob. Comput. **18**(8), 1870–1884 (2018)
19. Wang, Z., Schaul, T., Hessel, M., Hasselt, H., Lanctot, M., Freitas, N.: Dueling network architectures for deep reinforcement learning. In: International Conference on Machine Learning, pp. 1995–2003. PMLR (2016)
20. Wu, R.H., Lee, Y.H., Tseng, H.W., Jan, Y.G., Chuang, M.H.: Study of characteristics of RSSI signal. In: 2008 IEEE International Conference on Industrial Technology, pp. 1–3. IEEE (2008)
21. Yang, Z., Zhou, Z., Liu, Y.: From RSSI to CSI: indoor localization via channel response. ACM Comput. Surv. (CSUR) **46**(2), 1–32 (2013)
22. Zhang, B., Sifaou, H., Li, G.Y.: CSI-Fingerprinting indoor localization via attention-augmented residual convolutional neural network. IEEE Trans. Wireless Commun. **22**(8), 5583–5597 (2023)

# Automatic Marker Placement Method for Marker-Based Virtual Reality

Xiyu Bao[1], Meng Qi[2], Shiqing Xin[1], Chenglei Yang[1(✉)], and Yu Wang[1]

[1] Shandong University, Jinan, China
{201820489,wangyu}@mail.sdu.edu.cn, {xinshiqing,chl_yang}@sdu.edu.cn
[2] Shandong Normal University, Jinan, China
qimeng@sdnu.edu.cn

**Abstract.** Free walking in virtual reality is considered the most natural and effective way to explore virtual environments and enhance immersion and presence. Accurately tracking the user's position in a walkable physical environment can effectively avoid visual misalignment, collisions, and increase immersion. Feature-based tracking is the mainstream method, but indoor environments usually contain large areas of uniformity (e.g., white walls) or repetitive textures (e.g., ceramic tiles), which makes reliable feature detection and tracking challenging. In such environments, marker-based tracking can effectively overcome these challenges. However, this method requires complex manual layout of markers, which hinders its practical application. Therefore, this paper proposes an effective automatic marker placement strategy for specific physical environments and predefined paths, which can automatically determine the optimal placement of markers within given physical boundaries and constraints. We also design an evaluation method to assess the tracking accuracy of our approach. Experimental results show that our proposed method significantly improves tracking accuracy. This demonstrates that our method provides a practical and effective solution for accurately tracking the user's position in indoor environments that lack unique features.

**Keywords:** Marker-based tracking · Computational geometry · Optimal coverage · Virtual reality

## 1 Introduction

Virtual reality (VR) offers users an immersive experience in a virtual environment (VE). As VR continues to evolve, enabling users to move freely within the VE and simulate natural movements within the real environment (RE) is crucial for enhancing the overall experience [30,39,44]. Walking in VR is commonly combined with redirected walking, where users either walk freely in a physical environment [40] or on a predefined path [29,50].

To ensure that users can walk freely and safely in a walkable physical environment, the system must track the user's position. Feature-based tracking is


A. Soylu et al. (Eds.): MobiQuitous 2024, LNICST 634, pp. 447–469, 2026.
https://doi.org/10.1007/978-3-032-10554-7_24

the main visual tracking method that utilizes distinctive visual features (e.g., edges [5], corners [35], blobs [20], and patches [17]) within the RE to determine the user's position. However, indoor environments with large areas of uniform (e.g., white walls) or repetitive textures (e.g., ceramic tiles) pose challenges for feature-based tracking, leading to inaccuracies in determining a user's position [37].

To address this issue, marker-based tracking methods [1,6,15,34,36] have been introduced as promising alternatives. These methods utilize predefined markers placed within the RE to track user movements, thereby providing higher reliability and requiring lower costs and computational resources, as shown in Fig. 1(a). However, marker-based tracking requires complicated preparation making it impractical to use [13].

(a)

(b)

**Fig. 1.** physical environment with markers (red rectangle) in VR system. (Color figure online)

Huang et al. [12] proposed an automatic approach to optimizing marker placement. However, their approach requires a 3D scene model as input. While obtaining a 3D scene model of a physical environment can be challenging, the floor plan of the environment is relatively easy to acquire. The lack of effective solutions for markers placement strategy in the given floor plan of physical environments and other constraints hinders the widespread adoption of this tracking method. Addressing this gap is crucial to improve the capabilities of VR systems (e.g., redirected walking) in indoor physical environment that lack features.

In this study, we considered factors such as human height, marker constraints (e.g., position and size), the effective recognition range of markers, boundary of walkable physical environments (e.g., curved polygons with obstacles), and the predefined physical paths. We simplified the automatic placement problem into a optimal coverage problem for a 2D continuous space. The goal was to maximum the weighted area of walkable physical environment based on a specified number of markers.

We implemented an evaluation method to evaluate the effectiveness of our marker placement method. This method utilizes image recognition to calculate the bias between the virtual and physically objects. Using this method, we evaluated the performance of the proposed method under two conditions: unrestricted movement and walking along a predefined path.

The remainder of this paper is organized as follows: Sect. 2 discusses the marker-based tracking, marker type and identification, and optimal coverage problems. Section 3 describes the preliminaries. Section 4 offers a detailed description of the proposed placement method. Section 5 introduces a method for evaluating the effectiveness of different marker placements. Section 6 presents the user study and the results. Section 7 discusses the limitation of our study and considerations for future research, and Sect. 8 concludes.

## 2  Related Work

### 2.1  Marker-Based Augmented Reality

Research on markers has primarily focused on Augmented reality (AR) because one of the key challenges in AR is aligning virtual data with the physical environment. A marker-based approach addresses this challenge by using visual markers. This is similar to the core requirement for tracking the user's position in VR when enabling free walking.

Initially, markers were designed in various shapes such as circles [28], imperceptible patterns [18,35,37], and infrared markers [31,46]. However, the square-shaped marker became the preferred choice, following the introduction of matrix codes [33] and the ARToolkit [16]. Extensive research has been conducted to enhance the functionality of these markers [11,38].

These markers operate by recognizing the contour of the square and identify it as a marker once the internal pattern is recognized. They enable the augmentation of 3D objects with 3D poses, achieved by detecting the positions of the four vertices. Among these markers, ARToolKit [16], developed at HITLab, is widely recognized in the field of Human Computer Interaction (HCI). Additionally, ARTag [11] was developed to enhance the abilities of ARToolKit. T.U.Graz introduced the unobtrusive marker [45] to address realism issues. These studies were primarily aimed at enhancing marker functionality and usability.

To the best of our knowledge, there is limited research on the automatic placement of markers, given the floor plan of a specific physical environment. In practice, marker-based tracking requires extensive preparation and markers placement is typically performed manually. The entire process must be repeated multiple times to enhance effectiveness. In this study, we used QR codes, a common type of square-shaped marker, to evaluate our marker placement method.

### 2.2   Optimal Coverage for Continuous Space

Murray et al. [25] proposed a model formulation that represented the continuous space maximal coverage problem (CMCP). However, because of the nonlinearity and nonconvexity of the objective function, exact solutions for CMCP using standard computational packages are generally infeasible. Murray et al. [25] and Matisziw et al. [21] utilized regional geometry to identify optimal facility locations in space. Nevertheless, such geometry-based approaches only ensure optimality for limited cases and often require computationally intensive algorithms for general cases.

Murray and Wei [27] proposed the derivation of valid lower and upper bounds for the CMCP, however, an optimal solution to the problem remains elusive. Consequently, a commonly utilized approach to addressing the CMCP involves spatial discretization and formulation of the discrete Maximum Covering Location Problem (MCLP) [3]. Although this approach is computationally tractable and relatively easy to implement, it may introduce errors and uncertainties owing to spatial discretization. Moreover, variations in potential facility sites and demand could result in different outcomes using the MCLP, because it is known to be susceptible to the modifiable area unit problem [8,42], making it sensitive to scale and spatial units.

The challenge of optimal marker placement can be defined mathematically as a maximal coverage location problem (MCLP). The goal of the MCLP is to maximize the service coverage of regional demand, such as walkable regions in the physical environment, by strategically locating a certain number of facilities, which in this case are markers.

### 2.3   Solution for MCLP

To optimize continuous space coverage, a common approach is to discretize the demand region and transform the problem into a discrete location model that can be solved efficiently [3,42]. Various discretization methods have been used to abstract continuous space demand in coverage modeling. Two main schemes are often employed to represent a continuously distributed demand: a point-based abstraction [26,41] and an area-based representation [3,10,14,24,42,49]. An area-based representation scheme that involves overlaying coverage polygons to represent demand areas shows promise for reducing certain errors in representation when potential facility sites are known and finite [47]. Cordeau et al. [7] presented an effective decomposition approach to the MCLP based on branch-and-Benders-cut reformulation.

In this study, we designed a polygon division method to discretize the walkable physical environment (e.g., curved polygon with holes) to finite region set. This allows us to convert the problem into a MCLP. To solve this problem efficiently, we utilized the branch-and-benders-cut reformulation method [7] to find solutions for the MCLP.

## 3   Preliminaries

Although a physical environment may lack features, feature-based tracking remains the main tracking method, and on this basis, marker-based tracking is utilized to assist in improving tracking accuracy. Covering most areas of the walkable physical environment, rather than the entire area, is sufficient for practical use. The physical space occupied by markers should be minimized as much as possible, as placing too many markers requires a amount of human effort and space occupation. Considering the above, our goal is to maximize the area of walkable physical environments covered by a fixed number of markers.

**Fig. 2.** Real environment, the cross section (blue) at the height of user, and the effective recognition range (green) of ground marker and wall markers. (Color figure online)

In this study, we assumed that the users maintained a consistent height without squatting. As illustrated in Fig. 2, the markers (QR codes) were placed on either the walls or the ground and green regions were the effective recognition ranges of each marker. Those affixed to the walls were situated at the same height as the users. Participants were not permitted to angle their heads up or down. These assumptions ensure a fixed effective recognition range of each markers, which is further discussed in Sect. 7.

The cross section at height $H$ of the physical environment (blue plane) including the effective recognition range (green) of the markers are illustrated in Fig. 3. The effective recognition range is detailed described in Sect. 4.1. We define the boundary polygon of the physical environment as $P$, the height of the user $U$ as $H$, the size of the QR code as $L \times L$, the cross section of effective recognition range of marker on the wall $M_w$ at $z = H$ is approximately represented as a

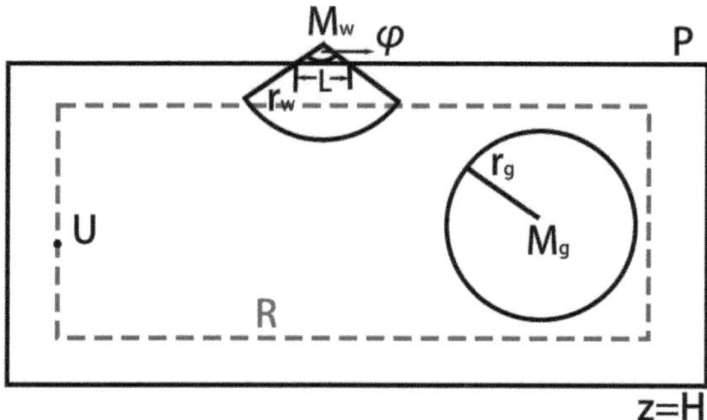

**Fig. 3.** A cross-section of the walkale physical environment $P$ at the height $H$ of the user $U$, including the effective recognition range of wall marker $M_w$ and ground marker $M_g$, and predefined paths $R$.

sector with angle $\varphi$ and radius $r_w$, and the cross section of effective recognition range of marker on the ground $M_g$ at $z = H$ is approximately represented as a circle of radius $r_g$. The physical paths (if they exists) are represented as $R = \{R_1, R_2, ..., R_n\}$.

## 4   Method

Our method was designed to determine the position of each marker (Fig. 4(a)) within a specified walking physical boundary (Fig. 4(b)) and a fixed number of markers, with the objective of maximizing the area covered by these markers in the walking physical environment. This is a MCLP and the notation for MCLP is as follow:

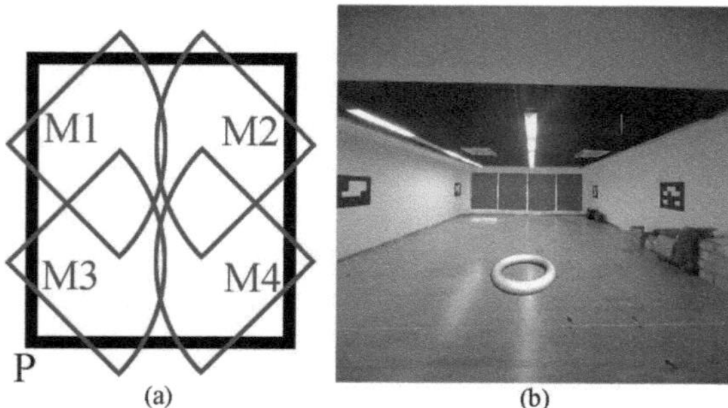


**Fig. 4.** (a) The optimal coverage layout for four markers $M1, M2, M3$, and $M4$ in the physical environment $P$ and (b) real environment with the placement of the four markers.

$i$ = index of potential marker locations (entire set $I$);

$j$ = index of object to be covered (entire set $J$);
$I(j)$ = set of markers covering object $j$;
$J(i)$ = set of objects can be suitably covered by marker $i$;
$d_j$ = set of weight of object $j$.

$$y_i = \begin{cases} 1, & \text{if marker is sited on location } i \\ 0, & \text{otherwise} \end{cases}$$

$$z_j = \begin{cases} 1, & \text{if object } j \text{ is suitably covered} \\ 0, & \text{otherwise} \end{cases}$$

The first step is to determine the covering boundary of a ground marker and a wall marker (Fig. 3), which is used to determine whether a marker suitably covers an object (point, line, or polygon). This step is detailed described in Sect. 4.1.

The second step is to determine object set $J$. The specified walkable physical environment is a continuous space, which means this problem is a continuous MCLP. Thereby, we converted the continuous MCLP to discrete MCLP by decomposing the boundary of physical environment (Fig. 5(a)) into discrete objects (Fig. 5(g)). This step is described in Sect. 4.2.

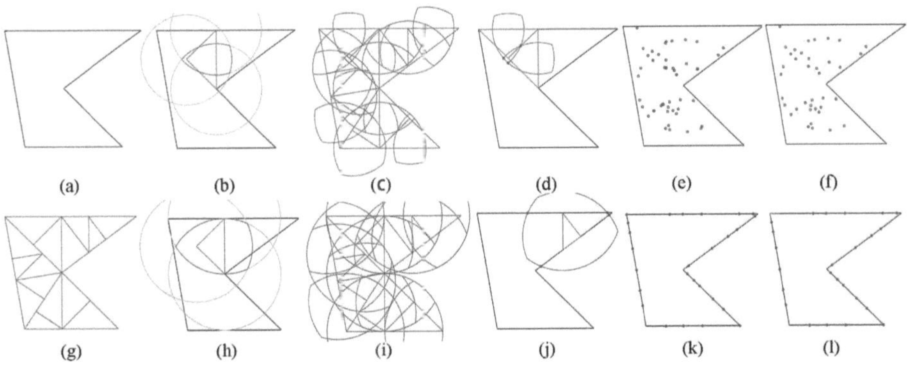

**Fig. 5.** (a) Physical environment, (g) object set. Ground marker location set for physical environment without predefined paths: (b) covering boundary of a object (triangle), (c) covering boundary of each object (triangle), (d) intersection points between two covering boundaries, (e) intersection points between each pair of covering boundaries, (f) final ground marker location set. Wall marker location set for physical environment without predefined paths: (h) covering boundary of a object (triangle), (i) covering boundary of each object (triangle), (j) intersection points between two covering boundaries, (k) intersection points between each pair of covering boundaries, (l) final wall marker location set.

The third step is to determine potential marker location set $I$. Since marker locations can be placed anywhere in continuous space, optimizing their configuration poses a challenge. To address this, a discrete set of critical locations (Fig. 5(f) and Fig. 5(l)) is derived by polygon intersection point set (PIPS) approach (or line-segment intersection point set approach) [23]. This approach computed the covering area (green) of each object (red) ((Fig. 5(c) and Fig. 5(i))) intersecting circles centered at the vertices of the object (Fig. 5(b) and Fig. 5(h)). The potential marker locations (Fig. 5(e) and Fig. 5(k)) are determined by finding the intersection points between two markers (Fig. 5(d)) or between a marker and a wall (Fig. 5(j)). This step is detailed described in Sect. 4.3.

Finally, the MCLP is solved using the branch-and-bound method, as outlined in [7], to determine $y_i$. This process is detailed in Sect. 4.4.

The whole process is shown in Algorithm 1 and Algorithm 2. In this study, we focused on two scenarios: users walking along predefined paths and walking freely. Algorithm 1 was designed for physical environment with predefined paths, whereas Algorithm 2 was designed for physical environment with predefined paths.

---

**Algorithm 1:** Marker placement algorithm with predefined paths

**Input**  : Polygon $P$, user height $H$, mark size $L$, and predefined paths $R$
**Output**: Ground marker set $M_g$, wall marker set $M_w$
1 Obtain $r_w$, $r_g$ and $\varphi$ based on $H$ and $L$.
2 Divide $R$ into segment set to form the object set $J$.
3 Obtain marker potential location set $I$ based on $P$ and $J$ by line-segment intersection point set approach [23].
4 Formulate MCLP to obtain marker set $y$ and divide $y$ into $M_g$ and $M_w$ based on marker type.

---

**Algorithm 2:** Marker placement algorithm without predefined paths

**Input**  : Polygon $P$, user height $H$, and mark size $L$
**Output**: Ground marker set $M_g$, wall marker set $M_w$
1 Compute $r_w$, $r_g$ and $\varphi$ based on $H$ and $L$.
2 Divide $P$ into polygon set to form the object set $J$.
3 Obtain marker potential location set $I$ based on $P$ and $J$ by PIPS approach [23].
4 Formulate MCLP to obtain marker set $y$ and divide $y$ into $M_g$ and $M_w$ based on marker type.

---

### 4.1   Effective Recognition Range of Markers

To determine the value of $r_w$, $r_g$, and $\varphi$, a pre-experiment was conducted. In our experiment, we used a PICO 4 Pro Enterprise VR HMD as our experimental equipment. Pico's local tracking system was used to determine physical location and directional information. PICO 4 supports a 105° field of view. During the pre-experiments, participants wearing PICO walked around a marker positioned on the ground (See Fig. 6(a)) and another marker placed on the wall

(See Fig. 6(c)). Within the PICO's field of view, participants could see that the marker was recognized as a QR code surrounded by a blue rectangle. During the walking task, participants were instructed to press the trigger when the virtual rectangle aligned with the boundary of the marker (See Fig. 6(a) and Fig. 6(c)), and their positions were recorded at that moment. If the virtual rectangle did not align with the boundary of the marker (See Fig. 6(b) and Fig. 6(d)), participants were instructed to continue walking without pressing the trigger. Subsequently, two scatter plots were generated for the two markers according to recorded positions, approximately forming shapes in Fig. 3, illustrating the effective range of the wall marker and the ground marker, respectively. In our study, $H = 1.8\,\mathrm{m}$, the side length of the QR code $L = 0.8\,\mathrm{m}$, $r_g = 1.8\,\mathrm{m}$, $r_w = 3.6\,\mathrm{m}$, $\varphi = \pi/2$.

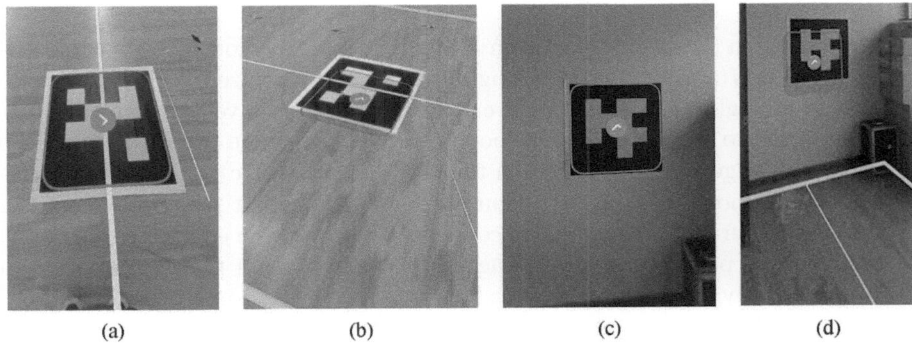

(a)        (b)        (c)        (d)

**Fig. 6.** The ground marker was accurately recognized in (a) and inaccurately recognized in (b). The wall marker was accurately recognized in (c) and inaccurately recognized in (d).

In this study, $d_j$ for scenarios with predefined paths was set to 1.0. For scenarios without predefined paths, $d_j$ was determined based on the distance between object $j$ and the physical environment boundary $P$. If the maximum distance between points in $j$ and $P$ exceeded a certain threshold, then $d_j$ was set to 0.5. Otherwise, $d_j$ was set to 1.0. This precaution was taken because in VR systems, for safety concerns, it is advisable to avoid directing users towards walls as much as possible.

## 4.2   Object Decomposition

There are two types of object in this study: polygons and paths. The decomposition method for polygons employs regular tessellation as described in [23]. For paths, the decomposition method involves repeatedly halving each segment until its length falls below a specified threshold.

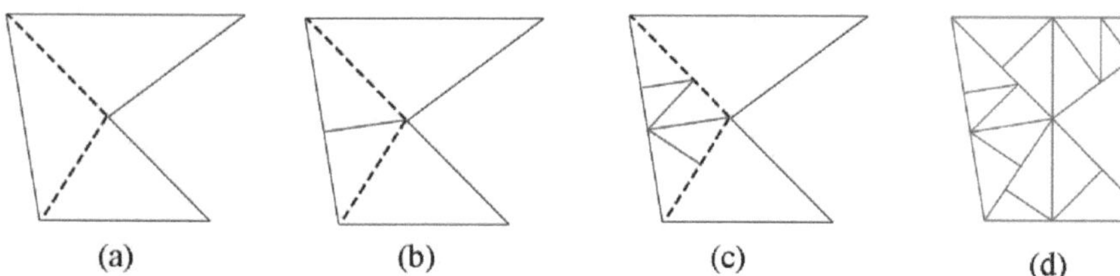

**Fig. 7.** Subdivision for a straight-line polygon: (a) triangulation of a straight-line polygon, (b) first subdivision of a triangle, (c) final subdivision of a triangle, (d) final subdivision of a straight-line polygon.

**Polygon Decomposition.** The decomposition of polygons are as follows:

- Triangulation is applied partition a straight-line polygon into multiple triangles (Fig. 7(a)), and then triangular division is utilized to divide it into smaller triangles. Each triangle is cut by connecting the vertex with the maximum angle to its perpendicular foot on the opposite edge (Fig. 7(b)) until the maximum edge length is less than the threshold (Fig. 7(c)). The final decomposition is shown in Fig. 7(d). Compared to the regular tessellation used in [23], the generated sub-polygons consistently have three edges.
- For a curved polygon, we use splinegon [9], an important representation form of curved polygon in industries, as input and utilize Voronoi-based decomposition (VBD) [4] to divide the polygon into five types of subregions Type 1-Type 5, as shown in Fig. 8(a). The subregions in VBD have better characteristics compared to other splinegon decomposition methods (e.g., horizontal visibility decomposition and bounded degree decomposition [22]). Each subregion is subsequently subdivided into smaller and more regular regions:
  - Type 1 formed by three diagonals (e.g., triangle). This subdivision process is similar to that employed for the triangles in the triangulation of a straight-line polygon.
  - Type 2 is formed by a diagonal and a curve, as shown in Fig. 8(b). Find the point on the curve that has the maximum distance to the diagonal. We then connect this point to the endpoints of the diagonal to divide a Type 2 into a Type 1 and a Type 2.
  - Type 3 is formed by two diagonals and a curve, as shown in Fig. 8(c) and Fig. 8(d): (1) If the curve is convex, as shown in Fig. 8(c), we connect the endpoints of the curve to divide a Type 3 into a Type 1 and a Type 2; (2) If the curve is concave, as shown in Fig. 8(d), we find the point on the curve that has the maximum distance to line segment connected by endpoints of the curve. We then make parallel lines for the line segment from the point to divide a Type 3 into a Type 1 and two Type 3.
  - Type 4 is formed by a diagonal and two curves, as shown in Fig. 8(e), Fig. 8(f), and Fig. 8(g): (1) If one of the curves is convex, whereas another is concave, as illustrated in Fig. 8(e), we find the point on the concave curve that has the maximum distance to the line segment connected by

endpoints of the concave curve. We then make parallel line to the line segment from the point to divide a Type 4 into two Type 3 and a Type 4; (2) If both curves are concave, as depicted in Fig. 8(f), the processing is the same as above. (3) If both curves are convex, as shown in Fig. 8(g), we connect the endpoints of each curve separately to divide a Type 4 into two Type 2 and a Type 1.

- Type 5 is formed by two diagonals and two curves, as shown in Fig. 8(h), Fig. 8(i), Fig. 8(j), and Fig. 8(k): (1) If both curves are convex, as shown in Fig. 8(h), we connect the endpoints of each curve separately to divide a Type 5 into a quadrilateral and two Type 2. The quadrilateral is divided into two Type 1 by connecting one of its diagonals; (2) If both curves are concave, find two parallel lines as illustrated in Fig. 8(d). If these two parallel lines do not intersect the other curve, as shown in Fig. 8(i), a Type 5 is devided into a quadrilateral and four Type 3. Otherwise, as shown in Fig. 8(j), we find the common tangent of two curves to divide a Type 5 into four Type 3; (3) If one of the curve is concave whereas another is convex, as shown in Fig. 8(k), we find a parallel line for concave curve and connect the endpoints of convex curve to divide a Type 5 into a quadrilateral, a Type 2, and two Type 3.

This process was iteratively repeated until the maximum edge length of each subregion was less than a specified threshold. The splinegon was finally subdivided into the following shapes: Type 1, Type 2, Type 3, and Type 4 (Fig. 8(l)). Each of these shapes has no more than 3 edges.

Subsequently, the object set $J$ was obtained based on polygon $P$ or predefined paths $R$.

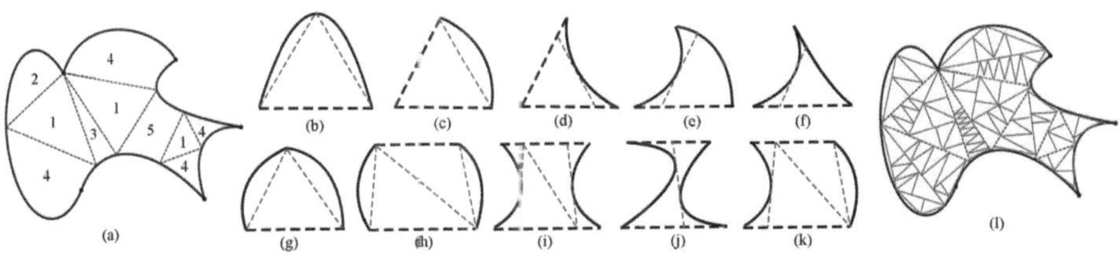

**Fig. 8.** VBD of splinegon (a), subdivision for type 2 (b), subdivision for type 3 (c)(d), subdivision for type 4 (e)(f)(g), subdivision for type 5 (h)(i)(j)(k), subdivision for splinegon (l).

**Path Decomposition.** The decomposition of paths are as follows:

- For the straight-line path, as shown in Fig. 9(a), we repeatedly cut each segment in half until its length is less than a threshold, as shown in Fig. 9(b).

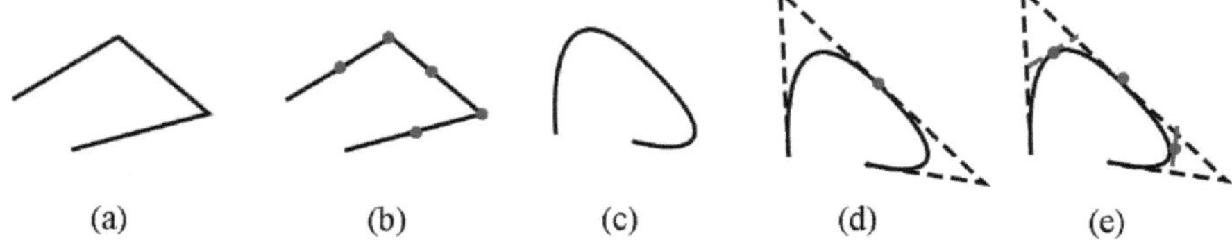

(a)          (b)          (c)          (d)          (e)

**Fig. 9.** Subdivision for straight-line paths and curved paths.

- For curved paths, as shown in Fig. 9(c), We use NURBS curve [32] as input and subdivide the NURBS curved path into triangular curves. In Fig. 9(d), the NURBS curve with inflection points is subdivided into two triangular curves at the inflection points. The positions of the inflection points are among the solutions of this equation

$$D'(t) \times D''(t) = 0$$

where $D'(t)$ is the first-order derivative, $D''(t)$ is the second-order derivatives, and $\times$ is the cross product of the two derivative vectors. The details of the computation of the inflection points for the NURBS curves can be found in [19]. We then find the point on each curve that has the maximum distance to the line segment connected by endpoints of the curve and cut the curve from the point until the length of the line segment of each curve is less than a specified threshold (Fig. 9(e)).

### 4.3   Optimal Marker Locations Set

Marker locations are permitted to be placed anywhere in continuous space that make determining the optimal configure challenging. To address this, a discrete set of critical locations is identified as optimal potential marker locations for different scenarios using methods outlined in [48]:

- In scenarios with predefined paths, markers only need to cover these paths instead of the whole walkable physical environment. The line intersection point set approach [23] was utilized to identify potential marker locations for achieving coverage along the predefined paths.
- Otherwise, markers need to cover the entire walkable physical environment. The PIPS approach [23] was employed to determine potential marker locations for achieving coverage across the walkable physical environment.

**Scenarios Without Predefined Paths.** The markers consist of ground markers and wall markers, each possessing distinct properties: the wall markers are positioned on the edges of polygons, with the requirement that the edges must be straight lines; whereas the ground markers are located within the polygon and do no intersect with any holes of the polygon. For a given object set $J$ and a polygon $P$, we compute the potential wall marker set and potential ground marker set separately, as the effective range of these two markers are differs. The process for physical environment without predefined paths is as follows:

- Ground markers: we obtain covering boundary $e_j$ for each subregion $j$ in $J$ (See Fig. 5(a)) by finding the overlap of circles with the center being vertices in $j$ and a radius of $r_g$, as shown in Fig. 5(b). The effective recognition range of a ground marker inside the covering boundary $e_j$ must fully cover $j$. All covering boundaries for each subregions in $J$ are shown in Fig. 5(c). For each pair of subregions, the intersection points are added to ground marker set $I_g$ if the intersection is visible to them (See Fig. 5(d)). The visibility algorithms for polygons can be found in [43], while the visibility algorithms for splinegons are detailed in [4]. We then obtain initial ground marker set $I_g$, as shown in Fig. 5(e). Finally, we remove locations where the minimal distance to $P$ is less than $L$ and merge each pair of locations where the distance is less than $L$, as shown in Fig. 5(f).
- wall marker: we first compute the covering boundaries of each subregions in $J$ (See Fig. 5(g)) by finding the overlap of circles with the center being vertices in $j$ and a radius of $r_w$, as shown in Fig. 5(h). All covering boundaries for each subregions in $J$ are shown in Fig. 5(i). For each subregion, the intersections between the subregion and straight-line edges of polygon $P$ are pushed into wall marker set $I$, as shown in Fig. 5(j). We then obtain initial wall marker set $I_w$, as shown in Fig. 5(k). Finally, we remove the locations where the minimal distance to vertices of $P$ is less than $L$ and merge each pair of locations which distance is less than $L$ as shown in Fig. 5(l).

Ground location set $I_g$ and wall location set $I_w$ are merged into the marker location set $I$.

**Scenarios with Predefined Paths.** The process for the physical environment with predefined paths is similar to the process described above. The main difference lies in the fact that in this scenario, the objects in object set $J$ represent the decomposition of predefined paths, whereas in the last case, the objects in $J$ represented the decomposition of polygon $P$.

### 4.4   Maximal Covering Location Problem

Once the object set $J$ and the potential marker set $I$ are obtained. We construct MCLP, which is formulated as the following integer linear programming model:

$$s.t. \max \sum_{j \in J} d_j z_j \tag{1}$$

$$\sum_{i \in I(j)} y_i \geq z_j, j \in J \tag{2}$$

$$\sum_{i \in I(j)} y_i \leq B \tag{3}$$

$$y_i \in \{0, 1\}, i \in I \tag{4}$$

$$z_j \in \{0, 1\}, j \in J \tag{5}$$

Herein, $B$ is the specific number of markers. In our study, we utilize an exact algorithm to address MCLP instances using effective branch-and-Benders-cut algorithms that leverage a combinatorial cut-separation procedure [7]. The result is an assignment of array $y_i$, indicating which marker location is employed.

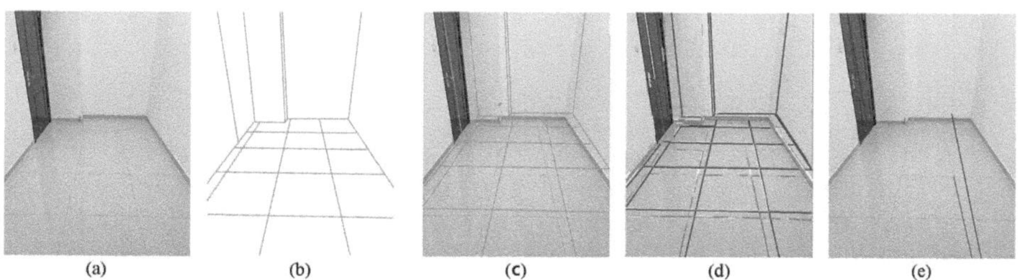

**Fig. 10.** Evaluation process: (a) physical environment, (b) virtual objects, (c) actual rendered virtual environment, (d) virtual lines (blue) and physical lines (red) detected by visual recognition, and (e) two pairs of virtual line and its corresponded physical line (the top-left pair on the door is an incorrect correspondence, while the bottom-right pair on the ground is a correct correspondence). (Color figure online)

## 5   Evaluation

To evaluate tracking accuracy, we constructed a AR system to measure the difference between user's physical position and virtual position during user walking. The use of user experience as a measure metric is not strict. Therefore, we rendered predefined virtual objects and used an automatic visual match to calculate the distance between the physical objects (See Fig. 10(a)) and virtual objects (See Fig. 10(b)) for each frame. Finally, an array of measured value was used to represent effectiveness of our methods.

To avoid extra physical characteristics, we used the margins between ground tiles, the vertical lines between walls, and the horizontal lines between the wall and tiles as physical objects. These line segments are easy to recognize. Virtual objects corresponding to these physical objects were rendered with specific colors different from those in the physical world. If a physical line and its corresponding virtual line were not aligned in a frame (Fig. 10(c)), it means that the virtual position in this frame was mismatched with the physical position.

The views in the HMD were recorded and stored as a series of pictures while the user walked. Each two frames ($f_{i1}$, $f_{i2}$) corresponded a pair of physical position $p$ and rotation $d$. In frame $f_{i1}$, the system did not render the virtual lines and outputted a picture of physical environment without virtual lines. In frame $f_{i2}$, the system rendered the virtual lines and outputted a picture of physical environment with virtual lines.

We used EDLines algorithm [2] in Python OpenCV to detect the lines in the former picture (See Fig. 10(a)) and latter picture (See Fig. 10(c)), respectively. The detected results are merged in Fig. 10(d), where blue lines represent virtual objects and red lines represent physical objects. Subsequently, we identified the corresponding physical line for each virtual line based on distance and parallel relationships. We then used the local outlier factor (LOF) algorithm to remove any unexpected correspondences, as shown in Fig. 10(e). Finally, we obtained the average value of the distance between the virtual and physical lines in each frame. The entire algorithm is presented as Algorithm 3.

---

**Algorithm 3:** Compute the difference between physical world and virtual world

---

    **Input**   : Image $Img_{phy}$, Image $Img_{vir}$, predefined color $C$
    **Output**: Distance $D$

1  Let $A$ be an array of distance between each pair of virtual line and its corresponded physical line.
2  Find all line-segments $L_{phy}$ in $img_{phy}$ by EDLines method.
3  Find all line-segments $L_{vir}$ with a specific color $C$ in $img_{vir}$ by EDLines method.
4  **foreach** $Line$ $l_v$ $in$ $L_{vir}$ **do**
5     Find line $l_p$ in $L_{phy}$ such that $l_p$ is the closest line to $l_v$ among all lines in $L_{phy}$ that are approximately parallel to $l_p$.
6     **if** $l_p$ $is$ $not$ $null$ **then**
7         Construct perpendicular lines from two endpoints $l_v^s$ and $l_v^e$ to the extending line of $l_p$, resulting in feet $l_p^s$ and $l_p^e$ respectively.
8         push $(|l_v^s l_p^s|+|l_v^e l_p^e|)/2$ to $A$.
9  Output average of values in $A$.

---

# 6  Experiment

In this study, we designed an experiment to explore the impact of our marker placement method in indoor physical environment lacking features. Whether to use markers is considered as one condition, and different scenarios are considered as another condition. This means that participants will undergo testing in four different condition combinations: (automatically placed markers, manually placed markers) × (with predefined paths, without predefined paths).

## 6.1 Study Setup

The research venue was a indoor environment featured white walls and ground tiles. We developed a AR system using the Unity engine. The VE included virtual lines with fixed coordinate and predefined color rendered in global world coordinates.

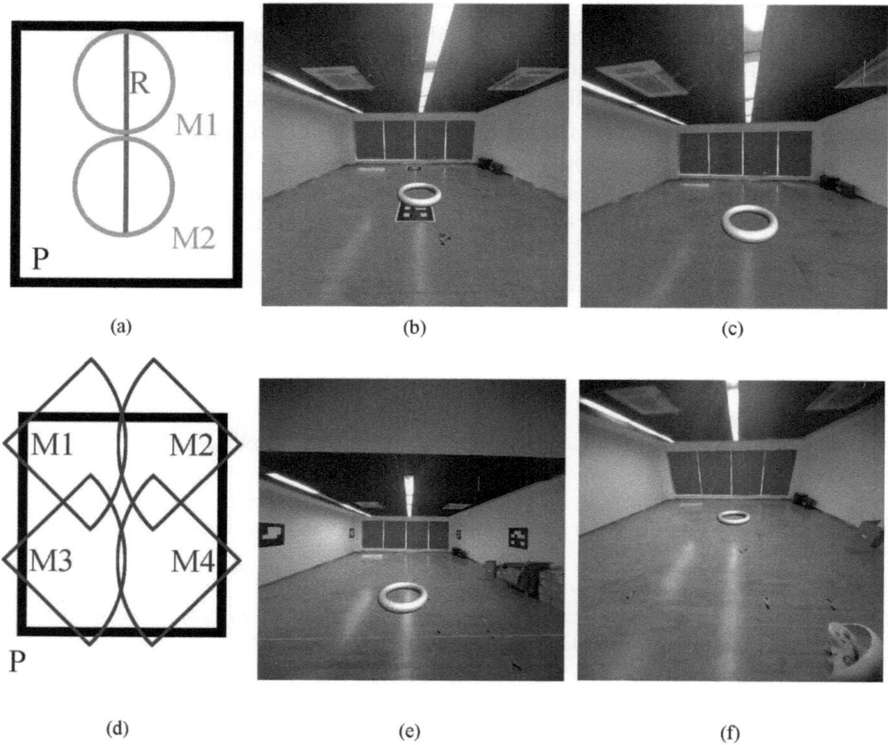

**Fig. 11.** First physical environment for experiment. (a) physical environment with predefined path (red) and effective recognition rage of two markers (blue) for $B = 2$, (b) virtual target and physical environment with markers, (c) virtual target and physical environment without markers, (d) physical environment without predefined path (red) and effective recognition rage of optimal markers (blue) for $B = 4$, (e) virtual target and physical environment with markers, (f) virtual target and physical environment without markers. (Color figure online)

## 6.2 Study Design

Each physical environment includes four conditions (automatically placed marker, manually placed marker) × (free walk, walking along predefined paths) as shown in Fig. 11. For each condition, we designed three predefined paths, resulting in three trials in each condition. Notably, to keep consistent of free walking under different scenarios (automatically placed marker, manually placed marker), the system automatically generated three random paths for each physical environment. The score of each trial was measured by Algorithm 3 (Fig. 12).

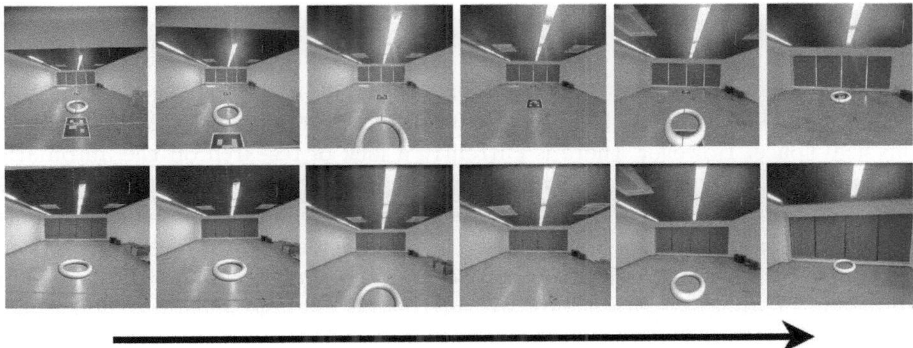

**Fig. 12.** Comparison between the automatic placement strategy and the manual placement strategy in a physical environment for tracking during user walking, with the first row showing walking with automatically placed markers and the second row showing walking with manually placed markers. The order of images from left to right is consistent with the user's walking process.

## 6.3   Study Procedure

The study lasted approximately 60 min for each physical environment. At the beginning of each trial, the participant pressed the trigger to start the trial, and a virtual white torus appeared on the path as the first target. The participant was instructed to walk towards the target. When a participant reached the target, it would be replaced by the next target. The participant was asked to stop, look around, and then walk towards the next target. The trial ended after the participant reached the last target.

## 6.4   Result

Table 1 displays the average and standard deviation of distances between the physical and virtual worlds. The results reveal the effectiveness of our method in reducing the average distance between the physical and virtual worlds by 33.06% in predefined path scenarios and 38.03% in free walking scenarios, as opposed to manual placement.

**Table 1.** Average (m) and standard deviation of measurement under different conditions.

|              | Predefined paths | Free walk       |
| ------------ | ---------------- | --------------- |
| Automatically | 0.0120 (0.0148) | 0.0135 (0.0140) |
| Manually     | 0.0363 (0.0198)  | 0.0355 (0.0206) |

## 7   Discussion

In recent years, multiplayer VR experience systems in large space have become popular. In such systems, users can roam in virtual reality by walking freely in physical space. However, there is currently a lack of research on the automatic placement of markers for tracking user viewpoints based solely on known 2D sketches of physical space, as well as evaluations of such tracking methods. This paper introduces this issue for the first time and attempts to provide a solution. Of course, further research is needed to improve accuracy and robustness. In addition, due to space limitations, we only tested a simple linear polygon scene. In this scene, the automatically generated layout effect is similar to the manually generated layout effect. The next step will be to test more complex scenes, such as curved polygons with holes.

In our experiment, the foundation of our model and the site we chose were almost featureless (with white walls and ceramic tiles on the floor). In fact, in practical applications, even in areas with fewer features (Fig. 1(b)), there are still some areas with distinct features (e.g., furniture). In the future of work, weighted fusion of markers and physical features is a more effective method.

Notably, the physical environment can be fully covered (Fig. 13) by setting the value of $B$ to 1, and subsequently running the MCLP algorithm multiple times. After each iteration of the algorithm, $B$ is incremented by 1. This iterative process continues until $\sum_{j \in J} d_j z_j = \sum_{j \in J} d_j$.

Sometimes, even if the participant is within the range of the marker, prolonged walking with their back to the marker may affect stability. In our study, $r_g$ and $r_w$ were small, so participants typically quickly passed through a range of markers, avoiding the aforementioned issues. It is worth exploring in the future whether long-term back or lateral marking walking will have an impact on stability.

In Sect. 3, we assumed that users were maintained consistent height (without squatting) and not allow to lower or lift their head. Because the effective recognition range of markers is related to $H$ and the angle between sight and ground. If this assumption was not made, the effective recognition range of the label was dynamically changing, and offline optimization planning could not be carried out. This can be considered in future work. In addition, in this study, we measured the fixed values of $H$ and $L$ to measure the values of $r_g$ and $r_w$. Intuitively, the effective recognition range of a marker in 3D space is a cone, but the specific mathematical relationship should be strictly derived.

**Fig. 13.** The physical environment is fully covered by markers when $B = 5$ and $\sum\limits_{j \in J} d_j z_j = \sum\limits_{j \in J} d_j$.

Notably, the boundary of the physical environment could be a curved polygon with obstacles. The markers could not be placed on the curved surface of the wall in this study because the recognition of curved markers required extra calibration. This can be considered in future work.

## 8   Conclusion

We introduce an automatic marker placement method that automatically determines the optimal marker placement within specified physical boundaries and predefined paths, thereby improving the accuracy of marker-based tracking methods in VR systems. Our method supports both straight and curved boundaries with holes, ensuring that it can adapt to a variety of physical environments. We also develop a comprehensive evaluation method to assess the tracking accuracy of different placement strategies. Experimental evaluations demonstrate that our proposed automatic marker placement method significantly reduces the tracking error. This result highlights the practicality and reliability of our method in accurately tracking the user's position within a VE, especially in situations where traditional feature-based tracking may be limited by uniformity or lack of features.

Our method has been used in VR systems with scripted redirected walking controllers to support users roaming larger virtual spaces by walking naturally in a limited physical space. In fact, the automatic placement of markers in a given physical environment is an interesting mathematical problem. The optimal placement of markers in physical environments with different surface representations and the recognition of markers on surfaces are both worthy research issues in the future.

**Acknowledgements.** This work was supported by the National Natural Science Foundation of China under Grant [number 62332017, 62277035, 61972233].

# References


1. Acevedo, P., Rekabdar, B., Mousas, C.: Optimizing retroreflective marker set for motion capturing props. Comput. Graph. **115**, 181–190 (2023)
2. Akinlar, C., Topal, C.: Edlines: a real-time line segment detector with a false detection control. Pattern Recogn. Lett. **32**(13), 1633–1642 (2011). https://doi.org/10.1016/j.patrec.2011.06.001
3. Alexandris, G., Giannikos, I.: A new model for maximal coverage exploiting GIS capabilities. Eur. J. Oper. Res. **202**(2), 328–338 (2010). https://doi.org/10.1016/j.ejor.2009.05.037
4. Bao, X., Qi, M., Yang, C., Gai, W.: Voronoi-based splinegon decomposition and shortest-path tree computation. Comput. Aided Geom. Des. 102316 (2024). https://doi.org/10.1016/j.cagd.2024.102316
5. Canny, J.: A computational approach to edge detection. IEEE Trans. Pattern Anal. Mach. Intell. **PAMI-8**(6), 679–698 (1986). https://doi.org/10.1109/TPAMI.1986.4767851
6. Celozzi, C., Paravati, G., Sanna, A., Lamberti, F.: A 6-DOF ARTag-based tracking system. IEEE Trans. Consum. Electron. **56**(1), 203–210 (2010). https://doi.org/10.1109/TCE.2010.5439146
7. Cordeau, J.F., Furini, F., Ljubić, I.: Benders decomposition for very large scale partial set covering and maximal covering location problems. Eur. J. Oper. Res. **275**(3), 882–896 (2019). https://doi.org/10.1016/j.ejor.2018.12.021
8. Cromley, R., Lin, J., Merwin, D.: Evaluating representation and scale error in the maximal covering location problem using GIS and intelligent areal interpolation. Int. J. Geogr. Inf. Sci. GIS **26**, 495–517 (2012). https://doi.org/10.1080/13658816.2011.596840
9. Dobkin, D.P., Souvaine, D.L.: Computational geometry in a curved world. Algorithmica **5**(1), 421–457 (1990). https://doi.org/10.1007/BF01840397
10. Drezner, Z., Suzuki, A.: Covering continuous demand in the plane. J. Oper. Res. Soc. **61**(5), 878–881 (2010). https://doi.org/10.1057/jors.2009.10
11. Fiala, M.: Artag, a fiducial marker system using digital techniques. In: 2005 IEEE Computer Society Conference on Computer Vision and Pattern Recognition (CVPR 2005), vol. 2, pp. 590–596 (2005). https://doi.org/10.1109/CVPR.2005.74
12. Huang, Q., DeGol, J., Fragoso, V., Sinha, S.N., Leonard, J.J.: Optimizing fiducial marker placement for improved visual localization. IEEE Robot. Autom. Lett. **8**(5), 2756–2763 (2023). https://doi.org/10.1109/LRA.2023.3260700
13. Huang, Y., Weng, D., Liu, Y., Wang, Y.: Infrared marker-based tracking in an indoor unknown environment for augmented reality applications. In: Yoshizawa, T., Wei, P., Zheng, J. (eds.) 2009 International Conference on Optical Instruments and Technology: Optoelectronic Imaging and Process Technology, vol. 7513, p. 75132V. International Society for Optics and Photonics, SPIE (2009). https://doi.org/10.1117/12.839662
14. Indriasari, V., Mahmud, A.R., Ahmad, N., Shariff, A.R.M.: Maximal service area problem for optimal siting of emergency facilities. Int. J. Geogr. Inf. Sci. **24**(2), 213–230 (2010). https://doi.org/10.1080/13658810802549162
15. Jun, J., Yue, Q., Qing, Z.: An extended marker-based tracking system for augmented reality. In: 2010 Second International Conference on Modeling, Simulation and Visualization Methods (WMSVM 2010), pp. 94–97. IEEE Computer Society, Los Alamitos, CA, USA (2010). https://doi.org/10.1109/WMSVM.2010.52

16. Kato, H., Billinghurst, M.: Marker tracking and HMD calibration for a video-based augmented reality conferencing system. In: Proceedings 2nd IEEE and ACM International Workshop on Augmented Reality (IWAR 1999), pp. 85–94 (1999). https://doi.org/10.1109/IWAR.1999.803809
17. Klein, G., Murray, D.: Parallel tracking and mapping for small AR workspaces. In: 2007 6th IEEE and ACM International Symposium on Mixed and Augmented Reality, pp. 225–234 (2007). https://doi.org/10.1109/ISMAR.2007.4538852
18. Lepetit, V., Fua, P.: Keypoint recognition using randomized trees. IEEE Trans. Pattern Anal. Mach. Intel. **28**(9), 1465–1479 (2006). https://doi.org/10.1109/TPAMI.2006.188
19. Li, Y.M., Cripps, R.J.: Identification of inflection points and cusps on rational curves. Comput. Aided Geom. Des. **14**(5), 491–497 (1997). https://doi.org/10.1016/S0167-8396(96)00041-6
20. Matas, J., Chum, O., Urban, M., Pajdla, T.: Robust wide-baseline stereo from maximally stable extremal regions. Image Vis. Comput. **22**(10), 761–767 (2004). https://doi.org/10.1016/j.imavis.2004.02.006
21. Matisziw, T.C., Murray, A.T.: Siting a facility in continuous space to maximize coverage of a region. Socioecon. Plann. Sci. **43**(2), 131–139 (2009). https://doi.org/10.1016/j.seps.2008.02.009
22. Melissaratos, E.A., Souvaine, D.L.: Shortest paths help solve geometric optimization problems in planar regions. SIAM J. Comput. **21**(4), 601–638 (1992). https://doi.org/10.1137/0221038
23. Murray, A., Tong, D.: Coverage optimization in continuous space facility siting. Int. J. Geogr. Inf. Sci. **21**, 757–776 (2007). https://doi.org/10.1080/13658810601169857
24. Murray, A.T.: Geography in coverage modeling: exploiting spatial structure to address complementary partial service of areas. Ann. Assoc. Am. Geogr. **95**(4), 761–772 (2005). https://doi.org/10.1111/j.1467-8306.2005.00485.x
25. Murray, A.T., Matisziw, T.C., Wei, H., Tong, D.: A geocomputational heuristic for coverage maximization in service facility siting. Trans. GIS **12**(6), 757–773 (2008). https://doi.org/10.1111/j.1467-9671.2008.01125.x
26. Murray, A.T., O'Kelly, M.E.: Assessing representation error in point-based coverage modeling. J. Geogr. Syst. **4**(2), 171–191 (2002). https://doi.org/10.1007/s101090200084
27. Murray, A.T., Wei, R.: A computational approach for eliminating error in the solution of the location set covering problem. Eur. J. Oper. Res. **224**(1), 52–64 (2013). https://doi.org/10.1016/j.ejor.2012.07.027
28. Naimark, L., Foxlin, E.: Circular data matrix fiducial system and robust image processing for a wearable vision-inertial self-tracker. In: Proceedings. International Symposium on Mixed and Augmented Reality, pp. 27–36 (2002). https://doi.org/10.1109/ISMAR.2002.1115065
29. Nescher, T., Huang, Y.Y., Kunz, A.: Planning redirection techniques for optimal free walking experience using model predictive control. In: 2014 IEEE Symposium on 3D User Interfaces (3DUI), pp. 111–118 (2014). https://doi.org/10.1109/3DUI.2014.6798851
30. Nilsson, N.C., et al.: 15 years of research on redirected walking in immersive virtual environments. IEEE Comput. Graphics Appl. **38**(2), 44–56 (2018)
31. Park, H., Park, J.I.: Invisible marker based augmented reality system. In: Li, S., Pereira, F., Shum, H.Y., Tescher, A.G. (eds.) Visual Communications and Image Processing 2005, vol. 5960, p. 59601I. International Society for Optics and Photonics, SPIE (2005). https://doi.org/10.1117/12.631416

32. Piegl, L., Tiller, W.: The NURBS Book. Springer, Heidelberg (1995)
33. Rekimoto, J.: Matrix: a realtime object identification and registration method for augmented reality. In: Proceedings of 3rd Asia Pacific Computer Human Interaction (Cat. No. 98EX110), pp. 63–68 (1998). https://doi.org/10.1109/APCHI.1998.704151
34. Retinger, M., Michalski, J., Kozierski, P., Drapikowski, P.: Ensuring high visibility of passive markers at fixed camera gain using divide and conquer method. IEEE Robot. Autom. Lett. **9**(11), 9741–9748 (2024). https://doi.org/10.1109/LRA.2024.3464368
35. Rosten, E., Porter, R., Drummond, T.: Faster and better: a machine learning approach to corner detection. IEEE Trans. Pattern Anal. Mach. Intell. **32**(1), 105–119 (2010). https://doi.org/10.1109/TPAMI.2008.275
36. Santos, P.C., Stork, A., Buaes, A., Pereira, C.E., Jorge, J.: A real-time low-cost marker-based multiple camera tracking solution for virtual reality applications. J. Real-Time Image Proc. **5**(2), 121–128 (2010). https://doi.org/10.1007/s11554-009-0138-9
37. Siltanen, S.: Theory and applications of marker-based augmented reality: licentiate thesis. Licenciate, Aalto University, Finland (2012). https://publications.vtt.fi/pdf/science/2012/S3.pdf. Project code: 78191
38. Siltanen, S., Hyväkkä, J.: Implementing a natural user interface for camera phones using visual tags. In: Proceedings of the 7th Australasian User Interface Conference - Volume 50, pp. 113–116, AUIC 2006. Australian Computer Society, Inc., AUS (2006)
39. Slater, M., Usoh, M., Steed, A.: Taking steps: the influence of a walking technique on presence in virtual reality. ACM Trans. Comput.-Hum. Interact. **2**(3), 201–219 (1995). https://doi.org/10.1145/210079.210084
40. Suma, E.A., Lipps, Z., Finkelstein, S., Krum, D.M., Bolas, M.: Impossible spaces: maximizing natural walking in virtual environments with self-overlapping architecture. IEEE Trans. Visual Comput. Graphics **18**(4), 555–564 (2012). https://doi.org/10.1109/TVCG.2012.47
41. Tong, D., Church, R.: Aggregation in continuous space coverage modeling. Int. J. Geogr. Inf. Sci. **26**(5), 795–816 (2012). https://doi.org/10.1080/13658816.2011.615748
42. Tong, D., Murray, A.T.: Maximising coverage of spatial demand for service*. Pap. Reg. Sci. **88**(1), 85–97 (2009). https://doi.org/10.1111/j.1435-5957.2008.00168.x
43. Toth, C.D., O'Rourke, J., Goodman, J.E.: Handbook of Discrete and Computational Geometry. CRC Press (2017). https://doi.org/10.1201/9781420035315
44. Usoh, M., et al.: Walking > walking-in-place > flying, in virtual environments. In: Proceedings of the 26th Annual Conference on Computer Graphics and Interactive Techniques, SIGGRAPH 1999, pp. 359–364. ACM Press/Addison-Wesley Publishing Co., USA (1999). https://doi.org/10.1145/311535.311589
45. Wagner, D., Langlotz, T., Schmalstieg, D.: Robust and unobtrusive marker tracking on mobile phones. In: 2008 7th IEEE/ACM International Symposium on Mixed and Augmented Reality, pp. 121–124 (2008). https://doi.org/10.1109/ISMAR.2008.4637337
46. Wang, T., Liu, Y., Wang, Y.: Infrared marker based augmented reality system for equipment maintenance. In: 2008 International Conference on Computer Science and Software Engineering, vol. 5, pp. 816–819 (2008). https://doi.org/10.1109/CSSE.2008.8

47. Wei, R., Murray, A.T.: Evaluating polygon overlay to support spatial optimization coverage modeling. Geogr. Anal. **46**(3), 209–229 (2014). https://doi.org/10.1111/gean.12036
48. Wei, R., Murray, A.T.: Continuous space maximal coverage: insights, advances and challenges. Comput. Oper. Res. **62**, 325–336 (2015). https://doi.org/10.1016/j.cor.2014.04.010
49. Yin, P., Mu, L.: Modular capacitated maximal covering location problem for the optimal siting of emergency vehicles. Appl. Geogr. **34**, 247–254 (2012). https://doi.org/10.1016/j.apgeog.2011.11.013
50. Zmuda, M.A., Wonser, J.L., Bachmann, E.R., Hodgson, E.: Optimizing constrained-environment redirected walking instructions using search techniques. IEEE Trans. Visual Comput. Graphics **19**(11), 1872–1884 (2013). https://doi.org/10.1109/TVCG.2013.88

# Establishing a Data-Efficient Witness Protocol for Connected Autonomous Vehicles


Siriboon Chaisawat[(✉)], Hye-young Paik, and Salil S. Kanhere

School of Computer Science and Engineering, University of New South Wales,
Sydney, Australia
{s.chaisawat,h.paik,s.kanhere}@unsw.edu.au



**Abstract.** With rapid advancements in automotive technology, autonomous vehicles are expected to operate widely on roads in the near future. This shift toward automation reduces human responsibility for monitoring surroundings, potentially leading to the Molly Problem, as defined by ITU-T, a scenario where no eyewitnesses are present at the scene. This presents a challenge in seeking alternative data sources to support investigations. Equipped with a range of sensors, vehicles functioning as witnesses or "witness vehicles" have gained attention in recent studies for supporting evidence gathering. However, casting a wider net to expand the potential pool and effectively identifying relevant witnesses within it is a challenge. According to existing works, witness vehicles are identified by those within a specific range receiving alert messages at the time of the incident. However, due to the dynamic nature of traffic and delays in accident detection and verification, actual witnesses may have already left the scene by the time these messages are broadcast. Without effective approaches for identifying actual witness vehicles, this could result in the collection of irrelevant data, further complicating the investigation process and posing privacy concerns for the data owners. To address these issues, we propose a "call-for-witness" protocol and four witness identification approaches: Proximity Assessment, Perception Field-Target Overlap Assessment, Visual Object Detection, and LiDAR-Guided Object Detection. The traffic authority can specify search queries, which vehicles use to perform local assessments, allowing them to determine if they possess data relevant to the incident. The implementation and evaluation were conducted on data collected from the CARLA simulator, which was used to model vehicle collisions with varying traffic densities. The results demonstrated significant improvements in reducing the amount of data and increasing the relevance of the data submitted to the traffic authority.

**Keywords:** Autonomous Vehicles · Witness Vehicles · Vehicle Collision Simulation




A. Soylu et al. (Eds.): MobiQuitous 2024, LNICST 634, pp. 470–490, 2026.
https://doi.org/10.1007/978-3-032-10554-7_25

# 1   Introduction

According to McKinsey [10], by 2030, 95% of new vehicles sold globally will be connected, making the driving task more automated and reducing human responsibility for perceiving surroundings. A report from the WHO [18] indicates that vehicles cause 3,700 fatal injuries and between 54,800 and 137,000 non-fatal injuries daily worldwide. The NHTSA [11] suggests that increasing the use of autonomous vehicles will improve overall traffic safety, potentially reducing crashes by 49%. However, as driving tasks become more autonomous with minimal human intervention, this raises new challenges, such as the "Molly problem" defined by ITU-T [6], where no human witnesses are present at road incidents. Additionally, identifying the liable party will become more complex since multiple sensors and software collaborate to support the vehicle's operation. Thus, liability can no longer be solely attributed to human drivers. Due to the lack of standard guidelines in vehicle digital forensics, several research works have focused on designing forensic frameworks to overcome both legal [15] and technical [5] challenges.

The role of vehicles serving as witnesses in road incidents has started to gain interest in recent studies [4,8,9,13,17]. New vehicle models are equipped with a range of sensors, such as 360-degree cameras, radar, and lidar, enabling them to perceive their surroundings accurately. This gives autonomous vehicles the capability to replace humans in witnessing incidents. However, after reviewing existing works on developing protocols for requesting vehicles as incident witnesses, several key issues were identified. Firstly, calling for witnesses is often seen as a real-time synchronous process. However, in practice, delays in incident detection and verification occur. Additionally, before vehicle data can be shared with the traffic authority, consent must first be obtained from the data owner, such as the vehicle owner. This indicates that the protocol is unlikely to be synchronous and occur in real time. Secondly, there is no mechanism to assess whether identified vehicles are actual witnesses. Most works simply assume that vehicles within the Dedicated Short-Range Communications (DSRC) range are witnesses, but due to the dynamic nature of traffic, the actual witness may already have moved out of range. Lastly, there is a lack of an effective approach to identifying relevant data among the sensor data possessed by the vehicle, which then results in a large amount of raw data being submitted, increasing the workload for the investigating authority and posing privacy risks due to unnecessarily sharing private information.

To address the aforementioned problems, we propose a call-for-witness protocol that supports message broadcasting over a wider area and for an extended period to ensure the reach of potential witnesses. For vehicles to submit data to the traffic authority, they must prove their relevance to the incident. To facilitate this, four self-assessment approaches are proposed based on the available vehicle sensor data. These approaches ensure that all submitted data comes from actual witness vehicles.

The subsequent sections are organized as follows. Section 2 provides a background on related actors, communication standards, key types of messages used in vehicle networks, and types of sensors equipped on autonomous vehicles. Section 3 discusses the challenges in vehicle digital forensics, reviews existing research works, and identifies research problems in the area. Section 4 provides an overview of the proposed call-for-witness protocol and the approaches for assessing a vehicle's relevance in incident witnessing. Section 5 discusses the technical components for each assessment approach. Section 6 presents the implementation and results from evaluating the proposed approach using the CARLA simulator. Lastly, Sect. 7 concludes the results and contributions of this study.

## 2    Background

This section provides an overview of the key actors in the vehicle network, the communication standards and messages crucial for vehicle safety and operation, and the sensors used by vehicles for comprehensive perception of their surroundings and accurate autonomous driving decision-making.

### 2.1    Key Actors in Vehicle Network

The primary actor in vehicle networks is the Connected Autonomous Vehicle (CAV), which is equipped with a range of sensors and software designed to perceive and respond to dynamic surroundings. Additionally, they are embedded with On-Board Units (OBUs) that support both short-range and long-range communications, enabling the real-time transmission and reception of safety and operational data.

The second actor is Road-Side Units (RSUs), which play an important role by serving as relay points for information exchange between vehicles and the traffic management center. They are equipped with hardware and software that support both DSRC and C-V2X communications.

Lastly, the traffic authority is responsible for overseeing the management of traffic, road infrastructure, and road users, with a focus on both operational efficiency and safety. In the event of an incident, the traffic authority, such as the National Highway Traffic Safety Administration (NHTSA), is responsible for collaborating with other entities, such as vehicle manufacturers and technical specialists, in investigating cases. Findings from case analyses are compiled into comprehensive reports and used to recommend improvements to vehicle safety guidelines, helping to prevent future incidents.

### 2.2    Communication Standards

C-V2X and DSRC are the two main communication standards in vehicle networks. C-V2X, primarily adopted in Europe, utilizes LTE and 5G to provide low-latency communication, high reliability, and extended range. This standard supports both direct communication (PC5 interface) for vehicle-to-vehicle (V2V) and vehicle-to-infrastructure (V2I) interactions, as well as network-based communication (Uu interface) for wide-area connectivity. On the other hand, DSRC is mainly used in America and operates over short distances with low latency. It implements IEEE 802.11p standards for wireless access in vehicular environments and operates in the 5.9 GHz spectrum with approximately 75 MHz bandwidth.

### 2.3   Key Communication Messages for Safety and Situational Awareness

The Basic Safety Message (BSM), introduced by SAE [14], is the fundamental message exchanged between vehicles for safety and situational awareness. Each vehicle uses a temporary ID, which is periodically changed to prevent tracking, to share messages containing details such as position, speed, heading, and brake status. Another important message is the Decentralized Environmental Notification Message (DENM), defined by ETSI [3], which is used for broadcasting information about accidents or road hazards to road users within the affected area. The message includes details such as event position, detection time, relevant area, and traffic direction. ITS Stations in the area, such as RSUs, can help disseminate the message by checking the validity of messages and forwarding them to the relevant area.

### 2.4   Sensors in Autonomous Vehicles

Autonomous vehicles are equipped with a range of sensors to provide a comprehensive and precise perception of their surroundings. The most common sensor is camera, which captures visual information of the environment. To achieve 360-degree perception, six to eight cameras are typically installed around the vehicle. Next is radar, which uses radio waves to measure distances and the relative speed of objects, functioning effectively under various weather conditions. Another sensor is LiDAR, which helps create a detailed 3D map of the environment by emitting laser pulses that reflect off objects. The point clouds generated can be processed using clustering techniques, allowing for the identification of objects and their positions. Global Positioning System (GPS) provides real-time positioning and navigation information essential for route planning and vehicle tracking, helping determine the vehicle's location relative to road maps and other geographic data. Lastly, Inertial Measurement Unit (IMU), consisting of accelerometers and gyroscopes, measures acceleration and rotational rates, aiding in determining the vehicle's current motion state and orientation.

## 3   Related Works

### 3.1   Challenges in Vehicle Digital Forensics

Vehicle digital forensics involves investigating data within vehicle systems and data exchanged between vehicles and external entities to understand incidents, such as road accidents or cyber attacks. Key steps in vehicle digital forensics include identifying relevant data sources, preserving evidence to prevent tampering or loss, analyzing data to extract correlations and identify potential causes of incidents, and documenting findings in a format suitable for further actions, such as legal proceedings or enhancing safety standards. However, vehicle digital forensics faces multiple technical and legal challenges.

The absence of well-established forensic guidelines for handling CAV-related incidents raises privacy concerns in accessing and collecting vehicle data for analysis. Additionally, to ensure data is admissible in legal procedures, the designed guidelines or framework need to ensure that properties such as confidentiality, integrity, availability, authenticity, non-repudiation, and privacy are achieved [15].

From a technical perspective, vehicle forensics presents multiple challenges. According to [5], vehicles' sensors generate approximately 4,000 GB of data per day. Handling this amount of data necessitates effective storage and access control to prevent unauthorized access and ensure the appropriate protection of sensitive log data. This issue complicates the correlation of logs from various sensors to extract critical information as part of investigations. In addition to the large data volume, the current embedded hardware and software components in autonomous vehicles still lack mechanisms to guarantee data integrity, raising concerns about potential data tampering before the data can be used as evidence.

### 3.2   Current Research Works in Vehicle Digital Forensics

A study [1] proposes solutions for vehicles to collaborate in verifying reported road events within VANETs. The threshold ring signature scheme is introduced to protect the privacy of participating vehicles by enabling anonymous message verification, where a subset of members collaborates to generate a joint signature. Additionally, an incentive mechanism encourages vehicles to respond to verification requests and provide accurate information.

Liability attribution in road accidents is another area of focus in multiple research studies. The paper [19] introduces a lightweight blockchain architecture for accident responsibility identification within the Internet of Vehicles (IoV), using two separate chains to improve storage efficiency and separate responsibilities. The Preservation Chain is responsible for storing operation-related data, such as driving records, communication logs, and maintenance records. In contrast, the Accident Identification Chain focuses on determining accident liability, involving entities like traffic authorities, law enforcement, insurance companies, and car owners. When an accident occurs, the Accident Identification Smart Contract (AISC) on the Accident Identification Chain activates a cross-chain interaction by requesting evidence from the Preservation Chain. Another paper [12] presents a similar framework for evidence collection and decision-making to support the identification of responsible entities in road accidents, acknowledging the limitations of current models that primarily hold drivers responsible. This framework introduces a partitioned blockchain system: the Operational Partition (P1), which maintains continuous records of the vehicle's behavior, maintenance history, and any operational instructions received, while the Decision Partition (P2) is activated only in the event of an accident, utilizing data from P1 to aid in the decision-making process regarding liability.

Preserving the integrity of vehicle-generated data has gained attention as it is crucial for ensuring the admissibility of digital evidence in legal proceedings. The paper [7] proposes a solution to address data tampering and forgery, ensuring that the integrity of vehicle-generated data is preserved for forensic purposes. Verifiable Delay Function (VDF) is introduced by requiring a predefined amount of time to produce proof on recorded data. This ensures that data is stored in chronological order and prevents input of fabricated data. Another study [5] designs a framework for maintaining driving logs—such as sensor data, perception, and planning—in a tamper-proof manner. Hash chains and Bloom filters are used to preserve the integrity and sequence of the collected logs. Encrypted logs are published to a remote cloud server, allowing authorized investigators to access them for analysis. The proposed system's performance in log proof creation and verification times is evaluated using the Waymo open dataset.

### 3.3   Witnesses Vehicles to Provide Supporting Data

The role of vehicles in witnessing incidents has recently been highlighted in research. A study [17] presents a framework in which a law enforcer or observer is assigned to collect incident-related data from impacted vehicles and digital witnesses, such as nearby vehicles and RSUs. A Restricted Boltzmann Machine (RBM) is utilized to extract relevant incident features, guiding the observer in requesting data from the relevant devices of accident vehicles. To ensure data integrity and authenticity, hashes of the data are published to a blockchain, while raw data remain private and accessible only when authorized stakeholders grant consent. For data collected from witness entities, short randomizable signatures are used to provide anonymity. However, the paper does not detail the mechanism used to identify digital witnesses and ensure their relevance before including their data in the investigation. Another study [4] introduces a blockchain-based framework designed to provide trust and verifiable event information for vehicle accident forensics. The process begins with accident vehicles broadcasting an "event generation" message over the DSRC range, with vehicles receiving this message considered as witness vehicles. A federated group of community vehicles with high reputation scores is then formed to verify data submissions from witnesses. A new block containing the incident-related data is confirmed through an n-of-m voting federated consensus and made available to the traffic authority. To prevent non-relevant vehicles from claiming to be witnesses and submitting data, the paper suggests limiting the response time after request messages are broadcasted for preventing multi-hop message forwarding. However, delays in detection and verification may cause actual witnesses to have left the scene and beyonding the DSRC range by the time these messages are sent, leading to the misidentification of non-relevant vehicles as witnesses. A study [13] proposed the WIDE framework, which requests vehicles in the vicinity of an accident to assist in determining the liable party. A two-level integrity assessment is introduced: the first level verifies the integrity of witness vehicle sensors by having them respond to challenges issued by RSUs to confirm their internal control states, while the second level employs Practical Byzantine Fault Tolerance (pBFT) to ensure data integrity during transit. The framework also introduces a blockchain-based reputation management system (BRMS) to evaluate witness credibility. However, it lacks a mechanism to confirm whether the identified vehicles actually witnessed the incident, and the paper acknowledges that witness privacy is not addressed. Another study [9] introduces a framework that leverages blockchain for real-time detection, verification, and data collection of traffic incidents. When a vehicle's sensors detect abnormal conditions, the sensor data are sent to a smart contract for evaluation against predefined criteria. If an anomaly is detected, an Accident Unique Identification (AID) is generated and broadcasted by the RSU, requesting nearby vehicles, i.e., witness vehicles, to analyze data collected during the incident. These vehicles then perform ring signatures on their conclusions and submit the data to the RSU. Upon receiving submissions from at least 2/3 of the witness vehicles, the RSU packages the data into a signature set and uploads it to the Traffic Control Center (TCC). The TCC verifies the signature set and applies improved clustering analysis to derive conclusions. However, similar to previous studies, this framework lacks a mechanism to verify whether the vehicles receiving the accident broadcast actually witnessed the incident. Additionally, since witnesses provide conclusions rather than raw data, there is uncertainty regarding the correctness of the derived conclusions. Another study [8] presents a system enabling incident witnesses to register and anonymously upload evidence. Witnesses use a master secret to generate pseudonymous identities and anonymous credentials, maintaining anonymity and ensuring unlinkability of submissions. Utilizing Ciphertext-Policy Attribute-Based Encryption (CP-ABE), only authorized staff with matching attributes can access uploaded data for analysis. Additionally, a state machine implemented through smart contracts facilitates transparent state transitions in the investigation process. However, due to the openness of the system design, any entity can claim to be a witness, placing the burden on the traffic authority to filter out data from irrelevant sources.

Reviewing of existing literature reveals a lack of effective approaches for assessing the relevance of vehicles as witnesses to road incidents. Without such an approach, substantial amounts of data from irrelevant sources may be submitted, which increases the workload for traffic authority in processing and filtering relevant information. Additionally, this poses privacy risks to data owners by unnecessarily sharing private data.

## 4    Solution Overview

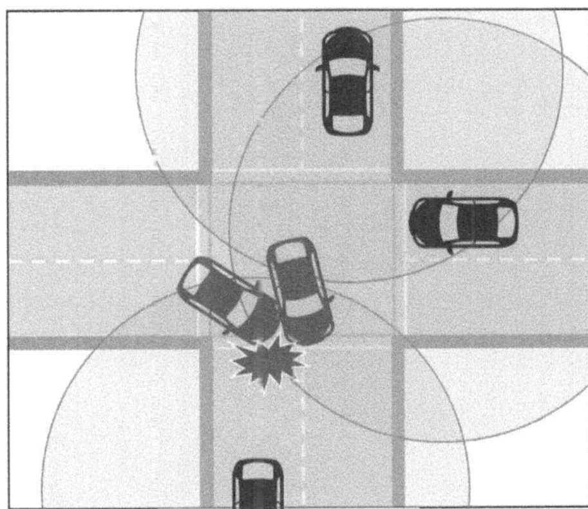

**Fig. 1.** Collision Scenario Between Two Vehicles with Nearby Vehicles Witnessing the Incident (Blue Circle Indicates Perception Range). (Color figure online)

### 4.1    Scenario and Assumptions

In this study, we focus on the scenario of two autonomous vehicles colliding with no human witnesses present, as illustrated in Fig. 1, with the following assumptions made. First, we assume that vehicles are likely to revisit the same routes over time. This assumption aligns with a study [2] that analyzed one week of travel data from 5,641 electric vehicles (EVs) in Shanghai, which found that approximately 15% of family-used vehicles exhibited flexible route choices, while 85% demonstrated a preference for stable routes. Factors influencing these patterns included departure time, travel distance, reliance on expressways, and travel direction (e.g., from suburban to central city areas). Therefore, call-for-witness messages can be configured to broadcast within areas surrounding the incident over an extended period, such as one week, to increase the likelihood of reaching vehicles that were at the scene. Second, due to the large volume of data generated by vehicle sensors, we assume this data can only be stored locally for a limited period, such as one day. After this period, the data is uploaded to the manufacturer to be stored for an extended duration in case it is needed for forensic analysis. Third, ownership of data generated by vehicles belongs to the data owner, which in this scenario is the vehicle owner. In order for vehicle data to be shared with external parties, explicit consent is required. Fourth, vehicles are assumed to operate at level 3 conditional driving automation, as defined by the SAE, where driving tasks are autonomously performed by the vehicle, while owners retain control over non-operational decisions, such as choosing to participate as a witness. Participation as a witness, in this scenario, is considered voluntary, with vehicle owners having the complete right to decide whether to engage in the process. Lastly, all vehicles are assumed to be equipped with DSRC and C-V2X technology, enabling support for both direct and network communication.

## 4.2  Process Overview

This section introduces the call-for-witness protocol. As illustrated in Fig. 2, the process involves five actors: the traffic authority, RSUs, witness vehicles, vehicle owners, and automobile manufacturers. The protocol is initiated when an accident is detected and reported to the traffic authority. The details of the subsequent steps are as follows:

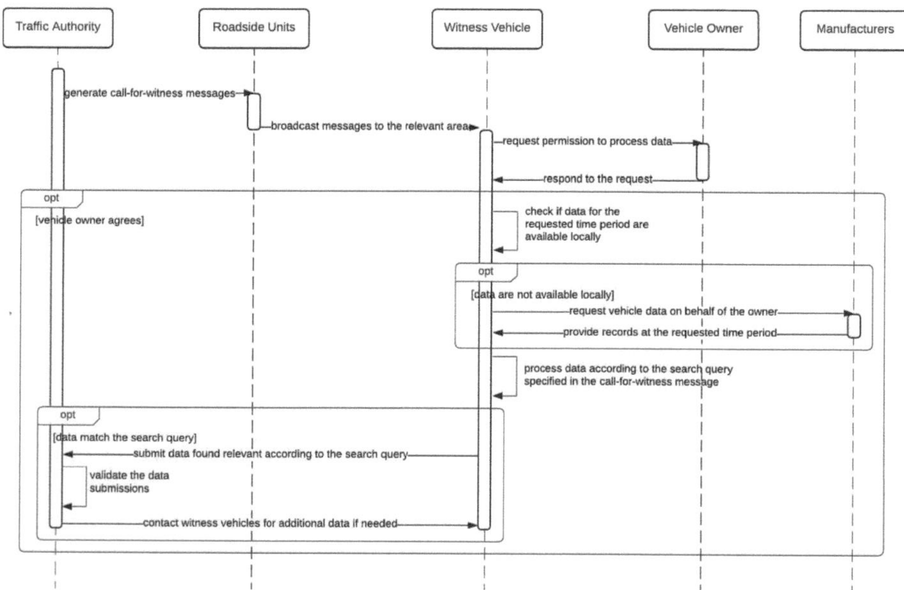


**Fig. 2.** Call-for-Witness Protocol

1. **Call-for-Witness Message Generation**: After a preliminary analysis of the data available at the scene, the traffic authority determines whether additional information is needed for case analysis. To request assistance from vehicles that witnessed the incident, a call-for-witness message extending the standard DENM message structure is generated. The à la carte container section of the message is customized to include queries tailored to the traffic authority's specific search criteria. Details about the message are further discussed in the Technical Components section.

2. **Message Dissemination**: The dissemination of the call-for-witness message follows the same steps as DENM message dissemination defined by ETSI [3]. In brief, any ITS Station with forwarding capabilities, such as an RSU or other type of ITS stations, can assist in relaying the message. This involves checking if its position falls within the relevant zone and forwarding direction, as well as verifying the message's validity. Vehicles within the DSRC range of these ITS Stations will receive the broadcasted call-for-witness message.

3. **Vehicles Receive the Messages:**
   (a) Upon receiving the message, the vehicle prompts the owner to decide whether they consent to process the data based on the search query in the call-for-witness message to determine if the vehicle was a witness to the incident. If the owner agrees, the vehicle proceeds to the next step of verifying data availability.
   (b) The vehicle retrieves data corresponding to the timeframe specified in the call-for-witness message. If the data is unavailable locally, the vehicle then requests the record from the manufacturer on behalf of the owner.
   (c) Four approaches are presented for vehicles to perform self-evaluation of their relevance to an incident: proximity assessment, perception field-target overlap assessment, visual object detection, and LiDAR-guided object detection. For each approach, the traffic authority provides a specific search query that the vehicle can use to evaluate its data. Details on each assessment approach are discussed in Sect. 4.3.

4. **Vehicles Respond to Traffic Authority**: If the results from processing the data match the query, the vehicle is considered a witness. It then sends the data to the traffic authority, and in this study, we assume that only visual evidence or camera images are requested for submission.

5. **Traffic Authority Validates Data Submitted:** The traffic authority validates whether the vehicles sending the data are actual witnesses based on the submitted data and may contact them for additional information if needed.

### 4.3 Approaches for Assessing Vehicle Relevance in Incident Witnessing

Illustrated in Fig. 3, four assessment approaches for vehicles to assess their relevance to a road incident are proposed, ranging from simple proximity assessment to more complex and precise methods, such as LiDAR-guided visual object detection. Depending on the data that the traffic authority has already acquired from the incident scene, they can select the appropriate assessment approach and define the search query in the call-for-witness message. Vehicles receiving the message will then use the specified query to perform a local evaluation on their data. The details of each relevance assessment approach are as follows:

1. **Proximity Assessment** Proximity assessment is the basic approach, where vehicles determine their relevance based on closeness to the incident location. Vehicles first need to retrieve their travel paths during the timeframe of interest (e.g., from 5 s before the incident to 5 s after). If there are any timestamps where the vehicle's position is within the specified range, the vehicle is considered a witness. Images recorded during this period is considered as evidence and encouraged to be provided to the traffic authority.
2. **Perception Field-Target Overlap Assessment** Perception field-target overlap assessment approach uses the camera's intrinsic and extrinsic parameters to calculate the projection region based on the camera's field of view and effective detection range. Calculating the effective detection range requires considering surrounding factors in the scene, such as lighting, weather conditions, and obstacles; thus, we assume this value has been evaluated and provided by the traffic authority. The target area, or Perception Area of Interest (PAI), is the geographical area where the traffic authority seeks to acquire visual data. For vehicles to perform this type of assessment, they must check if the projection from any of their cameras overlaps with the PAI. Images from cameras that meet this condition are then submitted to the traffic authority.
3. **Visual Object Detection** In the visual object detection approach, images from each camera angle recorded during the specified time period are input into an object detection model. The model analyzes these frames based on a given image query, which describes the search objects, actions, and context (e.g., reference objects). This approach ensures that only the images matching the query are returned.
4. **LiDAR-Guided Visual Object Detection** LiDAR-guided visual object detection approach incorporates LiDAR data with images from cameras, allowing for higher precision in locating and detecting objects. The search query used for this approach is the same as that for visual object detection, with the option to include the positions of search objects, if known.

## 5 Technical Components

As introduced in Sect. 4.3, this section provides detailed explanations for each relevance assessment approach.

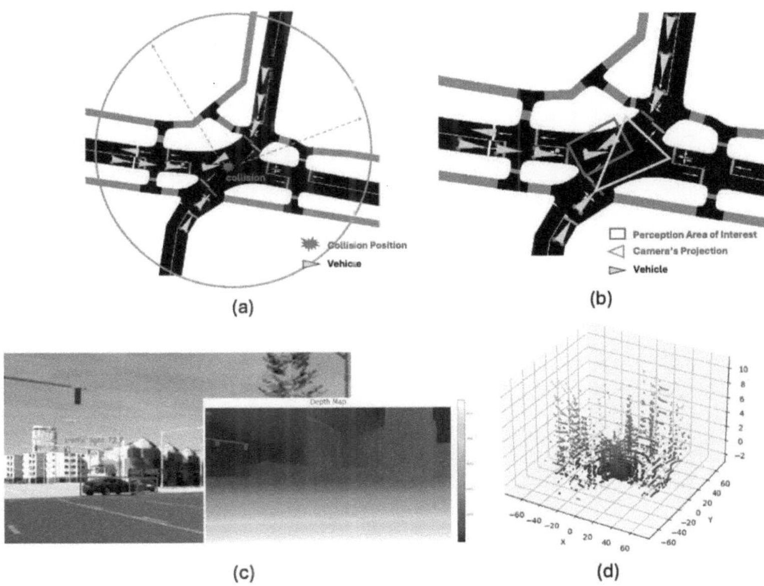



**Fig. 3.** Relevance Assessment Approaches: (a) Proximity Assessment (b) Perception Field-Target Overlap Assessment (c) Visual Object Detection, (d) LiDAR-Guided Visual Object Detection.

## 5.1   Relevant Assessment Approaches

**Proximity Assessment.** The search query for the proximity assessment includes both the search range from the incident location and the relevant timeframe. To conduct this assessment, the vehicle first retrieves its GPS records within the specified timeframe, then uses the Haversine formula to calculate the shortest distance between the vehicle's coordinates $(\text{lat}_v, \text{lng}_v)$ and the incident location$(\text{lat}_i, \text{lng}_i)$. By performing these calculations using vector operations, the vehicle can efficiently determine which timestamps fall within the specified range of the incident. Image frames captured at these timestamps are then retrieved and submitted to the traffic authority.

The following shows the Haversine formula, where $d$ is the distance between two geographical coordinates $(\text{lat}_v, \text{lng}_v)$ and $(\text{lat}_i, \text{lng}_i)$, and $r$ represents the Earth's radius, approximately 6371 km.

$$d = 2r \cdot \arcsin\left(\sqrt{\sin^2\left(\frac{\text{lat}_i - \text{lat}_v}{2}\right) + \cos(\text{lat}_v) \cdot \cos(\text{lat}_i) \cdot \sin^2\left(\frac{\text{lng}_i - \text{lng}_v}{2}\right)}\right)$$

**Perception Field-Target Overlap Assessment.** The search query for the perception field-target overlap assessment contains the interested timeframe,

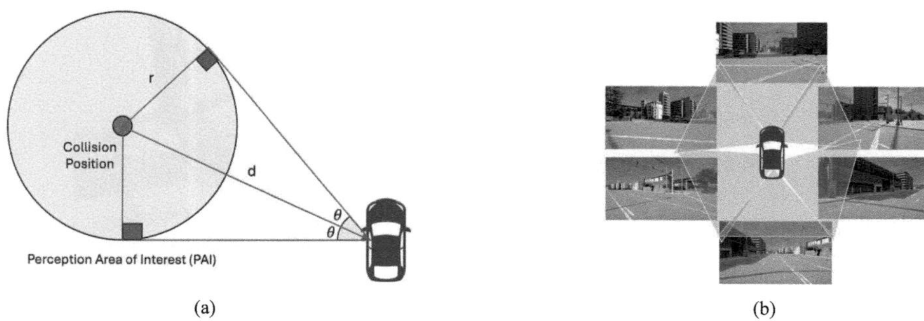

**Fig. 4.** (a) Perception Field-Target Overlap Calculation (b) Images Captured by Vehicle from Different Camera Angles.

effective detection range, and a list of geographical coordinates used for constructing the PAI. For the vehicle to perform this assessment, it needs to first check if there exists any timestamp within the given timeframe where the distance between the vehicle's position and the closest point on the PAI is within the provided effective detection range. As illustrated in Fig. 4(a), assuming the PAI is a 2D area of a circular shape (with elevation ignored) centered at the collision position and having a radius of $r$, the vehicle checks if distance from vehicle to the center, $d$, minus $r$ is within the given effective detection range. If this condition is satisfied, it indicates a likelihood that the vehicle's sensors could perceive the search data, and subsequent steps will then be performed. Next, the vehicle calculates a perception angle, $\theta$, that covers the observable area of the circle using the sine function. Since the circle is symmetrical, the total angle covering the area is $2\theta$. The calculation for $\theta$ is displayed as follows:

$$\theta = \arcsin\left(\frac{r}{d}\right)$$

To determine which cameras can capture images within the angle $2\theta$, the horizontal field of view, $\text{FoV}_{\text{horizontal}}$, must first be calculated using the camera's intrinsic parameters:

$$\text{FoV}_{\text{horizontal}} = 2 \times \arctan\left(\frac{\text{sensor width}}{2 \times \text{focal length}}\right)$$

For the cameras that have a $\text{FoV}_{\text{horizontal}}$ overlapping with $2\theta$, the images captured by these cameras are believed to contain evidence; thus, they are requested to be provided to the traffic authority.

**Visual Object Detection.** For the visual object detection approach, an image query and a depth difference threshold for identifying potential collisions between objects in the images are provided. In order for the vehicle to perform this assessment, the first step is to retrieve images that have been filtered using the perception field-target overlap assessment approach. Object detection is then performed on each image using a Convolutional Neural Network (CNN) to create feature maps. These feature maps are fed into detection layers that predict bounding boxes, object class probabilities, and an objectness score, indicating the likelihood of an object being present within each bounding box. Since multiple bounding boxes may be predicted for the same object, Non-Max Suppression (NMS) is applied to reduce redundancy by filtering out bounding boxes with lower confidence scores. The final output is a list of detected objects, visualized as bounding boxes with class labels and confidence scores. In addition to object detection, depth estimation is performed using CNNs to create a relative depth map from the image. Objects that appear at similar depths and have overlapping bounding boxes could indicate potential collisions.

Below is a simplified version of an image query for detecting vehicle collisions in the image.

```
SELECT frameID , cameraID
FROM images
WHERE cameraID IN ("front", 'front_left", "front_right", "rear",
"rear_left", "rear_right")
  AND object1.type = "sedan" AND object1.color = "blue"
  AND object2.type = "sedan" AND object2.color = "blue"
  AND INTERSECT(object1.bounding_box , object2.bounding_box)
  AND ABSOLUTE(object1.depth - object2.depth) < threshold
```

**LiDAR-Guided Visual Object Detection.** For the LiDAR-guided visual object detection approach, an image query is provided similarly to the previous approach, with the option to include the positions of target objects if known. This approach utilizes LiDAR data to improve object positioning accuracy and addresses partial visibility issues that may lead to object misdetection in the previous method. This approach involves several key steps. First, point clouds from the LiDAR sensor are clustered based on proximity and density to identify potential objects. Next, the 3D coordinates of these LiDAR clusters are transformed into a 2D coordinate system using both the extrinsic and intrinsic parameters of the sensors. The resulting 2D data then highlights Regions of Interest (ROIs) in the image, where these ROIs indicate a high likelihood of object presence. Lastly, object detection and classification are performed on these ROIs to predict bounding boxes, class labels, and objectness scores. If the positions of target and reference objects are provided in the search query, an additional step can be performed to compare the given positions with the LiDAR-detected object positions.

# 6    Implementation and Evaluation

(a)        (b)

**Fig. 5.** Traffic Simulation in CARLA Simulator.

## 6.1    Implementation

To implement the proposed approaches, CARLA, an open-source simulator for autonomous driving research, is used to simulate traffic and vehicle collisions, as displayed in Figs. 5 and 6.

To implement the proximity assessment, a search query is constructed by retrieving the collision position from CARLA's map. A Python script was developed to collect GPS data from each vehicle in the scene during a defined time period. Proximity checking is then performed by applying the Haversine formula to calculate the distance between the vehicle's position and the incident's position. For timestamps where the vehicles' positions are found to be within the given range, the corresponding six camera images at those timestamps are marked for submission to the traffic authority.

For the perception field-target overlap assessment, the PAI is defined by a set of coordinates on the CARLA map, representing the vertices encompassing the entire area of interest. In this experiment, an intersection is selected as the collision scene. Vehicle positions, headings, camera intrinsic and extrinsic parameters, and the effective detection range provided in the query are input into a Python script, which then checks whether any camera projections overlap with the PAI. The output returns a list of camera angles (e.g., front-left and rear-right) and the corresponding timestamps at which the overlap is detected.

For visual object detection, images from camera angles filtered by the previous approach are input into a Python script. This script utilizes a pretrained YOLOv3 model for object classification and MiDaS to estimate the depth of detected objects. The outputs from this step are then evaluated against the given image query to determine if they match the search criteria.

For LiDAR-guided visual object detection, DBSCAN is applied to cluster point clouds. Calibration parameters from the sensors, exported from CARLA, are used to transform the 3D LiDAR data into 2D coordinates. This transformation allows the mapping of LiDAR-identified ROIs onto image segments, where

(a)             (b)

**Fig. 6.** Collision Between Two Vehicles From Pre- to Post-Collision Moments at a 5-Way Intersection (Left Image) and a 3-Way Intersection (Right Image).

YOLO is subsequently applied for object detection and classification. The positions of objects in the image obtained from LiDAR are then compared to the search query. Images where matches are found are marked for submission to the traffic authority.

## 6.2   Experiment Setup

A 5-way and 3-way intersection in CARLA's Town3 were selected for simulating a collision between two vehicles under three different traffic densities—10, 20, and 40 vehicles per minute. All vehicles are set to autopilot to simulate realistic traffic dynamics. Each vehicle is equipped with GPS, LiDAR, and six cameras, each maintaining a fixed 65-degree field of view and producing images at a resolution of $1600 \times 900$ pixels. The system records data from each sensor every second. With this setup, we could evaluate the impact of traffic volume on the amount of sensor data generated and the effectiveness of the proposed relevance assessment approaches in each case.

To evaluate the proposed approaches, the following parameters were set for the experiment. The timeframe of interest was defined as 5 s before and after the incident, totaling 10 s. The search queries were configured with the following parameters: For proximity assessment, the range was set to 300 m from the incident position. In the perception field-target overlap assessment, PAI was defined by a list of four vertices covering the entire intersection, as shown in the yellow area in Fig. 7, with an effective detection range of 200 m. For visual object detection, the search query was structured as described in Sect. 5.1, with a depth difference threshold set to 300 units (based on the MiDaS scale) to capture cases of contact and near-contact objects, indicating potential collisions. For LiDAR-guided visual object detection, the search query was similar to the

**Fig. 7.** Perception Area of Interest (Highlighted in Yellow) and Incident Location (Marked by Red Cross) at a 5-Way Intersection (Left Image) and 3-Way Intersection (Right Image) (Color figure online)

previous approach, but the depth difference threshold was replaced with the known positions of objects in the scene.

### 6.3   Results Analysis

According to the scenario simulation, vehicles at a 5-way intersection tend to spend more time waiting for traffic lights, leading to a higher number of vehicles within the accident proximity. With proximity assessment, the number of images from vehicles that satisfy the search conditions at the 5-way intersection is greater compared to the 3-way intersection across all traffic density cases. Despite the larger number of images, many of these images are found to be irrelevant when compared to the ground truth. As shown in Table 1, this results in lower precision compared to the 3-way intersection.

Applying the perception field-target overlap assessment was found to significantly improve precision compared to the proximity assessment, without degrading recall. This approach can reduce irrelevant data submissions by 4.42 times for the 5-way intersection and by 3.19 times for the 3-way intersection.

Using visual object detection assessment significantly improved precision. However, according to the simulation, false positive cases were found at the 3-way intersection. This occurred because some vehicles were driving in close proximity to the impacted vehicles just before the collision, leading witness vehicles using the visual object detection approach to misinterpret these as collision incidents, as shown in Fig. 8(b). In contrast, at the 5-way intersection, no vehicles were found driving in close proximity to the impacted vehicles, resulting in no false positive cases. Therefore, precision reached 100% at the 5-way intersection but was lower in the 3-way intersection scenario.

Some images from witness vehicles capturing the collision at both the 5-way and 3-way intersections are found to be partially obstructed by objects and scene components, resulting in cases of false negative detection. This issue is particularly evident at the 3-way intersection, which has more limited viewing angles compared to the 5-way intersection, leading to lower recall rates when using the visual object detection approach. Incorporating LiDAR data can help reduce the number of false negative detections, improving detection by 1.29 times

**Table 1.** Evaluation Results of Relevance Assessment Approaches across Different Scenes and Traffic Densities

| Scene and Traffic Density (vehicles/min) | 5-way Intersection | | | 3-way Intersection | | |
|---|---|---|---|---|---|---|
| | 10 | 20 | 40 | 10 | 20 | 40 |
| Ground truth | | | | | | |
| No. of Relevant Vehicles | 5 | 7 | 12 | 6 | 8 | 10 |
| No. of Relevant Image Frames | 41 | 54 | 81 | 43 | 50 | 65 |
| Approach 1: Proximity Assessment | | | | | | |
| No. of Vehicles Meeting Criteria | 7 | 11 | 31 | 7 | 10 | 24 |
| Total No. of Image Frames | 354 | 521 | 1488 | 202 | 316 | 837 |
| Total Data Size | 700 MB | 1 GB | 4 GB | 400 MB | 630 MB | 1.7 GB |
| Precision | 11.58% | 10.36% | 5.44% | 21.28% | 15.82% | 7.77% |
| Recall | 100% | 100% | 100% | 100% | 100% | 100% |
| Approach 2: Perception Field-Target Overlap Assessment | | | | | | |
| No. of Vehicles Meeting Criteria | 5 | 9 | 16 | 6 | 9 | 13 |
| Total No. of Image Frames | 77 | 134 | 310 | 72 | 118 | 204 |
| Total Data Size | 150 MB | 270 MB | 620 MB | 150 MB | 250 MB | 400 MB |
| Precision | 53.25% | 40.30% | 26.13% | 59.72% | 42.37% | 31.86% |
| Recall | 100% | 100% | 100% | 100% | 100% | 100% |
| Approach 3: Visual Object Detection | | | | | | |
| No. of Vehicles Meeting Criteria | 5 | 5 | 7 | 6 | 6 | 6 |
| Total No. of Image Frames | 36 | 43 | 54 | 31 | 37 | 45 |
| Total Data Size | 75 MB | 85 MB | 100 MB | 60 MB | 75 MB | 90 MB |
| Precision | 100% | 100% | 100% | 96.77% | 91.89% | 86.67% |
| Recall | 87.80% | 79.63% | 66.67% | 69.77% | 68% | 60% |
| Approach 4: LiDAR-Guided Visual Object Detection | | | | | | |
| No. of Vehicles Meeting Criteria | 5 | 6 | 10 | 6 | 7 | 7 |
| Total No. of Image Frames | 39 | 48 | 66 | 34 | 45 | 57 |
| Total Data Size | 80 MB | 100 MB | 140 MB | 70 MB | 90 MB | 115 MB |
| Precision | 100% | 100% | 100% | 100% | 100% | 96.49% |
| Recall | 95.12% | 88.89% | 81.48% | 79.07% | 90% | 84.62% |

**Table 2.** Average Computational Utilization of Each Relevance Assessment Approach

| Assessment Approaches | Execution time | CPU | Memory |
|---|---|---|---|
| Proximity Assessment | 0.10 s | 0.0001% | 7.6 GB |
| Perception Field-Target Overlap Assessment | 0.11 s | 0.0001% | 8.5 GB |
| Visual Object Detection | 1.5 s | 65% | 40 GB |
| LiDAR-Guided Visual Object Detection | 10.3 s | 71% | 24 GB |

**Fig. 8.** (a) False negative collision detection from a witness vehicle's front camera at a 5-way intersection. (b) False positive collision detection from a witness vehicle's front camera at a 3-way intersection. (c) True positive collision detection at a 5-way intersection from a witness vehicle's rear right camera. (d) True positive collision detection at a 3-way intersection from a witness vehicle's rear right camera.

at the 3-way intersection and 1.14 times at the 5-way intersection. Despite the incorporation of LiDAR data for assessment, a small number of false negative detections are still present. This occurs when large and nearby objects, such as leading vehicles, block the laser beam scanning, limiting LiDAR's ability to detect collisions occurring behind these obstacles.

In terms of computational performance, as shown in Table 2, both proximity and perception field-target overlap assessments require similar amounts of CPU, memory, and execution time. In contrast, visual object detection and LiDAR-guided object detection consume significantly more CPU and memory. LiDAR-guided visual object detection, in particular, was found to have the longest execution time, taking approximately 10.3 s to process a single image frame—nearly seven times longer than visual object detection, which takes 1.5 s. Compared to the capabilities of Tesla's Full Self-Driving (FSD) computer [16], all the proposed assessment approaches are feasible to be executed locally within vehicles.

Lastly, in terms of data submission, the perception field-target overlap assessment can reduce data submissions by an average of 4.42 times at the 5-way intersection and 3.19 times at the 3-way intersection compared to the proximity assessment. Applying visual object detection further reduces the amount of data by 16.5 times at the 5-way intersection and 11.22 times at the 3-way intersection, with significant improvements in precision. However, recall is found to decrease, particularly in the 3-way intersection scenario, due to limited perception angles of the scene. Using LiDAR-guided object detection results in a substantial reduction in data submissions, by approximately 14.16 times at 5-way intersections and 9.21 times at 3-way intersections. Nevertheless, this approach still experiences some false negative detection cases, causing misidentification of relevant collision images.

## 7    Conclusion

In the near future, vehicles will become more connected and autonomous. With a range of sensors equipped, they will be capable of supporting traffic authority in gathering evidence for road incidents. The concept of vehicles acting as witnesses has been recently discussed in research; however, reviewing current literature shows a lack of effective approaches for determining the relevance of vehicles to an incident before considering them as witnesses. To address this problem, a call-for-witness protocol and relevance assessment approaches are proposed to enable vehicles to perform local checks on their data based on search queries defined by traffic authority. Based on the available vehicle sensor data, four approaches are proposed: Proximity Assessment, Perception Field-Target Overlap Assessment, Visual Object Detection, and LiDAR-Guided Object Detection. The experiment was conducted using data obtained from the CARLA simulator, where scenarios of collisions between two vehicles at 3-way and 5-way intersections with varying traffic densities were created. The results show that the proposed approach not only helps in identifying relevant data but also significantly reduces the amount of data vehicles need to share with traffic authority. Thus, the proposed solution can support traffic authority in evidence collection while protecting the privacy of vehicle data by ensuring that only relevant data are shared.

## References


1. Ahmed, W., Di, W., Mukathe, D.  A blockchain -enabled incentive trust management with threshold ring signature scheme for traffic event validation in vanets. Sensors **22**(17) (2022). https://doi.org/10.3390/s22176715. https://www.mdpi.com/1424-8220/22/17/6715
2. Deng, J., Gao, L., Chen, X., Yuan, Q.: Taking the same route every day? An empirical investigation of commuting route stability using personal electric vehicle trajectory data. Transportation **51**(4), 1547–1573 (2024)
3. ETSI: Decentralized environmental notification service (2022). https://www.sae.org/standards/content/j2735_202309/. Accessed 16 May 2024
4. Guo, H., Li, W., Nejad, M., Shen, C.C.: Proof-of-event recording system for autonomous vehicles: a blockchain-based solution. IEEE Access **8**, 182776–182786 (2020)
5. Hoque, M.A., Hasan, R.: Avguard: a forensic investigation framework for autonomous vehicles. In: ICC 2021 - IEEE International Conference on Communications, pp. 1–6 (2021). https://doi.org/10.1109/ICC42927.2021.9500652

6. ITU: The molly problem (2024). https://www.itu.int/en/ITU-T/focusgroups/ai4ad/Pages/MollyProblem.aspx. Accessed 16 May 2024

7. Li, J., Song, Z., Zhang, Z., Li, Y., Cao, C.: In-vehicle digital forensics for connected and automated vehicles with public auditing. IEEE Internet Things J. (2023)

8. Li, M., Chen, Y., Lal, C., Conti, M., Alazab, M., Hu, D.: Eunomia: anonymous and secure vehicular digital forensics based on blockchain. IEEE Trans. Dependable Secure Comput. **20**(1), 225–241 (2021)

9. Liu, X., Qiu, W., Ren, W., Xu, C., Choo, K.K.R.: An in-situ authentication with privacy preservation scheme for accident response in internet of vehicles. Internet Things **22**, 100728 (2023)

10. McKinsey: Unlocking the full life-cycle value from connected-car data (2021). https://www.mckinsey.com/industries/automotive-and-assembly/our-insights/unlocking-the-full-life-cycle-value-from-connected-car-data. Accessed 16 May 2024

11. National Highway Traffic Safety Administration: Parts: Partnership for analytics research in traffic safety (2024). https://www.nhtsa.gov/parts-partnership-for-analytics-research-in-traffic-safety. Accessed 16 May 2024

12. Oham, C., Kanhere, S.S., Jurdak, R., Jha, S.: A blockchain based liability attribution framework for autonomous vehicles. arXiv preprint arXiv:1802.05050 (2018)

13. Oham, C., Michelin, R.A., Jurdak, R., Kanhere, S.S., Jha, S.: Wide: a witness-based data priority mechanism for vehicular forensics. Blockchain Res. Appl. **3**(2), 100050 (2022)

14. SAE: V2x communications message set dictionary (2023). https://www.sae.org/standards/content/j2735_202309/. Accessed 16 May 2024

15. Sharma, P., Gillanders, J.: Cybersecurity and forensics in connected autonomous vehicles: a review of the state-of-the-art. IEEE Access **10**, 108979–108996 (2022). https://doi.org/10.1109/ACCESS.2022.3213843

16. Talpes, E., et al.: Compute solution for tesla's full self-driving computer. IEEE Micro **40**(2), 25–35 (2020). https://doi.org/10.1109/MM.2020.2975764

17. Tyagi, R., Sharma, S., Mohan, S.: Blockchain enabled intelligent digital forensics system for autonomous connected vehicles. In: 2022 International Conference on Communication, Computing and Internet of Things (IC3IoT), pp. 1–6. IEEE (2022)

18. WHO: Road traffic injuries (2023). https://www.who.int/news-room/fact-sheets/detail/road-traffic-injuries. Accessed 16 May 2024

19. Yao, Q., Li, T., Yan, C., Deng, Z.: Accident responsibility identification model for internet of vehicles based on lightweight blockchain. Comput. Intell. **39**(1), 58–81 (2023)

# Real-Time Obstacle Detection and Safe Operation for Industrial Autonomous Mobile Robots

Yuanhao Liu[1,2,3], Yinlong Zhang[1,2,4](✉), Shuai Liu[1,2](✉), Dapeng Lan[1,2], Chu Wang[1,2], and Wei Liang[1,2]

[1] State Key Laboratory of Robotics, Shenyang Institute of Automation, Chinese Academy of Sciences, Shenyang 110016, China
`{zhangyinlong,liushuai}@sia.cn`
[2] Key Laboratory of Networked Control Systems, Chinese Academy of Sciences, Shenyang 110016, China
[3] University of Chinese Academy of Sciences, Beijing 100049, China
[4] Guangzhou Institute of Industrial Intelligence, Guangzhou 511458, China

**Abstract.** To ensure the safety and stability of mobile robots operating alongside humans in industrial environments, the robot is typically equipped with vision and depth sensors to perceive the surroundings and required to maintain appropriate speed and safe distances by identifying obstacles ahead. However, the traditional vision-based obstacle detection methods suffer the drawbacks of unstable obstacle detection in complex environments and imprecise distance estimation of the obstacles. To address these issues, this paper proposes an innovative real-time obstacle detection and safe operation framework using the complementary RGB and depth measurements for industrial autonomous mobile robots. To enhance the effectiveness of obstacle detection and relative depth estimation, RGB and depth measurements are integrated in an innovative manner. The spatio-temporal hybrid deep learning network is built to segment obstacles and accurately determine their depth using the Euclidean clustering. An adaptive control strategy is designed to dynamically adjust the robot's speed, maintaining a minimal safety distance to ensure the safety of both the robot and the surrounding obstacles. Meanwhile, we implement a temporal information aggregation tracking model to detect falls among workers. Upon detecting a fall, the robot will immediately halt its operations. If the fall duration exceeds a predefined threshold, an alarm will be triggered to ensure worker's safety. The algorithm has been tested on a specially developed mobile robot platform. The experimental results highlight the competitive performance of our method.

**Keywords:** Industrial autonomous mobile robots · Safe operation · Obstacle detection · RGB-Depth measurements · Control strategies

This work was supported by the National Natural Science Foundation of China under contact 62273332, the Youth Innovation Promotion Association of Chinese Academy of Sciences under contact 2022201, Guangdong Basic and Applied Basic Research Foundation under contract 2023A1515011363. Liaoning Applied Basic Research Foundation under contract 2023JH26/10300028.



A. Soylu et al. (Eds.): MobiQuitous 2024, LNICST 534, pp. 491–506, 2026.
https://doi.org/10.1007/978-3-032-10554-7_26

# 1  Introduction

The integration of digital technology and robotic systems, driven by the emergence of Industry 4.0 and the continuous development of mobile intelligence, signifies the arrival of a new era in manufacturing. In recent years, the precise navigation and reliable operation of robots play a crucial role in ensuring production efficiency and worker safety, attracting widespread attention, especially in human-robot coexistence environments [1–4]. Across diverse industries, industrial autonomous wheeled robots are extensively employed for tasks such as assembly, picking and placing, and packaging. Their versatility, ease of programming, and cost-effectiveness highlight their immense potential in the present scenario. Typically, robots move along pre-planned paths to handle materials, such as carrying out goods handling tasks in warehouses, in order to enhance production efficiency and reduce labor consumption [5].

However, with industrial mobile robots developing towards digitization and intelligence, fixed-path task execution is no longer sufficient to meet the current production demands. Therefore, robots must move quickly and smoothly to improve production efficiency [6] while avoiding collisions with obstacles ahead, such as patrolling inspectors, fallen packages, and other automated guided vehicles (AGVs). This is especially important in human-robot coexistence environments. These collisions can result in personal injury and even lead to safety incidents like AGV fires, presenting a significant risk to production safety.

In recent years, various sensor application methods have been researched and developed to address the safe operation issues of industrial robots, primarily including three types, based on vision, radar, and ultrasonic sensors [7–12]. However, these technologies still exhibit limitations. Vision-based methods utilize visual sensors (stereo vision and RGB-D, etc.) to capture scene images and employ image processing algorithms to detect and recognize obstacles [13]. Radar-based methods utilize laser radar sensors to emit laser beams, measuring the distance and direction of detected obstacles. However, radar faces several challenges in obstacle detection, such as low resolution, vulnerability to environmental interference, inadequate reflection from certain materials, complex data processing, and high costs. In contrast, sound wave detection technologies, especially ultrasonic sensors, detect obstacles by measuring the propagation time and speed of sound wave pulses. Their sensitivity to environmental factors such as air density, temperature, and humidity results in relatively low accuracy, limiting their effectiveness in real-time obstacle detection for mobile robots. Taking into account the advantages and disadvantages of various methods, RGB-D sensors are particularly well-suited for obstacle detection and safe operation of mobile robots in human-robot coexistence industrial environments, owing to their low cost, high information capacity, and strong environmental adaptability.

Despite the significant advancements in RGB-D sensing technology for obstacle detection and safe operation of mobile robots, current methods still face inherent limitations, including detection failures, inaccurate distance estimation, and unreasonable control strategies, particularly in the application of industrial autonomous mobile robots operating in dynamic environments. Typically, current obstacle detection methods detect objects ahead using bounding boxes [14]. However, they often overlook factors like unexpected lighting changes, which can result in detection failures and collision incidents. Additionally, the use of detection boxes inevitably incorporates background depth information and may also include depth noise resulting from unexpected lighting conditions and hollow objects. When these rectangular regions are input into the depth image for distance estimation, such interference may mix with the actual depth of obstacles, compromising the accuracy of the relative depth estimation. Consequently, depending solely on the average depth or centroid depth of the obstacle region for distance estimation may prove to be unreliable in this context [15]. Moreover, current methods might not adequately adjust control strategies to account for the distance between the robot and upcoming obstacles in real-time. Such a simplistic braking operation could compromise system safety and elevate the risk of robot malfunctions or collisions with humans.

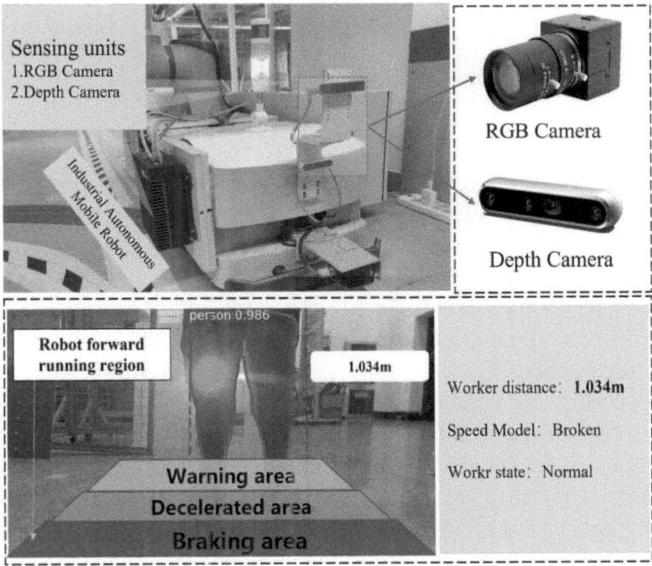


**Fig. 1.** Schematic diagram illustrating the safety awareness for industrial autonomous mobile robots. The robot is equipped with an RGB camera and a depth camera, capable of detecting and segmenting obstacles ahead, and measuring their relative distances to the robot.

To tackle these challenges, this study introduces a comprehensive RGB-depth fusion method aiming at improving the safe operation of industrial autonomous mobile robots, as illustrated in Fig. 1. Specifically, it employs an end-to-end deep learning model based on spatio-temporal hybrid detection techniques to tackle the inter-frame loss issue in obstacle detection by learning to capture long-range relationships in RGB imaging. Additionally, it utilizes a temporal information aggregation tracking model for worker fall detection to ensure their safety. Moreover, it applies a Euclidean point cloud clustering method in depth images to accurately estimate the relative distance of the obstacles. Finally, this method further integrates robot control strategies while comprehensively considering the distance and status of the obstacles.

(i)  We develop an innovative framework for industrial autonomous mobile robots focusing on obstacle detection and safe operation, integrating RGB-depth measurement technology.
(ii)  An advanced spatio-temporal hybrid forward obstacle detection model is designed to address the inter-frame loss issue in obstacle detection by capturing long-distance information. Meanwhile, a depth denoising method utilizing Euclidean clustering is employed to remove noise in the obstacle regions of depth images, consequently enhancing the accuracy of obstacle distance estimation.
(iii)  A safe operation strategy for industrial autonomous mobile robots is developed, allowing the robot to adaptively maintain a safe distance, thus ensuring the operating safety of both the robot and the workers. Meanwhile, we utilize a tracking model based on temporal information aggregation to monitor the falls of workers, thereby ensuring their safety.

## 2  Related Work

In the realm of industrial autonomous mobile robots, multimodal sensor fusion technology integrates RGB and depth images, merging the three-dimensional geometric features with the two-dimensional appearance characteristics. This significantly improves obstacle detection performance, particularly compared to single-sensor methods. Although it faces challenges related to bias and time costs in processing depth data, this fusion technology continues to ensure the safety, compliance, and human-robot compatibility of autonomous mobile robots during real-time obstacle detection.

Most existing methods [16–19] utilize dual branches to extract RGB and depth features, i.e., processing the color and texture features of RGB images and the geometric features of depth images separately, and integrating these features into a convolutional network. Enquan Yang et al. [20] employed an effective feature exploration method to achieve precise segmentation for the semantic segmentation of obstacles in indoor scenes. Tao Zhou et al. [21] proposed a novel framework called the Specificity-preserving Network (SPNet), which improves salient object detection (SOD) performance by exploring shared information and specific modality characteristics. Mingyang Wang et al. [22] introduced an attention-based multimodal RGB-D instance segmentation network called AMNet, designed for pixel-level obstacle segmentation. In [23], A. Q. Nguyen et al. presented a method employing affordable, compact RGB-D cameras for simultaneous fruit detection and distance estimation. The distance and size of the detected fruits are estimated based on their respective detection boxes in the depth images. In [24], Junhao Lin et al. proposed a new baseline model called the Attentive Trifusion Network (ATF-Net) for object detection in RGB-D videos. This model integrates the appearance information from RGB images, the spatiotemporal information from motion maps, and the geometric information from depth maps by designing three modality branches and a multimodal fusion branch.

While RGB-D sensors have enhanced the safe operation of industrial autonomous mobile robots, existing methods still encounter challenges in distance estimation and obstacle tracking. In addition, these methods do not fully account for specific application scenarios to industrial autonomous mobile robots. Specifically, some obstacle detection technologies use detection boxes to identify targets. However, they often overlook environmental factors like lighting changes, resulting in detection failures between frames. These rectangular regions contain background noise, and factors such as unexpected lighting and hollow objects may create depth noise [14]. Adopting an average depth or centroid point depth approach can result in inaccurate obstacle distance estimation [15].

## 3   System Overview

This study aims to enhance the obstacle detection and safe operation capabilities of industrial autonomous mobile robots using RGB-depth imaging, as shown in Fig. 2. We identify pixel-level obstacle regions via an end-to-end spatio-temporal hybrid deep learning model and utilize a temporal aggregation tracking model for worker fall detection. To accurately estimate obstacle distance, we utilize the Euclidean clustering method to filter noise in the obstacle pixel regions of depth images. Ultimately, the industrial autonomous mobile robot will adjust its speed adaptively based on the distance and status of the obstacles.

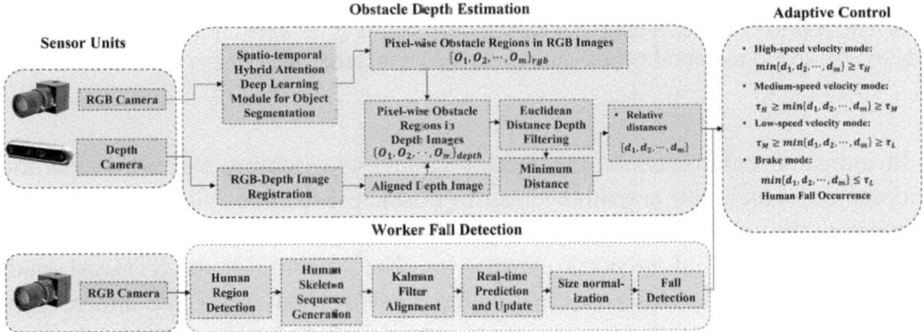


**Fig. 2.** The workflow of the industrial autonomous mobile robot obstacle detection and safe operation system. It consists of three modules: obstacle detection and relative depth estimation, worker fall detection, and adaptive robot control.

## 4   Method

### 4.1   Forward Obstacle Detection

In this work, we apply an end-to-end spatio-temporal hybrid deep learning model to detect obstacles in the robot's operating area. The model architecture includes three main components, such as the backbone network, the neck network, and the detection head, as shown in Fig. 3. The backbone network is based on the Darknet 53 feature extractor [25] and includes the basic convolutional unit (Conv), the Spatial Pyramid Pooling Fast (SPPF) module for fusing local and global features, and the C2f module which increases depth and receptive field, thereby enhancing feature extraction capabilities. The neck network employs a Path Aggregation Network and Feature Pyramid Network (PAN-FPN) structure to fuse feature maps of different scales, and utilizes the C2f module as the main feature extraction unit. The detection head employs a decoupled design to handle object detection, classification, and regression tasks separately. It outputs class probabilities, bounding box regressions, and confidence scores for the targets through convolutional operations and prediction layers, thereby completing the final object detection tasks.

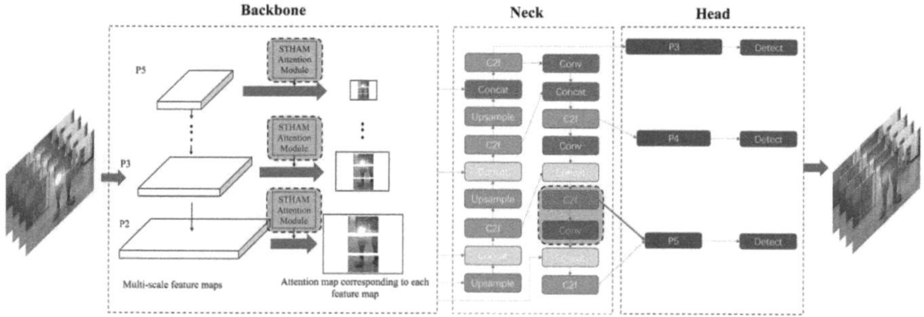


**Fig. 3.** The end-to-end spatio-temporal hybrid deep learning network. It mainly consists of two modules: the spatio-temporal hybrid attention module and the small object detection head module.

In industrial environments, unexpected changes in lighting and other conditions are common, which can potentially lead to obstacle detection failures. In this work, we integrate the spatio-temporal hybrid attention module (STHAM) into the backbone network as an enhanced attention mechanism. The structure of the STHAM module is illustrated in Fig. 4. This is a novel component that can aggregate and propagate information across the entire spatio-temporal domain, aiding subsequent convolutional layers in capturing global features more effectively. The STHAM achieves through a two-step attention mechanism, consisting of feature aggregation and feature distribution, which are used for global information and local information, respectively. In the feature aggregation phase, the module employs second-order attention pooling [26] to select key features within the spatial domain. Compared to traditional average pooling or max pooling, second-order attention pooling can capture and retain more complex relationships, thereby learning global contextual information and helping the network understand the overall semantic structure of the image. In the feature distribution phase, the module adaptively distributes features based on the local features at each position, rather than applying the same global features to every position as in SENet [27]. Typically, local features are extracted through local perception mechanisms, such as patching or convolution operations, and the attention mechanism selects the most relevant local information. This approach ensures that each position receives the necessary distinct features, thereby enhancing overall performance. Finally, the features learned by the global and local attention modules need to be merged for the final task. In industrial scenarios, the STHAM significantly enhances detection accuracy and robustness. It effectively handles complex scenes and diverse obstacles while maintaining low computational overhead, making the detection model more efficient and reliable across various environments.

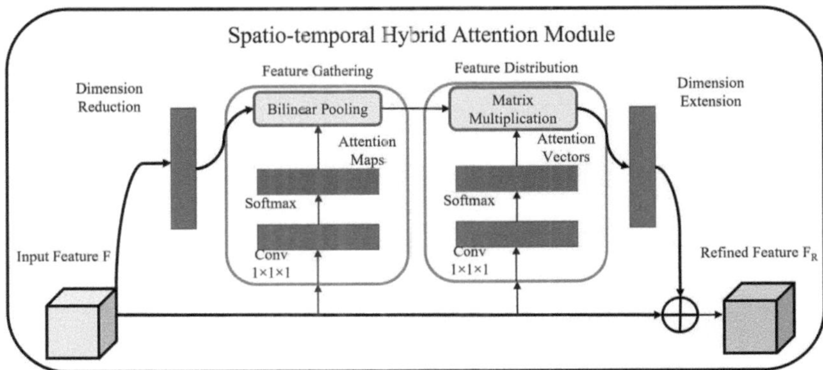


**Fig. 4.** The structure of the STHAM module. It includes two parts, such as feature aggregation and feature allocation.

Additionally, common challenges in object detection include missed detections and poor performance in detecting small objects. To address these issues and enhance detection performance for small targets, we add an extra detection head specifically designed for small objects, as shown in Fig. 5.

## 4.2  Obstacle Depth Estimation

In obstacle depth detection, we focus on obstacles within the operational area directly in front of the robot, confined to a trapezoidal range. Therefore, in the RGB image of the $i$-th frame, a trapezoidal region $\Phi_{i-RGB}$ is predefined, as shown in Fig. 1. Only obstacles within this region are considered, as external obstacles pose a lower collision risk to the robot.

In the $i$-th RGB frame, we detect obstacle regions $\{O_1, O_2, \cdots, O_m\}_{RGB}^{\Phi_i}$ and then use an RGB-Depth image registration model [28] to identify the corresponding regions in the depth map $\{O_1, O_2, \cdots, O_m\}_{Depth}^{\Phi_i}$. However, in $\{O_1, O_2, \cdots, O_m\}_{Depth}^{\Phi_i}$, depth noise may be present due to reflections, strong lighting, or hollow areas on objects.

In this study, we assume that the depth of each obstacle region varies only slightly in the depth image, a condition that is generally applicable to obstacle detection scenarios. However, in noisy depth images, depth values often fall into two main categories, true depth and noise depth, with significant size differences between these clusters. Clustering algorithms based on Euclidean distance are generally insensitive to the size, shape, and density of clusters. Therefore, we employ a Euclidean distance-based clustering algorithm for depth denoising [29].

We treat the pixel coordinates and depth of $\{O_1, O_2, \cdots, O_m\}_{Depth}^{\Phi_i}$ as three-dimensional data points $x$, considering all such points as a dataset $D = \{x_1, x_2, ..., x_n\}$.

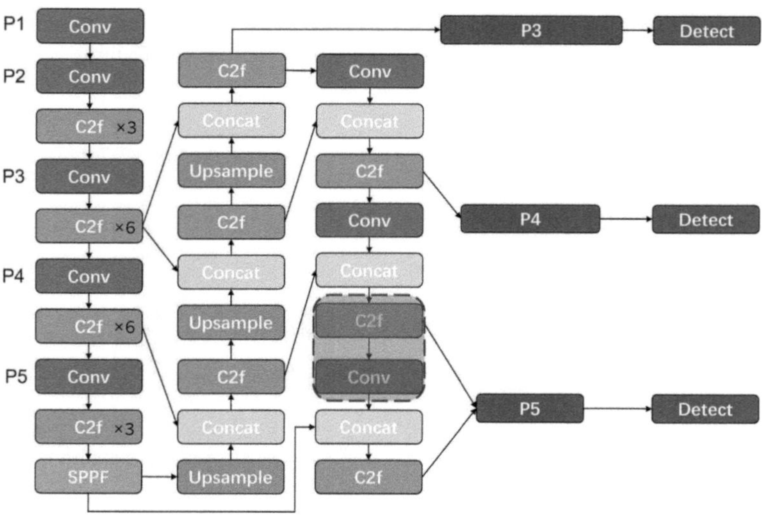

**Fig. 5.** The improved network includes a small object detection head, significantly enhancing its capability to detect small objects.

The Euclidean clustering algorithm first represents the depth point cloud dataset $D$ using a kd-tree, and then initializes an empty list of clusters and a queue for points to be examined. For each point $x$, it is added to the queue, and its spherical neighborhood points within a specified radius $l$ are searched. For each neighboring point, if it has not been processed, it is also added to the queue. After processing all points in the queue, the set of these points in the queue is added to the cluster list, and the queue is reset. This process is repeated until all points have been processed and included in the cluster list, resulting in a complete list of point clusters.

In $\{O_1, O_2, \cdots, O_m\}_{\text{Depth}}^{\Phi_i}$, after clustering the $k$-th region $\{O_k\}_{\text{Depth}}^{\Phi_i}$, we replace the depth values of noise clusters with the central value of the true depth cluster, effectively eliminating depth noise around the object contours. Subsequently, the minimum depth of the cluster centroids is considered as the actual depth of the obstacle.

### 4.3   Worker Fall Detection

Our fall detection and localization model consists of two stages: (1) the tracking stage, where the movements of each person in the video are identified and tracked, and (2) the classification stage, where it is determined whether each sequence of body frames indicates a fall.

In the tracking stage, the detection network first receives the complete frame sequence of the input video and generates bounding boxes representing human regions in each frame. Then, utilizing temporal sequence information, personalized human frame sequences are generated for each detected individual. To enhance localization accuracy, a Kalman filter [30] is employed to spatially align these human frame sequences. System performance is further enhanced by concentrating on the human body and eliminating redundant background information. In this stage, recursive estimation allows each new estimate to rely on the previous one, so only the last estimate needs to be stored. The error covariance matrix quantifies the difference between the system's current state and the expected result. With each new classification prediction, the system's observation vector is updated according to the detected person's movement to predict their position. To optimize the model's flow, a fixed-size video buffer is utilized to collect frames from the stream. When the buffer is full, predictions are executed by sending the set of frames for processing and classification. As new images arrive, the oldest images are removed and the latest images are added, ensuring a continuous flow for real-time classification. In this manner, the system can efficiently track and classify human movements, especially fall events, in a real-time environment.

In the classification stage, the human frames generated in the previous stage are first normalized in size to maintain a consistent aspect ratio for all images. This normalization is accomplished by adding reflective padding to preserve proportions, and then resizing the images to a given pixel square. Next, temporal alignment is applied on the normalized frame sequences for each individual to facilitate subsequent classification processing. For the classification model, we adopt a 2DCNN + LSTM approach [31], which integrates the tracking stage and the classification module. Considering the brief duration of fall actions, sequences of at least 8 frames are optimal for capturing fast movements. Additionally, short video clips comprising 1 to 7 frames can also recognize fundamental actions.

### 4.4 Adaptive Robot Safe Control

To enhance worker safety and robot efficiency, this study proposes an innovative adaptive safe control method that takes into account the distance between the robot and the obstacles ahead. The path area in front of the robot is divided into four zones: the braking zone, emergency zone, alert zone, and safe zone. Based on these zones, the robot's operating speed is automatically adjusted among high-speed, medium-speed, and low-speed modes. These adjustments not only improve work efficiency but also significantly enhance safety in the workplace.

For each RGB and depth image in the $i$-th frame, the $\min\left(\{O_1, O_2, \cdots, O_m\}_{\text{Depth}}^{\Phi_i}\right)$ in the obstacle area is initially determined. This minimum depth $\min\left(\{O_1, O_2, \cdots, O_m\}_{\text{Depth}}^{\Phi_i}\right)$ is then compared to a predetermined distance threshold to adjust the speed mode accordingly:

- If $\min\left(\{O_1, O_2, \cdots, O_m\}_{\text{Depth}}^{\Phi_i}\right) > \tau_H$, it indicates that the obstacle is within the safe range. The robot will maintain its current high-speed travel and illuminate a green LED.
- If $\min\left(\{O_1, O_2, \cdots, O_m\}_{\text{Depth}}^{\Phi_i}\right) \in [\tau_M, \tau_H]$ in the predefined trapezoidal area, it indicates that the obstacle is in the warning zone, prompting the robot to adjust its speed to medium and illuminate a yellow LED.
- If $\min\left(\{O_1, O_2, \cdots, O_m\}_{\text{Depth}}^{\Phi_i}\right) \in [\tau_L, \tau_M]$ in the predefined trapezoidal area, it means the obstacle is in the emergency zone. The robot will adjust its speed to low, and the LED will illuminate yellow.

- $\min\left(\{O_1, O_2, \cdots, O_m\}_{\text{Depth}}^{\Phi_i}\right) < \tau_L$ in the predefined trapezoidal area, it indicates that the obstacle is within the braking zone. The robot will come to a quick stop, and the LED will illuminate red.

It is important to note that when the obstacle ahead is identified as a worker, the robot will immediately adopt a gradual braking strategy to stop upon entering the predefined trapezoidal range, thereby ensuring the worker's safety. Additionally, when a worker's fall is detected, the robot will immediately implement the same gradual braking strategy.

## 5 Experimental Results and Analysis

### 5.1 Platform

In this work, our approach has been thoroughly evaluated on the development platform, as shown in Fig. 1. The dimensions of the robot are $850 \times 1850 \times 500$ mm, with a linear speed range of [0.1 m/s, 1.0 m/s] and an angular speed range of [0.1 rad/s, 0.5 rad/s]. In this work, the speed of the robot is divided into three modes: high speed, medium speed, and low speed. Specifically, the linear speed in high-speed mode is 1 m/s, in medium-speed mode is 0.5 m/s, and in low-speed mode is 0.1 m/s; the angular speed in high-speed mode is 0.5 rad/s, in medium-speed mode is 0.3 rad/s, and in low-speed mode is 0.1 rad/s. The sensor unit includes a monocular camera and a depth camera, both rigidly mounted on the industrial autonomous mobile robot. The obstacle depth estimation unit is an Intel RealSense D435i, which integrates an RGB camera and a depth camera. The resolution for both RGB and depth images is $1280 \times 720$, with a sampling rate of 30 Hz. The collected images are synchronized and processed by a laptop equipped with an Intel i9-11950H 2.6 GHz CPU, 32 GB of RAM, and an Nvidia GeForce RTX 3080 10 GB GPU.

### 5.2 Results and Analysis

To simulate an industrial indoor environment for the experiments, we have created a dataset containing common obstacles encountered by the robot. This dataset mainly includes items such as cargo (e.g., boxes and packages), tools (e.g., toolboxes, safety helmets, and workbenches), and mobile entities (e.g., workers and other AGVs). We have utilized RGB-D imaging technology to perform pixel-level segmentation of obstacles and label them as masks in the dataset. These obstacles are randomly placed along the predetermined path of the industrial autonomous mobile robot.

Typical results of obstacle detection and depth estimation are shown in Fig. 6. It can be seen that our method accurately detects and segments obstacle areas. Although environmental changes such as strong lighting can affect obstacle detection in some cases, like causing glare from the AGV and toolkit in Fig. 6, our method is made more robust by incorporating a spatio-temporal-hybrid attention mechanism, allowing for more reliable detection of obstacles ahead. Additionally, strong light and hollow objects can cause depth distortion, as seen with the workbenches and safety nets in Fig. 6. However,

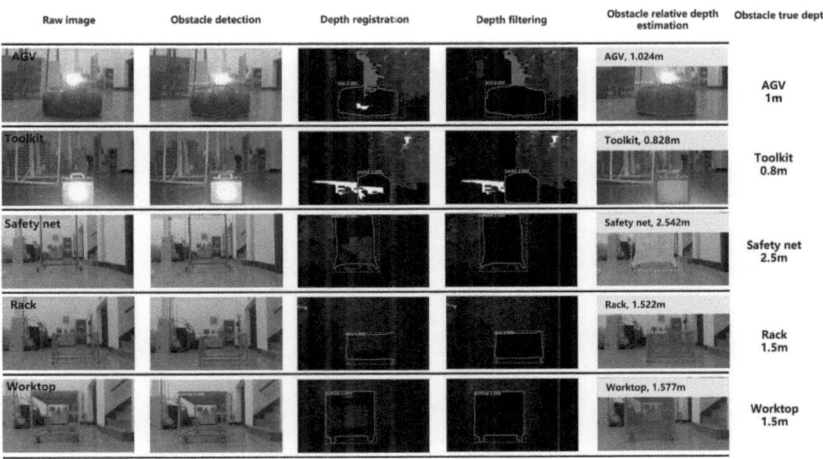


**Fig. 6.** Examples of relative depth estimation for some common obstacles (such as AGVs, workers, toolkits, and racks, etc.). Initially, the spatio-temporal hybrid deep learning model detects and segments obstacles in the RGB images. Subsequently, the depth registration model identifies the corresponding depth map and segments the obstacle regions in the depth image. After that, the Euclidean clustering method eliminates the depth noise in the obstacle regions. Finally, the relative depth of the obstacles is calculated.

the Euclidean clustering method we employ effectively filters out these depth noises and accurately computes the actual depth of the obstacles.

In comparison, the UEPAOA [14] can only identify obstacles using detection boxes, with poor robustness to environmental impacts. For instance, it may fail to detect a toolbox under unexpected strong lighting conditions, as shown in Fig. 7. Moreover, the UEPAOA [14] relies on the center point of the obstacle detection box to estimate depth, making it difficult to accurately measure the distance to obstacles with hollow structures and not accounting for the impact of lighting on depth map distortion. The scene with the worker and safety net in Fig. 7 further highlights the inaccuracies of the UEPAOA [14].

Compared to UEPAOA [14], ADPAR [15] can perform pixel-level obstacle segmentation, but it still lacks robustness in dealing with environmental changes. For instance, it may fail to detect a toolbox under strong lighting conditions, as shown in Fig. 7. It uses two methods to estimate the depth of obstacles: one based on the average depth within the detection box in the depth image and the other based on the average depth within the mask in the depth image. Although this approach can relatively accurately estimate the depth of objects, it does not account for the effects of lighting and hollow objects on the depth image. In the scene with the worker and safety net in Fig. 7, this impact is particularly evident (where [box] indicates the average depth within the detection box, and [mask] indicates the average depth within the mask). Compared to our method, ADPAR [15] exhibits a larger error in distance estimation.

To evaluate the performance of our system in obstacle depth estimation, we have utilized multiple evaluation metrics, such as mean average precision ($mAP$), mean inter-

**Fig. 7.** Comparative analysis of UEPAOA [14] and ADPAR [15] with our method for detecting obstacles and estimating depth. UEPAOA [14] may produce inaccurate depth estimates by solely calculating the centroid. In contrast, although ADPAR [15] can segment obstacles, it overlooks the hollow nature of structures and the impact of lighting on the depth map, which may create noise. Compared to these methods, our approach provides more accurate and precise measurements of the depth of obstacles.

**Table 1.** Comparison of our method with UEPAOA [14] and ADPAR [15] in terms of obstacle detection and depth estimation results

| Method | $mAP[\%]$ | $mIoU[\%]$ | $avg\_d\_err[m]$ |
|---|---|---|---|
| UEPAOA [14] | 87.29 | 83.46 | 5.46 |
| ADPAR [15] | 90.35 | 88.67 | 3.34 |
| Ours | 96.54 | 93.8 | 0.34 |

section over union ($mIoU$), and average depth error ($avg\_d\_err$). Our method was compared with UEPAOA [14] and ADPAR [15], with the results presented in Table 1. As shown in Table 1, our system demonstrates enhanced robustness, primarily due to the introduction of the STHAM module and the small object detection head. Furthermore, the depth denoising method significantly reduces the average error in obstacle depth estimation.

Our fall detection algorithm integrates time series information with a Kalman filter, allowing for real-time updates and predictions of personnel locations through recursive state estimation. This approach enables the rapid identification of fall events and their distinction from normal actions, as illustrated in Fig. 8. The detection model has been tested in complex industrial environments and is capable of accurately identifying fall events amidst various obstacles and equipment, even in chaotic and irregular backgrounds. Figure 8 illustrates several instances in which the model successfully identifies falls, thereby validating its robustness and reliability in real industrial settings.

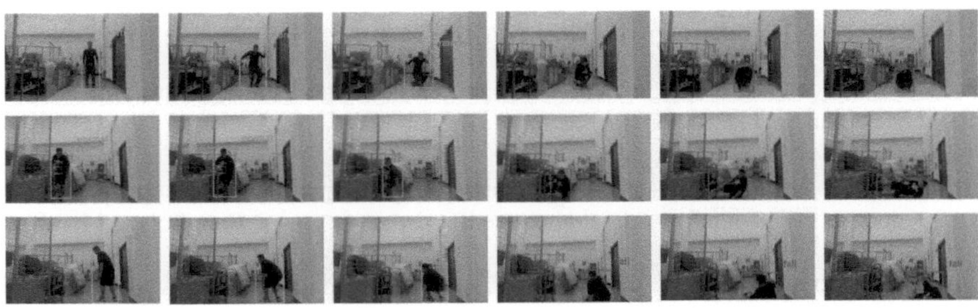

**Fig. 8.** Examples of fall detection. Our system can accurately detect instances of workers falling even in complex industrial environments.

According to the statistical results presented in Table 2, our fall detection network improves the $mAP$ and accuracy by 4.25% and 3.94%, respectively, compared to the OpenPose-YOLO [32] network. Additionally, it achieves improvements of 3.19% and 2.44% over the CNN network [33]. This enhancement can be attributed to the integration of time series information and the Kalman filter in our method, which allows for real-time updates and predictions of personnel locations. Additionally, the incorporation of long short-term memory learning enhances the recognition accuracy and robustness of fall detection.

**Table 2.** Performance comparison between our fall detection model and other models

| Method | $mAP[\%]$ | Accuracy[%] |
| --- | --- | --- |
| OpenPose-YOLO [32] | 90.29 | 90.42 |
| CNN [33] | 91.35 | 91.92 |
| Ours | 94.54 | 94.36 |

## 6  Conclusions

In this study, we have developed a obstacle detection and safe operation system for industrial autonomous mobile robots, integrating RGB and depth measurements, designed for human-robot coexistence environments. We have employed an end-to-end spatio-temporal hybrid deep learning model for obstacle segmentation and utilized the Euclidean clustering algorithm for accurate depth estimation of obstacles in the corresponding depth images. Finally, we have developed an adaptive control strategy for the robot to ensure the safety of both the robot and the workers. Meanwhile, we have implemented a temporal information aggregation tracking model to detect falls among workers. Upon detecting a fall, the robot will immediately halt its operations. Our system has undergone extensive testing on the development platform. The experimental results highlight the competitive performance of our method.

## References


1. Huang, J., Zeng, J., Chi, X., Sreenath, K., Liu, Z., Su, H.: Velocity obstacle for polytopic collision avoidance for distributed multi-robot systems. IEEE Robot. Autom. Lett. **8**(6), 3502–3509 (2023)
2. Zhu, W., Hayashibe, M.: A hierarchical deep reinforcement learning framework with high efficiency and generalization for fast and safe navigation. IEEE Trans. Industr. Electron. **70**(5), 4962–4971 (2022)
3. Kobayashi, Y., et al.: Robot navigation based on predicting of human interaction and its reproducible evaluation in a densely crowded environment. Int. J. Soc. Robot. **14**, 373–387 (2022)
4. Xue, B., Gao, M., Wang, C., Cheng, Y., Zhou, F.: Crowd-aware socially compliant robot navigation via deep reinforcement learning. Int. J. Soc. Robot. **16**(1), 197–209 (2024)
5. Zhang, F., Liu, J., Wu, R., Hou, B.: Design and research of workshop AGV system scheduling system based on intelligent fuzzy control algorithm. In: 2023 International Conference on Power, Electrical Engineering, Electronics and Control (PEEEC), pp. 679–683. IEEE (2023)
6. Yilmaz, A., Sumer, E., Temeltas, H.: A precise scan matching based localization method for an autonomously guided vehicle in smart factories. Robot. Comput.-Integr. Manufact. **75**, 102302 (2022)
7. Jahagirdar, A., Sathe, N., Thorat, S., Saxena, S.: Fire detection in nano-satellite imagery using mask R-CNN. Int. J. Signal Imaging Syst. Eng. **13**(1), 19–26 (2024)
8. Huang, W., Liu, H., Wan, W.: An online initialization and self-calibration method for stereo visual-inertial odometry. IEEE Trans. Rob. **36**(4), 1153–1170 (2020)
9. Wang, Z., Tian, G.: Object pose estimation from RGB-D images with affordanceinstance segmentation constraint for semantic robot manipulation. IEEE Robot. Autom. Lett. **8**(1), 595–602 (2023)

10. Zhao, L., Zhou, H., Zhu, X., Song, X., Li, H., Tao, W.: LIF-Seg: LiDAR and camera image fusion for 3D lidar semantic segmentaticn. IEEE Trans. Multimedia **26**, 1158–1168 (2024)

11. Li, C., Guo, S., Guo, J.: Study cn obstacle avoidance strategy using multiple ultrasonic sensors for spherical underwater robots. IEEE Sens. J. **22**(24), 24458–24470 (2022)

12. Krishnan, P.: Design of collision detection system for smart car using li-fi and ultrasonic sensor. IEEE Trans. Veh. Technol. **22**(67), 11420–11426 (2018)

13. Jagtap, S., Chopade, N.: Performance analysis of object detection and tracking methodology for video synopsis. Int. J. Signal Imaging Syst. Eng. **13**(1), 10–18 (2024)

14. Wang, D., Li, W., Liu, X., Li, N., Zhang, C.: UAV environmental perception and autonomous obstacle avoidance: a deep learning and depth camera combined solution. Comput. Electron. Agric. **175**, 105523 (2020)

15. Miranda, J.C., Arnó, J., Gené-Mola, J., Lordan, J., Asín, L., Gregorio, E.: Assessing automatic data processing algorithms for RGB-D cameras to predict fruit size and weight in apples. Comput. Electron. Agric. **214**, 108302 (2023)

16. Zhang, G., Xue, J.-H., Xie, P., Yang, S., Wang, G.: Non-local aggregation for RGB-D semantic segmentation. IEEE Signal Process. Lett. **28**, 658–662 (2021)

17. Yue, Y., Zhou, W., Lei, J., Yu, L.: Two-stage cascaded decoder for semantic segmentation of RGB-D images. IEEE Signal Process. Lett. **28**, 1115–1119 (2021)

18. Zhang, Y., Xiong, C., Liu, J., Ye, X., Sun, G.: Spatial-information guided adaptive context-aware network for efficient RGB-D semantic segmentation. IEEE Sens. J. **23**(19), 1115–1119 (2023)

19. Fu, Y., Fan, J., Xing, S., Wang, Z., Jing, F., Tan, M.: Image segmentation of cabin assembly scene based on improved RGB-D mask R-CNN. IEEE Trans. Instrum. Meas. **71**, 1–12 (2022)

20. Yang, E., Zhou, W., Qian, X., Yu, L.: MGCNet: multilevel gated collaborative network for RGB-D semantic segmentation of indoor scene. IEEE Signal Process. Lett. **29**, 2567–2571 (2022)

21. Zhou, T., Fan, D.-P., Chen, G., Zhou, Y., Fu, H.: Specificity-preserving RGB-D saliency detection. Comput. Visual Media **9**(2), 297–317 (2023)

22. Wang, M., Hu, L., Bai, Y., Yao, X., Hu, J., Zhang, S.: Amnet: a new RGB-D instance segmentation network based on attention and multi-modality. Vis. Comput. **40**(2), 1311–1325 (2024)

23. Nguyen, A., Nguyen, A., Nguyen, H., Luong, H., Dao, N.: Fruits detection and distance estimation using RGB-D camera for harvesting robot. In: 2021 International Conference on Science & Contemporary Technologies (ICSCT), pp. 1–6. IEEE (2021)

24. Lin, J., Zhu, L., Shen, J., Fu, H., Zhang, Q., Wang, L.: Vidsod-100: a new dataset and a baseline model for RGB-D video salient object detection. Int. J. Comput. Vision 1–19 (2024)

25. Farhadi, A., Redmon, J.: Yolov3: an incremental improvement. In: Computer Vision and Pattern Recognition, vol. 1804, pp. 1–6. Springer, Heidelberg (2018)

26. Lin, T.-Y., RoyChowdhury, A., Maji, S.: Bilinear CNN models for fine-grained visual recognition. In: Proceedings of the IEEE International Conference on Computer Vision, pp. 1449–1457 (2015)

27. Hu, J., Shen, L., Sun, G.: Squeeze-and-excitation networks. In: Proceedings of the IEEE Conference on Computer Vision and Pattern Recognition, pp. 7132–7141 (2018)

28. Halber, M., Funkhouser, T.: Fine-to-coarse global registration of RGB-D scans. In: Proceedings of the IEEE Conference on Computer Vision and Pattern Recognition, pp. 1755–1764 (2017)

29. Berthold, M.R., Höppner, F.: On clustering time series using euclidean distance and pearson correlation. arXiv preprint arXiv:1601.02213 (2016)

30. Khodarahmi, M., Maihami, V.: A review on kalman filter models. Arch. Comput. Methods Eng. **30**(1), 727–747 (2023)

31. Fischer, T., Krauss, C.: Deep learning with long short-term memory networks for financial market predictions. Eur. J. Oper. Res. **270**(2), 654–669 (2018)
32. Lina, W., Ding, J.: Behavior detection method of openpose combined with yolo network. In: 2020 International Conference on Communications, Information System and Computer Engineering (CISCE), pp. 326–330. IEEE (2020)
33. Casilari, E., Lora-Rivera, R., García-Lagos, F.: A study on the application of convolutional neural networks to fall detection evaluated with multiple public datasets. Sensors **20**(5), 1466 (2020)

# Simulating and Evaluating Search Strategies for Highly Accurate Localization Based on Wireless Technologies Using Autonomous Unmanned Aerial Vehicles


Eva Hetzel[1]([⊠]) , Nicolai Kröger[2] , Julian Sturm[3] , Oliver Zeidler[2] , Daniel Fraunholz[3] , and Wolfgang Kellerer[2]

[1] Karlsruhe Institute of Technology, KASTEL, Am Fasanengarten 5, 76131 Karlsruhe, Germany
`eva.hetzel@kit.edu`
[2] Technical University of Munich, Arcisstr. 21, 80333 München, Germany
[3] ZITiS, Zamdorfer Str. 88, 81677 München, Germany



**Abstract.** When persons are reported missing, the authorities are under severe time pressure to localize and safeguard them. This is especially the case, if the missing persons' lives might be threatened, e.g. if the night approaches and the outside temperatures are endangering survival over night. However, the localization of the missing persons can be quite challenging in many scenarios such as rough terrain where ground units of the authorities have limited access. In this paper, we therefore present a new approach with four different strategies for automated Search-And-Rescue (SAR) missions, i.e. the localization of missing persons' mobile devices using unmanned aerial vehicles. The strategies are compatible with multiple wireless technologies, e.g. cellular networks or WiFi. They are then evaluated with extensive simulations to cover a wide range of possible scenarios, including different search area shapes and sizes, missing persons' velocities, and equipment characteristics. The evaluation focuses on the required time to localize the device, the success rate of the SAR mission, and the running costs of the mission. Our results show that the missing person can be found quickly, within 20 to 30 min in most scenarios. For slow-moving persons, the time of localization could even be significantly reduced. Finally, we provide an overview of the advantages and disadvantages of each strategy. This allows to select the best one for a given scenario.

**Keywords:** Localization · Unmanned aerial vehicles · Search and Rescue · Wireless technologies


## 1 Introduction

Every day, there are between 200 and 300 new cases of missing persons registered in Germany [12] and even more in the USA (around 1500 per day in 2022) [9].



A. Soylu et al. (Eds.): MobiQuitous 2024, LNICST 634, pp. 507–531, 2026.
https://doi.org/10.1007/978-3-032-10554-7_27

Once a missing person is reported and if their life is assumed to be in danger or the person is a child, the authorities initiate a Search-And-Rescue (SAR) operation [12]. Especially if the missing person might be injured, e.g. if a hiker went missing or if the missing person is known to be suicidal, the authorities are under significant time pressure to find them. If necessary, they use thermal cameras, SAR dogs or helicopters in order to increase their chances of quickly finding the missing person [12]. Another tool which is available to the authorities in such an operation is the localization of the missing person's technical devices, such as mobile phones or wearables. The SAR mission can become increasingly difficult in mountainous terrain or in other regions that are hard to reach and search. The operational units need to drive around in cars or carry their technical equipment by foot when trying to locate a device, which can turn out to be inefficient and slow. Such a SAR mission can require a significant number of personnel and technical resources and become rather costly. According to a study by Röper et al. from 2020, operating a helicopter in an emergency services scenario can cost 70 euros per minute [23].

To address these issues, several papers in the literature examine the search for a person using drones in various ways. Exemplary, the authors in [15] introduce a probabilistic search approach where several drones are cooperating. In terms of technology, some of the work focuses on locating the mobile device of the missing person in a cellular approach with machine learning [1]. Others use different technologies such as optical approaches using cameras on the drones [24]. However, the approaches to locate the mobile device of a missing person are complex and computationally intensive. To perform the computations, either more equipment needs to be mounted on the drones or the information has to be transmitted to a centralized computation unit. SARDO, e.g., uses an Intel NUC board mounted on the drone to execute a convolutional neural network and find the future user trajectory [1,16].

Thus, in this paper, we introduce a new and less computationally intensive search approach to support the authorities in finding missing persons. The basic idea is to send out drones, equipped for device localization, to autonomously search for the missing person's mobile device. Since drones are not limited to streets and paths on the ground, they can search areas more efficiently and find the missing person, in the following also referred to as the target, faster than operational units on the ground, while on the other hand, they are limited in flight time and supported payload. The search pattern of the drones is determined by one of four search strategies. They consist of multiple steps that gradually delimit the area of possible target positions before estimating the final position more precisely. The operational units would then be able to look for the missing person through other approaches, e.g. with SAR dogs, at the same time.

These four strategies are then evaluated with extensive simulations to cover a wide range of possible scenarios. In particular, we consider different search area shapes and sizes, different target velocities, and characteristics of the equipment used. As mentioned before, the time to find a person is of utmost importance for the authorities to increase the chances of survival. Thus, the finding time is a key aspect of our results for each strategy. In addition, we analyze the costs and the success rate of a SAR mission. The main message of this paper is that the most suited strategy for a SAR mission with drones depends on the individual scenario. In particular, this paper contributes the following:

- We introduce the novel idea of end-to-end automation of SAR missions and design UAV-based approaches specifically fulfilling the requirements to achieve this high level of automation.
- We introduce four novel multi-stage search strategies using drones to localize the mobile device position of a missing person.
- We evaluate each of these strategies with extensive simulations in various scenarios. Based on these results, we compare the strategies and identify the most suited one for a certain scenario.
- We developed a framework to easily implement, evaluate and optimize further search strategies that are suited to more specific scenarios or operational needs.

The collection of location information can be seen as an invasion of privacy. However, our clear objective is to facilitate SAR missions and the strategies provided in this paper are only intended to be used by authorities that are looking for missing persons.

The remainder of the paper is structured as follows. In Sect. 2, background on technical aspects of locating devices for various technologies is given, followed by a discussion of related literature. Section 3 presents the four search strategies and explains them in detail. These strategies are then evaluated with simulations in Sect. 4. Finally, Sect. 5 concludes the paper.

## 2 Background and Related Work

The terms localization and positioning both refer to the estimation of the location or position of a target device, which has a transmitter and a receiver [7]. In this paper, the terms location and position are used synonymously, and the target, which is to be localized, is the device of a missing person.

The mobile stations used to find the position of the target are called reference stations. In this work, they are equipped with a transmitter and receiver [7] and mounted on unmanned aerial vehicles (UAVs). If there is no obstacle between the target and a reference station, they are in Line-Of-Sight (LOS). The quality of the location estimation can depend strongly on the LOS conditions and is best when there are no obstacles between the stations [20].

### 2.1 Proximity-Based Localization

The proximity-based localization is the simplest, but also the most inaccurate localization technique. For mobile networks, it is also called the cell identity (CID) technique, since for this method, the CID of the serving base station of the missing user equipment (UE) is provided [20]. With the CID, the service provider also transfers the location of the base station and the approximate area of its cell [5]. The localization result is then as accurate as the size of the cell, but it can be used as a first step in a localization process to limit the search area for further, more precise techniques. If the UE has previously lost the connection to the base station, the last cell it was using can be transmitted instead, which might further decrease the accuracy of this technique. For other technologies such as Bluetooth beacons or Wi-Fi networks, their respective serving area could be considered, but in theory these will be quite limited compared to cellular systems.

### 2.2   Multilateration

Multilateration is a range-based positioning technique, which uses the distances between the target and multiple reference stations to estimate the position of the target. For multilateration in a 2D space, at least three reference stations are necessary (trilateration). In three dimensions, there is a need for an additional reference station [7].

Three different metrics can be used to estimate the distances between the target and the reference stations: Received Signal Strength (RSS), Time of Arrival (ToA), and Time Difference of Arrival (TDoA) [31]. The following subsections describe RSS and ToA. With these metrics, a synchronization between the reference stations and the target is necessary. In this work, we assume to have this synchronization.

**Received Signal Strength.** The RSS indicates the signal strength of the incoming radio signal at a reference station on a logarithmic scale. The power balance Eq. 1 shows how the signal attenuation between the target and the reference station can be calculated from the RSS [7]:

$$RSS_i(dBm) = P_{t,i}(dBm) - L_{t,i}(dB) + G_{t,\theta,\phi,i}(dB) - L_{p,i}(dB)$$
$$+ G_{r,(\theta\pm\pi),(\phi\pm\pi),i}(dB) - L_{r,i}(dB). \tag{1}$$

The index $i$ stands for the $i$th reference station. $P_{t,i}$ is the transmitting power at the $i$th reference station. $L_{t,i}$ and $L_{r,i}$ denote the losses at the transmitter and receiver. $G_{t,\theta,\phi,i}$ and $G_{r,(\theta\pm\pi),(\phi\pm\pi),i}$ are the transmitting and receiving antenna gains. They depend on the radiation pattern and the direction of the antennas, where $\theta$ is the horizontal angle and $\phi$ is the vertical angle. The propagation loss $L_{p,i}$ is distance-dependent and can therefore be used to estimate the distance between the target and the $i$th reference station [7].

**Time of Arrival.** To estimate the distance via the ToA, the propagation speed of the radio wave is multiplied with the signal travel time [31]:

$$\hat{d}_i = c(\hat{\tau}_{ToA,i} - \tau_{ToT,i}) \tag{2}$$

where ToT stands for the Time of Transmission, the index $i$ denotes the $i$th reference station, and $c$ is the speed of propagation which can be assumed to be the speed of light in free space ($c = 2.99792458 \cdot 10^8$ m/s) [7]. $\hat{\tau}_{ToA,i}$ is the estimated ToA at reference station $i$.

## 2.3  Positioning and Localization for Devices

Locating a missing person via their mobile device is prone to the risk that they might not be carrying one. However, the omnipresence of mobile devices justifies the assumption that the missing person is carrying some kind of mobile device. Generally there are two options to estimate the position of a device as a third party. If the device cooperates, the third party can leverage existing positioning services such as GPS or vendor specific frameworks such as Google Play Services, which greatly improves the accuracy. Mobile networks, such as LTE or 5G, also provide specific protocols, i.e. the LTE Positioning Protocol (LPP), for the network operators to use device-assisted positioning methods. This is referred to as positioning.

If the device is unable to locate itself, or non-cooperative (e.g. because the third party is not the network operator), this is referred to as localization and other means are required to estimate the position. Especially smaller devices, such as Bluetooth or LoRaWan beacons do not offer device assisted positioning protocols and often have no way to measure their own position. In our scenario, we assume this case, where we need to rely on measurements performed by the authorities themselves, such as RSS and ToA measurements. This requires the availability of a persistent identifier in the radio communication, so that multiple measurements can be attributed to the correct devices.

An additional problem is to predict the frequency the target device uses. In mobile networks, this is based on the current or previous cell, which limits the options but still requires probing of different possibilities. For this reason, we propose a two-stage protocol with a larger first drone, that is able to carry multiple transceivers to parallelize the search and smaller drones that can be used once the target frequency is known. We call this larger drone 'Catcher', as its primary task is to catch the device's signal and share the information with the other drones. These smaller ones only need a single transceiver and can therefore significantly reduce the required payload and thus, increase the maximal flight time and reduce the cost.

In the following sections, some of the most prevalent radio technologies are presented and their suitability for our localization approach is discussed.

**Cellular.** Cellular technologies, such as GSM (2G), LTE (4G) and NR (5G) have seen widespread adoption, reaching about 6.4 billion subscriptions worldwide in 2022 with a forecast of 7.4 billion in 2028 [28]. Up until 5G, the permanent identifier (IMSI) could be obtained by any third party [25]. Together with the large transmit range of cellular devices, this is a prime candidate for localization.

**Wi-Fi.** Wi-Fi is another well established technology for wireless communication. While modern operating systems randomize the hardware addresses used in broadcasts, they mostly remain constant per network, making it possible to record multiple measurements if a known network can be spoofed [27]. The range is also sufficient, with around 100 m, and possibly more in Line-Of-Sight conditions [19].

**Bluetooth Low Energy.** While Bluetooth Low Energy (BLE) also has a wide adoption due to its presence in most mobile devices, it has multiple problems in the context of our use case. One issue is the limited range to around 10 m [19]. Like other technologies, more recent versions of BLE also try to increase the user privacy by regularly changing the address used in the broadcasts, making tracking infeasible if implemented correctly [3].

**Other Technologies.** While other technologies for medium to long range communications exist and might be applicable to searches, they have not seen widespread adoption in mobile devices. This includes low-power, low-bandwidth protocols such as LoRaWan and SigFox, but also satellite based protocols such as Starlink or Apple's "Emergency SOS via Satellite".

## 2.4   Related Work

The localization of mobile devices in SAR missions has already been studied in the literature. Albanese et al. [1] introduced an automated solution for SAR missions using UAVs called SARDO (Search-And-Rescue DrOne-based solution) in 2021. The main use case of SARDO is to find victims of natural disasters who cannot communicate with rescue teams because they are trapped beneath rubble. The authors of SARDO claim to be the first ones to provide a cellular SAR solution using drones, that can accurately localize missing persons' mobile phones. They use a concept they call pseudo-trilateration, where only a single UAV is used to estimate the user position. To process the distance measurements and predict future target positions, the authors use machine learning methods like neural networks. The SARDO authors assume that the target mobile phone is close enough to the UAV such that it can be identified and the pseudo-trilateration algorithm can start estimating the target position right away. In contrast, this paper considers entire SAR missions, where initially only a search area is known.

Compared to cellular solutions, other papers discuss different technologies. Schedl et al. introduced an automated SAR method using airborne optical sectioning, which makes it possible to find people with the camera of the drone and imaging techniques, even in occluding forests [24]. The method by Schedl et al. dynamically computes the flight path of the drone, depending on hints from a classifier, that suggest that a missing person might be hidden in a specific region. Like SARDO, Schedl et al. only use a single drone for their solution.

Ha et al. enhance the single-drone approach by introducing a search algorithm suggesting a hierarchical approach with two drones operating at different heights [15]. The drone flying at a high altitude performs a rough search of a larger area and then, based on a probabilistic search algorithm, suggests a smaller region for the drone flying at a low altitude to search. Flying at a high altitude allows the first drone to search a large area quickly, while the low altitude of the second drone allows for a precise search. The probabilistic search algorithm divides the area into smaller regions and assigns probabilities to them, thereby indicating the likelihood of finding the target within that region.

# 3  Simulation Model

This section introduces the four strategies for automated localization using drones. First, the drone movement patterns of the four strategies are explained. Then, the evaluation methods are described, which are used to evaluate and compare the four strategies. The description of the different types of drones and the selection of the most suitable ones for SAR missions can be found in the Appendix A.

## 3.1  Search Strategies

In the following, the four strategies are introduced. They all cover the period of time from the takeoff of the first drone until the precise localization of the target via trilateration. The input of the search algorithms is always the size, shape, and location of the search area. The search area can be found via proximity-based localization. If the algorithms do not fail, the output is a target location estimate. The strategies vary in their focus on either minimizing cost or minimizing the time necessary to locate the target and maximizing the success rate. Furthermore, they differ in the information that is assumed to be given, as the third strategy introduced takes advantage of the knowledge about the target's start position.

Each strategy uses a total of three drones of different types. At the beginning of the search mission, only one or two drones, depending on the strategy, are sent out to search the whole area. The four strategies mainly differ in this period of time until the first identification of the target. Once the target has been identified, the rest of the drones are called for the trilateration phase. In this stage, the strategies all use the flight patterns described for the naive strategy. These flight patterns cope with the mobile target escaping or evading the drones during trilateration.

**Naive Strategy.** The naive strategy forms the base for all four strategies. It uses one drone to find the initial search area, called the catcher drone, and two additional drones for trilateral localization in the next step. The catcher drone is selected to be a single-rotor drone, while the other drones are multi-rotor drones. The single-rotor drone has a very high flight range and endurance due to its possibility to be powered by fuel, therefore it is able to search large areas, e.g. an entire rural mobile radio cell. The multi-rotor drones then only have to fly for shorter amounts of time, since their target area is delimited drastically from the whole search area to the identify range of the catcher drone. Their task could also be performed by single-rotor drones, but since a shorter flight time and less payload are sufficient during the precise localization, the less costly multi-rotor drones are chosen. After the target is initially found, the single-rotor drone acts as one of the three drones necessary for trilateration.

For an efficient search of the area by the catcher drone, the area needs to be covered by circles with minimal overlapping. This is called the circle covering problem [2]. Fejes [10] proved in 1942 that the densest way of packing circles is in a hexagonal lattice, where the centers of the circles coincide with the centers of the regular hexagons and the radii are equal to the radii of the inscribed circles of the hexagons. According to [18], this approach can also be used for circle covering, but for the covering problem the circles do not inscribe, but instead circumscribe the hexagons. To find the points the drone has to visit, a hexagonal grid is used and the centers of the hexagons overlapping with the search area are selected. The drone heads for the centers of the hexagons by means of shortest distances, in a row-by-row manner. The first hexagon visited is the one closest to the current position of the UAV. This way, the entire area is searched very quickly and with almost minimal redundancy. Figure 1 illustrates the movement of the first drone along the hexagonal grid, simulated as a Python Matplotlib animation [29].

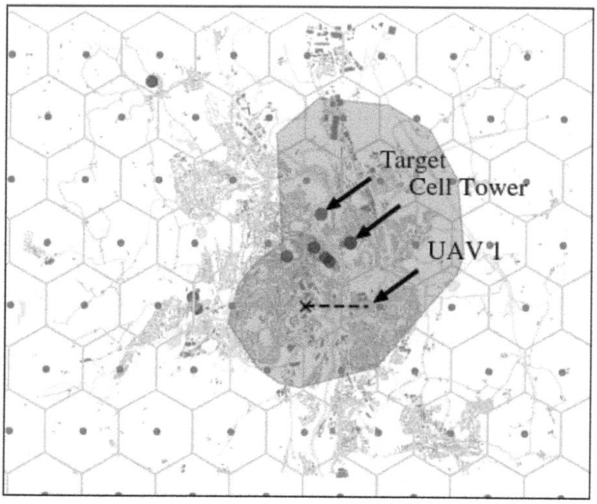


**Fig. 1.** Movement of the catcher drone (orange dot) along the hexagonal grid (gray). The transparent orange circle shows the identify range of the drone and the blue polygon depicts the search area. The dashed line indicates the direction of the drone towards the black cross. (Color figure online)

Once the catcher drone finds the UE, it keeps hovering at its current position and then calculates its distance to the UE. Now, the location of the UE can be narrowed down to a point on the circle around the catcher drone with its distance to the UE as radius. The second and third drone, the multi-rotor drones, are then called to the area around the catcher drone. They circle the catcher drone such that the entire area formed by its search radius is covered. In order to avoid getting the same result twice from both the second and third drone, one of them circles the catcher drone clockwise, and the other one counter-clockwise, so the target is approached from different directions. Once they detect the UE, they calculate their distances to the UE, similarly to the first drone. The position of the UE can then be estimated to be at the intersection of the three circles. For the estimate to be as accurate as possible, the distance measurements should be taken at the same time or shortly after one another, especially if the target is moving quickly, such that they are not outdated when calculating the circle intersection.

If the catcher drone was not able to find the target UE in its first round searching the area, because the target evaded the drone, the drone goes back to the first hexagon and visits all of the hexagon centers again, until the UE is in its reach. As long as the target is within reach of a drone, the drone is hovering. Since the distance between the hovering drone and the moving target might be changing, the distance has to be recalculated and updated constantly. If the target moves out of the reach of a UAV before the trilateration could be performed, the drone has to stop hovering and resume its search.

There are two cases to be distinguished: In the first case, one drone loses the target, but it is still in the reach of another drone. Then, the UAV that lost connection circles the other one until the target UE is back in its reach. In the second case, none of the drones have the target in their reach. In this case, the drones position themselves on a circle around the position of the drone which lost the target last. The idea behind this strategy is to cover all of the directions where the target could have escaped to. If the UAVs are too slow and not able to perform measurements on the target again, they start moving outward, away from the position where the target was last seen.

Figure 2 illustrates the movement of the drones in case two: First, the drones gather around the former position of the drone which had the target in its reach last. This position is marked as $x_1$ in Fig. 2. The dashed arrows show the movement of the drones and the dashed circles are their identify ranges. Secondly, they move outwards, if the target remains lost. This is depicted with the solid arrows and circles, showing the new position of the drones. As soon as one of the drones finds the target again, the remaining drones circle the one which has the target UE in its reach, as in case one. If the different kinds of drones have varying search radii, the smallest radius determines the distance at which the three drones surround $x_1$, the former position of the drone which lost the target last. The maneuvers that are performed in the cases where one or more drones lose sight of the target are independent of the search area and can therefore also be used if the target leaves the area after it was found by at least one drone at some point.


**Strategy with Two Catcher UAVs.** Compared with the naive strategy, the strategy described in this section uses a second catcher drone for the initial part of the search, i.e. to make the first contact with the target device. The reason for using only one single-rotor drone in the naive strategy was minimizing the cost of the drones and their equipment. Therefore, at first only one drone was sent out to find the rough position of the target UE. This strategy, on the other hand, aims

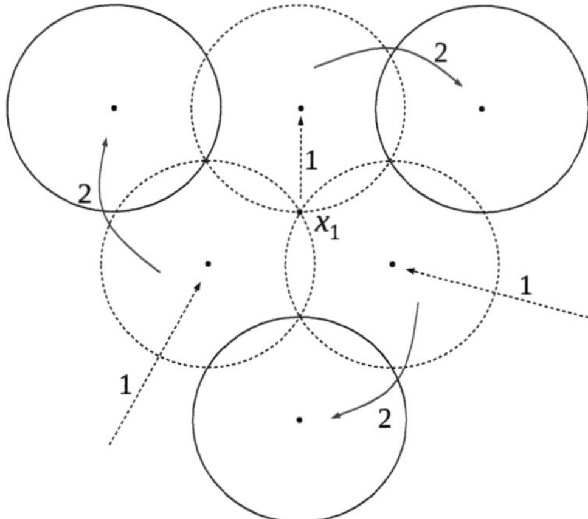



**Fig. 2.** Drone movement in the case of the target being lost by all three drones. $x_1$ marks the former position of the drone which lost the target last. First, the drones gather around $x_1$ (1) and then, if unsuccessful, they move outwards (2).

at being fast rather than cost-efficient. The purpose of the second catcher drone is to cover more ground at once and quickly search the area for the target UE. Once one of the catcher drones was able to find the target, only one additional multi-rotor drone is necessary for trilateration, since two UAVs are already airborne. Therefore, the total number of drones does not increase compared to the naive strategy. However, the equipment is more expensive and now two drones are required to have a high endurance and to carry large payloads.

The strategy for the initial search of the area is still based on a hexagonal grid, where the centers of the hexagons that are overlapping with the search area are visited by the catcher drones. The second catcher drone visits the centers in reverse order compared to the first catcher drone. Besides covering the search area up to twice as fast compared to the naive strategy with one catcher drone, depending on the starting points of the drones and their distances to the search area, it is also harder for a moving target to evade two UAVs coming from different directions than just a single one. Once one of the catcher drones finds the target, the second UAV takes on the role of a multi-rotor drone as in the precise localization step of the naive strategy and the third drone is called to aid in the trilateration. Both the second catcher drone and the multi-rotor drone circle the catcher drone that has found the target first. In this stage of the localization mission another advantage of the strategy with two catcher drones can be discovered: Since the catcher drone, which was not able to find the target first, is already in the search area and closer to the target than it was during launch, it can reach the other catcher drone much more quickly than a multi-rotor drone with the same start position in the naive strategy. This also reduces the risk of the target getting away while the second and third drone are still approaching.

The cases where one or more drones lose sight of the target are very similar to the naive strategy. If at least one drone still has the target in its reach, it is circled by the other drones. If the target was found by a catcher drone and then manages to escape all three drones, the position of the drone which had contact to the target UE last is surrounded as shown in Fig. 2. Assuming that the search radius of a catcher drone is larger than of the smaller drones joining for trilateration, this strategy provides more drones with a higher coverage compared to the naive strategy, also making it less likely to lose contact to the target.

**Strategy with Known Target Start Position.** The motivation of this strategy is that additional information leads to assumptions about the target position at the beginning of the mission and can be used to improve the drone movement and find the target more quickly. This additional knowledge could e.g. come from the person reporting the target missing at the police station.

In order to take advantage of the additional knowledge of the missing person's start position, the naive strategy is adjusted. The catcher drone which is sent out first immediately visits the hexagon which overlaps with the search area and contains the known target start position. From there, it continues its search, visiting the other hexagon center points in the same row-by-row manner as in the naive strategy. The drone approaches the hexagon center point instead of directly heading for the target start position, because it is assumed that the exact coordinates of the start position are not given and the target might have moved already when the person is reported missing. Furthermore, this allows for a smooth transition into the naive strategy. The other drones perform the same maneuvers as in the naive strategy.

If the target is assumed to be moving on streets because it is travelling by bike or car, this strategy might also improve the mission time until the target is found. Areas with a high street density or highly frequented crossroads can be chosen as a start position for the search. In the simulation, this use case is not considered explicitly.

**Random Strategy.** Besides the strategies based on a hexagonal grid for the movement of the first (two) drone(s), a strategy based on random search paths is also introduced. In this strategy, the naive strategy is altered such that the catcher drone moves towards random positions in the search area instead of following a hexagonal lattice. Once it reaches such a random position, the next one is chosen. The rest of the strategy remains the same.

The random strategy has no memory in the sense that it can be sure to visit every position in the search area. However, it could be advantageous over the other strategies, if the first UAV heads for the center of the area right away and can take advantage of the whole identify range of the UAV from the beginning instead of following hexagons at the rim of the search area in order to cover it entirely.

### 3.2   Evaluation Methods

The strategies are evaluated based on different aspects: probability of success, duration, and cost. Besides the evaluation of the differences between the strategies, the effect of parameter changes like target movement speed and drone identify range on the results are also studied. Furthermore, different search area shapes and sizes are investigated.

**Probability of Success.** The SAR mission can fail for various reasons. Those reasons are divided into two groups: The UAV-specific reasons and insufficient accuracy.

The group of UAV-specific reasons for failure are caused by characteristics from the hardware specifications of the UAVs chosen for a strategy. If one or more of the drones run out of power before the target is successfully located, the mission is considered a failure. Therefore, the cases in which a mobile target might evade or escape the drones have to be considered. If a drone can run out of power in a mission with an immobile target, the strategy needs to be adjusted. This issue could be addressed with changes in the flight maneuvers, start positions of the drones closer to the search areas or the choice of a more durable drone type.

The accuracy is measured in meters and describes the distance between the true location of the UE and the estimated location. It mainly depends on the localization method that is chosen, the LOS conditions, and the parameter that is chosen for the localization method, e.g. RSS or ToA, and their resolution. The accuracy of the strategies is not investigated with the simulation and has to be tested with experiments.

**Mission Time.** Duration refers to how fast the missing person's UE can be located. The start of a mission is defined to be the takeoff of the first UAV and the end is either when the target is successfully located or when the mission is interrupted, e.g. because of an empty battery or tank. Interrupted missions are not considered for mission time calculations.

**Mission Costs.** Cost considers the acquisition cost of equipment such as the UAVs and the technical equipment they are carrying as well as operating costs like electricity or fuel cost for the time of the search mission or maintenance and personnel costs. Therefore, cost also depends on the duration of the mission.

Table 1 summarizes the acquisition and operating costs of multi-rotor and single-rotor drones. The values are explained in detail in the Appendix B. The comparison shows that the acquisition costs of single-rotor drones and of their equipment in a SAR use case as well as the operating costs of single-rotor UAVs are significantly higher than of multi-rotor drones. On one hand, since especially the energy cost is dependent on the duration of the search mission, longer missions and therefore also flight times are expected to cause higher expenses. On the other hand, the use of more single-rotor drones, which might cause shorter mission and flight times, also causes higher expenses than the use of multi-rotor drones, due to the high acquisition costs and the higher energy costs per minute.

**Table 1.** Comparison of the costs of a multicopter with a single-rotor UAV. The single-rotor UAV is assumed to carry five SDRs.

|  | Multi-Rotor | Single-Rotor |
| --- | --- | --- |
| **Acquisition Cost in k Euro** | | |
| UAV | 3–3.6 | 15–180 |
| Equipment | 2.14 | 10.7 |
| **Operating Cost in k Euro/year** | | |
| Maintenance | 90 | 120 |
| Energy (in cents/min.) | 0.45 | 1.82 |

## 4   Simulation Results

This section presents the simulation results. First, the simulation assumptions and parameters are introduced. To evaluate the performance, the target speed, the UAV identify range and the scenario are varied. The scenario includes different search areas with varying shapes, sizes, and drone station positions. The performance of the strategies is discussed in comparison with each other.

### 4.1   Simulation Assumptions and Parameters

In order to evaluate and compare the strategies introduced in this paper, they are simulated as Python Matplotlib animations [29]. For each parameter set, the animation runs 1000 times to generate 1000 samples of a Monte Carlo simulation. In order to ensure the comparability between the four strategies, the same seed values are used for the target start positions and movement of the target across the four strategies. The strategies are tested in two dimensions, but can easily be expanded to three dimensions, if the ground is considered the fourth surface necessary for multilateration in three dimensions.

The drones are assumed to be placed on the roofs of public buildings like police stations or fire departments, such that they can start their missions autonomously at any time. To download and display the geospatial data of the search areas, the OSMnx Python package was used [6]. The OSMnx package allows to download street networks from OpenStreetMap as graphs.

The simulation is based on localization via cellular technologies and the cooperation of the service provider is assumed. Table 2 shows simulation parameters that are specific to the technical equipment. The speed chosen for the drones is not their maximum airspeed, but instead their cruise speed, which they can keep up for longer periods of time. The maximum airspeed is only used when the drones run out of power and have to return to their station quickly. The identify time is the time it takes for the equipment to identify the target, once it enters the range of a drone. Depending on the technology used for localization, it can be significantly higher for the first identification. The maximum flight times are assumed to be half an hour for the multi-rotor drones and four hours for the single-rotor drones.

**Table 2.** Assumed UAV simulation parameters for the two-step strategies.

| UAV Type | Speed | Identify Time | Max. Flight Time |
|---|---|---|---|
| Multi-Rotor | 17 m/s | 5 s | 30 min |
| Single-Rotor | 16 m/s | 30 s | 240 min |

Since it is necessary to get a permit to fly a drone at a height greater than 120 m in the EU [13], the UAVs are assumed to fly at a constant height of 120 m, although this does not apply to security authorities [14]. At a large height, the identify range of the drones is bigger than at a small height. At the same time, assuming the authorities still need to register drones that are flying at a high altitude, getting a permit before flying the drones in a SAR mission can cause a considerable delay. Therefore, we assume the maximal height allowed without a permit. The control range of the drones is assumed to be large enough such that all flight maneuvers are possible. The UAVs are assumed to have access to correct information about their own geographical locations at all times during the mission. The distance measurements are assumed to reflect the true distances, without non-LOS disturbances and measurement inaccuracies.

The two scenarios used for the performance evaluation are shown in Fig. 3. The scenario on the left, Fig. 3a, shows a mobile radio cell in Kempten. In this scenario, the cell of the cell tower the missing person's device is connected to determines the search area. The cell ID of the serving base station is assumed to be disclosed by the service provider after a request made by the authorities [5]. Kempten is a city in southern Germany close to the Alps. It was chosen as an example in this paper to stress the use case of a missing hiker that could be located with the help of UAVs. The approximate value of the cell area size can be found in Table 3. Figure 3b shows a different map section. It shows an area of woodland in the mountain range "Bayerischer Wald" between St. Englmar on the top left and Achslach on the right. This scenario was chosen to show the functionality of the search strategies in a larger area with bad cell coverage. Instead of searching a mobile radio cell for the mobile phone of a missing person, the drones search the woodland where the missing person is known to be with a high probability, e.g. because they were planning to go hiking there and did not return from their trip. Since there is no cell to be plotted in Fig. 3b, the search area is indicated with a blue line. In this scenario, the area to be covered by the drones is about three times larger than in the mobile cell scenario.

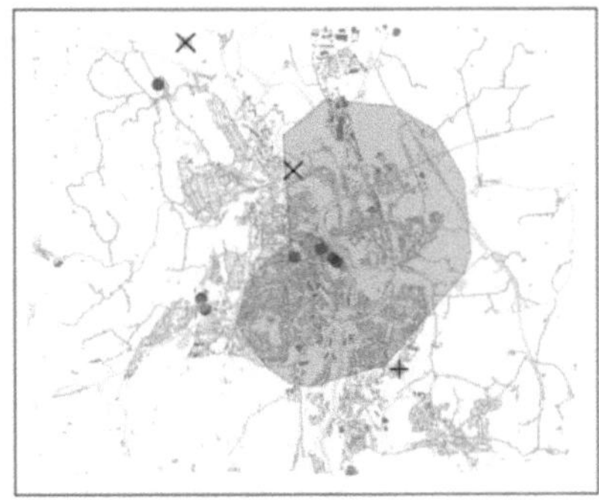

(a) Mobile cell scenario

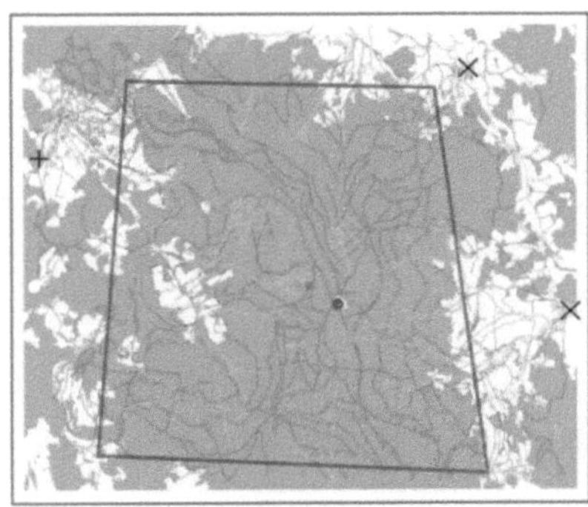

(b) Woodland scenario

**Fig. 3.** Search areas and UAV start positions of the two scenarios. The blue polygons show the search areas and the black crosses in yellow circles and the black plus signs in orange circles mark the UAV start positions of multi-rotor and single-rotor UAVs, respectively. (Color figure online)

**Table 3.** Search area shape and size scenarios used for the simulation, with the distances between the UAV start positions and the search area centroid.

| Scenario | Mobile Cell | Woodland |
|---|---|---|
| Search Area Size | $25.2\,\mathrm{km}^2$ | $77.8\,\mathrm{km}^2$ |
| Distance UAV 1 | $3.17\,\mathrm{km}$ | $6.71\,\mathrm{km}$ |
| Distance UAV 2 | $6.34\,\mathrm{km}$ | $6.81\,\mathrm{km}$ |
| Distance UAV 3 | $2.35\,\mathrm{km}$ | $6.80\,\mathrm{km}$ |
| Average Distance | $3.95\,\mathrm{km}$ | $6.77\,\mathrm{km}$ |

Besides the search areas of the different scenarios, Figs. 3a and 3b also show the UAV start positions. The black plus signs in orange circles show start positions of single-rotor drones and the black crosses in yellow circles show the ones of multi-rotor drones. In the case of the strategy with an additional catcher drone, the second catcher drone starts at the northern fire department in the Kempten scenario and at the fire department in Achslach on the bottom right in the woodland scenario. The individual as well as the average distances between the UAV start positions and the centroids of the areas are summarized in Table 3. The UAVs start from different positions, such that they are spread over a larger area and can assist in missions in other search areas as well.

In addition to the two scenarios, varying target speeds and UAV identify ranges were tested. The target speeds are chosen to represent different means of transport, specifically walking ($2\,\mathrm{m/s}$) and biking ($7\,\mathrm{m/s}$). The most important speed values for SAR missions are the small ones, because they are related to the use cases of missing hikers, disoriented or elderly people who were reported missing. The target is assumed to select a random destination position and head for the selected position at a constant speed until the destination is reached. It then (randomly) selects its next destination. If the target moves at a speed of at least 7 m/s, it has to use streets.

In order to test the compatibility of the strategies with different technical equipment with varying transmission powers, the UAV identify range values are varied. If the target is within the identify range of a UAV for a sufficient period of time, it can be identified by the equipment on the drone. Table 4 shows an overview over the values. Since the equipment carried by the single-rotor drones is assumed to have a higher transmission power and therefore a higher range than the smaller equipment on the multi-rotor drones, the multi-rotor range values were chosen to be approximately the single-rotor values divided by $\sqrt{2}$. Next to varying choices of technical equipment, the different UAV identify range values can also represent bad weather conditions or different drone heights. In rainy weather, the identify range might go down [17]. When the drones fly at a higher altitude and the transmission power is high enough, they might cover more ground at once [15]. Halving the identify range of the single-rotor UAV from 1000 m to 500 m quarters the area covered by the UAV at one moment in time. The same relation is also true for the multi-rotor drone. In the mobile cell scenario, the cell area is approximately $26.2\,\text{km}^2$. At a range of 1000 m/700 m, the three UAVs can cover up to 23.7% of the cell area at once. Lowering the range to 500 m/350 m leads to only 8.8% of the cell being covered, if the UAV ranges do not overlap and lie fully inside the cell.

**Table 4.** UAV identify range values used for the simulation.

| Radio Characteristics | Medium Gain | High Gain |
| --- | --- | --- |
| Single-Rotor | 500 m | 1000 m |
| Multi-Rotor | 350 m | 700 m |

## 4.2  Performance Comparison

This chapter presents the results of the Monte Carlo simulations regarding the success rates and the time it takes until the target is found.

**Scenarios.** Figure 4 shows the performance of the strategies in the two scenarios. The probability of failure and speed of varying configurations are depicted together in the form of cumulative distribution function (CDF) plots. The ticks on the x-axis show the mission time in seconds and the y-axis shows the probability of success. The mission time values of the failed missions are set to a value higher than the longest successful mission. Therefore, the total success probability can be read from the graph right before all of the lines jump to a success probability of 1. The rest of the graph shows, which configuration is more likely to lead to a fast success. The graphs with higher success probabilities at lower mission times show the better speed results. Since the takeoff time of the multi-rotor drones, which are mainly responsible for failed missions because of empty batteries, depends on the point in time when the single-rotor drone first identifies the target, failed missions can vary in their mission times. Furthermore, searching for a longer time does not necessarily increase the chances of finding the target, since it might have left the search area, becoming unlikely to find.

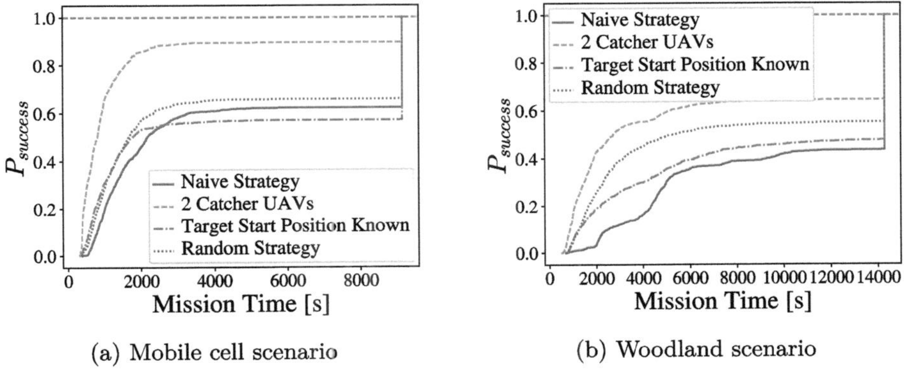


(a) Mobile cell scenario          (b) Woodland scenario

**Fig. 4.** Performance comparison of the strategies in the two search area scenarios. The target speed is fixed to 7 m/s and the UAV identify range to 1000 m/700 m.

The target speed is fixed to 7 m/s and the UAV identify range is 1000 m / 700 m. The strategy with an additional catcher UAV (orange) is the best strategy regarding success probability and speed, in both of the scenarios. The results of the other three strategies appear close to each other, especially in the mobile cell scenario. In the woodland scenario, the random strategy clearly is the runner-up regarding its success probability (red).

However, the strategy with known target start position (green) shows more completed missions at an earlier point in time in the mobile cell scenario. The strategy with known target start position appears to result in less mission time needed to find the target, but at the same time in a lower success rate than the one of the naive strategy. In the woodland scenario with a search area which is three times as large than in the mobile cell scenario, the random strategy (red) clearly shows a better performance than the other strategies with only one catcher drone. In this scenario, the strategy with known target start position (green) shows a clear improvement compared to the naive strategy.

**Target Speed.** When the target speed is reduced to 2 m/s, improved performance results can be observed across all strategies. Figure 5 shows an improvement of the success probability to up to 100% when decreasing the target speed to 2 m/s. In the case of a standing target with a speed of 0 m/s, the results are not displayed in the figure but were very similar. The strategy with known target start position (green) benefits the most from the lower target speed. Its success probability is almost doubled from approximately 50% at 7 m/s to 100% at 2 m/s and the mission duration is now comparable with the two catcher drone strategy (orange), which used to be the best strategy in this scenario. Both strategies are now able to find the target in 1000 s (17 min) in 90% of the cases, while the naive and random strategies take around 1700 s (28 min). In a scenario with an immobile target, the random strategy performs the worst out of the four strategies.

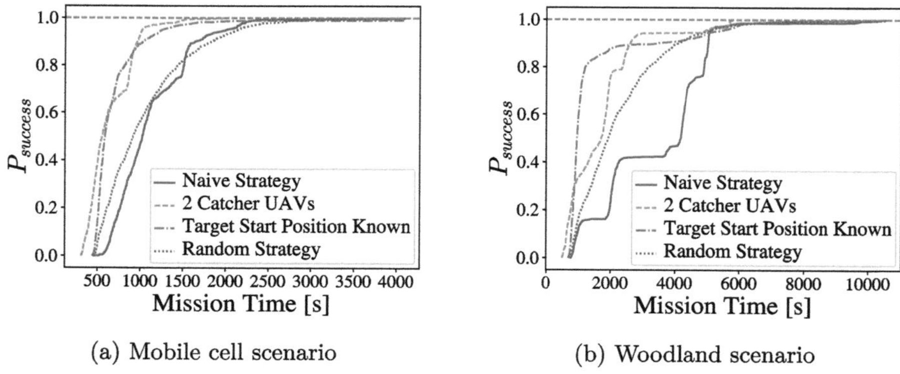

(a) Mobile cell scenario   (b) Woodland scenario

**Fig. 5.** Performance comparison of the strategies in the two search area scenarios at a lower target speed. The target speed is fixed to 2 m/s and the UAV identify range to 1000 m/700 m.

At 7 m/s, the strategy which is using two catcher drones from the beginning is the only one with a reasonable success rate (around 90%). This is displayed in Fig. 4a. At even lower target velocities, if the target is standing or walking, all strategies reach excellent success rates. However, the strategy with two catcher drones and the strategy with known target start position show better mission time values. If the target start position is not known and only one catcher drone is available, the naive strategy is a good substitute.

The woodland scenario also has much better success rate results at lower target velocities. Figure 5b shows, that even in a scenario with such a large search area, the success rate can be improved to almost 100%, if the target is moving at 2 m/s. In more than 90% of the cases, the target could be found with the strategies with two catcher drones and with known target start position in up to 2500 s (42 min), with the random strategy in up to 4000 s (67 min) and with the naive strategy in up to 5000 s (83 min). These values are much higher than in the mobile cell scenario (Fig. 5a) and it therefore takes all of the strategies longer to find the target in a bigger area, even at low target speed values. Figure 5b shows that in this configuration, the strategy with known target start position is clearly faster than the strategy with two catcher drones and the naive strategy shows the worst performance.

**UAV Identify Range.** Decreasing the UAV identify range leads to the strategy with known target start position being pushed to the bottom together with the naive strategy, as shown in Fig. 6. The strategy with an additional catcher drone (orange) shows the best performance out of all four strategies in all UAV range configurations, but does not achieve a success rate of more than 50%. Therefore, for the strategies to be of use in a SAR scenario, high identify range values need to be ensured.

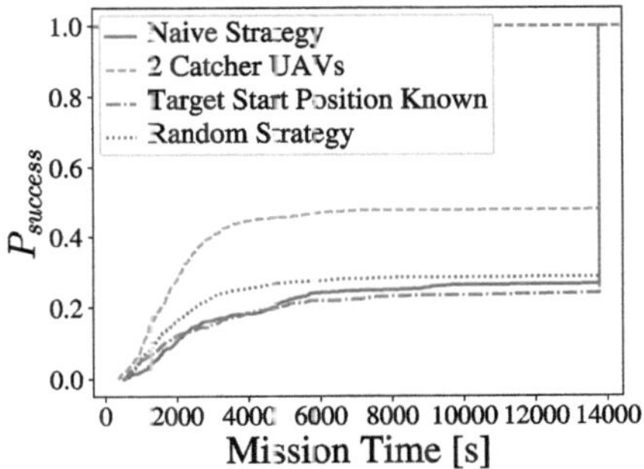


**Fig. 6.** Performance of the strategies with a UAV identify range of 500 m/350 m. The search area is the one of the mobile cell scenario and the target speed is 7 m/s.

## 4.3   Comparison of the Strategies: Summary

The results regarding the comparison of the energy costs of the strategies can be found in the Appendix C. The discussion shows that the strategy with two catcher drones can make up for the higher energy costs per minute by finding the target quicker. Comparing the strategies using only one catcher drone, the fastest and most successful ones are also the ones with the lowest energy costs.

To sum up, the success of the automated localization of a missing person's mobile device using UAVs depends on many parameters. One of the parameters, which has a big impact on the success rate and the time necessary to locate the target, is the target velocity. Under the simulation assumptions, the strategies show very promising results in the use cases of a missing hiker or an elderly person who wandered off. In those cases, if cost is secondary, the strategy with two catcher drones performs best. If the start position of the target is known, the corresponding strategy performs just as well and can be used to save acquisition costs. In the woodland scenario, it performs even better than the strategy with two catcher drones. Otherwise, if the target start position is not known and costs still have to be considered, the naive strategy also leads to good results, at the expense of the target not being found as quickly. In most of the cases, the target is found after half an hour. If the target is riding a bike, the only strategy with reasonable success rates is the strategy with two catcher drones. At even higher target velocities, the strategies are not reliable enough and cannot be applied.

The second parameter, which needs to be considered, is the identify range of the UAVs. It is crucial for the success of a search mission to use equipment with a high transmission power, such that the area covered by the UAVs is large. The size of the search area has a big impact on the time necessary to find the target.

Therefore, not only the success of the search mission depends on the given search area and parameter configuration, but also the selection of the most fitting strategy.

## 5    Conclusion

The search for missing persons proves difficult, especially in terrain that is hard to reach. Since there might only be a small period of time available to find the person unharmed and healthy, the authorities are under a lot of time pressure to find them. In order to support the authorities in such matters and make SAR missions faster, more efficient and more successful, this paper introduces four intuitive strategies for the automated localization of missing persons' technical devices using UAVs. The introduced strategies are evaluated with extensive simulations considering various scenarios and parameters. The results show that, in the case of a standing or walking target, the strategies are able to find the target with almost 100% certainty. They mainly differ in the time necessary to find the missing person and the necessary investments to buy the equipment. The strategy with two catcher UAVs could even find the target in more than 80% of the samples at a faster target speed. The random strategy also showed unexpectedly good results, especially compared with the naive strategy in many scenarios. Based on these results, the best suited strategy for a certain scenario can be selected.

The simulation framework is particularly designed to develop novel optimized search strategies for given real-world scenarios. This can be used to optimally plan the number of drones and their launch locations for an expected number of SAR missions or to perform on-the-fly mission planning. As future work, we plan to integrate an engine to generate and evaluate strategies based on evolutionary algorithms in real-time to provide increased mission planning capabilities.

## A    Selection of UAVs

Unmanned aerial vehicles (UAVs), more commonly known as drones, are aircrafts without human pilots onboard [21]. According to [32], UAVs can be categorized into the four major types multi-rotor, single-rotor, fixed-wing, and fixed-wing-multi-rotor hybrid.

During the localization, the UAVs need to be able to visit certain points in the search area and hover at those points in order to take measurements.

While flying, the drones need to carry varying technical equipment, depending on the technology used for localization and the task of the drone. Especially the drones deployed for the beginning of the search until the first identification of the target have to be able to fly for a longer time. In the next step, the search area is already delimited and the more precise localization can be performed much quicker. This is when the additional, smaller drones are used. There is no special need for very fast drones, since they have to scan the environment while flying and might even miss UEs if they pass by them too quickly.

Multi-rotor UAVs or multicopters are the most popular type of drone. The name usually specifies the number of rotors: Tricopters have three rotors, quadcopters, the most common multicopters, have four, those with six propellers are called hexacopters and octocopters have eight [32]. Multicopters are easy to manufacture and therefore the cheapest option. Furthermore, they can be controlled without special training necessary, they are agile, can hover, and are capable of vertical take-off and landing (VTOL) [21]. The biggest drawback of multicopters is that, on average, they can only fly for 20 to 30 min. This is due to the large amount of energy that is spent on stability in the air [32]. Multi-rotor drones are able to carry some payload, but the flight time is reduced with the amount of payload that is attached. Multi-rotor UAVs are therefore well suited for the task, but limited in their flying time.

Single-rotor drones resemble small helicopters. They have one large propeller at the top, which is lifting the drone into the air, and one small propeller at the tail, which is used for steering. Single-rotor UAVs can hover, are agile, are capable of VTOL, can fly for long times when powered by fuel or gas and carry heavy payloads. Because of the large rotor blades, single-rotor drones can be dangerous and their operation requires skill. Unlike the multi-rotor UAVs, single-rotor drones are expensive [26,32]. They are very robust and durable, while the possible flight patterns are similar to those of multi-rotor drones. If the flying time of multi-rotor drones is too short to identify the target, a single-rotor drone would be a fitting replacement. The multi-rotor drones can then be added for the precise localization, since they are more compact, cheaper and less dangerous than single-rotor drones, because their rotor blades are not as large.

Fixed-wing drones have wings and look like small airplanes. They are fast, built to fly long distances and stay airborne for a long time, if necessary for hours. One of the disadvantages of fixed-wing drones is their limited agility. They are not capable of hovering or VTOL and can only move forwards. Furthermore, there is a lot of space necessary for launch and recovery. The person flying the fixed-wing drone needs to be trained, and the drone itself is expensive, too [26]. Since fixed-wing UAVs cannot hover and their position is constantly changing, it is not possible to use them for taking measurements.

The fixed-wing-multi-rotor hybrid drones have propellers as well as wings and can hover, glide and are VTOL-capable, if not yet perfectly, since they are still in development [26,32]. The hybrid UAVs have very high endurance, range and speed [32]. To sum up the choice of UAVs, multi-rotor and single-rotor drones are selected to perform the tasks in the four strategies.

# B    Acquisition and Operating Costs

The costs for the UAVs and the equipment they are carrying are considered separately in this paper. Dileep et al. name a price range between 5 and 6k AUD for multi-rotor drones, which corresponds to around 3–3.6k euros, and a price range between 25 and 300k AUD for single-rotor drones, which corresponds to approximately 15–180k euros [8].

To provide numbers for the cost of the technical equipment carried by the drones, positioning in cellular networks is assumed. In this case, the multi-rotor drones can be carrying the USRP B210 board by National Instruments, which costs approximately 2.14k euros together with the steel enclosure kit, neglecting the cost of the antennas [22]. While the smaller multi-rotor drones only carry a single SDR, the larger drones have to carry multiple ones to efficiently search the radio spectrum for the device signatures.

According to Fritzsch et al., the operating costs of drones include energy and maintenance costs [11]. The cost of the maintenance of a multi-rotor drone found in the literature, 90k euros per year, is very significant [11]. The authors claim that the reason for this is that the maintenance of the drone is offered by the manufacturer and paid for in the form of a monthly service fee of 7.5k euros. Alternatively, an employee could be trained to maintain the drones. Then, the personnel costs together with the cost of the spare parts might be less than the 90k euros/year [11]. Since the single-rotor drone is more expensive than the multi-rotor drone, it is assumed that the spare parts of the single-rotor drone are also more expensive, which contribute to a higher maintenance cost.

The multi-rotor drone is assumed to carry two flight batteries with 274 Wh of energy each. Assuming electricity costs of 25.65 cents/kWh for retail [4], fully charging both batteries would cost 14.06 cents. With two fully charged batteries, the drone can fly for 31 min. It is assumed that the power consumption is steady during the whole flight of the drone and the electricity cost can be assumed to be 0.45 cents/minute. It is assumed that the single-rotor drone has a fuel tank that can hold up to eight liters of fuel. With a full tank, the UAV can fly for up to four hours. Assuming a price of 54.74 cents per liter of kerosine [30], fully refuelling the drone would cost 437.92 cents. If the power consumption of the drone is steady, the energy cost can be assumed to be 1.82 cents/minute.

# C    Energy Cost Comparison

This section compares the energy costs of the four strategies in varying search area configurations. For the comparison of the costs, successful missions as well as failed missions are considered. Failed missions cause energy costs just like successful missions and since in failed missions the drones keep flying until one of them runs out of battery or fuel, also considering failed missions works as a punishment for strategies with a bad success rate in the comparison.

To display the distributions of the energy costs over the simulation samples, Fig. 7 uses boxplots. For each sample, the flight time of every UAV is multiplied with the energy cost per minute, depending on the type of UAV. The blue, solid line of the plot shows the median of the resulting cost samples and the green, dashed line shows the mean. The boxes are limited by the first (lower) and third (upper) quartiles of the samples. The vertical lines, the whiskers, extend to the data points within 1.5 times the interquartile range, which is the difference between the values of the first and third quartiles. The circles mark the outliers.

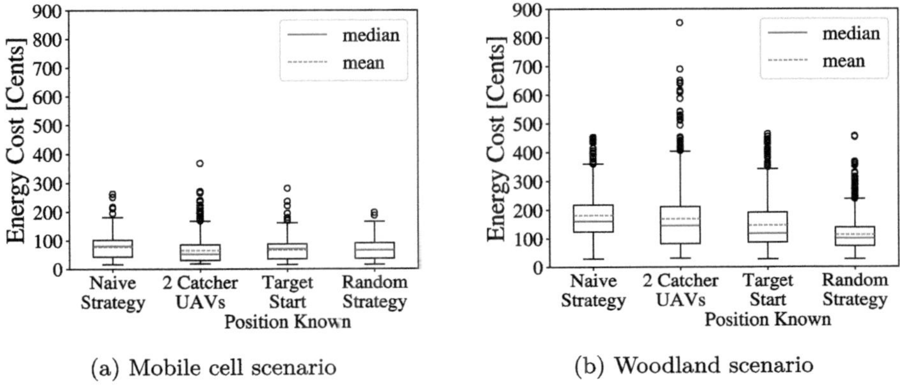

(a) Mobile cell scenario         (b) Woodland scenario

**Fig. 7.** Comparison of the energy costs per mission of the strategies in the two search area scenarios. The target speed is fixed to 7 m/s and the UAV identify range to 1000 m/700 m. The blue, solid line is the median and the green, dashed line the mean. (Color figure online)

Comparing the energy costs of the strategies in the four scenarios, the costs of the strategy with two catcher drones are surprisingly close to the costs of the other strategies. Figure 7 displays that in the mobile cell scenario, the median of the strategy with two catcher drones is even lower than of the other strategies. This shows that the time savings of this strategy are able to cancel out the higher energy costs per minute of the additional catcher drone. However, the strategy with two catcher drones shows a high number of outliers, which makes it harder to predict the energy costs of this strategy. In the woodland scenario, the energy costs are approximately doubled. Here, the random strategy results in the lowest energy cost value. The only strategy, which had a higher success rate than the random strategy in the woodland scenario, was the strategy with two catcher drones. In this scenario, the speed of the strategy with two catcher drones cannot make up for the higher energy costs per minute. Furthermore, the number of outliers is very high across all four strategies.

Especially at low target speed values (0 m/s and 2 m/s), which are not displayed in the figures, the strategy with known target start position is the least costly strategy. At 0 m/s, this strategy also shows almost no variance, since almost all targets are found immediately.

# References


1. Albanese, A., Sciancalepore, V., Costa-Pérez, X.: Sardo: an automated search-and-rescue drone-based solution for victims localization. IEEE Trans. Mob. Comput. **21**(9), 3312–3325 (2021)
2. Bánhelyi, B., Palatinus, E., Lévai, B.L.: Optimal circle covering problems and their applications. CEJOR **23**(4), 815–832 (2015)
3. Becker, J.K., Li, D., Starobinski, D.: Tracking anonymized bluetooth devices. Proc. Priv. Enhancing Technol. **2019**(3), 50–65 (2019). https://doi.org/10.2478/popets-2019-0036
4. BNetzA: Electricity prices for commercial and industrial customers in Germany in the years 2012 to 2022 (in euro cents per kilowatt hour) (2022). https://de.statista.com/statistik/daten/studie/154902/umfrage/strompreise-fuer-industrie-und-gewerbe-seit-2006/. (in German) statista. Accessed 25 Aug 2023
5. BNetzA: Technical guideline for the implementation of legal measures for the surveillance of telecommunications and the disclosure of information. TR TKÜV Edition 8.2, German Federal Network Agency for Electricity, Gas, Telecommunications, Posts and Railway (2023)
6. Boeing, G.: Osmnx: new methods for acquiring, constructing, analyzing, and visualizing complex street networks. Comput. Environ. Urban Syst. **65**, 126–139 (2017)
7. Campos, R.S., Lovisolo, L.: RF positioning: fundamentals, applications, and tools. Artech House (2015)
8. Dileep, M., Navaneeth, A., Ullagaddi, S., Danti, A.: A study and analysis on various types of agricultural drones and its applications. In: 2020 Fifth International Conference on Research in Computational Intelligence and Communication Networks (ICRCICN), pp. 181–185. IEEE (2020)
9. Federal Bureau of Investigation: 2022 NCIC Missing Person and Unidentified Person Statistics (2023). https://www.fbi.gov/file-repository/2022-ncic-missing-person-and-unidentified-person-statistics.pdf/view. Accessed 10 Jan 2024
10. Fejes, L.: Über die dichteste Kugellagerung. Math. Z. **48**(1), 676–684 (1942)
11. Fritzsch, B., Namneck, A., Schwab, A., Kirchner, L., Stonis, M.: Wirtschaftlichkeitsbewertung von Drohnen zum innerbetrieblichen Materialtransport. Logist. J. **11**, 2020 (2020). https://doi.org/10.2195/LJ_NOTREV_FRITZSCH_DE_202011_01
12. German Federal Criminal Police Office: The police handling of missing persons cases in Germany (2023). https://www.bka.de/DE/UnsereAufgaben/Ermittlungsunterstuetzung/BearbeitungVermisstenfaelle/bearbeitungVermisstenfaelle_node.html. (in German). Accessed 24 May 2023
13. German Federal Ministry for Digital and Transport: EU regulations on drones (2023). https://bmdv.bund.de/SharedDocs/DE/Artikel/LF/drohnen.html. (in German). Accessed 16 Aug 2023
14. German Federal Ministry of Justice: §21k LuftVO. https://www.gesetze-im-internet.de/luftvo_2015/__21k.html. Accessed 12 Oct 2023
15. Ha, I.K., Cho, Y.Z.: A probabilistic target search algorithm based on hierarchical collaboration for improving rapidity of drones. Sensors **18**(8), 2535 (2018)
16. Intel: Intel NUC Board NUC7i7DNBE Product Specifications. https://ark.intel.com/content/www/us/en/ark/products/130394/intel-nuc-board-nuc7i7dnbe.html. Accessed 12 Jan 2024
17. Joda, B., Zakari, D.M., Yahya, K.A.: Factors that impede transmission and reception of mobile cellular and global positioning system (GPS) signals in adamawa state. IOSR J. Electron. Commun. Eng. (IOSR-JECE) **13**(1), 13–24 (2018)

18. Kershner, R.: The number of circles covering a set. Am. J. Math. **61**(3), 665–671 (1939)
19. Lee, J.S., Su, Y.W., Shen, C.C.: A comparative study of wireless protocols: bluetooth, uwb, zigbee, and wi-fi. In: IECON 2007 - 33rd Annual Conference of the IEEE Industrial Electronics Society. IEEE (2007). https://doi.org/10.1109/iecon.2007.4460126
20. Mogyorósi, F., et al.: Positioning in 5g and 6g networks–a survey. Sensors **22**(13), 4757 (2022)
21. Mohsan, S.A.H., Khan, M.A., Noor, F., Ullah, I., Alsharif, M.H.: Towards the unmanned aerial vehicles (UAVs): a comprehensive review. Drones **6**(6), 147 (2022)
22. National Instruments: USRP B210 USB Software Defined Radio (SDR) (2023). https://www.ettus.com/all-products/ub210-kit/. Accessed 16 Aug 2023
23. Röper, J., Krohn, M., Fleßa, S., Thies, K.C.: Costing of helicopter emergency services-a strategic simulation based on the example of a German rural region. Heal. Econ. Rev. **10**, 1–15 (2020)
24. Schedl, D.C., Kurmi, I., Bimber, C.: An autonomous drone for search and rescue in forests using airborne optical sectioning. Sci. Robot. **6**(55), eabg1188 (2021)
25. Shaik, A., Borgaonkar, R., Asokan, N., Niemi, V., Seifert, J.P.: Practical attacks against privacy and availability in 4g/lte mobile communication systems. In: 2016 Network and Distributed System Security Symposium (2016). https://doi.org/10.14722/ndss.2016.23236
26. Tahir, A., Böling, J., Haghbayan, M.H., Toivonen, H.T., Plosila, J.: Swarms of unmanned aerial vehicles–a survey. J. Ind. Inf. Integr. **16**, 100106 (2019)
27. Tan, J., Gary Chan, S.H.: Efficient association of wi-fi probe requests under mac address randomization. In: IEEE INFOCOM 2021 - IEEE Conference on Computer Communications. IEEE (2021). https://doi.org/10.1109/infocom42981.2021.9488769
28. Taylor, P.: Statista: number of smartphone mobile network subscriptions worldwide from 2016 to 2022, with forecasts from 2023 to 2028. Online (2023). https://www.statista.com/statistics/330695/number-of-smartphone-users-worldwide/
29. The Matplotlib development team: matplotlib.animation (2023). https://matplotlib.org/stable/api/animation_api.html. Accessed 16 Oct 2023
30. U.S. Energy Information Administration: Kerosene - monthly price (2023). https://www.indexmundi.com/de/rohstoffpreise/?ware=kerosin&monate=60&wahrung=eur, indexMundi. Accessed 25 Aug 2023
31. Yan, J., Tiberius, C.C., Janssen, G.J., Teunissen, P.J., Bellusci, G.: Review of range-based positioning algorithms. IEEE Aerosp. Electron. Syst. Mag. **28**(8), 2–27 (2013)
32. Yinka-Banjo, C., Ajayi, O.: Sky-farmers: applications of unmanned aerial vehicles (UAV) in agriculture. Auton. Veh. 107–128 (2019)

# Simulation, Optimization, and Specialized Techniques

# Event-Driven Performance Evaluation of Statecharts and MicroPython on ESP32-C3 Platforms


Xinyu Tan[1,2] and Ismo Hakala[1,2]

[1] University of Jyväskylä, Jyväskylä, Finland
{xinyu.tan,ismo.hakala}@jyu.fi
[2] Kokkola University Consortium Chydenius, Kokkola, Finland



**Abstract.** Interpreter-based programming solutions for resource- constrained Internet of Things devices offer an innovative approach to integrating scripting languages into embedded development. While these methods have advantages, they also bring potential performance trade-offs due to the scripting overhead. Performance analysis of interpreter-based solutions is essential to assess their practicality on resource-constrained devices.

This study focuses on event-based performance by evaluating the performance of statecharts and MicroPython in handling event-based tasks. The evaluation, grounded in practical application scenarios, assesses event responsiveness and memory efficiency under both single-threaded and multithreaded environments.

The results demonstrate the feasibility of both Statecharts and MicroPython for resource-constrained devices. However, statecharts exhibit superior performance, characterized by faster event response, and a smaller memory footprint, making this approach particularly well-suited for more constrained environments.

**Keywords:** statecharts · interpreter-based · MicroPython · IoT · WSN · script language


## 1 Introduction

The Internet of Things (IoT) has revolutionized our interconnected world, enabling unprecedented data-driven innovation. Sensor nodes and other IoT devices are now integral to modern technology, playing an essential role in collecting, processing, and distributing real-time data. However, these devices often operate under significant resource constraints and in dynamic environments, requiring sophisticated software control mechanisms to manage various events and states effectively.

Programming these resource-constrained devices presents a unique challenge due to their limited ability to support traditional operating systems. To mitigate this problem, various programming approaches have been developed, including



A. Soylu et al. (Eds.): MobiQuitous 2024, LNICST 634, pp. 535–549, 2026.
https://doi.org/10.1007/978-3-032-10554-7_28

wireless sensor network-oriented operating systems and specialized code generators, all aimed at easing the programming process for these constrained environments.

The interpreter-based programming methodology, in which script codes are executed by an interpreter at runtime, has gained increased attention in IoT programming. This method supports dynamic script execution without the need for compilation, offering advantages such as the interactive debugging paradigm, rapid development, dynamic reconfiguration, and enhanced portability. Script languages, such as statechart script [6], JavaScript, Lua [10], and Python, are increasingly being adopted for use in resource-constrained IoT devices due to these benefits.

However, this methodology is not without drawbacks. Interpreters must perform intricate procedures to translate scripts into executable actions specific to the system, which can impact the overall system performance. Thus, a performance analysis of interpreter-based solutions is essential to assess their practicality and efficiency in resource-constrained devices.

Some studies, such as [11,17], have evaluated the performance of interpreter-based programming solutions on IoT devices. They often focus on computational efficiency using data-processing algorithms. These metrics, although insightful, do not fully capture the performance in the typical operational paradigms of resource-constrained IoT devices. In these devices, energy conservation is critical, as they often operate in sleep mode and are activated by external or internal event triggers. Therefore, event responsiveness is an essential measure of system performance, reflecting the system's real-time capability and energy efficiency.

This study undertakes a comparative evaluation of two distinct interpreter-based approaches, namely statecharts and MicroPython [2], to assess their performance in event-driven scenarios. A consistent experimental setup is maintained using the ESP32-C3 platform with FreeRTOS [1] to ensure a fair comparison and isolate the performance characteristics specific to the interpreter mechanisms. The methodology involves implementing event-driven tasks that mimic typical operational conditions of IoT devices in real-world applications. Furthermore, a traditional programming approach with C language and native system application interfaces (API) is employed in this analysis to provide a reference benchmark for the optimal effectiveness of the system.

The performance of these programming approaches is evaluated under two distinct scenarios: single-threaded and concurrent multithreaded tasks. The single-threaded task measures execution time as a baseline of event-responsiveness, while the multithreaded scenario assesses scalability by analyzing the growth in event-responsive time and memory usage with an increasing number of concurrent loads.

The primary contribution of this study lies in its event-driven performance evaluation of two distinct interpreter-based programming solutions: statecharts and MicroPython. The findings offer valuable insights for developers and engineers in identifying the most suitable programming language for their IoT applications.

The remainder of the paper is organized as follows. The basic concepts of statecharts and MicroPython programming solutions are briefly introduced in Sect. 3. Section 4 demonstrates the methodology of the experiment, detailing the task scenarios adopted in this research. The results of the experiment, along with the analysis and discussion, are presented in Sect. 5. Section 2 offers an overview of the works related to the topic. Finally, Sect. 6 concludes this paper.

## 2  Related Works

This section presents a literature review of interpreter-based solutions compatible with resource-constrained IoT platforms and the evaluation studies that assess the computational performance of MicroPython.

### 2.1  Interpreter-Based Solutions

Script languages have shown significant potential in software development due to their features, such as user-friendly syntax, rapid prototyping, and fast deployment. Some popular languages, such as JavaScript, Lua, and Python, have been further supported in the programming of resource-constrained IoT devices through specialized interpreter implementations. Furthermore, some IoT programming approaches incorporate state machine-based scripts for their visualized presentation and event-driven paradigm.

**JavaScript** was originally designed to automate small tasks within web-based applications operated on browsers. The resource-efficient interpreter implementations enable the execution of JavaScript on resource-constrained devices, providing an innovative alternative to programming IoT devices. JerryScript [4], a lightweight JavaScript engine developed by Samsung and currently managed by the OpenJS Foundation, exemplifies the adaptation of JavaScript to the constraints of IoT devices, balancing efficiency and functionality. Mongoose OS [3] is a framework for creating IoT systems. It leverages JavaScript's accessibility to streamline the development process of IoT applications. Furthermore, Espruino [19], a JavaScript interpreter, enables the implementation of JavaScript code on a variety of ESP-based platforms.

**Lua** is a lightweight, embeddable scripting language designed for embedded systems and client-server applications. Lua-RTOS [9] is an embedded interpreter with minimal resource requirements. Integrated as a component of the Whitecat IDE, Lua-RTOS facilitates the execution of Lua scripts on the ESP32, ESP8266, and PIC32MZ platforms. NodeMCU [16] is a Lua-based firmware for the ESP32 and ESP8266 modules, providing a programming experience similar to Node.js.

**State machine-based approaches** are popular in programming event-driven embedded programs. Conventional approaches convert state machine-based representation to system-specific languages, such as C and nesC, through code generators. Alternatively, some solutions, such as the statechart approach discussed in this paper, allow direct execution of state machine-based scripts on the target device via a compatible interpreter. SenOS [14] incorporates an FSM-based script, namely, the state transition table (STT). On the platform, STTs are interpreted as a series of library function entries linked to specific triggering events. Upon the occurrence of the event, the functions of the triggered entry are activated to complete the computational behavior of the system.

## 2.2  Related Evaluation Works

Scripting languages in embedded programming offers significant advantages, such as facilitating interactive debugging, providing a simplified syntax, and enabling rapid prototyping. However, the performance of these solutions raises concerns, primarily due to the overhead introduced by the interpreting processes. To address these concerns, several studies have conducted comparative analyses to assess the efficacy of interpreter-based solutions within typical IoT platforms.

Some studies that evaluated interpreter-based approaches focused on parameters such as execution efficiency in data processing algorithms. Research [11] conducted a comparative analysis between MicroPython and the C language that involved running the CRC32 and SHA256 algorithms on the ESP32 and STM32 platforms. The findings indicated that MicroPython performed significantly less than the C language in executing the data-processing algorithms. Another study [17] expanded the scope by comparing C/C++, MicroPython, Rust, and TinyGo on the ESP32 platform. This study involved running five different data-processing algorithms with varying input data lengths. The results indicate that MicroPython lagged considerably in data-processing tasks compared with the other languages tested.

Alternatively, a survey [5] offered a comprehensive literature review of JavaScript engines developed for resource-constrained MCUs. This survey evaluated six distinct solutions, examining them on several attributes, including supported platforms, memory footprints, the extent of ECMAScript support, the availability of framework tools, community activeness, and open-source licenses.

This paper, while related to the aforementioned studies, takes a different approach by focusing on the evaluation of the event-driven performance of interpreter-based programming approaches. The results reveal the efficiency of these approaches in programming resource-constrained IoT applications.

## 3  Overview of Statecharts and MicroPython

This section provides an overview of two interpreter-based programming solutions, statecharts and MicroPython, which will be subjected to comparative performance evaluation.

### 3.1  Statecharts

Statechart visual programming language [7,8] extends the finite state machine (FSM) formalism by incorporating hierarchical and concurrent state compositions. A state within a statechart can encapsulate subordinate state machines.

The states of these subordinate machines are referred to as *substates* of the composing state, which is termed the *superstate* of its substates. This structure can be applied recursively, i.e., a superstate can be a substate of a higher-level superstate.

The actions of the state graphs can be executed upon entering (*entry-action*), exiting (*exit-action*), and transitioning between states (*transition-action*). In addition, when the system is in a stable state, it can initiate long-term actions, referred to as *activity*. Activities represent continuous or ongoing actions performed while the system is in a particular state.

Statecharts, as suggested by [13,15], demonstrate the significant potential of programming IoT devices. The inherent event-driven paradigm of statecharts is particularly suitable for dynamic and frequently unpredictable environments typical in IoT scenarios. Moreover, statecharts represent system responses to events through graphical boxes and arrows, intuitively aligned with human cognitive patterns.

A previous study [6] proposed a statechart programming framework that facilitates the design of visualized statecharts in web-based editing software and subsequently generates statechart scripts for deployment on the target device. The frameworks implement the middleware, as shown in Fig. 1, that powers the execution of statechart scripts on resource-constrained devices through an interpreter. This executive methodology ensures that the computational behavior of the system remains unambiguous as in the original design. Statechart middleware is designed to support various platforms, including StateOS [18] and FreeRTOS.

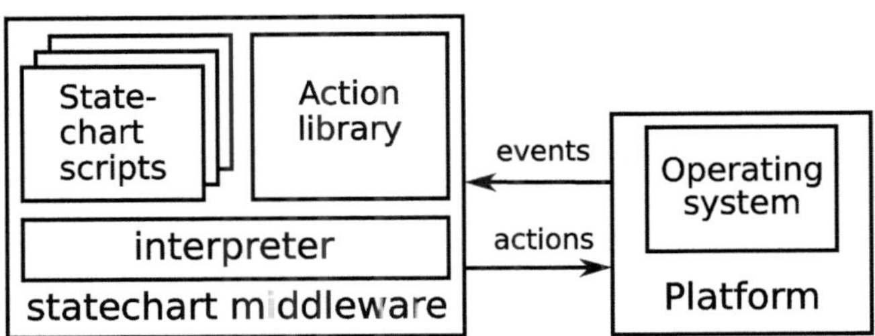


**Fig. 1.** Statechart middleware.

## 3.2   MicroPython

Python, an interpreted, high-level, object-oriented programming language, features dynamic semantics and a garbage collection mechanism. Its simplified syntax prioritizes cleanliness and straightforwardness, enhancing readability and comprehension. This design choice facilitates rapid development and iterative processes due to its interpreted nature and dynamic semantics.

MicroPython is a Python interpreter that facilitates the execution of Python scripts on microcontroller unit (MCU)-based platforms. This integration successfully extends Python's various benefits in embedded programming. Moreover, MicroPython provides additional library implementations for hardware operations, accommodating the unique requirements and limitations of resource-constrained embedded environments. The implementation of MicroPython supports popular IoT platforms through hardware-dependent firmware, namely *port*, including an ESP32-C3-compatible FreeRTOS-based port.

## 4   Experimental Setup

The experiment investigates the event-driven performance of the programming methodologies, statecharts and MicroPython, by subjecting them to two experimental tasks that draw inspiration from a real-world passive infrared (PIR) sensor-based, motion-tracking application [12]. Beyond these subjected programming solutions, the evaluation outcomes of the C language implementations with native system APIs establish a benchmark for optimal system performance.

The experiment is conducted on the ESP32-C3 platform, a single-core, 32-bit, RISC-V-based MCU with a custom version of FreeRTOS operating at 160 MHz. Compared to typical resource-constrained IoT and WSN devices, often equipped with only tens of kilobytes of RAM and flash, the ESP32-C3 is relatively resourceful, with 400 KB of data memory and 384 KB of flash. Both the statechart middleware and MicroPython port on the ESP32-C3 platform incorporate similar multithread APIs of FreeRTOS, establishing an ideal environment for conducting comparative performance evaluations.

Furthermore, to isolate the core performance differences, power-saving strategies for both the statechart implementation and MicroPython are disabled, ensuring the devices remain active throughout the experiment.

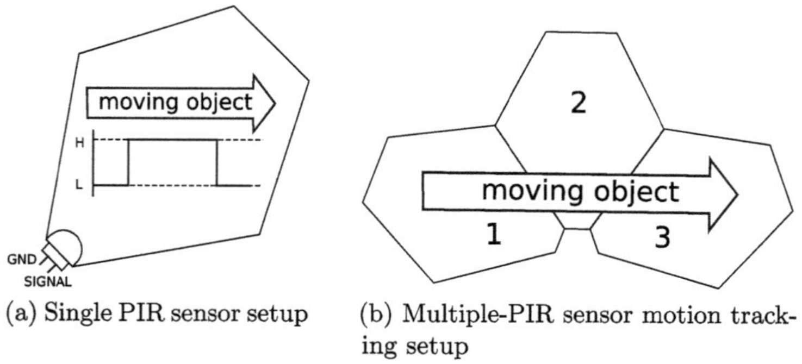


(a) Single PIR sensor setup     (b) Multiple-PIR sensor motion tracking setup

**Fig. 2.** PIR motion tracking systems.

## 4.1   Single PIR Motion-Tracking Task

In IoT systems, events are sourced internally or externally. A typical internal event type is a timer event initiated by a hardware time counter that triggers the event in the system upon reaching a predefined threshold. The external interrupt events caused by the transistor-transistor logic (TTL) level changes in a general-purpose input/output (GPIO) pin are typical external event sources that drive an IoT system.

The first experimental configuration investigates the event responsiveness of timer events and external interrupt events within a fundamental event-driven task. A single PIR sensor system, illustrated in Fig. 2a, is designed to capture motion within a limited area. The *SIGNAL* pin is pulled to a high TTL state as an output signal that indicates motion detection.

The operational processes of the task involve enabling the PIR sensor in a sampling period of one second. Upon motion detection, the PIR sensor is disabled until the end of the sampling period to avoid undesired interrupt events. Event responsiveness is determined by calculating the time elapsed between event occurrence and completion of the event response process.

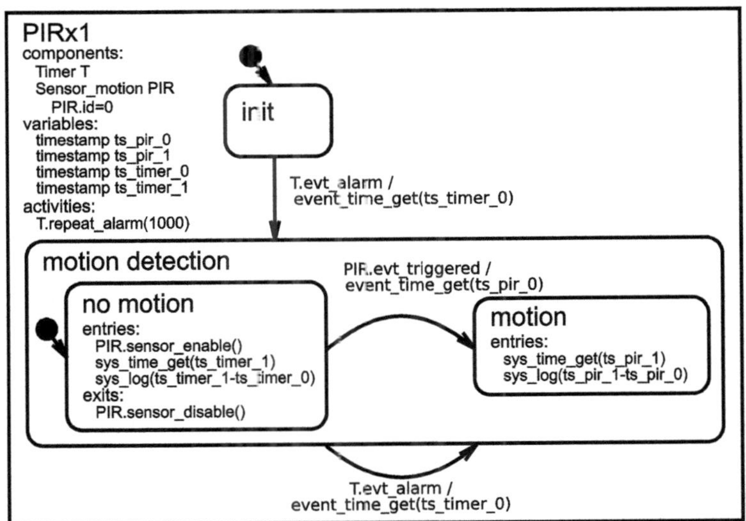


**Fig. 3.** Statechart diagram of the single PIR motion-tracking task.

The statechart diagram presented in Fig. 3 serves as a template for the implementation of the three programming solutions. The underlying principle is that all solutions apply to the same programming structure as depicted in this diagram.

Upon initialization, the root state activates a repeated alarm that generates a timer event every 1000 milliseconds. The system defaults to the state *init* until the timer event transitions the system to the state *motion detection*. Upon transitioning to the state *motion detection*, the system also enters its substate *no motion*. The entry actions of the state *no motion* enable the PIR sensor and evaluate the response time to the timer event.

In the state *motion detection*, the system's computational behavior is driven by the PIR event *PIR.evt_triggered* and timer event *T.evt_alarm*. In response to the PIR event, the system captures the event occurrence timestamp in the variable *ts_pir_0* within the transition action. Simultaneously, the PIR sensor is deactivated through the exit action of the source state *no motion*. Upon transitioning to the destination state *motion*, the current system timestamp is recorded in the variable *ts_pir_1*. The difference between these two timestamps, representing the event responsiveness of the PIR sensor event, is logged for subsequent analysis.

Upon the occurrence of the timer event, the system records the timestamp in the variable *ts_timer_0* within the transition action of the *motion detection* state. In the absence of motion detection, exiting the superstate *motion detection* triggers a simultaneous exit from the active substate *no motion*, consequently disabling the PIR sensor. Conversely, the system exits the substate *motion* without further actions when motion is detected. The event-reactive process is completed with the system re-entering the state *motion detection* and the substate *no motion* and re-enabling the PIR sensor. The timestamp at the end of this process is captured in the variable *ts_timer_1* to evaluate and log the elapsed time for further analysis.

The statechart solution accepts a similar design of the aforementioned statechart diagram in the supported design environment and transforms it into the statechart script. This script is then compressed and deployed to the statechart middleware within the target device.

In addition to statecharts, this single PIR motion tracking task is implemented in MicroPython and C language on a similar platform configuration. In MicroPython implementation, several programming methods are available, including the while-loop structure, multithreaded approach, and MicroPython kernel APIs. In this experiment, the MicroPython script implements an infinite while-loop structure with event flags controlled by corresponding event-callback functions. It is the most efficient approach among the alternatives due to its minimal requirement for additional context scheduling.

The C language version implements the infinite while-loop controlled by the native flow-control APIs in a single thread. This thread is blocked by the function *ulTaskNotifyTake* until the PIR or timer event occurs. In event callback functions, the function *xTaskNotifyGive* resumes the thread to perform associated event-reactive operations. This efficient strategy for event responsiveness provides a realistic benchmark for the following analysis.

### 4.2   Multiple PIR Motion-Tracking Task

To assess the scalability of programming solutions in concurrent multitasking settings, a multiple PIR tracking task is presented, as depicted in Fig. 2b, capable

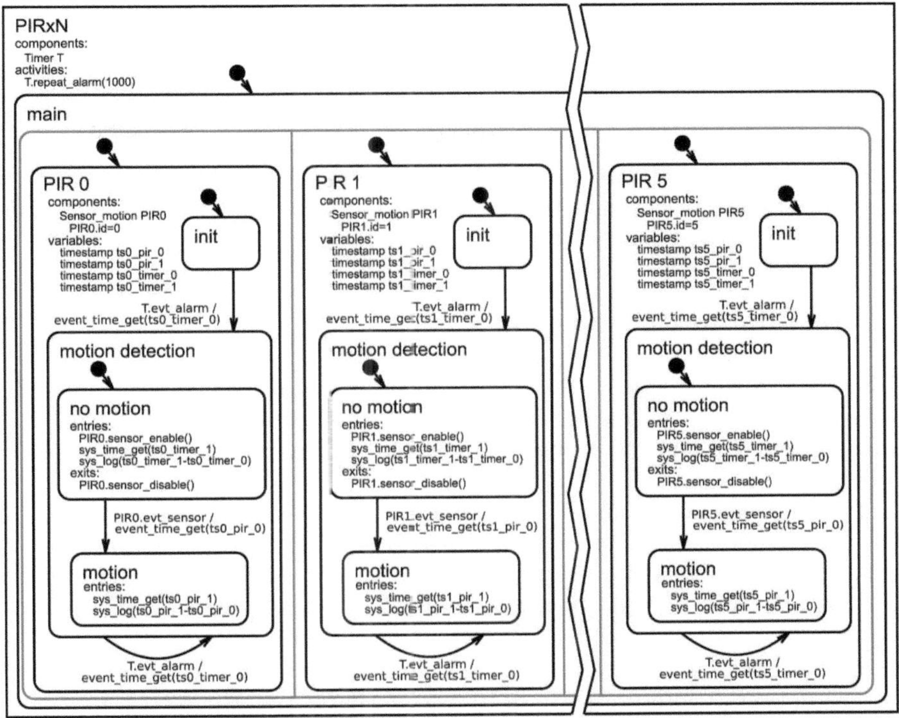

**Fig. 4.** Statechart diagram of the multiple PIR motion-tracking task.

of tracking a moving object in a broader area. This simulation involves the concurrent operations of up to six PIR sensors, each functioning similarly to the task scenario described in Sect. 4.1. The setup is designed to analyze how the system's responsiveness and memory consumption are affected by different numbers of concurrent threads, thereby gaining insights into the scalability of the system under diverse operational workloads.

In the statechart solution, depicted in Fig. 4, multiple state machines operate PIR sensors concurrently within the state *main*. Each state machine responds to its corresponding PIR sensor event. Furthermore, all state machines are synchronized by a common timer event.

In the MicroPython implementation, the concurrent management of PIR event handling threads is facilitated by the multithreaded library, _ *thread*. Each thread implements an infinite while-loop with a thread-locking mechanism that blocks the thread until the event callback releases the lock. The event response time of each thread is determined by measuring the elapsed time from the point of the event callback to the moment the thread is resumed.

Likewise, in the C implementation, handling multiple PIR event-driven threads is managed through the native multitasking interfaces. Each thread has an infinite while-loop. The control flow of the thread is through task notification APIs for the suspension and resuming of thread processes.

This experiment adopts a systematic approach that gradually increases the number of concurrent threads and analyzes the corresponding changes in event responsiveness and memory usage. By varying the number of threads from one to six and closely observing the consequent effects on these two parameters, the experiment seeks to evaluate the scalability and efficiency of the system under increased concurrent functionalities.

## 5    Results and Discussion

In Sect. 4.1, a single PIR motion detection task is implemented using three distinct programming approaches: statecharts, MicroPython, and C language. Two kinds of events, namely, PIR and timer events, trigger the event-reactive operations of the system.

Table 1 lists the executive time results of the event reactive operations of the three different programming solutions obtained by taking the average of 30 consecutive measurements. These results reveal a non-significant overall difference between the statecharts and MicroPython implementations in the event responsiveness of a single-threaded environment. Furthermore, both approaches perform slower than the native C language implementation due to the additional overhead of script interpretation in both statecharts and MicroPython.

The actions of statecharts are implemented as library functions middleware using system-specific language for faster execution. This approach avoids the overhead of full script interpretation required by MicroPython. However, benchmark results show that Statecharts exhibit response times to PIR and timer events that are very close to MicroPython.

This can be attributed to MicroPython's pre-compilation of Python scripts into bytecode, a low-level instruction set stored in memory before execution. While this approach incurs a larger memory footprint, it significantly boosts execution efficiency.

In contrast, Statechart middleware applies a dynamic interpretation strategy. Event-driven behaviors are interpreted only when the corresponding event occurs. This strategy minimizes memory usage during periods of inactivity but might introduce some interpretation overhead at runtime.

The memory usage of these implementations is presented in Table 2. The maximum used memory for each implementation is measured by the most engaged memory amount, as recorded by the system's dynamic memory manager. This measurement provides insight into the operational memory demands of each approach.

The ESP32-C3 implementation of the statechart interpreter, which operates with two principal threads, manages the event handler and statechart machines. The event-handling thread consumes a maximum of 1580 bytes of stack memory, while the statechart machine management thread has 1576 bytes. These memory footprints were calculated by subtracting the minimal free stack memory

**Table 1.** Mean values of event responses (n = 30) for the single PIR motion-tracking task using three programming approaches: statecharts, MicroPython, and C language.

| ($\mu s$) | PIR event | Timer event | |
|---|---|---|---|
| | | (motion) | (no motion) |
| Statecharts | 59.3 | 74.9 | 81.8 |
| MicroPython | 49.8 | 74.8 | 88.0 |
| C language | 5 | 7 | 9 |

(determined by the system function *uxTaskGetStackHighWaterMark*) from the allocated stack memory for each thread. Furthermore, to accelerate the script-reading process and boost event-responsive performance, the interpreter optionally preloads the statechart script (138 bytes) into data memory. Consequently, in this specific experiment, the statechart's total memory engagement amounts to 3294 bytes, including two interpreter threads, a statechart management data structure, and the statechart script.

The ESP32-C3 port of MicroPython requires a significant amount of data memory to preload Python scripts and their parsed bytecode as in-memory representations. With the allocated memory of operational threads within the interpreter, MicroPython requires a total of 3232 bytes of data memory. This is measured by the function *mem_alloc* of the garbage collector library *gc* in MicroPython.

The C language implementation also employs a single thread to manage event responses, resulting in a total memory footprint of 1580 bytes, calculated by subtracting the minimal free stack memory (determined by the system function *uxTaskGetStackHighWaterMark*) from the allocated stack memory.

The application footprints of statecharts and MicroPython implementations are determined by the size of the scripts deployed on the target device. The MicroPython script, which utilizes the text-based imperative Python language, has a footprint of 1606 bytes and tends to consume a considerable amount of memory, especially in the case of complex programs. By contrast, statecharts are characterized by their use of a concise and expressive modeling language. The statechart script is compressed into a binary-based format with 138 bytes in the target device, further enhancing memory efficiency for resource-constrained platforms. The C language has a conventional compiled hex image. By analyzing the mapping file, the size of the application-related functions is 764 bytes.

System flash shows the size of the compiled system image, which includes the interpreter implementation and the underlying ESP32 system. In the MicroPython ESP32-C3 port image, a significant portion of flash memory is consumed by the comprehensive Python interpreter, which is designed to support a wide range of Python features. By comparison, the statechart scripts adopt concise semantics and can be executed by a smaller interpreter structure.

In Sect. 4.2, a task involving the concurrent management of multiple PIR sensors was implemented using the three programming approaches. The goal

**Table 2.** The memory footprint results of the single PIR motion-tracking task using three programming approaches: statecharts, MicroPython, and C language.

| (byte) | max. used memory | app./script size | system flash |
|---|---|---|---|
| Statecharts | 3294 | 138 | 218284 |
| MicroPyth. | 3232 | 1606 | 1587840 |
| C lang. | 1580 | 764 | 195396 |

was to evaluate the scalability of each approach in terms of event responsiveness and memory usage under varying workloads of concurrent operations. Figure 5 illustrates the PIR event response time trend when multiple PIR threads are triggered simultaneously by individual PIR events, and Fig. 6 depicts the pattern of concurrent PIR threads processing a shared timer event. It is noteworthy that MicroPython exhibits a longer event response time in the multiple PIR motion-tracking task, even with a single thread configuration, compared to the results in the single PIR motion-tracking task of Table 1. This discrepancy is due to the overhead introduced by the multiple-threading library _thread used within the MicroPython implementation.

A notable observation is the significant increase in response time for the MicroPython implementation as the number of concurrent threads escalates. This is attributed to context switch operations within the MicroPython kernel, which can introduce substantial latency, potentially hindering the efficiency of event-response processes. This implies a comparatively diminished effectiveness of MicroPython in high-concurrency environments.

On the contrary, the increase in response time for statechart implementation is more gradual, indicating better scalability under similar conditions. This advantage originates from the fact that concurrent states within a statechart machine do not require individual stack memory for context management, unlike traditional multithreaded approaches. It eliminates typical context switch overhead, resulting in more efficient transitions between concurrent states.

The C language implementation, as expected, exhibits the most stable performance due to direct interfacing with the system's native APIs and lower-level operations.

The trend of increased memory usage in correlation with the number of concurrent threads, as depicted in Fig. 7, reflects the memory efficiency of the different programming approaches. Notably, the statechart approach demonstrates remarkable memory efficiency when managing concurrent tasks. This efficiency is primarily attributed to the statechart interpreter's ability to allocate only the minimal memory stack necessary for the context of concurrent states and their associated local variables. By contrast, MicroPython exhibits significantly higher memory usage, which is a potential limit factor in resource-constrained environments.

The ESP32-C3 has a sophisticated architecture integrating Wi-Fi, Bluetooth protocols, and comprehensive debugging interfaces. Threads on this system con-

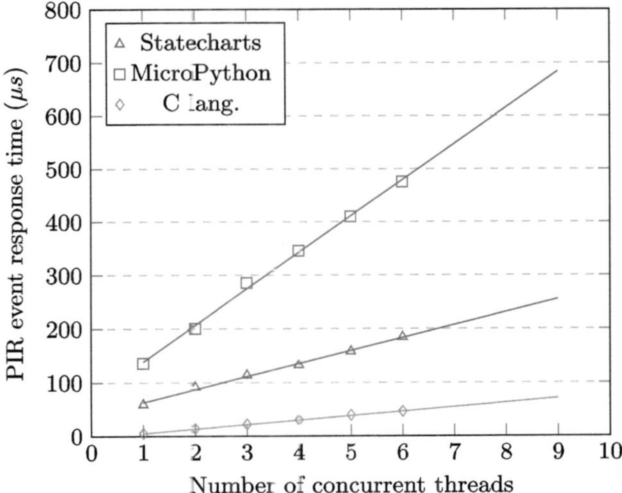


**Fig. 5.** Mean values of event responses ($n = 30$) for the multiple PIR motion-tracking task using three programming methods: statecharts, MicroPython, and C language. Trend lines illustrate the relationship between response time and the number of threads.

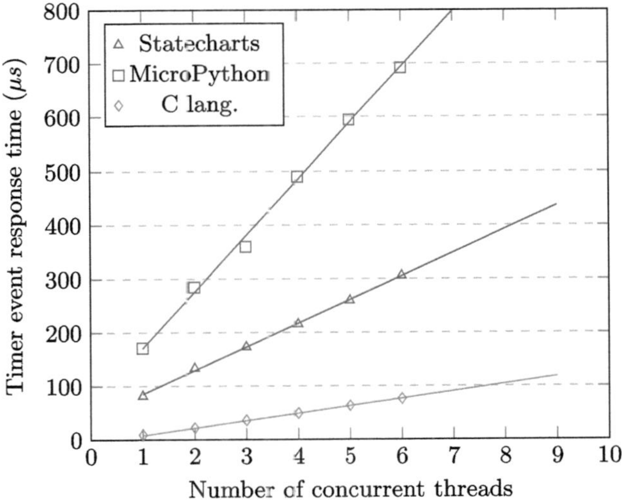


**Fig. 6.** Mean values of timer event responses ($n = 30$) for the multiple PIR motion-tracking task using three programming methods: statecharts, MicroPython, and C language. Trend lines illustrate the relationship between response time and the number of threads.

sume more stack memory than the typical lightweight systems in WSNs. We also implemented similar tasks using statecharts and C on FreeRTOS-based plat-forms (Xmega256A3, SAML21, SAMD51), achieving significantly lower memory footprints. However, these platforms aren't suitable for this experiment due to MicroPython's lack of official support for resource-constrained MCUs like the Xmega and SAML series and inconsistencies in the SAMD51 port that isn't FreeRTOS-based. Therefore, the ESP32-C3 offers a viable testing platform, as both statecharts and MicroPython can be implemented using a similar ESP32-FreeRTOS configuration, ensuring a consistent comparative evaluation.

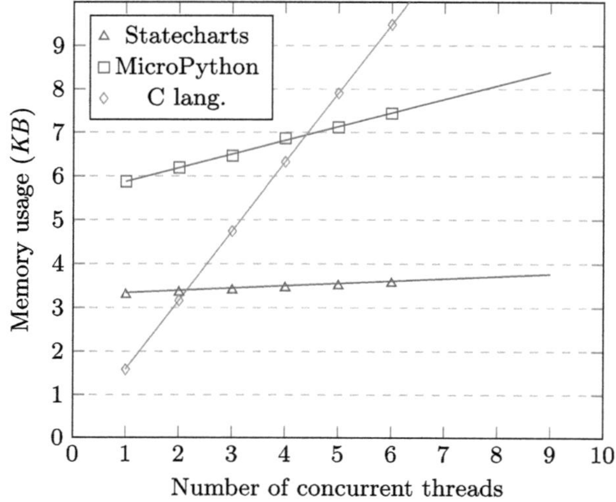


**Fig. 7.** Memory usages within the multiple PIR motion-tracking task using three programming methods: statecharts, MicroPython, and C language. Trend lines illustrate the relationship between memory usage and the number of threads.

In conclusion, the findings from this experiment demonstrate that both statecharts and MicroPython approaches are well suited to facilitate event-driven programming on the ESP32-C3 platform. However, the results of statecharts outperform MicroPython with better event responsiveness and memory usage efficiency. This efficiency makes the statechart approach a more effective solution in programming resource-constrained IoT devices.

## 6    Conclusion

This paper evaluates two distinct interpreter-based programming approaches, namely, statecharts and MicroPython, for programming resource-constrained IoT devices. The experiments focused on analyzing the event responsiveness and memory efficiency of the programming approaches through simplified event-driven tasks that originated from a practical IoT application. The findings indicate that both statecharts and MicroPython demonstrate a feasible capability to program event-driven tasks on resource-constrained IoT platforms. However, the statechart approach has superior efficiency, positioning it as a more viable solution for even more constrained embedded environments.

# References


1. Amazon Web Services: Freertos. https://www.freertos.org/. Accessed 09 Jan 2024
2. Bell, C.: MicroPython for the Internet of Things. Springer, Cham (2017)
3. Cesanta Software Ltd.: Mongoose OS (2013). https://mongoose-os.com/. Accessed 11 Aug 2023
4. Gavrin, E., Lee, S.J., Ayrapetyan, R., Shitov, A.: Ultra lightweight javascript engine for internet of things. In: Companion Proceedings of the 2015 ACM SIGPLAN International Conference on Systems, Programming, Languages and Applications: Software for Humanity, pp. 19–20 (2015)
5. Grunert, K.: Overview of Javascript engines for resource-constrained microcontrollers. In: 2020 5th International Conference on Smart and Sustainable Technologies (SpliTech), pp. 1–7. IEEE (2020)
6. Hakala, I., Tan, X.: A statecharts-based approach for WSN application development. J. Sens. Actuator Netw. **9**(4), 45 (2020)
7. Harel, D.: On the formal semantics of statecharts. In: IEEE Symposium on Logic in Computer Science, pp. 54–64 (1987)
8. Harel, D.: Statecharts: a visual formalism for complex systems. Sci. Comput. Program. **8**(3), 231–274 (1987)
9. Iberoxarxa team: Lua rtos. https://whitecatboard.org/software/lua-rtos/. Accessed 11 Aug 2023
10. Ierusalimschy, R., De Figueiredo, L.H., Filho, W.C.: Lua–an extensible extension language. Softw. Pract. Exp. **26**(6), 635–652 (1996)
11. Ionescu, V.M., Enescu, F.M.: Investigating the performance of micropython and c on esp32 and stm32 microcontrollers. In: 2020 IEEE 26th International Symposium for Design and Technology in Electronic Packaging (SIITME), pp. 234–237. IEEE (2020)
12. Jansson, J., Hakala, I.: Managing sensor data streams in a smart home application. Int. J. Sens. Netw. **32**(4), 247–258 (2020)
13. Kasten, O., Römer, K.: Beyond event handlers: programming wireless sensors with attributed state machines. In: Proceedings of the 4th International Symposium on Information Processing in Sensor Networks, p. 7. IEEE Press (2005)
14. Kim, T.H.: Design and implementation of a state-driven operating system for highly reconfigurable sensor networks. Int. J. Distrib. Sens. Netwo. **2013**, 7 (2013)
15. Mura, M., Sami, M.G.: Code generation from statecharts: simulation of wireless sensor networks. In: 2008 11th EUROMICRO Conference on Digital System Design Architectures, Methods and Tools, pp. 525–532. IEEE (2008)
16. NodeMCU team: Nodemcu. https://www.nodemcu.com/. Accessed 11 Aug 2023
17. Plauska, I., Liutkevičius, A., Janavičiūtė, A.: Performance evaluation of C/C++, micropython, rust and tinygo programming languages on esp32 microcontroller. Electronics **12**(1), 143 (2022)
18. Tan, X., Hakala, I.: Stateos: a memory-efficient hybrid operating system for IoT devices. IEEE Internet Things J. (2023)
19. Williams, G.F.: Making Things Smart: Easy Embedded JavaScript Programming for Making Everyday Objects into Intelligent Machines. Maker Media Inc. (2017)

# Simulating Urban Pedestrian Flows by Fusing Wide-Area Location Data and Spot Pedestrian Counts

Uegaki Masashi, Tatsuya Amano[✉], and Hirozumi Yamaguchi

Osaka University, Suita, Osaka, Japan
`t-amano@ist.osaka-u.ac.jp`

**Abstract.** This paper proposes a data-driven method to simulate pedestrian flow within a target area by integrating low-granularity GPS location data with traffic data measured by sensors at specific spots. The primary challenge addressed by this method is the combination of different data sources to enhance simulation accuracy. Our approach aggregates GPS data points into Points of Interest (PoIs) within the area and employs Gibbs sampling to estimate a two-dimensional Gaussian Mixture Model for departure and travel times between PoIs. This distribution enables the simulation to replicate realistic pedestrian movements between PoIs. Additionally, we incorporate spot traffic data measured by LiDAR sensors to adjust the simulated pedestrian counts, further improving the accuracy of the simulation. We evaluated the proposed method using GPS logs from a large public park, known for being a popular tourist destination, and spot traffic data measured by LiDAR at five locations within the park. The simulation effectively reproduced pedestrian flow patterns, achieving an average cosine similarity of approximately 0.8 between the actual and simulated time-dependent population density distributions. Furthermore, the method predicted visitor numbers at park facilities with a prediction error of 13.6%.

**Keywords:** Pedestrian Flow Simulation · Urban Mobility Data · LiDAR Sensing · Gaussian Mixture Model (GMM)

## 1 Introduction

In recent years, there has been a growing focus on understanding and analyzing human mobility data to revitalize local communities through tourism promotion and rediscovery of regional attractions. This data is crucial for assessing the area attractiveness, gauging public interest, and understanding demand, ultimately helping to guide tourists and residents to attractive local spots. The need to understand population movement trends during the COVID-19 pandemic, among other factors, has led to an increase in businesses providing anonymized and statistically processed location data obtained from smartphone applications and mobile communication logs [15]. This has resulted in a surge of applications

© ICST Institute for Computer Sciences, Social Informatics and Telecommunications Engineering 2026
Published by Springer Nature Switzerland AG 2026. All Rights Reserved
A. Soylu et al. (Eds.): MobiQuitous 2024, LNICST 634, pp. 550–569, 2026.
https://doi.org/10.1007/978-3-032-10554-7_29

utilizing large-scale location data, with potential uses in trajectory analysis, planning, congestion analysis, public transportation optimization, urban development, disaster prevention, and tourism [16,24].

Large-scale location datasets have become increasingly available [1,15,22,24]. These anonymized datasets are typically aggregated by mobile network operators and location data businesses from multiple sources, including GPS logs, Wi-Fi and Bluetooth scans, and cellular network connections. The growth of location-based services and partnerships with popular smartphone applications, where users have granted location permissions, has significantly contributed to this data availability.

While these datasets offer valuable insights into broad-scale movement patterns, they present challenges in capturing fine-grained movements within specific areas. Privacy protection measures, such as data anonymization, intentional error introduction, and sample deletion, often render individual user trajectories indiscernible. Moreover, data collected through smartphone applications may have inconsistent sampling rates due to power-saving features and varying GPS accuracy in different environments. Despite these limitations, these datasets provide unprecedented opportunities for understanding human mobility at a large scale, making them invaluable for urban planning, transportation optimization, and location-based services [2]. However, their coarse granularity necessitates novel approaches to extract meaningful and accurate information for specific local areas.

To address these limitations, we propose a novel approach that combines wide-area, low-granularity location data with high-precision spot-level traffic measurements. This combination leverages the strengths of both data types: the wide coverage and accessibility of low-granularity location data, and the high accuracy of spot measurements, which can be selectively obtained in areas of interest to enhance precision. By integrating these complementary data sources, we aim to enhance the overall accuracy of pedestrian flow simulations.

This study explores a method to simulate pedestrian flows within an approximately $1\,\mathrm{km}^2$ area by estimating origins and destinations (OD) using low temporal resolution location data. The proposed method aggregates location data to Points of Interest (PoI) within the area and employs Gibbs sampling to obtain two-dimensional Gaussian Mixture Models (GMMs) for departure times from PoIs and travel times between PoI pairs. GMMs enable efficient representation of complex movement patterns while preserving essential features of the large-scale location data, while the Gibbs sampling approach allows for continuous updating of the distribution as observational data is updated in real-time, making our approach adaptable to changing mobility patterns.

In the simulator, sampling from these GMMs provides the necessary departure times and movement speeds for pedestrians (mobile agents) from each PoI. Additionally, we incorporate spot-level pedestrian count data measured by stationary LiDAR (Light Detection and Ranging) sensors at multiple locations within the target area to calibrate the simulation's population density. This calibration process involves adjusting the overall distribution of simulated pedestrians to match the actual numbers observed at sensor-equipped locations, thereby improving predictions for the entire area, including locations not directly monitored by sensors.

The method was applied to Wakayama Castle Park in central Wakayama City, Japan, using wide-area low-granularity location data and spot-level pedestrian count data from LiDAR at five locations within the park, collected over approximately one week in December 2023. Wakayama Castle Park, located in a satellite city of Osaka, features diverse attractions including a castle tower, museums, and a zoo, providing a complex environment for pedestrian flow analysis. Comparison between actual measurements and simulated pedestrian flows revealed high accuracy, with an average cosine similarity of population density distributions of about 0.8. Furthermore, comparing the number of visitors to the zoo in the Wakayama Castle Park, manually measured, with the number simulated using data that excluded this information, showed a population error of 13.6% over the measurement period.

## 2   Related Work

Pedestrian dynamics, including evacuation behavior, have been extensively studied in recent years. A comprehensive survey by Haghani et al. [2] outlines the multifaceted nature of pedestrian flow analysis and utilization. This field encompasses various technologies, including data collection, individual pedestrian behavior modeling, crowd modeling, and application services such as behavior analysis, evacuation simulations, and land development planning. Existing approaches typically implement some or all of these aspects from diverse perspectives.

In data collection, approaches often employ sensing through video or wireless communication. For instance, [9] proposes a real-time counting system for pedestrians and bicycles using WiFi and Bluetooth. Additionally, [18] presents a technique for estimating crowd density from video footage, introducing a novel architecture called Switching CNN that leverages crowd density variations in images to enhance crowd localization and density estimation accuracy. The authors conduct performance evaluations using large-scale datasets. Our research group has also been conducting pedestrian flow analysis using a large-scale LiDAR platform in buildings [14, 21]. Other studies have collected and provided behavioral data from actual pedestrians through field experiments [19], or generated synthetic image datasets for use as training data in machine learning applications [3].

Individual pedestrian behavior modeling has seen numerous approaches over the years. The Social Force Model (SFM) [6] remains a well-known and influential model in this domain. Other approaches include agent models incorporating leader-follower dynamics and collision avoidance mechanisms [17]. Multi-agent simulations using microscopic behavior models have gained significant traction [8, 10]. Recent research has also explored decision-making models using Cellular Automata [7]. For a more comprehensive overview of these models, readers may refer to the survey by Vermuyten et al. [20]. Additionally, Gao et al. [11] provide an analysis of pedestrian flow from a deep learning perspective.

In a parallel approach, Makinoshima et al. developed a Bayesian Behavioural Model Estimation method for live crowd simulations aimed at indoor and constrained environments where individual movements can be monitored in detail. Their method focuses on leveraging real-time, site-specific crowd data to update behavioral models dynamically, providing high accuracy in long-term crowd flow forecasting [13].

When using simulators to reproduce pedestrian flows as faithfully as possible to real domains, these technologies are typically employed comprehensively, adjusting pedestrian patterns to match observational data obtained through the aforementioned sensing methods. For example, [12] proposes a method to reproduce pedestrian flows by fitting them to observed density data at various spots and density-velocity functions.

Our study addresses the challenge of utilizing privacy-protected GPS data with coarse spatio-temporal granularity. While this data preserves approximate movement patterns between PoIs, it necessitates a novel approach to accurately reconstruct pedestrian flows. Our key contribution lies in developing a method that integrates this low-resolution data with high-precision spot-level traffic measurements, enabling faithful reproduction of pedestrian dynamics on given road networks and PoIs.

## 3   Mobility Dataset

This research utilizes two types of mobility data with distinct spatio-temporal granularities and characteristics to simulate and reproduce pedestrian flows.

### 3.1   Wide-Area Location Data

This study utilizes privacy-safe GPS data (hereafter referred to as the location dataset) that has been aggregated from a wide area and from an unspecified number of smartphones, and has been appropriately anonymized and abstracted [1]. This data is collected primarily through GPS sensors in smartphones, supplemented by Wi-Fi positioning and cellular network triangulation when GPS signals are unavailable. The data is obtained with user consent through multiple smartphone applications in Japan, covering a range of services such as weather forecasts, news apps, and location-based services.

In recent years, user location data has been actively used, primarily by private companies. For instance, mobile carriers collect such data using their base station information and smartphone applications, while location data businesses, which have become increasingly common recently, collect data through smartphone applications of affiliated companies.

In either case, due to sufficiently long aggregation periods and spatial safety measures (such as noise addition through differential privacy, data sample deletion in sparse areas through k-anonymization, abstraction through meshing,

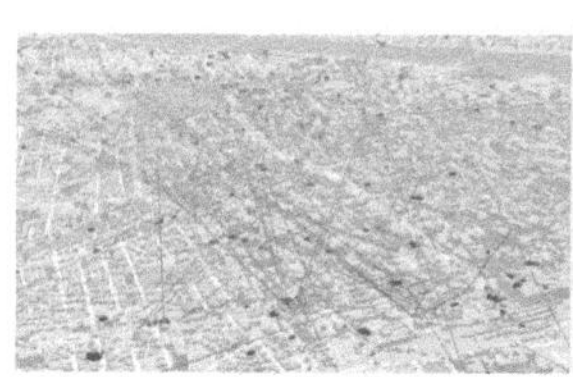
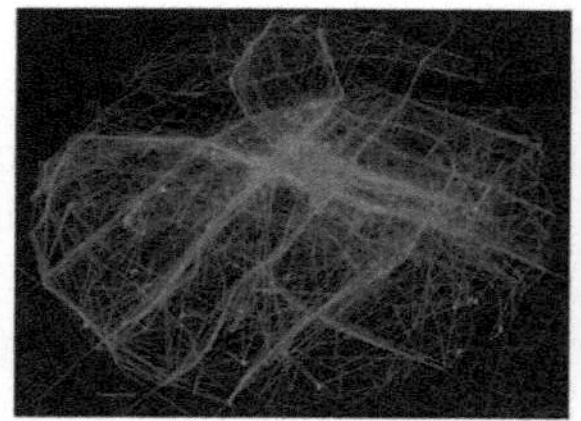
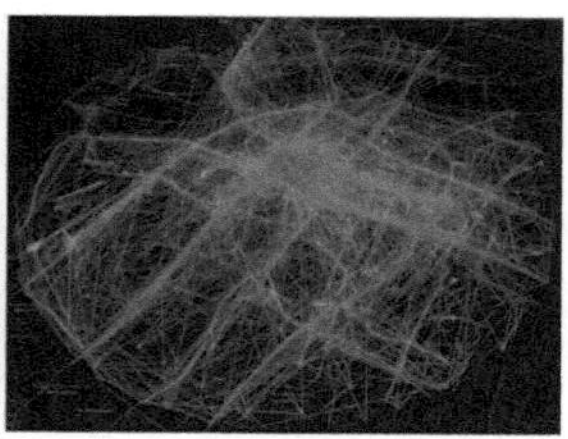

(a) Trajectories of four randomly selected users

(b) March 22, 2023 (typical day): 371 trajectories

(c) March 29, 2023 (peak visitor day): 679 trajectories

**Fig. 1.** Visualization of user trajectories: (a) Four randomly selected users over the entire data collection period, (b) and (c) Users visiting Wakayama Castle during the cherry blossom season.

etc.), the data is generally of very low granularity (for instance, if it's mesh data, the cell length is typically around one hundred to several hundred meters). While this low granularity poses challenges for direct reproduction of fine-grained human movements, it provides valuable insights into overall movement patterns within a given area.

The wide-area location dataset used in this study consists of a collection of records composed of tracking ID, latitude and longitude, and timestamp (to the second). We use data that passes through the central part of Wakayama City, Wakayama Prefecture, collected over two different periods.

One dataset was collected over a one-month period from March 18 to April 17, 2023, containing a total of 19,376,415 location records with 57,009 unique tracking IDs. The characteristics of this data are shown in Table 1 and Table 2. The tracking IDs are assigned based on certain identifiers related to users but do not represent unique users. The other dataset was collected over a one-month period from December 2, 2023, to January 1, 2024, containing a total of 15,772,338 records with 51,431 tracking IDs.

To illustrate the spatiotemporal distribution of the data, Fig. 1(a) shows the complete trajectories of four randomly selected users during the data collection period. In this figure, the trajectories of the four users are represented in blue, orange, purple, and green, respectively, allowing for a visual understanding of the visitation sequences at the PoI level.

Furthermore, to demonstrate the spatial range and volume of the data more clearly, Fig. 1 also visualizes the complete trajectories of users who visited Wakayama Castle Park on two specific days. Figure 1(b) shows the trajectories from March 22, 2023 (one week before the peak visitor season), while Fig. 1(c) displays the trajectories from March 29, 2023, which coincided with the peak visitor day during the cherry blossom viewing season, a major tourist attraction in Japan. The trajectory set in Fig. 1(c) is noticeably larger in volume and spread over a wider area centered around Wakayama Castle, reflecting the increased visitor numbers during this popular season.

**Table 1.** Distribution of Location Points per Tracking ID

| Metric | Value |
| --- | --- |
| mean | 339.9 |
| std | 1602.1 |
| min | 1 |
| 25% | 4.0 |
| 50% | 19.0 |
| 75% | 92.0 |
| max | 185068 |

**Table 2.** Distribution of Lifetime per Tracking ID

| Metric | Value |
| --- | --- |
| mean | 10 days 06:24:36 |
| std | 11 days 20:19:02.802025648 |
| min | 0 days 00:00:00 |
| 25% | 0 days 00:32:39 |
| 50% | 2 days 09:58:00 |
| 75% | 22 days 02:35:20 |
| max | 30 days 23:59:50 |

## 3.2 Spot Traffic Volume Data

In contrast to the wide-area location data discussed earlier, spot traffic volume data provides highly accurate, localized information about pedestrian movements. This type of data measures the number of people or vehicles passing through specific points and is often collected for traffic surveys and human flow analysis purposes. It is frequently gathered through manual counting or using devices such as infrared sensors, ultrasonic sensors, cameras, and LiDAR.

While spot traffic volume data offers high precision at specific locations, it lacks the extensive geographical coverage of wide-area location data. However, its accuracy makes it an invaluable complement to the broader, less granular wide-area data.

In this study, we installed LiDAR sensors at five locations within Wakayama Castle Park. These locations were chosen to cover the main pedestrian routes throughout the park, as shown in Fig. 2. The LiDAR devices were mounted on poles at a height of approximately 3 m above the ground and measurements were taken for 17 h daily, from 5 AM to 10 PM, over a period of 7 days from December 2 to 4 and December 8 to 11, 2023. We applied pedestrian detection and tracking methods [14, 21] to the 3D point clouds obtained by the LiDAR to aggregate the traffic volume (number of entrants and exits) at each spot.

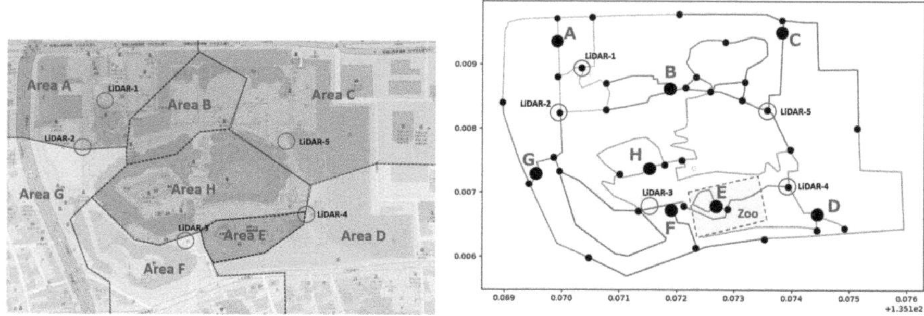


(a) Map of Wakayama Castle Park showing area divisions (A-H) and LiDAR sensor locations

(b) Road graph of the park with PoI A-H, walkable paths, and LiDAR sensor positions. The zoo area used for evaluation is highlighted with a red dashed rectangle

**Fig. 2.** Geographical representation and road graph of Wakayama Castle Park.

# 4 Method Overview and Preprocessing

## 4.1 Method Overview

This section presents our approach to simulating urban pedestrian flows by integrating sparse location data with pedestrian counts by LiDAR sensors. Our method extracts movement patterns from low-granularity location data and refines them using precise count data. The system input comprises wide-area location points, spot-level pedestrian counts, and geographical information including walkable paths and Points of Interest (PoIs). The output is a simulation scenario generating realistic pedestrian flows that align with both the broad patterns from location data and the accurate counts from count data. We begin with an overview of our method, followed by a detailed explanation of the data preprocessing steps.

Figure 2 presents the geographical representation and road graph of Wakayama Castle Park, the target area of this paper. Figure 2(b) illustrates the road graph with PoIs, walkable paths, and LiDAR sensor positions. The zoo area, highlighted with a red dashed rectangle, is used for evaluation purposes.

Our approach consists of four main steps: data preprocessing and segmentation, movement pattern extraction, initial simulation model generation, and model refinement. In the preprocessing stage, we transform raw location data into structured movement data based on PoIs. The movement pattern extraction step applies Gibbs sampling to estimate 2D GMMs for departure times and travel durations between PoI pairs, capturing the temporal patterns of pedestrian movements. The initial simulation model generation uses these estimated distributions to determine when agents should depart from each PoI and how long they should take to reach their destinations. Finally, the model refinement step adjusts the model to ensure consistency in arrival and departure numbers at each PoI and incorporates count data to improve accuracy.

## 4.2    Data Preprocessing

We now detail the data preprocessing steps, focusing on the location dataset. We define $L_{all}$ as the complete wide-area low-granularity location dataset, where each entry $i$ is represented as a tuple $(i.uid, i.lat, i.long, i.time)$. Here, $i.uid$ is the tracking ID, $i.lat$ is the latitude, $i.long$ is the longitude, and $i.time$ is the timestamp. From $L_{all}$, we extract a subset $L_{area}$ containing only the location points within the target area of Wakayama Castle Park. The geographical information of the target area is represented by a set of walkable paths $E$, as shown in Fig. 2(b). We define a set of PoI $P = p_1, p_2, ..., p_n$, which are key locations within the park such as the castle tower, gates, parking areas, and the zoo in the park. These PoIs serve as primary destinations or stay points for visitors. As shown in Fig. 2(b), the park is divided into a set of areas $A = \{A, B, ..., H\}$, with each PoI $p \in P$ associated with an area $a \in A$.

Our preprocessing of the location data begins with the identification of PoIs and the segmentation of the park into areas. We then process each location point in $L_{area}$. For each entry $i$, we perform map matching [23] to identify the nearest walkable path and associate each entry with an area and the nearest PoI, defining $i.area$ as the area containing the entry and $i.poi$ as the nearest PoI. This process utilizes the road network graph shown in Fig. 2(b), where nodes represent intersections or significant points, and edges represent actual walkable paths. To generate movement data, we consider consecutive entries $i$ and $next(i)$ with the same $i.uid$. We define a movement $m_i = (i.poi, next(i).poi, i.time, next(i).time - i.time)$, interpreting individual points as movements between PoIs. In the data cleaning phase, we remove outliers by excluding movements with durations exceeding three hours.

We then discretize the data to standardize its granularity. Departure times are discretized into 10-minute intervals, resulting in 144 slots per day, while movement durations are discretized into 1-minute intervals with a maximum of 180 min. The result of this preprocessing is a set of PoI-to-PoI movements $M$, where each movement $m \in M$ is represented as a tuple (departure PoI, arrival PoI, discretized departure time, discretized movement duration). This structured dataset serves as the foundation for generating a simulation scenario for pedestrian flow.

In the next stage of our method, we use this preprocessed data to extract movement patterns. For each pair of PoIs $p$ and $q$, we consider all movements $m_i$ where $i.poi = p$ and $next(i).poi = q$. We apply Gibbs sampling to estimate a two-dimensional GMM $G_{p,q}$ for the departure times and travel durations between $p$ and $q$. We also calculate $c_{p,q}$, the total number of movements from $p$ to $q$. These distributions and counts form the basis of our simulation model.

To generate agent behaviors in the simulation, we sample $c_{p,q}$ times from $G_{p,q}$ for each PoI pair $(p, q)$. This determines when pedestrians should depart from $p$ and how long they should take to reach $q$. However, this initial scenario may not accurately reflect real-world conditions, particularly at specific locations where we have pedestrian count data.

Therefore, in the final step of our method, we refine the simulation scenario using the count data. For each time slot, we calculate a single adjustment ratio based on the overall pedestrian flow across all LiDAR spots. We then apply this time-specific adjustment ratio to all movements in the scenario, ensuring that the simulated pedestrian flows better match the observed counts while maintaining the spatial distribution patterns derived from the location data. This approach allows us to correct for temporal discrepancies in the location data using the count data, without directly altering the estimated GMMs or individual PoI-to-PoI movement counts.

In the following sections, we will provide more detailed explanations of the movement pattern extraction, simulation scenario generation, and refinement processes.

## 5   Method Details

### 5.1   Predicting Pedestrian Flow Distributions Using Gibbs Sampling

This section elaborates on how we estimate the movement patterns between each pair of PoIs using the preprocessed data $M$ created in the preprocessing. We model these patterns as two-dimensional GMMs, capturing both departure times from the origin PoI and travel times to the destination PoI.

For each PoI pair $(p, q)$, we consider all movements $m_i \in M$ where $i.poi = p$ and $next(i).poi = q$. We then apply Gibbs sampling to estimate a GMM $G_{p,q}$ for the departure times and travel durations between $p$ and $q$.

Gibbs sampling allows for sequential estimation and updating of the GMM parameters, which is advantageous for datasets that are continuously updated and expanded in real-time. The process involves iteratively sampling the latent variable $z$ for each data point, indicating which Gaussian component generated that data, followed by sampling the mixture coefficients $\pi$, means $\mu$, and covariance matrices $\Sigma$ of the GMM.

To estimate the pedestrian flow distribution, we perform the following steps for each PoI pair $(p, q)$. First, we determine the number of Gaussian components $K$ in the mixture distribution from the pedestrian flow sample data. Then, we perform a fixed number of Gibbs sampling iterations to estimate the parameters of $G_{p,q}$.

Figure 3 illustrates the evolution of the Gibbs sampling process for a PoI pair with two distinct movement patterns. The x-axis represents the departure time from the origin PoI, and the y-axis represents the travel time to the destination PoI. As iterations progress, the estimated distribution increasingly reflects the two modes present in the data.

In each iteration of Gibbs sampling, we update the latent variable $z$ and the parameters of $G_{p,q}$: the mixing coefficients $\pi_k$, means $\mu_k$, and covariance matrices $\Sigma_k$ for each Gaussian component $k$. Below, we detail one iteration of Gibbs sampling for data $x$, with $n$ data points and $K$ clusters:

The iteration begins by calculating the probability $\eta_{i,k}$ that each data point $x_i$ was generated from Gaussian component $k$. This probability is proportional

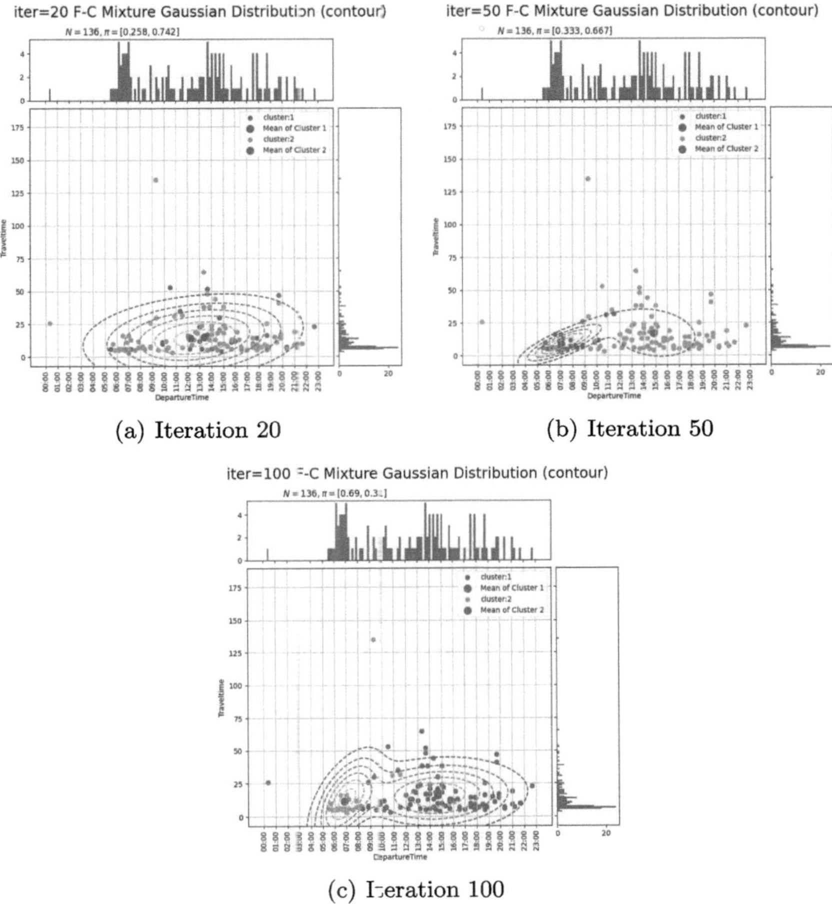

(a) Iteration 20

(b) Iteration 50

(c) Iteration 100

**Fig. 3.** Evolution of pedestrian flow distribution estimation using Gibbs sampling.

to the product of the mixing coefficient $\pi_k$ and the probability density of $x_i$ under the $k$-th Gaussian component, as shown in Eq. (1).

$$\eta_{i,k} \propto \pi_k \mathcal{N}(x_i | \boldsymbol{\mu}_k, \boldsymbol{\Sigma}_k) \tag{1}$$

We then normalize these probabilities to obtain a proper distribution over the $K$ components for each data point. Using these normalized probabilities (Eq. (2)), we sample the latent variable $z_i$ for each data point from a categorical distribution (Eq. (3)).

$$\eta_{i,k} = \frac{\eta_{i,k}}{\sum^{K} k' = 1 \eta i, k'} \tag{2}$$

$$z_i \sim \mathrm{Cat}(\boldsymbol{\eta}_i) \tag{3}$$

Next, we update the mixing coefficients $\pi_k$. We use a Dirichlet distribution as the prior, with parameter $\boldsymbol{\alpha} = (\alpha_1, \alpha_2, \ldots, \alpha_K)$. Equation (4) shows how we combine the observed information with the prior distribution parameters.

$$\alpha'k = n_k + \alpha k \tag{4}$$

Here, $n_k$ is the number of data points assigned to cluster $k$, $\alpha'k$ is the updated parameter, and $\alpha k$ is the prior distribution parameter. We then sample the mixing coefficients $\boldsymbol{\pi} = (\pi_1, \pi_2, \ldots, \pi_K)$ from the posterior distribution using the updated parameters, as shown in Eq. (5).

$$\boldsymbol{\pi} \sim \mathrm{Dirichlet}(\alpha_1', \alpha_2', \ldots, \alpha_K') \tag{5}$$

Following this, we update the cluster means $\mu_k$ and covariance matrices $\Sigma_k$. We use predefined hyperparameters $\beta_0$, $S_0$, $\mu_0$, and $\nu_0$, along with the data, to compute the updated parameters. Equations (6) through (9) demonstrate this process.

$$\beta_k = n_k + \beta_0 \tag{6}$$

$$\mu_k = \frac{\beta_0 \mu_0 + n_k \bar{x}_k}{\beta_0 + n_k} \tag{7}$$

$$S_k = S_0 + S_{\mathrm{data},k} + \frac{\beta_0 n_k}{\beta_0 + n_k}(\bar{x}_k - \mu_0)(\bar{x}_k - \mu_0)^T \tag{8}$$

$$\nu_k = n_k + \nu_0 \tag{9}$$

In these equations, $\bar{x}_k$ represents the sample mean of cluster $k$, and $S_{\mathrm{data},k}$ is the sample covariance matrix of the data points assigned to cluster $k$. $\beta_0$ is the prior sample size, $S_0$ is the prior scale matrix, $\mu_0$ is the prior mean, and $\nu_0$ is the prior degrees of freedom.

Finally, using these updated parameters, we sample new values for $\mu_k$ and $\Sigma_k$. Equations 10 and 11 show the sampling of the mean $\mu_k$ from a multivariate Gaussian distribution and the covariance matrix $\Sigma_k$ from an inverse Wishart distribution, respectively.

$$\boldsymbol{\mu}_k \sim \mathcal{N}(\mu_k, (\beta k \Sigma_k)^{-1}) \tag{10}$$

$$\boldsymbol{\Sigma}_k \sim \mathrm{Inverse\text{-}Wishart}(\boldsymbol{S}k, \nu_k) \tag{11}$$

We initialize the hyperparameters as follows: $\beta_0 = 1$, $S_0$ is set to the identity matrix, $\mu_0$ is a two-dimensional zero vector, and $\nu_0 = 2$ (the dimensionality of our data).

The use of GMM for modeling movement patterns offers several significant advantages. GMMs can effectively capture complex patterns that simple distributions cannot, such as multiple peaks representing different commute times.

They naturally account for uncertainties in location data and efficiently represent complex distributions with relatively few parameters. GMMs also provide interpretable results, as each Gaussian component can correspond to specific movement patterns like morning commutes or evening returns. Moreover, by using two-dimensional GMMs, we can capture correlations between departure times and travel durations, reflecting real-world phenomena like longer travel times during peak hours. This approach allows for efficient data compression and summarization, preserving essential features of large GPS datasets in a compact form. The flexibility of GMMs also enables easy extension of the model to incorporate additional variables or components as needed, making it a powerful tool for modeling diverse urban mobility scenarios.

## 5.2  Generating Simulation Scenarios from Estimated GMMs

We now describe the process of generating a simulation scenario using the GMM $G_{p,q}$ estimated for each PoI pair $(p, q)$ in the previous section.

The process begins with sampling from the estimated distributions. For each PoI pair $(p, q)$, we draw $c_{p,q}$ samples from $G_{p,q}$, where $c_{p,q}$ is the total number of movements from $p$ to $q$ in the original dataset $M$. Each sample $s_i = (t_i, d_i)$ is a pair consisting of a departure time $t_i$ and a travel duration $d_i$.

To align the scenario with typical simulation time steps, we discretize the continuous time values. The departure times $t_i$ are assigned to 10-minute time slots $T = \{1, 2, ..., 144\}$, representing the 144 10-minute intervals in a day. Similarly, the travel durations $d_i$ are discretized into 1-minute intervals $D = 1, 2, ..., 180$, allowing for a maximum travel time of 3 h (180 min). This upper limit is set based on the assumption that most pedestrian movements within our study area would not exceed this duration.

We then calculate movement speeds using the actual path distances between PoIs, rather than straight-line distances. For each sample $s_i$ between PoIs $p$ and $q$, we compute the speed $v_i$ as:

$$v_i = \frac{l_{p,q}}{d_i} \tag{12}$$

where $l_{p,q}$ is the actual distance between $p$ and $q$. These calculated speeds are then categorized into 11 discrete levels $V = 1.0, 1.4, ..., 5.0$ (km/h), covering typical walking speeds from very slow to brisk walking.

Using this processed information, we construct our simulation scenario $S$. For each time slot $t \in T$ and each PoI pair $(p, q)$, we generate a data entry:

$$S = \{n_{p,q,t,v} \mid p, q \in P, t \in T, v \in V\} \tag{13}$$

In Eq. (13), $n_{p,q,t}$ represents the total number of movements from $p$ to $q$ in time slot $t$, and $n_{p,q,t,v}$ denotes the number of pedestrians moving at speed $v$. Each element of this scenario represents the movement of individual agents (pedestrians) in the simulation. Specifically, $n_{p,q,t,v}$ indicates that $n$ agents will depart from point $p$ at time slot $t$, heading towards point $q$ with a speed of $v$. This scenario $S$ include the temporal and spatial patterns of pedestrian movements only based on the location data, providing a foundation for our urban pedestrian flow simulation.

### 5.3 Refining Simulation Scenarios Using Spot-Level Pedestrian Counts

After constructing the initial simulation scenario $S$, we perform a refinement step using the count data. To refine our scenario using the counts data, we introduce an adjustment step that considers the overall pedestrian flow across all LiDAR measurement points for each time slot. This step aims to correct potential temporal discrepancies in the location data while maintaining its broad spatial patterns. For each time slot $t$, we calculate a single adjustment ratio $r_t$:

$$r_t = \frac{\sum_{l \in L} L_{l,t}}{\sum_{l \in L} \sum_{p \in P_l} \sum_{q \in P} \sum_{v \in V} n_{p,q,t,v}} \tag{14}$$

In Eq. (14), $L_{l,t}$ represents the number of pedestrians observed by the LiDAR sensor at point $l$ during time slot $t$, and $P_l$ denotes the set of PoIs that contribute to the pedestrian flow past the LiDAR sensor at point $l$.

We then apply this time-specific adjustment ratio to create our refined scenario $S'$. For each PoI pair $(p, q)$ and time slot $t$, we compute:

$$S' = \{n'_{p,q,t,v} \mid p, q \in P, t \in T, v \in V\} \tag{15}$$

where $n'_{p,q,t,v}$ is calculated as:

$$n'_{p,q,t,v} = \lfloor r_t \cdot n_{p,q,t,v} \rfloor \tag{16}$$

This approach allows us to calibrate our simulated pedestrian flows based on the pedestrian counts while maintaining the spatial distribution patterns derived from our location data. By applying a uniform adjustment ratio across all locations for each time period, we correct for overall temporal discrepancies in the location data using count data. The resulting refined scenario $S'$ serves as the input for our pedestrian flow simulation, ensuring that the simulated flows accurately reflect both the broad patterns captured in the location data and the precise count data.

## 6  Evaluation

### 6.1 Simulation Setup and Movement Pattern Analysis

We implemented our proposed method using PTV Vissim [5] and Viswalk [4] to simulate pedestrian flows within Wakayama Castle Park, utilizing the datasets described in Sect. 3. Figure 4 shows a visualization of the simulation. The green areas represent PoIs, which serve as origin and destination points for pedestrian agents in the simulation.

**Fig. 4.** Visualization of pedestrian flow simulation within the park using VISSIM.

To evaluate the effectiveness of our proposed method, we conducted simulations using two scenarios: the initial simulation scenario $S$ (before adjustment with spot count data), and the refined scenario S' (after adjustment), as described in Sect. 5. This approach allows us to directly assess the effect of incorporating the spot count data on the accuracy of our pedestrian flow simulations. In this evaluation, the number of Gaussians ($K = 3$) and Gibbs sampling iterations (100) were determined based on empirical observations during our preliminary experiments. $K$ reflects typical movement patterns in urban parks, corresponding to major daily activities.

Figure 5 shows the estimated movement pattern distribution between PoIs A and B, while Fig. 6 displays the distribution between PoIs F and C. As seen in Fig. 6(b) the F-C route exhibits a bimodal pattern with peaks around 7 AM and 1 PM. This pattern likely reflects pedestrians crossing the park for commuting or lunchtime walks. In contrast, Fig. 5(b) shows a single peak after 2 PM for the A-B route, which is consistent with tourist visits to the castle tower.

## 6.2   Pedestrian Density Map Comparison

To initially evaluate our pedestrian flow simulation, we compared the simulated pedestrian movements with the original wide-area location data used to generate the simulation scenario. While this comparison primarily assesses the simulation's ability to reproduce the patterns in the training data, it provides valuable insights into the simulation's fidelity. A more rigorous evaluation using independent data is presented in the subsequent Sect. 6.3.

We constructed spatio-temporal pedestrian density maps for both the simulated and actual data. These maps represent the number of pedestrians in each of the eight defined areas (A through H) within Wakayama Castle Park for every hour from 6 AM to 10 PM.

We first analyzed the relative error between the simulated and actual pedestrian density map. For each area and each hour, we calculated the absolute

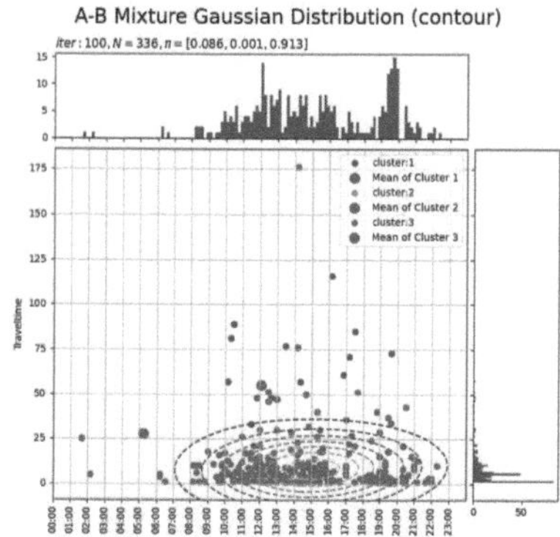
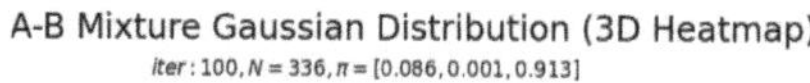
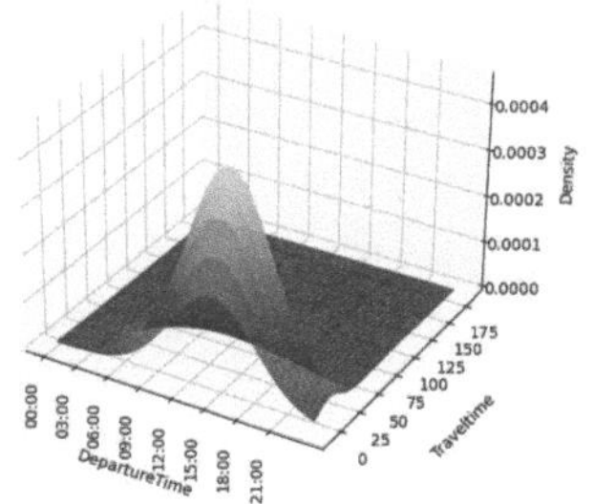

(a) 2D GMM distribution of departure times and travel durations

(b) 3D visualization of the estimated distribution

**Fig. 5.** Estimated pedestrian flow distribution between PoIs A and B.

difference between the simulated and actual counts, divided by the actual count. This metric helps identify specific times and locations where our simulation may be over- or under-estimating pedestrian numbers. Figure 7 presents a heatmap of these relative errors, both before and after adjusting our simulation using the spot traffic volume data. After incorporating count data, the average relative error decreased slightly from 0.81 to 0.79. More importantly, the error distribution became more uniform, indicating improved model consistency.

Next, we employed cosine similarity to measure the overall similarity in the distribution pattern of pedestrians across the park. For each hour, we treated the pedestrian counts across the eight areas as a vector and computed the cosine similarity between the simulated and actual vectors. This metric ranges from $-1$ to $1$, with 1 indicating perfect similarity in distribution patterns. Higher values suggest that our simulation accurately captures the relative distribution of pedestrians across different areas of the park, even if the absolute numbers might differ.

Figure 8 shows the hourly cosine similarity values over the course of the day, both before and after adjustment with the count data. After adjustment, the cosine similarity exceeded 0.8 for 10 h of the day, indicating a high degree of similarity between simulated and actual pedestrian distributions for most of the measurement period.

Our analysis revealed an intriguing pattern in the simulation accuracy across different times of day. While the overall accuracy improved after incorporating count data, we observed increased discrepancies during early morning and late night hours. This is evident in both the cosine similarity (Fig. 8) and relative error (Fig. 7) metrics. We attribute this phenomenon primarily to the varying sample sizes throughout the day. As a popular tourist destination, Wakayama Castle Park experiences significantly higher foot traffic during daytime hours, providing robust data for our model. However, the substantially lower pedestrian

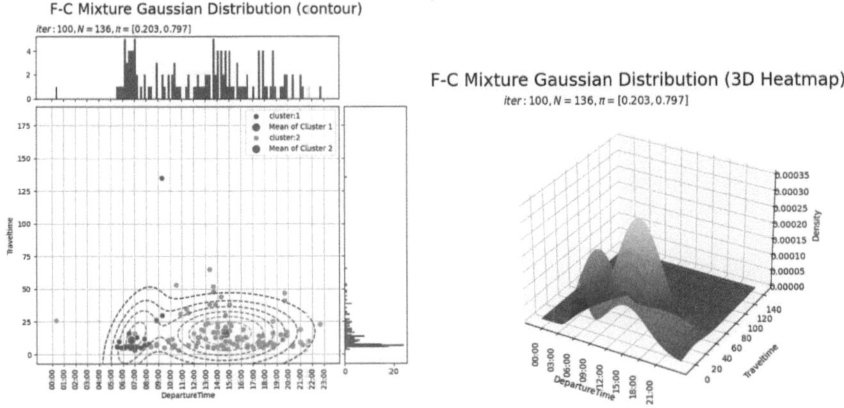

(a) 2D GMM distribution of departure times and travel durations

(b) 3D visualization of the estimated distribution

**Fig. 6.** Estimated pedestrian flow distribution between PoIs F and C.

counts during early morning and late night periods result in smaller sample sizes, making our similarity metrics more sensitive to minor discrepancies.

### 6.3   Visitor Count Prediction

To rigorously assess the accuracy of our pedestrian flow simulation, we conducted an evaluation using the same datasets described in Sect. 3, focusing on a critical area within Wakayama Castle Park that was not directly measured by our LiDAR sensors nor used in the simulation's calibration process. Specifically, we concentrated on the Wakayama Castle Zoo, an enclosed area within the park that serves as an independent validation point for our model.

We compared the simulated visitor numbers with actual counts at the zoo over a seven-day period from December 2–4 and December 8–11, 2023. This approach allows us to evaluate how well our model reproduces pedestrian flows in areas without direct measurement input, providing a robust test of its accuracy and generalization capabilities. The actual visitor count was measured by the staff of the zoo within the park.

Table 3 presents the comparison between the actual average daily visitor count and our simulated results.

For the Wakayama Castle Zoo, the actual average daily visitor count over the seven-day period was 1,306. Our simulation using only wide-area location data reproduced an average of 391 visitors per day, resulting in a substantial error of 70.1%. However, our proposed approach, which combines wide-area location data with count data from other areas of the park, significantly improved the reproduction to 1,129 visitors per day, reducing the error to just 13.6%. The error rate was calculated as the absolute difference between the simulated and actual values, divided by the actual value, expressed as a percentage.

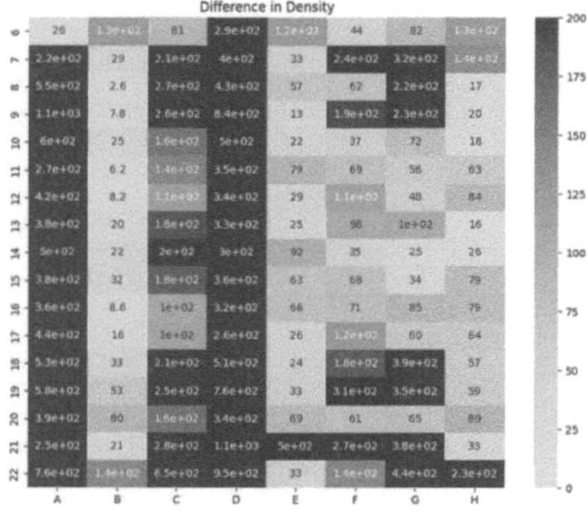

(a) Without adjustment using spot traffic volume data

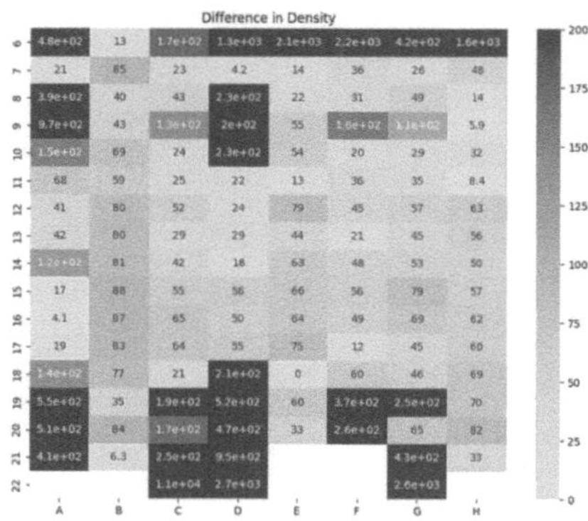

(b) With adjustment using spot traffic volume data

**Fig. 7.** Relative error between actual and simulated pedestrian counts at each PoI. The color intensity represents the magnitude of the error, with darker red indicating larger discrepancies between simulated and actual counts. (Color figure online)

**Table 3.** Daily visitor numbers for Wakayama Castle Zoo: Actual vs. Simulated

| | Actual | Simulated | |
|---|---|---|---|
| | | w/o spot-level counts | w/ spot-level counts |
| Visitors | 1,306 | 391 | 1,129 |
| Error (%) | – | 70.1 | 13.6 |

The significant improvement in simulation accuracy for the zoo area, which was not directly measured by our LiDAR sensors, demonstrates the effectiveness of our method in integrating different data sources. Location data, while providing broad coverage of movement patterns across the entire park, lacks precise scale information due to its coarse spatial granularity. It effectively captures the overall "shape" of pedestrian flows but fails to accurately represent the actual number of visitors. This explains the large error (70.1%) when using location data alone.

On the other hand, LiDAR sensors offer highly accurate pedestrian counts at specific locations. By integrating these precise measurements with the location data, our method effectively calibrates the scale of the movement patterns. This calibration process adjusts the overall distribution of visitors to match the actual numbers observed at LiDAR-equipped locations, indirectly improving predictions for areas not directly monitored by the sensors.

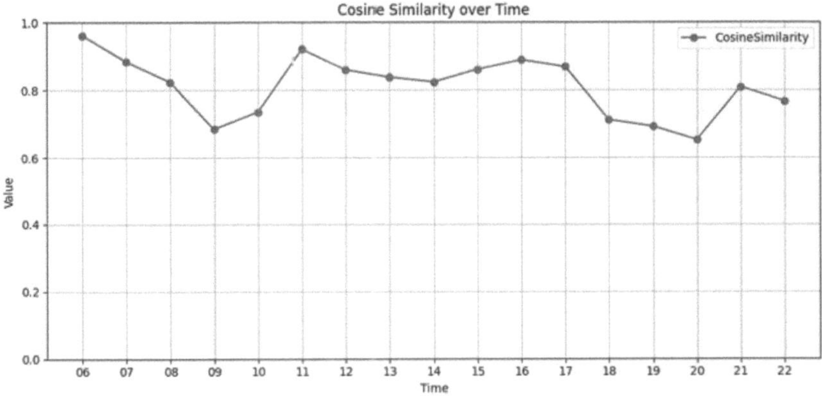

(a) Without adjustment using spot-level counts

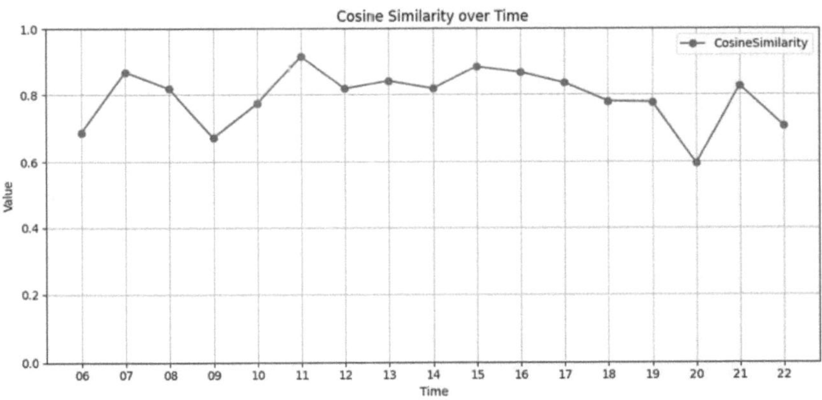

(b) With adjustment using spot-level counts

**Fig. 8.** Cosine similarity of population density map over time.

## 7   Conclusion

Our study demonstrates the effectiveness of integrating sparse location data with spot-level pedestrian count data to simulate urban pedestrian flows. The proposed method significantly improved the accuracy of visitor count predictions, reducing the error rate from 70.1% to 13.6% for the Wakayama Castle Zoo area.

However, it's important to acknowledge the inherent limitations of our approach. Our method relies on historical data patterns and is not designed to account for sudden, unpredictable events or rapid changes in pedestrian behavior. It cannot adapt in real-time to unexpected situations such as spontaneous gatherings or emergencies. Future work should focus on developing more adaptive models that can incorporate real-time data and respond to dynamic changes in urban environments. Additionally, extending the study to diverse urban settings and longer time periods would help validate the method's broader applicability. Despite these limitations, our approach shows promise in improving pedestrian flow predictions for typical scenarios, offering valuable insights for urban planning and event management under normal conditions.

**Acknowledgement.** This work was partially funded by NICT Commission Research 22608 and JST PRESTO Grant JPMJPR2361.

# References


1. Blogwatcher, I.: Blogwatcher location data (2024). https://www.blogwatcher.co.jp/. Accessed 20 Aug 2024
2. Dong, H., Zhou, M., Wang, Q., Yang, X., Wang, F.Y.: State-of-the-art pedestrian and evacuation dynamics. IEEE Trans. Intell. Transp. Syst. **21**(5), 1849–1866 (2020). https://doi.org/10.1109/TITS.2019.2915014
3. Fabbri, M., et al.: Motsynth: how can synthetic data help pedestrian detection and tracking? In: Proceedings of the 2021 IEEE/CVF International Conference on Computer Vision (ICCV 2021), pp. 10829–10839 (2021). https://doi.org/10.1109/ICCV48922.2021.01067. https://doi.ieeecomputersociety.org/10.1109/ICCV48922.2021.01067
4. Group, P.: Pedestrian simulation software PTV viswalk (2024). https://www.ptvgroup.com/en/products/pedestrian-simulation-software-ptv-viswalk. Accessed 20 Aug 2024
5. Group, P.: Traffic simulation software PTV vissim (2024). https://www.ptvgroup.com/en/products/ptv-vissim. Accessed 20 Aug 2024
6. Helbing, D., Molnár, P.: Social force model for pedestrian dynamics. Phys. Rev. E **51**, 4282–4286 (1995). https://doi.org/10.1103/PhysRevE.51.4282. https://link.aps.org/doi/10.1103/PhysRevE.51.4282
7. Huang, R., Zhao, X., Yuan, Y., Yu, Q., Liu, C., Daamen, W.: Modeling pedestrian tactical and operational decisions under risk and uncertainty: A two-layer model framework. IEEE Trans. Intell. Transp. Syst. **24**(5), 5259–5281 (2023). https://doi.org/10.1109/TITS.2023.3237335
8. Kaziyeva, D., Stutz, P., Wallentin, G., Loidl, M.: Large-scale agent-based simulation model of pedestrian traffic flows. Comput. Environ. Urban Syst. **105**, 102021 (2023). https://doi.org/10.1016/j.compenvurbsys.2023.102021. https://www.sciencedirect.com/science/article/pii/S0198971523000844
9. Lesani, A., Miranda-Moreno, L.: Development and testing of a real-time wifi-bluetooth system for pedestrian network monitoring, classification, and data extrapolation. IEEE Trans. Intell. Transp. Syst. **20**(4), 1484–1496 (2019). https://doi.org/10.1109/TITS.2018.2854895
10. Liu, S., Lo, S., Ma, J., Wang, W.: An agent-based microscopic pedestrian flow simulation model for pedestrian traffic problems. IEEE Trans. Intell. Transp. Syst. **15**(3), 992–1001 (2014). https://doi.org/10.1109/TITS.2013.2292526
11. Luca, M., Barlacchi, G., Lepri, B., Pappalardo, L.: A survey on deep learning for human mobility **55**(1) (2021). https://doi.org/10.1145/3485125
12. Maeda, K., Uchiyama, A., Umedu, T., Yamaguchi, H., Yasumoto, K., Higashino, T.: Urban pedestrian mobility for mobile wireless network simulation. Ad Hoc Netw. **7**(1), 153–170 (2009). https://doi.org/10.1016/j.adhoc.2008.01.002. https://www.sciencedirect.com/science/article/pii/S1570870508000048

13. Makinoshima, F., Takahashi, T., Oishi, Y.: Bayesian behavioural model estimation for live crowd simulation. In: Proceedings of the 23rd International Conference on Autonomous Agents and Multiagent Systems (AAMAS 2024), pp. 1355–1362. Richland, SC (2024)

14. Ohno, M., Ukyo, R., Amano, T., Rizk, H., Yamaguchi, H.: Privacy-preserving pedestrian tracking using distributed 3D lidars. In: Proceedings of the 2023 IEEE International Conference on Pervasive Computing and Communications (PerCom 2023), pp. 43–52 (2023). https://doi.org/10.1109/PERCOM56429.2023.10099061

15. Pepe, E., et al.: Covid-19 outbreak response, a dataset to assess mobility changes in Italy following national lockdown. Sci. Data **7** (2020). https://doi.org/10.1038/s41597-020-00575-2

16. Po, L., Rollo, F., Bachechi, C., Corni, A.: From sensors data to urban traffic flow analysis. In: 2019 IEEE International Smart Cities Conference (ISC2), pp. 478–485 (2019). https://doi.org/10.1109/ISC246665.2019.9071639

17. Robin, T., Antonini, G., Bierlaire, M., Cruz, J.: Specification, estimation and validation of a pedestrian walking behavior model. Transp. Res. Part B: Methodol. **43**(1), 36–56 (2009). https://doi.org/10.1016/j.trb.2008.06.010. https://www.sciencedirect.com/science/article/pii/S0191261508000763

18. Sam, D., Surya, S., Babu, R.: Switching convolutional neural network for crowd counting. In: Proceedings of the 2017 IEEE Conference on Computer Vision and Pattern Recognition (CVPR), pp. 4031–4039 (2017). https://doi.org/10.1109/CVPR.2017.429. https://doi.ieeecomputersociety.org/10.1109/CVPR.2017.429

19. Shahhoseini, Z., Sarvi, M., Saberi, M.: Pedestrian crowd dynamics in merging sections: revisiting the "faster-is-slower" phenomenon. XXPhys. A **491**, 101–111 (2018). https://doi.org/10.1016/j.physa.2017.09.003

20. Solmaz, G., Turgut, D.: A survey of human mobility models. IEEE Access **7**, 125711–125731 (2019). https://doi.org/10.1109/ACCESS.2019.2939203

21. Ukyo, R., Amano, T., Rizk, H., Yamaguchi, H.: Pedestrian tracking using 3D lidars – case for proximity scenario. In: Proceedings of the 2023 IEEE International Conference on Intelligent Transportation Systems (ITSC), p. 6 (2023)

22. Xie, P., Li, T., Liu, J., Du, S., Yang, X., Zhang, J.: Urban flow prediction from spatiotemporal data using machine learning: a survey. Inf. Fusion **59**, 1–12 (2020). https://doi.org/10.1016/j.inffus.2020.01.002. https://www.sciencedirect.com/science/article/pii/S1566253519303094

23. Yang, C., Gidofalvi, G.: Fast map matching, an algorithm integrating hidden Markov model with precomputation. Int. J. Geogr. Inf. Sci. **32**(3), 547–570 (2018). https://doi.org/10.1080/13658816.2017.1400548

24. Zhang, H., Zheng, Y., Yu, Y.: Detecting urban anomalies using multiple spatio-temporal data sources. Proc. ACM Interact. Mob. Wearable Ubiquitous Technol. **2**(1) (2018). https://doi.org/10.1145/3191786

# MDMV: A Malware Detection Method Based on Memory and Visualization on KVM


Xiangyi Wang[1,2,3,4], Jian Zhang[1,2,3,4(✉)], Lexin Jia[1,3,4], Zheng Meng[1,3,4], and Lingkai Xing[1,3,4]

[1] College of Cyber Science, Nankai University, Tianjin, China
`zhang.jian@nankai.edu.cn`
[2] College of Computer Science, Nankai University, Tianjin, China
[3] Tianjin Key Laboratory of Network and Data Security Technology, Tianjin, China
[4] Key Laboratory of Data and Intelligent System Security, Ministry of Education, Tianjin, China



**Abstract.** Malware keeps evolving and becomes more dangerous and harmful. Meanwhile, anti-analysis malware and evasive malware also increased, that caused traditional analysis platforms and detection methods gradually reduce their effectiveness. To solve these problems, we propose a malware detection method based on memory and visualization on Kernel-based Virtual Machine (KVM) called MDMV. MDMV employs KVM as the analysis platform, and dumps the physical memory of the virtual machine (VM) into snapshot files out of VM, which can capture the malware's footprint in memory. Then MDMV extracts and converts a key part of the dumped memory file to a grayscale image through Simhash, and utilizes local binary patterns (LBP) to further extract image features. These images are used to train a ResNet18 model enhanced with a self-attention module. Malware has difficulty disguising its footprint in the memory when it is running, therefor MDMV can resistant to evasive malware. MDMV exhibits strong transparency, security, and the ability to detect sophisticated malware. The best accuracy result on the experiment can reach 99.56% on our dataset, which samples are mainly collected from VirusShare. MDMV also has the ability to distinguish different malware families.

**Keywords:** malware detection · out-of-VM · KVM · memory snapshot · visualization · self-attention


## 1 Introduction

The continuously evolving malware presents a significant threat to computer systems. Malware often exploits vulnerabilities in computer systems, which carry out malicious activities and gain illegal financial benefits. Additionally, the evolution and diversity of malware variants have increased with maliciously used


© ICST Institute for Computer Sciences, Social Informatics and Telecommunications Engineering 2026
Published by Springer Nature Switzerland AG 2026. All Rights Reserved
A. Soylu et al. (Eds.): MobiQuitous 2024, LNICST 634, pp. 570–590, 2026.
https://doi.org/10.1007/978-3-032-10554-7_30

artificial intelligence (AI) technologies [12]. Every day, the AV-TEST Institute registers over 450,000 new malware [2]. The rapid technological evolution led to malware becoming increasingly sophisticated, diverse, and challenging to detect. Therefore, identifying malware quickly and accurately plays a critical role in cybersecurity.

Malware detection methods can be categorized into static and dynamic detection based on whether the malware is running during the feature extraction. Static detection methods do not require to execute malware and support rapid scanning. They concentrate on static features of malware such as MD5 values, byte sequences, assembly instructions, opcodes, etc. [1]. The combination of machine learning and deep learning has improved the efficacy of static detection. However, latest research indicated that some malware are designed to circumvent static detection. They can change the syntax and semantic information of their malicious code, encrypt or pack executable files [18], which makes them hard to be recognized. Additionally, some malware introduce random or constructed noise into their code [3], evading detection and degrading the performance of the detection model. Fileless malware also poses a challenge to traditional security measures, as they can only be captured and analyzed during their execution, which static analysis cannot achieve [13].

Dynamic detection methods require the execution of malware within a controlled, monitored environment. Many of them use sandboxes to trace dynamic characteristics, such as system calls, network, registry, file system, etc. [23]. Illegal and sensitive processes cannot fully hide their malicious behavior during execution, hence dynamic methods are more resistant than static methods. However, several malware have evolved countermeasures targeting dynamic detection [4]. They detect and analyze the environment during their execution to determine if they are in a sandbox, and may choose to terminate, suspend or modify their behavior accordingly. Some malware delay the execution of their malicious payload to evade immediate detection [6]. Additionally, some malware insert extraneous calls in their API invocation sequences, in order to disrupt the API calls fingerprint and evade detection [24]. These challenges necessitate more reliable and tamper-resistant dynamic features.

Some researchers adopted the approach of dumping the memory of processes in the operating system (OS), and converting them into images to determine whether they are malicious [13,19]. However, these forensic tools acquire memory in the same environment with the OS and applications, that can be interfered by malware [4]. Other dynamic analysis methods analyze the operating system's volatile memory acquired out of VM, without relying on in-guest components. They require memory dump files that contain the data stored in virtual or physical memory, and then reveal relevant features from the file [22]. Malware can not be implemented without leaving a footprint in memory, so these methods perform well in malware detection. However, they require a certain level of understanding of the current operating system, which diminishes the robustness of the method.

In this article, we propose a dynamic malware detection method called MDMV. It utilizes the KVM virtualization platform as an analysis platform, which offers isolation between VMs and the host. MDMV dumps the complete memory of the guest virtual machine out of VM, ensuring transparency by residing completely outside the guest OS. It utilizes the key part of the dumped memory as the footprint of malware, and applies visualization technology for obtained memory, implementing dimensionality reduction and feature extraction. First, MDMV executes a sample in the virtual machine, then utilizes libvirt to create a snapshot file of the VM's physical memory, like taking an X-ray for the current memory. Then MDMV obtains the key part of dumped memory that contains characteristics that reflect the VM's state. The obtained key memory is converted to a grayscale image through Simhash, and MDMV utilizes LBP to further extract features of the image. The acquired LBP images are used to train an improved ResNet18 model with a self-attention module, which can detect malicious samples. Experiments demonstrated that MDMV can effectively detect malware and categorize malware families. The main contributions are as follows:

1. We propose malware detection method based on KVM called MDMV. MDMV utilizes KVM as a memory snapshot platform to obtain the VM's physical memory. This method obtains memory out of VM without specific information of the virtual machine, and exists transparency, security and the ability to detect sophisticated malware.
2. MDMV extracts key parts of the memory and proposes a visualization method for them. It utilizes Simhash to generate fingerprints of the extracted key memory, and maps these fingerprints to grayscale images. It achieved dimensionality reduction and data standardization of memory snapshot file, effectively reducing the consumption, which demonstrates a balance of efficiency and capability.
3. MDMV utilizes LBP feature extraction method to enhance the origin Simhash image features, and improves ResNet18 model by adding a self-attention module. Experiments show that MDMV achieved good results in malware detection and family classification.

The organization of this paper is as follows: Sect. 2 introduces related studies with MDMV. Section 3 describes the architecture and workflow of MDMV. Section 4 presents the experimental results, and Sect. 5 summarizes this paper and discusses future work.

## 2   Related Work

### 2.1   Static Detection and Dynamic Detection

In the early stage of the research, Shafiq et al. [25] proposed a malware detection framework called PE Miner, which extracted structural features from PE files and used these features to identify malware. Subsequent researches have employed additional static features for malware detection, and the employment of AI technology enables processing increased number of features. Li et al. [16] proposed a method based on multimodal fusion and weight self-learning. They generated effective features by fusing multiple modalities of malware, such as byte, format, statistic, and semantic features. However, static detection methods are often limited in identifying metamorphic and polymorphic malware since they depend on known features and signatures [1]. There also exist techniques for generating adversarial malware, which can rapidly generate adversarial malware variants [15]. Static detections struggle to identify these samples.

Malware need to execute their malicious behaviors to launch attacks, and dynamic methods can capture the behavioral characteristics of malware. The Cuckoo sandbox is a widely utilized tool, which enabling researchers to gather dynamic features of malware. Zhang et al. [32] utilized Cuckoo to run samples and extracted content, strings and other information from collected API call sequences. They applied a hybrid CNN and LSTM model for detection. Further more, Zhang et al. [31] designed APIGRAPH to automatically extract API knowledge from API documentation. This knowledge was integrated into their malware detection models, effectively mitigating the problem of model aging and addressing the constantly evolving landscape of malware. However, these researches rely heavily on the report of the sandbox, and anti-sandbox samples may not perform their real behavior in Cuckoo to evade detection. There also exists black-box attacks against API sequences based malware detections [5].

## 2.2  Visualization

Some malware detection methods require a certain level of expertise in feature engineering and domain knowledge. To simplify the detection process, the incorporation of visualization has gradually increasing. In 2010, Conti et al. [8] proposed a method for converting binary fragments into grayscale images. It is regarded as the foundation of visualization in malware detection. Based on this idea, Vasan et al. [26] applied a color map and transformed malware binary files into color images. Their method was called IMCFN, and demonstrated that using color images to detect malware is more effective than using grayscale images. Ni et al. [20] proposed a malware classification algorithm called MCSC (Malware Classification using Simhash and CNN). MCSC disassembled malware to obtain their opcode sequences, then used Simhash to generate their fingerprints. Images were generated through Simhash values and standardized through bilinear interpolation. A CNN model was used to classify these images, effectively enhancing opcode sequence features through Simhash and visualization techniques. The trend of visualization is observed in both static and dynamic detection approaches. In dynamic detection, the application of visualization in memory-based methods is more prevalent. This aspect will be discussed in the next subsection.

## 2.3  Memory-Based Detection

System memory is a valuable repository of information regarding the state of a computer system. Details such as run processes, loaded libraries, and opened files can all be found in memory, that can be used for malware detection. In the early 21st century, memory forensics technologies emerged, that primarily analyze Windows systems' features such as the registry, system call table, Eprocess structures, etc. Volatility [29] is one of the most popular tools in this field. It supports analyzing memory dump files collected in various formats, and loading plugins for malware detection. However, implementing these functions requires semantic reconstruction, which necessitates prior knowledge of storage structures and the operating system. Moreover, the memory's address space structures of different architectures and different operating systems need to be given in advance, and adding new operating systems requires manual creation of their profiles.

To enhance the robustness of proposed method, Naeem et al. [19] dumped the processes's memory in the guest VM, and converted them into images. They utilized a CNN model to analyze the structural and statistical textural features of these images, and the outputs of the model were used to train a multilayer perceptron (MLP) model. They also employed an explainable AI-based approach for interpreting the model results, thereby enhancing their credibility. Dai et al. [9] converted malicious EFI memory files into grayscale images. To standardize these images for analysis, they employed bicubic interpolation, and used histograms of oriented gradients to extract image features. Their method showed that feature extractions are helpful for detecting images that are converted by malware. These methods gain the target processes in the memory, that contributes to more efficient detection with reduced resource consumption. However, their approach obtains process memory from in-guest, which makes it difficult for them to catch evasive malware, posing risks to integrity and reliability [30].

Capturing memory out of VM is a more effective strategy for malware detection. Landman et al. [14] proposed Deep-Hook, which obtained the volatile memory of the VM running on VirtualBox, and transformed byte sequences of whole volatile memory into an ARGB (alpha, red, green, blue) array to form images. The color images were used to train a CNN model. Later, Zheng et al. [33] proposed a visualized memory change area dimensionality reduction (VMCADR) method. They applied a memory difference algorithm to obtain the memory changed area, then used visualization technology to process memory change area files into grayscale images and RGB images for further classification. However, these approaches involve in reducing the entire VM's memory file, resulting in significant features loss, and may be influenced by similar or redundant regions. We believe that using information-rich areas for detection is a more effective approach.

# 3   Proposed Method

## 3.1   Overview

We propose a dynamic malware detection method called MDMV, which utilizes KVM as an analysis platform. This virtualization platform provides an isolation environment for the execution of samples and the acquisition of memory, avoiding interference from malware. Different from other memory-based detection methods, MDMV concentrates on the malware's influence on memory rather than targeting specific memory areas of processes. It does not require semantic information, nor does it need to hook or track the target program in memory. MDMV also effectively reduces the size of the generated memory dump and standardizes them to a uniform size for training.

The overflow of MDMV is shown in Fig. 1. In step 1, it runs the sample in VM. In step 2, it utilizes libvirt to get the dumped memory file of the whole VM on the memory snapshot platform. Then in step 3, MDMV extracts the key parts of the memory dump file, and converts them to grayscale image through Simhash in step 4. The image generates LBP image through feature extraction in step 5. Then MDMV repeats steps 1–5 and collects LBP images from different samples. The proposed deep learning model is trained by these images in step 6, and distinguishes images belong to malware in step 7.

## 3.2   Memory Data and Image Representation

On the KVM platform, the guest VM's virtual address is mapped to its physical address through a page table saved by CR3 register. This mapping often involves second-level address translation with shadow page table (SPT) or extended page table (EPT). It is a challenge for us to know the specific content in each virtual address without semantic reconstruction or process tracing. We extract a part of the memory area with distinguishable information to detect malware.

The memory dump file of a KVM virtual machine is stored in ELF format, and sequentially organized by the ELF header, program header for notes (PT_NOTE), memory, etc., as shown in Fig. 2. In memory, a standard page size is 4kb, and we analyze each page as a unit. Through analysis and experiments, we discovered that the initial portion of the memory dump file is information-rich, making it an effective choice as the key segment reflecting memory behavior. Our experiments have confirmed this observation. To avoid redundant information from the ELF header, we opted to use 16 MB of data starting from the 8th page of the memory dump for subsequent analysis.

Conti. et al. [8] made malware binary read as vectors of 8-bit unsigned integers and organized them into a 2D array. Based on this idea, we similarly processed the selected binary memory into a grayscale image. However, a challenge arised due to the large size of these grayscale images. Utilizing such large images for malware detection consumes considerable time and resources for model training. A similar issue raised at the method of converting binary data into RGB images [4]. Relevant experiment results are shown in Sect. 4. There is a need

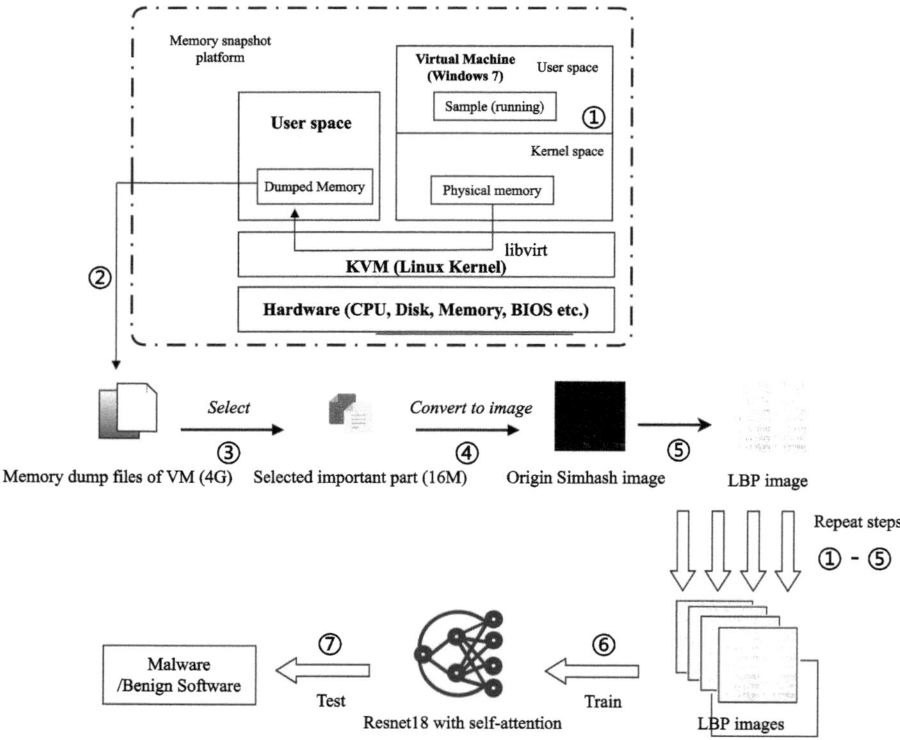


**Fig. 1.** Overflow of MDMV.

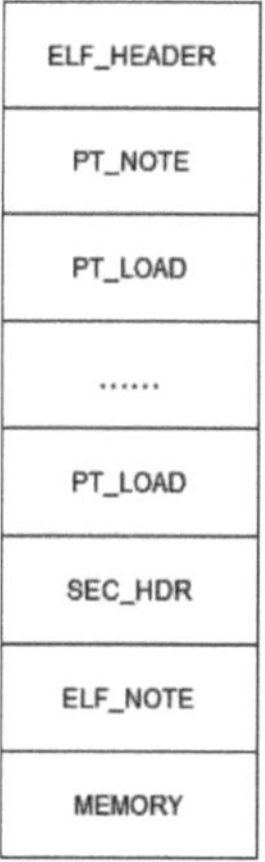


**Fig. 2.** The structure of dumped memory.

to explore alternative methods to describe the selected memory. The method should preserve features as much as possible without losing crucial information, and reduce the overall consumption.

Simhash is a locality-sensitive hashing algorithm used to compute hash values for data, enabling the assessment of similarity between them. Similar texts have a higher probability of being mapped to similar Simhash values. The Simhash algorithm can effectively achieve data dimensionality reduction while preserving key data features.

While other methods apply Simhash for extracting extract features in malware opcode sequences [20], MDMV employs Simhash to extract features of the binary sequence of the memory file, and then map the Simhash value into an grayscale image. Algorithm 1 describes how to extract the features from the binary file with Simhash and reflect the values to image. For each 1 KB of data in the selected memory snapshot, MDMV gets its SimHash value, and processes the value to produce a data pair $(x, y)$, where the values for $x$ and $y$ range from 0 to 255 as the horizontal and vertical coordinates of the image. This program is shown in Fig. 3. Figure 4(a) presents an example of Simhash grayscale image, which contains 16 MB data from the dumped memory. The generated grayscale image offers a detailed and streamlined depiction of the memory.

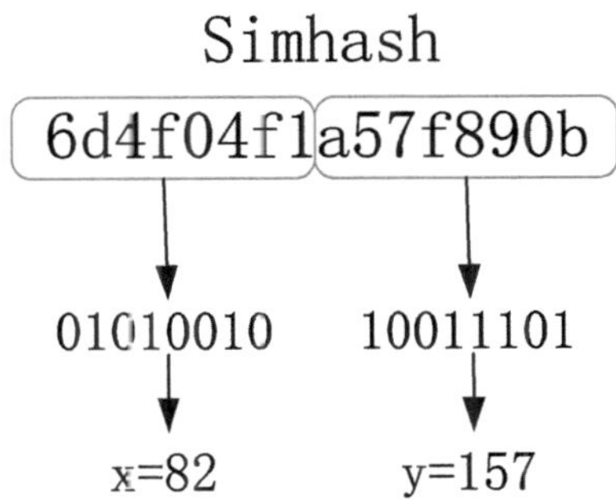


**Fig. 3.** Determining the horizontal and vertical coordinates in the image.

Our approach has achieved significant improvements compared to other methods that involve comparing the entire memory of the virtual machine. Table 1 offers a comparation for the average size of images and time consumption of different methods. VMCADR [33] compares the entire memory of the VM, which typically requires a considerable duration to generate the memory change area file. Its extended time is primarily due to the exhaustive memory comparison process. In contrast, MDMV generates a grayscale image mapped via Simhash in just around 24 s. The majority of its time consumption is dedicated to calculating the Simhash value.

---

**Algorithm 1.** Generate grayscale image with Simhash

---

**Require:** Memory dump file
**Ensure:** Grayscale image of size $256 \times 256$
 1: Initialize a two-dimensional int array *Image* with size of $256 \times 256$
 2: Read 16MB data orderly from the memory dump file after 7th page as sequence *Base*
 3: **for** each 1024 bytes(1 KB) sequence $S$ in *Base* **do**
 4:     Convert $S$ to a 1024-size ASCII string $S_a$. Every 8 ASCII characters of $S_a$ constitute a substring, and $S_a$ includes 128 substrings
 5:     Count the number of occurrences of every substring and assign weights
 6:     Use the MD5 algorithm to calculate the hash value of each substring of $S_a$, and get 64-bit hash $S_1,S_2,...S_n$
 7:     Initialize n 64-bit vector $T_1,T_2,...T_n$ with each bit of every vector to 0
 8:     **for** i **in** n **do**
 9:       **for** bit **in** $S_i$ **do**
10:         **if** the bit==1 **then**
11:           add the weight of the substring in $T_i$'s corresponding bit
12:         **else**
13:           subtract the weight of the substring in $T_i$'s corresponding bit
14:         **end if**
15:       **end for**
16:     **end for**
17:     Add $T_1,T_2,...T_n$ to vector $P$
18:     **for** bit **in** $P$ **do**
19:       **if** the bit $<0$ **then**
20:         set the value of the corresponding bit to 0
21:       **else**
22:         set the value of the corresponding bit to 1
23:       **end if**
24:     **end for**
25:     At this time, the SimHash value obtains 64 bits, and divide them into two 8-digit hexadecimal number. 4 bits convert 1 hexadecimal digit
26:     **for** bit **in** hexadecimal number **do**
27:       **if** the bit$>7$ **then**
28:         set the value to 1
29:       **else**
30:         set the value to 0
31:       **end if**
32:     **end for**
33:     Now each hexadecimal number converts to a decimal number. The decimal numbers are $x$ and $y$
34:     **if** $Image[x][y]<256$ **then**
35:       $Image[x][y] \leftarrow Image[x][y] + 16$
36:     **end if**
37: **end for**
38: Convert *Image* to a Grayscale image $G\_image$
39: **return** $G\_image$

---

**Table 1.** Average size and time consumption of different memory dimensionality reduction methods

| Method | Size(kb) | Time(s) |
| --- | --- | --- |
| **MDMV** | **6.44** | **24.2048** |
| VMCADR | 158.41 | 1956.2323 |

## 3.3   Visual Feature Extraction

Similar to other malware images mentioned in Sect. 2, the grayscale images transformed from the memory should also exhibit distinct visual characteristics. We further employ image feature extraction method to further highlight these characteristics.

Local Binary Pattern (LBP) [21] is an operation used to describe the local texture characteristics of an image. The LBP operator is defined within a 3×3 window, using the central pixel of the window as the threshold. The gray value of the adjacent 8 pixels is compared with this central pixel. If the value of a surrounding pixel is higher than the value of the central pixel, the pixel is marked as 1; otherwise, it is marked as 0. This process results in 8 points in the 3×3 neighborhood. An 8-bit binary number (256 possible values) is generated by comparing these points, thus reflecting the texture information of the area. We apply this feature extraction on origin Simhash images, in order to further enhance features. Figure 4(a), (b) display the origin image and LBP image.

(a) Origin                    (b) LBP

**Fig. 4.** The origin image and LBP image.

## 3.4   Deep Learning

ResNet was introduced in 2015 by He et al. [11], aims to overcome issues of gradient vanishing and exploding during training neural networks. ResNet introduced the concept of residual learning, incorporating a residual block in each module that includes a skip connection. This allows information to propagate directly to subsequent layers, preserving original features and preventing them from diminishing layer by layer. We choose ResNet18 as the foundational architecture for the deep learning model in MDMV.

Our goal is to learn the mapping features of the samples' footprints. Utilizing ResNet18 as a detection model might not adequately capture certain features in grayscale images, therefore we introduce a self-attention module. The structure of self-attention module is shown in Fig. 5. In this module, the matrices $Q$ (query), $K$ (key), and $V$ (value) are used in the computation, that are calculated based on the input matrix $X$ and the weight matrices $W_q$, $W_k$, and $W_v$. The calculation method is shown below.

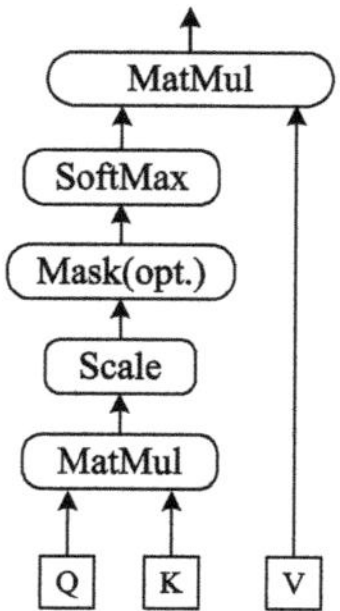


**Fig. 5.** The structure of self-attention module.

$$Q = XW_q \quad K = XW_k \quad V = XW_v \tag{1}$$

The output of the first convolutional layer serves as the input of the self-attention module. The output of the self-attention module is added to its input, and the combined values transfer to subsequent layers for further processing. The structure of our proposed model is shown in Fig. 6. Incorporating this self-attention module into ResNet18 enhances the model's ability to focus on the most relevant parts of the grayscale images, improving the model's performance in detecting malware.

## 4   Experiments and Results

### 4.1   Experimental Environment and Dataset

For our experiments, we utilized a computer environment equipped with an Intel(R) Core(TM) i7-7500 CPU at 2.70 GHz and 8 GB of DIMM RAM. The host machine ran the Ubuntu 20.04 (64-bit) operating system with a KVM virtualization platform. The guest virtual machine used the Windows 7 (32-bit, 4 GB RAM) operating system, version 6.1.7601. Windows 7 was selected as it allows the vast majority of malware to fully demonstrate their malicious

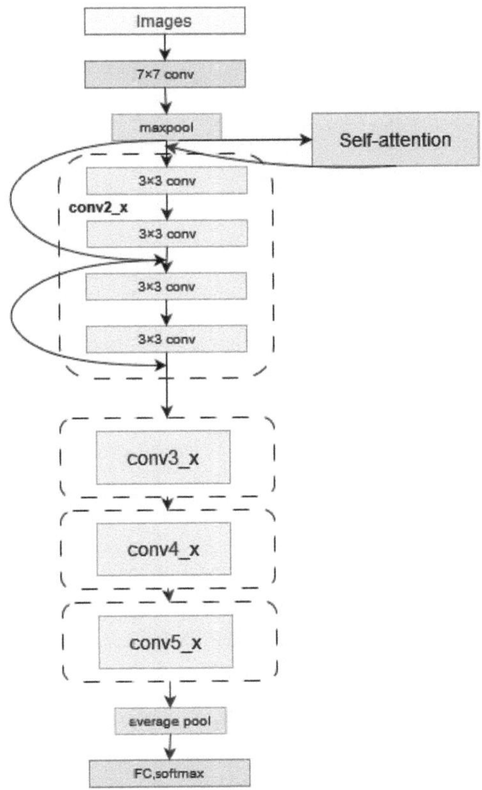



**Fig. 6.** The structure of proposed deep learning model.

behavior, while the advanced security mechanism adopted by higher version Windows system may affect the execution of samples.

We saved a snapshot of the guest VM immediately after the OS was successfully installed. During the experiments, each sample was run individually in the VM, followed by dumping the current memory to a file after 10 s of sample execution or upon triggering a system interrupt. This time frame allowed most software to load into memory and initiate operation. After each sample run, we restored the operating system using the origin snapshot of the VM to ensure system consistency.

The malware samples for the experiment came from VirusShare [27], that present encrypted and obfuscated samples. Some fileless samples were obtained from Kara et al. [13]. We downloaded the report corresponding to the MD5 from VirusTotal [28] to verify the validity of the sample, and selected the most prevalent type in the reports as the sample type. Types of malware samples are shown in Table 2. We collected benign samples from CNET [7] and the Windows system, which can run on Windows 7 (32-bit) system. There exists several benign software for file compression in the dataset, whose behavior may be similar to some malware. We extracted 1,113 abnormal physical memory snapshot files when the VM was running malware and 1,024 normal physical memory snapshot files when running benign programs. During each experiment, 80% of the collected data were used for training and 20% for testing separately.

**Table 2.** Type of malware samples

| Type | Quantity |
|------|----------|
| Trojan | 597 |
| Virus | 55 |
| Ransomware | 396 |
| Other | 85 |
| Total | 1113 |

The deep learning model was trained and tested using RTX 3090. We use accuracy, recall, and precision to evaluate the results of the experiments. Among them, TP, FP, TN, FN are used to respectively represent the real positive cases, false positive cases, real negative cases, and false negative cases. The accuracy, recall and precision are defined as follows:

$$Accuracy = \frac{TN + TP}{TN + TP + FN + FP} \tag{2}$$

$$Recall = \frac{TP}{TP + FN} \tag{3}$$

$$Precision = \frac{TP}{TP + FP} \tag{4}$$

### 4.2  Experiments and Results Analysis

**Different Detection Models.** We first validate the efficacy of using Simhash to convert memory dump file into images for malware detection. We used the original grayscale images for detection and trained on different models. The results are shown in Table 3. The selected models including machine learning models and deep learning models. We also conducted an ablation study on whether combining a self-attention module with ResNet18, and the results are also presented in Table 3.

The results validate that the Simhash-generated images from key memory data can be utilized for malware detection. Among the machine learning models, the Decision Tree exhibits the best performance, surpassing even some deep learning models. This can be attributed to the Decision Tree's ability to recursively select the best features to split the dataset, ensuring that valuable differentiation attributes are retained. Conversely, SVM relies on hyperplanes for classification, which may not always find an exact plane suitable for all datasets.

**Table 3.** Detection results of different models

| Model | Accuracy(%) | Recall(%) | Precision(%) |
|---|---|---|---|
| SVM | 86.24 | 100.00 | 79.21 |
| Bayes | 85.81 | 100.00 | 78.69 |
| Decision Tree | 94.98 | 94.17 | 96.17 |
| DenseNet | 92.14 | 85.83 | 99.04 |
| AlexNet(pretrained) | 95.41 | 95.42 | 95.82 |
| VGG19(pretrained) | 86.03 | 100.00 | 78.95 |
| **ResNet18** | **95.20** | **91.25** | **99.16** |
| **ResNet18+self-attention** | **98.91** | **98.75** | **99.16** |

When examining the deep learning models, the untrained AlexNet and VGG19 exhibited notably poor performance. Consequently, we opted to train and test these models using pre-trained parameters. All these deep learning models in our experiments performed less effectively than ResNet18, indicating the advantages of residual networks. In the comparison of ResNet18 networks, the addition of the self-attention module effectively improves accuracy. This improvement is likely due to the self-attention module's ability of enhancing the model's perception of image textures. Additionally, the self-attention mechanism provides the model with more grounds for decision-making, imparting a certain level of transparency to MDMV.

**Different Visualization Methods.** We will illustrate the rationality of choosing Simhash for visualization from the aspects of performance and efficiency. An important component of this evaluation involves comparing the file size and time consumption required to generate images using different visualization methods [4,8] for the same 16 MB data. Table 4 shows that the images generated by our method are smaller, requiring less storage space. However, our method takes longer time to generate images due to the calculation of Simhash values and mapping them onto images.

**Table 4.** Size and time consumption of different visualization methods

| Method | Size(kb) | Time(s) |
|---|---|---|
| **Simhash (ours)** | **6.44** | **24.2048** |
| Convert to Gray images [8] | 10076.16 | 0.7798 |
| Convert to RGB images [4] | 9971.52 | 0.6749 |

Based on the results from the previous subsection, we chose the ResNet18 model with self-attention module as the base model for further experimentation.

Since the converted grayscale images and color images are too large, we standardized the data to a size of 256×256 before training the model. Table 5 shows the average time for each visualization method to complete one training epoch. It also presents the detection results of these methods.

**Table 5.** Detection results of different visualization methods

| Method | One epoch time(s) | Accuracy(%) | Recall(%) | Precision(%) |
| --- | --- | --- | --- | --- |
| **Simhash (ours)** | **5.3087** | **98.91** | **98.75** | **99.16** |
| Convert to Gray images | 177.7184 | 80.08 | 100.00 | 66.45 |
| Convert to RGB images | 139.7296 | 96.54 | 92.38 | 98.98 |

It is evident that these two visualization methods posed challenges during model training, even though they exhibit faster visualization speeds. After standardization, these large images still consume longer training time than our Simhash images. Experimental results suggest that scaling images results in greater feature loss compared to using Simhash. Considering the balance between speed and feature preservation, our proposed method is both reasonable and necessary. It demonstrates a favorable balance of efficiency and capability. This balance is crucial for practical applications, ensuring that the model is not only efficient in terms of computational resources but also retains the necessary details for malware detection.

**Different Feature Extraction Methods.** We further enhance the detection ability of MDMV through feature extraction. Besides LBP, we also selected two feature extraction methods for comparison. The Histograms of Oriented Gradients (HOG) [10] method is based on calculating a histogram of normalized local directional gradients in a dense grid. The image is divided into small cells, and a one-dimensional gradient direction histogram is computed by accumulating gradient directions within each cell. These cells are then grouped into larger blocks, normalizing all cells within each block. The normalized block descriptor is called the HOG descriptor, and these HOG descriptors are combined to form the feature vector.

The Haar-like feature [17] is commonly used in the field of computer vision. It involves templates of white and black rectangles. The feature value is determined by sliding these templates over the image, calculating the sum of the white rectangular pixels and subtracting the sum of the black rectangular pixels. The Haar eigenvalue reflects the gray level changes in the image. The deep learning model used for detection were both ResNet18 with self-attention module. The results are shown in Table 6.

LBP, HOG, and Haar-like are three feature extraction methods that respectively describe images from the aspects of texture, gradient, and rectangular features. Our experimental results show that LBP and Haar-like methods have

**Table 6.** Detection results of different feature extraction methods

| Method | Accuracy(%) | Recall(%) | Precision(%) |
| --- | --- | --- | --- |
| Origin | 98.91 | 98.75 | 99.16 |
| **LBP** | **99.56** | **99.58** | **99.58** |
| HOG | 98.03 | 97.50 | 98.73 |
| harr-like | 98.81 | 98.43 | 99.05 |

good detection performance, while HOG features even diminish detection accuracy comparing to the origin Simhash images. Analyzing the principles, the binary sequences extracted by Simhash are mapped to specific points in the grayscale image in our experiments. LBP features compare the grayscale points with their surrounding values, effectively highlighting and reinforcing points with different values. HOG focuses on identifying changes in gradient or edge directions, which may be challenging to discern in our images with subtle gradient changes. Haar-like images perform well, but the improvement in performance is not as pronounced as LBP images. Overall, we choose LBP as the feature extraction method for MDMV. This decision is based on its effectiveness in extracting pertinent features within the grayscale images produced by Simhash, thereby enhancing the overall accuracy of malware detection.

**Different Malware Detection Methods.** We compare MDMV with other static and dynamic malware detection methods in this subsection. First, we constructed our dataset and then uploaded malicious samples to VirusTotal and analyzed them through 48 antivirus engines. The detection rates from the top 6 antivirus engines are shown in Table 7, demonstrating the standards of the samples in this dataset. It can also be seen that a single antivirus engine still faces false negatives on our dataset.

**Table 7.** Detecting rate of top 6 antivirus engines

| Antivirus engine | Detection rate(%) |
| --- | --- |
| Microsoft | 97.10 |
| FireEye | 96.61 |
| Kaspersky | 96.37 |
| Avast | 96.37 |
| APEX | 95.04 |
| Tencent | 92.85 |

Then we selected detection methods based on static binary images, dynamic API calls, and dynamic process memory collected in VM respectively. These detection methods were introduced in Sect. 2. The comparison of them is shown in Table 8, and the experimental results are presented in Table 9.

**Table 8.** Comparison of different detection methods

| Method | Static/Dynamic | Feature acquisition | Transparency | Influence on system | Security |
|---|---|---|---|---|---|
| IMCFN | Static | - | - | - | Low |
| Zhang et al. | Dynamic | In-VM | Medium | Medium | Medium |
| Bozkir et al. | Dynamic | In-VM | Low | High | Low |
| **MDMV** | **Dynamic** | **Out-VM** | **High** | **Low** | **High** |

**Table 9.** Detection results of different detection methods

| Method | Accuracy(%) | Recall(%) | Precision(%) |
|---|---|---|---|
| IMCFN [26] | 91.12 | 91.37 | 91.12 |
| Zhang et al. [32] | 93.22 | 89.36 | 92.64 |
| Bozkir et al. [4] | 96.30 | 100.00 | 91.89 |
| **MDMV** | **99.56** | **99.58** | **99.58** |

From the experimental results, the static method [26] does not perform well, which can be attributed to the presence of encrypted and obfuscated samples in the dataset. These factors make it challenging to effectively represent the features of images converted from malicious codes. The effectiveness of API-based method [32] remains limited, and the CPU and storage have occupied a lot of resources in reproducing this method. The process memory based method [4] also applied image feature extraction to generate feature vectors, and its performances are comparable to its in the original research. However, during the process memory collection, some process of samples could not be found in the system and collected through Procdump. These samples may be process-injection malware, that cannot be found by Procdump. This issue makes this process memory based method has difficulties in accurately describing our dataset. In contrast, the memory we extracted from the VM provides a better reflection of the impact of malware. This is one of the reasons for choosing VM's memory for malware detection, as it offers a more comprehensive and accurate representation of malware behaviors.

**Different Families.** We have demonstrated the effectiveness of MDMV in malware detection and will further investigate its applicability for malware family classification. For this purpose, we selected three malware families for classification: CryptoRansomware, Locker, and Zeus. The quantities of samples from each family are shown in Table 10.

**Table 10.** Type of malware families

| Type | Quantity |
| --- | --- |
| Zeus | 213 |
| Locker | 165 |
| CryptoRansomware | 231 |

CryptoRansomware is a type of ransomware that uses encryption algorithms to lock victims' files, rendering them inaccessible. Locker is another ransomware variant that tends to lock down the entire system rather than just encrypting files. Zeus is a long-standing trojan, which spreads through malicious links and exploits vulnerabilities to steal sensitive information. These malware families exhibit distinct behaviors. To adapt our model for family classification, we modified the softmax layer of the model for multi-class classification.

The results of classifying different families through MDMV and IMCFN are shown in Table 11. Compared to IMCFN, MDVV demonstrates superior effectiveness, as static detection has difficulty in identifying encrypted or obfuscated code. Meanwhile, the similarities between CryptoRansomware and Locker make it challenging for IMCFN to distinguish these two families. In contrast, our behavior-based method demonstrates a higher accuracy in distinguishing them.

**Table 11.** Classification result of different family classification methods

| Method | Accuracy(%) | Recall(%) | Precision(%) |
| --- | --- | --- | --- |
| IMCFN | 80.84 | 81.45 | 80.84 |
| **MDMV** | **96.77** | **96.77** | **97.07** |

## 5 Conclusions and Future Work

We propose a malware detection method called MDMV, which utilizes the KVM as the analysis platform. MDMV captures the physical memory snapshot of a virtual machine and extract the first 16 MB of this file. It uses Simhash to the selected memory into a grayscale image which preserves key memory information. MDMV further processes this image using LBP to extract features. We employ a ResNet18 model enhanced with a self-attention module to determine whether the sample corresponding to the image is malware or not. MDMV achieves a detection accuracy of up to 99.56% and demonstrates effectiveness in classifying malware families. MDMV exhibits stronger robustness and transparency than traditional memory forensics methods, because it does not rely on high-level semantic information. By preserving the malware's footprint in the memory snapshot, MDMV can reveal malicious behaviors effectively. Additionally, extracting memory from outside the VM avoids issues with malware evasion that can occur when collecting process memory in VM. In future work, we will further explore the structure of memory, and MDMV on different Windows systems and platforms. We will also research on reducing computational resources, so as to make MDMV effect in real world.

**Acknowledgments.** The authors would like to thank anonymous reviewers for their helpful comments and suggestions. The work of this paper was supported by the National Key R&D Program of China (2022YFB3103202).

# References


1. Alshamrani, A., Myneni, S., Chowdhary, A., Huang, D.: A survey on advanced persistent threats: techniques, solutions, challenges, and research opportunities. IEEE Commun. Surv. Tutor. **21**(2), 1851–1877 (2019). https://doi.org/10.1109/COMST.2019.2891891
2. AV-TEST: AV-test - the independent it-security institute (2023). https://www.av-test.org/en/statistics/malware/
3. Biggio, B., et al.: Poisoning behavioral malware clustering. In: Proceedings of the 2014 Workshop on Artificial Intelligent and Security Workshop, pp. 27–36. Association for Computing Machinery, New York (2014)
4. Bozkir, A.S., Tahillioglu, E., Aydos, M., Kara, I.: Catch them alive: a malware detection approach through memory forensics, manifold learning and computer vision. Comput. Secur. **103**, 102166 (2021). https://doi.org/10.1016/j.cose.2020.102166
5. Chen, X., et al.: Malader: decision-based black-box attack against API sequence based malware detectors. In: 2023 53rd Annual IEEE/IFIP International Conference on Dependable Systems and Networks (DSN), pp. 165–178 (2023). https://doi.org/10.1109/DSN58367.2023.00027
6. Chen, X., Andersen, J., Mao, Z.M., Bailey, M., Nazario, J.: Towards an understanding of anti-virtualization and anti-debugging behavior in modern malware. In: 2008 IEEE International Conference on Dependable Systems and Networks With FTCS and DCC (DSN), pp. 177–186 (2008). https://doi.org/10.1109/DSN.2008.4630086
7. CNET: App for windows (2023). https://download.cnet.com/windows/
8. Conti, G., et al.: Automated mapping of large binary objects using primitive fragment type classification. Digit. Investig. **7**, S3–S12 (2010). https://doi.org/10.1016/j.diin.2010.05.002, the Proceedings of the Tenth Annual DFRWS Conference
9. Dai, Y., Li, H., Qian, Y., Lu, X.: A malware classification method based on memory dump grayscale image. Digit. Investig. **27**, 30–37 (2018). https://doi.org/10.1016/j.diin.2018.09.006
10. Dalal, N., Triggs, B.: Histograms of oriented gradients for human detection. In: 2005 IEEE Computer Society Conference on Computer Vision and Pattern Recognition (CVPR 2005), vol. 1, pp. 886–893 (2005). https://doi.org/10.1109/CVPR.2005.177
11. He, K., Zhang, X., Ren, S., Sun, J.: Deep residual learning for image recognition. In: 2016 IEEE Conference on Computer Vision and Pattern Recognition (CVPR), pp. 770–778. IEEE (2016). https://doi.org/10.1109/CVPR.2016.90

12. Kaloudi, N., Li, J.: The AI-based cyber threat landscape: a survey. **53**(1) (2020). https://doi.org/10.1145/3372823
13. Kara, I.: Fileless malware threats: recent advances, analysis approach through memory forensics and research challenges. Expert Syst. Appl. **214**, 119133 (2023). https://doi.org/10.1016/j.eswa.2022.119133
14. Landman, T., Nissim, N.: Deep-hook: a trusted deep learning-based framework for unknown malware detection and classification in linux cloud environments. Neural Netw. **144**, 648–685 (2021). https://doi.org/10.1016/j.neunet.2021.09.019
15. Li, K., Guo, W., Zhang, F., Du, J.: Gambd: generating adversarial malware against malconv. Comput. Secur. **130**, 103279 (2023). https://doi.org/10.1016/j.cose.2023.103279
16. Li, S., Li, Y., Wu, X., Otaibi, S.A., Tian, Z.: Imbalanced malware family classification using multimodal fusion and weight self-learning. IEEE Trans. Intell. Transp. Syst. **24**(7), 7642–7652 (2023). https://doi.org/10.1109/TITS.2022.3208891
17. Lienhart, R., Maydt, J.: An extended set of haar-like features for rapid object detection. In: Proceedings of the International Conference on Image Processing, vol. 1, pp. 900–903 (2002). https://doi.org/10.1109/ICIP.2002.1038171
18. Muralidharan, T., Cohen, A., Gerson, N., Nissim, N.: File packing from the malware perspective: techniques, analysis approaches, and directions for enhancements. ACM Comput. Surv. **55**(5) (2022). https://doi.org/10.1145/3530810
19. Naeem, H., Dong, S., Falana. O.J., Ullah, F.: Development of a deep stacked ensemble with process based volatile memory forensics for platform independent malware detection and classification. Expert Syst. Appl. **223**, 119952 (2023). https://doi.org/10.1016/j.eswa.2023.119952
20. Ni, S., Qian, Q., Zhang, R.: Malware identification using visualization images and deep learning. Comput. Secur. **77**, 871–885 (2018). https://doi.org/10.1016/j.cose.2018.04.005
21. Ojala, T., Pietikainen, M., Maenpaa, T.: Multiresolution gray-scale and rotation invariant texture classification with local binary patterns. IEEE Trans. Pattern Anal. Mach. Intell. **24**(7), 971–987 (2002). https://doi.org/10.1109/TPAMI.2002.1017623
22. Or-Meir, O., Nissim, N., Elovici, Y., Rokach, L.: Dynamic malware analysis in the modern era–a state of the art survey. **52**(5) (2019). https://doi.org/10.1145/3329786
23. Parildi, E.S., Hatzinakos, D., Lawryshyn, Y.: Deep learning-aided runtime opcode-based Windows malware detection. Neural Comput. Appl. **33**(18), 11963–11983 (2021). https://doi.org/10.1007/s00521-021-05861-7
24. Rosenberg, I., Shabtai, A., Elovici, Y., Rokach, L.: Adversarial machine learning attacks and defense methods in the cyber security domain. ACM Comput. Surv. **54**(5) (2021). https://doi.org/10.1145/3453158
25. Shafiq, M.Z., Tabish, S.M., Mirza, F., Farooq, M.: PE-miner: mining structural information to detect malicious executables in realtime. In: Kirda, E., Jha, S., Balzarotti, D. (eds.) RAID 2009. LNCS, vol. 5758, pp. 121–141. Springer, Heidelberg (2009). https://doi.org/10.1007/978-3-642-04342-0_7
26. Vasan, D., Alazab, M., Wassan, S., Naeem, H., Safaei, B., Zheng, Q.: IMCFN: image-based malware classification using fine-tuned convolutional neural network architecture. Comput. Netw. **171**, 107138 (2020). https://doi.org/10.1016/j.comnet.2020.107138
27. VirusShare (2023). https://virusshare.com/
28. VirusTotal (2023). https://virustotal.com/

29. Volatility: Volatility. volatility framework - volatile memory extraction utility framework (2023). https://github.com/volatilityfoundation/volatility
30. Xu, Z., Ray, S., Subramanyan, P., Malik, S.: Malware detection using machine learning based analysis of virtual memory access patterns. In: Design, Automation & Test in Europe Conference & Exhibition (DATE), pp. 169–174 (2017). https://doi.org/10.23919/DATE.2017.7926977
31. Zhang, X., et al.: Slowing down the aging of learning-based malware detectors with API knowledge. IEEE Trans. Dependable Secure Comput. **20**(2), 902–916 (2023). https://doi.org/10.1109/TDSC.2022.3144697
32. Zhang, Z., Qi, P., Wang, W.: Dynamic malware analysis with feature engineering and feature learning. In: Proceedings of the AAAI Conference on Artificial Intelligence, vol. 34, pp. 1210–1217 (2020)
33. Zheng, L., Zhang, J.: A new malware detection method based on VMCADR in cloud environments. Secur. Commun. Netw. **2022**, 4208066 (2022). https://doi.org/10.1155/2022/4208066

# Collection Scheduling with Memory Constraints for Low Earth Orbit Satellite Constellations


Saumya Jaipuria[1] , Ansuman Banerjee[1(✉)] , and Himadri Sekhar Paul[2]

[1] ACMU, Indian Statistical Institute Kolkata, Kolkata, India
ansuman@isical.ac.in
[2] TCS Research, Kolkata, India
himadriSekhar.paul@tcs.com



**Abstract.** In recent years, the remote sensing infrastructure is slowly shifting towards satellite constellation systems from monolithic satellites. A constellation offers high-fidelity (both in time and space) distributed sensing capability. The prospect of using a small satellite constellation as a commercial infrastructure for serving a multitude of applications for multiple users, is quickly becoming a reality. However, such infrastructures demand handling of high volume of sensor data with high velocity. In addition, commercial exploitation also requires capability to handle variable sensing demands depending on user requirements. Therefore, it is a challenging problem to efficiently utilize on-board sensing resources to make the infrastructure commercially attractive. In this paper, we present the sensing task (*aka* collection) scheduling problem under limited storage constraints in satellites. We present an integer linear programming (ILP) based solution and show that it produces higher throughput in comparison to state-of-art collection scheduling methods, through extensive simulation. Further, we present a linear relaxation and randomized rounding based heuristic, with guaranteed approximation bounds, and show experimentally that it is comparable with the optimal solution.

**Keywords:** Satellite Constellation · Low Earth Orbit Satellites · Scheduling


## 1 Introduction

In recent times, monolithic heavy satellites are being replaced by constellations of smaller, lighter satellites for remote sensing and imaging applications. Small satellites are resource constrained and thus pose severe challenges in delivering remote sensing services under latency constraints. In the traditional approach, satellites act as passive sensing devices which are used to image specific areas on the Earth surface and transmit all data back to Earth bound ground stations following the Bent-pipe architecture [9]. Smaller satellites, being lighter, can fly


© ICST Institute for Computer Sciences, Social Informatics and Telecommunications Engineering 2026
Published by Springer Nature Switzerland AG 2026. All Rights Reserved
A. Soylu et al. (Eds.): MobiQuitous 2024, LNICST 634, pp. 591–613, 2026.
https://doi.org/10.1007/978-3-032-10554-7_31

in Low Earth Orbits (LEOs) and therefore with low periodicity around the Earth (approximately $90mins$), and offer high resolution imaging capabilities owing to their state-of-the-art sensing payloads. However, restricted viewing angle of on-board sensors [23] and their proximity to surface, allows a relatively thin swath of earth surface for imaging. To observe a wider swath, a constellation of small satellites is employed for performing the job collectively. Such collaborative sensing requires identifying fragments of the area to be observed and assigning each fragment to an appropriate satellite for imaging. In this paper, we present an observation scheduling algorithm for a satellite constellation following the traditional bent-pipe architecture, under on-board data storage constraints.

Modern small satellites are capable of generating high data volume at very high speed. For example, ERS-1 launched by the *European Space Agency* generates hundreds of MBs of raw SAR (synthetic aperture radar) data every 10 secs [8,17]. However, on-board storage of ESR-1 is limited, prompting its mission to activate SAR imaging only when it is near a ground station in order to minimize storage requirement. The huge data generation capability of on-board sensors consumes memory at a commensurate rate, which is an added challenge. Planning a satellite constellation observation schedule involves identification of swaths, assigning and scheduling swaths to satellites for imaging, and timely transportation of image data to ground stations. An added challenge comes from the fact that communication opportunities with the ground stations are not continuous, they appear at intermittent points on the LEO routes, depending on their movement trajectory and ground station locations. Further, limited on-board storage and communication constrains the data capture capabilities of small satellite constellations today and is a topic of active research.

A well-defined mission demands observation points and its communication windows with the ground stations to be fixed a-priori so that memory requirements can be determined during the design. However, as we move towards commercialization of the remote sensing infrastructure, the observation areas are no longer pre-defined, but dynamically generated based on user demands. In fact, in a commercial infrastructure, all infrastructure components evolve - number of satellites and their trajectories change, the number of ground stations change, while communication technology and bandwidth evolve as well. Commercialization demands a dynamic mission control. In this paper, we address the problem of synthesizing a schedule of collection and data download for small satellite constellations over short schedule horizons, with an aim to maximize the collection objectives, while honoring the different limitations imposed by the technology and infrastructure. We propose a heuristic to solve the problem at low resource cost and with high accuracy.

The mission of a small satellite constellation is to collect observation data in a distributed manner. A typical mission involves specifying an area on the Earth's surface as 'Region of Interest' (RoI). Individual satellites are then commissioned to observe parts of the RoI based on their pre-decided trajectories. One of the popular approaches to determine the mission of a satellite is using discretization of space, known as *tessellation* [25] which breaks each RoI into sub-regions, and then *scheduling* [15] to assign satellites to sub-regions. An important challenge today is to design a schedule for directing individual satellites to maximize the number of individual sub-regions collected, given different constraints. This is the main problem addressed in this paper. In this work, we propose an integrated collect-communicate-download schedule for satellite constellations. Our contributions include:

- An integer linear programming (ILP) model for optimal schedule construction.
- A heuristic based on randomized rounding over a linear relaxation of the ILP, with a detailed analysis on its performance with respect to the optimal.
- An analysis of several special cases.
- Simulation results for a comparative performance study of different methods.

The rest of the paper is organized as follows. Section 2 includes a formal presentation of the scheduling problem, followed by the ILP formalization of the optimization problem involved in Sect. 3. In Sect. 4, we discuss some special cases of the problem. A randomized rounding based approximation algorithm is presented in Sect. 5. In Sect. 6, we present results of our simulation experiments. We present some related work in the next section. Section 8 concludes the discussion.

## 2   Problem Definition

In this paper, we address the scheduling problem associated with distributed sensing and data collection by a constellation and transfer of the same to ground stations. In this section, we present our system model. We consider a version of the problem where both space (*i.e.* the RoIs) and time are discretized. Each sub-region after tessellation can be observed or sensed within one time instant by a satellite. Let $\mathcal{A} = \{A_1, A_2, \ldots A_n\}$ be a set of tessellated sub-regions. Each sub-region $A_i$ is denoted by the latitude-longitude coordinates, $(\phi^{(i)}, \lambda^{(i)})$ of its center. Let, $\mathcal{S} = \{S_1, S_2, \ldots S_k\}$ be a set of $k$ satellites, where each $S_j$ is defined by its trajectory or track $R_j$ over the Earth. $S_j \in \mathcal{S}$ has onboard memory capacity to store $M_j$ units of collection. In this paper, for simplicity of illustration, we treat observation of one sub-region as one unit of collection task.

A trajectory of a satellite $S_j \in \mathcal{S}$ is represented by an ordered sequence of latitude-longitude co-ordinate pairs over time, *i.e.* $R_j = \left( (\phi_0^{(j)}, \lambda_0^{(j)}), (\phi_1^{(j)}, \lambda_1^{(j)}), \phi_2^{(j)}, \lambda_2^{(j)}) \ldots (\phi_t^{(j)}, \lambda_t^{(j)}) \ldots \right)$ corresponding to the points that the satellite goes over in its route at each discrete time instance. At a time instant, a satellite has the opportunity to collect data from zero or more sub-regions. A satellite does not need to be at the nadir of a sub-region to target its sensor head perpendicularly to observe it, sensing can also be done from an angular view, termed as the *look angle* for the region. Look angle for sensing is bounded and the maximum look angle is defined on the sensor. We call such a case as a *collection opportunity*. The act of performing the sensing task is termed as a *collection task* and a collection task can happen only when certain other conditions (discussed later) for collection are satisfied. Therefore only a subset of the collection opportunities can be translated into collection tasks. The objective of this work is to propose a collection schedule to appropriately assign collection tasks to each satellite, following a set of constraints with an optimization objective of maximum collection.

In addition, the infrastructure also includes a set of ground stations denoted by $\mathcal{B} = \{B_1, B_2, \ldots B_m\}$, each associated with its location coordinates, *i.e.* $B_k = (\phi^{(k)}, \lambda^{(k)})$. The ground stations serve as the data sinks for the satellites. The communication link between a satellite and a ground station is transient, and is established when they are in direct view of each other. One way to model this is to define a spherical region around a ground station [21]. When a satellite enters this region, communication between them is possible, which essentially implies that a communication link is set up when the distance between the satellite and the ground station is below a defined threshold. In this work, for the sake of simplicity, we discretize the communication instances as well, subject to the distance threshold constraint, as explained later. Further, we assume the satellite-to-ground communication happens in pre-defined frequency radio bands [20], in accordance with the capabilities of the communication devices. This implies that when multiple entities need to communicate with a single entity, the communication bandwidth is shared, either by Frequency Division Multiplexing (FDM) or Time Division Multiplexing (TDM). This effect is modelled in our formulation as effective data transfer rate. The effective rate is maximum at instances only when a satellite has the opportunity of an isolated communication with the ground station. The rate falls to half when two satellites simultaneously communicate with the ground station, and so on. For small satellites, on-board resources are limited. Storage constraint limits the data collection capability of the satellites, since a satellite can perform only a constant number of collections, limited by its storage, until it can transfer the data to a ground station and then reuse its onboard storage for further collections. However, as mentioned above, a satellite can only intermittently connect to ground stations. In addition, the communication bandwidth with the ground stations is not only constrained, but is shared among multiple satellites which may attempt to transfer data simultaneously to the same ground station. In this work, we ignore constraints arising out of kinematics [10] of satellites.

The problem addressed in this work is to schedule collection and data transfer events for each satellite in the constellation under the constraints outlined above. We denote this as the *Small Satellite Scheduling under Memory Constraint* problem ($S^3MC$). To model the problem, we assume that the volume of data collected by a satellite for a sub-region is constant and is used as an unit for data volume associated with storage and communication. As discussed, the model allows multiple satellites to connect to a ground station and the communication channel being shared among them. The data transfer capability of each satellite is also bounded. Let $U_j$ be the maximum data transfer capacity of satellite $S_j$. Similarly, each ground station also has a maximum data acceptance capacity and let $D_k$ denote the corresponding value for ground station $B_k$.

**Table 1.** Collection and communication opportunities as an example

| Time | Satellite | RoI | Look-angle | Time | Satellite | LoI | Look-angle |
|---|---|---|---|---|---|---|---|
| 0 | $S_0$ | $A_0$ | $0.25°$ | 4 | $S_1$ | $B_0$ | $-$ |
| 0 | $S_0$ | $A_4$ | $0.5°$ | 5 | $S_0$ | $A_1$ | $0.5°$ |
| 1 | $S_1$ | $A_1$ | $-0.25°$ | 5 | $S_0$ | $A_3$ | $0.75°$ |
| 2 | $S_0$ | $A_2$ | $1.0°$ | 6 | $S_1$ | $A_0$ | $0.5°$ |
| 2 | $S_1$ | $A_0$ | $-0.85°$ | 6 | $S_1$ | $A_2$ | $0.0°$ |
| 3 | $S_0$ | $A_5$ | $1.0°$ | 7 | $S_1$ | $B_0$ | $-$ |
| 4 | $S_0$ | $B_0$ | $-$ | 8 | $S_0$ | $B_0$ | $-$ |

The trajectory of a satellite can be pre-computed with reasonable accuracy for a limited duration from its state at the starting time of the duration concerned. Let $H$ denote the scheduling horizon. In other words, our objective is to schedule the collection and download events for the interval $[0, H]$. One of the requirements of remote sensing is to download all collected data. Therefore, the schedule needs to include download events corresponding to the collection events in the schedule such that all collections are downloaded to ground stations by the end of the horizon. It may so happen that there may exist a collection opportunity for a sub-region within the scheduling horizon, but after that either no download slot is available or a download slot cannot be allocated for the collection to be downloaded within $H$. With the pre-computed trajectory information, the collection opportunities of the satellites can be predetermined. Also the communication windows among satellites and ground stations can be pre-computed. We present this information as a table $\mathcal{T}$. The schema of the table is $\langle \text{Time} \in [0, H], \text{Satellite} \in \mathcal{S}, \text{sub-region or ground station} \in \mathcal{A} \cup \mathcal{B}, \text{look angle for sub-region or - otherwise}\rangle$. Table 1 shows an instance of such a table in the example scenario below. The first tuple $\langle 0, S_0, A_0, 0.25°\rangle$ denotes satellite $S_0$ has a collection opportunity for sub-region $A_0$ at time instance 0 with a look angle of $0.25°$. Similarly, $\langle 4, S_0, B_0\rangle$, denotes satellite $S_0$ has a communication window with ground station $B_0$ at time instance 4.

## 2.1   An Example

To illustrate the model, we present a small system consisting of 2 satellites, $\mathcal{S} = \{S_0, S_1\}$, each with storage capacity of 2 units and employed to observe 6 sub-regions $\mathcal{A} = \{A_0, \ldots, A_5\}$. The satellites can download the data collected to one ground station $\mathcal{B} = \{B_0\}$. Based on the trajectories of the satellites and the latitude-longitude coordinates of the ground station, Table 1 shows the collection and download opportunities for the satellites. Also, let the maximum data transfer capacity of the ground stations be two data units per time instance. In case of parallel connections with multiple satellites, the data transfer capacity is divided among the contenders. For example, at time instance 4, both $S_0$ and $S_1$ are connected simultaneously to the ground station $B_0$. The scheduler can either allow one of the satellites to utilize the full downlink data transfer capacity of the ground stations, or allow each of them to transfer one data unit.

Each satellite's schedule is a sequence of events of collection and download. For example, according to Table 1, satellite $S_0$ has a collection opportunity for intervals $[0, 3], [5, 5]$ and a download window for intervals $[4, 4], [8, 8]$. At a time instant, a satellite can have more than one collection opportunity, as shown in Table 1. At time instant 0, satellite $S_0$ can either collect data from sub-region $A_0$ or from $A_4$. As mentioned earlier, to collect data from a sub-region, the satellite need not be directly above it, the sensor head can be adjusted to get an angular view (look-angle). For example, at time instant 0, $S_0$ needs a sensor head movement of $0.25°$ and $0.5°$ to collect data from $A_0$ and $A_4$, respectively, while at time instant 6, $S_1$ is directly above sub-region $A_2$ and does not need to adjust the sensor head to collect data. The sub-regions $A_4$ and $A_5$ have only one collection opportunity each, by satellite $S_0$ in the first collection window. So, if $S_0$ collects any data from any two sub-regions from $A_0$ and $A_2$, in the first collection window, $A_4$ and $A_5$ will have no other opportunity to get collected. Consider a schedule in which $S_0$ collects $A_4$ and $A_5$ and $S_1$ collects $A_1$ and $A_0$, and during the shared data transfer window only $S_0$ is allowed to download its collected 2 data units. In that case $S_1$ has its memory full and would not be able to collect $A_2$ which is visible to $S_1$ only in the second collection window. Therefore $A_2$ will not be collected. In another possible schedule, $S_0$ collects $A_4$, $S_1$ collects $A_0$ and then during the download window $S_1, S_0$ downloads the 2 data units. In the second collection window, $S_0$ collects either $A_1$ or $A_3$ and $S_1$ collects $A_2$. In either case, 2 sub-region ($A_5$ and $A_1/A_3$) cannot be collected.

## 3    ILP Model Formulation

The Small Satellite Scheduling under Memory Constraint ($S^3MC$) is NP-hard, the proof follows from a reduction from the Multi-Robot Task Allocation (MRTA) problem [5]. We omit the hardness proof here due to paucity of space. In the following, we present two variations of the problem. In the following, we first present an Integer Linear Programming (ILP) formulation of the problem. We consider a discrete version of the problem model where both space and time are discretized. Here we present an ILP based model which incorporates two sets of indicator variables, the $x$-variables of the form $x_{ij}^t$, indicating collection events for sub-region $A_i$; and the $y$-variables of the form $y_{ijk}^t$, indicating download events of collected data. The indicator variables are defined as follows.

**Indicator Variables:** The indicator variable $x_{ij}^t$ indicates whether a region $A_i$ is collected by the satellite $S_j$ at instance $t$. The variable can be set only when satellite $S_j$ has a collection opportunity for $A_i$ at time instance $t$, *i.e.* some collection opportunity represented by the record $\langle t, S_j, A_i, \alpha^\circ \rangle$ is present in the table $\mathcal{T}$.

$$x_{ij}^t = \begin{cases} 1 \cdots & \langle t, S_j, A_i, \alpha^\circ \rangle \in \mathcal{T} \text{ and this opportunity} \\ & \text{is included in the schedule as a collection task} \\ 0 \cdots & \text{otherwise} \end{cases}$$

Similarly, the indicator variable $y_{ijk}^t$ models the data download event for the sub-region $A_i$ to the ground station $B_k$ by satellite $S_j$ at instance $t$. A necessary precondition of setting this variable to 1 is that the corresponding collection event for $A_i$ by satellite $S_j$ must have been executed before $t$. The other precondition is that there is a communication window between $S_j$ and $B_k$ at time instance $t$, i.e., the task $\langle t, S_j, B_k, - \rangle$ is present as a download opportunity in table $\mathcal{T}$.

$$y_{ijk}^t = \begin{cases} 1 \cdots & \text{sensor data for } A_i \text{ is transferred to ground station } B_k \\ & \text{by satellite } S_j \text{ at time } t \text{ and } \langle t, S_j, B_k, - \rangle \in \mathcal{T} \\ 0 \cdots & \text{otherwise} \end{cases}$$

**Constraints:** We now define the system constraints on these variables.

*At-Most One Collection for Each Instant for a Satellite:* Each satellite might have multiple collection opportunities at an instant, but it should collect data for at most one of these sub-regions.

$$\sum_{i=1}^{|\mathcal{A}|} x_{ij}^t \leq 1 \quad \forall t \in [0, H],\ S_j \in \mathcal{S} \tag{1}$$

*At-Most One Collection for Any Sub-region:* To avoid redundant collection for a sub-region, each sub-region is required to be collected at-most once within the scheduling horizon $H$. This also indirectly implies minimization of system resources for the collection activity. For every sub-region $A_i \in \mathcal{A}$,

$$\sum_{t=0}^{H} \sum_{j=1}^{|\mathcal{S}|} x_{ij}^t \leq 1 \tag{2}$$

*Download Validation:* A region $A_i$ can be downloaded by satellite $S_j$ at time $t$ only if it has been collected once before, at some time $t'$, $0 < t' < t$. Also there should be only one download instance for each collected region. For all instances $t \in [1, H]$, for all satellites $S_j \in \mathcal{S}$, and for every sub-region $A_i \in \mathcal{A}$,

$$\sum_{k=1}^{|\mathcal{B}|} y_{ijk}^t \leq \sum_{t'=0}^{t-1} x_{ij}^{t'} \tag{3}$$

*Limited Onboard Memory Capacity:* At any instance, the accumulated collection cannot exceed the satellite memory capacity. At any time instance $t$, the accumulated collection of satellite $S_j$ can be computed as the number of sub-regions collected by the satellite till time $t$ minus the number of sub-regions whose data has been downloaded. Both collection and download are in terms of the number of sub-regions. For every satellite $S_j \in \mathcal{S}$ and for all time instances $t \in [0, H]$,

$$\sum_{i=1}^{|\mathcal{A}|} \sum_{t'=0}^{t} x_{ij}^{t'} - \sum_{i=1}^{|\mathcal{A}|} \sum_{k=1}^{|\mathcal{B}|} \sum_{t'=0}^{t} y_{ijk}^{t'} \leq M_j \tag{4}$$

where, $M_j$ denotes the storage capacity of $S_j \in \mathcal{S}$. The summation over the $x$-variables in the LHS of the equation corresponds to the data units for the sub-regions collected till time $t$. The summation over the $y$-variables counts the number of data units downloaded till $t$. The difference represents the residual data units which need to be stored on-board and therefore denotes the memory requirement at time instance $t$. The residual data at every time instance must be bounded by the onboard memory capacity of the satellite.

Transfer of All Collected Data: Also, all data collected needs to be downloaded to ground stations by $H$. For every satellite $S_j \in \mathcal{S}$ and all sub-regions $A_i \in \mathcal{A}$,

$$\sum_{t=0}^{H} x_{ij}^{t} = \sum_{k=1}^{|\mathcal{B}|} \sum_{t=0}^{H} y_{ijk}^{t} \tag{5}$$

*Bounded Data Down-Link Capacity of Ground Stations:* Each ground station has a maximum capacity per time instance to receive data from satellites. Let $D_k$ denote this quantity for ground station $B_k$. For all time instances $t \in [0, H]$ and for every ground station $B_k \in \mathcal{B}$,

$$\sum_{i=1}^{|\mathcal{A}|} \sum_{j=1}^{|\mathcal{S}|} y_{ijk}^{t} \leq D_k \tag{6}$$

*Bounded Up-Link Data Transfer Capacity of Satellites:* Each satellite has an upper bound on the number of data units per instance of time that it can download to a ground station. Let $U_j$ denote this quantity for satellite $S_j$.
For every satellite $S_j \in \mathcal{S}$ and time instance $t \in [0, H]$,

$$\sum_{i=1}^{|\mathcal{A}|} \sum_{k=1}^{|\mathcal{B}|} y_{ijk}^{t} \leq U_j \tag{7}$$

**Optimization Objective:**

Maximize the number of collections,

$$maximize \sum_{t=1}^{H} \sum_{i=1}^{|\mathcal{A}|} \sum_{j=1}^{|\mathcal{S}|} x_{ij}^{t}$$

The above constraints can be solved by a standard ILP solver [24]. A solution from the ILP solver gives us the collection download schedule for the satellites with the maximum number of collections within the given horizon.

**Table 2.** Mission plan for satellites corresponding to two different scheduling horizons

| Scheduling Horizon = 8 | | Time | Scheduling Horizon = 7 | |
| --- | --- | --- | --- | --- |
| Schedule for $S_0$ | Schedule for $S_1$ | | Schedule for $S_0$ | Schedule for $S_1$ |
| COLL $A_4$ | | 0 | COLL $A_4$ | |
| | COLL $A_1$ | 1 | | COLL $A_1$ |
| | COLL $A_0$ | 2 | | |
| COLL $A_5$ | | 3 | COLL $A_5$ | |
| COMM $B_0$ : 1 unit | COMM $B_0$ : 1 unit | 4 | COMM $B_0$ : 2 unit | |
| COLL $A_3$ | | 5 | | |
| | COLL $A_2$ | 6 | | COLL $A_2$ |
| | COMM $B_0$ : 2 units | 7 | | COMM $B_0$ : 2 units |
| COMM $B_0$ : 2 units | | 8 | | |

### Example (contd.)

For the example in Sect. 2.1, the optimization must select a subset of collection opportunities from Table 1 such that all collections can be downloaded to the ground station within the scheduling horizon. For a scheduling horizon of 8, the opportunities (collection and download) from Table 1, selected as part of the overall collect download schedule, is presented in Table 2. Here the *COLL* and *COMM* keywords denote collection and communication/download tasks respectively. However, if the scheduling horizon is specified as 7, the download opportunity $\langle 8, S_0, B_0 \rangle$ goes out of scope. Consequently, although the collection opportunity $\langle 5, S_0, A_3, 0.75° \rangle$ can potentially be included as part of the final schedule, $S_0$ does not have any download opportunity available after time instance 5 within the scheduling horizon. The final plan is shown in Table 2.

## 4   Special Cases

In the section, we discuss some special cases of the $S^3MC$ problem.

**Special case 1: Unbounded Storage:** Consider unbounded onboard memory capacity of each satellite. Thus, the constraint on the optimal schedule is affected only by the constraints on the data download opportunities of the satellites with respect to the trajectory, up-link and down-link capacities. The hardness proof for this variant follows from MRTA as well. We now consider a more general case with bounded storage. As a special case to this, consider unbounded communication link capacity. Unbounded download link capacity enables satellites to download all data collected up to the earliest point of link establishment with the ground stations. We consider two variations based on the distribution of collection points for this special case.

**Special Case 2: Unbounded Link Capacity:** Consider the case when onboard memory of each satellite is finite, while the download link capacity is unbounded. Again there are two possibilities.

*Case 2.1: Disjoint Tracks:* Let us first consider the case where the collection opportunities are such that the collection points are disjoint among satellites in the constellation. Since any collection point can be observed uniquely by one satellite only, a collection schedule for each satellite can be generated independently, such that number of collection points is maximized in the schedule. This variation can be solved in polynomial time by assigning each satellite to opportunities on it's route till its memory is exceeded and then assigning the collections to ground stations en route and continuing this.

*Case 2.2: Overlapping Tracks:* Now, let us consider the other case where the collection opportunities are non-disjoint among the satellites. Unbounded download link capacity essentially allows us to model intervals between two communication link establishment events of a satellite as a knapsack. The problem now is to select appropriate collection events and place them in one of the sacks (or intervals) such that number of collections is maximized. The hardness of this case follows from a reduction from the knapsack problem, which is known to be NP-hard [11].

**Special case 3: At most one collection opportunity per time instant for each satellite:** Consider the case where we restrict each satellite to have at most one collection opportunity at any time instant. Therefore, we can ignore the look-angle for the sub-region. Removing multiple collection opportunities per time instant creates an interesting case, which as we show is solvable in polynomial time, using a classical max-flow formulation [12].

**Table 3.** Collection and communication opportunities

| Time | Satellite | LoI | Time | Satellite | LoI |
|------|-----------|-----|------|-----------|-----|
| 0 | $S_0$ | $A_0$ | 4 | $S_0$ | $B_0$ |
| 1 | $S_0$ | $A_1$ | 4 | $S_1$ | $B_0$ |
| 1 | $S_1$ | $A_0$ | 5 | $S_0$ | $A_4$ |
| 2 | $S_0$ | $A_2$ | 5 | $S_1$ | $A_3$ |
| 2 | $S_1$ | $A_1$ | 6 | $S_0$ | $A_1$ |
| 3 | $S_0$ | $A_3$ | 6 | $S_1$ | $A_0$ |
| 3 | $S_1$ | $A_2$ | 7 | $S_1$ | $B_0$ |
|   |   |   | 8 | $S_0$ | $B_0$ |

The constraints described in Eqs. 2–7, can be encoded into a flow network by designing it as layers and applying flow capacity across edges. The first layer is composed of nodes each representing one sub-region. This layer is followed by two identical layers, each composed of nodes which represents instances of communication opportunities. For example, if a satellite $S$ has a communication opportunity at time $t$, then the second and the third layer contains one node corresponding to this communication opportunity $(S, t)$. Similarly, the fourth layer is composed of nodes of the form $(B, t)$, corresponding to the communication opportunities.

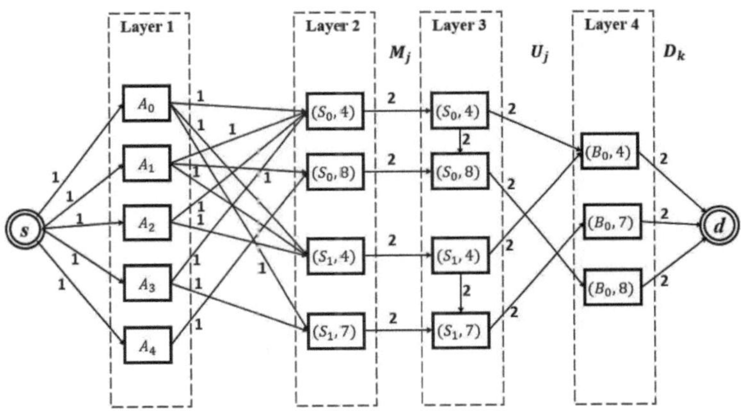


**Fig. 1.** Network Flow model of opportunities described in Table 3.

However the interconnections between these layers are different. A node of the second layer is connected with all the sub-region nodes of the first layer, such that the sub-region has a collection opportunity by the corresponding satellite and the satellite had no other communication opportunity since then (Eq. 3). The edge capacity is set to 1 to denote the constraint of at-most one collection per sub-region (Eq. 2). The nodes in the third layer denote storage states of the satellites. A node of the second layer is connected with the corresponding node in the third layer to model the data storage in memory and the edge capacity is marked as the memory capacity of the satellite. The nodes in the third layer corresponding to a satellite are also connected in series, such that a node is only connected to one which is following it immediately by its time-stamp value. The edges have capacity equal to the memory capacity of the satellite. These intra-layer edges denote in-memory storage of data and are therefore limited by the memory constraint (Eq. 4). The fourth layer of nodes corresponds to communication with ground stations and models simultaneous data transfers from multiple satellites. A node in the third layer connects with a node in the fourth layer if there is a communication available at the time instance between the satellite and the ground station as represented by the nodes involved. Edges between third and fourth layers have up-link capacity of communication with ground stations (Eq. 7). The nodes in the fourth layer are connected to the sink node with down-link capacity of the ground station as the capacity on the edges (Eq. 6). Fig. 1 shows a construction of the flow network for opportunities described in Table 3. Once the flow network is constructed, any standard flow solution [12] gives us a schedule with maximum possible (optimal) collections.

### 4.1 General Case: Non-sub-modular

As mentioned earlier, $S^3MC$ is NP-hard. We now design an approximation algorithm that can closely approximate the ILP solution since ILP does not scale. In this context, we first analyze the sub-modularity properties of $S^3MC$, as in [19]. The sub-modularity property ensures that several classical algorithms can be applied to achieve good approximations. However, the general problem of maximizing collection with a fleet of satellites having limited storage capacity with limited down-link and up-link, turns out to be non sub-modular, as discussed below. We first reproduce the definition of sub-modularity from [19] (Fig. 2).

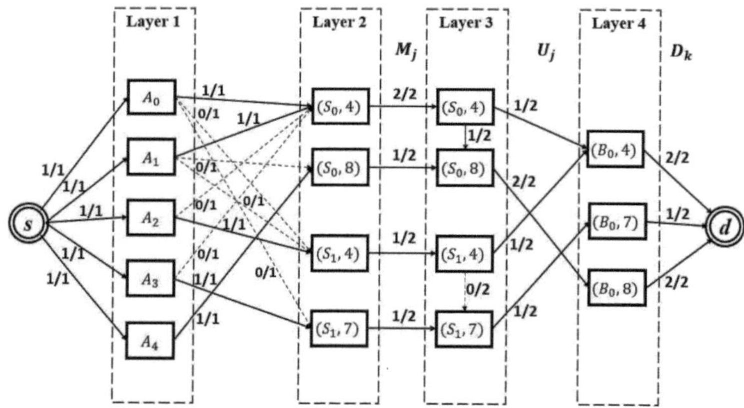


**Fig. 2.** Maxflow solution for network model of Fig. 1.

**Definition 1.** *Given a finite set of elements $\mathcal{G}$ (ground set), a function $f : 2^{\mathcal{G}} \to \mathfrak{R}$ is sub-modular if for any set $A \subseteq B \subseteq \mathcal{G}$ and for every element $e \notin B$, the following holds,*

$$f(A \cup \{e\}) - f(A) \geq f(B \cup \{e\}) - f(B)$$

Let us denote an element $e_{ij}$ as an assignment of a sub-region $A_j$ to satellite $S_i$ for collection. The ground set is given by $\{e_{11}, e_{12}, e_{21}, \ldots e_{|\mathcal{S}||\mathcal{A}|}\}$. Every possible collection assignment, therefore, can be expressed as $\mathcal{E} \subseteq \mathcal{G}$. By the definition of the problem, it is sufficient to assign a sub-region for collection to at least one satellite. We denote by $f(\mathcal{E})$ the number of unique sub-regions scheduled for collection. Consider the following counter-example to show that the function $f$ is non-sub-modular. Specifically, we consider a system with two satellites $S_1$ and $S_2$ with one unit storage, and two sub-regions to collect, $a_1$ and $a_2$. The satellite tracks are such that all downloads happen after collections are over. This generates the ground set $\mathcal{G} = \{e_{11}, e_{12}, e_{21}, e_{22}\}$. We construct two schedules $A = \{e_{11}\}$ and $B = \{e_{11}, e_{21}\}$, and hence $A \subset B$. Also $f(A) = 1$ and $f(B) = 1$ since one region $a_1$ is collected for both $A$ and $B$. Let us consider the event $e_{12}$ to show that $f$ is not sub-modular. Since storage capacity of both the satellites is 1 unit $f(A \cup \{e_{12}\}) = 1$ since $S_1$ can store only 1 collect. On the other hand $f(B \cup \{e_{12}\}) = 2$ as two satellites are involved in this assignment and two collects for $a_1$ and $a_2$ can be stored.

$$f(A \cup \{e_{12}\}) - f(A) < f(B \cup \{e_{12}\}) - f(B) \text{ and } A \subset B$$

and hence $f$ is not sub-modular.

## 5    LP-Relaxation

In this section, we present a randomized rounding based approximation algorithm [19] on top of a linear relaxation of the problem in Sect. 3. The relaxed version of the problem has the same set of constraints as in Eq. 1–7, but the indicator variables $x$'s and $y$'s are no longer forced to be integer decision variables, rather they can take any value in the interval $[0,1]$. In this LP-relaxed version of the problem, these variables are denoted as $\bar{x}$'s and $\bar{y}$'s respectively. The LP-version of the problem can be solved in polynomial time. Then we apply randomized rounding on the solution obtained from the LP solver. Essentially the value of $x^t_{ij}$ is treated as the collection probability of sub-region $A_j$ by satellite $S_i$ at instance $t$. The generation of the final schedule from this solution is presented as Algorithm 1, termed the Approximate Collection Schedule (ACS).

A solution is feasible if it satisfies the onboard memory constraint of the satellites along with down-link / up-link capacity constraints. The solution obtained after randomized rounding is not guaranteed to satisfy these constraints since multiple variables may be set to non-zero values, while satisfying other constraints, hence, the need for the feasibility check. This feasibility condition is given as the until condition in ACS. We continue till a feasible solution is found. Appendix A presents a formal analysis and proof of correctness of the algorithm.

**Input**   : $\mathcal{S} = \{S_1, S_2, \ldots S_k\}$ : Set of satellites
**Input**   : $\mathcal{A} = \{A_1, A_2, \ldots A_n\}$ : Set of sub-regions
**Input**   : $\mathcal{B} = \{B_1, B_2, \ldots B_m\}$ : Set of ground stations
**Input**   : $\mathcal{T}$ : Table containing collection and communication opportunities
**Input**   : $H$ : Scheduling horizon
**Output**: $\mathbf{Q}$ : Schedule for the constellation
**begin**
  **do**

1      $(\bar{x}, \bar{y}) \leftarrow \mathtt{LP\text{-}Solver}(\mathcal{S}, \mathcal{A}, \mathcal{B}, \mathcal{T}, H)$, a linear relaxation of the scheduling problem;

2      $\hat{x}_{ij}^t \leftarrow 1$ with probability $\bar{x}_{ij}^t$ else $0$ ;

3      **for** $t \in [1, H]$ **do**

4        **for** $t' \in [0, t-1]$ **do**
         $\mid$ **if** $\hat{x}_{ij}^{t'} \neq 0$ **then** $\bar{X} \leftarrow \bar{X} + \bar{x}_{ij}^{t'}$
       **end**

5        **if** $\bar{X} > 0$ **then** $\hat{y}_{ijk}^t \leftarrow 1$ with probability $\frac{\bar{y}_{ijk}^t}{\bar{X}}$ else $0$
     **end**

  **until** $(\hat{x}, \hat{y})$ *defines a feasible solution*;

6   **for** *each* $\hat{x}_{ij}^t == 1$ **do** $\mathbf{Q} \leftarrow \mathbf{Q} \cup (\mathrm{COLL}, t, S_j, A_i)$ **for** *each* $\hat{y}_{ijk}^t == 1$ **do** $\mathbf{Q} \leftarrow \mathbf{Q} \cup (\mathrm{COMM}, t, S_j, B_k)$ Sort $\mathbf{Q}$ on $t$ in ascending order;

**end**

Algorithm 1: Approximate Collection Schedule (ACS)

## 6 Experimental Results

In this section, we present our experimental results to show the performance of the proposed algorithms. All experiments were conducted on a machine with AMD Ryzen5 5600 processor and 125 GB RAM. The LP and ILP formulations were solved using the Python PULP Library [1]. Our experimental results compare the performance of the three algorithms. The ILP solutions from the Python ILP-solver [1] for the formulation presented in Sect. 3 are shown as *ILP*, while the solutions from our proposed heuristic presented in Sect. 5 are shown as *ACS* in the figures. Additionally, besides the *ILP* and *ACS* algorithm described above, *InfMem* (our implementation of [3]) serves as a baseline where the satellites are assumed to have unbounded memory and up-link capacities and the ground stations have unbounded down-link capacity.

In all the tables, columns under *Avg collections* denote the average number of collections made by each of the 3 approaches for different satellite and sub-region count. The columns under *Max memory used* denotes the peak number of collections present in the memory of a satellite over the scheduling horizon, following the schedule generated by a specific approach. Our experiments were conducted in two different modes. In the *simulated mode*, communication and computation opportunities were generated randomly. In the *realistic mode* the satellites were instantiated from TLE (Two-Line Element [26]) data published by *Planet Labs* [18] and observation regions were generated around random city locations selected from the city database [22].

**Table 4.** Varying memory capacity of the satellites

| # Sub-regions | Avg Collections | | | Peak memory used | | | # ACS iterations |
|---|---|---|---|---|---|---|---|
| | ILP | ACS | InfMem | ILP | ACS | InfMem | |
| 60 | 26 | 26 | 37 | 2 | 2 | 8 | 8 |
| 80 | 28 | 27 | 41 | 2 | 2 | 8 | 2 |
| 100 | 30 | 29 | 48 | 2 | 2 | 8 | 5 |
| 60 | 36 | 36 | 37 | 4 | 4 | 8 | 1 |
| 80 | 40 | 40 | 41 | 4 | 4 | 8 | 1 |
| 100 | 46 | 46 | 48 | 4 | 4 | 8 | 1 |
| 60 | 37 | 37 | 37 | 6 | 6 | 8 | 1 |
| 80 | 41 | 41 | 41 | 6 | 6 | 8 | 1 |
| 100 | 48 | 48 | 48 | 6 | 6 | 8 | 1 |

As mentioned earlier, each satellite can have multiple collection opportunities at any time instance with different look angles. For our experiments, we bound the maximum collection opportunities per instant to 5.

*Varying Memory Capacity: InfMem* being a less constrained version of *ILP*, gives the maximum possible collections that can be made satisfying Eqs. 1, 2, 3 and 5, assuming the satellites have unbounded memory capacity. In Table 4, for the first 3 rows, satellites have memory and up-link capacities of 2 units each, and the ground stations have down-link capacity of 4 units each. Similarly, for rows 4–6 it is 4 units each and for rows 7–9 it is 6 units each. The number of satellites and ground stations is 4 each, and the scheduling horizon is 30 units. The number of sub-regions is varied from 60 to 100 with a step of 20. As the memory capacity of the satellites changes from 2 units to 6 units, the number of

**Table 5.** Varying the scheduling horizon

| H | # Sub-regions | Avg Collections | | | Max memory used | | | # ACS iterations |
|---|---|---|---|---|---|---|---|---|
| | | ILP | ACS | InfMem | ILP | ACS | InfMem | |
| 30 | 110 | 48 | 47 | 49 | 4 | 4 | 9 | 2 |
| | 130 | 49 | 49 | 50 | 4 | 4 | 9 | 1 |
| | 150 | 57 | 57 | 58 | 4 | 4 | 11 | 1 |
| 40 | 110 | 67 | 67 | 68 | 4 | 4 | 10 | 1 |
| | 130 | 66 | 66 | 68 | 4 | 4 | 10 | 4 |
| | 150 | 68 | 68 | 69 | 4 | 4 | 10 | 1 |
| 50 | 110 | 87 | 86 | 88 | 4 | 4 | 9 | 5 |
| | 130 | 90 | 89 | 92 | 4 | 4 | 10 | 10 |
| | 150 | 89 | 88 | 91 | 4 | 4 | 8 | 178 |

collections increases, as it has more capacity to store data between two successive communication tasks. When each satellite has a memory capacity of 6 units, its solution (in terms of number of collections) is same as the baseline, however, unlike *InfMem*, *ILP* and *ACS* solutions never exceed the memory capacity.

*Varying Scheduling Horizon:* Table 5 shows the effect of varying the scheduling horizon. The number of satellites and ground stations are both taken as 4. The scheduling horizon is varied from 30 to 50 with a step of 10. The number of sub-regions is taken from the set $\{110, 130, 150\}$. The memory and up-link capacity of the satellites is 4 units each. The down-link capacity is 6 units each. As the scheduling horizon increases, so does the number of collection and communication opportunities, which in turn increases the number of collections made.

**Table 6.** Average number of collections

| # Sat | # Sub-regions | Avg Collections | | | Exec time (in s) | | | Peak memory used | | | # ACS iterations |
|---|---|---|---|---|---|---|---|---|---|---|---|
| | | ILP | ACS | InfMem | ILP | ACS | InfMem | ILP | ACS | InfMem | |
| 8 | 150 | 132 | 130 | 133 | 27.9 | 25.7 | 9.1 | 4 | 4 | 13 | 9 |
| | 200 | 114 | 113 | 115 | 39.9 | 35.9 | 12.2 | 4 | 4 | 10 | 2 |
| | 250 | 121 | 121 | 124 | 52.8 | 47.1 | 15.1 | 4 | 4 | 11 | 2 |
| | 300 | 120 | 120 | 122 | 66.7 | 60 | 18.6 | 4 | 4 | 13 | 1 |
| | 350 | — | 125 | 128 | 81.7 | 76 | 21.7 | 4 | 4 | 16 | 7 |
| | 400 | — | 128 | 133 | 97.6 | 88 | 24.9 | 4 | 4 | 17 | 2 |
| | 450 | — | 135 | 140 | 112.8 | 102.1 | 28.3 | 4 | 4 | 20 | 1 |
| 10 | 150 | 150 | 147 | 150 | 35.3 | 32.8 | 11.5 | 4 | 4 | 18 | 9 |
| | 200 | 154 | 153 | 155 | 49.7 | 44.2 | 15.1 | 4 | 4 | 17 | 2 |
| | 250 | 145 | 144 | 147 | 66.2 | 64.7 | 19.3 | 4 | 4 | 16 | 18 |
| | 300 | 152 | 152 | 155 | 84.2 | 83.8 | 23.6 | 4 | 4 | 18 | 23 |
| | 350 | — | 152 | 154 | 102.8 | 92.4 | 27.6 | 4 | 4 | 18 | 1 |
| | 400 | — | 150 | 153 | 121.6 | 113.7 | 31.8 | 4 | 4 | 17 | 6 |
| | 450 | — | 152 | 156 | 140.8 | 129.9 | 35.9 | 4 | 4 | 18 | 4 |
| 12 | 150 | 150 | 148 | 150 | 43 | 43 | 14.1 | 4 | 4 | 18 | 25 |
| | 200 | 174 | 174 | 176 | 62.3 | 55.8 | 18.8 | 4 | 4 | 17 | 3 |
| | 250 | 187 | 187 | 192 | 70.2 | 56.3 | 18 | 4 | 4 | 20 | 7 |
| | 300 | 180 | 179 | 183 | 103.6 | 101.1 | 28.8 | 4 | 4 | 18 | 17 |
| | 350 | — | 182 | 186 | 126.4 | 113.8 | 34.1 | 4 | 4 | 18 | 1 |
| | 400 | — | 174 | 178 | 150 | 135.7 | 38.7 | 4 | 4 | 16 | 1 |
| | 450 | — | 185 | 188 | 176 | 160.5 | 44.7 | 4 | 4 | 18 | 1 |

*Varying Number of Sub-regions:* In Table 6, the satellite constellation size is chosen from the set $\{8, 10, 12\}$, and the number of collection sub-regions is varied from 150 to 450, with a step of 50. The number of ground stations is taken as 4. Each satellite is assumed to have a memory capacity and up-link capacity of 4 units. Similarly the ground stations have a down-link capacity of 4 units each. These values are taken arbitrarily to record one set of experiments. We have repeated the experiments varying these values, however, the results we show here are for the above setting of the parameters. The scheduling horizon is assumed to be 60 units. Table 7 shows the results for larger instances. The number of sub-regions is chosen from $\{1000, 1200, 1400\}$. The number of satellites and ground stations is taken as 15 and 4 respectively. The memory and up-link capacity are 4 units each and down-link capacity is 8 units.

*Summary of Our Findings:* From the results we can see that *InfMem*, having lesser constraints in comparison to *ILP*, is able to generate a solution faster, however the generated solution might not actually be feasible as it might assign more collections to a satellite than its memory capacity. For example, in the first row of Table 6 where $|\mathcal{S}| = 8$ and $|\mathcal{A}| = 150$, execution time for *InfMem* is 9.1s, which is less than the execution time of *ILP* (27.9s) and *ACS* (25.7s), however, the peak memory required to follow the schedule generated by *InfMem* is 13, which exceeds the memory capacity of the satellites, that is, 4 units. *ILP* generates an optimal solution for the problem, however, it does not scale when the problem size increases and times out (as shown in Table 6) since it is unable to produce a solution within the allotted time, which is varied across the instances depending on the problem size. *ACS* consists of solving the LP formulation followed by randomized rounding. Rounding the LP solution randomly might generate an infeasible solution. We keep on rounding the LP solution randomly until we find a feasible solution. In Table 6 it is shown that, as mentioned in Lemma 1–3, on an average the number of times the feasibility check fails (# *ACS* iterations) is small. Both LP and randomized rounding are polynomial time solvable. Since the number of times this rounding is repeated is also small, we get a near optimal solution in lesser time.

**Table 7.** Number of collections

| # Sat | # Sub-regions | Avg Collections | | | Exec time | | | Peak memory used | | | # ACS iterations |
|---|---|---|---|---|---|---|---|---|---|---|---|
| | | ILP | ACS | InfMem | ILP | ACS | InfMem | ILP | ACS | InfMem | |
| 15 | 1000 | 461 | 461 | 469 | 1 h 26 m 59 s | 1 h 24 m 49 s | 5 m 39 s | 4 | 4 | 7 | 1 |
| | 1200 | 436 | 436 | 451 | 1 h 53 m 37 s | 1 h 51 m 51 s | 6 m 43 s | 4 | 4 | 8 | 1 |
| | 1400 | 441 | 441 | 447 | 2 h 16 m 37 s | 2 h 15 m 55 s | 8 m 4 s | 4 | 4 | 5 | 1 |

# 7   Literature Review

The task scheduling problem for satellite constellation involves selecting data collection opportunities that maximizes observation objectives while simultaneously obeying system constraints. The problem is well studied in the context of a single, agile satellite and more recently for multi-satellite systems. Authors in [6] present a Lagrangian relaxation based solution to scheduling for COSMO-Skymed, a three satellite SAR constellation. Authors in [7] improve this result to cater to a larger system and higher planning horizon. This work presents a mixed approach of dynamic programming with MILP to solve the multi-objective scheduling problem in reasonable time [4] and this also shows significant improvement in quality of solution over their earlier graph based approach [3]. In [10], the author classifies the scheduling algorithms into two broad categories, namely feasibility and infeasibility based interpretations. The author also proposes a maximum independent set based heuristic and shows that the approach scales well for large constellations. More recently, in [14] authors introduce a consensus-based task pruning method for the MILP formulation of the scheduling problem. This method aims to enhance computational efficiency in assigning observation tasks to multiple satellites within a given time horizon.

State-of-the-art solutions for collection scheduling assume constraints only corresponding to the satellite kinematics. With increasing adoption of small satellites in remote sensing infrastructures, scheduling problems also need to address the complexities arising due to limited resources on-board satellites due to the small form factor, in addition to the constraints imposed due to intermittent connectivity to ground stations. This paper attempts to address the collection scheduling problem in its full generality, with a model of the relevant constraints that appear in a practical constellation planning and deployment task. We propose an ILP based formulation along with a randomized rounding based approximation approach with guaranteed approximation ratio. A similar randomized rounding technique was explored in a different context in [13,19].

## 8    Future Scope and Conclusion

In this paper, we present a memory-constrained data collection problem for a satellite constellation. We carry out simulations to observe the performance of our proposed algorithms and show that we are able to generate schedules close to the optimal one for moderately large configurations for which an ILP solution cannot be generated. For larger problem sizes, our method performs well in comparison to the baseline heuristic. On some instances, the approximation algorithm takes quite a substantial amount of time due to the feasibility checks we make during the randomized rounding procedure. We plan to address this with better approximation algorithms in future.

Orbital Edge Computing [2] has come up as a promising option in recent times to improve resource utilization of space-based remote sensing infrastructures, specifically the ones based on small satellite constellations. Therefore, the scheduling problem must also consider optimizations involving on-board data analytics. Real-time requirement on data gathering and its analysis are practical requirements for many applications and need to be addressed as part of this resource utilization problem. Within a satellite constellation, the problem of resource optimization can also factor in the possibility of distributed data analytics and its influence on the collection scheduling problem. We plan to augment our framework with the consideration of satellite onboard compute facility and thereby, develop an integrated collect-compute framework for better resource utilization and collection maximization.

# Appendix A: Analysis of ACS Algorithm 1

Let $Pr(e)$ denote the probability of event $e$. The probability of the decision variables $x$'s to be set to 1 are $Pr(\hat{x}_{ij}^{t} = 1) = \bar{x}_{ij}^{t}$ (line 1 of Algorithm 1). If, for a given $(t, S_j)$ more than one $x_{ij}^{t}$'s are set to 1, then one of them is selected randomly, and the others are reset to 0. Similarly, if more than one $x_{ij}^{t}$'s are set to 1 for a given $A_i$, then one of them is selected randomly and others are reset to 0. We compute the probability with which a region is downloaded. According to the constraints in Eq. 3, a region can only be downloaded after it has been scheduled for collection. Therefore, the indicator variable signifying a download event for region $A_i$ by satellite $S_j$ to ground station $B_k$ at a time instance $t$ is set with probability $\bar{y}_{ijk}^{t}$, provided that the region is scheduled for collection at least once in a time instance prior to $t$ and can be computed as,

$$Pr\left(\hat{y}_{ijk}^{t} = 1\right) = Pr\left(\hat{y}_{ijk}^{t} = 1 \;\middle|\; \sum_{t'=1}^{t-1}(\hat{x}_{ij}^{t'} = 1)\right) \cdot Pr\left(\sum_{t'=1}^{t-1}(\hat{x}_{ij}^{t'} = 1)\right)$$

$$= \frac{\bar{y}_{ijk}^{t}}{\bar{X}}\bar{X} \;=\; \bar{y}_{ijk}^{t}$$

where, $\bar{X}$ denotes the sum of $\bar{x}_{ij}^{t}$ for which the corresponding $\hat{x}_{ij}^{t}$ is set to 1. If for a given region $i \in \mathcal{A}$, more than one $y_{ijk}^{t}$'s is set to 1, one of them is selected randomly, and others are reset to 0.

**Lemma 1.** *The schedule obtained by Algorithm 1 satisfies the memory constraints of the satellites in expectation.*

*Proof.* Memory requirement for a satellite is essentially the residual collected items with the satellite. The expected residual collection at any point of time during the scheduling horizon is expressed as Eq. 4 and therefore the memory requirement at time $t$ is

$$\sum_{i=1}^{|\mathcal{A}|}\sum_{t'=1}^{t}\hat{x}_{ij}^{t'} - \sum_{i=1}^{|\mathcal{A}|}\sum_{k=1}^{|\mathcal{B}|}\sum_{t'=1}^{t}\hat{y}_{ijk}^{t'}$$

Therefore, the memory requirement in expectation,

$$E\left[\sum_{i=1}^{|\mathcal{A}|}\sum_{t'=1}^{t}Pr\left(\hat{x}_{ij}^{t'} = 1\right) - \sum_{i=1}^{|\mathcal{A}|}\sum_{k=1}^{|\mathcal{B}|}\sum_{t'=1}^{t}Pr\left(\hat{y}_{ijk}^{t'} = 1\right)\right]$$

$$= \sum_{i=1}^{|\mathcal{A}|}\sum_{t'=1}^{t}\bar{x}_{ij}^{t'} - \sum_{i=1}^{|\mathcal{A}|}\sum_{k=1}^{|\mathcal{B}|}\sum_{t'=1}^{t}\bar{y}_{ijk}^{t'} \;\leq\; M_j \quad \dots \quad \text{(by Eq. 4)}$$

$\square$

**Lemma 2.** *Algorithm 1 ensures that the memory used by any satellite $S_j \in \mathcal{S}$ does not exceed $\frac{1}{2}\left(\sqrt{\frac{|\mathcal{S}|}{M_j}} + 1\right)\left(\sqrt{\frac{|\mathcal{S}|}{M_j}} + 2\right)$ times its memory capacity with high probability.*

*Proof.* The algorithm generates a schedule which satisfies the memory constraint of the satellites in expectation (Lemma 1).

$$E\left[\sum_{i=1}^{|\mathcal{A}|}\sum_{t'=1}^{t} Pr\left(\hat{x}_{ij}^{t'} = 1\right) - \sum_{i=1}^{|\mathcal{A}|}\sum_{k=1}^{|\mathcal{B}|}\sum_{t'=1}^{t} Pr\left(\hat{y}_{ijk}^{t'} = 1\right)\right] \leq M_j$$

The $x$ and $y$ variables are independently rounded, therefore each term in the expression is also independent. Applying the Chernoff Bound [16], we have,

$$Pr\left(\left(\sum_{i=1}^{|\mathcal{A}|}\sum_{t'=1}^{t} \bar{x}_{ij}^{t'} - \sum_{i=1}^{|\mathcal{A}|}\sum_{k=1}^{|\mathcal{B}|}\sum_{t'=1}^{t} \bar{y}_{ijk}^{t'}\right) > (1+\gamma)M_j\right) \leq e^{-\frac{\gamma^2}{2+\gamma}M_j}$$

where $\gamma > 0$. To make the upper bound as low as possible, we take $e^{-\frac{\gamma^2}{2+\gamma}M_j} \leq e^{-\psi}$, where $\psi = |\mathcal{S}|$ *i.e.* the number of satellites in the constellation. This implies,

$$\psi \leq \frac{\gamma^2 M_j}{2+\gamma} \implies M_j\gamma^2 - \gamma\psi - 2\psi \geq 0$$

$$\implies \gamma \geq \frac{\psi + \sqrt{\psi^2 + 8M_j\psi}}{2M_j}$$

In practice, $M_j \gg \psi$, then $M_j\psi \gg \psi^2$. We set,

$$\gamma = \frac{\psi + \sqrt{M_j\psi + 8M_j\psi}}{2M_j} = \frac{1}{2}\left(\frac{\psi}{M_j} + 3\sqrt{\frac{\psi}{M_j}}\right)$$

Therefore, $1+\gamma = 1 + \frac{1}{2}\left(\frac{\psi}{M_j} + 3\sqrt{\frac{\psi}{M_j}}\right) = \frac{1}{2}\left(\sqrt{\frac{\psi}{M_j}} + 1\right)\left(\sqrt{\frac{\psi}{M_j}} + 2\right)$.

Thus, the memory required to store collected data does not exceed $\frac{1}{2}\left(\sqrt{\frac{\psi}{M_j}} + 1\right) \cdot \left(\sqrt{\frac{\psi}{M_j}} + 2\right)$ times the memory capacity of a satellite with high probability. $\qquad\square$

**Lemma 3.** *A data element scheduled for download is also scheduled for collection at some earlier time instance with high probability.*

*Proof.* The expectation that a data element $A_i$, collected by some satellite $S_j$, is scheduled for download at $t$ is given as

$$E\left[\sum_{k=1}^{|\mathcal{B}|} Pr\left(\hat{y}_{ijk}^{t} = 1\right) Pr\left(\sum_{t'=1}^{t-1} \hat{x}_{ij}^{t'} \geq 1\right)\right]$$

$$= \sum_{k=1}^{|\mathcal{B}|} \bar{y}_{ijk}^{t} \sum_{t'=1}^{t-1} \bar{x}_{ij}^{t'} \geq \left(\sum_{k=1}^{|\mathcal{B}|} \bar{y}_{ijk}^{t}\right)^2 \quad \cdots \quad \text{(by Eq. 3)}$$

So, the expectation is linked with the LP-solution value assigned to $\bar{y}$ variables and therefore has high lower bound only when those are assigned high values. $\square$

**Theorem 1.** The $S^3MC$ problem can be solved by $ACS$ with an approximation ratio of $1 - \sqrt{\frac{2M}{\mathcal{OL}}}$, where $\mathcal{OL}$ is the optimal value of the relaxed $S^3MC$ in LP form and $M$ is the total available storage in the constellation.

*Proof.* ACS returns the expectation of the objective value as:

$$E\left[\sum_{t=1}^{H}\sum_{i=1}^{|\mathcal{A}|}\sum_{j=1}^{|\mathcal{S}|} x_{ij}^{t}\right] = \sum_{t=1}^{H}\sum_{i=1}^{|\mathcal{A}|}\sum_{j=1}^{|\mathcal{S}|} Pr(\hat{x}_{ij}^{t}=1) = \sum_{t=1}^{H}\sum_{i=1}^{|\mathcal{A}|}\sum_{j=1}^{|\mathcal{S}|} \bar{x}_{ij}^{t}$$

Each $\bar{x}_{ij}^{t}$ is an independent random variable in $[0,1]$. Applying the *Chernoff Bound Theorem* [16], we have

$$Pr\left(\sum_{t=1}^{H}\sum_{i=1}^{|\mathcal{A}|}\sum_{j=1}^{|\mathcal{S}|} \bar{x}_{ij}^{t} < (1-\delta)\mathcal{OL}\right) \leq e^{-\frac{\delta^2}{2}\mathcal{OL}}$$

where $0 < \delta < 1$. Let $\mathcal{OP}$ denote the optimal solution to $S^3MC$. $\mathcal{OP} \leq \mathcal{OL}$. Therefore,

$$Pr\left(\sum_{t=1}^{H}\sum_{i=1}^{|\mathcal{A}|}\sum_{j=1}^{|\mathcal{S}|} \bar{x}_{ij}^{t} < (1-\delta)\mathcal{OP}\right)$$

$$\leq Pr\left(\sum_{t=1}^{H}\sum_{i=1}^{|\mathcal{A}|}\sum_{j=1}^{|\mathcal{S}|} \bar{x}_{ij}^{t} < (1-\delta)\mathcal{OL}\right) \leq e^{-\frac{\delta^2}{2}\mathcal{OL}}$$

In order to make the upper bound of the probability as small as possible, we take $e^{-\frac{\delta^2}{2}\mathcal{OL}} \leq e^{-M}$, where $M = \sum_{j=1}^{|\mathcal{S}|} M_j$, which implies that the upper bound converges quickly to 0 as the storage capacity of the constellation grows. Accordingly, $\delta \geq \sqrt{\frac{2M}{\mathcal{OL}}}$ since the number of sub-areas to collect is typically much larger than the storage capacity of a small satellite constellation. Therefore $0 < \delta < 1$. So, the approximation ratio is $1 - \sqrt{\frac{2M}{\mathcal{OL}}}$. $\square$

# References


1. Optimization with pulp. https://coin-or.github.io/pulp/
2. Arechiga, A.P., et al.: Onboard image processing for small satellites. In: IEEE National Aerospace and Electronics Conference, pp. 234–240. IEEE (2018)
3. Augenstein, S.: Optimal scheduling of earth-imaging satellites with human collaboration via directed acyclic graphs. In: AAAI Spring Symposium Series (2014)

4. Augenstein, S., et al.: Optimal scheduling of a constellation of earth-imaging satellites, for maximal data throughput and efficient human management. In: Proceedings of the International Conference on Automated Planning and Scheduling, vol. 26, pp. 345–352 (2016)

5. Aziz, H., et al.: Multi-robot task allocation-complexity and approximation. In: Proceedings of the 20th International Conference on Autonomous Agents and MultiAgent Systems, AAMAS 2021, pp. 133–141. International Foundation for Autonomous Agents and Multiagent Systems, Richland, SC (2021)

6. Bianchessi, N., Righini, G.: A mathematical programming algorithm for planning and scheduling an earth observing SAR constellation. In: Proceedings of the 5th International Workshop on Planning and Scheduling for Space (2006)

7. Bianchessi, N., et al.: A heuristic for the multi-satellite, multi-orbit and multi-user management of earth observation satellites. Eur J. Oper. Res. **177**(2), 750–762 (2007)

8. Chan, Y.K., et al.: Design and implementation of synthetic aperture radar (SAR) field-programmable gate array (FPGA)-based processor. Appl. Sci. **12**(4), 1808 (2022)

9. Durresi, A., Sridharan, M., Liu, C., Goyal, M., Jain, R.: Congestion control using multilevel explicit congestion notification in satellite networks. In: 10th International Conference on Computer Communications and Networks, pp. 483 – 488 (2001). https://doi.org/10.1109/ICCCN.2001.956308

10. Eddy, D.: Task Planning for Earth Observing Satellite Systems. Stanford University (2021)

11. Feng, T., et al.: The dynamic and stochastic knapsack problem with homogeneous-sized items and postponement options. Nav. Res. Logist. **62**(4), 267–292 (2015)

12. Ford, L.R., Fulkerson, D.R.: Maximal flow through a network. Can. J. Math. **8**, 399–404 (1956). https://doi.org/10.4153/CJM-1956-045-5

13. Jaipuria, S., Banerjee, A., Bhattacharya, A.: Roadside traffic monitoring using video processing on the edge. In: 16th International Conference on COMmunication Systems & NETworkS, COMSNETS 2024, Bengaluru, India, 3–7 January 2024, pp. 542–550. IEEE (2024)

14. Kim, S.J., Kim, C.H., Choi, H.L.: Observation task scheduling of satellite constellation with consensus-based task pruning. In: AIAA SCITECH 2024 Forum, p. 0746 (2024)

15. Mitrovic-Minic, S., et al.: Collection planning and scheduling for multiple heterogeneous satellite missions: survey, optimization problem, and mathematical programming formulation. In: Modeling and Optimization in Space Engineering: State of the Art and New Challenges, pp. 271–305 (2019)

16. Mitzenmacher, M., Upfal, E.: Probability and computing: randomization and probabilistic techniques in algorithms and data analysis. Cambridge University Press (2017)

17. Paek, S.W., et al.: Small-satellite synthetic aperture radar for continuous global biospheric monitoring: a review. Remote Sens. **12**(16) (2020)

18. PlanetLabs: Planet labs public orbital ephemerides. https://ephemerides.planet-labs.com

19. Poularakis, K., et al.: Service placement and request routing in MEC networks with storage, computation, and communication constraints. IEEE/ACM Trans. Netw. **28**(3), 1047–1060 (2020)

20. Roy, S.S., Nagasekhar, T., et al.: Dual band (SX) ground station antenna for low earth orbit (LEO) satellite tracking application. IEEE Access **10**, 80910–80917 (2022)

21. Sante, R., Bhosale, J., et al : Design and development of automated groundstation system for beliefsat-1. In: Proceedings of the International Conference on Paradigms of Computing, Communication and Data Sciences: PCCDS 2022, pp. 591–605. Springer, Cham (2023)
22. SimpleMaps: World city database. https://simplemaps.com/data/world-cities
23. US Geological Survey: Look angles and coverage area (2023). https://www.usgs.gov/centers/eros/look-angles-and-coverage-area. Accessed 19 Oct 2023
24. Virtanen, P., et al.: Scipy 1.0: fundamental algorithms for scientific computing in python. Nat. Methods $17(3)$, 261–272 (2020)
25. Walker, J.G.: Coverage predictions and selection criteria for satellite constellations. Royal Aircraft Establishment (1982)
26. Wikipedia: Two Line Element set. https://en.wikipedia.org/wiki/Two-line_element_set

# Smartphone Contact-Object Estimation by Acoustic Sensing Focusing on Abstraction Level


Haruya Nishi[1]([✉]), Shigemi Ishida[1], Tomoki Murakami[2], and Shinya Otsuki[2]

[1] Future University Hakodate, Hakodate, Hokkaido 041-8655, Japan
{g2123046,ish}@fun.ac.jp

[2] Access Network Service Systems Laboratories, Nippon Telegraph and Telephone Corporation, Chiyoda City, Japan



**Abstract.** Searching for the smartphone lost in a house is a time-consuming task because we usually rely on a ringing sound as a target signal. To support the smartphone search lost in a house, we are developing a smartphone search assistant system that estimates the smartphone's surrounding conditions based on acoustic sensing with a smart speaker. In this paper, we focus on smartphone contact-object estimation. Several studies have reported smartphone contact-object estimation using supervised machine learning (ML). However, the ML-based contact-object estimation fails when a smartphone is on an unknown object. There are too many objects in a house, which makes it impractical to train the object estimation model with all the objects in a house. Therefore, we propose a smartphone contact-object estimator that considers the abstraction level of estimation results to support unknown objects. Our estimator is based on two key ideas: (1) We prepare for estimator neural networks for multiple abstraction levels and switch the neural network model to a higher abstraction level when the estimation is unconfident. (2) We train the neural networks using information derived from the neural network corresponding to other abstraction levels. Experimental evaluation revealed that our proposed contact-object estimator successfully estimated a contact object with an accuracy of 0.991.

**Keywords:** Acoustic sensing · untrained object estimation · hierarchical neural network


## 1  Introduction

Many smartphone users often lose their smartphones in their houses [1]. We usually search for a lost smartphone relying on a ringing sound as a target signal


This work was supported in part by the Japan Society for the Promotion of Science (JSPS) KAKENHI Grant Numbers JP21K11847 and JP20KK0258 as well as the Cooperative Research Project Program of RIEC, Tohoku University.





A. Soylu et al. (Eds.): MobiQuitous 2024, LNICST 634, pp. 614–630, 2026.
https://doi.org/10.1007/978-3-032-10554-7_32

by making a call to the lost smartphone from another device, which is inefficient due to the dependence on the human senses. When the lost smartphone is covered by something or is under something, a smartphone search might be more difficult.

We are developing a smartphone search assistance system that employs acoustic sensing to estimate the smartphone's surrounding conditions using a smart speaker [2]. Figure 1 shows an overview of the smartphone search assistance system using a smart speaker. We define the smartphone's surrounding conditions as the room where the smartphone exists, the contact-object, and the cover state. Users can feel easier to find the lost smartphone with the smartphone's surrounding condition information.

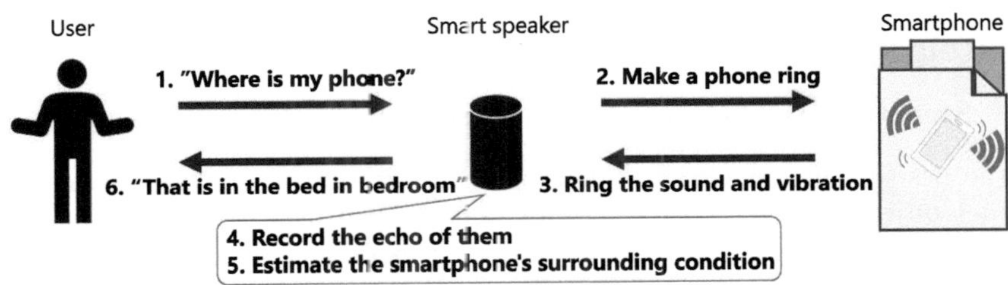


**Fig. 1.** Overview of smartphone search assistance system.

In our previous work, we presented a smartphone cover-state classification method, which estimates one of the smartphone's surrounding conditions [2]. In this paper, we present a smartphone contact-object estimator, i.e., the second one of the smartphone's surrounding conditions.

Several studies have reported smartphone contact-object estimators using a supervised machine learning (ML) model. However, these estimators need to learn almost all objects in a house for smartphone search because they cannot handle untrained objects. Untrained objects are always mistakenly estimated as one of the trained objects. Estimation mistakes confuse a user to find a lost smartphone.

In contrast, we present a smartphone contact-object estimator that considers the abstraction level of estimation results to support unknown objects. Even if the object estimation fails, more abstract descriptions such as *the smartphone is on clothing* can be a hint to search for the lost smartphone. Our estimator switches the estimation model to one of a higher abstraction level to provide a hint for the search on estimation failures. The estimation failures are detected based on the confidence of an estimation result derived from the ML model.

Specifically, our contact-object estimator employs two approaches to improve the estimation and generalization performance: (1) We prepare for multiple neural network estimation models corresponding to abstraction levels and switch the model based on the estimation confidence. (2) We build a hierarchical neural network to share information among estimation models of different abstraction levels during model training. In this paper, we define three abstraction levels: object, material, and soft-hard levels.

To verify the effectiveness of our estimator, we evaluated the estimation and generalization performance of the above two approaches using data collected in a practical environment. The results show that our estimator effectively estimated contact objects with an estimation accuracy of 0.991 for 21 objects.

The rest of this paper is organized as follows. Section 2 describes related work of contact-object estimation and neural networks with a hierarchical structure. Section 3 describes our smartphone contact-object estimator that considers the abstraction level, followed by evaluation experiments in Sect. 4. Finally, Sect. 5 concludes this paper.

## 2   Related Work

### 2.1   Smartphone Contact-Object Estimation

To the best of our knowledge, this is the first attempt to estimate smartphone contact objects using a smart speaker. There have been smartphone contact-object estimators using smartphone built-in sensors such as a microphone [3–5], an accelerometer [6], a camera [7], and a combination of multiple sensors [8].

The microphone-based approach estimates a contact object using variation sound based on the acoustic characteristics of the contact object. Hwang et al. [3] estimated 12 contact objects such as a clothing pocket, desk, and chair with an accuracy of 0.910 based on the vibration sound difference of the contact objects. Ali et al. [5] also estimated 24 contact objects that usually exist both in a work office and home with an accuracy of 0.865 with the considerations of the effect of background noise. Hasegawa et al. [4] estimated 18 contact objects such as a clothing pocket, a wooden desk, and a smartphone stand with an accuracy of 0.821 based on the high-frequency components of the echo of a phone's beep sound.

The accelerometer-based approach estimates a contact object using the smartphone vibration characteristics affected by contact objects. Cho et al. [6] estimated six contact objects such as a sofa, bag, and hand with an accuracy of 0.850 based on the movement of a smartphone, which moves largely on the smoother surface of contact objects.

The multiple sensor-based approach estimates a contact object using smartphone built-in sensors such as a microphone, accelerometer, and magnetic sensor. Darbar et al. [8] estimated 13 contact objects with an accuracy of 0.917 using a rule-based hierarchical inference model based on microphone, magnetic sensor, and proximity sensor.

Although these studies have successfully estimated contact objects, no considerations on untrained objects have been taken. In a practical environment, there are many candidates for a contact object. Training with all the candidates is impractical.

## 2.2   Hierarchical Neural Networks

Hierarchical neural networks have been reported mainly for image classification tasks to improve performance [9–15].

Wang et al. [9] proposed scene classification using two abstraction levels, i.e., instances and parts. Instances represent all objects except the background, while parts represent components within instances. For example, an image containing multiple people is subdivided into instances of each person, which has parts such as a head, arms, and chest, for scene classification. Image classification is performed using based on both instances and parts.

Novack et al. [10] aimed to improve classification accuracy for unknown images by leveraging existing label hierarchy information and an implicit semantic hierarchy based on zero-shot image classification utilizing GPT-3. The implicit semantic hierarchy assumes a hierarchical structure exists between classes, even if the hierarchical structure is not explicitly defined in the dataset.

These studies demonstrated that hierarchical neural networks trained with labels of hierarchical structure improved classification performance. In this paper, we represent objects at different abstraction levels and utilize a hierarchically structured neural network. We train the hierarchical neural networks considering the hierarchical object representation.

## 3   Smartphone Contact-Object Estimator Considering Abstraction Level

### 3.1   Approach

The primary idea of our method is to take *abstraction levels* of objects into contact-object estimation. Estimation mistakes confuse a user to find a lost smartphone. Our method outputs information with a higher abstraction level when estimation confidence is low. As shown in Fig. 2, we can describe an object at different abstraction levels. For example, *a button-down* is *clothing* and *a soft object*. Our estimator outputs clothing when the estimation result of *a button-down* is derived with low confidence.

In this paper, we define three abstraction levels: object, material, and soft-hard levels. We employ the following two approaches.

1. Estimation output with high confidence: We prepare for estimation models corresponding to abstraction levels. Our contact-object estimator calculates estimation confidence and marks estimation results invalid when estimation confidence is lower than a threshold. The final estimation output is the valid estimation result from the lowest abstraction level. In this paper, the lowest abstraction level is the object level, followed by material and soft-hard levels. When the estimation confidence at the object level is above the confidence threshold, for example, the estimation result at the object level is used as the final output. When the estimation confidence at the object and material levels are lower and higher than the threshold, respectively, the estimation result at the material level is the final output. The confidence threshold for each abstraction level is set on the training of the estimation model.

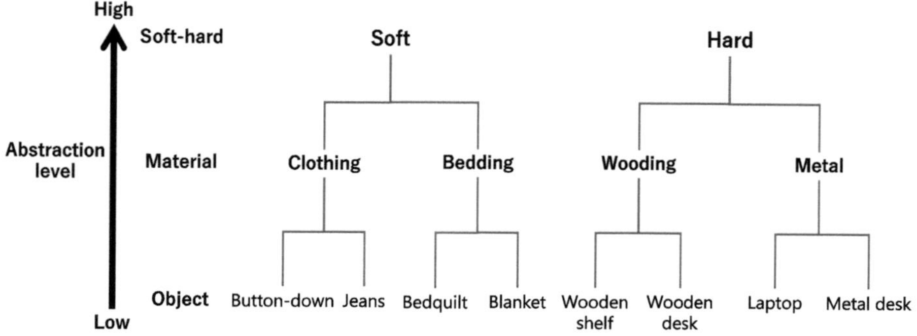



**Fig. 2.** Example of hierarchical representations of objects.

2. Information sharing between different abstraction levels on estimation model training: We use neural networks as an estimation model for each abstraction level. In the estimation model training, we transfer a part of the neural network model to another estimation model corresponding to different abstraction levels. In this way, we can include the feature extraction layers of the estimation models at different abstraction levels as part of the neural network, improving estimation accuracy. This approach is based on an intuition that we can estimate *a button-down* easier when we know the object is *clothing*.

### 3.2   Design Overview

Figure 3 shows an overview of our smartphone contact-object estimator considering abstraction level. Our contact-object estimator consists of three blocks: a data collector, feature extractor, and hierarchical estimator. The data collector collects sound signals caused by smartphone vibration using a smart speaker built-in microphone. The feature extractor converts the sound signals into a mel-spectrogram, which is used as a feature vector for contact-object estimation as a classification task in the contact-object estimator. The hierarchical estimator consists of three estimation neural network models corresponding to three abstraction levels. The estimation result is taken from the results of the three models based on estimation confidence described as $C_i$ in Fig. 3.

The neural network models in the hierarchical estimator share some layers. During the model training, we transfer these layers to share information trained for contact-object estimation at each abstraction level.

The following subsections describe the details of each block.

### 3.3   Data Collector

The data collector collects sound signals caused by smartphone vibration using a microphone embedded in a smart speaker.

Sound signals used for the estimation model training are to be collected in daily life before a smartphone is lost. We assume that a smart speaker is

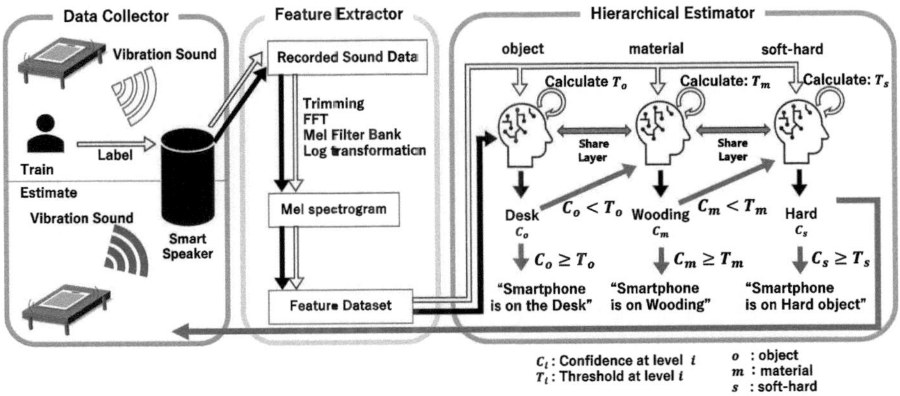


**Fig. 3.** Overview of smartphone contact-object estimator considering abstraction level.

connected to the smartphone, where we install a data collection application. The smart speaker collects vibration sound on everyday notifications. The smart speaker records vibration sound for 3 s immediately after the start of vibration, which is the same procedure presented in [5]. The data collection application then asks a user about the smartphone contact object to collect training label.

Sound signals used for the contact-object estimation are collected when a user asks the smart speaker to find a smartphone. The smart speaker sends a command to the smartphone to vibrate and collects the vibration sound.

### 3.4  Feature Extractor

The feature extractor calculates a mel-spectrogram from the recording data passed from the data collector.

First, we extract vibration sound data from the recording data. Because the starts of the recording and vibration are not precisely synchronized, the feature extractor trims off the first part of the recording data. The feature extractor extracts sound data between 100 and 1600 milliseconds from recording data, obtaining 1500-millisecond vibration sound data. The vibration length depends on the smartphone and might be less than 1500 milliseconds. If the vibration length is less than 1500 milliseconds, the feature extractor trims off non-vibration sound sections and repeats the vibration sound, obtaining the 1500-millisecond sound data.

Next, the feature extractor applies fast Fourier transform (FFT), mel filter bank, and logarithmic transformation to the vibration sound data to derive a mel-spectrogram in a logarithmic scale. Typical examples of mel-spectrograms are shown in Fig. 4. Figure 4 shows mel-spectrograms when the contact objects are bedquilt and metal desk. The mel-spectrogram represents the sound power in each frequency band at each time. We can see that the mel-spectrograms depend on the contact object.

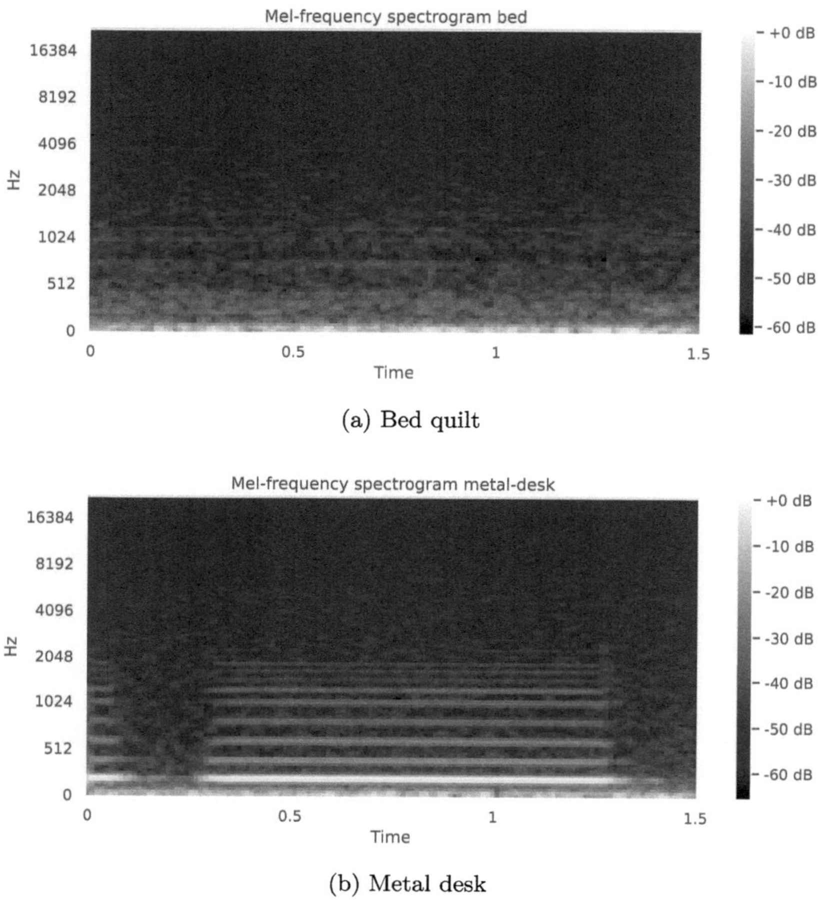

(a) Bed quilt

(b) Metal desk

**Fig. 4.** Example of mel spectrograms of different contact objects.

In this paper, the feature extractor calculates a mel-spectrogram from the 1500-millisecond data sampled at 44.1 kHz. We use an FFT window size of 2048 and shift the window with an overlap size of 512. The number of channels in the mel-filter bank is 128. We obtain the sound power information for each FFT window, resulting in a mel-spectrogram dimension of $128 \times 130$.

## 3.5   Hierarchical Estimator

The hierarchical estimator estimates a smartphone contact object based on a mel-spectrogram obtained in the feature extractor. The hierarchical estimator consists of estimation models corresponding to each abstraction level. Each estimation model outputs an estimation result and the estimation confidence of the contact object at a specific abstraction level.

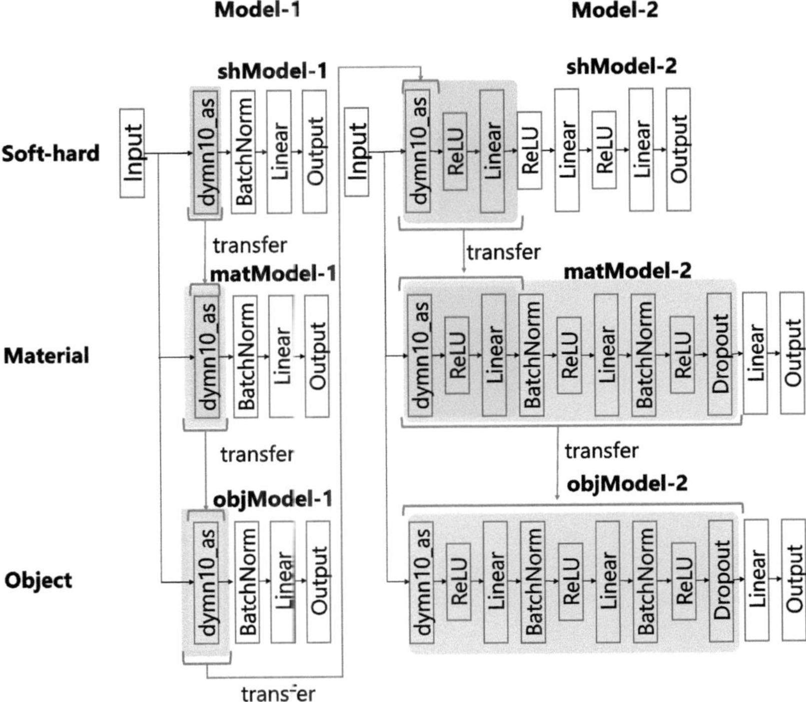


**Fig. 5.** Overview of the structure and training of neural network in hierarchical estimator.

Figure 5 shows the structure and the training overview of neural networks used in the hierarchical estimator. The neural network consists of Model-1 and Model-2, each of which includes estimation models corresponding to each abstraction level. Model-2 is used for contact-object estimation at each abstraction level, while Model-1 is an intermediate model used to train Model-2. Model-1 is discarded after the training.

The neural networks are trained in two rounds. In the first round, we train neural network models in Model-1 from the higher abstraction level. The model information at the higher abstraction level is transferred to the model at the lower abstraction level in the training. In the second round, we train neural network models in Model-2 from the higher abstraction level. We train the models with fine-tuning based on Model-1 or the higher estimation model in Model-2.

The actual training procedure is below. In this procedure, estimation models at soft-hard, material, and object levels in Model-$i$ are represented as shModel-$i$, matModel-$i$, and objectModel-$i$, respectively. We use the dymn10-as deep neural network model from Schmid et al. [16] as a pre-trained model. dymn10-as is the fine-tuned ImageNet architecture trained with acoustic event dataset AudioSet.

1. shModel-1 training:
   We train the shModel-1 that consists of dymn10-as, BatchNorm, and Linear, i.e., Fully-Connected, layers.
2. matModel-1 training:
   We transfer the dymn10-as in the shModel-1 in this step. We extract the dymn10-as in the shModel-1 and append new BatchNorm and Linear layers, building a matModel-1 model. The matModel-1 is then trained.
3. objModel-1 training:
   We transfer the dymn10-as in the matModel-1 in this step. We extract the dymn10-as in the matModel-1 and append new BatchNorm and Linear layers, building an objModel-1 model. The objModel-1 is then trained.
4. shModel-2 training:
   We transfer the dymn10-as in the objModel-1 in this step. We extract the dymn10-as in the objModel-1 and append multiple new ReLU-Linear layers, building a shModel-2 model. The shModel-2 is then trained.
5. matModel-2 training:
   We transfer the feature extraction layers in the shModel-2, i.e., dymn10-as with ReLU and Linear layers, in this step. We extract the feature extraction layers in the shModel-2 and append new BatchNorm, ReLU, and Linear layers, building a matModel-2 model. The matModel-2 is then trained.
6. objModel-2 training:
   We transfer the matModel-2 except output layer, i.e., dymn10-as followed by BatchNorm, ReLU, and Linear layers, in this step. We removed the matModel-2's output layers and append new Linear layer as an output layer, building a objModel-2 model. The objModel-2 is then trained.

After the model training is completed, we determine confidence thresholds for each estimation model in Model-2. As shown in Fig. 3, the confidence thresholds are set at each abstraction level. We first input all the training data into each estimation model in Model-2, deriving estimation results and estimation confidence. We then filter incorrect results out. The confidence threshold is calculated for each estimation model as the mean of the confidence values corresponding to the remaining, i.e., correct, estimation results.

In this paper, we define the estimation confidence as the maximum output value of the Linear layer, i.e., the final output layer of each model in Model-2. The output of the linear layer is a set of real numbers for each class. For example, because the material-level estimation is a seven-class classification task, the linear-layer output is expressed as $[-2.02, -1.53, 0.45, 5.71, 0.05, -0.42, 1.05]$. In this example, the estimation confidence is the maximum output of 5.71.

The hierarchical estimator chooses the estimation results of Model-2 as an overall contact-object estimation result based on the estimation confidence at each abstraction level. Let $T_s, T_m, T_o$ be the confidence threshold at soft-hard, material, and object levels, respectively, and $C_s, C_m, C_o$ be the estimation confidence values at soft-hard, material, and object levels, respectively. The output of the hierarchical estimator is determined as:

1. When $C_o \geq T_o$:
   The hierarchical estimator outputs the objModel-2 estimation result.

2. When $C_m \geq T_m$:
   The hierarchical estimator outputs the matModel-2 estimation result.
3. When $C_s \geq T_s$:
   The hierarchical estimator outputs the shModel-2 estimation result.
4. When $C_s < T_s$:
   The hierarchical estimator retires the overall estimation process from the beginning. The data collector collects vibration sound data again, followed by feature extraction and object estimation. If $C_s < T_s$ in the re-estimation again, the hierarchical estimator outputs *unknown*.

When the output of the hierarchical estimator is *unknown*, the smartphone search assistance system, shown in Fig. 1, provides information only about the cover state and the smartphone-located room.

## 4   Evaluation

We evaluated our smartphone contact-object estimator using the data collected in a practical environment. We first evaluated the estimation accuracy of the estimation models of each abstraction level as a micro-level evaluation. We then evaluated the overall contact-object estimation accuracy, i.e., smartphone contact-object estimation based on estimation confidence, as a macro-level evaluation. Finally, the estimation accuracy against untrained objects was evaluated.

### 4.1   Experiment Setup

Figure 6 shows the data collection experiment setup. A target contact object was put on a metal desk with a height of approximately 70 cm. We put an ASUS Zenfone 8 smartphone face up on the target object and installed an audio-technica AT2050 microphone approximately 1 m away from the object at a height of approximately 70 cm. We set the directionality of the microphone toward the smartphone. The microphone was connected to a ZOOM H6 audio recorder. Note that the oversized target objects that could not be placed on the metal desk were directly placed on a wooden floor.

Figure 7 shows the list of target contact objects in this experiment. We used 21 contact objects, which can be described in 7 materials. Based on the material, we assigned a label of soft or hard to each object.

We collected vibration sound data in the following procedure. The sound data was collected while changing the position and orientation of the smartphone for each trial to emulate different contact conditions.

1. Place the smartphone on the contact object.
2. Start recording.
3. Activate vibration for one second.
4. Take the smartphone off from the contact object and place the smartphone again to change the position and orientation of the smartphone.
5. Repeat steps 3 and 4 for 50 times.
6. Stop recording.

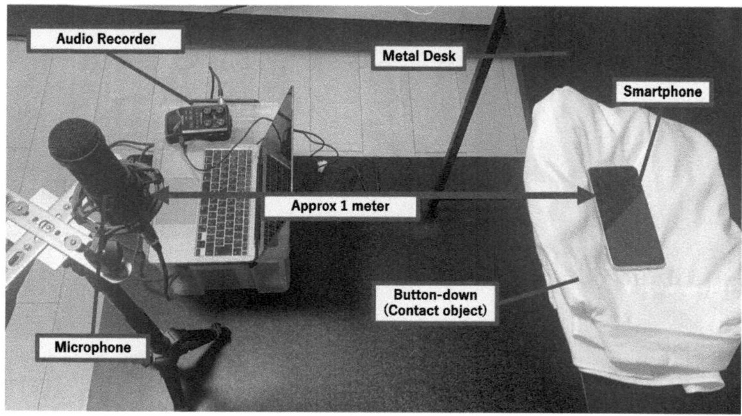



**Fig. 6.** Experiment setup.

| | 1 | 2 | 3 | 4 | 5 | 6 | 7 | 8 | 9 |
|---|---|---|---|---|---|---|---|---|---|
| soft-hard | Soft | | | | | | | | |
| material | Clothing | | | Bedding | | | Memory-foam | | |
| object | Button-down | Jeans | Sweat shirt | Blanket | Bedquilt | Pillow | Mousepad | Chair | Sofa |

| | 10 | 11 | 12 | 13 | 14 | 15 | 16 | 17 | 18 | 19 | 20 | 21 |
|---|---|---|---|---|---|---|---|---|---|---|---|---|
| soft-hard | Hard | | | | | | | | | | | |
| material | Paper | | | Metal | | | Wood | | | Plastic | | |
| object | Thick-book | Thin-book | Cardboard | Metal desk | Laptop | Steel shelf | Wooden desk | Wooden shelf | Floor | Accessory case | Plastic container | Plastic shelf |

**Fig. 7.** Target contact objects in this experiment.

In total, we collected the recording data of 50 trials for each object. At the beginning of each trial, we made a sound of 2000 Hz pure tone for 100 milliseconds as a trial onset marker. Referring to the trial onset markers, we split the recording data for each trial.

To demonstrate the effectiveness of the proposed contact-object estimator, we compared the estimation accuracy between the following two methods. We calculated the F-score for each label and calculated the harmonic mean of the F-scores for all labels, deriving the estimation accuracy.

1. Proposed method The method presented in Sect. 3. For the proposed method, we evaluated the F-score with a hold-out method, which randomly splits the dataset into training and test datasets only once, because of the long training time.
2. SVM method The smartphone contact-object estimation method presented in our previous work [2]. The SVM method uses a support vector machine (SVM) classifier with mel-frequency cepstral coefficients (MFCCs) as features instead of a mel-spectrogram. We prepared for estimation models for each abstraction level and separately trained the estimation models. We evaluated

the SVM method with the harmonic mean of estimation accuracies derived with 10-fold cross-validation.

## 4.2  Estimation Accuracy of the Estimation Models at Each Abstraction Level

To evaluate the performance of the estimation models at each abstraction level, we compared the estimation accuracy of models in Model-1 and Model-2. The collected data were randomly sorted and split in the ratio of training : validation : test = 6 : 2 : 2. We then trained and evaluated the estimation models at each abstraction level.

Figures 8 and 9 show the confusion matrices of contact-object estimation results for each abstraction level using models in Model-1 and Model-2, respectively. From Fig. 8, we can see that Model-1 successfully estimated the contact objects at the object and material levels. On the other hand, there were incorrect estimations at the material level, especially for soft objects such as memory foam.

Referring to Fig. 9, we can confirm that Model-2 demonstrated a high degree of success in estimating objects at all abstraction levels. Particularly at the material level, Model-2 appears to have outperformed Model-1.

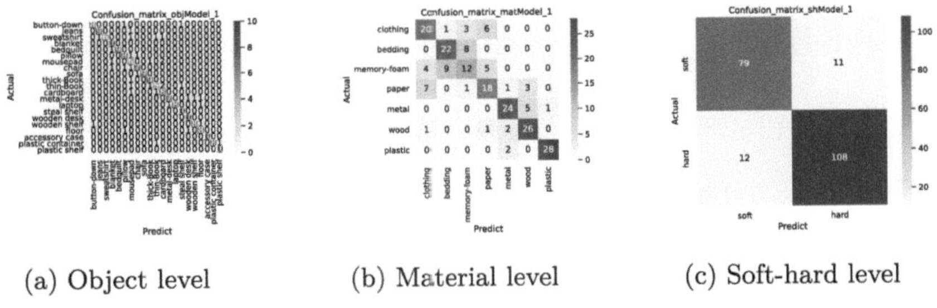

(a) Object level        (b) Material level        (c) Soft-hard level

**Fig. 8.** Confusion matrices of contact-object estimation results by Model-1.

Table 1 shows the estimation accuracy of the estimation models at each abstraction level. The table also shows the estimation accuracy of the SVM method. As shown in Table 1, the proposed method, i.e., Model-2, showed the highest accuracy among the SVM, Model-1, and Model-2 at all the abstraction levels. At the material and soft-hard levels, Model-2 greatly improved the estimation accuracy compared to Model-1. The 2-round training successfully captured the information of other abstraction levels, resulting in higher accuracy.

The estimation accuracy of the models in Model-1 was lower than that of the SVM method at the material and soft-hard levels, as shown in Table 1. This was mainly caused by the limited amount of training data against the complicated neural network. The related studies [6] and [8] have also shown the difficulties

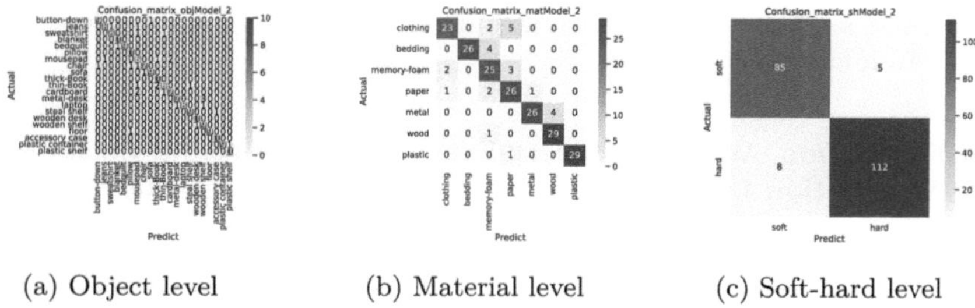

(a) Object level          (b) Material level          (c) Soft-hard level

**Fig. 9.** Confusion matrices of contact-object estimation results by Model-2.

**Table 1.** Estimation accuracy at each abstraction level

| Abstraction level | SVM | Model-1 | Model-2 |
|---|---|---|---|
| Object | 0.843 | 0.824 | 0.857 |
| Material | 0.850 | 0.714 | 0.876 |
| Soft-hard | 0.881 | 0.890 | 0.938 |

in the recognition of soft and hard. Our 2-round training approach was effective in training the soft-hard classifier with the limited training data.

The above results confirm that the estimation model training using the information derived from other abstraction levels improved the estimation accuracy.

### 4.3  Overall Estimation Accuracy

To evaluate the overall performance of contact-object estimation, we evaluated the estimation accuracy of contact-object estimation based on estimation confidence. For each trial of the collected data, we obtained a final estimation output from the estimation results at each abstraction level derived in the previous subsection. The output of the hierarchical estimator was determined based on the estimation confidence according to the estimation procedure presented in Sect. 3.5. We then calculate the harmonic mean of the F-score for estimation results at each abstraction level.

Table 2 shows the overall estimation accuracy of the SVM and Model-2, i.e., the proposed method. The table also shows the estimation completion rate, which is the rate of test trials whose estimation confidence exceeded the confidence threshold. Table 2 shows that the estimation accuracy of the proposed method was higher than that of the SVM method at all the abstraction levels. Comparing the estimation accuracy of the SVM and the proposed method, we can confirm that the proposed method improved the overall estimation accuracy.

In Table 2, the estimation completion rate of the SVM and Model-2 at the object level was 43.5% and 51.4%, respectively. This result indicates that we derived a high accuracy for more number of test trials by the proposed method compared to the SVM method. The total estimation completion rate can be calculated by summing the estimation completion rates at all the abstraction levels. The total estimation completion rate of the SVM method and Model-2 was 78.1% and 71.9%, respectively. Both methods could estimate the contact object for more than 70% of the trials. At material and soft-hard levels, the estimation completion rate of SVM was higher than that of Model-2. Model-2 discarded estimation results at these abstraction levels when the confidence level was low, resulting in high accuracy.

**Table 2.** Overall estimation accuracy and estimation completion rate

| Abstraction level | Accuracy | | Estimation completion rate | |
|---|---|---|---|---|
| | SVM | Model-2 | SVM | Model-2 |
| Object | 0.967 | 0.991 | 43.5% | 51.4% |
| Material | 0.877 | 0.909 | 19.2% | 10.5% |
| Soft-hard | 0.954 | 1.000 | 15.4% | 10.0% |

Comparing Tables 1 and 2, we can confirm that the estimation accuracy for both SVM and Model-2 was improved at all the abstraction levels. The estimation output decision based on the estimation confidence successfully improved the estimation accuracy at each abstraction level, not depending on the estimation model.

The above results confirm that the contact-object estimation based on estimation confidence improved estimation accuracy.

### 4.4 Estimation Accuracy Against Untrained Objects

Our final goal is to realize a contact-object estimator that supports untrained objects. We evaluated the contact-object estimation accuracy when the smartphone is on an untrained object. We performed Leave-One-Object-Out (LOOO) cross-validation in this evaluation. For each of the 21 objects, we used one object as test data and used the remaining data of 20 objects as training data to derive the harmonic mean of F-scores. Note that the training data was again randomly split in the ratio of training : validation = 8 : 2 for the neural network training.

First, we evaluated the estimation accuracy without the confidence-based decision. Table 3 shows the estimation accuracy of SVM, Model-1, and Model-2 against untrained objects without estimation confidence-based decision. We excluded the estimation accuracy at the object level because the object-level estimator always outputs an incorrect estimation result as we used supervised learning algorithms. The estimation accuracy of the proposed method, i.e., Model-2, was 0.521 and 0.872 at material and soft-hard levels, respectively, which were higher than those of the SVM of 0.330 and 0.812. We can confirm that Model-2's generalization performance was higher than that of the SVM at all the abstraction levels. Comparing the estimation accuracy between Model-2 and Model-1, we can also confirm that the Model-2's generalization performance was also higher than that of Model-1. Our 2-round training with the hierarchical neural network improved the generalization performance and improved the object estimation performance against untrained objects.

**Table 3.** Estimation accuracy of contact-object estimation for untrained objects without confidence-based decision

| Abstraction level | SVM | Model-1 | Model-2 |
|---|---|---|---|
| Material | 0.330 | 0.483 | 0.521 |
| Soft-hard | 0.812 | 0.813 | 0.872 |

Next, we evaluated the overall estimation accuracy against untrained objects. Table 4 shows the overall estimation accuracy, i.e., estimation accuracy with the confidence-level decision, against untrained objects. The estimation accuracy of Model-2, i.e., the proposed method, was 0.580 and 0.836 at the material and soft-hard levels, respectively, which were higher than those of the SVM of 0.338 and 0.740. We can confirm that Model-2's generalization performance was higher than that of the SVM method at all abstraction levels.

**Table 4.** Overall estimation accuracy against untrained objects

| Abstraction level | Accuracy | | Estimation completion rate | |
|---|---|---|---|---|
| | SVM | Model-2 | SVM | Model-2 |
| Object | – | – | 21.0% | 7.8% |
| Material | 0.338 | 0.580 | 20.0% | 46.2% |
| Soft-hard | 0.740 | 0.836 | 25.0% | 5.8% |

At the object level, the estimation completion rate of the proposed method was 7.8%, which is lower than that of the SVM method of 21.0%. For untrained objects, estimation completion at the object level means incorrect estimation. The lower completion rate of the proposed method at the object level indicates high robustness against untrained objects.

At the material level, the estimation completion rate of the proposed method was higher than that of the SVM method. The proposed method performs better in capturing features of hierarchical object representation, which resulted in the higher estimation completion rate for untrained objects.

On the other hand, at the soft-hard level, the estimation completion rate of the proposed method was lower than that of the SVM method. In total, estimation was completed for $7.8 + 46.2 + 5.8 = 59.8\%$ trials in the proposed method, while $21.0 + 20.0 + 25.0 = 66.0\%$ of estimation trials were completed in the SVM method. Note that estimation completion does not indicate correct estimation. In the proposed method, we sacrificed unsure estimation results, which resulted in high accuracy and low estimation completion rate. There might be room to improve the soft-hard estimation of the proposed method while keeping estimation accuracy.

The above results confirm that our contact-object estimator, employing a hierarchical neural network and considering abstraction level, improved the estimation accuracy against untrained objects. We think the estimation accuracy was still insufficient for practical use, especially at the material level. We are working to more improve estimation accuracy against untrained objects.

## 5   Conclusion

In this paper, we proposed a smartphone contact-object estimator for an in-home smartphone search support system. Machine learning-based contact-object estimators have been proposed, though, they have difficulties in estimation against untrained objects. We therefore proposed a contact-object estimator considering abstraction level to support untrained objects. The proposed method relies on two approaches: (1) We prepare hierarchical neural networks for multiple abstraction levels and switch the neural network to a higher abstraction level when the estimation is unconfident. (2) We train the neural network using information derived from other abstraction levels. We conducted experimental evaluations and confirmed that our contact-object estimator estimated contact objects with an accuracy of 0.991 for 21 objects, demonstrating the effectiveness of the above two approaches. We are planning to work on contact-object estimation considering other surrounding conditions such as a cover state.

## References


1. TrackR: Survey on what you are looking for (2013). https://prtimes.jp/main/html/rd/p/000000006.000022312.html
2. Nishi, H., Ishida, S., Murakami, T., Otsuki, S.: Smartphone cover-state classification via acoustic sensing for smartphone search in indoor environments. In: 2023 IEEE 12th Global Conference on Consumer Electronics (GCCE), pp. 429–430. IEEE (2023)
3. Hwang, S., Wohn, K.: VibroTactor: low-cost placement-aware technique using vibration echoes on mobile devices, pp. 73–74 (2013)
4. Hasegawa, T., Hirahashi, S., Koshino, M.: Determining smartphone's placement through material detection, using multiple features produced in sound echoes. IEEE Access 5, 5331–5339 (2017)
5. Ali, K., Liu, A.X.: Fine-grained vibration based sensing using a smartphone. IEEE Trans. Mob. Comput. 21(11), 3971–3985 (2021)
6. Cho, J., Hwang, I., Oh, S.: Vibration-based surface recognition for smartphones. In: 2012 IEEE International Conference on Embedded and Real-Time Computing Systems and Applications, pp. 459–464 (2012)

7. Yeo, H.-S., Lee, J., Bianchi, A., Harris-Birtill, D., Quigley, A.: SpeCam: sensing surface color and material with the front-facing camera of a mobile device. In: Proceedings of the 19th International Conference on Human-Computer Interaction with Mobile Devices and Services, Vienna Austria, pp. 1–9. ACM (2017)
8. Darbar, R., Samanta, D.: SurfaceSense: smartphone can recognize where it is kept. In: Proceedings of the 7th Indian Conference on Human-Computer Interaction, IndiaHCI 2015, pp. 39–46. Association for Computing Machinery, New York (2015)
9. Wang, X., Li, S., Kallidromitis, K., Kato, Y., Kozuka, K., Darrell, T.: Hierarchical open-vocabulary universal image segmentation. In: Advances in Neural Information Processing Systems, vol. 36, pp. 21429–21453 (2024)
10. Novack, Z., McAuley, J., Lipton, Z.C., Garg, S.: Chils: zero-shot image classification with hierarchical label sets. In: International Conference on Machine Learning, pp. 26342–26362. PMLR (2023)
11. Gargiulo, F., Silvestri, S., Ciampi, M.: Exploit hierarchical label knowledge for deep learning. In: 2019 IEEE 32nd International Symposium on Computer-Based Medical Systems (CBMS), pp. 539–542 (2019)
12. Giunchiglia, E., Lukasiewicz, T.: Coherent hierarchical multi-label classification networks. In: Advances in Neural Information Processing Systems, vol. 33, pp. 9662–9673 (2020)
13. Maltoudoglou, L., Paisios, A., Lenc, L., Martínek, J., Král, P., Papadopoulos, H.: Well-calibrated confidence measures for multi-label text classification with a large number of labels. Pattern Recogn. **122**, 108271 (2022)
14. Wang, R., Ridley, R., Qu, W., Dai, X.: A novel reasoning mechanism for multi-label text classification. Inf. Process. Manage. **58**(2), 102441 (2021)
15. Zou, X., et al.: Segment everything everywhere all at once. In: Advances in Neural Information Processing Systems, vol. 36 (2024)
16. Schmid, F., Koutini, K., Widmer, G.: Dynamic convolutional neural networks as efficient pre-trained audio models. IEEE/ACM Trans. Audio Speech Lang. Process. **32**, 2227–2241 (2024)

# Author Index

MIX
Papier aus verantwortungsvollen Quellen
Paper from responsible sources
FSC® C105338

If you have any concerns about our products,
you can contact us on
**ProductSafety@springernature.com**

In case Publisher is established outside the EU,
the EU authorized representative is:
**Springer Nature Customer Service Center GmbH**
**Europaplatz 3, 69115 Heidelberg, Germany**

Printed by Libri Plureos GmbH
in Hamburg, Germany